The Original Patriots:

Northern California Indian Veterans of World War Two

Chag Lowry

Published by Chag Lowry
Eureka, California

**The Original Patriots:
Northern California Indian Veterans of
World War Two**

Published by Chag Lowry
P.O. Box 185, Eureka, California 95501
ova@humboldt1.com

Front cover:
Stanley Lowry at a Memorial Day Parade in Susanville, California in 1998. United States flag shown on the cover was flown on the destroyer the USS *Dewey* during the battle on Iwo Jima in February of 1945.

All photographs by Chag Lowry unless otherwise noted.
Book design by Robert Marcus Graphics
Maps adapted from U.S. military sources by Robert Marcus Graphics

ISBN-13: 978-0-9791709-0-4
ISBN-10: 0-9791709-0-7

Printed in the United States of America.

First printing. April, 2007

www.originalpatriots.com

For my son Trey and his generation.

May they never experience war.

This first printing of

The Original Patriots: *Northern California Indian Veterans of World War Two*

is sponsored by the following:

The Susanville Indian Rancheria

The Yurok Tribe

The Bear River Band at Rohnerville Rancheria

The Morongo Tribe of Mission Indians

The Smith River Rancheria

The Elk Valley Rancheria

The Table Bluff Reservation–Wiyot Tribe

The Tyme Maidu Tribe

The Mooretown Rancheria

Table of Contents

Introduction 6

The California Gold Rush and Indian Boarding Schools 9

Indian Boarding Schools 11

Reservations and Political Definitions 15

World War One 16

The Origin of World War Two 21

The European Theater 23

Neil McKinnon (Yurok) 25

Frank Richards (Tolowa) 30

Sharon Wasson (Paiute) 36

Wally Scott (Yurok) 40

Ulysses Davis (Hupa/Yurok) 44

Floyd Richards (Tolowa) 46

John Peconam (Mountain Maidu) 47

Glenn Moore, Sr. (Yurok) 57

Leland Washoe & Jim Washoe (Washoe/Pit River) 61

Charles Lindgren (Yurok) 65

Johnny Smith (Mountain Maidu/Pit River) 67

Chuck Donahue (Yurok/Karuk) 71

Frank Martin (Koncow Maidu) 72

Tommy Merino (Mountain Maidu) 74

Lena Swearington (Karuk) 78

Stanley Lowry (Mountain Maidu/Pit River) 85

Frank Ames (Yurok) 91

Al Valadez, Sr. (Paiute/Mountain Maidu) 93

Frank Dowd (Yurok) 97

Alfred McCovey (Yurok) 100

The Home Front 104

Chuck Williams (Yurok) 104

Vernon Numan (Paiute/Shoshone) 110

Dee Rouse (Yurok) 112

Jimmy James (Yurok/Hupa) 116

Bill Evans (Paiute/Pit River) 120

Don Preston (Pit River/Paiute) 122

Louie Melendez (Paiute) 125

The Arsenal for Democracy 130

Georgiana Trull (Yurok) 130

Edith Fogus (Hupa) 132

Josie Valadez (Paiute/Pit River/Maidu) 134

Josephine Peters (Karuk/Yurok) 137

The Pacific Theater 139

Mervin Evans (Pit River/Shoshone) 142

Ned Crutcher (Paiute/Shoshone) 147

Lee McCardie (Hupa/Yurok) 153

Lee Hover (Karuk) 154

Gene Ryan (Mountain Maidu/Pit River/Washoe) 160

Frank Grant (Karuk) 164

James Campbell, Sr. (Hupa) 168

Archie Thompson (Yurok) 174

Jack Madero (Paiute/Mountain Maidu) 176

Jack Risling (Karuk/Yurok/Hupa) 178

Harold Blake (Yurok) 185

Les Ammon (Hupa) 187

Elmer Rossig (Wiyot) 189

Ed Mitchell (Yurok) 191

Kenny Childs (Yurok) 195

Dave Risling (Karuk/Yurok/Hupa) 197

Kenny Sanderson (Yurok) 204

Bill Rossig (Wiyot) 207

Willard Carlson (Yurok) 210

Darrell McCovey (Yurok) 214

Wilbur Smith (Paiute/Maidu/Pit River) 217

Reuben Green (Tolowa) 222

Grant Hillman (Karuk) 225

Francis Allen (Pomo) 231

Charlie Bowen (Mountain Maidu) 236

Wally Griffin (Yurok) 241

Leonard Lowry (Mountain Maidu/Pit River) 245

In Memoriam 249

In Remembrance 256

Epilogue 259

Notes 264

Bibliography 266

Introduction

In January of 1941 my grandfather Stan Lowry and his younger brother Leonard decided to join the United States Army. They had hoped to serve together in the same company as brothers. Although World War Two hadn't yet reached America, my grandfather and great-uncle had a strong desire to become soldiers.

They began their basic training at a small base named Fort Ord in central California. The United States was drawn into the war after the Japanese Navy attacked Pearl Harbor, Hawaii, on December 7, 1941. It was feared that the Japanese might next invade California, and Stan and Leonard were part of an Army division that was deployed up and down the state's coastline.

The invasion never materialized, and Leonard was then selected to attend an officer candidate school at Fort Benning, Georgia. Stan went to a base in Texas and eventually made staff sergeant before going overseas. These two brothers had joined the Army hoping to watch over each other. Instead, they fought in campaigns half a world apart; Stan in Europe and Leonard in the Pacific. Stan was in the 99th Infantry Division and Leonard was in the 32nd Infantry Division.

By the end of the war my grandfather had earned a Silver Star and a battlefield commission to second lieutenant in the Battle of the Bulge and commanded men in combat in the battle of the Ruhr pocket in Germany. My great-uncle Leonard earned a Silver Star, was promoted to captain, and commanded men in combat on Papau New Guinea and on the Philippine islands of Leyte and Luzon.

Because of his leadership and bravery during both World War Two and later during the Korean War, Leonard is the most decorated Native American soldier in United States history. He is also one of the most decorated American soldiers in history.

The battles they went through, whether it was on an island in the Pacific or in a village in France, were often dirty, terrible and extremely traumatic.

As a young boy I always enjoyed watching older Native men and women at gatherings and ceremonies. I am of Yurok, Mountain Maidu, and Pit River Native American ancestry. My mother is Yurok, and our Yurok homeland begins at the Pacific Ocean and follows the Klamath River through ancient redwoods and towering mountain passes.

My father is mountain Maidu and Pit River. My Maidu and Pit River homelands span the high deserts of northeastern California, and I was raised on the Susanville Indian Rancheria among my father's family in the small town of Susanville located in Lassen County in California.

There was one gathering in the fall that occurred every year where I closely observed the older Native men. My parents would load me and my brother and sister into our car and take us to a potluck. When we arrived and walked in my grandfather Stan Lowry and his brother Leonard would be speaking with my great-uncle Bob Aguilar and their cousin Mervin Evans; they would be sitting on metal chairs set next to plain tables in a nondescript building located on the Lassen County fairgrounds. Other Native men and their wives sat at nearby tables and spoke while drinking hot coffee and eating food piled onto white paper plates. There was one table loaded with fried chicken, potato salad, green beans, pies, cakes and Kool-Aid. Even at a young age I could tell these were strong Indian men who seemed to have a mysterious connection that I couldn't quite recognize or grasp.

After a while I would go play with my cousins and run around outside. Sometimes we would pass through where these men were sitting. I would hear phrases from their conversations, phrases such as "veterans," and "battles," and "rights." These men would also hold themselves in a distinct manner. I could never put my finger on it, but they were somehow bonded together in a way that I found fascinating.

I remember them talking about Thomas Tucker; he was of Mountain Maidu ancestry and was the first soldier from Lassen County to die in combat in France during World War One. I also remember they spoke of their time in the Second World War in subdued tones. Most often these men would be telling each other funny stories or talking about sports. They would ask one another about their families and share stories about vacation trips. But their story about Thomas Tucker and the glimpses into their war time experiences were what stayed in my memory over the years.

That gathering my family attended is known as the Susanville Indian Veterans' Reunion. It has been held every year since 1946 to the present. All of those older Native men were veterans of the United States military. Most were veterans of World War Two. Some served in the Korean War, some served during peacetime, and some, including my late uncle Mike Lowry, were in the Vietnam War.

It is a rare occurrence for any World War Two combat veteran to speak of his experience. The battles they went through, whether it was on an island in the Pacific or in a village in France, were often dirty, terrible and extremely traumatic. So these Indian Veterans' Reunions were unique not just because it was Native men who talked about their time in the war; they were unique because it was World War Two veterans who were sharing their stories in a public setting.

As I grew older I wanted to understand more about the Second World War. But what I learned didn't include the histories or the stories of Native Americans who served this country. They didn't exist in movies or books about the war. However, I alone had a total of 14 family members who were in the military during that conflict. My parents knew of several Indian families where three or four brothers all served in the war. As I reached my early 20s I started to think about those Native veterans I had observed as a young boy.

What were their stories? What about the war histories of the rest of northern California's tribes? Did they send their sons and daughters into battle as well? What countries did they travel to? Were they treated with respect in the service? Why would anyone choose to fight and possibly kill other people for any reason?

My journey for answers to these questions began when I was 24 years old. I started to audiotape interviews among my family members who served in the war. I then interviewed family friends and ended by interviewing as many Native veterans in northern California whom I could contact. Although many veterans had passed away I was able to reach an astonishing number of people.

I started this book with the intention of focusing solely on the World War Two experiences of these Native men and women. Following research and several interviews it became clear that I had to start at that time of first contact between northern California Native people and non-Native settlers and miners in the mid-1800s. These Native men and women are only one or two generations removed from the terrible trauma of the California Gold Rush.

The state of California is only 157 years old. Northern California was one of the last places in the continental United States where indigenous cultures were invaded by European and American settlers. My great-grandparents on both sides of my family were born and raised prior to contact with non-Native people.

Toward the end of the Gold Rush the Indian boarding school era began. Starting in 1880 and lasting into the 1930s, hundreds, possibly thousands of Native children from northern California were forced from their homes into re-education centers to be violently assimilated into "American" society. At this time the racist idea abounded that Native people were doomed to die out if they stayed "uncivilized" and "heathen," so they needed to be taught a new way of life. Both sides of my family are survivors of these American policies of genocide and forced assimilation.

When America joined the Allies in World War One in 1917 several dozen men from indigenous tribes in northern California served in the Army. They went to boot camps and sailed overseas to fight in France against the Germans. They saw the slaughter in the trenches and they fought with bravery and determination. And they did this without the benefits of United States citizenship.

When America joined the Allies in World War Two in 1941 my grandparent's generation of Native people joined the fight. Nazi Germany and Imperial Japan were ruled by men who believed in racial superiority and their armies ruthlessly slaughtered millions of people. The indigenous people of northern California recognized this danger and they fought and sacrificed to help defeat these nations. They deserve to be recognized whether they saw combat or not. They deserve to be included in the history of "The Good War" and they deserve to be seen as a part of "The Greatest Generation."

Why did they serve? After their families survived such heinous policies of death and cultural destruction, why would this generation choose to serve in the United States military? Why would they do such an unbelievable thing as to fight on continents thousands of miles away for American democracy when it often didn't apply to them? These questions and more led me through seven years of searching among my people and my neighbors.

They deserve to be included in the history of "The Good War" and they deserve to be seen as a part of "The Greatest Generation."

These interviews are only a small part of the life experiences of these people and their cultures. They do not represent the entire history of the people, families and tribes featured. They only represent what each person chose to share at that particular moment in time. Many of these veterans were sharing their war histories for the first time, and several have passed away since we spoke. I deliberately used the terms "Native," "Indian," "Native American" and "Indigenous" as common definitions for these veterans and their cultures throughout this book.

I only included information on events and places that these men and women encountered during their part of the war. This book does not encompass the entire conflict. It is safe to state that Native people from tribes throughout the United States were present from the beginning to the end of the war, and much more work needs to be done to help bring those histories to light.

I would like to thank the Susanville Indian Rancheria, the Yurok Tribe, the Bear River Band at Rohnerville Rancheria, the Morongo Band of Mission Indians, the Smith River Rancheria, the Elk Valley Rancheria, the Table Bluff Reservation-Wiyot Tribe, the Tyme Maidu Tribe and the Mooretown Rancheria for supporting this book about our veterans. Thank you to Libby Maynard and the board of the Ink People Center for the Arts. Thank you to my friend Peter Pennekamp and to the Humboldt Area Foundation for supporting this book. I am very appreciative of my good friend Bill Merkle for all those discussions we had over the years about a war we never experienced.

Special thanks to Jeanne Riecke, Ruth McCardie,

Dewey Myers, Hank Crutcher, Leif Hillman, Melody George, Wes Crawford, Joanne Scott, Dion Wood, Virginia Aguilar, Gene Brundin, Marlette Grant Jackson, Gina Campbell, Hearldine Campbell, Charlene Storr, Dena Magdaleno, Christine Law, Mary Jane Risling, Fawn White, Cathy Dowd, Seth Martin, Stacey Canez, Shirley Weaverling, Sherri O'Rourke, Roberta Lindgren and Diana Ferris for their help in providing contacts, research and photographs. Any mistakes in this book are my own.

I found a lot of pride within these Native people; pride of America, our flag, the Statue of Liberty and our freedom.

I located as many Native veterans as possible and am indebted to their family members who helped me so much. My grandparents truly showed me the way throughout this endeavor. Many veterans chose to speak with me because they knew either my late grandfather Stan Lowry or they knew my late grandmother Evelina Hoffman on my mother's side.

Thank you to my father Ike Lowry and to my mother Sandra Hoffman Lowry for your enthusiastic support of this work. There were many times when you kept me going through this journey. I am proud to say I am your son. Thank you to my father-in-law Leonard Haff for helping edit my manuscript. As a father, a grandfather, a teacher and a Marine you make your family proud. I would also like to thank all of my family and friends who listened to me and responded to endless questions about veterans.

My most special thanks and love go to my wife Rebecca for always encouraging me during this amazing project. You enabled me to finish this book.

I found a lot of pride within these Native people; pride of America, our flag, the Statue of Liberty and our freedom. I also found pride of Native religion, heritage and family. I heard some amazing oral histories and stories filled with courage, heroism, sacrifice, honor, pain and death.

I hope you will appreciate this unique glimpse into the lives of men and women who are truly special. I thank them for their willingness to share, their abilities to forgive and their hope in future generations.

Stanley Lowry ca. 1943-4.
Photo courtesy of Ike Lowry.

Leonard Lowry in 1946.
Photo courtesy of Virginia Aguilar.

The California Gold Rush and Indian Boarding Schools

That a war of extermination will continue to be waged between the races, until the Indian race becomes extinct, must be expected.

California's first Governor Peter H. Burnett, January 7, 1851

The national myth taught in American schools and accepted by many is that the California Gold Rush was a grand exodus of peaceful people looking to find gold and strike it rich. The reality is that many of the miners who invaded California from the years 1848 to 1880 were vicious, greedy men who slaughtered thousands, possibly tens of thousands, of Native people. Northern California in particular was one of the last lawless places in the country where murder could take place on a large scale.

Few women accompanied these miners; they raped many Native women throughout the state.[1] After the first few years of the Gold Rush, miners were often employed by big companies and they used water cannons that literally tore down mountains and washed tons of silt into riverbeds and creeks to find nuggets. They destroyed Indian cemeteries, sacred sites and villages while looking for gold. They used tons of mercury in sluice-boxes to find gold then dumped the toxins wherever they wanted. This mercury lies at the bottom of many of California's lakes and in the San Francisco Bay right now.[2]

The "Indian War" in California is a lie. There were no "wars" between the settlers and Indians. A war can be defined as armed hostilities between nations. A war involves armies with soldiers and weapons. It involves formal declarations by nations stating their cause. What happened in early California was not a military war; it was ethnic cleansing at its worst.

White settlers and militias often waited until Native people were conducting a ceremony, when they were all together in one place and had no weapons, then they descended upon them massacring babies, women, children, old people and adults. They often struck at night because they were cowards. These scenes were repeated throughout northern California under the blanket of federal and state policies.

"The Indian problem" was discussed by several prominent California leaders at a state constitutional convention in September of 1849 at Monterey. [3] Among those present were men such as John Bidwell, Mariano Guadalupe Vallejo, Elam Brown and John Sutter along with over 40 other delegates from throughout the state. Many of these delegates were born in different parts of the country and they were lawyers, farmers, merchants, bankers, military officers and printers. [4]

The first California Legislative session was held in March of 1850, and most of these same men now participated as State Senators and Assemblymen. An act titled Senate Bill 54, *An Act Relative to the Protection, Punishment, and Government of Indians* was introduced by Senator Bidwell on March 16. It was tabled on March 30. [5]

On April 13, 1850 Assemblyman Brown introduced Assembly Bill 129, *An Act for the Government and Protection of Indians.* The Legislature passed the bill on April 19 after lowering the number of whip lashes Indians would receive for punishment from 100 to 25. The Governor signed it into law on April 22, 1850 just four months before California became the 31st state in the Union.[6]

What happened in early California was not a military war; it was ethnic cleansing at its worst.

This act allowed thousands of Native people to be bought and sold as slaves from 1850 on. Many were sold to vineyards and wealthy landowners for cheap labor in California's Central Valley and elsewhere. In northern California boys sold for $50 apiece and girls sold for up to $100 apiece.[7] The Civil War erupted in 1861. When the Civil War ended in 1865 Native people were still being used as "indentured servants."[8] An estimated 10,000 Native people may have been indentured or sold between 1850 and 1863.[9] *An Act for the Government and Protection of Indians* was not completely repealed until 1937.[10]

White men often stole young Native girls and forced them to become their wives. With no knowledge of English and no way to contact their families, many of these young Native women had to stay "married" and make the best of their situation.[11]

The highly informative report titled *Early California Laws and Policies Related to California Indians* was compiled and written by Kimberly Johnston-Dodds and published by the California Research Bureau in September of 2002. It contains the specifics of *The Act for the Government and Protection of Indians,* along with information about other statutes and legislation passed regarding California's indigenous people.

The report also lists the amount of money appropriated and paid out by the state of California for the murders of Native people in each county. This report, located online at www.library.ca.gov, also lists the amount of money the United States Congress appropriated and paid for the murders of Native people in California's counties. Bounty hunters in every county could bring in a human head, hands, "redskins" or other body part to local court houses and claim bounties ranging from 50 cents to five dollars per dead Indian person.

In 1855 alone California and the Federal government paid over $60,000 to Humboldt and Klamath counties for "expeditions" against Native people.[12] This was just for two counties in the entire state. Newspapers from the time did not hide their contempt for indigenous people; editors often called for complete extermination of Native cultures. They did try to hide the truth behind these massacres and murders by calling them "skirmishes," "raids" and "battles."

They also followed the pattern established since the first colonies were formed back East; they dehumanized indigenous people by calling them racist names such as "heathens," "diggers," "savages," "brutes," "squaws," "braves," and "redskins." Researchers can locate these papers on microfilm at universities such as Humboldt State and historical societies throughout California. One of the few times a massacre was written about and questioned was in the spring of 1860.

In the 1860s and 1870s the U.S. Army created a fort system throughout the state and many served as concentration camps for Native people.

The writer was Bret Harte. He wrote about the massacre of Wiyot babies, women and elders during a religious ceremony held on an island near Eureka, California. The people who did this in the dead of night were members of Eureka society. This article was wired to San Francisco and eventually reached the papers in New York. The New York Tribune and the New York Times featured the story on March 26, 1860. Many citizens in the U.S. were outraged when they found out. Bret Harte soon left northern California fearing for his life.[13]

This is but one example that the massacres in California were deliberately kept secret from the general public by creating the fake "Indian War" illusion. Although newspaper editors called for the genocide, and they happily reported when militias and soldiers destroyed Native villages and people, no photographic evidence exists (to my knowledge) of any of these atrocities.

Why not? Because the perpetrators in California wanted to hide what they did from the rest of the country. Putting a photograph of dead Indians alongside a story would humanize the subject. How could they lie about a picture of dead children and women? Writing about "dangerous savages on the warpath" created a different mental image in the minds of readers. The written word is not infallible. It can be manipulated to create a false history, or at least a distorted history. And this is what has happened to the written history of early California.

In the 1860s and 1870s the U.S. Army created a fort system throughout the state and many served as con-

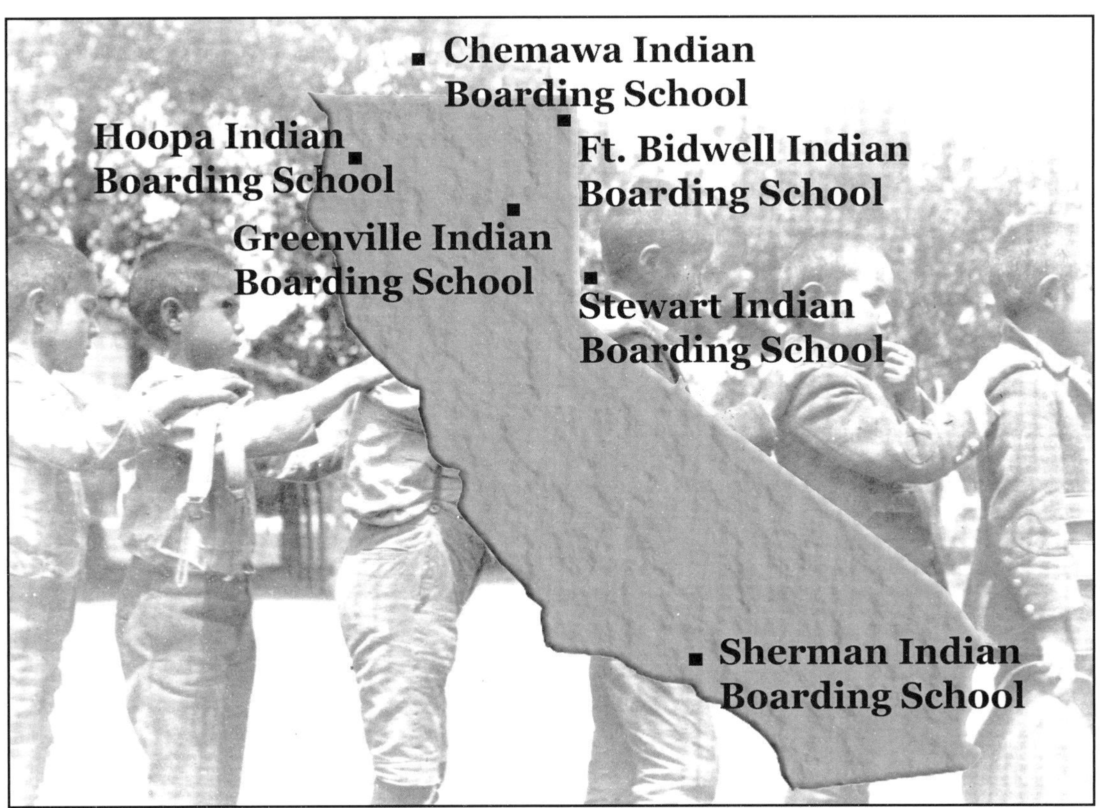

Indian Bording Schools of California.
Map researched by Chag Lowry.

centration camps for Native people. The term concentration camp is not used here lightly. Hundreds, perhaps thousands, of Native people died at camps such as Fort Humboldt in Humboldt County, Fort Ter-Wer in Del Norte County, Fort Jones in Siskyiou County, Fort Wright and Fort Bragg in Mendocino County, and Fort Reading in Shasta County.

Native survivors of massacres were often taken to these camps and forced to stay in squalid areas with little food or water. They were shot if they tried to escape and many Native women were raped at these places by soldiers. Hundreds of Native people also died while being force-marched, often in chains, from fort to fort under the orders of U.S. soldiers. Some Native people and communities resisted these attacks. They did fight back when they could. There are oral histories of this resistance among our Native people, but these histories are few in number.

The genocide and terrorism of this time is unparalleled in American history. It is also unacknowledged in most history books, documentaries and movies. California's Native people know this history. We whisper it among each other in our homes and say silent prayers at ceremonies for what was lost. Only in the last 25 years have people such as Jack Norton, Cliff Trafzer, Robert Heizer, Joel Hyer, Byron Nelson, Protap Chaterjee, and Robert and Jeannette Costo written books to document this tragedy.

In early 1851 three federal Indian commissioners traveled among California's indigenous people supposedly offering treaties of peace. A total of 18 treaties were signed by several Native communities and the commissioners which promised Native people large tracts of land for reservations, provisions, and security in return for their acknowledgement of United States territorial rights over much of the state.[14]

A total of over 7,400,000 acres were to be contained within these reservations under these treaties, which would have accounted for over seven percent of the state of California. In June of 1852 the United States Senate held a secret session and rejected the treaties because of pressure from California's state representatives.[15] The Senate's actions remained secret until 1905. California's indigenous people were never informed of this deception. Those few that did know of the treaties were most likely murdered in subsequent years by militias or settlers.

Despite all of this death, deceit, and destruction, by the 1890s there were still areas where indigenous people, perhaps a few thousand in total, struggled to continue their ways of life. Many of these places were in northern California. Native people still spoke their languages, created baskets and regalia and still held their ceremonies when they could. But this way of life was still considered a threat to California and the United States. It needed to be completely eradicated.

A cheaper, less contentious way to exterminate these Native cultures was soon discovered. It cost too much money for the U.S. Army and militias to keep hunting down and killing Indians in remote areas and national opinion was finally turning against the physical destruction of Native people. People in cities started writing letters to newspapers denouncing this practice.

Native people in the U.S. did not have United States citizenship rights until 1924.

So government agents and social workers began stealing and forcing Indian children to attend boarding schools far from their indigenous homelands. Schools such as these were now being used with success throughout the country. Within one or two generations indigenous knowledge would be eliminated through forced education and the Natives themselves would be assimilated into American society. This would be the final solution to the national Indian problem.

Indian Boarding Schools

The subject of Indian boarding schools is a wide-ranging topic that warrants more research and dialogue among Native people, scholars, educators and the general public. These places are better named as re-educa-

The author's great-grandmother Edna Evans Lowry poses with her cousins Oliver Evans (in middle) and his brother Willis Evans at the Stewart Indian Boarding School in 1904. Oliver later fought in World War One and his photo is featured on page 19.
Photo courtesy of Virginia Aguilar

Native boys dressed as soldiers holding wooden guns as part of a military exercise at the Hoopa Valley Indian Boarding School in 1904.
Photo courtesy of Chag Lowry.

tion centers, as this was their intent. For the purposes of this book, I will alternate this term with the commonly known term of Indian boarding schools.

The first off-reservation boarding school for Indians was located in Carlisle, Pennsylvania. In 1879 former U.S. Army officer Richard Henry Pratt founded the Carlisle Indian School in an old Army barracks with the motto of "Kill the Indian and save the man." The goal was to forcibly assimilate Native children into white society.[1] Dozens of other Indian boarding schools based on military-style regimentation were established throughout the country during the 1880s and 1890s. They were often housed in old military barracks. There were eventually over 300 of these schools in the country.

This re-education system represented cultural genocide against Native societies; generations of young Native children had to attend these schools and traditional knowledge was rapidly lost. Canada also had residential schools for indigenous children that were very similar to the American model and Australia had a boarding school system for Aborigine children.

Young girls in dress uniforms at the Hoopa Valley Indian Boarding School ca. 1922-3.
Photo courtesy of the Indian Action Council.

In virtually all cases, the parents could do nothing as their children were forcibly taken away. Native people in the U.S. did not have United States citizenship rights until 1924. They could not represent themselves in a legal courtroom to stop their children from being taken. Children as young as four and as old as 18 were made to attend schools in America that were often located hundreds of miles away from their families.

They were punished for speaking their language, denied their religion, forced to cut their hair and had to wear uniforms. The wearing of uniforms and dresses at these boarding schools is particularly insidious. These uniforms and dresses represented the death of one's old identity and the assimilation into a new one. This new identity was based on self-hate, self-doubt, confusion, fear and terror.

The clothes, which represented an alien culture and felt so different, were literally on the skin of these kids every day. It inhibited their movements and forced them to lose their individual personas. These children were the future mothers, fathers, doctors, craftsmen, basket weavers, mid-wives, scientists, astrologists, fishermen, singers, traditional dancers, botanists, hunters, teachers, storytellers, sport heroes and medicine people for their respective cultures. The clothes denied these identities.

Hundreds, perhaps thousands of children died at these schools due to disease, malnutrition, physical and sexual abuse, torture and neglect. Kids sometimes went for years at a time with no visits allowed by family members. Siblings were often split up and attended different sites.

Many young people died of broken hearts at these places. Although cemeteries were created at some schools, there are few written records of exactly how many children died while in the boarding school system. There are also no memorials for these children at the sites of most of these centers.

Students at the schools were taught a variety of vocational skills based on the racist notion that Indians could not excel at higher education. It also filled the need for cheap labor at nearby farms, ranches, and vineyards, and for white homeowners who wanted servants. Boys were taught ranching, farming, painting and other labor-intensive skills. Girls were taught sewing, cooking, house cleaning and other domestic skills.[2]

The men and women who taught at these places were not teachers and administrators as we view them today. Many were racist and had no compunctions about beating their students until they stopped speaking their Native language and stopped "acting Indian." It is also unclear how much sexual abuse occurred at these places.

Young boys in uniforms at the Hoopa Valley Indian Boarding School in 1924. They are from different tribes and cultures throughout northern California.
Photo courtesy of the Indian Action Council.

Toward the 1920s and 1930s the boarding school system slowly evolved. Conditions at the schools were less harsh due to public pressure against the appalling conditions at several sites. Native children could make the choice if they wanted to attend boarding schools. Despite the disturbing history of these places they were still the only educational option available to Native people at the time so many children attended.

The involvement of Native men in the U.S. Army during World War One also helped force some changes in American policy toward Native education and Native citizenship. Some Native people were even hired to teach and administer at these schools during the 1930s.

Many indigenous kids chose to attend the boarding schools during the Depression because of unemployment on reservations. Their families could not afford to house or feed them. California's boarding schools stopped issuing military-style uniforms around 1935. The men and women featured in this book attended during this time of transition in the Indian boarding school system. Some of these schools still exist today although they are radically different in scope and intent.

Much of the knowledge about Indian boarding schools in California is contained in the memories of people in their 70s, 80s, and 90s. As I conducted my interviews among Native veterans I was struck by how many attended at least one of these re-education centers. Did the wearing of uniforms and the military-style structure of the boarding schools contribute to their decision to join the military? This certainly wasn't the intent behind the creation of the schools, but was it a factor?

Here in California there were six Indian boarding schools where children and teens were sent prior to World War Two:

The Hoopa Indian boarding school opened in 1893 on the Hoopa Reservation. It was located on the site of Fort Gaston. Fort Gaston was established in 1859 as a military concentration camp for Indian people from throughout northern California.[3] Gold miners and white settlers wanted land claims and demanded that Indians be exterminated. Survivors of massacres were force marched and detained at Fort Gaston. Countless Indian women were raped at the fort. Fort Gaston was closed in 1892. The Hoopa boarding school made the transition into a regular high school sometime in the 1930s. Today, the Hoopa High and Elementary schools both sit near where Fort Gaston and the Hoopa boarding school once existed.

The first Indian boarding school in southern California was established in Perris, California in 1892. By the fall of 1902 the site was changed to Riverside, California and the Sherman Institute, also known as the Sherman Indian Boarding School, was created.[4] In 1942 the Sherman Indian Boarding School dedicated their high school annual to the United States war effort. The Sherman Indian School still exists today as one of the oldest operating Indian boarding schools.

Boys standing in line as punishment at the Hoopa Valley Indian Boarding School in 1924.
Photo courtesy of the Indian Action Council.

Greenville Indian Boarding School in 1924.
Photo courtesy of David Schafer.

Fort Bidwell was a military post established near the present day town of Alturas in northeastern California in 1863 or 1864. The post was closed in 1893 and the Fort Bidwell Indian boarding school was created using the old military barracks as student dormitories. Indian children from northeastern California attended this little-known boarding school that was located on the Fort Bidwell Indian Reservation. The school was shut down in 1930 and the barracks were destroyed.[5]

The Greenville Indian boarding school was built in 1898 and was used from 1900 to 1930 as a boarding school for Native children from the local area. The author's great-grandparents Robert and Edna Lowry met each other at this boarding school.

The Indian Training School was established in 1880 near the present day city of Salem, Oregon. It was renamed the Chemawa Indian School in 1885 after moving to a different location. In 1927 it became an accredited four-year high school. Over the years hundreds of Native youth from tribes in Washington, Oregon, Alaska, New Mexico, Idaho, Montana, Arizona and California have all attended and graduated. The Chemawa Indian School still exists today as the oldest continuously operated Indian boarding school in the country. It is run by the Bureau of Indian Affairs (BIA).[6]

The Stewart Indian boarding school was located near Carson City, Nevada. It was opened in 1890. Native students from California, Nevada, New Mexico, Arizona, Idaho, Oregon and other states attended over the years. Stewart, like the rest of the Indian boarding schools, was known for fielding very competitive sports teams throughout its existence. It was permanently closed in 1980 after BIA funding was cut.[7]

The Stewart Indian School's band in 1953-4.
Photo courtesy of Ned and Wilma Crutcher.

The author's grandfather Stanley Lowry (at right) stands with William B. Meyers at the Sherman Indian Boarding School in 1928.
Photo courtesy of Ike Lowry.

Indian Training School in Chemawa, Oregon.
Photo courtesy of the Pacific University Archives, Harvey W. Scott Memorial Library.

Reservations and Political Definitions

In California there are Reservations and there are Rancherias. A Reservation is land held in trust status by the United States federal government for the use, possession and benefit of a federally recognized tribe.[1] In California a Rancheria is land held in trust by the United States federal government for the use, possession and benefit of California indigenous Native Americans who comprise a federally recognized group. By 1930 over 30 Rancherias had been established in California through acts of Congress.[2] The term Rancheria is derived from the Spanish word ranchero, which means a small collection of dwellings or temporary rural settlements.

The main practical difference between a Reservation and a Rancheria is that on a Rancheria you will often find members of different cultural groups who must work together as one political entity. It can happen that only one cultural group of people may reside on a Rancheria. On a Reservation you will most likely find members of one cultural group who must work together as one political entity.

Both Rancherias and Reservations have sovereign status as nations and both work on a government-to-government basis with the United States. This tribal sovereignty has rarely been respected by the United States either politically or socially. Reservations and Rancherias in northern California can have a tribal council usually comprised of seven elected tribal members. These council members can represent their constituents while meeting with the United States Congress. They may also conduct local business and have unique responsibilities as a political entity.

A Native person who does not live on their federally recognized Reservation or Rancheria still has the same inherent sovereign rights as those who live on them. These inherent rights can include the right to vote in tribal elections, access to health care, quality education, affordable housing, access to fishing and hunting lands and other rights. A tribal council is supposed to protect their member's interests at all times when making local decisions and while dealing with the U.S. government, although this does not always happen.

It is important to note that these are inherent rights; these are not rights bestowed upon Native people by the United States government. These rights have been maintained through the treaty process between Native tribes and the United States and upheld numerous times in the United States judicial system.[3]

There are many Native people in northern California who are members of cultural groups with no political recognition by the United States government. This means they lack a political process in which to protect their inherent rights. Several of these groups are attempting to gain or regain their federal trust status as tribes but this process can take many years and isn't always successful.

Native Americans have a unique status among all American citizens. Our sovereign rights can be easily misunderstood and sometimes even feared. What must be remembered is that Native veterans who served in World War One and World War Two fought and helped preserve the sovereign United States and they helped preserve the sovereignty of their own people.

Native Americans have a unique status among all American citizens. Our sovereign rights can be easily misunderstood and sometimes even feared.

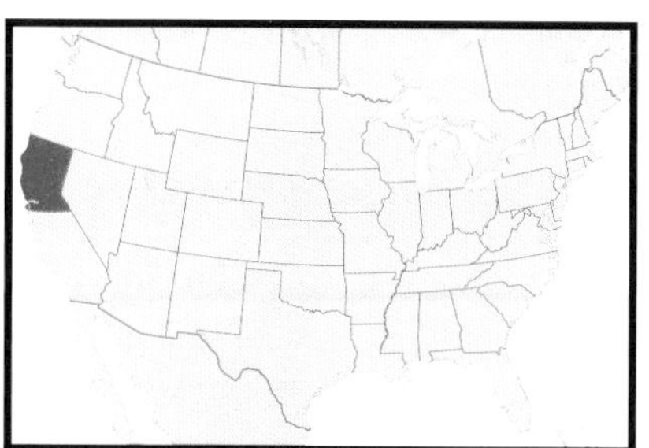

Map of United States with northern California highlighted in red.

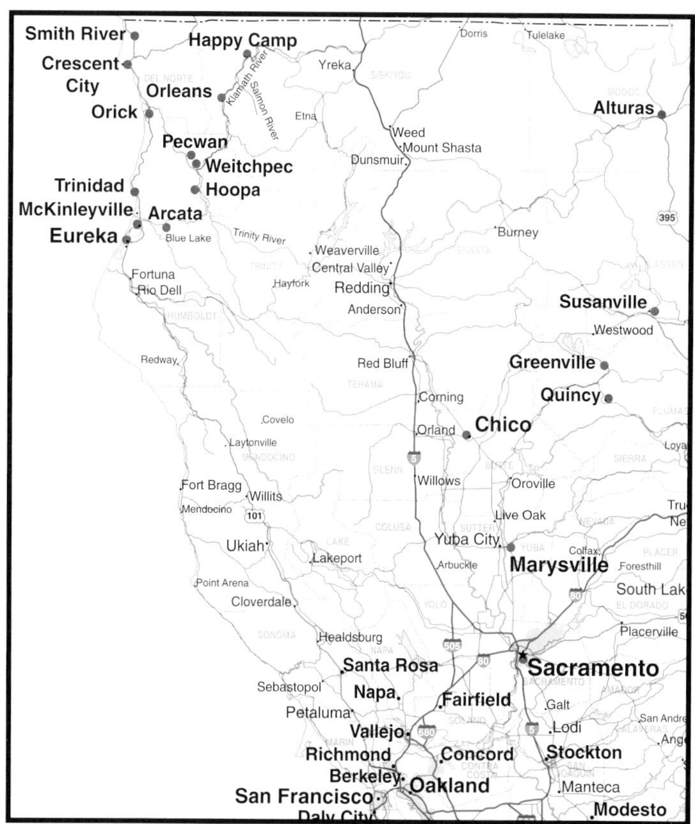

Map of northern California hometowns of veterans featured in this book.

World War One

World War One occurred from 1914 to 1918. It was fought in Western and Eastern Europe, the Middle East, on the Mediterranean Sea and on the Atlantic Ocean. Many countries took part on the side of either the Allies or the side of the Central Powers.

Britain, France, Italy, and Russia were among the nations that helped comprise the Allies. Germany, Austria-Hungary, and Turkey were known as the Central Powers. During the course of the war there were many other countries such as Japan, Italy, Romania and Bulgaria that took part on either side of this terrible conflict.

Barry Phillips (Yurok) in 1917-18.
Photo courtesy of Barry's sister Dee Rouse.

Why did the war start in the first place? The assassination of Archduke Franz Ferdinand on June 28, 1914 provided the spark. Ferdinand was the heir to the throne of Austria-Hungary. He and his wife Sophie were killed in the city of Sarajevo by a young Serbian man named Gavrilo Princip.[1]

Princip had wanted to kill the Archduke for some time, and he was guided by a group of people who wanted to combine Serbia with other Baltic states to create a Slavonic nation. The killings caused Austria-Hungary, with Germany's backing, to try to punish the state of Serbia. Serbia received the backing of Russia, and this caused a chain reaction among European countries to pledge support for either the Allied side or the Central Powers side. Each alliance had to save face and continued to threaten each other while mobilizing their military forces.[2]

The war rhetoric heightened until Germany invaded Belgium, France, and Luxembourg on August 3, 1914. Then the Great War began. During the four years of this conflagration over 8 million soldiers and sailors died and over 20 million were wounded. There were over six-and-a half million civilian deaths due to this war. These numbers are debated estimates.

The United States did not participate in World War One until the spring of 1917. President Woodrow Wilson had pledged to stay neutral during this "European conflict," and many Americans agreed with him. In 1915 Wilson was occupied by events in Mexico. Francisco "Pancho" Villa, a Mexican revolutionary, had begun to conduct guerrilla raids into New Mexico in which several Americans were killed.

John Lopez (Tolowa) served in the U.S. Navy during World War One.
Photo courtesy of Frank Richards.

Wilson had supported another revolutionary, Venustiano Carranza, as the president of Mexico, and Villa did not like this action. After the raids Wilson created the famous "Punitive Expedition" that was directed against Villa and his followers. This expedition was comprised of U.S. Army soldiers and was commanded by General John Pershing with the goal of capturing Villa.

Pershing's soldiers pushed deep into Mexico in pursuit of Villa but never captured him. Among Pershing's soldiers was George Patton, who would later become a famous American general in World War Two. Distrust between the U.S. and Mexico was heightened due to this incursion.

During the early years of World War One American banks and firms continued to loan millions of dollars to both the Allies and the Central Powers, although much more was loaned to the Allies. In order to keep doing business with the Allies America needed to be able to use the seas for merchant shipping. During most of the war Germany followed a policy of unlimited submarine warfare that resulted in the sinking of several ships that carried American citizens. This greatly angered the United States but Wilson still didn't declare war.[3]

Andrew James (Yurok) in 1917-18.
Photo courtesy of Jimmy James.

In January of 1917 Germany's Foreign Minister Alfred

Zimmermann sent a secret telegram to the German Minister in Mexico. It contained instructions for the minister to propose a Mexican-German alliance and a Mexican declaration of war against the United States. This would then occupy the United States with a threat from the south and turn their attention away from the European conflict. [4]

Bert Numan (Paiute) in 1917-18.
Photo courtesy of Vernon Numan.

The Carranza government in Mexico was not receptive to the telegram's proposals, and the British government intercepted the telegram and gave it to President Wilson. Wilson released the telegram to the American public in March of 1917. On April 2, 1917, Wilson went before Congress to ask for a declaration of war on Germany. Congress voted to authorize war on April 6, 1917, officially drawing the U.S. into the fight on the Allied side.[5]

In the early stages of the conflict in 1914 neither side could attain a decisive victory, so a line of trenches were built in the Western battlegrounds in France. The fighting bogged down into a series of battles in which tens of thousands of young men died for a few hundred yards of territory at a time. The armies on both sides were not trained for this type of trench-warfare.

Frederick Riecke (Yurok) in 1917-18.
Photo courtesy of Jeanne Riecke.

The trenches these young men had to live in were filthy, disgusting, disease-riddled burrows. Soldiers died by the thousands because of diseases such as typhus. New weapons of war were now used and the men had to face screaming artillery shells, machine gun fire and poison gas attacks. The soldiers died and were wounded in droves. By the time the U.S. entered the war both the Allies and the Central Powers were in dire straights. Each side had lost almost an entire generation of their men in the fighting.

On May 18, 1917 Congress passed the Selective Service Act.[6] Over the next two years almost three million men were drafted for service in the Great War. Among these were over 6,000 Native Americans from tribes throughout the country.

Irving Numan (Paiute) in 1918.
Photo courtesy of Vernon Numan.

Thousands more voluntarily enlisted for military service during the war. An estimated total of almost 13,000 Native American men served in the military during the war. Various estimates state that 20-to-30% of the known total adult male Native American population served in the war.[7] These men were integrated with white soldiers in training camps, unlike African-American soldiers who were segregated. Several dozen Native men from the Mountain Maidu, Yurok, Karuk, Hupa, Paiute, Wiyot, and Pit River cultures of northern California served in the military and in combat.

Indian men went to training camps all over the country and were generally accepted by non-Native soldiers. In fact, many soldiers believed in the stereotype of the "Indian Warrior," and Native men were supposed to have extraordinary fighting abilities due to their Indian ancestry. Officers wanted Indian soldiers because they believed they would be more blood-thirsty in battle.[8]

The "Stoic Indian" stereotype was also common; Indian soldiers would be able to withstand the horrors of trench-warfare better because they wouldn't have any emotional response to the fighting. These stereotypes were perpetuated in books about the American West that were popular at the time.

Lewis Sanderson, Sr. (Yurok) in a studio photograph taken in France in 1918. Lewis saw action in the battle at St. Mihiel. Four of his sons served in World War Two. His son Kenny Sanderson is featured on page 204.
Photo courtesy of Alverna LaFranche.

When the American Expeditionary Force (AEF), commanded by John Pershing reached France in 1917 there were Native Americans among those first Army units. Native Americans fought in every major battle until the end of the war. Native men served in some of the most dangerous areas of the fighting as scouts, snipers and messengers. Many Indian men from different tribes were highly decorated by both the United States and by France for bravery in combat and for carrying important messages under heavy fire to headquarters.

George Roberts (Tolowa) in 1918. George also served in the Army in World War Two. He and Gus Brundin are brothers.
Photo courtesy of Gene Brundin.

Native men fought in battles at Chateau-Thierry, in the Aisne-Marne offensive, in the St. Mihiel offensive, in the Argonne Forest during the Meuse-Argonne offensive, and in countless other unnamed places all along the Western Front. Native Americans served in the United States Navy during the war and there were also Native American supply clerks, cooks, truck drivers, and medics.[9]

Toward the end of the war several Native soldiers of Choctaw ancestry used their indigenous language while relaying battle commands over telephones lines. They did not use a code, but their German enemy could not decipher the messages. Other Native soldiers from the Cheyenne, the Sioux, Osage, Comanche and possibly other tribes also spoke in their native languages to relay vital battlefield information during the last two months of the conflict. This method of transmitting messages was of invaluable benefit to American units.[10]

Norman "Happy" Gorbet (Maidu) and August "Gus" Brundin in 1918 in France. They were related by marriage and lived in Crescent City.
Photo courtesy of Gene Brundin.

Native American men contributed mightily to the Allied victory over the Central Powers. When the final armistice was signed with Germany on November 11, 1918 Native soldiers took part in the celebrations. There were many who did not live to see this day. An estimated five percent of all Native servicemen died in action during the war, higher than the one percent rate for the entire AEF.[11]

"Gus" Brundin (at left) with two American soldiers and one French soldier (second from right) in France during World War One.
Photo courtesy of Gene Brundin.

What was accomplished by the Great War? Millions of soldiers, sailors, airmen and Marines lost their lives on both sides. Millions more were wounded. Millions of civilians were killed, wounded, and displaced. Most of the countries involved earned little in terms of social, military or economic gains. At the end of the war the victorious Allies punished Germany with harsh terms in the Treaty of Versailles. Germany had to give up territory and disassemble much of their military apparatus. They also owed the Allies a huge amount of money and supplies.

Robert Spott (Yurok) served as a message courier for the Army in France. This was a very dangerous assignment as messengers were specially targeted by German snipers. He earned a Croix De Guerre, which is the French government's highest honor for bravery in combat. It is hanging right below his portrait in this photo.
Photo: Del Norte Historical Society

Germany's civilian population believed that their Army was close to winning the war when it ended. When the Treaty of Versailles was announced there was immediate confusion, anger and resentment in Germany.

The myth of the infamous "stab in the back" by civilian Treaty negotiators began to circulate, and this helped lay the foundation for World War Two.

The most astonishing fact regarding Native American participation in World War One is they were not American citizens. Native Americans were not given United States citizenship until 1924, six years after the war ended.

Grover Knudsen (Yurok/Karuk) in a studio portrait in France ca. 1917-18. Photo courtesy of Gene Brundin.

In his excellent book *American Indians in World War I: At Home and At War* Thomas Britten describes the confusion many local draft boards had when confronted with Native men who wanted to enlist in 1917. Were they eligible to join? Many Native American men were drafted and went into the service even though they knew they weren't American citizens.

Although Britten points out that several thousand Native people were given citizenship prior to 1924 through such legislation as the Dawes Act of 1897 or through intermarriage between a Native woman and a non-Native citizen, the majority of the people in the United States did not consider Native Americans as citizens.

The majority of the citizenry in the United States at this time still considered Native people as less intelligent, less cultured and less human than white people. So this legislation was practically ignored and did not confer "citizenship" upon indigenous people. Natives at this time didn't consider themselves as full citizens either, not while white people were still stealing their lands, their children and their cultural knowledge under the various guises of archeology, anthropology and education in full view of the general public.

At the time the Dawes Act was passed in 1897 Native people still had communal ownership and ties to millions of acres of land throughout the country. This legislation was designed to end those communal ties. The main force behind this act was a woman named Alice Fletcher. She was a Harvard-trained archeologist who believed that Native people could never become "civilized" if they were allowed to live on communally-owned reservations or lands.[12]

Brothers Grover (at left) and Walter Knudsen pose with their niece Edna. Photo courtesy of Gene Brundin.

The Dawes Act was designed to break up reservation lands into individually owned 80-acre allotments or 160-acre family-owned allotments. Native people under the age of 18 received 40-acre allotments.[13] Fletcher and others believed that Indian people could only evolve if they learned how to individually own land and learn to farm on it.[14] After all the allotments on a reservation were handed out there would be millions of acres of surplus land. This surplus land was then stolen by unscrupulous land sharks and businessmen. Plus, Indian people now had to pay taxes on allotment land they had always lived on.

Oliver Evans (Pit River/Shoshone) in 1917. Photo courtesy of Virginia Aguilar.

Many did not understand the tax system and had their allotments taken away in lieu of taxes by corrupt state surveyors. The allotment system lasted until 1934. From 1887 to 1934 Native people lost over 86 million acres of land in America. Two-thirds of the allotted land now belonged to white people.[15] This deception and fraud is what returning Native American World War One veterans faced as they came home.

In 1924 the United States Congress finally passed the Indian Citizenship Act as a blanket measure that gave all Native Americans citizenship rights. This act did not convey white acceptance of Native religions, cultures or people but it was a step in the right direction toward that elusive equality which Native people still fight for today. Even after the end of World War Two states such as Arizona, Utah and New Mexico denied Native people the right to vote clear into the 1950s.

They lost oral histories, ceremonial songs, traditional healers, medicinal knowledge, native languages, family histories, fathers, sons, brothers, uncles, nephews and friends.

When an indigenous person died in combat in France during World War One their tribal community lost a great deal. They lost oral histories, ceremonial songs, traditional healers, medicinal knowledge, native languages, family histories, fathers, sons, brothers, uncles, nephews and friends. These Native communities lost potential social, political and cultural leaders.

Many Native people returned home scarred emotionally, mentally and physically from this war. They were never the same. This was the sacrifice that Indian people gave for the United States of America during World War One. The question remains why Native men from small villages in northern California chose to sacrifice their time, their energy and in many cases their lives for a war fought on a continent thousands of miles away. These men have long since passed away, but I was able to ask this question to many of their family members and many of their tribal members who knew them.

The answers given were all the same, "These men were patriots." Imagine that.

Thomas Reed (Yurok) in a studio photograph taken in France in 1917-18. Thomas is the author's great-great-uncle.
Photo courtesy of Patty Gibbons.

Thomas Tucker (Mountain Maidu) was the first soldier from Lassen County to die in combat in France.
Photo courtesy of Ike Lowry.

Walt McCovey, Sr.(Yurok) at right and Sergeant S. Stanton were stationed on the U.S. and Mexican border prior to World War One. Walt was shipped overseas to fight in France and was wounded in combat. On the back of this photo Walt had written "We are some soldier boys." Walt is the author's great-great-uncle.
Photo courtesy of Walt McCovey, Jr.

The Origin of World War Two

The end of World War One saw tens of thousands of German soldiers return home bitter and disillusioned. They had no education and no employment. Among these ex-soldiers was a man named Adolf Hitler. Many soldiers and citizens believed the myth that the German Army was not defeated on the battlefield, but rather they had been "stabbed in the back" on the eve of victory by corrupt German politicians. Most of these soldiers organized themselves into groups collectively known as the *Freikorps,* a type of irregular force that pitched street battles against communists and others in the 1920s and early 1930s.[1]

France and Belgium suffered tremendous losses during the war. Much of the fighting had occurred in these two countries and they faced years of rebuilding. Allied countries such as Britain and Russia lost millions of young men while fighting Germany, Austria-Hungary and Turkey. One country that had joined World War One on the Allied side was Japan. Despite this alliance Japan did not really trust the West or Russia and after the war they began to plan to build up their military forces.

The United States had lost thousands of soldiers as well but their industrial capabilities and their homeland were untouched by the war. Although President Woodrow Wilson labored hard to create the League of Nations and the Treaty of Versailles, the U.S. Senate rejected both the League and the treaty. [2] After Wilson died President Warren Harding helped foster an isolationist policy in America to keep the country out of European politics.

In 1929 the Stock Market crashed in the United States. Millions of people lost their life savings and their jobs as banks and businesses closed. Although economic conditions improved by the late 1930s there was still high unemployment until the start of World War Two in Europe. The Depression also affected the economies of countries in Europe and Asia throughout the 1920s and 30s.

Among the hardest hit was Germany. The country was struggling to pay war reparations and unemployment was rampant. In the 1920s more and more Germans began to listen to the hate-filled speeches of Adolf Hitler.

Hitler was thrown in jail in 1924 for a failed *Putsch* (revolt) against the government and it was there he dictated the book *Mein Kampf* (My Struggle). Although Hitler was Austrian by birth his message appealed to many German citizens. In this book Hitler laid out his opinions on Aryan supremacy, the need for *lebensraum* (living space) and his hate for Jews and communists.[3] Hitler only spent nine months in a comfortable cell after his failed *putsch.* He then began to attract more and more support in the next decade from Germans as well as from people in other countries throughout Europe.

In 1933 Hitler was named Chancellor of Germany. He appealed to many people in Germany as a strong leader who could restore social order. Other politicians thought they could control him once he was in power, but Hitler proved to be ruthless in using his SS men to consolidate his strength and eliminate opposition. The SS *(Schutzstuffel)* were Hitler's personal army and they were loyal to their Fuhrer to the death. The concentration camp named Dachau was opened in 1933 and guarded by the SS.[4]

In the 1920s more and more Germans began to listen to the hate-filled speeches of Adolf Hitler.

Hitler used laws such as the Enabling Act of 1933 and the Nuremburg Laws of 1935 to give himself dictatorial powers and to restrict the rights of all German citizens. The Nuremburg Laws also stripped Jews of their citizenship and denied them to right to marry Aryans. In 1934 Hitler assumed the role of President and took the title of *Fuhrer,* the absolute leader in his Third Reich.[5]

Hitler used military brinkmanship in March of 1938 to bring about the *Anschluss* (union) with Austria. In September of 1938 Hitler was able to force a conference between Britain, France, Italy and Germany in which his demands to occupy the Sudetenland region in Czechoslovakia were appeased. In November of 1938 the Nazis launched a brutal series of attacks on Jews in Germany known as *Krisstalnicht.* They murdered over 90 people, injured hundreds, burned synagogues and vandalized Jewish schools, cemeteries and businesses.[6] Although this overt action shocked the world community it was only a harbinger for Jews of the horror yet to come.

In March of 1939 German troops took control of the rest of Czechoslovakia but the rest of Europe still did not act against Hitler's aggression. Italian dictator Benito Mussolini had his fascist government sign the Pact of Steel treaty with Germany in May of 1939. Mussolini was the original fascist and he wanted to grab military glory along with Hitler. On September 1, 1939 German forces launched a *blitzkrieg* (lightning war) against Poland. France, Britain, Australia and New Zealand declared war on Germany on September 3.[7] World War Two in Europe had finally begun.

During the worldwide Depression military leaders in Japan became more powerful and in 1931 the country had invaded Manchuria. In July of 1937 Japan went to war against China and quickly gained control of much of that country's resources. One of the most heinous atrocities of World War Two occurred in the Chinese city of Nanking from December of 1938 to February of 1939 when Japanese forces occupied the city. They systematically raped at least 20,000 Chinese women and murdered as many as 300,000 Chinese people in two months. [8]

In September of 1940 Japan signed the Pact of Steel treaty with Germany that created the Axis Powers along with Italy. During this time the United States and Britain had conducted negotiations with the Japanese government in an attempt to avoid hostilities. Both sides offered proposals they knew would be rejected by the other and the U.S. and Britain imposed a crippling economic and oil embargo in response to Japan's military aggression. Hardliners in Japan lead by new Prime Minister Hideki Tojo advocated quickly going to war with America and Britain. President Franklin Roosevelt and his government had recognized the growing threat and in July of 1941 had directed General Douglas MacArthur to mobilize troops in the Philippines to prepare a defense of those islands.[9]

In September of 1940 Japan signed the Pact of Steel treaty with Germany that created the Axis Powers along with Italy.

On December 7, 1941 Japanese forces launched a surprise attack on the United States at Pearl Harbor on the Hawaiian island of Oahu. They also attacked U.S. forces on Wake Island and the Philippines on the same day. Of the 96 ships anchored at Pearl Harbor, 18 were sunk or damaged and 3,748 U.S. servicemen were killed or wounded along with 103 civilians. The United States declared war on Japan on December 8. Japan's Axis allies Germany and Italy declared war on the United States on December 11[10] World War Two was now a global conflict.

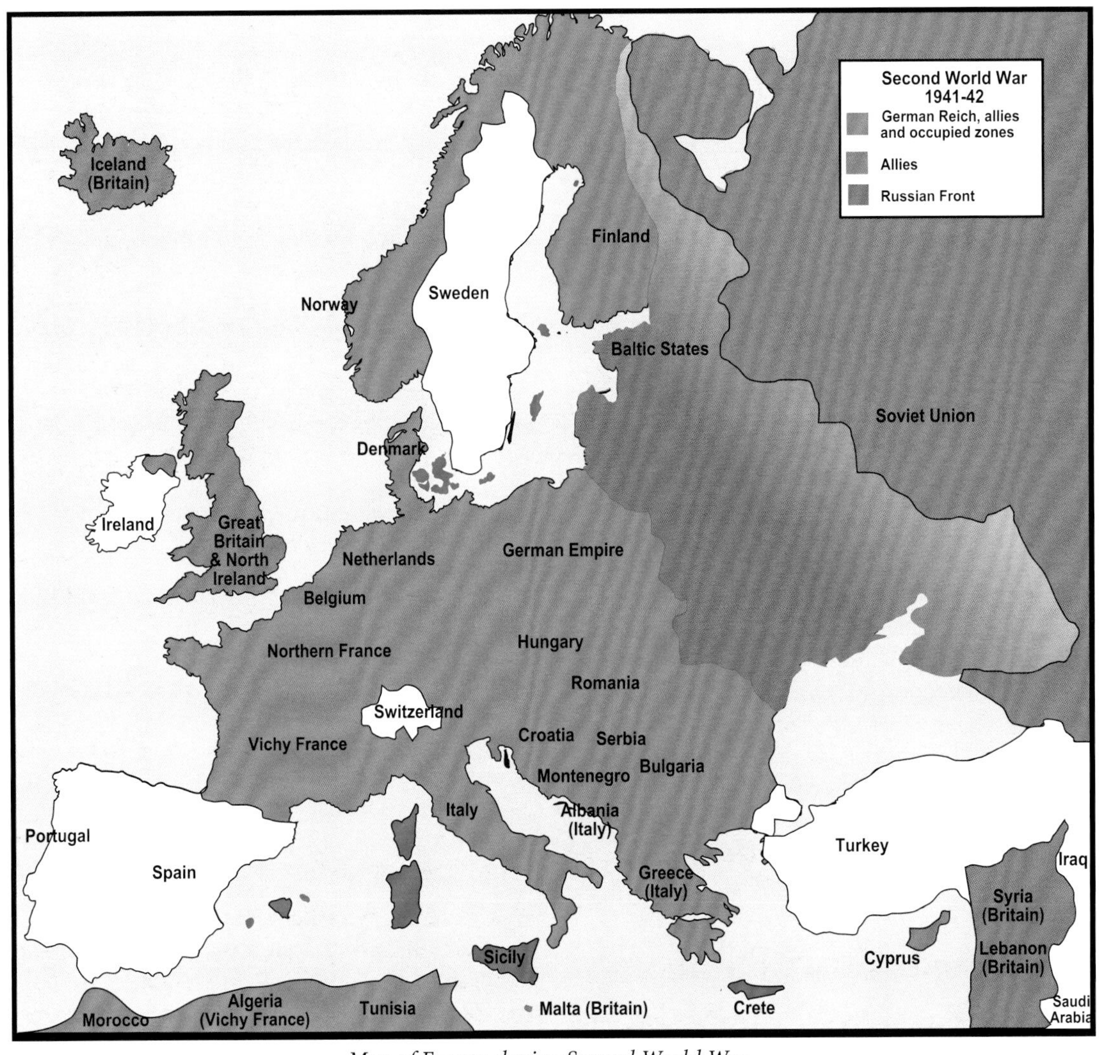

Map of Europe during Second World War.
Based on U.S. military information on wikipedia.com.

The European Theater

The Air War Over Europe

After 1942 the United States and Great Britain could field bombers with fighter escorts for a strategic bombing campaign to strike at Germany and her allies. The US Eighth Air Force used the B-17 Flying Fortress and the B-24 Liberator for bombing missions. Each of these airplanes were four-engine bombers that could reach targets throughout continental Europe. One of Germany's major mistakes of the war was not to build their own strategic four-engine bomber.[1]

Over 13,000 B-17 bombers of different variations were constructed in the United States. They could seat a crew of ten and had a range of about 2,000 miles with a top speed at just over 300 miles an hour. The B-17 could hold over 15,000 pounds of bombs and had a ceiling of 35,000 feet.[2]

The B-24 Liberator had a range of just over 3,000 miles and could carry a bomb load weighing over 13,000 pounds. The Liberator could seat a crew of ten and had a top speed at just over 300 miles an hour. It had a ceiling of 30,000 feet. More than 18,000 Liberators of different variations were built; more than any other U.S. plane.[3]

The Army Air Corps was renamed the Army Air Force in June of 1941. The Air Force was a part of the Army in World War Two and became a separate branch of the military after the war. The German *Luftwaffe* (Air Force) used the first jet fighters late in the war, among them the Messerschmitt Me-262. They did not make a strategic difference during the conflict but they helped usher in a new age of aviation technology. After the war almost every Allied country attempted to find German flight engineers who could be put to work to bolster that country's military capabilities.

Crew members such as **Neil McKinnon, Frank Richards, Sharon Wasson** and **Wally Scott,** who flew aboard the B-17 Flying Fortress and the B-24 Liberator, faced an incredibly dangerous mission every time they took to the air. They faced the threat of enemy fighters and anti-aircraft flak over thousands of miles of hostile territory while flying with huge bomb loads. If shot down and captured, crew members faced years of imprisonment in POW camps. In 1943-4 the completion rate for 25 operational missions was at 35 percent.

The Land War in Europe

On November 8, 1942 Operation Torch commenced with the landing of over 100,000 Allied soldiers on the beaches in Algeria and Morocco in North Africa.[4] The combined Anglo-American landings were designed to give American troops some experience against German forces and to open a second front against the Axis to help relieve the Soviet Union in their struggle against the Nazis. Months of fierce desert fighting occurred and ended in May of 1943 with an Allied victory.

On July 10, 1943, the US Seventh Army under Lieutenant General George Patton and the British Eighth

DAWN of
YOUR FUTURE
U. S. ARMY AIR FORCES
—Enlist Today!

Recruiting poster.
Library of Congress, Prints and Photographs Division, (LC-USZC4-3309).

Army under General Bernard Montgomery invaded Sicily in Operation Husky. More than 180,000 troops and over 2,500 ships were used in the invasion.[5] Hard fighting in the rugged Sicilian terrain ended with the Germans and Italians retreating to mainland Italy by August of 1943.

The Italian Campaign featured some of the most brutal and bloodiest fighting in the entire war. The Italian government had deposed dictator Benito Mussolini and surrendered by September of 1943 so Hitler decided to reinforce the country with more German divisions. Battle after battle ensued for months, with the German forces fighting behind formidable lines of defense such as the Gustav Line near central Italy and later behind the Gothic Line in northern Italy.[6]

From late 1943 through 1944, Allied forces won hard-fought battles at places such as Salerno, Naples, at the Anzio beachhead, and at Monte Cassino throughout Italy. Although Winston Churchhill once described Italy as "the soft underbelly of Europe," it was anything but. **Ulysses Davis** and **Floyd Richards** took part in some of these battles. The US 82nd Airborne Division was deployed during the battles at Naples and during the landings at the Anzio beachhead, and **Jim Washoe** was a part of this force.

In 1945 at the end of the war in Germany elements of the 82nd Airborne were called on to help occupy the American sector in Berlin. It was here they earned the name "America's Guard of Honor."

On June 6, 1944, American and British forces landed in Normandy, France as part of Operation Overlord. The largest amphibious operation in history had begun. The night before, 3,000 landing craft, 2,500 other ships, and 500 naval vessels such as escorts and bombardment ships had left English ports carrying hundreds of thousands of men. That night over 800 aircraft carrying parachutists or towing gliders flew to the Normandy landing zones. Over 12,000 aircraft would support the D-Day operation.[7]

The American 82nd and 101st Airborne divisions dropped behind enemy lines in France and suffered many casualties but secured their objectives. The British Sixth Airborne Division seized its objectives and also captured bridges over the Caen Canal and Orne River. During the 6:30 a.m. landing on June 6 the British and Canadians on Gold, Juno, and Sword beaches defeated Nazi defenders, as did the Americans at Utah. The American First Division at Omaha Beach confronted the most fortified of the German defenses and lost many men before securing their beachhead. The Allies suffered almost 5,000 casualties by the end of D-Day.[8]

John Peconam was at Utah Beach, **Leland Washoe** waded ashore Omaha Beach, **Charles Lindgren** fought at Omaha Beach and **Johnny Smith** parachuted behind enemy lines as part of the 82nd Airborne Division during Overlord.

There were more than 60,000 nurses who accepted commissions in the Army and served in every theater of the war. The Army Nurse Corps received full military status in 1944. Army nurses served near the front in both Europe and in the Pacific.[9] Women such as **Lena Swearington** helped evacuate and care for wounded soldiers aboard planes and hospital ships during World War Two.

In September of 1944, as part of Operation Market-Garden the 505th Parachute Infantry Regiment made its fourth jump at Groesbeck, Holland in the largest airborne assault in history. The 101st and 82nd Airborne divisions and the British 1st Airborne Division all took part. **Chuck Donahue** and **Frank Dowd** were members of the 82nd Airborne and both participated in Market-Garden.

The Allied plan was to invade Germany through the lower Netherlands after capturing bridges over the Lower Rhine and other rivers. Unfortunately, the British parachutists landed in an area recently occupied by two SS Panzer divisions. Over 3,000 British soldiers and many Americans died or were wounded during the operation.[10] In 1945 at the end of the war in Germany elements of the 82nd Airborne were called on to help occupy the American sector in Berlin. It was here they earned the name "America's Guard of Honor."

The Battle of the Bulge lasted from December 16, 1944 to January 15, 1945. The battle occurred during perhaps the coldest winter in modern history in the Ardennes Forest on the German and Belgian border. The German code name for the Battle of the Bulge was "Watch on the Rhine." Hitler hoped to split the Allied forces by isolating the British in the north and sending his armies to capture the supply port of Antwerp on the Belgian coast.

At 5:30 a.m. on December 16, three German armies launched the attack in an all-out artillery barrage along an 85-mile-long front. Although they had complete surprise against 6 American divisions the line only bulged back a little during the battle. The Germans lost 100,000 soldiers killed, wounded or captured. There were over 20,000 American casualties.[11]

The Rhine River was the last natural defense barrier for Germany. On March 7, 1945, American forces captured the Ludendorff Bridge, which spanned the Rhine River at Remagen, Germany. Hitler ordered a frenzied attack that included the launch of several V-2 rockets to try and topple the bridge but the rockets missed and the Americans kept the site. This enabled the Allies to send their troops and equipment further into Germany on a much faster timetable.[12] Adolf Hitler committed suicide on April 30, 1945. Germany surrendered to the Allies on May 8, 1945.

The village of Berchtesgaden located in the Bavarian Alps is where Adolf Hitler and many high-ranking Nazi leaders had villas. Hitler's villa was named the *Berghof,* and a secret stone fortress known as the *Aldershorst,* or Eagle's Nest, was located higher up the mountain from the *Berghof.* The Nazis had over half a million bottles of rare wine, ports and champagne stolen from France hidden in the Eagle's Nest. Other Nazis, including Hermann Goring and Heinrich Himmler, also had villas with cellars filled with stolen wine from the German occupation of France.[13] The Nazi regime also stole art, sculptures, gold, jewels, books and other items of value from countries they invaded and occupied during the war.

The Nazi regime in Germany built hundreds of concentration camps in Germany and in countries they occupied during World War Two. They also built death camps with the express intent of murdering Jews, homosexuals, Gypsies, political dissidents and other enemies of the Third Reich. Over six million Jews were put to death and over five million other people died in camps run by Nazi Germany.[14] Several of the men interviewed for this book witnessed the appalling conditions in some of these camps.

Tommy Merino, Frank Martin, Stanley Lowry, Frank Ames, Al Valadez, Sr., Frank Dowd and **Alfred McCovey** all fought during the Battle of the Bulge and participated during the final push into Nazi Germany and its surrounding territories.

Neil McKinnon

Neil McKinnon and I met at his house on August 23, 2002. Neil was a member of the Army Air Corps and served on a B-17 Flying Fortress in the 303rd Bomb Group of the 360th Bomb Squadron in the Eighth Air Division.

I was born in 1923 at an Indian house right below Weitchpec. My parents were Neil and Nettie. She made a lot of baskets.

I'm Neil the second. I went to school at Weitchpec one year and then I went to Morek. The Morek school was at least three miles away and we walked there every day.

Did you have any brothers or sisters?

There were five of us altogether. There were two sisters and two brothers. I'm next to the youngest. We went to school together most of the time. The Morek school had 25 or 30 kids at one time. There were mostly Yurok kids and a couple of white kids.

What type of work did your father do?

He worked around the place and he worked on the road. After that he was a mailman for years.

Did you ever sit and watch your mother make baskets?

Oh yeah, I watched her a lot of times. She'd get her own material. She made baby baskets, caps, open work baskets...she made all kinds of baskets, just oodles of them! She taught a few people.

What did you do for fun when you were little?

I don't know, all we did around the house was work. We had fun too. In those days we'd go up the hill in the wintertime with our guns. There was no TV, no electricity, nothing up there. We fished, but not for fun, we fished to eat.

Where was your father from?

From Weitchpec; so was my mother. My father was from right above Pearson's store right on that point. I went to school at Hoopa for a little while then I went to Sherman.

When you went to Hoopa was it a boarding school?

It was a regular school. My sister and brother went there when it was a boarding school. They had to stay there at least six months. I don't know what year they changed it to a regular school. It was a long ways away; we had to go by horseback to get them to a car then they'd take them to Hoopa.

Neil McKinnon (bottom row, far right) and his B-17 crew, ca. 1944. Photo courtesy of Neil McKinnon.

Did your mother or father speak the Yurok language?

My father did. My mother didn't speak it but she understood every word. My father could speak it. He didn't speak it at the house, just when somebody came by.

So you went to Hoopa for a little while?

Yeah, about a year and a half, then I went to Sherman, then the war broke out. I was at Sherman and then I worked at an aircraft plant then I went in the service.

When you were at Sherman and you went to school half a day and had trade half a day, so what was your trade?

They took me to welding. It was a pretty big welding shop. There must have been 20 of us at a time they'd teach. They had a good apprentice school, for that anyway.

Then were you drafted?

Yeah, I was drafted down in San Diego. (Neil worked at the Solar Aircraft Corporation as an acetylene welder from 1942 to 1943.) I was 19 years old. The first place they shipped me was to Fort Ord for a couple days then they shipped me to Fresno.

Boy, that was hot there! I went to Colorado. They taught us how to work on guns and ball turrets. They taught us how to release bombs.

Before you went to Colorado, did you choose to be in the Air Corps, or did they select you?

I asked to be, so I got my choice! I was working in an aircraft factory so I wanted to be the Air Corps. I didn't want to crawl around on the ground with the infantry if I could help it.

When you were at the base in Colorado did they separate you into gunners and bombers?

They called us armor gunners. We learned how to work machine guns and release bombs. They were 50-caliber guns. We learned how to take them apart and put them together blindfolded. If we got out someplace in the dark they wanted us to be able to put them together without seeing.

Neil McKinnon ca. 1944-5.
Photo courtesy of Neil McKinnon.

You wouldn't believe how people learn how to do that. You take it apart and put it together, take it apart and put it together. That's what they train you to do. It got boring, but it would have been handy.

When they taught you how to shoot the 50-caliber were you on a shooting range or in a field?

We first started on a shooting range but at the end they took us up in a little airplane. That was the fun part. It was a tiny airplane, like those Zeroes. You could sit in the back and shoot. It was the first time I'd been in an airplane in my life!

They got us up there and said the target was going by and I didn't shoot. I'd never been in an airplane before! It just peeled off and I so I started shooting at the target. We went about three or four times in that plane. We just learned how to lead your target and shoot. That target was about a thousand yards away.

That was in Las Vegas at Elliot Field. At Colorado we just went to armament school for a couple months at Buckley Field. After Las Vegas they shipped us to Utah for about a week. We had summer clothes because Las Vegas was so hot.

At Utah we were standing in snow! We about froze there for three or four days. From there they shipped us to Texas to get with our crews. Texas was where we did our main training before we went overseas. We had the whole crew then. That's when I was with the B-17.

Do you remember the first time you went inside a B-17?

Not really, because everybody was doing the same thing. You just went on with the bunch.

How many people are on a crew for the B-17?

It started out with 10, then they ended up taking one guy off. They had two waist gunners on either side. After we got overseas they took one guy off so that dropped it down to nine. There's the pilot, co-pilot, engineer, navigator, bombardier, radio operator, ball-turret gunner, waist gunner and the tail gunner.

Did you volunteer for the ball-turret or did they choose you?

They chose me! It was three feet in diameter and you have guns on each side of you. It had some kind of secret sight that helped you. And it was cold down there! You had an electric suit on but your breath would create a chunk of ice that'd go down to your chest. That was just from breathing.

What was the highest altitude you'd reach?

31,000 feet; most of the time we flew at the 25-to-27,000 range. They figured out the little shells could only go up a certain amount of feet. The bigger shells would get you up there. When we got up to 31,000 feet most of the fighters couldn't get up there because the United States had something on their plane that could make it go higher.

So after your time in Texas where did you go for your missions?

They shipped us to England in a big boat. It was the Queen Elizabeth. We left from Texas to Nebraska, then they shipped us to New Jersey. They didn't even have us get in a barrack because the ship was waiting for us.

They put us on a ferry to get us to the ship. I missed seeing the Statue of Liberty; we were so tired when we got there we slept about 20 hours. They had us running to get that ship and goddammit; I missed the Statue of

Liberty when we got out in the harbor.

It took us three-and-a half days to get across but we were on the ship for eight days. We weren't the first ones to get unloaded. There were 25,000 guys on that ship. It would go this way then that way so the submarines wouldn't get it. All the crew was together. The enlisted men had their quarters and the officers had their own.

Did you ever see any other Indian men in boot camp or anywhere else?

There were a few, there wasn't too many. There were two or three in boot camp.

Where did you come in at England?

Scotland was where the ship came in. We stayed about six months at Molesworth in England. We flew everywhere. Poland was our longest mission. I have the list of all our missions here. We bombed part of France where they had factories. We mostly bombed in Germany.

What type of fighter escort did you have?

P-51s and P-38s. We formed up six to a squadron and 18 to a group.

You must have flown through a lot of anti-aircraft flak?

Oh yeah, sometimes we went through flak for 45 minutes, it was just black! In Berlin they just shot up in the air. It was just perfectly black but you'd fly right through it. It felt like hail hitting you, but a lot wouldn't reach us.

The airplanes would go this way, then that way, a few hundred feet high and a few hundred feet low so they couldn't just get a bead right on you. But a bomb run, that's the spookiest part. You just held level then. When those bombs dropped you felt a big relief because then you could maneuver again.

Since you were in the ball-turret that must have been really intense because you could see everything...

Oh yeah, I was all by myself down there. You could see everything good there though. After about four or five missions you could tell where you were by all the rivers and such. We weren't very high then but you could still see a long ways.

Did you have radio contact?

Yeah, we had radio contact attached on our neck. We could talk to the pilot or somebody.

Did you ever run into German aircraft on any of your missions?

A few times. We'd look out and a few times they came in and hit us, but all the guys next to us were getting the heck shot out of them. If you flew a tight formation they'd leave you alone.

If you flew out of formation they'd strafe you with their machine guns. That's why you'd fly as close as you could together. Even then they came and got you a little bit but in a tighter formation you had less of a chance of getting shot at from the airplanes.

You must have watched your fighter escorts engage...

Oh yeah, they were right across from us. I saw them quite a few times. You can see the flash from the ground when they (anti-aircraft guns) shoot at you. I could see everything.

What types of anti-aircraft guns were shot at you?

Well, they were five-inch shells and three-and-a-half inch shells. The five-inch shells went up higher.

On your missions, what were your duties as the ball-turret gunner?

To shoot at airplanes. If something happened to the bombs, if they couldn't release the bombs, I was supposed to know how to get rid of them manually by turning them loose. If something happened with the wire system my specialty was to get in there and turn them loose. They don't want you to haul them back, they want you to drop them someplace. But I never had to do that. We always got rid of them first.

> *Sometimes we went through flak for 45 minutes, it was just black!*

Was there ever a time when someone on your plane was hit by flak?

Oh yeah, the pilot got hit once. He got hit in the head but didn't tell us until we got back to the base. He didn't want us to worry about it. We got shot up once really bad. A dud hit us and went right through the plane.

It was a five-inch dud that just missed me by about two feet. The radio operator was going to fall out, he was hanging down at the bottom and looked around; nobody else was jumping so he pulled himself back in!

He was ready to bail out...

He thought we were going down for sure. But it never caught fire and didn't explode. That was a dud, we looked at it. It hit right in the dead center of us. That wasn't our day.

You were telling me about one of your missions...

Well, at Pennemunde, I didn't know it until way after the war was over, but it looked like a black field to bomb; we bombed it two times. The Germans were ahead of us in making the atomic bomb at the time.

They (US intelligence) knew about it and we went and bombed it all out. It killed 100 scientists in one raid. They were way ahead of us in making the atomic bomb. I didn't know about it until after the war, I read it in a book. We destroyed all those scientists in there.

What were some of your other missions like?

That was the most important one, I think! We had to get rid of those guys. We mostly bombed oil fields. When we bombed Berlin, we just bombed Berlin to discourage the people. That was their main city.

It was to hit their morale. One time we had 1,800 planes hit Berlin. You could see them all over! When there was nothing else to bomb we bombed Berlin. We bombed their officer's quarters out.

Can you describe how you shot in the ball-turret?

I didn't have to shoot it very many times. Above me those guys would shoot, bang, bang, bang, bang and it would vibrate! I didn't have to shoot many times. The ball-turret would go around and around. You had little handles to turn it this way and that way. You had your triggers right on top. If you hit your target real good you'd lead into it. They didn't bother us too bad.

Other guys got shot up bad. One time the group next to me lost seven planes. When we got back to England seven planes were gone. I've seen seven planes go down myself. I saw this fighter plane coming; he must have been shot, he hit into a bomber, and then they went down and hit another bomber.

We called B-24s flying coffins! We thought ours was a lot tougher than a B-24. A B-17 could land on the water without breaking up, but a B-24 would break up.

I saw seven go down that day myself. There was a plane behind us, all of a sudden there was a puff of smoke, there was nothing left, just a puff of smoke. I've seen guys bail out. They'd open their 'chutes too quick. The airplane's on fire and I saw them going down with their 'chutes on fire. I don't blame them, they're not used to jumping out so they'd pull the cord without dropping far enough. That's terrible, to see something like that.

You were able to deal with seeing such terrible things?

It didn't seem to bother me. Some guys would really get bothered. That's just the way it was. Some guys would get all shook up when they got back.

What's the difference between a B-17 and a B-24?

We called B-24s flying coffins! We thought ours was a lot tougher than a B-24. A B-17 could land on the water without breaking up, but a B-24 would break up. A good pilot could land on the water after running out of gas.

We used to see some guys land on the water. Then they'd have to get out in life rafts. We circled guys that went down a few times. We'd have more gas than the rest of them so we'd circle and pinpoint them. England had a good rescue service. They'd come right out and get those guys.

What was the air base like that you were stationed at?

We just had these little round billets. I don't think we were on just one plane, we had a squadron. Our group was named the Hell's Angels. They had pictures in the movies of the Hell's Angels. I was in the 303rd Bomb Group in the 360th Squadron. The other guys next to us were the 359th and 358th.

You probably got to be pretty close friends with your crew?

Heck, we lived together for about three or four months at least. That's my crew right there (He points to a picture on the wall). I was the youngest guy on the crew. There's only two of us alive.

After you flew your missions, did your crew ever talk about what you saw, or if you had a close call?

When we came back from a mission they took us back to a little room and debriefed us. They asked us what we saw. That was intelligence. They gave us a shot of whiskey, a double shot if you wanted it. Sometimes I took more than that, some of the other guys didn't drink, so I took theirs!

The medical department gave us that. It would relax you, I guess. It never really got to me though. Some of the other guys would come back and boy, they'd talk about this close call or that.

What was the time length between each of your missions?

Sometimes it was two or three days, sometimes it was the next day. It all depended on where they wanted you to go.

When did you become a staff sergeant?

That was after five or six missions, I think. You had to be a buck sergeant before you could fly. Germany respected rank. If you're a sergeant you get treated different in prison camp. That's why you were a buck sergeant when you start flying. They respected rank. They treated you a little better.

It says on your records you were awarded the Distinguished Flying Cross...

After so many missions they automatically give it to you. They figure you went through so many missions you must do something to make it! I think they gave us three dollars more per paycheck if they gave you that medal.

Where were you when the war ended in Germany?

I was in Colorado both times, when it ended in Japan and ended in Germany. They had shipped me back to Colorado. We flew back in a cargo plane. We came through the United States on a train. They sent me to Santa Monica for 10 days and I stayed in a rich hotel! Then they shipped me back to Colorado.

What was the mood like when the war in Japan ended?

There were three of us in town. They were going to have a big parade. We had a five-day pass and stayed in town and didn't get out until everything was all over!

How long were you overseas in the war?

About five months. They shipped me back around October. When you finish 25 missions they send you back, but they ended up extending it to 30. They figure 25 missions are about all you can handle.

I went on 32 missions. When I first went over there, they told us only five percent of the flyers were finishing their missions. That wasn't a very good average.

That was because...

Planes were getting shot down. 90% probably survived by bailing out, but only five percent would finish their missions. In war times there would be four crews where we were at, and at the end of the day we were the only crew left.

Most of them survived, but they didn't come back. What they did at the base, they knew they weren't coming back, so they'd clear out all their stuff before we got back. So it was just empty when we got back. All their clothes were gone and everything.

Where were you discharged?

At McClellan Field in Sacramento. I had volunteered to take B-29 school; I wanted to go back overseas. They sent me to Colorado to go to B-29 school but the war was over. We didn't have to go to school anymore. Finally I had so many points they discharged me.

Did any of your family serve in the war?

Just me.

Did you ever write home?

I wrote once in a while. I wrote just enough to let my mother know I was thinking of her someplace! You had to have your lieutenant sign it so you weren't telling any secrets. I had a partner who signed mine in some lieutenant's name and I signed his!

When you were in England did you visit any towns?

I went to London. We went to little towns within 12 or 15 miles in between our missions. Everybody had a bicycle. It had nice rolling hills. There were no cars over there, everybody had a bicycle. I probably ended up in London about five or six times. We'd hit a certain bar we knew.

When you were in London did you see the damage caused by the bombing?

Oh yeah, I saw a lot of damage. It was like the Fourth of July at night time there. Those buzz bombs would come over. You could see them coming, and everybody would shoot the heck out of them. Everybody would run for their shelters.

We were brave enough to get out and look and people yelled to get into the shelter. Those buzz bombs that came over had motors on them; you could hear them shut off and no one knew where they'd hit, then boom!

Then the V-2s came over. You never heard them until they were already there. I had a friend who had a girlfriend. He took her back to this building. The next time he went down there that building was just flat.

She had left about 10 minutes before the bomb hit. That V-2 just flattened it. We were lucky to go to London. Most of the crew wouldn't go. That first night we went we stayed in this hotel. A bomb hit and knocked all the windows out of the building. They wouldn't go to London anymore!

There were a lot of Indian men from this area who went in the service...

From everyplace, I don't know why, they wanted to join in. They just wanted to join. Like my son, he joined for Vietnam. He said that's where the action was.

Your family must have been happy when you came home...

Oh yeah, they were. They were living in Morek. That's about 15 miles downriver from Weitchpec.

What type of work did you do after the service?

Woodwork, logging, falling trees. I fell tree for 41 years, almost all in this area and mostly on the Klamath River. I worked with quite a few people; Frank Ames, Glenn Moore. A lot of other Indians worked there.

Did you mostly work in the redwoods?

About half the time, but mostly among fir. For the last 20 years I worked in the redwoods.

Taking down a redwood, is that a challenge?

Oh yeah, every tree is different. You'd get your saw as level as you could. If you cut it crooked the tree will fall awkwardly. Every tree is different. When I first started I had an eight-foot bar. The motor alone weighed 110 pounds, plus the bar and chain. I came down to smaller saws in the last few years. The last tree I fell for pay was in 1990.

I notice you make gambling drums, how long have you done that?

Probably 10 years. I make earrings too. Some guys came by and show me the principles, and you learn as you go along. You improve yourself and do it quicker and better.

When you were young, did your family take you to the ceremonies?

At McClellan Field in Sacramento. I had volunteered to take B-29 school; I wanted to go back overseas.

Yeah. My father was a dancer. He danced in the Brush Dance and Deerskin Dance. He sang in the Brush Dance. Have you ever been to a Deerskin Dance? He was a flute carrier in the Deerskin Dance. The only place that had a Deerskin Dance was in Hoopa.

They had one in Johnson's (Wautek) but mostly in Hoopa. I remember him carrying the flint. He sang all kinds of songs in the Brush Dance. Only two guys sing in the Deerskin, and it's the same in the Jump Dance; two guys sang.

When I was little I danced in one Jump Dance, one Deerskin Dance and a couple Brush Dances. I remember dancing at Johnson's when I was a little guy. They said you have to learn how to dance. I went to Hoopa and danced in the Jump Dance when I was in high school.

Would they have stick games after?

Most of the time. I never played; I was a little kid playing on the sandbar or something.

They'd have Indian card games too?

Oh yeah, that's the best time. I watched them. I know how to play the game. Those old timers, when they sang they kept time with the drum. The guy that had the cards, he kept time by using his body and threw out the cards with the time.

The guys now don't keep time with the music. Those old timers kept time with the music, with the beat, and they threw their sticks out. I've made some pretty good drums. I have drums here, and drums over there (in his house).

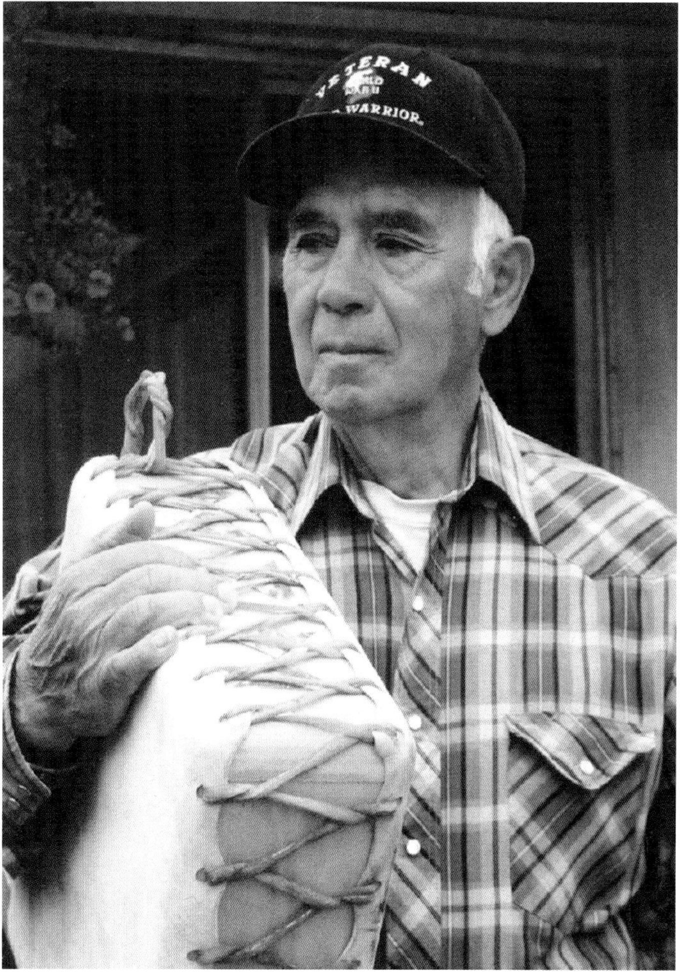

Neil McKinnon

How long does it take for you to make a drum?

It's hard to tell. It takes quite a while if you only make one at a time.

Has anyone ever asked you to tell your story, for a newspaper, or any other history project?

No, this is my first time being interviewed like this.

Is there anything you'd like to share that I didn't ask you about your time in the service?

You didn't ask if I had any girlfriends!

I won't ask that! Do you think it's important for the public to know what our Indian people did for this country in the service?

Well, they should know, but you know how it is now. They should realize Indian people fought for our country just like they did. And it was taken away from us and we still fought for it.

Neil McKinnon continues to make drums and other pieces of woodwork related to his Yurok ancestry. Neil had his discharge papers and official list of missions his crew completed. Here is the list of missions and targets they bombed, all in the year 1944: May 4/ Abortive Sortie; May 12/ Merseberg; May 19/ Berlin; May 20/ Orly Air Drome; May 24/ Berlin; May 25/ Blainville; May 27; Mannheim; May 28/ Cologne; May 29/ Posen; May 31/ Gilze-Rijen; June 2/ Dannes; June 4/ Le Tourquet; June 6/ Caen; June 7/ Conde Sur Noireau; June 8/ Orleans; June 12/ Cambrai-Epinov; June 13/ Evreux-Fauville; June 14/ Creil; June 15 La Possonniere; June 16/ Juvencourt; June 21/ Berlin; June 22/ Lille; June 29/ Haiterblick; July 5/ Gilze-Rijen; July 9/ Chateadun; July 13/ Munich; July 17 Peronne; July 18 Pennemunde; July 20/ Dessao; July 23/ Creil Air Drome; August 3/ Crepieul; August 4/ Pennemunde.

Frank Richards

Frank and his wife Lestie Richards live in the small town of Smith River. Frank is of Tolowa heritage. I drove with Frank on a foggy day to the Smith River cemetery and we talked in my car. Afterwards he showed me where many Tolowa veterans lay in their final resting place and told me war stories about many of them. This interview occurred on March 22, 2000.

I was born in the old Richards house right over here about quarter of a mile away. My grandfather Ed and his wife Ida Richards owned the house. My dad was born at Yontocket (a Tolowa village site) over across the river. My mother Ada was born at what is now known as Ship Ashore. I was born in 1925.

Where did you first go to elementary school?

In this little Indian school right up over here; Ocean School was the name of it. My sister Marian and I both went there. All the kids around here, all of my relatives and friends, we all went there for a long time.

Then we went to the school near the little town of Smith River. I started there in the sixth grade, my sister Marian was three or four years behind me. We were the first two Indians students to go there, as far as I remember.

My cousin Ray Moorehead went a few years later. We got along pretty good with everyone, of course back in the 1850s and 1860s there were bad problems, you know. But a lot of older Indian people actually worked for some of the Caucasians on the ranches here. A lot of my family from here and around the reservation went to Del Norte High School. I only went there one year with my cousin Edwin.

The following year some of our relatives and people from this area were at Sherman Indian School so I went down there. We stayed there for three months. We were supposed to have written permission and enough money to come home. We had to leave at night, sort of escape you might say!

When you first got to the school, what was your first impression of it?

Well, they run it pretty much like they would in the service, actually. They had roll call, bed checks and all that. If a person really wanted to apply themselves they could have learned something. I went to the bakery school for a while, for half a day, and then the regular class the other half.

They had a small farm there. Some kids worked in the barber shop or as auto mechanics. It wasn't all that bad. Of course, it's pretty flat and hot country for somebody who was born and raised in Del Norte County!

There were no redwoods, just orange groves. We couldn't take very much of that, but we got to meet Indian people from a lot of different tribes, from Arizona and New Mexico. Lots of people were from Chiloquin, Oregon, and some were from Klamath.

Most of what I saw was a lot of buildings and lots of heat; I just couldn't take that. We could leave the school if we had written permission and enough money to get home. One day Ray Moorehead got his and went home.

My cousin Edwin and my good friend Charlie Whipple and I talked about it and one night after roll call we went out through the window with our suitcases and headed for Smith River! We caught a Greyhound and came home.

What was a typical day like there?

If you wanted to be there it wasn't bad. We had lots of roll calls, and we'd form up out in the front of the school and march to dinner, or to class, just like the military. The boys and girls were separated.

When you came back to Smith River what did you do?

I went to work for Tyson mines just east of the little town of Smith River. I was too young to work underground so I pushed a cart around for 85 cents an hour for probably about a year. I was getting ready to go in the service; all of my relatives and most of my friends were in the service by then, most of them were in the Army, so I thought I'd go in the Army.

Then I got a notice saying I was going to be drafted, this was only three months after I turned 18. So I went in the Army. I went to San Francisco first, then down to the Presidio in Monterey. While I was there they had us try out for different aptitude tests, and to check to see if you were healthy, to see if you had good teeth, good ears, and were young and dumb I guess!

Later they told us we were trying out for the Army Air Corps. So from there I went to Buckley Field, Colorado and took basic training there in a couple feet of snow, which wasn't fun, everyone was sick.

We got out of that school then went to Lowery Field, which wasn't far away. I took armament and some gunnery there. By then we were actually seeing our first airplanes. Then some of our class went to Florida.

I got to come home once while we were there. When I went back we went to Westover Field in Massachusetts, and that's where they brought all the people together; the pilots and navigators and bombardiers all met there and that's where we met our crew. Then we went to Georgia and we trained together.

When you were in training, did you ever practice jumping out of a plane?

No, we practiced that on the ground. They had an old plane on stilts out in water and you practiced that way. Our training was a little different from the infantry. For instance we didn't train with hand grenades or M1 rifles.

Targeting Germany- A B-24 releases a bomb load during a mission by the 47th Bomb Wing near Wiener Neustadt. Bombs visible on right. Photo courtesy of Frank Richards.

What we took was 50-caliber machine gun training, turret training and bomb sighting. I learned about bomb racks too. In armament training I learned about all the turrets. I could have had my choice of any of the turrets but I took the ball.

When you were in training did you ever meet other Indian men?

There were a lot of Indians in the Air Corps and some in the WACs (Women's Auxiliary Corps). I don't remember any of their names, but they were from all different tribes. Our training consisted of a lot of gunnery, and of course the pilots were doing their thing.

We had a lot of air-to-air gunnery, air-to-ground, and they even had us ride around in the back of a truck shooting a shotgun at different targets that would pop up. After a while we went up to Mitchell Field in New York and stayed there a short while. We went to New Hampshire and got new clothes. We figured we might be going to Alaska by the heavy clothes they gave us, but they were high altitude clothes.

When we left New York we circled the Statue of Liberty; that was fun! Everything was fun back then, you're young and didn't know what you were getting into. We went to Bermuda and stayed there a week. There were about 14 new airplanes, some of them were B-17s. I was in a B-24.

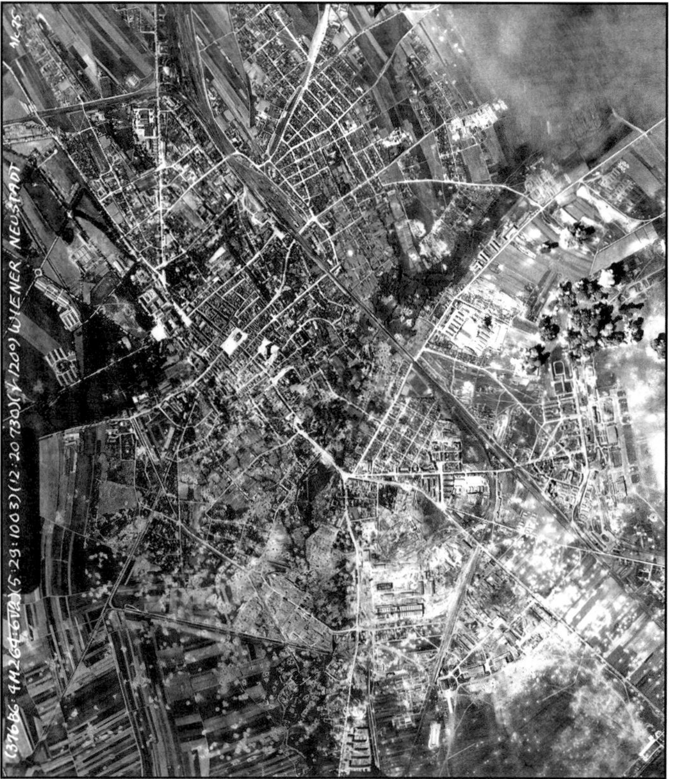

Aftermath of the Raid- White pockmarks dot the landscape in Wiener Neustadt. Note the exploding bombs at right. Photo courtesy of Frank Richards.

We went to the Azores. When we flew in we were in fog but we had a good navigator and we came right in. We left there and stopped at two places in North Africa; French Morocco and Tunisia were the places we stopped.

By then we were seeing evidence of the war, there were all kinds of destroyed equipment and airplanes. We went across to Italy and stationed there. I remember seeing the airplanes when they came back from their missions; they came back pretty well shot up. We flew missions out of Italy until the end of the war.

I was in the ball-turret in the B-24. You sat in this little ball. I was actually too big to be a ball-gunner. You were supposed to wear a parachute and get into the thing. The ball had a door that was big enough to fall out of if you had to.

There was a safety belt you were hooked up to, if you had to get out you'd just reach back there and unhook the belt. Then you unlatch the door, it was a flyaway door that would take off into the wind. Then you'd push out and be clear.

But I was too big; I just wore my parachute harness. I left my parachute pack up inside the plane. It would be completely worthless because there wasn't enough time to reach it. I was pretty lucky, we never had any fighters come in on us. We'd see them in the distance, and we'd see them take off from their airfields.

Our main problem was anti-aircraft flak. When you get near the target the bombardier would actually control the plane, he'd have the controls. You're flying straight and level then; this is the last few minutes of the bomb run. He takes over the plane completely.

You're flying straight and level, you can't break formation. By then the planes are bouncing around with all the concussion going on. You can't leave, there's flak up ahead of you. Most of it was 88-millimeter anti-aircraft from the ground.

You see all these black puffs of smoke and you have to go through it, you can't leave. So that's what we did. I can remember that at least one time we had the Tuskegee airmen fly cover for us. They were good. They say that they never lost a bomber to German fighters while they were on a mission. They had something to prove.

Can you describe the first time you actually sat in a turret?

Well, that was actually in the States during training. It was a shut-off feeling because you're down by yourself; you're the only one on that particular plane that's by yourself. See, the nose-gunner has company, the top turret gunner is right behind the co-pilot and pilot, the radio operator is directly below him. Then the flight engineer is usually close to where the pilot is. The tail-gunner is in back and he has company.

When we got into the anti-aircraft flak I could get out of the turret if I wanted. The enemy fighters aren't going to come into their own flak. A lot of times when you see enemy fighters out in the distance the radio operator would get back to the waist window and man the hand-held gun on that side. The flight engineer will take the gun on the other side.

What made you decide to be in the bottom turret?

To start with, nobody else wanted it! I was too big but I wanted to go with my crew and I wanted to fly. I didn't realize what I was getting into, I guess. Of course, we were young people, and in any branch of the service they'll tell you this. You don't really think about it too much, you're scared, but you don't really think about it.

What year did you go in the service?

I went in the last part of 1943. It was December of '43.

I got credit for seven sorties. That was enough!

Will you describe what you did on a mission?

The first thing was they got us up early in the morning with whistles and bugles! Six of us enlisted men stayed in a big pyramid tent. Our officers stayed right nearby. They were good guys. We'd go to the mess hall and a lot of the older guys said we had to eat or we'd be air sick. I never saw so much spam in my life! They had it fixed every way you could think of; with pineapples, or raisin sauce, boiled, baked, you name it!

Then we went to the briefing room. They'd tell us the target and tell us how bad the anti-aircraft flak was going to be, and whether or not to expect fighters. We'd take off from our field and meet at a rendezvous point and form up our formation.

We'd meet other groups that had done the same thing. Our flight cover was mostly P-51 fighters. Then we'd take off together toward the middle of the Adriatic. Then we'd head north to wherever our target was, either over Austria, Germany or northern Italy. We never put on our heavy clothes to start with, or our parachute.

You have no need for a parachute if you're too low. Your clothes start going on as you gain altitude. We'd be at maybe 10,000 feet then the pilot would call and tell us to put on our oxygen masks. Those were uncomfortable. We had flak suits and flak helmets. The flak suit was overlapping steel.

When I wasn't in my turret I was sitting on the ammunition boxes by the waist gunners. By the time we were coming back from a run you'd have ice form on the oxygen mask. Most of our targets were train yards, shipyards, ball-bearing factories and oil refineries.

My bomb group hit the Romanian oilfields before I had joined. I talked to a lot of the older guys that were there before me when they were bombing that place. My main problem was anti-aircraft fire from the 88-millimeter guns; I never had to fire at any fighters. We were

SQDN.	LEAD BOMBARDIER	AIMING ACCURACY		PATTERN DENSITY		ADJUSTED TOTAL
		DISTANCE	%	400'x800'	%	
514th (•)	KRYSA	85'	100.0	13 of 15	86.7	96.7%
513th (o)	McORRY	460'	90.0	17 of 18	94.4	91.1%
512th (▲)	LOGAN	345'	100.0	8 of 19	42.1	85.5%
515th	See additional plot for this Sqdn.					71.8%

Bomb statistics from one mission for the 47th Bomb Wing at the Sulm Railroad Bridge in Austria.
Photo courtesy of Frank Richards.

up there pretty high.

By the time I got there we had the skies pretty much under control. What amazed me is how the Germans never gave up until the very last. They were gung-ho until the very end, I'm sure the ground men will tell you that. They didn't quit; they didn't know what the word meant, I guess.

Were there any times when your bomber was hit by flak?

Frank Richards (top row, second from right) and his B-24 crew. Photo courtesy of Frank Richards.

One time we went on a mission going through Brenner Pass, which is in the Alps. The Germans had brought in railroad guns on these flatcars. We caught hell going up there. When the flak goes off real close you can feel it.

The planes get hit, sometimes not bad. I can only remember one time where we got the order to prepare to bail out of the hatch at the back of the bomber. It's only about three by four feet wide.

What always amused me were the guys saying they'd never bail out. You should have seen them line up when our bomber got in trouble! We had opened the door lock but never went. All the gunners said that flak was worse than fighters.

Your heart must have been pumping hard!

Yeah, but when you're thinking you're going down with the plane you don't give it much thought. You remember that people have done it before. You only have one parachute though! I don't think that young people think about dying. You're scared, but you don't think about it.

Where did you stay and sleep in between missions?

We stayed in those pyramid tents. The only shower was clear across the field. I was in the 376th, 514th, then there was the 12th, 13th, 14th and 15th squadrons all there. Everybody got along good. We were all there for the same reason.

Can you describe the B-24?

To me it was a better plane. It was a little faster, a little better bomb load. According to what I've heard since the war, you had a little better chance getting home in a B-24 than a B-17. Of course if you're a '17 man you'll say different!

But the '17 was harder to get around in. It's a pretty plane. I like the B-24. Some of the ones we flew were named *Boomerang* and *Lucky Patches,* and others I can't remember. They carried mostly 100 or 500 pound bombs and fragmentation bombs.

I've seen one blow up when we were in training. In training, one crew would land a plane and another would get in. The mechanics overseas took better care. They'd work all night on one to get it ready for you.

In the last part of the war they sent some up without guns as long as they carried bombs. A bomb has a little propeller and a fuse on each end when they're in the rack. They have an arming wire that is hooked onto the bomb rack that goes down and out and through these little propellers.

When the bomb leaves this arming wire stays. The bomb drops and the propeller start spinning. When they wind out they pull off

Frank Richards in 1944. Photo courtesy of Frank Richards.

and they're armed and ready to go. You could also set bombs; in other words you could have it drop clear down through several stories of a building and have it explode at the bottom. Or you could have it blow up at the top of the building.

Frank Richards

Would you see the bombs as they fell from your position?

Yes, they go with the plane for a little while. Then they start dropping behind. You got a real good lurch if you dropped all the bombs at once. We would be at about 15 to 20,000 feet mostly. It depended on the target.

You knew you were helping out with the effort. Of course you think about civilians; women and kids, you know. But usually the bombs hit pretty accurately. We bombed during the day and the British were bombing at night. They were getting hit day and night themselves.

What were the names of the German fighters that would come after bombers?

Me-109s mostly, and Fw-190s were the worst ones. Right at the end of the war they had Messerschmitt Me-262s. They were the first jets. The Tuskegee airmen shot some of them down. When I came back to the States I came home on leave first.

We came in at Virginia. I came home then I went back to Hastings, Nebraska. We stayed there and then they were going to ship us to Texas to B-29 school. But before we even got there they dropped the first atom bomb on Hiroshima.

That canceled all the schools. So we stayed in Brownsville a while. They lost my records along with a few other guys so we stayed in a little longer. Then I went to Maryville to get my discharge. I got out in 1946. I spent most of that time riding around the country and looking it over. I never did see anything that looked like the redwoods.

What was it like when the war was over and you were shipped home?

It was good. When we came back, we came back with our whole bomb group. As we were getting ready to leave Italy, you probably heard about Axis Sally on the radio? She was always talking about how they (the Axis) knew everything we were doing.

She said 'We heard you're going home, our U-Boats are still out there so you'll probably never make it.' She was always saying things like this. 'Your wives are running around over here while you're fighting,' all that kind of stuff. I guess they had Tokyo Rose in the Pacific.

What was your reaction when you heard about the atomic bomb being used?

I was pretty happy. Everybody was pretty happy about that. I think that the U.S. argument was that it saved a lot of lives of boys who were going to have to go into Japan. That troop train that I was on when we heard, half the outfit had their bottles out! The MPs tried to keep them quiet!

That must have been a great feeling though…

Oh yeah. I went to work in the woods with my dad after the war. I got married to my wife Lestie. She had four brothers that were in the war and a brother who got killed in Korea. He was the one who introduced us.

We got married in 1951 in Reno. We went through Charlie Bowen's country! I didn't know him then, but soon after that I did. I never talked about the war until maybe the last ten years. I used to wonder why, but you're just damn lucky to be alive.

Frank and Lestie Richards have two children and five grandchildren. Frank worked in the timber industry for 50 years. He enjoys watching his grandchildren play in sport events such as basketball and football.

Sharon Wasson

I attended the 2002 Susanville Veteran's Reunion on October 12 where I met with Sharon Wasson. We sat at a table in the Veteran's Memorial building and he spoke about his time in the service. Sharon has volunteered at the registration table for the Veteran's Reunions for many years. He is a relative of Mervin Evans and is of Shoshone and Paiute ancestry.

I was born in 1924 in Hoopa. My father Tom Wasson was a clerk for the (Bureau of Indian Affairs) Agency there. His mother was Shoshone and his father was half-white and half-Paiute from McDermitt in Nevada.

My mother was Sadie Dyer. She was from a little town called Yerington in Nevada. She was Paiute. We lived in Hoopa for about two years. My father was a clerk in Hoopa. Then we went to San Francisco.

Did you have any brothers or sisters?

I just found out I had an older brother that died as a baby in Hoopa. Then I had a brother and sister. I'm the oldest of the three.

How long did you live in San Francisco?

We went there in 1926 and left in 1934.

Do you remember what it was like in San Francisco?

When we played the Indian school there at Stewart it was an all-Indian affair!

Oh yeah, foggy and rainy! I was very fortunate because my father was a pitcher for a Bay Area baseball team. All summer long they'd play baseball games on Saturdays. It was semi-pro.

Where did you go to school there?

Oh, just grammar school. Then I got tuberculosis and spent 14 months in a hospital there. I finished kindergarten and first grade in the hospital.

After your time in San Francisco where did your family go?

We came here to Susanville for six months. My father's dad died in 1934 so that's why he came back. They were putting up the theatre here and my dad got on as a laborer. Apparently he had his application in with the Indian Service and he got a job as a clerk in Carson City in December of '34. So we moved over there until I went in the service in 1942.

So you went to a regular high school?

Yes. I played football and basketball and did a little boxing my senior year.

Were there any other Indian kids in your class?

Yeah, I think there were five of us on our football team. When we played the Indian school there at Stewart it was an all-Indian affair! There was a lot of built-in competition there. You could kind of say it was the haves and have-nots. At the Indian school they were sent there because of economic problems at home.

Did your family have a hard time during the Depression?

No, because dad worked all through the Depression. My mom stayed home as a housekeeper.

Do you remember where you were when Pearl Harbor happened?

Yeah, we were cutting a cottonwood tree in the front yard in Carson City. We heard it on the news. We didn't have TV in those days. I wasn't into politics or anything. I spent five years in the Boy Scouts.

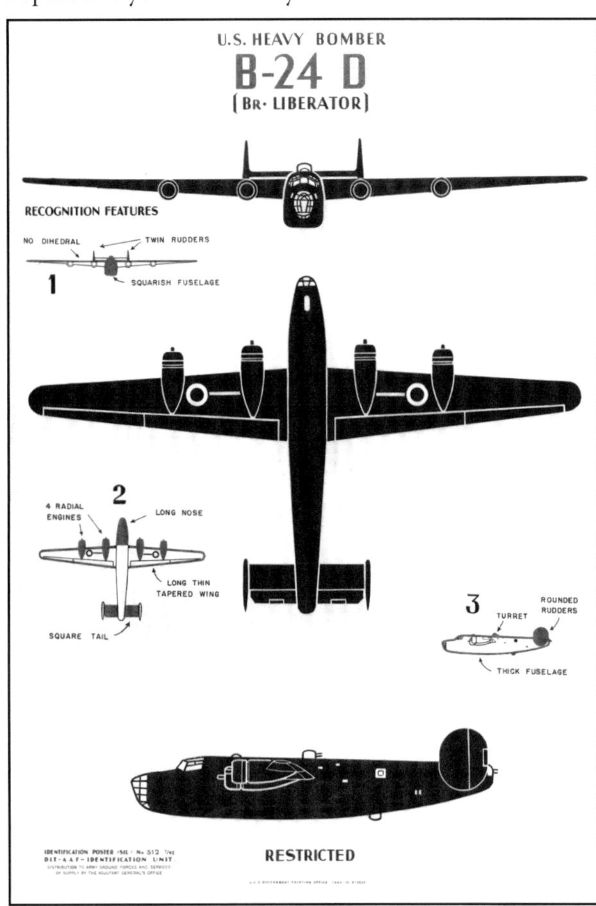

Library of Congress, Prints and Photographs Division, (LC-USZ62-103754).

What did you think after Pearl Harbor happened?

Well, they had a poster on the wall at the high school. It was a P-39. I wanted to be a pilot! I was drafted into the Air Corps. They sent us to Sacramento for swearing-in then we went to Monterey for the exams.

Did you travel with any other Indian men?

Harrison Thomas was there. When we took our eye exam in Sacramento he couldn't see the big 'E.' We didn't know he couldn't see! He was from the local area here.

After your time in Monterey where did you go?

They sent me to Mississippi for basic training.

Do you remember the name of the camp you went to?

Never forget it! Keesler Field in Mississippi. They had basic training then they'd send us to different schools by the scores that we had (on the exams). I spent six weeks in aerial gunnery school. I learned the 30-caliber and the 50-caliber hand-turrets.

Can you describe your first time in a plane at Laredo?

It was fun! There were no fancy aerobatics but I liked it.

Did you go up as a crew?

No, it was all individual at that school.

Can you describe how it was to shoot a 30 or 50-caliber?

I can't describe it. It had a hell of a kick but it was mounted so solid you could feel it shake, but that was it. That's flexible gunnery.

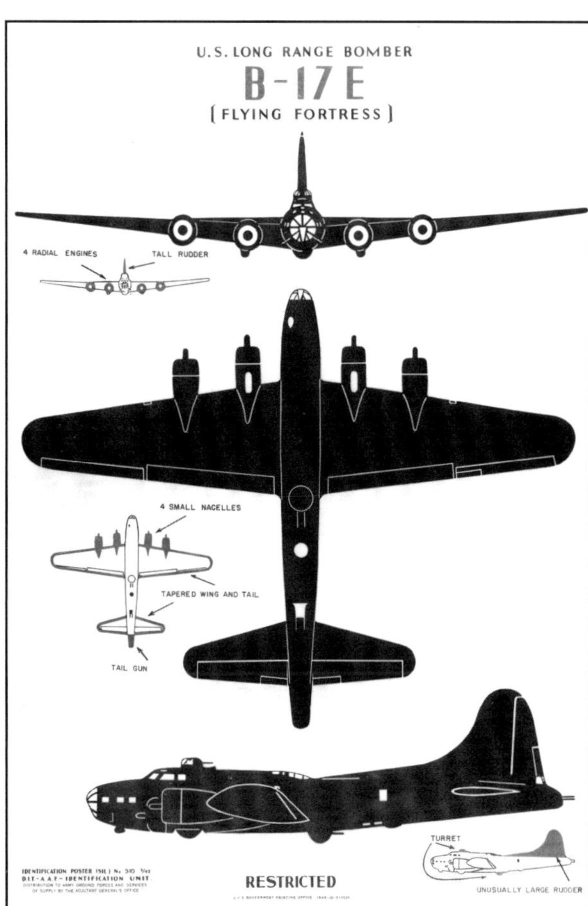

Library of Congress, Prints and Photographs Division, (LC-USZ62-103751).

Was it loud?

Not really, not in the airplane. It would be in a room like this, but up there the noise just dissipated. You get used to it.

So you did that for six weeks?

Yeah, they had a track and there would be four of us on the back on the flatbed of a truck taking our turns. They had these skeet traps where they'd shoot over you. That was fun. We had 12-gauge shotguns, we were moving and the target was moving. You can't pay for that kind of training! It was fun!

Did you ever see other Indian men during basic?

Not in basic. I did meet a fellow from south of Hoopa. It was probably in gunnery school. Wallace Scott was his name. We weren't in the same group. He took his training as a radio operator then I lost all contact with him.

After your training at Laredo where did you go?

They sent me back to Mississippi for mechanic school. It was a B-24 school and we learned about the B-24. I think that was 19 weeks. All I remember is the heat down there!

What was life like at the camp, did you ever get to go on leave?

Oh yeah, I went to New Orleans a couple times. There was nothing there that really interested me. They had a little town across the border; Biloxi. It was a nice clean little town about 20 miles away. It was fun to go there. Keesler Field was dirty; you had to have over 120,000 guys there.

Did anybody treat you any different because you were Indian?

No.

You were just another soldier?

Yes.

Can you describe the B-24?

Well, it's an air-cooled four-engine. There's a lot of hydraulics involved in the flaps and the gear.

Where did you go after that school?

That's when we organized the crew. We weren't assigned to any group yet. There was just one more month of training down in Tucson. That was nice down there in the wintertime. We took one month of B-24 flight training then we got together as a group just north of El Paso.

They had an Air Force base north of El Paso by Alamogordo. We spent two months there. That was where we formed our group. When we finished our training there we were sent overseas. We picked up our plane in Kansas and flew it down to east Palm Beach.

We thought we were going to India because we never heard of B-24s in England. But there it was. It took us 20 days to get to England. We were based 40 miles northeast of London.

We thought we were going to India because we never heard of B-24s in England. But there it was. It took us 20 days to get to England.

So you were part of the Eighth Air Force?

Yes, there were three divisions. One had a triangle with their letter code, one had a circle with their letter code, and ours had a square with a P. They didn't have that in the beginning. When we got there that's the way they had it set up.

What was the base like where you stayed?

We were lucky, we had Quonset huts. I think there

were three crews to each one. It could have been four crews with double bunks. There were six of us in our crew.

What was your position on your crew?

On the B-24 I was a left waist-gunner. The radio operator used the other gun when he wasn't on the radio. On the B-17 they had the engineer on the top turret. That's where I was on the B-17.

What was your first mission?

It was a short one across the Channel. I can't remember all of them now. They had their headquarters and did all the planning there. They had to make sure all the new crews could gel. It depended on where they needed us.

On our fourth mission we had an aircraft blow up right off our right wing. It just disintegrated right there…direct hit.

Do you remember the name of your plane?

The pilot called it *Rhapsody in Rivets.*

That's a good one!

That's the B-24. When we went to the B-17 the crew chief named it after his wife, he called it *Bashful Maryanne.* I have a book about them.

Do you remember any of the countries you flew over?

Well, you can't see the boundaries. We knew what the targets were. We flew over Denmark a couple times, but I don't think we dropped any bombs in Denmark when we flew down toward Berlin.

After D-Day our targets were military targets in France until our troops went in. Then we went back to hitting oil refineries. That's what most of our targets were.

Can you describe how your squadron would form up for a mission?

We took off in single file to the assembly area. There were four squadrons in a group formation. We'd be in a half-mile line and there were about a thousand bombers.

Did you ever see any German fighters?

We saw two fighters on one mission. They stayed way in the back firing their cannons at the rear ship. Then on our 31st mission about 30 fighters hit the back of us.

They knocked 12 of us down. One fighter came right by our wing but he came up so fast I didn't have time for a shot. Our gunner didn't tell us there was a plane in the area on our intercom.

That must have been very intense…

Those 30 fighters had it in for that one group. They almost knocked that group out of the air.

What were the American fighters that escorted you?

We couldn't tell because they didn't fly with us. They traveled faster than we could. We had plans where we had fighter cover from different fighter groups. One group would be there and when their gas got low they'd bring in another one.

Can you describe what it was like to have anti-aircraft flak shot at you?

There's nothing you can do about it. On our fourth mission we had an aircraft blow up right off our right wing. It just disintegrated right there…direct hit. We had flak in all our missions.

They had a technique where they'd shoot the guns up at our altitude and hope to hit something. They didn't try to follow us. They'd pick a designated area over the target and shoot. It worked sometimes.

Did your plane ever get hit by flak?

The bombardier got hit in the neck. That was the only time anybody got hurt in our crew. It was a small piece, and he got a Purple Heart for it.

So you were never in any danger of being shot down?

Every time they shot at you, you were in danger. But the odds weren't that high they'd hit an airplane. But with 500 guns, that makes a pretty dark cloud over the target.

There was a pretty high casualty rate for the bombers…

There was at the beginning, but when I was there the Germans were out of oil and couldn't supply their airplanes. So in essence they were grounded in 1944. But they were working on those jet airplanes.

On our last mission I got to see some of those, but they didn't attack, they were just training. They moved at high speeds. We flew at about 200 miles per hour. Those things could fly 400 miles an hour, which was fast in those days.

What was the main altitude you flew at?

It varied on the target. We were under 9,000 feet when they had that battle in Holland. When the weather cleared we went in at 9,000 feet. I don't think we went over 24,000 feet. It would vary on the weather. That's all figured out before the mission.

After the mission would they debrief you?

Yes, when we landed.

What did you do there?

Had a shot of whiskey! Some of the pilots didn't drink, so we'd get to drink their whiskey too! At the beginning we didn't pay any attention to it, but by the last we thought it was good stuff!

How many total missions did you go on?

We went on 35.

When you came back to base knowing you'd lost some planes, was that hard on your crew?

Not really, because we never did get to know each other that well.

How did your crew handle the pressure of going on

dangerous missions?

You might make it; the chances are you would. There was no fighter opposition to really speak of. But with that flak you could never tell.

Did you have missions over Berlin?

No, we had missions about 40 miles away from Berlin. That was a hot target, really well defended.

Did you have missions over other cities?

Oh yeah, but it depended on what the mission was. We went after several railroad yards, I can remember that. During the invasion we hit bridges to keep the Germans from bringing equipment in. It was all planned ahead.

You mentioned your crew switched from a B-24 to a B-17?

In one week!

Was there any difference between the two?

Oh yeah, the B-24 is mostly hydraulic and the B-17 is almost all electric. The B-17 was a big glider, actually.

Which plane would you say was safer?

The B-17. You could knock a wing section off the B-17 but the B-24 couldn't fly if that happened. The B-24 was a more advanced plane. I was a turret-gunner on the B-17.

What was that like?

It was good for sightseeing! I didn't have to shoot much.

Can you describe how you would come back to base and land?

On D-Day we landed at a different base. We flew the first mission in the morning and for some reason we couldn't get back to our base so we landed at another field. We got back, loaded up and went off again, but we couldn't drop our bombs because of a cloud cover. We couldn't see the ground.

What was your second mission on D-Day?

We were supposed to hit Caen, but we couldn't drop our bombs. That would have helped the invasion because that was a critical landing area.

What type of bombs did you carry?

It depended on the mission. One was a 2,000-pound bomb. We could only pack two. They filled the bomb bay. That's when we were trying to destroy those bridges after D-Day. The rest were usually 500-pounders.

You must have been pretty close with your crewmembers, what States were they from?

Oh yeah, our radio man was from Pennsylvania, our tail-gunner was from Kansas, the nose-gunner was from St. Louis, one waist-gunner was from New York, one waist-gunner was from Philadelphia…

And you're from California!

Yeah!

Sharon Wasson

After your 35 missions what did you do?

I applied for pilot training. The war in Europe ended so the government didn't know what to do with us. They put us through six weeks of flight training and sent us to Houston. Then the war ended.

We were in a small base in Texas. I had enough points to get out, so I got out. I went right to college in Reno. I didn't really have much to work towards. I played basketball and football. I eventually went into flight engineering.

I went to work for a company in Oakland and flew for that company until 1985. I flew almost 25 years as a flight engineer. Most of the work was hauling supplies for the Navy and the Air Force. We supported the defense line around the United States. We'd haul cargo for the government. Half my flying was for that, and half was overseas. I retired early and moved back to Susanville.

How long have you been coming to the Veterans' Reunions?

Since they first started. We originally planned to have them moved to other communities but it didn't work that way, so we've been having them here ever since. We've lost over half of the group.

What was your brother's name?

Glen. He volunteered to join the Marines. He had to lie about his age, so we used to joke that sometimes he was my older brother and sometimes he was my younger brother!

Do you remember what Division he was in?

He was in the Twenty-First Marines. I don't know what division that was, but he got shot-up three times. He talked about Tinian, Iwo Jima, and Guam.

Why do you think so many Indians served in the war?

That's a good question, I don't know why I served! Everybody else knows why they served! But now that I'm thinking about it, we're taking a horrible beating from the Bureau of Indian Affairs in Winnemucca.

We've got something they want and they're doing everything they can to take it. The BIA wants to take our land. So a man should know what the issues are before he does anything like that (volunteer for the service).

A man can't take anything with them when they die. If they can't take anything when they die, how can they say they own it? That's the truth.

Do you think we should learn about Indian people?

Yes, because our way, our religion, this is the way I had it explained to me: The Earth is our Mother, the Sun is our Father and we're all part of God's Creation. We live by His laws. Men make rules, God makes laws.

Sharon Wasson resides in Susanville and enjoys visiting with other Indian veterans. He is working on documenting the economic and political situation between the Shoshone people and the BIA.

Wally Scott

Wally Scott is of Yurok ancestry and he met with me on November 19, 2003 at his home in Arcata. He was a member of the Army Air Corps during World War Two.

I was born on September 16, 1923 so that makes me 80 years old! I was born at Luffenholtz up by Trinidad. My father was Walter and my mother was Mabel Stevens. She was Yurok and her father was Indian but we don't know what tribe.

She was born in the Blue Creek area. My father was Scottish and Irish. He was raised at the west end of Blue Lake in that area. From what I know his family came through Nova Scotia from Ireland and Scotland. I was too young to talk to my grandparents when they were alive.

I had one sister but she's gone now. My aunt Minnie took me to Blue Lake. She was a white woman and was married to Oliver Scott who was Hupa Indian. That's who raised me. I was raised all my life in Blue Lake. I left there in 1957. That's my hometown.

What was life like for you at Blue Lake when you were young?

Oh, it was good. During the Depression we used to go fishing and we raised gardens and had apple trees. I worked for my uncle cutting wood where the Rancheria is now. We'd get 10 cents a cord and that was good money! We'd go weed or garden somewhere and get a dime a row. The rows were about two miles long but a dime was a lot of money in those days.

Did you live near any other Indian families?

No.

Do you remember name of the elementary school you attended?

It was Blue Lake Elementary. There were maybe 15 or 20 kids in the class. I never got in any trouble. Some of those kids were outlaws! One of them was a good friend of mine. He was Portuguese. I always got along good.

And after that school where did you go?

Arcata High. We had a bus ride from Blue Lake. There weren't too many people in Blue Lake, maybe a thousand. Then in the 50s they started logging and there were all kinds of people there.

Do you remember the names of any of the Indian kids who went to Arcata High with you?

There was Harold Anderson from Orleans and he was killed in the war in a B-17. Then Wally Griffith, and a Lindgren, and Lee Swanson, Lee Hover...There were quite a few at that time. We all played sports.

Did you have any favorite sports?

Baseball! I played shortstop. I played for the second Humboldt Crabs team here after they started and I played semi-pro baseball. When I got out of high school I went to San Francisco because I had a cousin down there.

I worked at a meat packing factory and I played baseball with them. They had a lot of major leaguers that played with them. In those days baseball players didn't make a lot of money like they do now. So when spring came they sent me by Santa Rosa for spring training and then to Salt Lake City for Class C baseball.

Do you remember where you were when the war broke out?

I was back here working at Samoa at the mill when we heard about December 7.

Were you drafted?

Yes. You know, a young guy doesn't know any better, but I wanted to see something different besides Humboldt and San Francisco! They sent me to Monterey and then to Mississippi. Then they shipped me to gunnery school in Laredo, Texas. From there I went to Sioux Falls, South Dakota for radio school. When I was through with that I went overseas.

So you were in the Army Air Corps?

Yeah, the Army Air Corps.

Were you selected or did you volunteer to be in the Air Corps?

At Biloxi they put me in the Air Corps and sent me to aerial gunnery school and then to radio school to learn about Morse code.

What was it like to go to all those different bases?

I wasn't there at Mississippi very long. They were really getting us in and out. It was really hot at Laredo. Then we went to South Dakota. It would be three in the morning and we'd have to stand at attention in 15-degree weather. But it was all right. I never went to the towns or anything.

Can you describe the gunnery school?

Well, we started with BB guns and then we started skeet shooting with shotguns. At the end we'd go up in planes. There would be a guy with a big sack behind his plane. We'd be in a little plane and shoot at it with 30-calibers. I thought gunnery school was fun. But you had to watch out for rattlesnakes in the prairie!

What did you do in radio school?

It was mostly radio silence when we were overseas. We didn't use it very much or the Germans would know where we were!

All right. So the Army selected you to be on the radio?

I think they gave us some tests to see if we'd qualify to work on the radio. I must have done all right because I had no idea about Morse code! We'd go through classes and hear it over and over.

At nights I'd go over it in my head. I got it down pretty pat. I got to where I take 20 or 30 words a minute with code. There was one Mexican guy who could take 60 words a minute! After the message was over he'd still be writing. Some guys are just born with it and could do it but I couldn't.

Obviously you could or they wouldn't have picked you...

Yeah, a lot of guys flunked out. They couldn't even get five words a minute. They couldn't understand that sound.

Did you ever come across any other Indian guys in the service?

Oh yeah, I met several of them. I remember one guy from Oklahoma; his name was Oliver Redwing. We went to Hollywood on New Year's Eve to this bar. There were a bunch of Marines there. Oliver wasn't a very big guy but he wanted to go beat up those Marines! I said he was crazy, that those Marine had been overseas, but he wanted to fight them!

There was another Indian guy overseas who I met one day. We were talking, he was a big guy and he was a gunner. We got to talking and he said after their next mission we should go to a town that had a bar and drink some beer.

I said sure, and we went on our mission and he was right off our wing. I remember we were going over Paris and we heard a big explosion. That was the end of him; he'd got shot down on his first mission. God! He was a nice guy. I think he said he was Osage but I can't remember his name.

Wally Scott ca. 1942-3.
Photo courtesy of Wally Scott.

So after your training you went to England?

Yeah, we came over in a brand-new B-17 at the end of 1943. We left Nebraska and flew to New York, then to Maine, then to Goose Bay then to Iceland. From there we flew down to Northern Ireland. Then they put us into bomb groups. They were losing so many guys you'd never know who you'd be flying with.

One night you'd come into the barracks and it would be full. The next day there'd be nobody, maybe just a few guys. We lost a lot of men. The last mission I did was on D-Day. I looked down and it seemed like there were a million boats! We finally found out what was going on. They'd kept it a secret.

I was based at a place called Polebrook; it's about 60 miles north of London. There were based all over there.

I was with the 351st bomb group. It's a famous bomb group because Clark Gable was in it.

What was it like at Polebrook?

Luckily, we had barracks better than those poor guys in the infantry. We had a couple hangars where guys would work on the planes. It was a regular air base. I went to London a couple times and there was a town north of us named Peterborough. It was a pretty good-sized city.

Me and another guy were there and I met a guy from Arcata. He said there was another man from Arcata named Kenny Gieger. We were going to meet each other but he got shot down that next day! So we never did meet. But Kenny made it and he's living here in Oroville now.

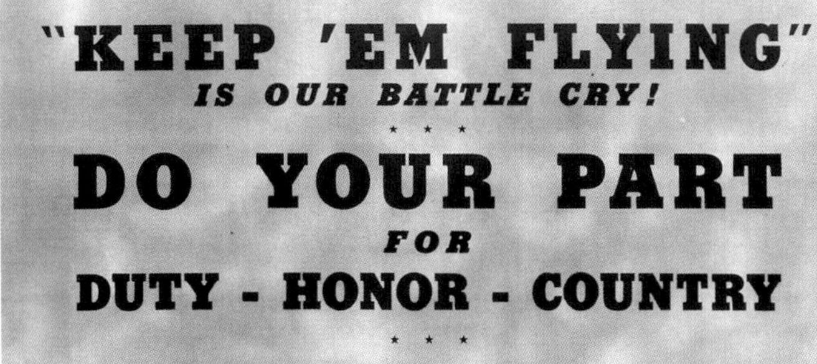

Recruiting Poster
Library of Congress, Prints and Photographs Division, (LC-USZC4-2747)).

Do you remember the name of the first B-17 you flew in?

We called it the *Yankee Rebel.* It was old and beat up but it was a good plane! I also remember the *393 Cuban Queen.*

You went on a lot of missions, can you describe what it was like before you went?

Well, there was a briefing room with a map and they'd tell you where you're going. They'd make a big joke; they'd say we'd be escorted across the English Channel by English Spitfires. After that we'd be escorted by Me-109s and Fw-190s.

Those are German fighters! A big joke, you know! One guy got mad and 'Come with us you SOB!' We were usually at around a 28,000 foot altitude. The heaters never worked but we had woolen clothes on and big gloves.

I remember one time a guy took his glove off. He was ejecting a shell off the 50-caliber. He put his finger on the metal and it froze right to the metal! I had to go back there and pull his finger off that metal.

You mentioned when you were in England you had to live through the V-1 and V-2 attacks, can you describe them?

Oh man, you couldn't hear those V-2s coming. I was down by London about 20 miles away. I was teaching these kids how to work the radio. You could hear the V-1 bombs coming. They had a motor, but those V-2s were rockets. Those were scarier. They did damage to London but they weren't accurate. They'd hit pretty close but I never went to go look!

You ended up as a staff sergeant or a technical sergeant?

As a tech sergeant.

How many missions did you complete before you were raised in rank?

Oh, I don't remember.

When you went on a mission would they tell you what country you'd target, and where did you go?

Yeah, they'd show you on that map. We hit Auckland, Frankfurt, Hamburg, Berlin, Schweinfurt, and we went to Czechoslovakia once. We hit Paris in France, that's where that Indian guy got killed.

They told us that Ford Motor Company had a big ball-bearing plant and not to drop a bomb near it. Another guy told us that he'd had the same order while flying somewhere over Germany. Geez!

When your bomb formation flew what did it look like?

We had six high, one lead, and one low. Sometime we'd only have enough planes to have six out.

Which was the greater danger, flak or German fighters?

There was usually pretty heavy flak but then those German planes came in and knocked the hell out of you. After going through that flak here they'd come. We were no match for those fighters until we had our own fighters over there. We shot some of them down but those 109s got a lot of us.

What would you be doing during a mission?

Mostly sit there with the radio in case any messages came through. On the bomb run they had stuff that looked like tinsel. We had a little door and I had to dump that stuff out. It was supposed to foul up their radar. It looked like Christmas tinsel. On the way back we'd get weather reports on the base.

How long would a mission last?

It would depend on the target. Some took several hours. Short ones didn't take very long. They had submarine pens right across the Channel and those took three or four hours. Those were on the French side of the English Channel.

You mentioned that you flew during D-Day, can you describe that?

Like I said there were all those ships. We got hit pretty heavy by flak over there but not by fighters. Our Air Force had those fighters killed off. I saw those boats down there but I didn't know what was going on until we got back to England that night.

That was the end of my career. Then I came home and trained for B-29s. The war ended just as I was ready to go. So I lucked out there.

Why did they transfer you back, was it because you finished a certain number of missions?

Yeah. Like I said, I taught there for a while. These new kids came in and I taught them how to use the radio. Then they shipped me back here. I volunteered to go on the B-29s. I didn't like it here (at the base). You had to salute the officers. In the Air Corps you never saluted. You'd laugh at people who saluted. But here you had to salute.

It must have been traumatic on the B-17, how would you and your crew get through that time and time again?

I don't know, you had to do it! You're scared of it, you're scared, but then after it's over you go downtown and drink some beer and get over it. If you're still there.

It must have been hard to deal with the fact that some guys didn't come back from a mission...

Yeah, one time this ball-turret gunner under the plane never came up. So we looked under there and all that was left was one bulb. The poor guy got blown right out of there. This wasn't my plane but it was in our group.

Do you remember any names of other planes?

No. Those old planes were all drab brown and didn't have any Plexiglas windows. There were all open and man it was cold! Later on they put that Plexiglas in for the waist gunners and on top.

Were you one of the first groups to go over to England?

No, there were guys there before us. I don't know when they started that bomb group but we were in the middle.

Wally Scott

You were given some pretty high honors for your time over there, do you remember when you were awarded those?

No, they gave that to those guys who flew over there.

When you were given the awards did they mean anything to you?

No.

You were just trying to make it through another day?

Yeah.

Now that you can look back on your time in the service, what are your feelings about that?

I'm glad I did it. It was supposed to be the war to end all wars. We tamed the Germans but look at the world in upheaval now. Maybe all those lives were wasted for nothing.

How about when you learned about what the Germans had done to Jews and Gypsies and others in the camps?

You want to know what I think about that? I think about the American Indian; he went through a Holocaust too and they never made a big deal about that. They still don't.

We got killed off, for Christ' sake. They killed the Jews

and there's a big deal about it. We never had a Holocaust; it was legal to kill us off. That's what I feel about that.

Did anyone in your family share stories about what happened to Indian people here during the Gold Rush?

Yeah, my uncles told me stories. I was awful young when they told me. We'd sit on the beach in Orick and they'd tell me stories.

What do you think the United States could do to make things better with Indian people?

Well, give them an education and an opportunity. A lot of Indians are stuck on the reservation. My wife and I went up to Canada and they had a conference with Indians from Canada, South America and everywhere.

I think about the American Indian; he went through a Holocaust too and they never made a big deal about that. They still don't.

It's terrible how they are still getting pushed off their land. One guy from South America spoke in his own language and told how they lived off the land but these big oil companies came in and pushed them off. Even those Canadian Indians aren't treated right.

It seems like there will always be a struggle for Native rights...

It sure as hell does.

What type of work did you do after your time in the service?

I worked in the woods most of my life. I worked near Orleans and Hoopa. I went to Oregon and Alaska. In those days there were lots of saw mills. I worked in Orleans with a bunch of goofy Indians!

What does it mean to you to be a member of the Yurok culture?

I'm glad I am one. I wish I knew more. I've read books on it. I went to Humboldt State and this one professor said we were Digger Indians and we lived off roots. I said wait a minute, we had salmon and all types of food. I mentioned all our history, and said we didn't live on roots. He said I was right.

I'm glad you said that, those teachers need to be educated!

He didn't know, he read it in a book. This was when I went to school there in 1942 and there were only 400 kids or so. Not like today where there are 7,000.

How many children do you and your wife have?

Two of my own and six step-children. My wife Joanne is well-educated and she's a registered nurse.

How does it make you feel when you see Indian people who work to continue their indigenous traditions?

I went to a conference in Seattle. There were a lot of young Indian people there. They're really getting into their culture.

What would you tell young Indian people today?

Try to learn your language. Try to find out from your elders what they know and what's going on. They'll tell you.

Have you ever been interviewed like this about your time in the service?

No, I never have.

Well, I appreciate you sitting down with me and sharing.

Thank you for coming over.

Wally and his wife Joanne reside in Arcata, Ca. They continue to attend Native gatherings and education conferences.

Ulysses Davis

1918-2006

Ulysses Davis was kind enough to talk with me about his experiences in the war on November 29, 2001. He was of Hupa and Yurok ancestry and lived in Hoopa, Ca. In his younger years Ulysses Davis was a dancer and singer in the traditional Brush Dance ceremonies. He was a well-known and respected member of the Hoopa community. I was surprised to learn that Ulysses knew my grandfather Stan and great-uncle Leonard from when they attended the Sherman boarding school in Riverside together.

I was born on July 24, 1918. My father's name was James Davis and my mother's name was Maggie Henry. I went to grade school in Hoopa until the eighth grade. Then I went to Sherman in Riverside in 1934 and graduated in 1938.

It was a trade school where you could learn just about any trade you wanted. I took blacksmithing and welding. After blacksmithing went out I went into transportation and trucking. After I graduated I went to Reno, Nevada to get into trucking.

I did that for a year. Then I went to work on the Shasta Dam for a few months. I got into the Teamsters Union there. I drove a truck at the Dam on the construction site. When I left the Shasta Dam I went into the Army.

When I came back from overseas I went to the Bay Area to look for a trucking job. Down there I went into a trucking outfit that got their freight from the train system. From there I transferred to another outfit and stayed there until 1951.

I went to another company and stayed there for 31 years. I worked for one company for 31 years and then retired. I went all over the state of California with a truck. The last trip I took was to Grant's Pass, Oregon. I used to call my truck *Old Betsy.* I shut her off the last time in Eureka in 1980.

Who did you know at Sherman?

There were several people I knew down there. Leonard Lowry and Stanley Lowry were my good friends. We had boxing class there. Leonard went on to the Northwest Middleweight championship, I believe. The last time I saw him was in Reno in 1941 or 1942. I was a boxer; it was something I was good at.

What year did you go in the Army?

In 1942 at the Presidio in Monterey. I took my basic training at Camp Roberts. I also went to camp in North Carolina and at a camp in New Jersey. From there we went to North Africa. One guy thought we were going to England, but I told him we were going southwest.

The next morning they said we were going to Africa. We landed in Casablanca. That was in early 1943, I believe. I was with the Second Armored Division. A bunch of us were transferred out and made up a transportation outfit. We went back and forth from Casablanca to Tunisia. After that was over I went into Sicily.

After the Sicilian campaign they took us back to Africa. We got ready for the invasion at Salerno, Italy. I went in with the British and stayed there for a while. We went back to North Africa and regrouped then they sent a bunch of us to England.

We stayed in England and sat out the invasion of France. We went over later. I went through Belgium and southern Germany. When the war ended I was in Innsbruck, Austria.

What did Casablanca look like?

It was surprising, it wasn't that bad. I thought the desert would be worse. It wasn't too bad. We arrived there in January and it was pretty stormy. It could have been worse. From there I went to Sicily. My duties were to haul troops in amphibious boats. They called them "ducks." I took troops in on these. I also hauled war material like howitzers.

I went with the British to Salerno, Italy. At our first landing there was a sniper. There was a big building maybe a hundred yards long and pretty tall. That sniper was in a little dugout up there. He was picking off wounded men on stretchers. One of our guys, a sergeant, went looking for him. He came up to him around a corner. That sniper threw his gun out and said 'Comrade.'

The sergeant filled his stomach full of Tommy-gun shells, for shooting those men on stretchers. Otherwise they would have taken him prisoner. But that sergeant killed him and left him there. That's just part of the war, the things you run into. We lost a lot of men from mines. Lots of men hit mines and were blown up. I saw a horse step on one and he was gone.

We were near a potato field with our camp. They had a British artillery outfit right next to our camp. Afterward I was thinking that if the Germans had found that out they could have wiped all of us out with their artillery!

What did you do when you went through France?

I went through parts of France after they had liberated it and helped haul supplies to different places. We would start at Cherbourg and truck supplies wherever they sent us. We'd ride back in transport carriers.

Lots of men hit mines and were blown up. I saw a horse step on one and he was gone.

What was Austria like?

That was a pretty hilly country. There were a lot of steep hills. The turns were awful sharp in the mountains. I didn't meet any of the civilians because we weren't supposed to fraternize. The houses all looked really clean, and we could see some of the people, but we didn't get to meet them. We were busy transporting supplies. This is hard to remember about, it was a long time ago!

I was a line corporal and had a crew. One time someone overturned a truck, and someone else came and took the ordnance from the back. There was a guard at a bridge, and he told me where the truck went.

I didn't know what to do so I took that ordnance back. This guy didn't have any paperwork to do that, and that was a dangerous thing to do. When new guys would come in the outfit they were non-commissioned officers.

I didn't get promoted anymore because then we had more officers than we needed. I was satisfied with where

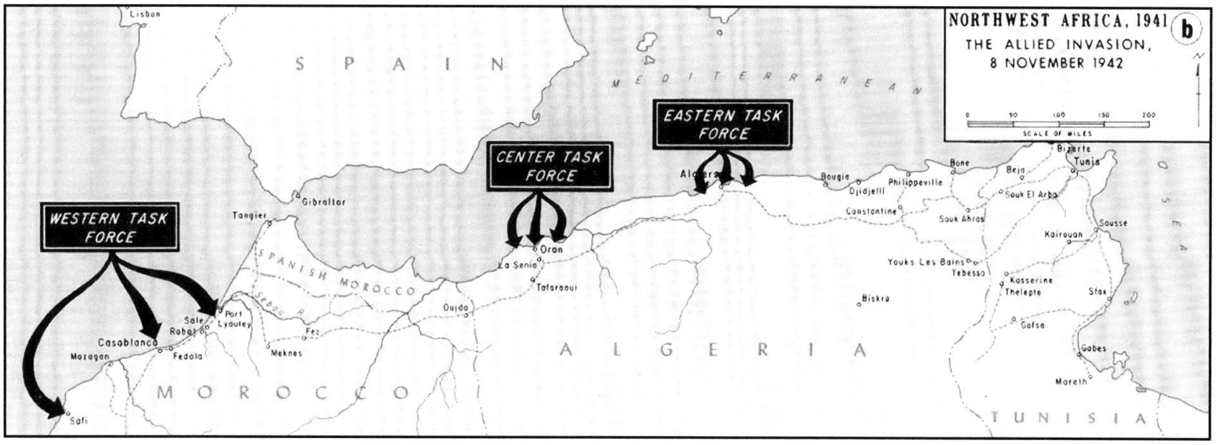

Operation Torch.
From U.S. military sources on wikipedia.com

Ulysses Davis

I was. I knew as much as any officer. My duties were more or less to oversee the truck drivers and my squad of trucks. After the war someone said, 'Oh, you were just a truck driver.' But a truck driver over there was responsible for a lot.

Floyd Richards

Floyd Richards was born on September 19, 1922 in Smith River, California. He is of Tolowa ancestry and is Frank Richard's uncle. Floyd joined the Army in November of 1942 and went to boot camp in Monterey, Ca. He went to camps in Oklahoma, Louisiana, Texas and Virginia before being shipped to North Africa.

Floyd was a member of Company K, 349th Infantry in the 88th Infantry Division. The 88th Division fought in some of the most terrible battles in World War Two in Italy. Their battle campaigns included Rome-Arno, the North Appennines, and the Po Valley. In the hard fighting in Italy soldiers of the 88th Division and other divisions had to crack the German's Gustav line, a defensive belt of fortified positions manned by battle-hardened German soldiers. Members of the 88th Division are credited with being the first to enter Rome.

Elements of the 88th Division also helped attack and eventually pierce the German's Gothic line of defensive positions in the fall of 1944. At the end of the war the division crossed the Po River and were driving toward the Alps when Germany surrendered. For his efforts as a soldier in these campaigns Floyd earned three Bronze Stars. Floyd was a staff sergeant while in Italy.

Floyd Richards in Italy ca. 1943-4.
Photo courtesy of Floyd and Elinor Richards.

Floyd received a Purple Heart for wounds in combat at a special ceremony in Smith River in the late 1990s over 50 years after the war. His records had been lost and encouragement from his children spurred him to work with a local veteran's agent to retrieve his records and re-submit them for the recognition. Floyd's health prevented him from giving a full interview but he was willing to provide information about part of his experiences so readers

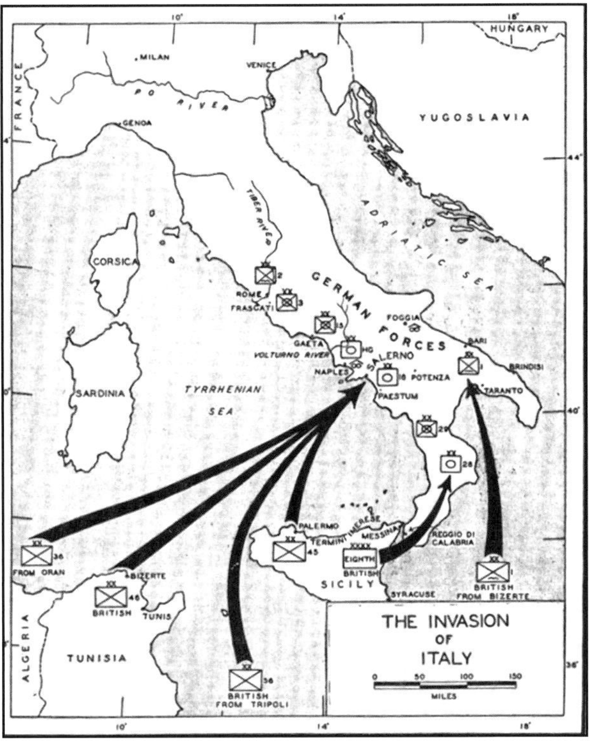

Map of the invasion of Italy, 1943
Map from U.S. Army, www.army.mil.

Floyd Richards

can gain some awareness of the Italian Campaign during World War Two.

Floyd and his wife Elinor have four children and numerous grandchildren and great-grandchildren. After the war he worked in construction and in the logging industry. Floyd's family and his community are very proud of his service to his country.

John Peconam

John Peconam is of Mountain Maidu heritage. He is one of the Indian men I grew up admiring at family gatherings and reunions. John and his wife Vi live in Richmond, Ca. John was a Military Policeman in the U.S. Army during the war.

They invited me to their home and I spoke with John on October 18, 2002. The five-hour trip to visit them went by very fast because I was so excited that John would share with me. We sat at their kitchen table after a great dinner and dessert and talked.

I was born November 26, 1918 in Susanville. My mother's name was Isabel and my father was Earl Peck. He was from Alturas and my mother was from Susanville. I'm from the Mountain Maidu tribe on my mother's side.

Her mother was Roxie Lamb. My mother died at my birth, so the family gave me the Peconam last name, since that's who raised me.

Who raised you?

Inez Peconam. She was my mother's sister. Her husband was Jerry Posey. He was Swiss-Italian. I was adopted by them.

Did they have any children?

No, it was just me.

Ah, an only child, so you got all the dessert?

I sure did!

Where did you go to elementary school?

At Lincoln school. I was the only Indian there.

What was that like, to be the only Indian kid?

Well, as a young kid I didn't pay much attention to it. We got along great. From there I went to Washington school until sixth grade, then another school through eighth grade. I went to high school in Susanville.

What sports did you play in high school?

Well, I played football, a little wrestling, played baseball, and that's it. I played several positions in football. I played tackle and defensive end, and while I was in high school I was a reserve for the junior college. I played high school and junior college football from when I was a freshman.

I went to junior college in Susanville. It was all right (at the high school). I found it a little difficult. It was kind of hostile between whites and Indians there. I was a senior before any Indian kids came to school.

Leonard Lowry graduated out of Sherman and he came back to Susanville and went in as a senior there. And then Johnny Evans came in. Jack Madero came in to the junior college for a while. There were only four of us that I can remember.

Did you get to know your grandmother Roxie?

Oh yes, I stayed with Roxie many times. At that time she was very active. She was very nice. We'd go pick acorns. My dad would drive us out in the truck and we'd get out. We'd get acorns and I used to help her around her place. I used to stay with her when my mom and dad were out working.

Did you gather anything else with her?

Willows and choke-cherries. She used the willows to make baskets. She was quite a basket maker. She liked the choke-cherries because she'd pound the seeds out and make a pudding or bread out of it.

It was food for her. I used to do a lot of hunting. I

owned my own .22 when I was 11 years old. I used to go hunt rabbits and especially ground hogs. Those were quite a luxury.

So she liked to eat ground hogs?

Yes, and she liked porcupines. She used the quill in her work. She'd take the tail and make a hairbrush out of it. She'd take the quills and decorate her garments with them. She'd cut the points off. I remember watching her cook.

She used to do all her acorn pounding in a little stone mortar, and her grinding with a pestle. She would make acorn bread that she would cover with leaves and cook outside on the ground. It was delicious, big, brown acorn bread.

She would make acorn bread that she would cover with leaves and cook outside on the ground. It was delicious, big, brown acorn bread.

Did she ever speak the Maidu language?

All the time. She tried to teach me but I wasn't interested. I was going to a white school and that's what I had to do. I thought it was a waste of time for me at that particular time, as a young kid.

Did she live by herself?

Most of the time, yes.

Did any other older Maidu people visit with her?

She lived by the Morales family. She stayed in one house and they stayed a couple hundred yards away. They helped care for her. By the time I was 16 or 17 I moved away and then went in the service.

I went overseas and then came back to visit her. She always spoke in Indian. At that time she was blind. She could only see figures. She'd send someone to the store, even me, to buy something for her. She'd give me the money, maybe 50 cents or something, and I'd have the change and she'd take it and say, 'Come on, you're cheating me!'

How old did she live to be?

Vi: A hundred and eight.

Do you remember what type of baskets she'd make?

Here's a picture of her. She made a lot of little baskets. That basket there is real fine, like something your great-grandmother made. She did a little beadwork, that's hers too. That buckskin dress, she made.

When did you first start going to the Bear Dance?

When I was about 10 years old. It was down by Johnsonville, and then there was one in Greenville. I know we went in the old model-A Ford we had to one in Genesee Valley. Vi and I have gone to quite a few.

What does the Bear Dance mean to you?

That's a good question, I've never thought about that. I think it's a tradition that should be always kept, and I think the younger people should get involved in it more.

It seems like you were the only Indian kid that stayed in Susanville, and all the others went to boarding schools...

I never went to a boarding school.

Why is that?

I take that back, I went to Fort Bidwell. But I was only there two weeks. That was the worst two weeks of my life! I'm seven years old and in the second grade. We had these stiff uniforms they'd give you. I had a bunk bed and had a hell of a time crawling into it. They had this instructor who took care of that room. He carried a buggy whip. If you did anything he'd hit you on the legs.

The first job I had was to milk a cow. Everybody had to work, we went to school four hours a day and then had to work. I didn't know if you pulled the tail on the damn thing or what! But Sidney Benner was there. He was older.

Stan was there. He was a little older and fell right in with the group. If it wasn't for Sidney helping me and showing me how to milk the cow...They waited, and the cow gave so many pounds of milk, and if you didn't get that poundage or better you weren't doing your work right.

I enjoyed the school part of it. Edith Bowen was teaching there at that time. She was nice. She treated me like a human being. Anyway, I had to work on a manure wagon, where the wheels turn the spikes. Here's a seven-year-old kid on the end of that thing pitching manure; I could have fell in the damn thing. But anyway, Posey and my mother came up and took me out. I was in there exactly two weeks.

Why do you think they took you out?

Well, Posey didn't want me to go to school there. He wanted me to go to a public school. So I came back and went in the elementary school.

Do you remember how you went to Fort Bidwell?

Yeah, a lady from the Indian Agency in Susanville took me.

Were any other Indian kids with you?

No, just by myself.

That must have been pretty scary!

It was scary, all the way. I didn't know, I got up there and the first thing these kids do is try you out to see if you're a bully or a crybaby. I wasn't there maybe 24 hours before I got in my first fight.

Do you remember when they gave you your uniform?

Yeah, the first night you got there. If it fit you it fit you. If it didn't...but they were pretty much the same.

Where did you sleep at night, can you describe that?

In a dorm. There was a big long dorm, just like an Army barracks. It was two beds high. When you went to wash they had a long trough with little faucets along there.

Did boys of all ages stay in that barrack?

No, there were age groups. There were probably 30 kids to a barrack. I wouldn't have known one from another; we were all Indians as far as I was concerned.

Do you remember the names of any other kids?

Well, Sidney was there and Stan was there. I don't remember any others. I wasn't there long enough to know too many of them.

Were there girls at the school too?

Yeah, there were girls there. They lived across the little parade ground there. If I remember right, they wore a skirt with a blouse and a jumper.

Did you ever have to do any marching?

No.

What would be a typical day?

Well, the first thing we'd do is clean up then go to breakfast. My schedule was to go to the barn. The guy would tell you what to do. I had this cow I needed to milk. I got so I could do it. I always needed help and Sidney Benner was there to help me.

After that we'd clean the stall. On that manure wagon I was on there were three of us. There was an older boy that drove the horses, then there was the boy who pitched the manure onto the wagon, and then I pushed it off into the wheel when it was moving along. Then when lunchtime came along we went and got cleaned up and went to school. Then when we came back we had dinner and it was time to go to bed.

Do you remember if any kids spoke their Indian language?

No. I associated with more of the Indians when we were in the classroom. Then of course they did the reading in English.

What was Fort Bidwell like?

Well, there was the town of Fort Bidwell there. There was a lane that went up to the school. There were the barracks that were in a line and they had a small parade ground in the middle. The farmland was all on one end.

The buildings were a kind of dark gray; it looked like a prison. To me, not being around that type of living, I was homesick, scared, and happy when they came to pick me up from there.

Did you ever see any of the kids get punished?

No…I did see them get slapped enough.

So that would have been around 1925?

1924 or 1925.

They did away with that school in 1930…

I don't know. I remember when Vi and I went up there to show it to her. There were a few Indians living there, but there was no school.

Was the junior college you went to called Lassen Community College?

Yes.

You were probably one of the first Indians to attend…

I was told I was the first Indian that graduated out of Lassen Union High School and the junior college. I graduated from the junior college in 1940.

Do you remember where you were when you heard about Pearl Harbor?

Yeah. I went into the service and went to boot camp at Camp Roberts for 13 weeks. This was on an 18-month enlistment. Then they were forming an Army Military Police (MP) unit, so they had a specification that you had to be 170 pounds. That didn't mean anything, they took you anyway. I applied for it and passed the physical exam.

I was in Las Vegas at the airport to fly to Reno when they called all personnel back over a loudspeaker. Pearl Harbor was attacked.

Then they asked you a couple questions and I passed that. They brought a cavalry company from Camp Riley who had already been through that and brought them to Camp Sibert, Nevada. They shipped us to Camp Sibert. That was where we started learning the MP routine.

The instructors there were retired civil officers and retired FBI men along with regular Army officers. We learned surveillance, traffic, report writing, fingerprinting and then through the regular Army we learned guns and guard work and all that. While we were there my 18 months were just about up and we were getting ready to go on furlough.

John Peconam in 1946.
Photo courtesy of John Peconam.

I was in Las Vegas at the airport to fly to Reno when

they called all personnel back over a loudspeaker. Pearl Harbor was attacked. So they came and rounded us all up, took us back, put us in trucks and over a period of 24 hours we were in San Francisco. We came to Fort Mason and lived in little tents.

Our job there was to take these young commanding officers and raise hell with them to see that they wouldn't break down.

We did guard work on the piers. I had Pier 45 which is the end of Fisherman's Wharf. This was to keep all the civilians out; they had a barbed wire fence across all of it. Each pier had an MP stationed to it. I was there about three months.

Then we were moved to Oakland where we did police work. Then from Oakland I went to Fort Benning, Georgia. That was where I learned to become a sergeant. Our job there was to take these young commanding officers and raise hell with them to see that they wouldn't break down.

How would you do that?

By having inspections and seeing if their shoes were polished; we had white gloves and went through their barracks and went under the bed then under the springs for dirt. We went through their pockets. In close order drill we'd yell at them.

We didn't beat them or anything, I'd yell at them for a while then another sergeant would come over and yell at them; we'd just keep going at it. You could pick out the weak guys. You could tell the ones who were officer material right off the bat, but that wasn't our job.

Then I came back and did some more duty in Oakland then I went to Fort Lewis in Washington. We went to another Military Police outfit there and trained. Then we were called...there was 15 of us. We were all called together and told we would never go overseas because we were such a valuable team.

The companies we trained passed with real high grades. While we were there I was a swimming instructor! Each and every one had to learn to tread water and swim through fire and stay afloat for 15 minutes. This was in February at American Lake; there was ice on the damn lake!

We got pass that and we were shipped to Camp Milestandish out of Boston. They were getting ready to go overseas. So the 15 of us thanked God, we were supposed to go to Camp Kilmer in New Jersey with another training outfit.

So we took all these men down to the boat, and the first name they called was mine! Then they went right down the list and called all the rest of them! So we went out and formed into a convoy and proceeded to Europe.

We had one destroyer with the group we were in and

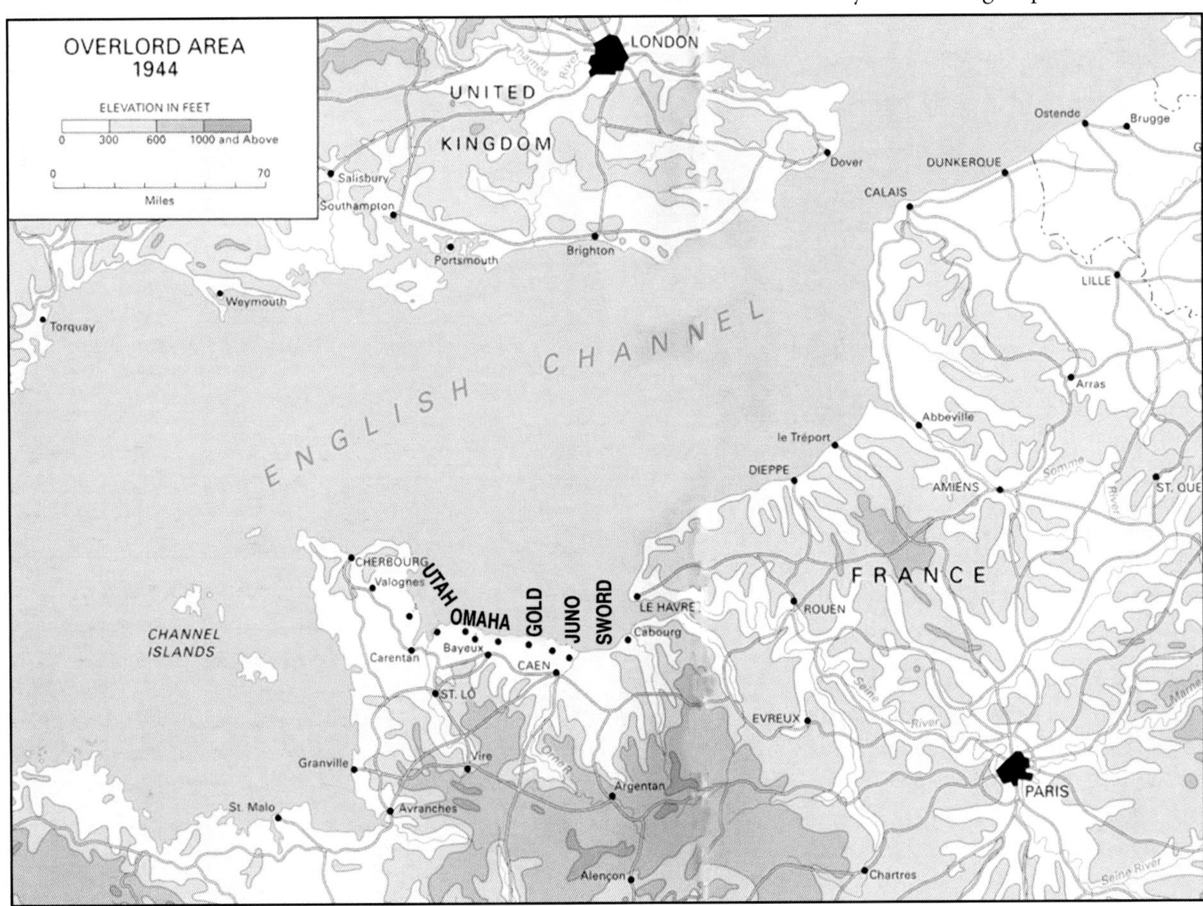

Allied code names for beach targets in Normandy.
Map adapted from U.S. Army, www.army.mil.

they had these Canadian torpedo boats. Somewhere out in the ocean they had a submarine scare. It was foggy. When they had these submarine scares they'd form a smoke screen and then the ships disperse. When they had a submarine scare we'd come to the top on deck. You figure there are maybe 3,000 men on a damn boat and we're sleeping in these damn holes.

There were all-metal bunks set 18 inches apart. It's like rain in there all the time from our breathing. Well, we never saw the ship but we did see black smoke. We didn't know if it was one of ours or not. But when we got out of this scare we were all alone.

Then all of a sudden here came all the ships forming into another convoy. We went into Greenock, Scotland. We were loaded into a train and went down into England. We were billeted there for about three months. We had combat training there.

Going back a little, you decided to join the service way before Pearl Harbor, why did you do that?

Oh yeah, there was a draft (after Pearl Harbor). I had a buddy with two young kids and he was drafted. So one of the people on the draft board that we knew let me take his place so he wouldn't have to go. He never did go.

What was your friend's name?

Clyde Beatty.

And he lived in Susanville too?

Yeah, and later he moved to Chico.

He must have been very appreciative of what you did...

Well, I don't know, it was just that we were good friends. We hunted a lot together. He may have never went anyway but he was within the draft age.

When you heard over the loud speaker that Pearl Harbor was attacked, do you remember what you felt?

At that particular time it wasn't announced there was a war on. It was that we were being attacked. Pearl Harbor was being attacked and all personnel were called back. You're all excited, here you want to go home and you're being picked up and taken back to camp.

You didn't have time to think about anything. Then when they announced there was a war on...I felt it was my duty. I was trained to go. I was trained to do what I was supposed to do and I was willing to go.

And how old were you at that time?

Between 21 and 22.

So you made it England, where did you stay?

We stayed in a little town called Sully Hull. We were just a quiet company. We were allowed to move around. We were billeted in homes. We never trained outside of calisthenics and a little close order drill in that area.

From there we were moved to a place called Starport, which was a big Army camp in England. This was where we started to do more combat training and so forth.

What was your combat training like?

Same as it was in boot camp, rifle, drills, marching. One thing that I always remembered was they had a picture of the beach. I don't know if it was Normandy beach or whatever but they took each platoon and on this picture there was a big gun emplacement. It was 16 feet from the bottom of the sand up to that area there, and there was a cliff.

They said our platoon would go in there as close to the beach as we can; we had these great big spikes to push into the chalk cliffs to try to eliminate that gun emplacement. Well, when we were going over there my platoon got that, but we were lucky, when they were bombarding from the ships they knocked the gun out.

So what we did, we got up there and we stayed at the bottom of the cliff. Then we followed the cliff around and moved with the infantry. Then we went into the town of St. Gilles and into an apple orchard. That was where we stayed, in the apple orchard between the hedgerows with the Germans on one side and us on the other. We lived in foxholes. We never saw any combat. Shells would come over.

Then we went into the town of St. Gilles and into an apple orchard. That was where we stayed, in the apple orchard between the hedgerows with the Germans on one side and us on the other.

John and Vi Peconam

That was your first time in combat, what day did you go onto Normandy, you said it was D-plus one?

Yeah. That's not one day, that's one hour after the first wave...We were so scared, you wanted to get where you were supposed to go. I guess being scared gets you so that you're not scared. I mean, you're moving all the time. You don't think about it until you're stationary.

What type of craft did you take to get to the beach?

Hell, I don't know...An LST, where they lower the front down. My unit, we had one man wounded and that's all. We lost some after, but not right then. We were on the beach for three days before we moved. We moved around, we got up to the gun emplacement. We moved as a unit, not as individuals.

When you went up the beach to the gun emplacement, were there Germans there?

Yeah, they were dead. The first dead Americans I saw were floating when we lowered the boat to come out. I saw a lot of dead Germans after we got on top up there.

Do you remember what beach that was?

Utah.

Do you remember what division you were in?

We were special troops moving in with the 103rd or the 83rd, I don't know. Of course, after they got situated we were the ones that put up the signs that said go this way or that way.

We were to collect all guns, cameras and binoculars in the village.

How would you go about doing that, did you have maps to look at?

Yeah, we had maps. Lots of times we were ahead of a unit and we had little round signs with an arrow on it. To go forward the sign was up, to go back the sign was down. For instance, they'd move a corps over here then our job was to see that all the traffic is on the right of this new position. Lots of times we'd take coffee cans or they'd give us these cans that were already perforated with holes in them and you'd put a candle in them to show the way.

You were putting up these signs in hedgerow country?

Yeah, then we pulled out of there and moved down to Muraz and then to St. Lo, then from St. Lo to...I can't remember all those little towns.

What kind of weapons did you carry while you were doing your duties?

I carried a .45 and a Garand rifle. I wanted something, if I had to shoot, I wanted something to shoot away with. We also had six hand grenades per person but never really used them. We did get into a few skirmishes. One was at St. Lo; I got hit in the leg but it was a minor scratch. I was lucky; I got hit three times but not enough to get me a 23% disability.

What happened that first time you got shot?

There was a sniper. Nobody was around and we were in a jeep. My leg was out and moving...of course they got him. The guy in the back of the jeep in back of us saw the spit of the gun, the little puff, and they pulled over and got the guy. We stopped at a medical station, took a rod, put a little cotton on it, put some iodine on it and cleaned it. It was just a muscle.

Did you ever have any close combat?

No.

When you moved as part of your mission, would you move in pairs?

We moved with five to a jeep. We always had a control center. They'd tell us where to go. They'd designate us a small village. Our job in these villages was to work with the *FFI,* which was the Free French unit, I don't know what the 'I' stands for, but to work with them to clean out any German snipers. (*FFI* stood for French Forces of the Interior, which was the organization of fighting groups within occupied France).

We were to collect all guns, cameras and binoculars in the village. In France and Germany each little town had a square. Each little town would have a town crier who would go around and give the news.

At this village we had a boy who could speak French and German really well. I had two men wounded and I decided we'd have them (the French) do that. He told them what we wanted and they would bring in all the weapons they could and then go look for more. Meanwhile, we'd find the most important guy we could, a doctor or a mayor, and we'd bring him into the house there and shove him around.

We had this red ink there, and we'd mess his hair up, pull his clothes out, and bang our hands together a lot. We'd tell them if they didn't bring in the rest of the weapons we'd shoot him. You'd be surprised at all the other stuff that'd come in.

Then we'd give him a pound of sugar or some coffee and send him home. That was the only way we could get these weapons out of people's hands. Then the GI maintenance would come up, load all that stuff up, and take it back.

Can you describe what the French resistance people looked like, or how you would meet with them?

Well, they usually wore a banner on their arm. In most towns that were taken they were there. The ones that were with the Germans were gone. We were in one little town, and the (French) guy takes me to a garage and there were three women there.

All their hair was cut off and they'd been beaten. There were three graves that they'd dug. They were shacking up with German officers. We couldn't stick our nose into this, because there weren't enough of us.

We just had to walk away. We heard the shots. But they (the *FFI*) did a great job of helping cleaning out the Germans. We'd give them supplies and they'd tell us who was a German sympathizer.

So you'd do this before other units came in?

Yeah, we were ahead of a lot of units. We were ahead of the infantry a lot of times. One particular time we were moving the 12th Corps into Germany and we were supposed to get at this intersection; some other guys were supposed to lay out the track and we were supposed to take these guys and move them to a new area.

We pulled up there and we could hear the Germans talking in their tanks. We were just a block on the other side of us. They knew we were coming because they were moving out!

That must have been very intense...

Oh, it was scary as all hell! Here's five guys... But I don't know, it's not like the infantrymen that go out and shoot each other all the time. You'd see these infantrymen go out, and they'd be calm. They'd come back and you'd see them. But I guess we had a lot of scary moments, some tense moments...that never really bothered us.

This unit was moving in, the first in this particular area, and they were driving with little tiny lights on the jeeps. There was a whole unit coming in, and somebody had turned off one of the lights, so they got off wrong. We heard them going up, we knew the sound of American trucks, so we got up there and the other four (MPs) got on the side of the road away from the trucks with their guns, and I had a flashlight.

I stopped the jeep and went over there. I didn't know the new password to give them, because we were out there. Anyway, I told them what we were there for. This guy had a canvass over him and he had a map. He asked me to show us where we were. He pulled the canvass back and I shined the flashlight in there, and this was Tommy Whitmeyer, who I had gone to school with and played foot ball with from Susanville!

This was about one in the morning. So we turned them around and got them going on the right road. This was about six jeeps and 15 trucks. The next morning, we hadn't slept, but we told the captain where the Germans were. But as we looked around, we saw we had turned them around in a minefield! There was a big sign saying 'Achtung! Mines!' We turned them around and got them out of there!

The scariest part of that, after we moved the Corps, we dug in foxholes to sleep; they had what we called *Midnight Charlie,* which was a German observation plane. The anti-aircraft opened up on it. That's what really scared me, because all this flak started falling down and it hit in this water and started sizzling. You could actually see it. They shot from different directions and that thing flew right over us.

And this was in Germany?

Yes.

Going back, after you went through St. Lo, where did you go?

We went through southern France and past the Maginot Line. We went up past that and into Luxembourg. We moved a lot of units in and out of there. It was wintertime then, with snow.

Did you have snow gear?

No, but we met a medical outfit moving through and I talked to their supply man. They were the best-equipped people I ever knew, they had overshoes...He gave us blankets, he gave us wool sweaters, and we were well-supplied.

We stayed in a summer tourist's hotel there in Luxembourg. We had one conflict there. There was a young German soldier up in the belfry of a church. There was an artillery outfit across from us. This kid put his rifle out to aim at someone and one of my guys saw the rifle barrel. He never fired because the captain sent 10 men up there and they captured him. I don't know what they did with him.

When the big push came we were with the 6th Armored. We'd watch these tanks go out. Each tank had a little banshee siren on them, and they'd wail. They had these minesweepers, they were tanks with a long wide rod on each side, like a bulldozer, but they had chains on them that would beat the ground as they'd go to explode mines.

I saw tanks I couldn't believe. They looked like somebody drilled them full of holes. A tank-retriever would be pulling this tank back that was burnt and looking like a woodpecker got to it, but this was metal.

You mentioned that at night you could tell the difference German and American vehicles, what would a German vehicle sound like?

Well, it was just a different sound. Some of them have a missing cylinder; there was no rhythm to it. Most of their vehicles were the old-type chain driven vehicles. We'd knocked out a lot of their factories; the Air Force did a hell of a lot of damage to them. They even used horses to pull wagons.

He pulled the canvass back and I shined the flashlight in there, and this was Tommy Whitmeyer, who I had gone to school with and played football with from Susanville!

What would American vehicles sound like?

Just like vehicles now.

What was the country of Luxembourg like?

It was very forested and very hilly from where we were. There may have been areas of farmland, but we never saw that. And it was wintertime.

Was it cold?

Oh! The day we got in there it was 40-below. We were there for a while; this was when Bastogne was going on, during the Battle of the Bulge. We got orders to take small tanks through Luxembourg on the road. We're on the jeep leading and we came to this field that was all plowed out. There was snow everywhere.

I stopped the jeep and told this commander this wasn't right. It was a trap. He got up on the tank and said 'No, go on.' So we went through, the Germans let us through. Then they knocked out the first tank, and the one in the middle, and the one in the back. They isolated maybe 25 tanks.

They couldn't move, they couldn't fire, because the snow was banked up. We abandoned the jeep and worked our way back through the snow because the firing was only on one side. We got back and by that time the captain had got on the radio and called for help. More tanks came and a plane came over.

The hospital at the camp where we stayed had a big tent, like a circus tent. They had stretchers and under those there was a stovepipe. This was how they kept from freezing to death. I was on a jeep by this bridge when a plane bombed it and was hit by a piece of concrete, so I had to go to the hospital to have it removed.

Then we went into the Bulge. Our duties were to bring troops in. They wanted to try to relieve Bastogne. The Germans had them cornered from three ways and were moving in on them. Our big problem there was artillery, ours and theirs. It would hit into the trees and splinter them. There were mines too.

Do you recall the mood of the soldiers when you were moving into Luxembourg, did you think the war was almost over?

I saw them piled up on the road like cordwood, 20 feet high and twice as long as this house; dead prisoners waiting for grave registration to put them in trucks.

We never thought about that. After Luxembourg we moved into the southern part of Germany. At that time we knew the war was pretty much over because we'd see these lone German soldiers AWOL. We never stopped, we never kept a soldier.

We didn't have room for them. But we'd check their packs and take their guns and any ammo and let them go on. That was our first sign. Then we started seeing civilian prisoners walking. Their camps had been overrun by the Americans and they were moving home.

What did they look like?

Oh, skeletons. I mean, we'd see them with their entrails hanging out. And you can't give anyone food, because if you give one food and drive away the others would attack him and kill him.

The Germans, we saw prisoners hanging on telephone poles like Christmas ornaments. You wanted to help them but you couldn't do it. You just had to harden yourself to it and keep going. It was the same way with the dead on both sides.

So civilians you saw were Jews?

They were Jews, there were Hungarians, there were Poles, and probably even German sympathizers.

Did any of them wear the striped uniform?

Yes. They didn't have any way to get out of them.

That must have been really terrible to see...

Yes, it was. But like I say, you have to harden yourself to that.

Now that you've had time do you think about it, or do you not think about it?

Well, at night. I'm sleeping and have nightmares. It scares the hell out of me. I took some pictures at this German town. They killed about 500 people, the Germans did. They just threw them on the ground and covered them up with a bulldozer with dirt.

Well, we found them. We made the German civilians dig them up and lay them out. I took pictures of that; babies, women, boys, old men, old women. We had a bulldozer come in and dig a big, long trench. Then the grave registration put them in body sacks; one man, one woman, and so forth. If they had a name or found something on them they'd put that in there.

I know this is hard to remember for you, but when you were going through Germany, and you saw the civilians coming from the camps, did you see them from inside a camp, or from the roads?

I saw them on the roads. I saw them piled up on the road like cordwood, 20 feet high and twice as long as this house; dead prisoners waiting for grave registration to put them in trucks.

Did you or any of your men speak to them?

No, we were told not to.

Where were you when the war ended?

I was in Czechoslovakia. We were supposed to lead a unit that was going to bring some horses. All we knew was they were valuable horses. We were supposed to escort them to Munich and loaded them up. I guess the Americans would take them home.

But the war ended. Then we went back to this little town, then we got called back to Munich, and we were put on trains back to Camp Lucky Strike. When we were at Camp Lucky Strike in France we got a jeep and went back to Utah beach, which was about 20 miles away. There were five of us.

On this trip back we pulled up to where that gun emplacement was . The beach had moved away from it a little. But we were looking down and they had long sticks with a big white ribbon or rag stuck in the ground. We asked a sergeant stationed there in an engineer outfit what they were.

Those were unexploded mines, and it looked like a field of daisies. That really scared me. We came through that. Just think how many were killed by mines going off, and these were mines that didn't work, maybe sand got under the trip mechanism.

That must have been really sobering...

Oh boy, that's the one that scared me more than anything else. One of the guys said 'You know someone's up there watching after us.'

So you served with the same five guys the whole time?

Well, there were two teams of us working pretty close together. Our group would go in and stay a week, then the others would, and vice versa. We went into this one town, I don't know the name of it, and this group was there four days and we went in to relieve them.

They loaded up their jeep and told us what to look for and what to watch. Then they pulled over on the side of the road, the road we came in on, and hit a mine. It broke one man's back, and his legs. This other time, see, GIs would build little fires in their coffee cans to warm their food or whatever, and there were piles of coal in all these little towns.

The Germans would take this coal, dig it out and make a paste, put an explosive in there, and cover it over. It wasn't enough to kill you but it was enough to put you out of condition. I saw that happen.

You mentioned that you spent some time in Paris, was that after the war? What was Paris like?

Oh, Paris is Paris anyway it is! They had their galley up there with nothing but show girls. And lots of bars, you couldn't walk into a bar without some girl trying to pick you up.

The Army had a camp with some buildings that they confiscated. We didn't mingle with them too much because we were the guys stopping their trucks. Often times we'd work without an MP sign on us, just in our GI clothes.

Did you get to see the Eiffel Tower?

Yes, the Eiffel Tower, and the Seines River, but we didn't have too much time. Then we went to Camp Lucky Strike and then came home.

When did you get to visit Switzerland?

That was after the war when we were in Germany. We got 30-day leaves so a buddy and I went to Switzerland and bought watches, then came back and sold them.

You had mentioned there was a family that wanted to meet you because you were Indian?

That was Posey's family in Switzerland. There were two brothers that came from the same village that Posey was. We stayed there at the hotel but we ate with this family. They cooked everything in a fireplace in this great big kettle.

They cooked these diced potatoes and they'd break an egg, stir it, and pour coffee and goat's milk in it and heat it up. They laughed when they first saw me, they had expected to see an 'Indian' not a GI!

Did you ever go through any of the big German cities?

I went through Berlin after the war, it was just rubble, and I went through Frankfurt. Berlin was occupied after the war. That's where we sold our watches, to the Russians. Russian soldiers were paid in American scrip.

So while we paid 10 dollars for a watch, they didn't know how much they had, they'd just take the watch and we'd have a sack of money! And doughnuts, that was the most costly thing. We bought them from the canteen.

We'd make a deal with the cook and he'd give us six dozen doughnuts. We never got anything for the doughnuts, but we could move through their areas without being stopped. On the side of the road there would be a whole trainload of stopped vehicles.

So you were going into the Russian zone?

You had to go through them to get to the American zone.

So you bought them off with doughnuts...

We bought them off with doughnuts!

John Peconam

What were these Russians like?

They were just ordinary people.

Were they pretty friendly to you?

These ones were. From what I had heard, they were the most undisciplined soldier there was, their idea of an attack was to just go! I never saw this, I just heard it.

How did you get home?

We came on a boat. It was like a luxury liner and we slept in better bunks. It was a nice trip home, everything was lit up and they had music going. We landed in New York and from there we went to Camp Kilmer.

We stayed there to get new clothing and have our papers signed. Then we went on a C-47 in bucket seats and flew to Sacramento. We stopped in Tennessee, and from there to Palm Springs, then on to Sacramento to Camp Beale just outside of Marysville. Then I was discharged.

What was your rank when you were discharged?

Staff sergeant. I was a sergeant in Oakland.

We'd make a deal with the cook and he'd give us six dozen doughnuts. We never got anything for the doughnuts, but we could move through their areas without being stopped.

I was wondering when you met Vi?

When we were running convoys. We would bring a group of trucks from Stockton to be shipped overseas. We had a control station in Hayward. The MPs would take the trucks from civilians and we would take them to San Francisco.

We had a route down Seventh Street and then over the bridge. We never let any civilians cars break us up. Well, Vi was out there waving. She worked in a soda fountain there on the street. Vi and a cousin of hers and another girl worked there. Every time we went by they would wave. The whole company was stationed in Oakland at that time.

(Patton) and his driver pulled up and he had his dog and his ivory-handled pistols.

And when were you married?

December 23 in 1943 in Reno. I met her about six months before. Two weeks after we were married I was shipped to Boston; then I didn't see her until two years later.

Did you write?

Once in a while.

What was it like to get her mail?

Great!

Vi's giggling over there...

John: Yeah!

Vi: You better say great!

So the two of you met because of the war...

Vi: Yeah, he used to take the convoys right past where I worked. We'd all run out there flirting and waved at the fellows. And I waved at him and he turned the jeep around and came back! That was it.

And now it's almost 59 years later.

Vi: 59 years.

What was it like for you to have your new husband go off to war?

Vi: I missed him, of course. But I worked for the Army base, the Oakland depot, and Western Union. I kept busy.

What was the mood like for you here at home when you heard the war ended?

Vi: I was waiting to hear from him and I got a telegram telling me he'd be home. When he got there we were excited. Then a year later we had our daughter.

A baby boomer!

Vi: Yes, a baby boomer. We also have a son, six grandchildren, and five great-grandchildren.

It sounds like your family is pretty proud of your time in the service.

Vi: Oh yes.

Why do you think so many Indian people were in the service?

Well, most of the Indians were so proud they went into the Marines. I knew of a unit with the 93rd Signal Corps attached to the 12th Corps and they had some Indians in there, but I never met any of them. I saw a general. He was from back East. The tribe he belonged to begins with an 'O.' He was the 12th Corps artillery general.

I did guard duty in front of his bivauc in England. He needed somebody to listen to his speech. He had to deliver a speech. I told him I couldn't leave my post. He said that was all right and he came outside! He said his speech and I told him it was very good. We got to talking about where I was from and what school I went to. I told him I was Indian and what tribe I was.

And that's when you asked if he was Indian?

You could tell he was Indian, he looked liked the Indian off the nickel! He was tall and straight. He said he went to school with the ROTC, and from there he went to military school. He was a quiet guy, he was something like Patton, he'd sit in his jeep and not say a word, but he'd take everything in.

Did you ever see Patton?

Yes. The first time I saw him was in England. That's when we knew we were going overseas. He gave a speech at the camp I was in. He told us that the American soldiers were going into a part of the country where if you didn't look out, they would hit you with a sack of shit!

That's just how he spoke, you know. That was the first time we listened to him. Another time, we were on an intersection, and thank God we had just looked at our maps to see where all these units were and what roads they should take. He and his driver pulled up and he had his dog and his ivory-handled pistols.

We all saluted. A major with him asked us where this particular spot was and how to get there, and we rattled it off just like that. About four days later our captain came over and congratulated us for being so precise with the directions.

The captain said, 'I told him all our men are like that!' And then I saw him in Luxembourg again, but that was at a distance. He was killed in Luexmbourg by a car sliding into him. He's buried there.

Would you say he was an inspiring General?

He must have been. Now (General) Bradley, we had a Puerto Rican sergeant at a control post and our guys happened to be there when a command car came through with two flags flying on it, and he wouldn't stop.

This sergeant took three shots at that command car and Bradley got out! The sergeant said, 'I told your driver to stop and he didn't, I have witnesses.' Bradley gave us a pack of cigarettes! I can't say I smoked with the man but he gave us some cigarettes.

When did you first attend the Veterans' Reunions?

The second one they had. Let's see, all the guys were

there; Stan, Mervin, 'Doggie,' Leonard, the Jacksons, Herman Williams…

Was it nice to be around other Indian vets?

Yes, I enjoyed it.

John, have you ever been interviewed or asked about your time in the service by someone other than your family?

No.

Did you ever talk about your experiences in the war?

The grandkids would ask me. I told Johnny the last time he asked me about medals and heroes and so forth. I said that everybody who was over there fighting, as far as I'm concerned, is a hero.

John and Vi Peconam continue to attend the Bear Dance held near Susanville, which is held on the Roxie Peconam campground, named after his grandmother. John is a second cousin with Gene Ryan, a first cousin with Jack Madero, and is a member of one of the largest Mountain Maidu families in all of northern California.

Glenn Moore, Sr.

Glenn Moore Sr. was a good friend with my grandfather Stan. They knew each other from their time at Sherman and they visited each other often over the years. When I first met Glenn he recognized my last name and called me "That little Maidu boy."

I didn't know at the time that he knew my grandfather. Glenn is of Yurok ancestry and has been a traditional singer and dancer in the Brush Dance ceremonies of the Yurok people for many decades. He and his wife Dorothy agreed to meet with me at their house on November 8, 2001.

I was born on the Klamath River near a little village called Sregon. There's a big rock known as Moore's Rock a little ways from Sregon, that's where I was born. I was born in 1920, but the BIA (Bureau of Indian Affairs) has me born in 1919. I don't have a birth certificate so I went by that age.

I was in a big family. There were 11 children altogether. I had an older brother named Bennett. He was in the infantry at the end of World War One. He and his uncle Homer Cooper went to Fort Lewis in Washington, I think that's what it was called. While they were in basic training the war ended.

When World War Two came along I was already in the service. At that time they told you if you're drafted they put you where they want you. If you enlist you get to choose where to go. I was visiting my brother Bennett when he told me this. He had been in the Army infantry during World War One.

In the second war he was in the Navy, and had traveled all over the world. He was a quiet man. He was killed in New Guinea in 1942. He had been drafted and they had sent him to the same base there in Washington that he had been in during World War One. He wrote to me when I was at school at Lowry Field in Colorado.

I was in armament school. He had said he was going to go to the Pacific. I wrote back a little bit. The last time I saw him he had told me to enlist in the Air Corps, not the infantry. So that's what I did, I enlisted in the Air Corps. I listened to my older brother.

But going back to his story, it wasn't very long when I received his letter. He had been shipped out. I then got a telegram from the Red Cross that he was killed in New Guinea. So I came home and helped my mother take care of things.

Where did you go to school when you were young?

My mother and father couldn't read or write. If I got a bad report card they couldn't tell the difference! I got by. I got to Sherman and that wasn't too bad. You go to school half a day and then work in the shop half a day.

I never got good grades there, either. At armament school, which was a pretty tough school, it had to do with all the weapons on an airplane; whether it was bombs, or later on, rockets and sights on the bombers. They had a special bomb-sight school right across from us. That place was guarded 24 hours a day. We didn't have anything to do with the bomb sighting. They had other guys go over there. We had 50-caliber machine guns and 20-millimeter cannons. They even had a 37-millimeter cannon on an Air Cobra. I don't think it worked out very good.

We had to synchronize the guns. The bullets had to go through the propellers, so it had to be synchronized. Otherwise you'd shoot the props off.

Anyway, when I was going to school there at Lowry Field I would see these yard birds, they called them yard birds; they would be walking outside picking up cigarette butts and filling up the coal buckets. They burned coal in the classroom stove. I talked to some of those guys; they had washed out of school and were waiting to go in the infantry or as engineers. As soon as they got enough of them they shipped them out.

I got to thinking about what my brother had said, and decided I better study. I had a hard time; some of those guys went to college and it was easier for them. We had to synchronize the guns. The bullets had to go through the propellers, so it had to be synchronized. Otherwise you'd shoot the props off. That had to be pretty precise. There's a lot of math involved. There was electrical work too.

So anyway, we finally graduated. The course usually took about nine months but I think they cut it way down. While I was going to school there I was waiting for a furlough. I didn't have any money but I was lonesome, I wanted to come home.

My folks didn't have any money and I didn't want to bother them. Lowry Field is a little east of the Rocky

Mountains near Denver. I used to look up at the white mountains. I used to hitchhike a lot.

I thought I would hitchhike up over those mountains. I was watching this list where they put people's names down for a furlough. About that time we were listening to the radio that Pearl Harbor was bombed. They had all military personnel back to their units. So they tore up that list and we were in for the duration.

I enlisted for three years. When I enlisted, during World War One they treated the draftees so bad... I used to work with a fellow named Tim Safford. He was in the infantry, he went to France. He said when they went on the troop trains going East they wouldn't even let the draftees out of there.

Glenn Moore, Sr. ca. 1942-3.
Photo courtesy of Glenn and Dorothy Moore.

If they did get out, they had guards watching them. The enlistees did whatever they wanted. So when World War Two came along, they wanted to do away with that and kind of make up for it. So then the first three months I got 21 dollars a month and the draftees got 31 dollars a month. They were treated pretty well, too.

When I got through school they were shipping everybody out. Some went to Hamilton Field; others went all over the United States. My barracks were getting empty; I wondered when they were going to ship me out, you know.

Finally, they said to report to this hangar. It was three miles down the way. They said I was going to be an instructor. I couldn't even recite a poem in front of a classroom, how the hell could I be an instructor? I lost some sleep over that! They sent me to another month of school.

I started teaching small arms and ammunitions. I just studied that part of it. I had a hard time, but I got better. On the Fourth of July they opened up Buckley Field farther east. Fighters used to go out there and practice their gunnery. So anyway, I went to Buckley Field. Some went to Yale.

There were only three armament schools; Yale, Buckley Field and Lowry Field. Lowry Field was for the heavy bombers like the B-24 and the B-17s. They taught air gunnery there, too. Fighters had a kind of simple bomb run because they didn't carry too many bombs. I was in a fighter-bomber, the P-38s, P-51s and P-47s. The fighter-bombers were kind of in-between the fighters and bombers.

I stayed there a couple years then I got kind of tired doing the same thing. By that time I was teaching electrical wiring for armament controls. I got transferred over to a mobile unit and went to California. I was training with this P-38 mobile unit.

These guys had been there for a year before I got there. They had come from Maine. I joined them as the armament man. We traveled all around, mostly on the West Coast. Then they told us we had to go overseas. We went to Denver to our headquarters. I was on detached service the rest of the time.

We went overseas to England and were attached to the Eighth Air Force. The Eighth Air Force had P-38s. They flew the escorts. We went to quite a few English bases there. We had a P-38 that was all stripped down in a trailer. Those guys rigged the trailer so it could ship out.

There was one big Royal Air Force base about half-

Glenn Moore, Sr. (bottom row, far left) and members of his company in Paris in 1944.
Photo courtesy of Glenn and Dorothy Moore.

way up England; they had all the big bombers. Those bombers look small compared to what they have now. But they were losing officers and good pilots. Every day somebody else would go down.

There were fuel tank problems; there were belly tanks and other tanks on the plane, and you have to remember to switch the tanks when you get a warning. Some of the guys would forget to switch the tanks and they ran out of fuel. Things like that happened.

Do you remember which ship you were on when you went to England?

The Queen Mary. I don't remember the ship I came back on, it was a small American ship. Coming over, we crossed the North Atlantic up near Iceland in March. I remember it was cold outside.

Were you in England during the buzz bomb attacks?

I was in London when those came over. A lot of the buildings had been hit pretty badly. There was rationing and you couldn't hardly get good food. This was in early 1944. When we got to London we got to the train depot.

London is spread out several miles. It isn't like New York. The reason I heard that London was built this way was New York is built on solid rock and they could build big skyscrapers and London is built on softer ground so they spread it out. We'd go out in the country and there'd be these little tunnels with small trains. Those trains would go underground and you could travel all over in those tunnels.

There was a big racetrack where the King and Queen would watch horse races. The whole thing was full of American military vehicles. That was where we bivouacked. The first night they put us in a tent. All the tents were tied next to each other.

We went to bed. About two or three in the morning we could hear that siren toward the English Channel. Pretty soon it got louder. They relay them. It was a German bomber. This guy was sitting there at night with a cigarette in his mouth. They had told us not to light cigarettes at night.

We heard that bomber coming in and everybody dove away. One guy had been taking a leak and he ran right into all the ropes that held up our tents and fell into them. A bomb landed not far away, but it had sounded like it was coming right for us. That was our first night there!

We got used to it after a while. We were down toward South Hampton. They used to say that the south end of England was about ready to sink, they had so much equipment there before the invasion. We were at a southern air base three or four days before the invasion. They painted all the American planes with stripes.

The night before the invasion, we didn't know about it, but you could just feel it was happening, it was eleven o'clock in the evening and still light. All these planes came flying overhead. Cherbourg was over this way, and all the planes going that way flew right over the top of us.

We must have stood there for an hour, maybe two hours, and those planes kept coming. And England is not mountainous like it is here; you can see a long ways in any direction. Any way we looked we saw running lights. They rumbled over us. I'll never see anything like that in my lifetime again. The next day they said those planes flew 11,000 missions.

Glenn Moore, Sr.

Our P-38s would come in shot up. They would radio in if they were having problems. The fire trucks would get ready. This one guy came scooting down sideways and skidded along. We saw his prop come flying off. Usually the pilots would scramble out of their planes because the gas tanks might blow. But this guy sat on the wing, pulled a cigarette out and lit his cigarette. The firemen came and took him in.

At Normandy they lost a lot of men on Omaha Beach. Some of the guys told me that the landing crafts would come up to the beach and there were bunkers on top. It reminded me of Agate Beach near Patrick's Point. There were big cement bunkers with 88-millimeter cannons in there. Every time a landing craft would come in they would open up on them with those cannons.

We were inside those bunkers; we walked around in them and looked around. You could look right down on the beach. What also happened, there was another smaller beach next to the main one. There was deep water in between the two beaches. So the guys with full packs would jump out and go right to the bottom. Finally they had enough guys that drowned lying on the bottom that other guys could walk on top of them and get to shore.

I think we lost almost 3,000 casualties that first day. Then the engineers had dozers and they'd get shot, another engineer would get in and go a little further, then they'd get shot. That was a pretty tough time. I went by the grave there and it was all fresh at the time. Now, you see pictures with nice rocks, and it looks pretty. Back then, it was all bare ground and fresh crosses, these little wooden crosses with no paint on them.

The first town we came into was St. Lo. It was just flattened out, no buildings or anything

The first town we came into was St. Lo. It was just flattened out, no buildings or anything. Everything was made of bricks over there. Those French people were digging around where they used to live.

People always talk about the first time you see somebody that's the best impression you get of them; at St. Lo there was a trench with a board across it and some captured Germans were sitting there on the board with their behinds toward us going to the bathroom. That was the first time I ever saw a German. I saw a lot of German prisoners.

How long after D-Day did your unit arrive at Normandy?

It was about a month after. We landed at Omaha Beach. We went through Paris after St. Lo. We got to stay in a big fancy hotel. We thought for sure we'd get to eat steak and have hot baths. There was nothing to eat, we ate our K-rations on a big fancy table and there was only cold water! We could hear shooting at night but we didn't go look around.

When we were in France we were transferred to the Ninth Air Force. That was a fighter-bomber group. They had the smaller planes and were giving ground support to Patton. They took those air bases as soon as the Germans left them.

It shortened their flights. By that time Patton was moving pretty fast, so they sent us back to get ready to go to Japan but they dropped the bomb. I ended the war as a staff sergeant. I was discharged in November of 1945. I had enlisted in September of 1941.

When did you meet your wife?

I came home on a furlough. I grew up down the river. In 1934 or '35 they put the road in. I left for Sherman in 1936. In the summer time I'd come back and work in the woods. Then we'd go back to Sherman. There would be two Greyhound busloads that would go down. After Sherman I went in the service.

So I never went to school here in Hoopa where she did, so I met Dorothy in 1945. They had a hall dance and then had a Brush Dance. They always say that's where our Indian men meet their wives, at the Brush Dances. She was between the two Gray boys, Albert and Walter. She was singing; she was a good singer.

What does the Brush Dance ceremony mean to you?

Well, I saw my first Brush Dance around 1932 or '33 down at Requa. At that time it was Prohibition. There were a lot of bootleggers around. There were a lot of drunk Indians, men and women. There were a lot of fights. So it wasn't very good at that time. It didn't dawn on me what the Brush Dance meant to us.

I think that was about the lowest part of our culture during that time. As I've gone around the country talking to other Indian people we talk about how the same thing happened all over. It didn't just happen to us here; in some places it was worse.

Anytime there was a ceremony going on they deliberately had whiskey and booze around. If they destroyed our culture they'd have us clipped, you know. That's how they do it; if they destroy what you believe in they have you. After the war I finally realized that was not the way it was supposed to be. A lot of us growing up were used to seeing that, and we kind of got the wrong impression.

But back then there were still a lot of old people who could tell us what things really meant. The Brush Dance is a healing dance. I talked to old people here, they said families would live in an Indian house, and if they had a sick baby they'd call a Brush Dance. They'd take the top of their house off and have a Brush Dance. They could have it anyplace.

It must make you feel pretty good to see your family in the dances today?

Oh yeah, we've been trying to teach the young people that it's a religious ceremony. I shared my songs with young Glenn. He used to sing my songs then he sang his own songs. At the first Deerskin Dance he was so small he couldn't hold the pole, he was straddling it.

He was helping sing even then. I like the way he's turned out. I don't know if the ceremony will ever reach like it was in prehistoric times. We hear things, you know, like the Maidu have, about the power they had.

I don't know if we'll reach that because it's changed. You can imagine; I was born in 1920. The people I talked with, they were born in the 1840s. I knew those guys; they were still living when I was just old enough to know what's going on. So the big change that came to us here was in the 1850s to the 1870s when gold was discovered.

So that's when our life changed. Booze came in, white men married or took Indian women, and they moved out of their Indian homes. They'd wear white man's clothes and speak differently. Sometimes I wonder if it might have been a relief to some, because our Indian laws were so strict.

But that power they had, they did things that are hard to believe now. You know how we passed knowledge on, an old man would tell his grandson, like I do with Curtis here, but in those times that was interrupted.

In the old times there were fewer distractions. An old man can teach his grandson or somebody, and that person would learn. The way we lived, we lived in an Indian house. There was the main house, where they cooked and stored food. The men stayed in a sweathouse. When a boy comes along they put him where the men stay.

I was talking with Georgiana about this. They would take a very young boy, so by the time he was a teenager he was very well-educated in the Yurok ways. He was taught how to hunt or be a doctor. The old people had a way how to judge people. They would pick someone and then teach them.

Glenn Moore Sr. and his wife Dorothy continue to encourage their grandchildren in learning about Yurok tradition. Glenn still participates in the ceremonies held by the Yurok, Hupa, and Karuk people. His wife Dorothy worked as a welder at the dock facilities in Eureka during the war.

Leland Washoe

1924-2005

Leland Washoe was very kind and spoke with me and my brother Skip on October 30, 2001 at his home in Greenville, Ca. It was a cold, rainy, wintry day. Leland was a minister with the Indian Mission Church and descended from the Washoe and Pit River people. He lived among the Mountain Maidu people most of his life.

Where were you as you prepared to assault Omaha Beach at Normandy?

All the troops were getting ready at this big seaport in England, and that's where they put me into the 1st Division. I stayed with them until the war was over. We prepared to invade and I was in the second wave.

When I got in there was hardly anybody there. It was pretty well banged up in there when I went in with a buddy of mine. I saw some of my buddies that didn't make it. Shells came in and severed their heads off.

So me and my buddy, after we hit the beach, we were on our stomachs. Shells were coming in. We happened to look back. Right behind us there was a big half-track loaded with dynamite. The crew was tying their best to get it out. Before they could it just went up, it just blew up.

The blast took me and my buddy off the beachhead and lifted us way into the air; it was that powerful. My and my buddies were still on our stomachs with some other fellows. Here came this officer; he was roly-poly but mean. He told us to get moving and get all these trucks going and clear it out. I never saw the guy before but he was mean!

How far away were the German soldiers?

They were from this table to the end of the fence outside (about fifty feet). They were looking down on the beach in fortified gun emplacements. You could see them; we'd run out there, look around, pull out a gun and fire, then run back.

We were supposed to get support from the Air Force but they messed up and missed their targets. The Navy gave us support. They gave us the best support. The bombers didn't hit where they were supposed to. The only way we could knock them out was with line troops.

When that half-track went up I never realized all the damage it did inside of me. When I came out of the service they said I was A-1. When we had our examinations they left our shoes on. But my ankle and my insides were all torn up. I've been living with it for 50 years. My stomach isn't down where it's supposed to be.

The blast took me and my buddy off the beachhead and lifted us way into the air.

I have a hard time breathing because my diaphragm is damaged. They wanted to operate on me but they said it was 50-50, so I'm going to just live my life this way. They did give me the Purple Heart. They gave it to me on the records but they never sent it to me. I also received the rest of the campaign medals, and I believe we were supposed to receive the Bronze Star, but I don't know.

It didn't mean that much to me; your life means more. But it was good to answer the call and go fight for your country. I feel good about what I did. I always look at it this way; there's always someone who was worse off than me. Some guys didn't have any limbs or had no arms. They would be lying in a basket until they came and took them away.

What type of weapons did you have?

We had hand grenades. You'd have to pull that pin out and then hold it for a little while then let it go. Once you pull that pin you better get rid of it! I had four grenades on me when I went in. We had all the types of rifles; the BAR, the 30-caliber artillery piece, 50-calibers mounted on our equipment, and some type of automatic gun, but I don't remember the name of it now.

It was supposed to be equal to the burp gun that Germany had, but it wasn't as good as a burp gun. With a burp gun you can set it and you're here, and the other guy would be over there, and it would sound like he was somewhere else. They could change the sound or something like that.

You didn't know where they were coming from. We had the regular M-1, the Garand, which was the standard. It was a good gun. The rules were it's your baby, and you take care of it. You keep it clean and keep your life, or you let it get dirty, and it will stick on you and you lose your life. You had to keep that M-1 clean or when you needed it wouldn't work. I had a 30-caliber, the little field piece, that's what I had.

When you took some Germans prisoner, what did they look like?

They had pretty colorful uniforms. They had those wool-type hats beside their helmets. I didn't see them wear their helmets unless they were in combat. Otherwise

Leland Washoe

they were marching with those wool hats on. There was another thing, and this is the honest-to-God truth, but those Germans had canteens filled full of blood.

That's what they drank, and I don't know what for. They had blood in their canteens, and talk about something tough to smell, but they carried it right with them. I don't know what type of blood it was. It must have been some type of animal blood, or some type of a goulash with blood in it.

We made our way up the little draw there up to the top where it's leveled off. That's where everybody was dug in; the 1st Division and some of the other outfits. The 2nd Division didn't come in until midnight. When the next morning came all you could see were people dug in. We didn't go very far in.

That first night we were dug in by hedgerows. I didn't feel very bad. A lot of guys were right alongside there. We had a lot of scouts. I saw some guys on their knees near there looking over the side. I thought they were alive, but they were dead. Snipers had picked them off. That made me see things differently.

There was a church with a high steeple nearby. My buddies were saying, 'You better get down, Chief, get down. Someone up there is shooting at you.' I didn't know it, so they must have been pretty bad shots because I didn't get hit!

So we dug in and went through the night like that. The next day there was six of us left out of the company. We had to get replacements for all the rest. The first sergeant was there, a few other fellows and myself.

This is a funny thing, that one buddy I was with, the one who I went in on the beach with, he was a painter. I never saw him again after that night. I don't know what happened to him. I think there might be two of the guys who were with me that might still be living today. They were younger than I was.

How old were you at that time?

I was 18. (Leland was 18 when entering the service, 20 when at Omaha Beach).

When you were by that church, did you have to fire on it?

Oh yeah, and you wouldn't believe it, but those snipers were French girls. The Germans used French girls. They were hidden up there firing on us. We moved a little farther to the left and dug in an apple orchard.

We didn't move very far because they were firing on us, they had us pinned down all the time. We stayed there one night and we moved back toward the beachhead. We lost some people there that night. You could see the Navy shooting those big shells.

There were flares coming down. We had a chaplain, and he got in one of the foxholes. He didn't get hit. We got up the next morning and somebody noticed that those girls made a mistake. Those French girls were underneath a type of dam made of willows, like the type a beaver makes. It didn't take long to ambush them out of there and clean them out.

It took a long time to get rolling, so we kept supplies going all the time. We were there for a few months before we could go through St. Lo. There was really nothing left of St. Lo when we went through. We went to a seaport, I can't remember the name of it; it was toward Utah beach. From there we came back through France.

We went through Paris, then through Germany. We went through Belgium and then went to the Elbe River in Germany. The Germans were right on our backs. At Belgium they told us to pull back but we couldn't.

All that equipment and tanks were too heavy. We always moved things at night. We helped with building bridges for bridge crossings. We'd build pontoon bridges. We also helped haul infantry troops and howitzers in the amphibious ducks.

Can you describe what the amphibious ducks looked like?

It really looks like a duck when you think about it. It's an all-terrain vehicle that can go in water and on the ground. It looks like a big duckbill. I drove them; they're easy riding.

Did you ever have to do any fighting when you went through the towns in either France or Germany?

Just one time… one time. There was a little town in Germany. The infantry had gone through all right, but then the Germans had slipped back in and infiltrated the town again. That's the only time we ever had to do hand-to-hand fighting.

There were a bunch of us fellows with some infantry and the Germans had seen they were outnumbered. They came out with a white flag. Their officers were there too. So we took it in good faith they wanted to surrender. But when we got up close to them their officers gave the command to fire on us.

They killed everyone except me. I hit the ground pretty quick. I was the only one left. I yelled to my buddies in the back that I was coming back and to cover me. They covered me and I got back. We had to retake the town before we ever got going. That's the only time I fought like that. Of course, on the beachhead I had plenty of that, more than I ever want.

That must have been very traumatic for you.

Oh, it was. I can't say I wasn't scared. When I hit the Normandy beachhead I was scared. But I told you about the half-track blowing up. When that happened, something came over me and I really got mad.

I was ready to go then. In our training they tell you to either kill or be killed. That's how they train you. They also told us that we are at war. They told us that even babies are the enemy, because one day they'll grow up and fight your son or your relatives.

As you were going through France, what was the weather like?

It was raining. The rain really came down heavy. When it did break, it would be hot like it is here. When we took our basic training in Liverpool it rained every day.

It was foggy, boy, you couldn't see anything there. It didn't matter if it was raining; you had to get out there and maneuver in the hills or wherever. We had good raincoats.

When the Battle of the Bulge happened, where were you located?

I was right there about 10 miles from Belgium. We were dug in right there. The infantry went alongside us. Our division was on the left-hand side of Tommy Merino. His division was on the right-hand side of me.

The 28th Division really got raked over the coals there. They lost a tremendous amount of people. I was lucky that they didn't stick me in that division or I might not have made it back. Even as it is, I thank God that I made it back.

Did you ever get a leave while you were in France?

Yes, I went to Paris with a buddy. Our outfit was close by. They told us to watch out and take care of your self. My friend and I went to the underground city in Paris. It was just like regular buildings but underneath they had decorated stores there.

Jim Washoe
Leland's brother Jim served in combat as a member of the 82nd Airborne Division in Italy. Jim's family is very proud of his service to his country.

We had just got down there and were going to have a beer, when here came the MPs. They told us to get out of there by the morning. So me and my buddy got going early in the morning and got back to our outfit.

Before we left I went to some stores up top and bought some perfume and other things to send back home. I boxed it up and sent it back home. Other than that I wasn't able to bring anything back home.

Did you ever come across any of the concentration camps?

Yes, our whole outfit did. We saw those big places. It's not a very pleasant place, I'll tell you. I don't know how they could do that, to put that many people in those places and burn them. A lot of the camps were over there toward where the Bulge happened. I could see how big they were, and see how they operated.

Just to think about what they did is stunning. They put thousands and thousands and thousands of people in there, mostly Jewish people. Even today I'm puzzled about that because the German Jews were supposed to be the most intelligent people over there.

The buildings reminded me of dry-kill. You know how we have long buildings here to dry your lumber? Those buildings were long and all hooked up to gas. We just laid a man to rest here on Saturday. He was an old soldier.

As a soldier, I was really excited when I first saw those 1st Division soldiers. They were all decorated, and I wanted to wear the uniform really bad. But after I hit Normandy and saw all those guys die like that, I thought that I didn't want it that bad.

He went through a camp. He worked with me here. He could have told you about it. His funeral was on a cold, windy day. I was holding the post flag. My other friend carried the American flag. It was all I could do to hold that flag.

Where were you when the war ended in Europe?

On the Elbe River. I don't know the name of the little town but we were right there. The word came over one of those PA systems. It stunned me; that the war was over. I wasn't even thinking about it being over.

Boy, you should have seen the rest of those guys, they were jumping and shouting, and threw their guns away! As a soldier, I was really excited when I first saw those 1st Division soldiers. They were all decorated, and I wanted to wear the uniform really bad. But after I hit Normandy and saw all those guys die like that, I thought that I didn't want it that bad.

When they trained us to fight, for some reason in my heart I still had compassion. I just didn't see it that way. I can't do that. You can't help it. When the war in Japan ended I was on a ship that was headed there. So the ship turned around and headed to New York.

I was pretty glad to see that Statue of Liberty, I'll tell you. I didn't see it when I had left. I came back to the same camp in New York from where I had left. You're used to eating Army chow, and then they put all the milk you can drink and all the steak you can eat in front of you, it was really wonderful.

What did you do after the service?

I came back to Marysville and got my discharge at Camp Beale. I came home here and saw an old Indian lady named Emma Tom. I met her when I was really young. She always called me 'Niki-heskum." She had given me a little bible before I went across the ocean.

I carried that bible with me in my front pocket. I came back with it and she was still there. She liked to make Indian bread. She would sing songs while making it. She lived for quite a while after I came back. I had no intention of settling down here, I intended to go to Loyalton where I enlisted, but I got a job and ended up staying here all my life!

I worked at a big sawmill over here until they closed it down. I worked at a mill in Quincy, then in Loyalton, then here in Crescent Mills. After that I retired and went to work for the Forest Service. This was my last year doing that.

Where were you born and raised?

I was born in Quincy. After a few years there my uncle moved with me here to Greenville to fall timber. He had a heart attack in the woods and didn't make it. I went to the Sherman Institute after that. I was about 12.

My cousin Wilber Smith and his sister went with me to Sherman. I stayed there until Pearl Harbor. When Pearl Harbor broke out we went different ways. I went in the Army and Wilbur went into the Navy.

What was the experience like for you at Sherman?

I didn't have any problems. I went to church. I became the boy's advisor after a while. I worked at a job near there, in a place called the Shamrock Café owned by some Irish people. Every night they would have food they couldn't sell, like doughnuts and pastries, that they'd let me take home.

So when I got back to the barracks all the boys would clean that food out! When I graduated they gave me a certificate. I had worked in the cabinet shop. That was my trade. When I went in the Army and was taking my aptitude test I lucked out. I started drilling guys right away.

There were a lot of Mexican guys there at the Presidio and no one to take care of them so they left it to me to drill them. I showed them left foot, right foot, and all that. I got my experience in this from the band at Sherman. I had played in the band so it was easy for me.

After that they shipped me to Wyoming for basic training. There were a lot of Indians there. I didn't run into anybody from my area. After Wyoming they sent me to Camp Reynolds, Pennsylvania. From there I went to New York. I had a friend whose folks owned a bar there in New York. He was Czech. We'd go out at night. At that time New York was big. I don't know about now, it must be really big!

The only time I ran into another Indian man and talked was on the ship over to England. That was an English ship we were on. We came in at Liverpool. I was a replacement. We took training there because it was a duplicate of the Normandy beachhead.

Can you tell me about your affiliation with the Indian Mission Church?

I've been there through quite a few Indian ministers. You know Frank Mullen? His father was the one who and kept it going for a long time. Most of them have passed on. Today I'm down there as a pastor trying to hold it together.

A lot of the congregation had to relocate to find jobs. We had a revival there last month. We had a big camp there this summer. There were Indian folks from Arizona, Canada, and all over the country. I feel that we're here on this Earth…we all have to try to get along.

Were you ever married?

I was married sometime after the war. There were four or five of us couples that got married in Reno. My wife's name was Marguerite. She passed away in 1974 of leukemia. She was Tommy Merino's sister. We had eight children and12 grandchildren.

In movies and war films you never see any Indians, what do you think of that?

Well, I don't believe it's right that we keep them out of these movies because they were there too, with the rest of those people. The only war movies I see Indians in are the old-fashioned wars, with bows and arrows. I thought they had Ira Hayes in a movie, didn't they?

He was in the movie* Sands of Iwo Jima *briefly. But that movie was mostly about John Wayne. John Wayne never served in the military, so what do you think about him pretending in all those war movies?

Well, I don't think about John. They said he was prejudiced against Indian people. I don't think too much about him.

You been involved in the VFW, what are your duties there?

Right now there's an old veteran down here; he's in a wheelchair and doesn't have transportation. I'm trying to work that out. If any veterans want to go to church I'll take them. I'll help them out any way I can. You do what you can.

I participate in the parade on Memorial Day. I've been carrying the American flag for years. I participate in the Indian veteran's reunions when I can make it. It's good to be around other Indian veterans, I really love it.

I had a good experience down at a gathering at D-Q University near Davis; there was an Apache fellow there with his wife. He was quite a soldier. They cooked lamb stew and hominy. It was good! Organizations are good for our people. Otherwise they try to separate us. I've never had any trouble blending in with people.

Why do you think it's important for young people to know what veterans did during the war and after?

I think it's good for them to know that veterans are fighting for the rights of their people. You're fighting for peace and democracy. But some of that is slipping away. Most of the soldiers will tell you that we're losing some of what we fought for.

Here's an example, the medals that our VFW organization gets used to be made in the United States. But now companies in Korea and China or somewhere else makes them for us. If you have a real soldier, a person who really knows America, they won't take them.

That's what happened to our post here. They ordered medals for the fellows who'd earned them, but they all came from Taiwan. The commander got mad and sent them back. It was the same thing at a convention. They want American medals made here. You have to reason with things like this. I was taught that God created us to reason with one another.

Leland Washoe was a highly-respected member of the Crescent Mills and Greenville community. His family is very proud of his service toward his faith, his country and his people.

Charles Lindgren

1923-2003

I saw a picture of a young Charles 'Chuck' Lindgren in uniform in my local paper for a Memorial Day spread on the weekend of 2001. His picture intrigued me, who was this smiling soldier, and where was he now? I found that Chuck lived in Trinidad, near his family's ancestral Yurok village of Surai. I asked if he would like to talk to me about his experiences. He said he would and I met him on November 11, 2001.

Charles Lindgren ca. 1942.
Photo courtesy of Roberta Lindgren.

I was born in 1923 to Axel and Georgia Lindgren here in Trinidad. They were good parents too. I went to grade school here in Trinidad. There were 10 children in the family and I was right in between! I went to high school in Arcata. Then my mom said, 'You have to work.'

So I did. I gave her a check every other payday. I got paid on the 10th and the 26th. I worked out at Big Lagoon for Louisiana Pacific. I had a good boss; he gave me nine hours every day until they closed down. I had a log roll on me in 1970 and that's what retired me.

Logging is dangerous work, isn't it?

Yes, but a person has to work. I wanted to own something, to hell with someone else buying it for me. I worked in the woods all my life. When I was young I set chokers. You show up every day. I was also a heavy loader. If there was a Saturday and they needed someone to work, I said sure. That's time-and-a-half. I worked hard all my life. My father worked in the woods too.

What was life like for your family here in Trinidad?

We'd go down to the beach and fish. My grandmother would dry the fish. We ate prepared acorns and dry seaweed. My grandmother would say, 'It's low tide we have to go get seaweed!'

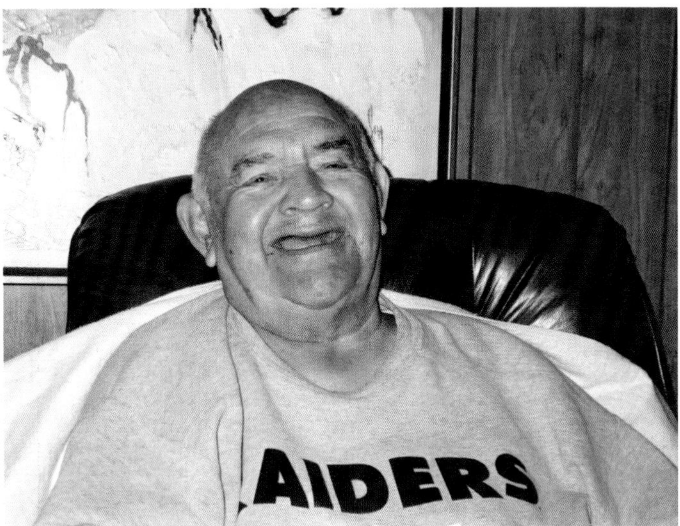

Charles Lindgren

She'd take her *lap-sa* and gather seaweed in it. I really liked the seaweed. She would know what time of the day to go gather. If there's sand in the seaweed it's no good. There was never any sand in mine! She'd make the big seaweed cakes and dry them out on boards.

Did anyone in your family speak in Yurok?

They all did. I could understand a little. I used to go to the Brush Dances. I liked to go but I can't now because I'm in a wheelchair.

When did you graduate from high school?

In 1943. Uncle Sam said 'I want you!' I went to boot camp down by Fresno. After that they shipped me up to Washington. We walked up Mount Rainier and trained in the snow. I stayed there for two or three months.

Then where did you go?

I went to New York. When we left on a troopship to England I stood on the deck. I could see the Statue of Liberty getting smaller and smaller. We were zigzagging to keep away from submarines. A lot of those boys were just blue and vomiting. I stayed in England for 13 months.

What did you do there?

We built landing strips. I was in the Army Corps of Engineers. I had gunnery training; they showed you how to operate a 50-caliber. They trained you to shoot a target. It would be maybe 100 yards away. There would be a tracer at every 50 bullets. The tracer was red so you could see where you're hitting.

One time in England three of us went out and had a few beers. We came back to our tents. One of them called out, 'Air raid, air raid!' You have to get out when they say that. The sergeant came out and hollered at us, 'You can't say air raid when there's no air raid!'

So he took us over to the kitchen and made us peel potatoes. I was just peeling forever and my friends were too. I never peeled so many potatoes in all my life! We had three garbage cans full of potatoes. One time this guy who was a gunner was sick. We were all in the mess hall eating. The guy came in and asked, 'Who wants to go for a ride to Germany as a tail-gunner?'

I thought, hell, I'll go. Boy, I wouldn't want to do that again! That's scary, having those Germans shoot at you. There was a fighter coming by and I just opened up on that son-of-a-gun and everything on it just went to pieces. When you're the tail gunner you're sitting there ready to shoot.

They shot a lot of flak at us. That flak would go right through the plane. I don't know how high we were. That was a B-26 that I was in. They had the B-26 and the B-17 over there. I don't know what the fighters were. But when we went out there was a fighter on each side and one in the back. They were a lot faster than we were. I never did go anymore!

And this was before you participated in the Normandy Invasion?

Yes. I was one of the first to go ashore from our craft at Normandy (on Omaha Beach). Those poor boys in the craft behind me, those damn Germans dropped a bomb right on them. I bailed off our craft. I was wet clear up to my waist.

I didn't change my clothes for three days. I didn't fool around after I hit the water. I did wonder about my mother. I thought of her, and then I ran like hell up to the bank. I was carrying the barrel of a 50-caliber, and the kid behind me was carrying the tripod.

I told him not to forget me, and keep coming. He said, "Chuck, I wouldn't do that.' By God, when I needed him to come around and help set up the gun, he did. We set the gun down and fixed it up. I could see those damn Germans on that bank.

I didn't aim or anything. I just sat the gun down and let them have it. You could see them just rolling out of those foxholes and bunkers. You shoot anything you see. I also had a pistol. I could shoot older people but I wouldn't shoot a kid.

How many people were in that landing craft with you when you were approaching the beach?

I couldn't tell you. It was jammed full. There were a

lot of kids in there. I was only 19 years old.

After you had set your gun on the beach, what did you do?

Well, three days later we came out. They let us sleep in a building one night. We went toward St. Lo in France. Do you know where that is? That was a hell of a battle.

They'd take over in the daytime then we'd take over in the night. That went on for days. I don't know how I made it through that, to tell you the truth. But I never got hurt. I came home and mom was still there.

She must have been pretty happy to see you!

Oh my, she was. I think I went to bed and stayed there for two days.

So your job in the war was to handle the 50-caliber and set it up in battle?

Yeah. You have to have a lot of ammunition. The ammunition would come all rolled up and it would come out ready to shoot. I was just a corporal, but they said I knew what the hell was going on. My friend was a PFC (Private First Class). He packed the ammunition. Boy, I shot a lot of rounds. Every so often someone would bring more ammunition. The gun was loud.

Did you ever have to do hand-to-hand fighting?

Oh, yeah. It seemed like we always beat them. We had more ammunition. It was traumatic. I always think, 'Goddamn, how did I make it through that?' The good Lord must have had His hand over me.

What was the weather like?

It was foggy and rainy in France, like it is here. It also snowed some.

What was it like eating K-rations?

No good! But I had to eat. Boy, they were no good!

Where did you go after that?

We went across France toward Germany. One time in Germany there was a bridge that went across this river. The company commander asked if anyone knew how to use dynamite. This was another time where I volunteered.

I had used dynamite back home in the woods, blowing out stumps near Big Lagoon. So I raised my hand and said I could. He told me to go down and blow these big concrete pyramids out so tanks could go through. You had to watch out for mines they had left.

If you see any wire you'd have to take them out. But I loaded them up and blew them out. The Germans were coming around and shooting, and dropping bombs from planes. We also crossed the Rhine River and I made it to Munich, Germany. It was a pretty good-sized city. We never had any transportation to go anywhere. All I wanted to do was go home, because I was thinking about my parents.

And you were in Munich when you heard the Germans had surrendered?

Yes. In December of 1945 they asked us, 'Who's going home?' And we all raised our hands! I went down to Marseilles, France. We had Christmas dinner there. But there were these three French girls that wanted to come to the United States. I was hoping they'd hurry up and get us out of there because I didn't want them! We finally got out of there. Boy I was happy to get away from those girls!

Where did you come in to dock?

In New York; there were a lot of people there.

Your parents and family must have been very happy to see you when you got home...

Oh yes. My brother Glen got killed in the service. He died over in the Pacific.

After the war, did you go back to logging?

Yes, I had to work. That's all I knew. I worked in the woods for 27 years.

I was wondering what you think of our American flag?

I don't like to see them burn it. A person that does that is no good.

Why did you go in the Army?

Well, Uncle Sam said so. You have to go. You have to serve.

One time in Germany there was a bridge that went across this river. The company commander asked if anyone knew how to use dynamite. This was another time where I volunteered.

Chuck Lindgren is fondly remembered by his family and friends as a fun-loving uncle and companion. His family and friends are very proud of his service to his country and his people.

Johnny Smith

Johnny Smith is of Mountain Maidu and Pit River heritage. He was very gracious and spoke about his time in the service on October 28, 2001 at his home in Greenville. It was getting dark on a cold evening and he had just finished stacking a cord of wood when I arrived.

I was born in April, 1921 high on a ridge near the Ingle Mine (near Greenville). That's where my dad worked. He was a blacksmith, and his first shop was right on the crown of the hill way up in the wilderness. It was in 1931 or '32 when they closed it down.

I had to go to Lincoln School here in the valley. Mostly Indians went to that school. There were very few white children who went there. We got along pretty nice together. We didn't know anything about racism at that time.

I never had any brothers but I had three sisters. My parents were Seymour and Louise Smith. Dad was Maidu and mom was Pit River. I went to the Greenville High School here and I ran track and played in the band. I played the drum and cymbals.

We had quite a large band for a small school. We had

a great music teacher. We had a really nice time. Tommy Merino also played the drums. He and I worked on a ranch while we went to high school. We milked 25 cows in the morning before school. At night we'd ride the saddle horses to watch the show. It was a good life. It seemed like when we were young we didn't have time to get into mischief. We were always busy.

Did you ever go to the Bear Dance when you were young?

Oh yeah, dad used to be the bear a lot of times. They used to have them at the end of the valley here and also at other places here in Greenville. There were quite a few when I was young. To me, it's something that should never be stopped.

Johnny Smith in Arkansas in 1942.
Photo courtesy of Johnny Smith.

It's good education for the younger generation. They should try to accept the way the older Indians used to think. If they're interested they should participate.

When you were in high school did you hear about what was going on in Europe?

We heard about a lot. They would tell us about things. It seemed to me that when we were young we didn't take heed of things. When the war did start I was piling lumber in the lumberyard. My partner was drafted. He was at least 35 years old.

That's when I came to my senses. This was serious. If they got him then we'd have to go. All you do is keep working and prepare yourself. One of these days that letter will get to you. It finally came! I had to take a physical in Monterey.

Were you married before the war?

Yes, I married Gladys in 1940. It was pretty hard to be apart from her. But they drill you so much it becomes your life. You think about home; it's human nature. But you had to think about other things, you had to.

I went to Little Rock, Arkansas for boot camp. I was in the Army. It was hot! I didn't mind the training because I was in pretty good shape from handling lumber. My training never bothered me. If I had to do it I had to do it. I just did what they said. I never ran into another Indian man until I went to Fort Benning, Georgia. That man was from around Maine.

They needed volunteers for the Airborne. They showed you the nice boots, nice jump pants, nice jump coat and a scarf. You also got 50 dollars more in pay. So I decided I'd take it. When they wanted volunteers I stepped out there. There were only two of us that volunteered. That's when they sent me to Fort Benning.

What did they train you to do?

They trained me how to land from an airplane. They put you on a platform and had you jump and turn, jump and turn. They'd show you how to roll. There was a lot of running and boxing. We had a regular carbine.

The M1 was a great rifle too. I took care of it. They told you that it's your baby! They made you run on big poles, climb a rope and do lots of push-ups!

Will you describe the first time you jumped out of a plane?

First they took us down to where all the planes were. They had C-47s and put you in a big room. There were different groups of guys. They had 24 of us facing each other. The only thing that bothered me was they told us that WACs had packed the parachute.

Before, that was your own responsibility. You packed the 'chute. But when the time comes it wasn't that way! That bothered me. They would show you how the 'chute works and how not to get the line tangled up. That's the only thing that bothered me, was to have someone else pack the 'chute. You'd be a goner before you could even start!

But you made it!

Yeah, I made it. When I jumped it didn't bother me. The guy behind you would check to make sure you're hooked up all right, and so on. On your first jump you're tumbling then you look down and wait for that 'chute to pop.

I had my hand right on that reserve 'chute. You're trained real well and you feel good when that 'chute opens. Then you have to feel for the wind when you come down. You have to turn and always look straight ahead. They train you so good that you go right into your role. But sometimes the wind will turn you and you belly flop! When you come down, you hit with a bang! You hit pretty hard.

After that they had us practice a night jump. To me the night jump was a lot easier than a day jump. That wasn't too bad. It was exciting, but a lot of boys got hurt. A lot of them hurt their back, or broke their legs. You had to have five jumps to qualify. Then you get your wings, and your patch, and the fancy stuff!

What was it like to take a ship across the Atlantic?

Oh, I know what a sailor feels like! That was a ride! We were three days out from the Azores Islands and we were on the tail end of the convoy. Our ship got torpedoed. It was just about dusk when it happened.

To this day I don't know why, but I was in the second hold, and I started up and got halfway up the ladder to get on the deck when it happened. I don't know why I came up. It was one of those things, you know?

The first thing I saw was sailors running when the ship got hit. I got up on top of the deck and hung onto the railing. The ship started to tip. The captain came over and said not to jump. He said the ship could tip 45 degrees and not tip over. But man, you had to hang on for dear life. There was a lot of water and it was heavy. The sailors got down there and shut down the hole.

We lost several men. There were so many guys panicking and running. I was all right and the men in my bunk were all right. That was a Victory ship but I can't remember the name of it.

We made it to the Azores Islands and stayed there four days. The convoy left us there and then sent a destroyer back to get us. On the fourth day there was an English ship that came by. Man that ship stank! It was called the *Acheron Newcastle.* I learned to eat porridge on that ship. You'd put chow on the table and everything would slide off and fall to the floor. I laugh about it now. That was quite an experience.

What division were you in?

At first I didn't know. When you're going over there they don't tell you. After I got ready to go to France they said I was a replacement for the 82nd Airborne. Some men were replacements for the 101st Airborne; some were in the 82nd. I was in the 325th Glider Infantry Regiment.

Can you describe what the glider was like?

The glider has no motor and they put 12 of us inside. It has a rope attached to the glider. The C-47 plane winds up and pulls that glider, then pop! It shoots the glider out like that. I was sitting right behind the co-pilot. He was wringing wet with sweat. I was sweating it out too.

It was just like being in a kite. There was just a little ply board seat, aluminum tubing and cloth covering it. It was so narrow you'd sit knee-to-knee in that kite. Some of the boys got sick, and you're sitting there and can't do anything. You just take it.

Oh man, I'm telling you, I sure felt sorry for those boys. I did the best I could; it didn't bother me. I would sit there and not feel anything. I didn't feel the hype. But there would be some guys next to you that would get scared, and that's real scary.

Eventually they eliminated the gliders. There were too many guys that got killed. We were just really lucky. The Germans had some big ties in the trees on the ground at the drop zone. They had some really good intelligence.

How did they know before you got there?

It was just like that Japanese woman (Tokyo Rose) that would come on the radio and say where the airborne would go. That scared us if they zeroed in on you. It made you think a lot.

Were you fired on when you were in the glider?

Yes, by 88-millimeters. That's a wicked gun. When you hear one of those you think, 'This is it.' We were just lucky to make it. We were really lucky when we landed.

It was a rough landing. I'm glad they took the gliders completely out.

They didn't use them anymore. That was the only time when I was with the group we used it. They would take all the guys they wanted for this destination or that destination. They were serious. Everybody was on the team and every man worked together. We had to go and meet the German resistance. That was tough.

The ship started to tip. The captain came over and said not to jump. He said the ship could tip 45 degrees and not tip over.

They were seasoned. It wasn't easy. You have to give them credit. They were in machine-gun nests. There was one hill where they had pillboxes. That was hard to take out but we got it. We also got the machine-guns and then we'd go on.

If Uncle Sam wants something, he's going to get it. You have to do it or else! That took about four days. We cleared the way for the next group to come in. Then they'd take us out to find another place to break through. After that we went to a marshaling area. We'd get orders to go different places.

Did you ever have to fight up close with the Germans?

Not real close. I missed the fighting where you had to have hand-to-hand combat. After Normandy they had called for volunteers to build bridges. I had handled dynamite before I went in the service and it was on my record. They asked me if I knew about it. I did so I helped clear the way for bridges to be built.

Our next jump mission was in Germany. That was tough. The weather was cold. Good thing we had a lot of tough boys! I didn't realize we had so many tough boys. They had endurance. You'd be tired and have to keep going. They would get mad and angry and just go. I thought I was tough.

And these men were all part of the 82nd Airborne?

You bet. Most of our outfit was from Chicago. They were mean, tough guys! We were behind the line and it took four or five days to get back. There were quite a few of us. We had to fight our way back. They'd have that little burp gun, it was wicked. It would cut your leg off so fast. You'd hear it shoot and that was that. You had to have eyes all the way around on your head and you made sure to listen while walking.

And you parachuted this time?

Yes, we parachuted. They gave us pictures of the area, and approximately where gun emplacements would be. They dropped us about 700 or 800 feet above the ground. If you get up too high the shrapnel from the guns would get you. It was amazing; it was just like buckshot.

I remember on that jump, I could picture this valley where I live. It went by in just a flash. I could see my home. It was amazing. I always tell people it was quite an experience but I wouldn't take a million dollars to do it again! After that they held us back. Other groups went out.

Johnny Smith

Did you become close to the other men in your company?

We were really buddies. We hung right together; we were there for each other. We were real friends. It was just like your family; you get so attached to them.

It must have been very traumatic to lose a buddy.

Yes, just like you and me, we're talking here. In the moment we walk from here to there, you're down. It's that quick…It's hard to take.

What would you eat while in combat?

You didn't have time. You would snack. You had hardtack and have this bar of candy and some water and that would fill you up.

When would you sleep?

You'd sleep standing up or sit down and sleep when you could. I weighed 120 pounds when I came home. I weighed 157 pounds when I went over.

Did you ever do anything really fun while you were overseas?

Well, there was this one time in Paris after the war. The Eiffel Tower was supposedly off-limits. They had the stairs boarded up. It was a time of war and no tours were allowed. Seven or eight of my buddies and I decided there was no harm in climbing the Eiffel Tower.

I almost got about halfway up when all of a sudden these MPs spoke over the microphone. They said to get down now; we were going to the stockade if we didn't. Oh man! So we came down. It took a long time. I took my time climbing down.

Did you have to spend some time in the stockade?

Yeah!

Was it worth it?

I think so!

Where were you when the war ended in Germany?

I was headed to Japan on this ship. The captain announced the Japanese surrendered. Oh boy, talk about the men on that ship. They just about tore things apart! They turned us around for New York. I had never seen so many dollar bills before. The men had started gambling. Oh man!

I sat up four days because I wanted to see the Statue of Liberty. I took my seat. I didn't move. My buddy would get me things so I didn't have to leave. Then I would get him something. We wanted that place where we could see the Statue of Liberty….it was quite a sight. It was exciting, it was really exciting. We came in at Pier 19 in New York. From there I went to Fort Bragg, North Carolina. That's where I got my discharge.

How did it feel when you took that first step onto the pier?

Oh! You're thinking, 'I'm home, I'm home.' It makes you feel so good. There were so many Red Cross people there. They gave us coffee and doughnuts. It was great. When you're walking to your destination the first thing you run into are all these young women. They want souvenirs! I had some of these lapel pins in my pocket. They would come up and ask for a souvenir and I'd give them one.

Did you get to walk through New York?

Before I went over I had. I walked through Times Square and to all the bars. I didn't have to buy anything. Someone was always there to get me something.

So you were never treated any different because you were Indian?

When I went to Little Rock for basic training I noticed how they treated dark-skinned people. It was the same thing in Georgia, but in Georgia my buddies put a stop to that. There was a bus driver that told me to get in back.

I said, 'Oh no, sir, I'm sitting right here, sir.' All my buddies were right there, all six of us. They said to sit right there. That bus driver said he wouldn't take us. But my buddies said to stay right there, and I did.

That's when I found out how people back east treated dark-skinned people. They were serious, they meant it. I always figured, 'Heck, I'm here, I'll fight you.' It didn't bother me a bit.

There was another time during the war; I was in Reams, France. I was on a leave with some buddies. The night before we got there some paratroopers were in town. They had killed a couple of black guys.

There was this black soldier in the saloon we were in that said he was going to kill a couple paratroopers today. We had just walked in and didn't know anything about it. He came at my buddy and my buddy had to pop him, and down he went. He started to come around and we took off.

Why do you think the Army segregated black soldiers, but not Indian soldiers?

Well, to me, there weren't that many Indians. I was the only Indian in my group. I think that's the reason. Most of the guys would find out I was Indian and call me 'Chief.' I always had a good time with them. I often wondered about my buddies, but I've lost track of them. It was quite an experience.

How did you get back home?

I rode the bus from North Carolina to Reno, Nevada. From there I made it back to Greenville. A lot of people here in Greenville greeted me. They would say 'Hi.' This little town was grateful. I was really glad to see Tommy Merino in Taylorsville. We had written letters to each other.

When did you start attending the Indian Veteran Reunions in Susanville?

I attended the first one. It's been going for a long time. It's great to be around other Indian veterans. You know they were there. It's a good time and they're really interesting.

Going through this experience, did it make you think about life in a different way?

On a mission they would say, before we left, there would be a 90 percent casualty rate, and a lot of you guys aren't coming back. It was kill or be killed. You had to do it. You don't want to, but you have to. It made me think, 'Why did I do this before? When I get home, I'm going to do something different.'

Johnny Smith carries his VFW Post flag at ceremonies and gatherings. He is a retired logger and cowboy. He and his family conduct the Seymour Smith Run every year near Greenville to honor his father who loved to run.

Charles "Chuck" Donahue

1926-2006

Chuck Donahue was born in July of 1926. He was of Yurok and Karuk ancestry and was very proud of his heritage. He preferred to talk about his decades of experience fishing on the Klamath River more than anything. He also liked to catch eels and hunted in the woods almost his entire life. He was friends with many of the Native veterans included in this book, and held a special respect for "the Colonel,'"Leonard Lowry.

Chuck was a member of the 82nd Airborne Division during World War Two. He saw some terrible things during Operation Market-Garden. He landed along with other American soldiers and endured heavy fighting. Chuck carried a Browning Automatic Rifle (BAR) during most of his time in the service. The loss of life on both sides was something he did not like. He asked if it would be all right if he did not give a taped interview; he just wanted a little something to be included about him to go alongside his fellow Indian veterans.

Chuck Donahue worked as a timber faller for many years in Del Norte and Humboldt counties after the war. He liked to create traditional gambling drums and other regalia for the Brush Dances. He participated as a singer and dancer in Brush Dance ceremonies as well. His children and numerous grandchildren and great-grandchildren are very proud of his service to his country and to his people.

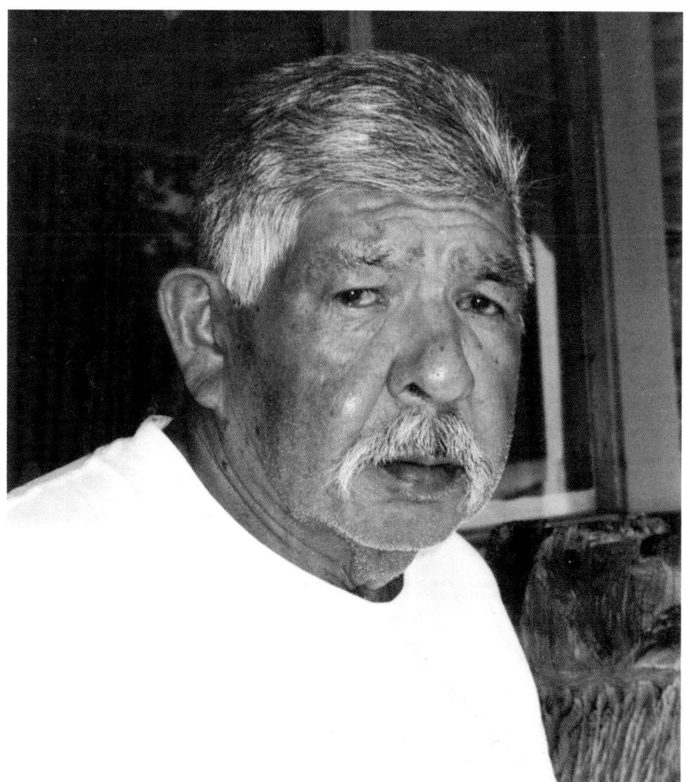

Chuck Donahue

Frank Martin

1911-2007

I met with Mountain Maidu elder Frank Martin at his son Seth's house in Oroville, California on February 3, 2002. I first met Frank at an Indigenous language conference in 1999. Frank had traveled there with Tommy Merino and other Maidu speakers. At the conference Tommy and Frank spoke about Maidu culture and history.

Tommy stated they had known each other for over 50 years. On their ride to the conference they had talked about their wartime experiences with each other for the first time ever. They were both members of the Third Army and both were in France and Germany at the same time in the war, although neither knew it. Tommy told this story to the audience and I remembered it, so I made the effort to find Frank to see if he would share some more about his time in the war.

There were German soldiers waiting for our men (at Normandy). I went there on the third day. I helped clear mines. I studied for that.

Frank Martin 1943.
Photo courtesy of Seth Martin.

I was born in 1911 here in Butte County in Enterprise. My mother comes from the Davis clan. My grandmother was Mary Atkins. Frank Martin was my father; he was Koncow Maidu. Nancy Martin was my grandmother on the Martin side.

I graduated from Enterprise in the eighth grade. I went to Stewart in the seventh grade. I came back to Enterprise and graduated from eighth grade and then I went to Sherman. I graduated from Sherman in 1932. They had their own cadets there. I was in charge of the cadets at the school. They were kind of respected by the Army.

Where did you go to boot camp?

I was inducted and discharged from Camp Beale, California. When I got to Camp Claiborne in Louisiana they put me down to go to officer's training. I didn't want to go so they sent someone else in my place.

How did you get to Europe during the war?

I took the Queen Mary and we went to Scotland. We unloaded there and trained there. I was in the 398th Combat Engineers. I was in an engineer outfit and we were under Ike. We hit the beaches first because we were construction engineers. We would help rebuild docks and railroads. Later I was under Patton in the Third Army.

I understand you were at the Normandy Invasion in France?

There were German soldiers waiting for our men (at Normandy). I went there on the third day. I helped clear mines. I studied for that. They had these little personnel bombs that would jump out of the ground. There was also the butterfly bomb.

You couldn't deactivate that one. If you touched it and tried to bring the wing down it would blow. They had to blow those up. If you kicked it, it would blow your leg off. The Germans also had bombs they dropped from airplanes. They wouldn't blow up, but some did. I ran something similar to a Geiger counter to look for those and the personnel bombs on roads.

What was the weather like in France?

It was kind of hot, but it kind of cooled down after a while. I went into Cherbourg after that to help rebuild the dock. I had German soldiers working for me. I had a squad of them in Cherbourg. I was an expert in booby traps; I trained for that.

I taught some people how to do that. At Cherbourg there was a seawall where they shot the Buzz bombs; they had it booby-trapped and I cleared it out. After you find one trap you're all right! You'd be sick until you found the first one, that's all I know!

Where else did you travel?

When the Bulge started they sent us up to the front. My outfit was in the southern edge of the Battle of the Bulge. When the Germans came in they created a crease in our lines, but Patton cut it off. That's why they call it the Bulge.

Before we crossed the Rhine we bivouacked in the Black Forest. There were deer and everything in the forest was clean. Germany had beautiful forests. When we crossed the Rhine we were in platoons. They had blown up the bridges. Before Germany surrendered they put me in the English 95th; I was under Montgomery!

Did you ever see General Patton?

Yeah, I saw him. He was a soldier. My own opinion is he was killed by the politics of the United States government. That's just my own opinion. I saw Ike too. I saw him in England.

This is a hard question, but did your outfit ever come across any of the concentration camps?

(After a long pause). I smelled them. We could smell them for miles. We could smell the burning Jews. I had a Jeep of my own and I took officers to meetings. We could smell them. I saw the camps but I never went in them.

Did you ever serve with other Indian servicemen?

Yes, I had an Indian friend who was shot in the guts in the Bulge. It crippled him. He died a while back. I had a friend from Utah; we buddied around but I was more or less alone when I drove that Jeep.

Were you ever shot at?

I was shot at and missed over there, but when I came back here and joined some Indian political organizations I was shot at too! What the hell!

Did you ever write home to anyone?

I wrote to my mother from over there. I told her to give me some of the addresses of the people over here so I could write to them.

How did you come home?

I came back on the Queen Mary. They were going to try to send me to Japan but I had enough points. When the war (in Japan) ended I was at Camp Beale.

You are very involved with the Bear Dance and your Indigenous culture. You also served this country with honor. What are you most proud of?

I'm proud of my people; that's what I'm proud of. People ask me that question, and that's what I tell them.

Did you have any family that has served in the U.S. military?

Yes, there was Ralph Martin, he was in Korea. I had some cousins that served in World War Two.

How do you feel about the U.S. Army?

In order to have a future for our children, we have to have the Army. Years ago, the Army also had the first germ warfare against my own people. My own Maidu people, there were thousands of us.

We're down to a few hundred now. They gave them blankets with diseases on them. That destroyed our people. I think about the Army. Today, the BIA and the BLM (Bureau of Land Management) has destroyed the unity of our people.

Can you understand the Koncow Maidu language?

Yes, I can understand the language from around here. I can understand Mountain Maidu from near Genesee (by Greenville). My mother and my aunt would get together and they would speak. My father was killed because of gold in this area.

My mother married a man with the last name of Jackson and we moved over there. So I can understand some of the language from up there. I have a book on the language and some of the people are teaching it here.

To me, the Bear Dance is a spiritual way of life. It's also a protection for our society and our ancient people; not only for here, but for all the red people on this continent.

What does the Bear Dance mean to you?

To me, the Bear Dance is a spiritual way of life. It's also a protection for our society and our ancient people; not only for here, but for all the red people on this continent. That Bear Dance isn't like this TV here! It's real.

The Bear Dance is a spiritual meeting to bless all creation. Years ago in the beginning of creation, the bear taught us, and we worked with the bear. That's why we have the Bear Dance because the children can be on one side of the creek and gather berries, and the bear will be on the other side left alone.

The Creator has blessed that area. We call the Creator Wona-mee in our language here. That means everlasting life. I have the hide here, but I've never danced as the bear. I do carry the spiritual flag in the Bear Dance.

The flag is a spiritual sign of creation. It's created out of *yo-o*, which is a plant, a flower, a seed. It's something spiritual. The flag represents Mother Earth. When we gather together as friends it becomes blessed. When you come there, there are no enemies.

Frank Martin worked in the logging industry until age 72. He sang and participated in the Bear Dance for several decades. He was well-respected throughout northern California for his efforts to pass on his knowledge of the Koncow Maidu culture.

Frank Martin

Tommy Merino

1920-2004

I spoke with Tommy Merino at his home in Taylorsville on Memorial Day, May 28, 2001. Tommy was a Private First Class in Company A, 11th Infantry Regiment, 5th Infantry Division, Third Army during the war. In his portrait photograph he is holding his original card with a prayer for good weather written on it. This card was handed out during the Battle of the Bulge among Patton's Third Army.

When I graduated from high school I wanted to get in the Army band. The reason I wanted to get in the Army band was because I played in my high school band for four years. We went to San Francisco in 1939. We played there for seven days at Treasure Island. Every student had to play individually in front of the judges.

We tied for second place out of 11 western states. It was a marching band, for four years we marched so no one got out of step, so when I went in the Army it was automatic and everything was good. I didn't have to fight the system. And Johnny Smith, he played in the band and when he went in the service everything was automatic! I went to Greenville High School. I graduated in 1939.

Where were you born and raised?

I was born three miles from Taylorsville in a canyon. The times were tough then, so my grandmother took me in and raised me. Her name was Sadie Blueskin Rodgers. She was our Indian doctor. She raised me and put me through high school.

She was blind. She spoke a little English, but mostly she spoke the Mountain Maidu language. That's how I know the language. I went to boarding school at Stewart, Nevada. Then I came back home and went to school here in Indian Valley.

My mother couldn't read or write so I had to learn the hard way. We had no tutors. I went to a one-room school where they taught all eight grades. There was no running water at the school. I graduated from the eighth grade in that one little school.

When I was little I used to go hunting with my grandfather Paul Rodgers. I used to watch him and watch him. A deer would come and go, and come and go, then when he was ready he killed his deer, fixed it all up and brought it home.

Do you have any brothers or sisters?

I have a half-brother that lives in Susanville. And one brother lives here about five miles away. I have a sister that lives in Marysville. I'm the oldest, the big brother!

How old were you when you went to the boarding school at Stewart?

I was there three years at Stewart. I was pretty young. They punished us out there for speaking your language. All the other kids from all over the U.S. and I would go outside in the sagebrush and talk. We'd never say a word in the school. That's how we kept our language going.

How would they punish you?

They'd put you to work scrubbing floors. Anything they could do, like packing wood, anything to make you work. We wore all blue clothes, kind of like a uniform. We had kind of dark blue outfits, a shirt, pants and a bib overall.

What was it like being raised around other Mountain Maidu people?

Well, there were certain Bear Dances that I went to and certain ones I didn't. The ones I went to my grandfather and grandmother took me.

What is the meaning behind the Bear Dance?

Well, they start here next week. This is the time they start. It's a religious belief. We've come through the winter and everyone has survived. The rattlesnake and the grizzly bear have come through the winter. There are no more grizzlies here so now we use the brown bear. So you make prayers to them.

Some people do it a different way. I do it a certain way because my grandmother did it for years and years. I was listening to this tape I had of my grandmother talking about the Bear Dance. During the war years the dances had ceased. They were talking on the tape about when the last Bear Dance was held before the war years. They said it was at my grandmother's place.

When did you get married?

My wife and I were together since we got out of high school. She and I got married in 1942. Her name was Ivy Smith. I was in the service so if I got killed my wife would get something. I was on leave and we got married in Nevada.

The second daughter we had, she was about a year-and-a-half old when I came back from overseas. I had never seen her. My wife was carrying her when I had left. I lost my wife two-and-a-half years ago. We had a lot of years together, going to reunions and such.

Where were you when the war broke out?

I was right here in Indian Valley. Everything was going on when I went to high school. It wasn't World War Two; it was Hitler and his big movements all over in Europe. I went in the Army in 1941. In 1945 the Red Diamond Division was sent home. We stopped at Camp Campbell, Kentucky.

We were there for about two weeks. Then they shipped everybody home for 30 days. Then the Diamond Division was going to go to the Pacific. Over in France my captain had told me that my records were fouled up. He said, 'Don't do anything over here. Your division is going to the Pacific. Once you get back there tell them.' I figured I would go to headquarters and tell them they have my paperwork fouled up while I was on leave.

So I was on leave. I had my old Chevrolet and my wife and I were heading to Quincy. I got to the where the road makes a 'Y' and it broke down. This was early in the morning. I asked a man to send a mechanic down to the 'Y.' So late in the afternoon the mechanic came. We were up on the hill in the shade. The mechanic said, 'What are you doing up there?'

I said, 'Get this old car fixed up, I want to get to Quincy.'

He said, 'To heck with Quincy, the Japs surrendered today!'

I was there at the 'Y' when the Japs surrendered. So we had two bars between here and the 'Y.' I had my uniform on. Everything was open.

I went on into Taylorsville, there were bonfires, and people everywhere were celebrating! I never got drunk though. I had a few beers but never got drunk! It was a great feeling. The worst part of it was I had to go all the way back to Camp Campbell, Kentucky to get discharged.

I had to stay two months before they released me. So I came back on a train and got into Reno, Nevada. Now I'm a union man. The whole town was on strike. Buses, restaurants, you name it, everything was on strike. I don't go across any kind of a picket line. I went to a store and bought some apples and oranges and started walking.

I was by the University of Nevada there in my uniform and waved a little bit. A car pulled over and took me to Stead Air Force base. I was there by the road when another car pulled in and the man said 'Where you going?'

I said, 'I'm going to Greenville, California.' He was going there too! My wife didn't know I was coming home.

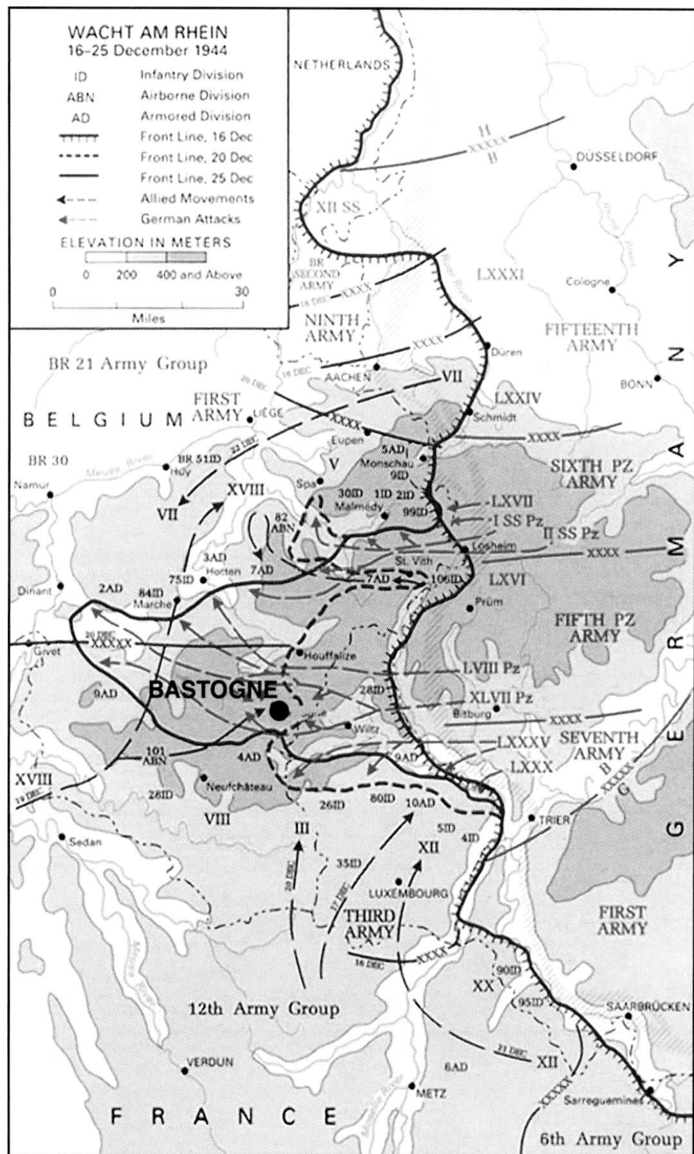

Map of Battle of the Bulge
U.S. military sources on wikipedia.com

I wasn't sure when I was coming home!

What branch of the service were you in?

I was in the Army in the 5th Infantry Division, which is the Red Diamond Division. I started my basic training in Monterey. Most of us were shipped all over the country from there. I stayed there for a month. Then they shipped me to Marysville, to Camp Beale. That camp had just opened. Two of us were shipped there. We got to talking. I asked him what he did. He said, 'I was in a band, I play the trumpet.'

He asked me what I did. I said, 'I was in a band and I played the drums.' You know what was going on, they shipped us to Camp Beale to form a drum and bugle corps! They didn't ask if anyone played an instrument, they just picked people to go, that's how the Army operated.

So when I got there, we got the corps formed. I have a picture of it. Our job was to get up early in the morning and go through the camp playing and waking everybody up! I came home on a furlough and the corps pulled out.

And several forts that were part of the Siegfried Line that had never been taken in history; Patton went right through them.

To this day I don't know where that unit went. So what happened to me, they shipped me to camp in Pennsylvania. I was with the combat engineers there. Our job was to make bridges at night. Each guy had to learn to make things in the dark.

We finally got our shipping orders to camp in New York. We did some more training there. Then we went overseas. We went in the Queen Mary and landed in Glasgow, Scotland.

We landed in deep water because the German U-boats were around. We went ashore on smaller ships. The two Queens traveled separately; there was the Queen Elizabeth and the Queen Mary. There was no convoy because they were too fast for the U-boats. They turned every minute or so. But the smaller troopships, a lot of them were sunk. They had to have convoys to follow them, but the U-boats would still sneak in on them.

Where did you go after that?

Well, we got on what they call the 'limey' trains, the little trains that the British have over there! When we got to England we had non-commissioned officers. They completely changed the training that we had learned in the U.S.

They told us that with what we learned in the States we'd be dead before we got to the firing lot. They said, 'Some of you were probably hunters in your youth. You act like you were hunting deer.' So that's what we did. From there we got ready and D-Day hit. It was several days after D-Day when our Division moved in.

We hit Utah beach where the rest of them went through. We were in England on D-Day. We didn't know if we were going in or not. You never know, everything was a secret. From Normandy we went into Saint Lo, France.

That's where our outfit really got into the battle then. From there it was all the way to Germany. General Patton had practically all the tanks. Everybody said we rode; we didn't ride, we walked. If Patton told us we have to be somewhere at all costs by night, we'd be there. There was no backing up.

What was the weather like?

In England it rained a lot. When we hit Metz that's when the storms were worse. Our Third Army went all the way to Germany. When the Battle of the Bulge happened it pulled the Third Army out of Germany into the Bulge. That's when the weather was cold. I belong to the Battle of the Bulge Association and they claim that was the coldest spell in Germany.

Hitler had it all figured out. What went wrong; he was battling on two big fronts. The Russians were fighting on the other front. Hitler wanted to go to the city of Antwerp and cut the U.S. and its Allies in two. It didn't happen.

The other bad thing before this happened in the valley near Metz. It was a political war, of course. They fouled Patton up with his tanks. We sat in that valley for days with no gas for our tanks.

As far as you could look there were tanks and we couldn't move. Then finally something happened and we got that gas and headed right into Germany. And several forts that were part of the Siegfried Line that had never been taken in history; Patton went right through them. Some of them were almost seven feet through with armor and steel, you could never blow them up.

But what he did was go right around them. We went right over those big tank traps. The heavy equipment outfit would go out and make room for our tanks to move. We went through a lot of small towns but we bypassed quite a few too. We had a lot of opposition from the Germans. You were never quite safe.

I was in a scout group. We scouted at night. We could hear the Germans talk in the night. That's as close as we got because of all the snow. When we slept there were two guys in a foxhole; you take turns every half-an-hour taking a nap.

But if you both fell asleep you froze to death. You had to have your gun under your body. You sit on it or lay on it otherwise it would freeze. It was really cold. I felt sorry for the engineers. I was shipped over as an engineer.

We were in England and this captain stood on a table and yelled for the combat engineers. We raised our hands. He said, 'You're combat engineers today but tomorrow morning you're infantrymen.' So everything we learned over in the States we never used. I was in the service for a little over four years.

I wore this diamond on my hat here. At a conference down at D-Q University a month ago I wore the hat. There was a man from the Tule Indian Reservation there. He said, 'Are you a diamond man?"

I said, 'Yes, I'm a diamond man.' He said, 'I wore the red diamond too.' Now that's the first Native American man I've ever met that also wore the diamond. I went to the diamond reunions but never saw another Native American.

That must have really been something....

Oh, it was really something. We know there's an Indian man in either Upper or Lower Lake that wore the diamond. There was an Indian man in Susanville that drove Patton's tanks, although I never met him.

Did you ever see General Patton?

Oh yes. He's the only general that wore the ivory-handled pistols. He is also the only general that was right up on the front lines with the men. He was in a jeep. Other generals were 50 or 60 miles behind giving orders. He was a front-line general. He was proud. I feel that Patton was one of the top generals in the United States.

What kind of impact did he have on the soldiers there?

When he said to move everybody moved. No matter what he said, they did it. We figured we were under a man that knows what he is doing. He studied the history of all the great leaders, even the Native American leaders. He was a professional general. He is buried among his men that were lost in the Battle of the Bulge (in Luxembourg). That's where he wanted to be.

You must have been really close to the men you shared a foxhole with?

Yes, we're just like brothers. Everybody supported each other. You also had to make sure that you knew the guy you were with, because there were so many Germans that were in there. They spoke perfect English and they wore the same uniforms that we did. Nobody knew who was who.

So you made sure that you knew the guy in the foxhole; he had to be somebody you trained with, you've been with, not a stranger. If somebody you didn't know slipped in the hole to replace someone who was killed, well, you were taking a long chance.

They looked like a GI but they may not be. They had a lot of those guys coming through there like that. We were taught a little German, French and Russian. We didn't know a lot, but enough to get by. Just like the Indian language!

What were you thinking when you were moving at night and could hear the German soldiers talking?

When you start hearing them in the distance you try and shy away. You're in the snow and you can hear them. It's freezing, but you try and walk slow and not make noise. There were a lot of people that have asked me, 'Weren't you afraid you would get shot?' Gee, you never thought of that. Never. I didn't anyway.

I talked with Leonard and Stanley and all of them. They said the same thing. You never thought of being killed! I was wounded. The whole countryside blew up one time. We had hit a mine of some kind.

I got wounded in the right shoulder and my left foot. I didn't know I was hit, it was so cold. We had a little station in back. We got some hot coffee and warmed up. When I warmed up, my right arm couldn't move. A guy came over and looked and said, 'Heck, you're all full of blood. You're going to have to go back to the medics.'

So they took me back to the medics and took my shirt off, my back was all busted up. They sewed it up as best they could in the field, you know. I still carry shrapnel in my left foot today. Around 1948 or '49 I applied for a job at Collins Pine and had to have a physical.

The doctor said to strip down, I stripped down. He said, 'You've been in the service, haven't you?' I said, 'Yeah.'

He said, 'Put on your clothes, you're hired.' Just like that. I said, 'How did you know I was in the service, how did you recognize the markings?' He said, 'I was over there too.'

I worked at that job for almost a year. Then Elmer Peck, he's a Navy veteran, he was going into construction. He took me to a site near Genesee and introduced me to the boss there. I went to work the next day and worked 16 years there!

Tommy Merino (sixth from left with drum) and his Army band, ca. 1943.
Photo courtesy of Tommy Merino.

What type of food did you eat in the service?

We had what you call K-rations. A small box of stuff, it had small cans of meat and hard crackers. Then you had what they call a D-ration. It was one hard chocolate. You could carry it all day and it wouldn't melt.

If your regular ration didn't come in that's what you had to live on. Once in a while you'd have a hot meal. But you're moving so much it was hard to get a hot meal.

You're carrying everything with you and couldn't build a fire. When we would get in a larger group sometimes there would be a stove and a fire. But us infantrymen kept moving.

After you got wounded how long did you stay in the hospital?

I didn't stay in a hospital at all. It wasn't really a hospital where I stayed, it was an emergency set-up. I was there about a week then they shipped me right back to the front lines.

Was your shoulder all right?

No, it wasn't. I didn't have broken bones, but it wasn't all right. I didn't pay attention to it. A while back at the Veteran's Hospital in Reno, my shoulder was bothering me, so they looked at it.

Tommy Merino

They said they would give me a shot. It was almost three months before they called me to get the shot. That was two months ago. It didn't really help.

If you had a choice, would you do it all over again?

I imagine I would. When I went in the service it was a challenge for me. I had been in a band so I had no problems in basic training. But when I came out of the service that was the bad part. I had served my time for the United States.

I could have been captured; I was wounded in the service. I felt there was something wrong with our government because I couldn't buy a can of beer when I got out of the service. It was against the law for me as an Indian, so I got on the bandwagon with different Indian organizations to have that law repealed.

But right today as I'm talking to you, there are places in this country that wouldn't serve Indians. That's really wrong. So I would go back in, but I've been a fighter against the system ever since I got out. I became an area commander for the American Legion in 1969 for the northern part of the state of California.

I had a team that worked with me. Every meeting would have 200 to 300 veterans in them. I would always tell them how I couldn't buy a beer when I got back from the war. So I would try to educate them, because they didn't even know that was going on. Not that I really drank, but that law was wrong.

What would you tell Indian children about education?

Learn to study, do your homework. The main thing for the younger people is this: all I had was a high school education, but you can't make it today with that. You have to have some knowledge of computers and that type of skill.

I think it's really important for them to learn their native languages. If you don't know your language, a lot of ceremonies can't be conducted. There are some things you can do, but other things you can't.

Tommy Merino participated in the Bear Dance ceremony in Taylorsville every year until his passing. He was a founding board member of D-Q University near Davis, California and a teacher of the Mountain Maidu language. He was often asked to give a blessing in his language at community gatherings and events in Indian Valley.

Lena Swearington

1914-2005

I was able to visit with Lena Swearington at her daughter Shirley Weaverling's home on May 18, 2004 in the tiny town of Dunsmuir, California. Lena is of Karuk ancestry, and she served in the Army Nurse Corps in Europe during the war. She was discharged as a captain and is one of the highest-ranking Native American women that served during World War Two.

My parents were Peter and Susie Grant; my father was from Butler's Flat down the Salmon River. My mother was Karuk from Cottage Grove; there's a new bridge about 18 miles down the river and Cottage Grove is by there. Frank Grant, Sr. was my father's brother. My mother had a big family; they lived on the other side of the river by Cottage Grove.

I had four sisters and three brothers. I'm the second oldest, I was born in 1914 at home in Happy Camp! We lived right in the town. They had a good school there. We walked to the school when we were old enough. My father was a miner because they did a lot of mining in Happy Camp at that time. Later on he worked on the road. He worked on a gold mine down by Independence.

When you were little did anybody in your family speak the Karuk language?

My mother and her sisters did; they all spoke it but none of us ever learned. We grew up listening to them but never learned it. What good would it do out in the world? I intended to go out into the world and become a nurse ever since I was very young.

Why did you want to be a nurse?

I just wanted to! I don't know, but it always struck me as something to do.

Were there other Indian families nearby?

They were all like us. There was a lot of inter-marriage. There are very few full-bloods left, and some say they are but they aren't.

Did your mother or any of her sisters make baskets?

Mom was an excellent basket maker. I never tried it though.

How many years did you stay in Happy Camp when you were little?

I left when I was just going on 13.

And that's when you went down to the Sherman boarding school?

Yes. It was the only place we could go to get an education, plus we didn't have to pay for it. They were collecting kids from up and down the river. My sister Agnes and I were eligible so papa put us on the list and we went.

So this was in 1927?

Yes.

Do you remember how you got down there to Sherman?

We went by car to Dunsmuir and then got on a train. It wasn't very comfortable but kids don't care what they ride in!

Do you remember if you were scared?

I don't think I was scared; I knew I had to go and was just wondering what it was all about. How would you feel if you were sent away all of a sudden?

I think I would have been scared, so you must have been pretty brave!

Well, we met these other kids and got acquainted so it wasn't that bad. I don't remember being scared.

When you were down at Sherman did you get to meet kids from other tribes?

Oh yes, they made them from all over, even from back East. They had three dormitories; one for the little kids, one for intermediate and one for high school. At first they put me in the intermediate then they put me in with the high school girls. They had three boys' and three girls' dormitories.

It was just a regular building. Upstairs they had a great big hallway and on each side they had beds lined up. Downstairs on the back it went into a big room. We called it the music room. That was it.

Were you able to stay with your sister?

Yes, we stayed in the same building.

Did you have to wear the same style of dress?

No, only on Sundays when we had regiment and then we had to wear skirts and black shoes. We'd have to wake up at seven in the morning.

Lena Swearington ca. 1942-3.
Photo courtesy of Shirley Weaverling.

Did you have half a day of school and half a day of vocational?

We went to school first; we had four classes of all the basics. Then in the afternoon we went to the different places. For the girls you could go to the laundry, the hospital or the sewing room. I was in the sewing room most of the time. I went from practical sewing to fine embroidery and then to making suits.

The first things we made were pajamas and shirts. I don't know how I did it! We even put cuffs on them and everything. I learned and I didn't mind it.

I know different Indian people had different experiences at these schools, would you say you had a good experience?

Yeah, I was always amenable. I didn't mind doing things. If we got demerits we had to go to the basement and sew material together to make rugs. Then our matron would send them out and sell them. They were big heavy rugs; that was our punishment.

What would you be punished for?

Oh, for not being on time. I was only punished twice. On Sundays for regimental we had to be on time. We had a great big parade ground and we had to parade. We'd march up the end and march back. We'd go four-by-four in a straight line. They'd sit up on the stand and watch us.

Lena Swearington (second from left) and a crew of Army nurses with two pilots during the war ca. 1943-4.
Photo courtesy of Shirley Weaverling.

The teachers?

The superintendent.

Why do you think they had you do that on Sundays?

Because a lot of people came and watched the parade. We were in regiments.

Did you ever get to go off of the school grounds?

They'd take us in a bus. I remember going up to the Los Angeles playground in the snow, and they took us to a lake once. I didn't go very much. I stayed close.

How many years did you go to Sherman?

Four.

Did you ever come back home during that time?

Once, for the summer.

The other three summers you stayed down there?

Yes, we stayed and worked. The summer after I graduated I was old enough to stay and work. I stayed down there and worked for two years in L.A. Then I went home for two years. I thought I had to give up my goal to become a nurse because they only took you into nursing when you were 18 and I wasn't old enough because I was 16 when I had graduated.

I wanted to go right then but maybe it was a good thing I didn't. After I worked down there for two years I came home for two years. We had a good doctor here and he talked me into going to school. He knew I wanted to become a nurse and he set it all up. My grades were always good so he sent them over to Bacome, Oklahoma. That's near Muscogee. They had a junior college, a high school and grade school too.

Did your parents encourage you to do this?

Well, they didn't have to. I was determined. They never said anything, but I think they were proud of me. I was the only one that went on.

So you went to Oklahoma, how did you get there?

I went by bus. They had dormitories and an orphanage, and that first summer I stayed in the orphanage!

Were there any other Indian girls at that school with you?

I think it was mostly an Indian school with some others there. They had a lot of good teachers; I'm glad I went.

Did you ever feel like you were treated any different because you were Indian?

I've never felt that at that school or at any place. I never thought 'Indian and White.' We never called ourselves Indians, we just lived. If anyone asked if I was Indian I told them I was half-Indian. I never claimed to just be Indian. Why claim one and not the other?

How many years did you go to that school?

Just two.

Did you go through a graduation ceremony?

No, because it was just a two-year school. You just got a certificate. After that the superintendent gave me a watch and a ticket and I was on my way to Arizona! I went to Sage Memorial Hospital; it was set up in Navajo country.

It was just a small place but we had quite a few of us taking nursing. We had to do everything from the floor up! It was all training; manual and book work. We worked on the wards too. In the mornings we had our book work and in the afternoons we worked in the wards, so we had lots of training.

Was it mostly Indian people who were patients?

Yes, but everyone came there because it was a good hospital and the doctors were very good. We had all kinds of training in nursing. When we finished and got our caps we went to Phoenix for the state boards.

Was that an exam?

Yes, a very strict one.

What did you have to do to pass the state exam, did you have to study?

No, we had it all already! I wasn't dumb, that was one thing!

Oh, I can tell that!

I got along pretty good. Then I came back and I took a job in the hospital and got paid for it. It wasn't very much but in those days you didn't get very much pay, but you had a place to stay and eat.

When you passed that test you were a licensed...

I was an RN; a registered nurse. My job was at that same hospital because they were short of nurses at that time. The operating nurse was a good friend of mine so we kept up and knew what was going on. There's a whole world out there and you have to keep up with it. You can't ignore it. You have to live with it.

About what year was this?

I got the license in 1940 and stayed there until 1941. In '41 Roosevelt had called all the young men to get a year's training. So my brother Peter was in the CCC. He was halfway through. Then they called the Red Cross nurses in to train.

So a friend and I joined up right across the street and then we joined the Army. We expected to go to the same place but she was much more ahead of me as an operating nurse because she'd been there a few years. We told the doctor we had signed up and he said we'd be separated. He didn't want us to join. He wanted us to stay.

I wanted to join because my brother was already doing this. So I went to Albuquerque and I don't know where my friend went. I went to Kirtland Field in Albuquerque.

Why did you want to join the Army?

Well, I guess for adventure! I didn't know what was going to happen but everything was building up. Everybody knew; you can't shut out the world. We knew what Hitler was doing all this time. We knew what Roosevelt was doing and we knew why he was doing it. It's a good thing he did.

So you went to an Army base?

It was a bomber base for the 54th. We worked in the hospital. I was attached to the hospital. We worked like at any hospital. Later on in my experience the hospitals didn't have enough. But the Army always had sufficient stuff to work with.

How many other nurses and doctors did you work with?

I don't remember, but we were sufficient.

What were the type of injuries that would happen on the base?

There weren't very much because not much was going on.

Was this before or after Pearl Harbor?

I joined up in June of 1941. My brother had joined up earlier. We were just going in to see how it would be to work with the Army. So Pearl Harbor came. But the night before this our bombers took off.

I joined up in June of 1941. My brother had joined up earlier. We were just going in to see how it would be to work with the Army. So Pearl Harbor came.

They were moving to Hawaii because there was something going on with the Japanese. They were on their way to Hawaii and were just landing when the Japanese hit them. Their airplanes just blew them out of the air. A lot of those people that we knew went down. We had the nicest Chaplain who was Catholic; he was so good and he took care of the boys. He'd come and see them every day and we got to know him real well.

He got killed that first day. That made us all the more determined. Everybody knew we were in for the duration. We didn't know how long it would be.

Do you remember how you heard Pearl Harbor was bombed?

I went to church, and then was out for a walk when the radio came on that Pearl Harbor had been bombed. We all gathered around and listened for news.

After that happened did you stay at that base for long?

At that time I was just in the Army attached to the Air Corps. There were some girls there from Texas. This one friend of mine and I heard they were starting this Air Evacuation and they were calling in nurses to train and become eligible. They were doing this in Sacramento at Mather Field and we decided we'd like to try it so we moved there.

This wasn't a fighter base or anything, it was just a little place. So we got there and then when they were ready for us we went to Kentucky! We were in the same group. We went through different places and went through basic.

Basic training?

Like the guys went through!

Describe some of that...

We went down to Fort Knox; it was pouring rain with mud all over. We only had little pup tents. The sun came out eventually. You had to crawl under this barbwire and they were shooting their guns over you. If you put your head up...I think they were shooting blanks and every so often real ones. A fellow we knew was killed doing this. I guess he raised his head and that one bullet got him.

We were scared to death. Some of those guys were on catwalks and they'd throw these firecrackers at you. We crawled clear over with our heads down. Then we had to go for a long hike and we had to train with the rifle too. I don't know why we had to go through all that; it was the same as the guys.

Did you ever shoot a weapon before?

You don't have a gun onboard a plane! I don't know why they had us do that.

But you got through it...

Oh yeah! Then we went back to Bowman Field in Kentucky. We would get litters and put people on them. We'd practice with each other. Then one night we were ready to fly out from Bowen Field. We were leaving that night.

We were in the air and all of a sudden I started feeling terrible. They put me in a litter! Then we landed and they said to see the doctor but not to go to the hospital because they were going to leave that night. I had to walk clear across the base to get to the doctor and then I had to sit and wait for an hour. Finally the doctor came and said 'Get this girl to bed!'

We were on the Ille de France; it was a big French ship they loaned us. It was all stripped down. There was a whole army of 7,000 people onboard.

I had a big fever; I had developed pneumonia just as I was going overseas! I didn't get to go with my friend and I was mad! I wanted to go; I knew all the girls real well and didn't know the others. They came and told me good-bye and that made me feel worse. They took off to New York and sailed the next day.

Did you ever get in contact with any other them after the war?

No.

After you got well what happened?

I went back to Bowman and they attached me to another squadron. There were 24 nurses in a squadron along with a head nurse. I had already gone through all the training and didn't have to do a lot of it. So they sent me to the general hospital in Louisville and that's where they were so short of nurses and so short of supplies it made you feel awful. There was so much to do and not enough people. The nurses were all leaving.

How long were you there?

It seemed like a long time but I guess it wasn't. Eventually we sailed for England and landed in Scotland.

Did you sail out of New York?

Yes. We were on the *Ille de France;* it was a big French ship they loaned us. It was all stripped down. There was a whole army of 7,000 people onboard. Everybody got seasick! This was in February. Even I got seasick. We were going north but that's where the German subs were so they detoured us toward the Azores.

It turned nice and sunny. Everybody was out and they were all green! I felt so sorry for the poor guys down below. They'd come up so sick for just a breath of fresh air. Some of them just stayed on deck and slept there!

So we sailed up the coast to Scotland and then we took a train to England. They were already bringing wounded into England from France. We went back up to Scotland and flew from Prescott in Scotland to Newfoundland, then on to New York. I only went to New York once. We'd fly from Prescott to Newfoundland then someone there would take over on the plane.

When you first reached England where did you stay?

Greenham Common. It was by Reading. It was an air base in England. We each had a technician, an enlisted man who was very capable. This was in 1943. England was pretty open. You could see green fields from the air. When you're down on the ground you'd come to these little towns or villages. We used to ride our bikes around the country and visit the old churchyards.

We stayed in Scotland for about six months. I enjoyed Scotland too. We were in Glasgow. They were flying from Prescott, which was the biggest airfield right on the coast, over to New York.

And they were ferrying wounded soldiers?

Yes. We took turns on the planes. I went out once when the plane just before me was shot down. This was wintertime in 1944. They were all killed of course, the patients and the nurse on the plane, and when we flew out the pilot went clear down to the ocean looking for debris. They couldn't find any. It was sad when you think of all those who were on their way home and they went down and were killed unnecessarily. The German submarines were very good up there in the North Atlantic at that time.

Do you recall the first time we went on a plane with wounded soldiers?

No. But we went to Iceland and landed then we went on to Newfoundland and changed personnel. The ones there that were rested went on to New York.

There would be one nurse on a plane?

Yes, and a technician.

What type of planes were you in?

You know, the TWA had passenger planes so these were converted. TWA and United had converted planes. Some of the planes were C-47s. That's what they were flying from the first aid stations to Scotland.

How many plane rides or missions were you on?

I had my flight book for a long time but I don't know where it went! I had all my stuff in there, who I flew with and how many...I couldn't tell you but we had kept track of all our flights. Then we went back down to England after D-Day and then into France.

What type of uniform did you wear?

We had flight suits. We wore caps and a jacket that were darker blue. We wore a shirt and tie.

Tell me about the time that you were on a flight and a German fighter plane came along...

I wasn't on a flight, I was stationed in Orleans opposite this cathedral. We were all loaded up with 24 patients ready to take off and the alert came on that fighter planes were coming in. They said to get under the plane. I said 'Where are the patients going? If they're going to stay in the plane I'll stay with them, I'm not going to desert them now.'

So we heard the planes coming in really fast. They strafed the field but fortunately we weren't on the field, we were off on the end. And they came in and it felt like they were gunning up my back! Oh! I don't know what we would have done if they had veered to our side. I guess we'd have been sitting ducks.

They were all scared but they said we were all clear. We took off and flew over to England and deposited them in a hospital. They only had surgeons stationed at different places and different hospitals. These men had come right off the battle lines and went to a first aid station. Then we picked them up and took them to a hospital, or if they were ready, we flew them on home. After you discharge them you're free to catch a plane going back to your base.

And you were never afraid of flying?

No! I don't know why! I was flying over the English Channel from England once after I dropped off my patients in a little plane. The pilot flew right down next to the water. There was a mechanic who was white in the face. He said to me 'If our tail hits that water we'll go down!'

It didn't bother me; I figured if the pilot could do it, I could do it! Anyway, after he said that I remembered that's how Glenn Miller went down. They were flying too close to the water because the weather was bad. They went down and he was killed in the Channel.

Was there ever a time when you were overseas when you were treated differently because you were a woman?

There were quite a few of us around. I think it all depended on how you were going to act. If you were to act smarty you would get treated badly. But if you were friendly and nice they appreciate that. All the soldiers did. It wasn't hard being friendly to those guys because you knew they risked their lives every day. If they were hurt they didn't blame anybody, they just took it.

Can you describe some of the wounds the soldiers had after combat?

Well, they were taken care of at the aid stations. They were all covered; a lot of them had broken arms but they could walk. There were some that had head injuries and they couldn't walk, and there were some who had leg and back injuries. But we didn't see any of the gory stuff.

They were taken care of before they got on the plane. We watched their temperatures and their blood pressure, and we watched how they reacted in the air. One boy was airsick on the plane and he couldn't turn. We cleaned him up as best we could.

Lena Swearington

Were there any times when soldiers passed away while they were on the plane?

No.

Did you ever get to talk to any of the soldiers?

Some were very talkative, but most were very quiet; at least the ones I took care of were. There was this German Colonel who was flying back to wherever they took Germans into custody in the States. He was going back and I don't think he had a guard. He couldn't move but I thought about him when we were up in the air.

What was the name of the squadron you flew with?

I was with the 816th squadron. There were 24 of us with the chief nurse. We flew with the Ninth Air Force.

How long would your flights be in the air?

Sometimes they seemed long. It was about six hours. Of course they had to watch for German subs. Like I said, that one plane went down just before we flew out. They told the pilot to look for debris but there wasn't any. The water was rough.

And that plane was taken down because a German sub fired on it?

That's what they said.

Was there ever a time when you were afraid?

Really afraid? I don't think so.

Why do you think that was so? Was it something inside you?

I always went to church. I always knew that God was watching over us. My mom was the same. I know she was praying for me too. I had a lot of friends. It was nice to know you were safe. I always felt no matter what happened, it wasn't me, it wasn't my time.

I always knew that God was watching over us. My mom was the same. I know she was praying for me too. It was nice to know you were safe. I always felt no matter what happened, it wasn't me, it wasn't my time.

I think that's what a lot of those boys felt too. If they were going to die, they were going to die. They went into the battle thinking maybe they wouldn't come back and a lot of them didn't. I always felt secure.

During your time as a nurse was there ever a time when you saw any Indian soldiers?

If I did, I didn't know they were. There were so many others who were dark. There were Spanish and Portugese…Nationalities were never important to me; they were all people.

Tell me a little about that time you flew all the way to New York…

I only went once. We had to land in Maine first on account of the bad weather in New York. That's where we left our patients. I went to New York on a regular plane. I stayed overnight and flew out just as soon as we could catch a plane. They had planes hauling things going back.

When we were in the service the officers always got a lot of alcohol and we got a carton of cigarettes every month. We got some scotch, some gin and some wine. A lot of us girls would get together and give it to the enlisted men and they'd have a party! I never smoked and I only drank a little wine. We felt like we were helping them to relax a little and they were glad to have it.

You probably made their day!

Yeah! I did keep a bottle of scotch. I carried it to New York; how I don't know! But I wrapped it up and sent it in the mail to Pop. He hoarded that stuff for a long, long time! He and a friend would have a drink every now and then. He really had a good time with that.

Did you ever have time to write home?

Yeah, we used that little V-mail. Peter always wrote to me. Pauly was up in the Aleutians and he wrote to me too. He had laryngitis up there and almost died. His sergeant wrote to me about that. Then he wrote to me when he was all right. You couldn't mention where you were or say what you were doing because that would give secrets away. I always wrote to mom.

What type of food would you eat in the service?

Well, it wasn't as great as people may think! The Navy had the best food, I don't know why! I remember once they had a whole load of butter on this ship and before they could ship it out it got all rancid. There were little things like that. Sometimes when we were out we had to use our rations. It was just some crackers and a little meat but it wasn't that much.

When you were on your base in Scotland or England and it was time to eat where would the nurses sit? Were you able to sit amongst the soldiers?

No, we stayed by ourselves. Most of the time our squadron rented a hotel and there would be two to a room. We did this in Scotland and down at Greenham Common too. So we had our own cook.

Were you and the nurses able to get information on how the war was going?

We always knew what was going on. We'd hear it on the news and you could hear more on the base. I could keep track of Peter by following the news.

Toward the end of the war when the Allies were liberating the concentration camps did you hear about that? Did that information come out fast?

Well, when we were in France we heard a lot about how they treated them and what they did. This was just from the French people that were with the Allies. We heard a lot through the grapevine. The grapevine's always good no matter where you are. We heard about a lot of the bad stuff that was going on but there was nothing we could do about it.

When were you in France?

We were over there a little while after D-Day. We stayed in Orleans in a big hotel. We stayed there until the war ended. We flew on planes from there. That's where I was when that plane strafed us.

What was it like to meet some of the French citizens?

We met a girl who was very friendly. She could speak English and she was a sister of this French doctor. We didn't see him much but he had a family and she took care of them. We used to go to their home for dinner. She was very nice.

I don't remember meeting anybody else who was close. Most of the French you met needed so much. One thing they wanted were cigarettes. I never kept those.

Where were you when the war ended?

We had moved to a chateau just outside of Paris. It was all ours! It was beautiful. No matter where you stayed they had gotten rid of a lot of stuff. After the war they had to recover a lot. Most of the French were poor because they'd given their all.

Do you remember the day when the war ended?

We heard it on the news. Everybody went to Paris to celebrate but I didn't go. You could hear all about it so what was the use in going?

How long did you have to stay in France after the war ended?

They were taking everybody home. The girls all went home early but I was going to stay in. Then the ones who were left intended to go to the Pacific. We all went down to Marseilles and stayed there for a long time. Then the war ended over there and we had to wait for a boat home. Finally in October or November we got a ride home.

Did you come through New York on your way home?

Well, it was rough going after we got out of the Mediterranean and went into the Atlantic. The meals were excellent! They had steak and everything. Everybody was sick again! I was determined not to be sick, but I was. I didn't go to bed; I sat out on the steps. The waves would hit over the sides.

As we got closer to home it was calmer. It was early in the morning when we sailed up the Potomac to New York. It was so good to see America again! And there was the Statue of Liberty standing up there giving us a big welcome home!

I really enjoyed that. It really made me feel good. And that was that! All the girls who lived in California flew back. I went from Sacramento to home again. Then I got the urge to go to Hamilton for six months. I was still in the service and I went to Florida to a base there for six months. I worked in the hospital. The war was over for about a year now.

After your time in Florida where did you go?

I got married; I flew over to Sacramento and we went to Reno to get married. I got out of the service because I was married. My husband Jim had been in the service. I met him at Hamilton Field. We were divorced 12 years later. I have two children and two grandchildren and seven great-grandchildren!

After your time in the war what did you do?

I went home and had my children and took care of them. We moved back to Happy Camp in 1947. For a while we didn't have a doctor there. The trouble was, people found out I was a nurse and they started coming to me! I'd call this doctor in Yreka and he'd tell me what to do or to send them to him.

Finally we had a doctor come and live there and he was good. They contacted me and asked if I wanted to work with him. The kids were halfway grown by that time so I went to work with him. Then another doctor came in and I worked with him.

I worked until 1971. When the doctors weren't there people would come at night and knock on my door. Then they built a clinic and I didn't have to work anymore.

It must make you feel good to know that you helped heal all those people over the years...

They remember me!

We had moved to a chateau just outside of Paris. It was all ours! It was beautiful.

Lena's family is very proud of her service to her country and her people. During the duration of her time as a nurse she helped hundreds of patients and their families.

Stanley Lowry

1917-2000

My grandfather Stan Lowry was of Mountain Maidu and Pit River descent. He was the third of eleven children born to Robert and Edna Lowry. Robert and Edna met at the Greenville Indian boarding school. My grandfather and I spoke on January 29 and again on April 15 of 2000. He passed away in the summer of 2000.

I was born in Milford (near Susanville). I stayed there until I was six. I remember we had two or three horses on our farm; we had a peach orchard, an alfalfa field, chickens and one old sheep.

It hated me, every time I would come out there to the corral. One time I was making fun of it, there was a log out there and I slipped and fell right in front of the sheep! He started to butt me, he didn't have horns and wasn't hurting me, but I was yelling and my mom came running out there to chase him away.

I was seven when we moved to Susanville. Prior to us getting in the war we had a Depression. People at home learned to live without a lot of stuff. There was already a ration for gas, different foods; this country was almost ready for war.

Leonard and I volunteered; I was 22 and he was 19 years old. We left in 1941, January 8 for Fort Ord. 18 men left Susanville for Fort Ord. January 8 is my son Ike's birthday. Leonard and I volunteered right off the bat. We knew we'd get drafted anyway. If we volunteered we might get to pick where we wanted to go.

Did you go to the same boot camp together?

Yeah, at Fort Ord, we were there about three months then we went on our first maneuvers up in the state of Washington. We came back then we went from Fort Ord down to Camp San Louis Obispo. From there we went out in the Mohave Desert for training. Leonard went to OCS in Georgia then from there he was sent to Australia and he fought all the way up through the islands.

I went to Mississippi, then I went to France and Belgium and fought at the Battle of the Bulge, from there we kept going through Germany, all the way through

Germany, and in the spring we hit a river which separates Germany from Czechoslovakia.

We were going to cross that and we would be liberating people, but we didn't! If we'd liberated, women would be out there with wine and everything, but the war ended. We had to come back and that was that.

You both went into the Army thinking you would be able to serve next to each other, instead, Leonard went to the Pacific Theatre and you went to Europe...

He went to Fort Benning, Georgia to be an officer. At that time the officers that graduated with him were sent to the South Pacific. In the first place, young Indians wherever they fought were probably the best fighters this country had. When we first went into war, there was a bunch of California Indians at Fort Ord.

In the face of obstacles ~ COURAGE
UNITED STATES ARMY

Recruiting Poster.
Library of Congress, Prints and Photographs Division, (LC-USZC4-2289).

Most had been in government boarding schools. They already knew how to left face, right face, keep time and all that; in no time they had arm bands that say corporal or sergeant and they'd be marching these white guys around. Another thing Roosevelt initiated during the Depression was the CCC camps. That was the Civilian Conservation Corps.

Did you ever go to a CCC camp?

Oh yeah. The camps were in the national forests. You keep the forest clean, burn the dead trees and fight bugs. They were all over. Even the Indians had their own CCC camps. We had one up in Chiloquin, Oregon, one in Warm Springs (in Oregon) and one in Yakima (in Washington). Most of the Indian CCC men came from the West Coast, but a lot came from Minnesota or near there.

The first one I went to was in Warm Springs. They came here and got me, my dad, Calvin's dad and a bunch of old men. We all got on that bus. We stayed at the Klamath Reservation overnight; from there we made it up to Warm Springs. About 20 miles from Warm Springs there was a railroad.

After the first payday all the old married men hopped a freight train and went home. I was there in the summertime then school would open at Riverside, so I'd hop a freight train to go there. It was all Indian people at the camps.

It was a good life, a clean life, we were disciplined. So we were ready. We were healthy from marching up and down the hills. It didn't take much to go from a CCC boy into a soldier. We could take the big marches in the Army.

The CCC camps helped white people too because they had their own, but what we had over them was government school where we learned military training. Sherman, these other military...I mean Indian schools, had their own guard, with real rifles and bayonets.

Indians were ready to go up the grade; PFC, corporal, sergeant, staff sergeant, when they got to combat. A lot went to Fort Benning, but a lot became officers like me through battlefield commissions.

The Germans always thought the Americans were soft, but we had millions of boys in the CCC camps; they were in shape, they weren't soft. So when we met the Germans we were well-conditioned.

Did you have any other Indian vets that served right with you?

Yeah, we had several Indians in the division but there weren't any in our regiment. I was in the 99th Division of the 393rd Regiment, Second Battalion, Company F, Second Platoon. We killed and captured more Germans than any of them!

When we first got there, it was so cold; there was three or four feet of snow. People got trench foot so we were called the 'Trenchfoot Division.'

Then later on, we were such a new division, a young division, we were called the 'Battle Babies.' We had a good division. We went right up against the Siegfried Line. There were Germans in those great big bunkers; we had a hard fight with them.

Even though everyone knew you were Indian, you weren't treated different in the Army?

No, no. When I first went in the Army at Fort Ord, there were a few of us (Indian soldiers) in every company. They would call us 'Chief' or something, we stopped that quick.

Did you ever meet with any of the civilians in the war? How did they treat you?

The civilians, they were pretty much like American

people. German people are more like Americans than any other country over there. I didn't like England too well, they were prejudiced. France was all right. But the Germans, when the war ended, they were the nicest people. They knew all about Americans.

They knew about Jessie Owens, the great athlete, they loved Jessie Owens, or Joe Lewis, even if he did beat up Max Schmelling. But they were just like, you walk down the street here, you could feel the same way. Those other countries, you go down the street, they'd all have walls, you know, they'd never talk to you. If they had a gate or fence, they'd be behind it; they'd never talk to you.

What types of weather did you fight in?

Well, the Bulge was snowy, cold, it felt like 30 or 40 below zero. See, Leonard fought in Korea; that was cold, freezing, fighting the Koreans and Chinese. He always used to say, 'Oh, you didn't have it very rough over there.'

I had a guy in my outfit that went to Korea in the same division that Leonard did, the Second Division. He said the snow and the cold was similar except over in Korea they were prepared for it; they had clothing and everything. But we didn't have it, there were guys walking around in the snow barefoot.

When you first went in, what was your rank?

I was a yard bird first. We got inducted in Sacramento then we went to Carmel by Fort Ord. The first night there, when we got up in the morning, somebody stole my pillow case. So I had to go over to headquarters.

For losing my pillowcase I was fined nine cents and put on KP (Kitchen Patrol). Washing those big garbage cans, that's the only time I ever spent on KP in the service. So I was a yard bird, I wasn't even a Private. I was lower than a Private! Yard bird was a nickname.

So what was your rank when you retired?

Second lieutenant. That's another thing, Leonard got to go to school and he became what they call a '90-day wonder.' After 90 days they become officers. I got mine on the battlefield, a battlefield commission.

You said once you were wearing beaded buckskin moccasins, was that during the War?

Yeah, my sister Viola sent me some beaded moccasins. We were at a place in Germany called Geisterheim, near a peak. I took a squad with me, we went way up the top of the peak, we went through the German line; we had a radioman with us.

We could watch the Germans, what they were doing down below us. We could see their tanks moving out. We were giving information back to our battalion and our regiment. We were giving all the information about what the Germans were doing.

When I first went in the Army at Fort Ord, there were a few of us (Indian soldiers) in every company. They would call us 'Chief' or something, we stopped that quick.

Our general was there; we were telling where the German tanks were. Out in the open field was a little shack, some of our patrol stayed there. I saw some German tanks pull up to that shack, here came part of our outfit with their hands up; they took them right down below where we were with our radio. When the word got back there, another regiment went up there; they didn't even know we were there.

We were from the 393rd, they were from 395th. They came up the hill, we saw them coming, and we waved them up the hill. They tried to capture some of us! The captain, I told him 'Look, I'm American Indian, with the 393rd.'

I was even wearing beaded buckskin moccasins. I said 'I'm Indian!'

They didn't believe it. They called the artillery, and put the artillery in the hills where we were. We couldn't even dig in the ground, we didn't want to make any noise and it was mostly rocks anyway. We hid underneath the big boulders. Then the artillery started hitting up there.

Stanley Lowry (in center) and his buddies at Ford Ord, Ca. in the spring of 1941.
Photo courtesy of Virginia Aguilar.

The only way we could get it to stop, I had my radioman call clear back to division headquarters to stop that artillery. This captain made three of us hold up our hands, I said, 'We're 393rd, our regiment is right down there, I said, 'What, do I look like a German?'

He still didn't believe it. He started getting rough, then I told him, I said, 'I have a sergeant up there with an automatic rifle, I've got you zeroed, you keep getting me mad and I'll move my hand and say good-bye to you.'

They finally cut us loose. That's when General Laur found out we were up there, and had been up there for several days. That's when I got my Silver Star, for being up there and sending all that information on German movements back to the camp.

I know you had hand-to-hand training. Did you fight hand-to-hand also?

Not really. Most of the time you never saw the enemy. You just knew where they were. Just call artillery, put artillery on them. And never even see them. Sometimes we'd see the convoys, the trucks moving people back and forth.

And we were observers, when we see the Germans move we'd call artillery. We had an artillery officer nicknamed 'High Pocket,' he was deadly with that. He would put one smoke shell over there, and call battalion; we'd have 16-battalion guns behind us and just tear up the country there.

Stanley Lowry (bottom row, third from right) and "his boys" from the 99th Division at Camp Van Dorn, Mississippi ca. 1943.
Photo courtesy of Ike Lowry.

That's what I would do. Use whatever support weapons we had. If we were moving out somewhere and got stopped by a machine-gun nest, instead of charging like the Marines did, we'd just disappear, and I'd call for artillery support. If that wasn't enough, we'd call for the Air Force.

We were moving across one river, we tried to put some boats across the river; there was ice on it though. There was a city right across from it, a big city. 200 SS troops had taken over the city. They had hung the mayor of the city because he wanted to surrender. So, when we started to come across, they fired on us and we lost some men.

We moved back and called the Army Air Force. Here comes the Air Force, from England. In 18 minutes over that city, they just wiped it clean, and killed thousands of Germans; men, women, children and those soldiers. In just 18 minutes.

If I was stopped by machine-gun fire, I would call for mortar fire; they would fire a round and hit, I would correct it then knock out a machine-gun or whatever. I would always use whatever I had. Instead of sending men in I would hold them back and plaster the Germans with mortar or whatever until they were ready to give up.

Did you ever come across Panzer units?

Oh yeah, they hit us a lot. That's the German armored outfit. When we first went up fighting them, their tanks were so much bigger than ours we couldn't hardly hurt them. After five months, we got the new General Pershing tank then our tanks were knocking them out.

Did you ever come across German SS units?

Yes, they were special, almost like the Marines. The SS were rounding up Jews and putting them in concentration camps. They were bad. Every time we'd catch SS, I had one kid from South Carolina, he had a bayonet, and he'd put in right in their butts and march them back, when we took prisoners.

He didn't know how to read or write when he entered the Army, after the war he used that G.I. money and went to school; last I heard he was a professor at a University in South Carolina.

Were there SS that wouldn't surrender, that fought until they died?

Yeah, we had to dig them out. Throw grenades at them and bring them out. The SS had their own crest and they had things on their collars that showed they were SS. They were tough; the whole German army was tough.

They were exceptionally well-trained. If the Germans weren't fighting on all the fronts, like in Russia and the others, I don't know if we would have won. We might have had to resort to the A-bomb. They could have held us off or pushed us back if things were different.

Did you ever fight against any famous German generals?

Von Rundstedt. He hit us the hardest. He had 30 divisions. He pushed us back. (Field Marshall Karl von Rundtedt was the Commander in Chief of the Western

Forces for Germany). Once, we had to make a stand.... Our general came by and said this was it. He said to hold at all costs. He put barbed wire behind us, usually it's in front; then he had engineers put in a minefield! We had to stay there.

Behind this ridge there was a depot, if the Germans got into that and refueled.... a lot of their Panzer tanks would get up right close to us and run out of gas, then their crews would get out and get back toward their line.

When they did that, we'd sneak down there and look inside them; they'd be full of canned fruit, cherries, apricot, canned goods, and chocolate, bars of chocolate. We'd go and raid that then we'd throw a grenade in, the kind that burns; a phosphorus grenade.

You fought in small towns and villages, right?

Oh yes, we went through little towns and villages. In most cases we'd have artillery. Any time we'd come to a town we'd send a patrol and they would get fired on, our artillery officer would call them back and he'd lay the artillery right on them and slaughter them. It was terrible, every time we would knock a town out we had to go through there, Once we saw a woman sitting there holding a dead baby, there wasn't a dry eye out of all of us.

When you went through these towns, did you ever come across any concentration camps?

Oh yes. I went through quite a few. The people were skeleton-like, and there were ovens where they burned them....Some of the camps were there in Germany. (Stan went through a Dachau subcamp near the town of Mulhdorf, and observed the Buchenwald system of camps right after the war ended).

Did you ever learn any German language?

We'd say "Hands up, hurry!" (In German). One of my boys, he was on patrol and went into a little opening and there was about 15 Germans sitting there cleaning their weapons, he couldn't think of anything but 'Stick 'em up!' And they did!

One time we saw these two Red Cross airplanes come flying in, then we saw them flying out, the Germans were shooting, but they shot high over their heads, I could see the tracers go up high, they missed them on purpose, but you had some scared Red Cross girls! But the thing about the Red Cross was, you'd take over a place and it wouldn't be long before they were there with coffee and donuts.

They were right there with us. There were a lot of funny things that happened during the war. I can remember those. The really tragic and bad things I've blanked out. We went through and saw some terrible things. Something about that, your mind just blanks it out.

Did you ever capture any German soldiers?

Oh yeah, we had German prisoners that went with us. The Germans, they stayed right with us. We had good food. We were heading toward Russia. They thought we would keep going and get in a fight with the Russians, and they would be there to help us.

The Germans would help fight the Russians. They wanted us to. The Germans were scared to death of the Russians. I crossed the Rhine River on the Ludendorff Bridge. I crossed that on my birthday, the 11th of March, 1945.

Did you ever capture German officers?

Oh yeah.

Stanley Lowry ca. 1943-4.
Photo courtesy of Ike Lowry.

What were their ranks?

I don't remember. We captured thousands of Germans before the war ended. They would yell, 'We're coming in!' Then they'd walk in laughing and grinning, happy to surrender.

You were a second lieutenant after a while. How many men were under your command?

About 50.

That's who you gave orders to.

Yeah. I got to be a lieutenant and still had the same platoon. Same guys. Actually, I took those boys, trained them in Mississippi. And camp in Texas, that's where we shipped out from. I took those boys with me, I only lost five killed, and maybe 10 badly wounded; you know, lost a leg or an arm.

Whenever one of them died, I was right there talking to them or something, you know. See, when we got to Belgium, the first night we camped. They were just

Stanley Lowry

started a cemetery, just had three or four crosses. We were gone for 90 days, and we came back for a rest. As far you could see were crosses...all Christian, but some were Hebrew.

The best thing that ever happened to me, we were in central Germany in a city that was pretty bombed out; the boys went through and found a great big safe in either a post office or a bank. The boys got some C-4 and blew the door open.

There was all kinds of money in there. We had millions of dollars worth of money. There was American money, British pounds, Italian lire, German marks and French francs. They asked if I wanted some. I said yes, I was going back to Paris for R and R. I said I'd take francs. They gave me two little suitcases full of francs. I took them with me. A bunch of us officers took a jeep back to France from Germany.

I had just got a package from home, from my sister Viola. The guys wanted me to open it because they thought there were cookies or something else in there to eat. I didn't want to open it because there was deer meat jerky in there!

Finally we stopped in Paris, France. It was a nice warm day and they had these little tables set out there on the sidewalks where you could eat or drink. I finally told those guys to come over to the table. I opened that package and there were some big pieces of jerky in there. They were serving beer nearby, so we could have jerky and beer.

But those guys didn't know what the jerky was. Finally one tall guy said he knew that it was jerky. I asked him where he ate jerky. He said in California. I asked him where at in California, and he said in Susanville! His last name was Clement, and his father owned a second-hand store on Weatherlow Street. Boy, we all ate that jerky and drank beer!

So while I was there, a Frenchman came up. He said he wanted me to come with him. The Frenchman and his wife had a restaurant there. A bomb had come down through the restaurant to the basement and exploded. It had torn up everything.

The war wasn't over and they couldn't open the restaurant. I asked them how much would it take to replace it. They said a lot of money. I held up one of those suitcases and asked would that be enough? They said yes! There was one million francs in there. They said that would do just right. They said to come with them.

We went to a place similar to a City Hall, and they gave me a quarter-interest in the restaurant. The wife, the man and his eight-year-old son were there. Then they took me to a bank there and told me to put the other million francs I had in the bank there.

So I put the money in the bank there. The war wasn't over yet, we still had far to go, so I left my money there. I more or less forgot about it until I got home. I thought, God, I have a million francs over there!

So after 50 years with all the interest there's millions of francs over there! I always thought if I had the chance to go over there and get it I'd send the money home and put it in the bank here! But in 50 years I never went over there. I imagine that boy is still alive over there. So you're sitting here talking to a millionaire!

What year were you discharged?

I went in in '41 and came out in '45. I couldn't stay in; I'd had enough. We came in at New York. I had to take a bunch of troopers to take care of the payroll and everything, and the New York harbor...seeing that big band around the Statue of Liberty with the girls all out there... People were handing us milk; the Red Cross handed us milk. We never had it over there.

We wound up having six people; I took them to El Paso, Texas. Took a slow train through Arkansas. I took care of them and everything. Seemed like I'd never get home. Went to Marysville, in California.

Gene Ryan, he's another one of my cousins. He lives in Redding now. We came into Susanville and where the Bank of America is, there used to be the Lassen Industrial Bank. Right next to there was a bar called the *Band Club.*

And me and Gene Ryan, we went in there, and there was a sign on the door that said, 'No dogs or Indians allowed.' We pushed the damn door open; we went in there and grabbed a barstool and Wham! We hit that beer, knocked all the whiskey and glasses and everything; we just tore that place up.

Who owned it was Charlie Evans who used to be a logging contractor here, he used to work with a lot of Indians. We tore up as much as we could of that bar, me and Gene went outside there, waiting for the cops to come.

But Charlie Evans showed up. He knew who we were. We showed him the sign, 'No dogs or Indians allowed.' He tore that son-of-a-bitch sign down and said 'God!'

Right then and there he fired his manager of the bar. We really tore that place up. Gene was a big guy too; he was a pretty good fighter. Hell of a welcome, to come home and find a sign that said, 'No dogs or Indians allowed,' you know.

Are you proud of how you served your country during World War 2?

Oh yes, but I changed my tune when I went to Wounded Knee, but that's another story....

Stan Lowry lived in Susanville all his life. Stan fought for this country in World War Two; in 1973 he went to the Pine Ridge Reservation in South Dakota to help with the Indian occupation at Wounded Knee. The occupation helped to show the world about the crimes the U.S. Government was committing against American Indians.

Stan stayed active with the Indian Veterans' Association. He marched in Veterans' parades with pride in Susanville for over 20 years. His favorite hobby in his later years was fishing in the lakes near Susanville. He enjoyed participating in the Bear Dance and in his younger years he dressed to represent the grizzly bear.

In the summer of 1998 my Grandpa Stan's staff sergeant from World War Two named Eli Heitic traveled with his two sons from Ohio to Susanville to visit with Stan and his family. It was the first time they had seen each other since the war. When asked why he did this, Mr. Heitic replied, "Stan's a good man. If I had to go through the war again, I'd go with him all the way. He was like my big brother."

Frank Ames

1919-2002

I met with the late Frank Ames Sr. on February 20, 2002 at his home in Hoopa. He was of Yurok ancestry. I am a good friend with Frank's granddaughter Stacy Canez and she went with me to the interview.

I didn't know it, but Frank knew my grandfather Stan on my father's side from when they attended the Sherman Indian School. When Frank was very young he was a neighbor with my great-grandmother Lena Reed McCovey on my mother's side. They were neighbors in the Yurok village of Pecwan. The Indian community is a small world!

I was born in Requa on the Klamath River on January 19, 1919. I turned 83 not too long ago. My parents lived in Pecwan down the Klamath River. My father's name was Jackson Ames; he came from Bluff Creek and moved to Pecwan.

My mother was Caroline Jake Ames. She was from Blue Creek on the Klamath River. Then they moved to Johnson's (also known as Wautek). I stayed in Pecwan until I went to school. I went to grade school right in

Frank Ames

Johnson's, a few miles down from Pecwan. We had to walk.

There weren't too many cars so we had to walk. That was our school. Emma and Jack Norton were our teachers at Johnson's. One time Emma opened her milk backward and it spilled; she didn't know what she was doing, and she was the teacher!

When you were very young, did you ever go to any of the Brush Dances?

Oh yes, I hate to brag about it, but I was a singer in the Brush Dance, the Jump Dance and the Deerskin Dance. My dad was a singer in the Deerskin Dance. I played in the stick games. Sometimes I played on the end and other times I played in the center. I played a lot of times here in Hoopa.

Frank Ames ca. 1945
Photo courtesy of Frank Ames.

Where did you go to high school?

At Sherman Institute in Riverside. It's about six miles south of Riverside. I finished high school there. I went around 1938 or '39. After that I joined the service. I knew Glenn Moore and all the Moore boys. He was my buddy and we stuck together. We would go through some other schools when Sherman played them, and get in an argument, and we'd fight them.

There was Glenn, Ed and Don Moore all down at Sherman. We kind of grew up together. My brother Leonard Ames went to Sherman too. They gave us a chance to go through all the different trades. I liked cutting hair as a barber. It was a clean, good job. I stuck with that. I liked to box. I went all over to box. We went to Long Beach and I boxed. I had a lot of fun. I'm 83 years old and I'm still in good shape.

When I was in the service I boxed in Texas, Louisiana and in Juarez, Mexico. We were just across the border. I liked athletics, maybe that's why I'm in pretty good shape now. That's my life history!

I got to travel a lot of places, not of my own accord, but when you're in the service you can. I also traveled when I was in Sherman Indian School. I went to San Francisco when I joined the service and from there I went to Louisiana. I went to Dallas after that, then to New Jersey, then to New York. Then I went overseas. We stayed in England for a while.

How did you get to England?

I went over on the Queen Elizabeth. They tried to bomb the ship. I was with my crew 30 feet under the water in that big boat. We were lucky they didn't sink us. When we were in England one time I saw these people pushing a cart, and all these other people would look in there.

I went over there and looked in the cart to see what everybody was interested in. There was a black baby laying in there, that's what people were looking at. England was where our troops went first. You could tell there were a lot of places that were bombed. We got along with everybody over there.

After your time in England what did you do?

We went through France. We went through Germany. I had a partner whose name was Frank. He was a big guy. We stuck together through the war. We went through Frankfurt, which was a big town. The civilians were on the run.

When the war ended, all these officers came out of this forest with their hands up. I took a Luger pistol from an officer. I still have it. We were on our way back, this is a true story, we were on a train, and these German people gave us some vodka. We drank a whole bunch, it tasted awful, but we drank it anyway because we were so happy!

And you were in the Army?

Yes, I was. I forgot which division I was in. I was in the regular Army. I carried an automatic machine gun. I was a technician corporal. I don't remember any of the towns in France because we were on the go. We went right through France and on to Germany. When we were in Germany they were sending these Buzz bombs into England. They were just like a little plane.

Back in England we were on a 40-millimeter gun, and everybody was supposed to know where their position was. I was on a lateral position. One time we all saw this Buzz bomb, and we all jumped on our guns. I ended up pumping the bullets off, and kept going.

There was a big mountain ahead of us and it burst into flames. I don't know if anyone was around there or not but it burst into flames. It was just like a little airplane. This is that German Luger that I took away from that German officer. It's a nice gun. I've had it a long time.

Did you ever come across other Indian men in the service?

Oh yes, there were quite a few, especially in New York. They were nice people; Indians got along good. They were from different places.

Were you treated any different in the service because you were Indian?

No, I would say we were just like everybody else. It was wartime, and everybody had to do what you had to do in the service. One thing though, when I was in Louisiana, this guy told me something. I boxed him, and I mauled him and stepped on him when I was done!

Did you ever write home when you were overseas?

No, I didn't have time enough to write home. We just toughed it out over there. I think everybody knows that during wartime some of the boys didn't come back. I came back. I was lucky, you might say. During the service I got along with everybody. I like to get along with people; I've had a lot of fun that way.

Did you ever have to fight hand-to-hand against the Germans?

No, when we were going through the war was drawing to an end. All the people liked us. That's the way it went all through Germany. Everything was going our way. Everybody was glad to go home and there was no more fighting. When the war ended we were passing though towns and traveled on the autobahn.

Did you ever walk through any of the concentration camps?

No, I never went through. I was lucky. We saw bodies of humans. They were piled up inside this room; there were women and children. We got to see it anyhow. We were allowed to see them. That was when we went through Germany.

I saw lots of death. One time this (German) guy was in a foxhole, and my partner said, 'You're the SOB that killed my brother,' and he just riddled him right there with a machine gun.

It must have been pretty traumatic to see some of the things you saw.

Oh yes, it was. For instance we came through a town, and this one guy came up to us. We almost shot him. He looked like a German; he had German clothes and everything. But he was American. He was a prisoner there. He was telling us about how they walked the prisoners 25 miles and whoever couldn't make it, they just riddled them with bullets right there. That's what he was telling us.

Can you describe how you came home?

On the way back I got to New York, this is the best part, everybody was happy to come back to the United States. I got a half-gallon of milk that I drank all by myself. The rest of my buddies all took a gallon of milk and drank it all! And incidentally, the Statue of Liberty was there, and that's what everyone was happy about.

I went over on the Queen Elizabeth. They tried to bomb the ship. I was with my crew 30 feet under the water in that big boat.

I was sure happy, because I'd never seen it other than in a picture. But I did see it! But milk was the best thing too. From New York, we flew to Dallas, Texas. We finally came to Camp Beale and then I came home.

I bet your parents were really happy when you came home.

Oh yes, they were very happy. I came on a bus to Hoopa, and then I went on a smaller bus to Pecwan and Pecwan Creek. I lived just across the creek. I was really lucky that I went overseas and came back, and nothing ever happened to me.

What type of work did you do after the war?

I've done woodwork all my life. Falling trees and bucking trees. I worked with my brother Howard and a lot of other people, too. I worked in the woods in Humboldt and Del Norte counties. I stayed in camp in Del Norte. I worked in Redwood Creek, and in Hoopa here. I worked until I couldn't work anymore!

Thank you for talking with me.

Thank you for letting me talk a little bit about myself. You might say I'm lucky to be here, I've been hurt working in the woods. I think I had a good life.

Frank was a retired logger and enjoyed spending time with his family and friends. He and his late wife Ruth Jackson-Ames had seven children, 22 grandchildren, and 19 great-grandchildren.

Al Valadez, Sr.

Al Valadez, Sr. and his wife Josie live just up the road from my childhood home in Susanville. They both served in the war effort. Al fought under General Patton in the Third Army in Europe and Josie served as an aircraft welder in San Diego. Al was very kind and spoke with me at his home on January 9, 2003.

I was born on December 9, 1922 right here in Susanville. My father's name was Domingo Valadez and my mother's maiden name was Bernice Brown. My father was from El Paso, Texas.

How did he come out this way?

Oh, I don't know. He came over this way like anyone else wanting to see what's over the next hill. My mother is from right here in Susanville. My grandpa had a place right here in the valley. Up toward Rice Canyon is where we have my grandpa's land and a family cemetery.

They used to call my father Charlie Paiute, but his last name was Brown. His wife's name was Ellen. My grandfather was of Paiute ancestry and my mother was part Maidu from over toward the Greenville area.

Did you know your grandparents well?

Oh yeah, I used to come to town with them every day. They'd come to town in a wagon. That was the big event of the week! There were nine of us in the family. There were five brothers and four sisters. I was the next to the oldest. My grandfather was a rancher. During the summer months he was a guide and took people up trails to Mount Lassen. I guess he liked it.

So I had an early education about the city; I didn't like a lot of it because there were too many people and everybody was in a hurry.

Did your grandmother know her Indian language?

Oh yeah, she spoke it and my mother did too. My grandpa conversed with them too. But like most kids I went to go play and didn't learn the languages.

Which languages were these?

Maidu and Paiute.

Do you remember if what differences there were between languages?

Yeah, there were different pronunciations. They had different sounds to them.

When you were young where did you live?

Up that little road by Rice Canyon. It was pretty much a farm environment. We had horses and wagons. We'd hunt rabbits and other animals to provide meat for the table. We had to go to where the creeks and rivers were to go fishing. We went as far as Feather River. At that time they didn't have that dam.

Did that dam change the depth of the creeks?

It sure did. Down at the bottom of that lake is a crossroads. There used to be a settlement down there. My mother told me that they used to live at that settlement there when she was little.

Did your family ever collect acorns or anything like that?

Oh yeah, and we hunted a lot. There used to be four houses out there in the Rice Canyon area where our family lived. They were all my aunts and uncles there.

Were there ranches owned by white families nearby?

Yes, quite a few lived in the valley. They'd raise their cattle and whatever else they needed for food.

Where did you go to grade school?

When I was old enough I went to Stewart Indian School over in Nevada. I was probably seven or eight when I first went there. I went there for about four or five years. Then our family moved into town and I went to regular city schools.

How did you get to Stewart?

My folks took us there. We went there for the school year and they'd come bring us home at the end of the school year. Almost all nine of us kids went there. The younger ones stayed here in Susanville.

What was Stewart like for you?

It was a boarding-type school where a lot of parents took their kids to get an education. There were boys and girls dormitories. After school was out for the summer they'd come get us and we'd come home.

Did you have to wear a type of uniform?

Yeah, they'd have us wear these knickers. You know those short pants? Nobody liked them because if you fell you'd skin your knees. Nobody liked those knickers. They were a kind of uniform-type thing. They had caps if you wanted to wear them. Most everybody had a cap or a hat.

We went to school the full day. The younger ones didn't go as long. They went maybe half a day at most. Us younger ones would get off at noon. It was our fun time then! We went to set traps for rabbits. We had our own track in that area. We'd go running.

When you were at Stewart did they have trades?

Yeah, but most of us spent time playing until we got older. I liked running. I did a lot of running in that time period. At that time I did a lot of draft-type drawing. But then my parents moved to Portola, California and took me there and I went to grade school and high school there in Portola.

I got a chance to go to school in San Francisco because I liked engineering. There was a college that had an engineering and business branch so I took the engineering part since I liked it. After that I went in the service. After the service I came back here and went to the junior college.

So I had an early education about the city; I didn't like a lot of it because there were too many people and everybody was in a hurry. I came from a small place like Susanville so it was kind of frightening, but you get used to it. I did a lot of drafting in high school so I liked that engineering work.

When you were at Stewart were there other Indian kids from this area?

There were quite a few from here, from Modoc and from Lake Almanor. There were some from southern California. There were a lot from Nevada. Most were from California and Nevada.

Do you recall when Indian kids might have spoke in their language at Stewart?

Oh yeah, I remember that. I know some say they didn't allow it but a lot of the kids were the same tribe and they spoke. Some of the schools did try to stop that. That's wrong to keep kids from speaking their own tongue.

Where were you before the war started?

I was going to engineering school in San Francisco. We all came back home. There weren't many Indian kids that went to school in that area. There were Chinese and Japanese kids at the school and they'd ask where Susanville was. They'd ask if it was way up in the mountains and I'd tell them yes, it was up in the good country!

Were you drafted or did you volunteer for the war?

I volunteered down in San Francisco in early 1942. I got my draft notice when I was already in.

By volunteering did you get to choose where you wanted to go?

Yeah. They had three or four rows for the Army, Navy, Marines or Coast Guard. There were some people I knew. There were some guys from Chester and Westwood and we all went in the Army. I knew those guys from when we played football.

Where did you go to boot camp?

I went to the Presidio and then they shipped us to a different area. I spent part of my time at Camp Beale. I was always interested in engineering so I went with the engineers. The engineers built roads and designed building. I was always interested in architecture. We had 13 weeks in the boot camp.

After boot camp, is that when they put you in your division?

In fact they put me in two different divisions. I went into the 101st Airborne but I got hurt on my third jump. I twisted my knee badly and couldn't walk. They put me in the quartermaster corps but I didn't like that so I went into the regular infantry with the field artillery.

Were there any other Indian people or black people in the quartermaster corps?

There were Hispanics from southern California.

Did you know Spanish?

I could understand it but couldn't speak it well. My dad spoke it with my uncle.

What were your duties with the field artillery?

Each artillery piece has several people that man them and supply the ammunition. We all had a role to take. It was a 105-millimeter piece. We had other types of mortars, 60 and 80-millimeter mortars, also in our unit. We learned all of them.

Did any of your brothers join the service?

Yeah, my older brother Dave had went in before me. He went into the 82nd Airborne Division. He tried to get me into it but they wouldn't take brothers into the same division. Another brother Joe was in the Marines.

There was nothing but the Marines for him! He went on Iwo Jima. That was the last of four islands he fought on. He passed away a few months ago. I had another brother in the Air National Guard stationed near the Great Lakes.

How did you get across to Europe?

We went over on the Queen Elizabeth. I didn't like the ocean because it made me seasick! To this day I don't like the ocean. We docked in Scotland and we came down to England. We stayed at a marshalling area until they sent us to France.

Al Valadez, Sr.

We were only in England for less than six months. It was different for them (the English) to see Indians in the service. A long time ago Indians didn't have to go to war but we went anyway. I did get to go to London and all the big cities.

They had those buzz bombs going. You could hear their engines cut off and they'd go down. We watched them going over. They'd make a whistling sound and go down and blow something up.

Your division went in after the Normandy Invasion…

Yeah, we docked in at a little town near Cherbourg. Not right at Cherbourg but at a smaller town. Things were going hot and heavy. I was in the 69th Division as part of the Third Army. I have all my information in a little booklet somewhere. It was quite an experience. I was lucky enough to dig my foxholes deep enough so I didn't get hit.

I carried a BAR, a Browning Automatic Rifle. You let it off at three or four rounds at a time. They also had you carry an M1 Garand Rifle. They taught us how to use different weapons. The BAR was a little heavier than a regular M1 but I liked it because it had more rounds in it.

So your company must have had to fight in a lot of small towns?

Oh yeah, a lot of fighting in small towns. That's when you have to watch it because you don't know where your enemy is; they could be hiding anyplace. To us, our enemies were the Germans, but you had a bunch of people who didn't like Americans. They learned later on they were wrong.

We'd try to find a barn or anything in order to stay in instead of having to dig a foxhole! Especially when the ground was frozen.

Was there any time you got to go on leave?

Oh yeah, after 90 days we got a leave. We got to go back to London and into parts of Sweden and other parts of France. I went to London and Paris and to those Scandinavian countries. They all wondered why I was fighting for a white man's country. I said that's where my people come from.

The white man was the one that came there and interfered with us. They couldn't understand that. 'Then I'd fight for them?' they'd ask. I said I didn't care; if somebody shoots at me I'll shoot back. I think they finally understood the situation.

What was Paris like?

Oh, it's a city! It has cobblestone streets and roads. You can imagine how long it would take to build those streets and alleys with those cobblestones.

How did the French citizens treat the American soldiers?

They figured we came over to help and they treated us pretty well, especially the young ladies! We were always interested in the young ladies anyhow; we were young! We went up the Eiffel Tower. It was like being up in the air.

I got up to parts of Norway and Sweden. I went through Belgium and Holland. All the young ladies would flock over to see what the Americans were like. This was right in the middle or later part of the war.

After you went through France where did you go?

We went into Germany. We had a lot of opposition there. The Germans didn't like us and we didn't like the Germans. Hitler and his group especially didn't like us. It was an experience. I can't remember all the cities and towns we went through.

Did your company take part in the Battle of the Bulge?

We were in the Third Army which was Patton's Army and we went right through there. He was kind of a brash A-hole, that's what everybody called him. But he was pretty fair. It was like a big deal for him to talk to us but it didn't mean anything to me. He had two legs and two arms like anyone else; he was no God to me.

What was the weather like while you fought in Germany?

Snow, and cold and wet! About that time they finally shipped some rubber galoshes to us. Other than that we had old leather boots that soaked up water. When they got wet they stayed wet. Those galoshes were like a Godsend! I had purple feet there a couple of times. We'd get about three or four feet of snow. It was a mountainous area.

Your company must have gone against the SS and Panzer divisions?

Oh yeah, those Panzers had big tracks three or four feet across. They were big enough and heavy enough to crush anything. They'd almost crush our tanks if they maneuvered them the right way.

It must have been terribly intense to go through fighting like that?

Well, you don't get used to it but you have to keep moving. We (the Third Army) went through Bastogne. The Third Army had to help out. They had artillery and everything all around them. Those bastards of Bastogne!

When you were moving through the cold country did you have to stop and build foxholes?

Ha! We'd try to find a barn or anything in order to stay in instead of having to dig a foxhole! Especially when the ground was frozen. You'd think you could dig a foxhole in that damn ground? When it's frozen you can't. We kept on going and some of us got close to Italy. We kept going until we got close to Czechoslovakia.

Did you ever meet the Russian soldiers?

Oh yeah, and they didn't like us because all the women were coming over to the American side. We couldn't help that.

What was the mood like when you heard the war ended?

We celebrated for a week! In our area we had three schnapps distilleries. Every day somebody would take a trip through there and get some for us guys. Some of it was good and some of it was bad.

Was there ever a time when you were going through Germany that your company came across any of the concentration camps?

We went through three of them. You'd be surprised, it was supposed to be a civilized society but it didn't seem to matter to those Germans. I think at the end of the war they knew they were going to lose anyway.

We went through several of them. You'd be surprised at the way those people looked...skin and bones...I couldn't believe it. You had to see it to believe it. It was supposed to be a civilized society...

That must have been really terrible to see...

Oh yeah, you have to see it to believe it, that's all there is to it. We saw some bad things. At the concentration camps they fed the people after everyone else ate, and a lot of times there wasn't anything left. You see those people and they're just skin and bones.

It made you angry when you saw that, and they had a lot of those concentration camps. They were trying to get rid of the Jewish people and they had a bunch of them in those camps. I don't know how many camps there were but there were quite a few of them. They said the Jewish people were inferior but the Jews are more humane.

When you went through those camps did you stay very long?

Well, we stayed in the area but they didn't keep us there very long.

I understand this is a hard question to answer, but how were the camps built and what did they look like?

They had barracks and had quite a few people in them. A lot of them had these ovens to get rid of people; they'd throw them in the ovens and burn them up. If you don't think that made the GIs mad...it sure did. You can't realize how some people who are supposed to be civilized...the Germans wanted to get rid of all the Jewish people.

Al Valadez, Sr. joined his wife Josie during her interview which is located in the chapter titled The Arsenal for Democracy in this book.

Frank Dowd

Frank Dowd is of Yurok ancestry and was raised in the Yurok village of Weitchpec near the confluence of the Klamath and Trinity Rivers. Frank is a traditional Brush Dancer and has participated in the Brush Dance ceremonies since a very young age. He is my great-uncle by marriage, and we spoke at his home in Crescent City on October 17, 2001.

I went to elementary school in Weitchpec. I was born in 1925 to Bill and Eliza Dowd. I went to high school in Hoopa and then went to Sherman in 1941 and then the war broke out. I went in the service in 1942. I was in Sherman for about a year.

What was it like growing up in Weitchpec?

We would fish and hunt. My dad taught me. I was really young when we went fishing. We would mostly hunt deer. There were 11 kids in the family and I was the second to youngest. I first started going to the Brush Dance when I was a kid.

Why do you participate in the Brush Dance?

You feel good when you dance. I feel good when I see my relatives doing the same thing. My uncle Sam Jones had a lot of Brush Dance songs. It makes me feel good when I see people doing things for the Indians.

You jumped once a week. You had to have five jumps to qualify. A lot of guys didn't make it. They would get scared and not jump out of the plane.

Has anybody ever talked to you about your time in the service?

No, this is the first time anyone's ever come to me and asked me questions.

Why did you decide to join the service?

I really don't know why. I was in school then went in the service. I had a brother that served in Japan. His name was George and he was in the Army. He made it back. I went to Camp Roberts for basic training. It was pretty hard. You're not used to that.

Frank Dowd (at right) and a buddy ca. 1943-4.
Photo courtesy of Kathy Dowd.

They have to qualify you if you wanted to be a medic, or a tanker or whatever. I chose to be a paratrooper. You could make more money! You get so much on top of your base pay. You had to go through more training in Fort Benning, Georgia.

What would you do on a particular day in Fort Benning?

You had to get up early in the morning for your basic training. You jumped once a week. You had to have five jumps to qualify. A lot of guys didn't make it. They would get scared and not jump out of the plane.

Can you describe the first time you jumped out of a plane?

They took you up early in the morning. You're all in line and hooked up. They tap you on the back and away you went. You had to learn how to pack your own 'chutes.

Frank Dowd

You had a spare 'chute in front. I can't describe that feeling when you jump. It just takes your breath away and away you go!

You count to about 10, if your 'chute doesn't open, you pull the spare. When the 'chute opens you get a big jerk. If you're straps aren't on tight you get burned. You can maneuver yourself this way and that. When you land you have to watch how your chute goes. You learn how to fall and roll over when you hit the ground.

What was your division?

After I got through with my basic training I got a leave. I didn't make it back in time. The outfit I was with went over to France in the invasion. I didn't get to go. When I got back they shipped me to New York. I stayed there and they shipped me to England.

That's when I learned I was part of the 82nd Airborne. I was in the 505th Parachute Infantry. I think I was in the 2nd Battalion. I was a replacement after they had got back from the invasion in France. We were preparing for another jump, but didn't know where. It was early in the morning when we did have to jump.

There were maybe three or four outfits jumping. They had switched us with these English paratroopers and they got wiped out when they jumped. I don't know why they switched us but they did. We jumped where the English were supposed to jump and they jumped where we were supposed to. You could see all the flak coming at us in the plane.

How many men were in the outfit in the plane?

There were 12 on each side, so there were 24 of us, I believe. I don't remember any of the names of the guys. You weren't supposed to be real close to each other. They trained us that way. You might do something you weren't supposed to do and get shot yourself, I guess.

We jumped into Holland (as part of Operation Market-Garden). I only jumped that one time in combat. The Germans had broken through in the Bulge and killed a lot of people, so they took us by truck to go stop them.

When you jumped into Holland how did your group get back together?

We jumped alongside each other and landed in these big fields with hedges. We would jump then another wave would come in. We were in the first wave so not very many of us got hit. I know one guy got killed right in front of me.

He was a big guy, and it was by a hedge and there was a farmhouse where the Germans were shooting from. He was right in front of me and they hit him. He dropped and everybody concentrated on that house and peppered that house. That was the first time I fired my rifle at somebody. They took some prisoners out of that house.

That must have been traumatic to see someone die like that...

That's why they taught you not to get close. I saw the prisoners being sent to the rear. You have to learn how to survive for yourself. The Germans looked just like you see in the movies.

Then where did you go?

We started across Holland. I remember one time where we went across this river in amphibious boats and some men were killed while crossing. You just did your job. They pulled our outfit out of Holland and sent us near St. Vith (during the Battle of the Bulge.) They loaded us on trucks; we didn't know where we were going.

We stayed there in the snow for a long time. The town had mountains on both sides. We were up in the mountains. They put us on an outpost. There were about five or six Indians and we were always picked to go out on patrols. Our sergeant was from Montana. He made it back; I can't remember his name. The staff sergeant was killed.

You actually got to serve with other Indian men?

Yes. They were in our outfit. It seemed like to me that they would always pick us to go on patrol. Our sergeant was pretty good; we always made it back. One time we got broken up somehow. It was nighttime, I remember him yelling for us all to get back. No one got killed though. I don't believe we ever got shot on those patrols. They were from all different areas in the States.

There was a road that came up the hill from that town. We were on the outskirts of that town. There were

Frank's brother George Dowd ca. 1942. George served in the US Army in the Aleutian campaign and was mistakenly captured at one point in combat by other Army soldiers. They thought he was Japanese until a buddy of his vouched for him.
Photo courtesy of Kathy Dowd.

no houses. There were two of us in a foxhole. One of us had to keep awake. I remember this one guy who really liked women.

His mother sent him things to give to women. I used to laugh at him about that. He got killed there. It snowed on us a lot, maybe a foot or more. We had K-rations; I don't remember having a hot meal. I don't know how long we stayed there; it must have been a couple weeks or maybe longer.

What was the fighting like?

Well, these Germans, they would run right up against our guns. They didn't care if they died or not. Some of them seemed like they were drunk. They would holler and run right at you. I had a rifle but we also had machine guns.

Well, these Germans, they would run right up against our guns. They didn't care if they died or not. Some of them seemed like they were drunk.

We had to kill a lot of people, sometimes it was close. We just did our duty. You had to do what you had to do or you get killed. You were trained. If the Germans are shooting at you, you had to shoot back to survive.

We looked at the German weapons sometimes. One time we were sitting there looking at things and this one guy grabbed something and said, 'What is this for?' It was a flare, and goddamn, he pulled it open and it shot in the air. About five or six mortar rounds came in there. You could hear them coming so we got out of there!

What was it like to fight in the snow?

We had white rain clothing. It was cold. Sometimes when we moved we could ride on tanks. I had to shoot the 50-caliber machine gun a few times on the tank. I shot at German infantry. My feet got frozen one time. I had to go to the medics because I couldn't feel them. They were numb. My feet still give me problems; they're cold all the time.

After you were relieved what was that like?

Boy, you were glad to get out! We ended up in Berlin after the war was over. We helped occupy the American section. We just had to be there, you could go anywhere in your section.

You had to report in at certain times. I was there about four months until I came home. It wasn't very bombed out where we were. I also got to visit Paris in France. I came back on the Queen Mary.

When did you meet Aunt Venola?

I knew who she was, but we got married after the war. I worked for Simpson timber about 20 years. I fell timber, set chokers...whatever needed to be done. I worked in construction for about 15 years after that.

As an Indian veteran, are you proud of the way you served in the war?

Yes, you just tried to get back. That's the main thing, coming back.

Frank Dowd and his wife Venola live in Crescent City, Ca. Frank is retired and he and Venola still attend and participate in the Brush Dance ceremonies every year. He also supports Venola with her duties as a member of the United Indian Health Services Board of Directors.

Alfred McCovey

Do you know any Indian veterans?' I asked my cousin Diana Ferris. She smiled and said, 'My dad, he was in the service.' I couldn't help but be shocked, another relative of mine that was in the war? Sure enough, Diana's father Alfred "Big Boy" McCovey was in the U.S. Army.

What's more, he lived right next to Frank Ames, who I had interviewed shortly before. What's more, he is married to one of Frank's sisters. I had thought it was a small world when I talked with Frank. I traveled to Alfred's house in Hoopa on June 13, 2002. It was a hot summer day, and we talked about his experiences and how we were related.

I was born in Johnson's (along the Klamath River) in 1925. My parents were Sadie and Charlie McCovey the second. His dad was Charlie the first.

Did you have any brother and sisters?

Yes, five brothers and six sisters; it's a big family. I'm in the middle. I spent a big part of my life in Johnson's. I only went to grade school in Pecwan at the school there. After we moved from Johnson's we lived in Notchko, that's where my dad built his house there. It would be five miles to walk to school and five miles to come home. We were young then and it didn't make any difference. (Notchko is a Yurok village).

Did your family do a lot of fishing on the Klamath River when you were young?

Yes, my dad did. He fished for salmon and eels.

From France we went straight to the front lines in Germany. Just that experience alone, seeing everything bombed out alongside the ride, it makes you think about a lot of things; to see that and know you're heading for the front.

Did anyone in your family make baskets?

Yes, my mom and grandmother made a lot of baskets. My grandmother's name was Elsie. We lived pretty close to her at Johnson's and at Notchko. My mom made a lot of eel baskets. My dad used them. They were big baskets with kind of a mouth on them. We'd put them in smooth water where it kind of riffles, and the eel would get suctioned into the basket.

When daylight came we'd get the basket out. Sometimes there would be 75 or 100 in there and we'd sell them for 10 cents apiece. Now you pay about two dollars apiece for them. My dad also hunted for deer.

He'd leave at first daylight in the morning, then at 10 or 11 at night he'd come home with a deer on his back. At Notchko we lived off the land. We had two fields of gardens; we ate the deer meat, the eels and salmon. We never had it rough when it came to eating, there was always something there.

When you were young did your family attend the Brush Dances?

Oh yes, they held them in Johnson's, and up here at Hoopa. I never saw the Jump Dance, but I went to a lot of the Brush Dances.

Did your mother and grandmother speak the Yurok language?

Oh yeah, they spoke it all the time. The only way I could understand my grandmother was when she'd speak a little English. My dad was half-Indian and half-white, but he could understand it.

How are you related to my grandmother Evelina Hoffman?

She's a first cousin. My dad (Charlie), Uncle Bill (Evelina's father), Uncle Walt and Uncle Ike were all brothers. The McCovey name came from Charlie McCovey the first. He was from back East and was in the Merchant Marine.

He came over here and married a full-blooded Yurok woman. We don't know if we have relatives back East through the McCovey name. There could be a lot of McCoveys we don't know about!

After you were done with eighth grade where did you go?

Well, I went down to Sherman, but I didn't like it there. My brother put me on a bus and sent me back home, so that's as far as I got through school.

What didn't you like about Sherman?

When I first got off the bus and looked around at it and I just didn't think much of it. I didn't want to be there so far away from home. It was a different climate.

Then what did you do?

Well, after I turned 17 my brother and I went to Oregon, lied about our age, and went to work in the woods for different companies. From then on I worked in different places until they drafted me into the service. When I got out of there I came back and worked in the woods; I set chokers, peeled, and did different odd jobs. I did that for the biggest part of my life.

Logging is pretty dangerous…

It is, a lot of guys try to get in a hurry and try to do things too fast. That's when some guys get killed. I used to take my time. As long as I did the work, that's the main part.

You were probably in really good shape from working in the woods.

Oh yeah, I used to work 10 hours a day.

When you were working in the woods before the war did you hear about what was going on with Japan and Germany?

I didn't pay much attention to it then. I know my two brothers Darrell and Stanley were over at Pearl Harbor (during the war). I went in and took my basic training at Fort McClellan in Alabama. I came home on leave then went right back and they shipped us over to Maryland.

Then they put us on a ship and we went to Italy and then France.

What did you do in Italy?

Boy, that country is something else. They had us there for a while. You'd go out for a hike in good weather for a little while and then it would pour down rain. I was pretty close to Naples. We boarded a ship there and went to France.

From France we went straight to the front lines in Germany. Just that experience alone, seeing everything bombed out alongside the ride, it makes you think about a lot of things; to see that and know you're heading for the front. We got to the front at night and there was about a foot of snow on the ground.

They told us there was a German patrol coming across our area that night, but we didn't know where. We heard guns going off, and we heard people moaning out there. Some of the old-timers had seen these Germans coming and shot them down. Those guys were groaning out there all night, it was terrible.

When did you become a glider man?

When we got to France, we didn't know where we were going. There were a bunch of trucks out there, so we asked them if they were coming for us. They said yeah, they were taking us to the 101st Airborne.

We didn't know a damn thing about the Airborne! But that's where they put us. They asked if we wanted to be a paratrooper or a glider man. I said I would be in the glider. I guess being a paratrooper was a lot safer than the glider; paratroopers had two 'chutes, one in back and one in front. Gliders don't have anything. You're riding around in a big box up there!

Did you have any training in a glider?

Yes, it wasn't bad. We were young and it was kind of exciting to fly around up there. We trained overseas. We were in France after the Normandy Invasion. The company we went into had just a few men left. Guys would tell us how when they hit the beachheads they got hit so badly they were about wiped out.

What type of plane were the gliders attached to?

A big plane towed them. We were behind that. The gliders were off the ground before the big planes got up. After they got so far up they cut the rope or whatever it was holding them and they would be off. There were 12 people in a glider. I didn't have go into combat in a glider, those things were just…

Where at in Germany did you go?

I don't remember where the front was. We were by Bastogne somewhere. When we came back off the front lines we went near Hitler's home at Berchtesgaden. You've seen those pictures of Hitler's home? We were guarding 500 SS troopers there who were supposed to be Hitler's toughest men.

They wouldn't let us go into Hitler's home; only officers could go in there. I was right there; we could see it. That was in the mountains. He had the Eagle's Nest up there, with an elevator that came from the top of the mountain. That was quite a place up there.

Did you ever have to be in hand-to-hand fighting?

No, on the front lines the Germans would be maybe 500 yards away. You could see them walking around. We used a lot of artillery; you could hear them going off all the time. I would be in a foxhole with another guy on the front.

The foxholes you dig in basic training would be just a round hole where one guy could fit in, but the foxholes on the front would be big squares with logs on top of them, and brush to conceal yourself.

They wouldn't let us go into Hitler's home; only officers could go in there. I was right there; we could see it.

That first night we crawled in there and didn't know what to do. Those guys we relieved were so glad to get out they just left everything! The next day we saw everything around and it wasn't so bad, but getting there at night we didn't know where anything was.

That must have been pretty scary!

It was!

And how old were you then?

I was 18.

How old were most of the men with you?

They were all pretty young, except for the guys that had been in combat before I got there. I learned a lot from some of the guys who had landed on the beachhead. They told me what they went through, you know. That helped me out.

Did you ever come across any other Indian men?

No, I was the only one in my outfit.

Were you ever treated different because you were Indian?

Not really, I got along pretty good with everybody. I made friends with the guys. I knew if I got in trouble I'd have to show I could fight back. Some guys would get smart with someone else and they'd get scared and back off, but I wouldn't! If I have to fight I'm going to fight! That's the McCovey blood in you!

How many of your brothers also served?

Five of us served. Two in the Navy and three in the Army. Only Darrell is still living. He and Stanley were in the Navy, and Howard, Allen and I were in the Army.

Did you ever write home?

I wrote home to my mother. All of us made it back.

I bet your mom must have been really happy!

Yeah! I had come back on leave to Klamath and Uncle Bill brought me over to Orick. I walked on in over the hill to Notchko and was about halfway down the hill and started hollering. I guess they recognized my voice, so my oldest brother came running down, jumped in the boat and came across the river where I was at and picked me up!

Oh, we were both happy to see each other, you know. I was so glad to come home. That was Allen. I was back on leave for 10 days. You know, I was pretty young and

Alfred McCovey

never did travel except to Oregon.

When I went down and got to San Francisco and got on a train I thought, 'Geez, I don't even know where I'm going!' So I saw some guys there with their duffel bags, they were the guys I had been training with, so I caught up with them and we went to the same place. That was quite an experience there!

You had mentioned you guarded some SS soldiers, what was that like?

Well, we had these towers built and we'd go up and guard them. We had machine guns and spotlights, and you'd watch a certain area. They told us if Germans ever came close to the fence open up on them. They said those SS were Hitler's toughest men, but when you're locked up everything changes, you know.

What was the food like when you were on the front lines?

We had those K-rations, those little boxes of food. I guess everything had to be good because that's the only thing you got to eat!

Did you lose some weight while you were over there?

No, I kept the weight on pretty good. All through training and over there I stayed about 155 pounds. When you get out of basic you've trained so much you're in good shape.

Did your uniform and boots hold up while you were on the front?

Yes, but with all that snow your feet were pretty cold. The boots weren't leather.

At the end of the war, you were near Berchtesgaden, where did you stay?

We stayed in some buildings there. I was cleaning this pistol there one day and I don't know what happened, but I shot my hand clear through. I didn't hit a bone or anything, but I was in the hospital for two weeks until it healed.

What was the hospital like?

Well, there were guys hopping around on crutches, and they packed me in on a stretcher! There wasn't anything wrong with my legs! The only thing, when I was there on the bed they put a guy next to me who was burned.

Oh, I couldn't handle that when they came to dress him. I asked them to move me or move him because I couldn't handle the smell. That was the only bad experience in the hospital.

I was also wondering if your unit ever came across any concentration camps...

Well, just before the war ended we were in a place where the Germans burnt the Jews. We were down looking in a cellar and we opened up these doors and saw that, and boy, we closed those doors pretty fast.

You know how when people get burnt, that's what was in there. That's the only experience I had being in a concentration camp. I don't remember where that was. It was in a camp. It's been so long ago....

What do you remember about coming home after the war ended?

When we came back we landed in New York. We were in a big parade up Fifth Avenue. Then we went to camp. They said if we wanted to stay in New York for the weekend we could go, or if we wanted to go home, to stay in camp and get ready. I stayed in camp because I wanted to leave. We flew from New York to Oakland. I went to Camp Beale and got my discharge there.

When we came back from overseas I came on the Queen Mary. I was standing on the deck and heard somebody call out 'Hey Big Boy!' I never saw the person though; there were 10,000 people on that ship. I told my buddy next to me that somebody knew me pretty well to call me by that. I never knew until after we got out of the service that it was Puzzy! (Frank Dowd).

That's a neat story, how did you make your way from Camp Beale back home?

That was kind of a weird experience. After I got out of Camp Beale my buddies and I spent all our money drinking. They took off on their way, but here I was broke! Where the heck am I going now? I went to Red Cross and told my story. They said they'd give me a place to sleep.

I walked and walked and made it there. They gave me 10 dollars. At that time, a round-trip bus ride to Eureka cost six dollars. I made it up, and it wasn't even a week later when my mother got a letter from them wanting the 10 dollars! I said to hell with them if they can't even help a serviceman get home for 10 dollars.

Alfred McCovey ca. 1943-4.
Photo courtesy of Alfred McCovey.

Can you describe when you came home?

Oh, it was the happiest day of my life, getting back to my whole family except for my brothers still in the service. I worked in the woods in this area…I don't know how many years. Then I worked at the mill here in Hoopa until they sold it. I worked with mostly Indian men from around here. One of my brothers was killed in the woods.

I was looking at your discharge papers, and under 'race' they marked you down as 'white.'

Yeah, I didn't know that, but my oldest boy said look at that, they marked you down as 'white.' They could have marked me down as 'other.'

How does that make you feel?

I don't feel very good about that.

Why do you think so many Indian people served in the war?

Well, most were drafted. My brother was 16 and he lied about his age, he put our grandmother down as his mother so he would look older.

Is there anything else you'd like to share?

Well, I was glad I went in the service because I got to travel. When I was over there I got a leave and went to Switzerland. That's someplace I would have never seen otherwise. I was so young I didn't care to see too much, though.

I mostly went to the bars! Switzerland had big lakes and elevators into the mountains. That's the cleanest country I've been in. I got to see different things I would have never seen when I was in the service.

Alfred "Big Boy" McCovey and his wife Maude had six children and also have over 40 grandchildren and great-grandchildren. He enjoys spending time with his family and staying close to home.

The Home Front

The Japanese attack at Pearl Harbor spurred the United States to mobilize all aspects of society toward war. For each airman, soldier, sailor and Marine at the front there were dozens in training back home. **Vernon Numan** was among those who were preparing to go to war. There were instructors in the Army, the Navy, the Air Force and the Marines who might not have seen combat but were instrumental in training those who fought. **Chuck Williams** was one such officer and instructor. There were also those men in the armed forces that worked with experimental aircraft, who built naval ships and who manufactured ammunition. **Jimmy James** and **Bill Evans** helped the war effort in this capacity.

In May of 1942 the Women's Auxiliary Army Corps (WAAC) was created after much debate in Congress to work with the Army to provide skills, knowledge and training from women for the national defense. In 1943 the Women's Auxiliary Army Corps was converted into the regular Army as the Women's Army Corps (WAC).

WACs served as clerical workers, teachers, stenographers, telephone operators, mail carriers, motor pool drivers and signal operators. Women were also assigned as weather observers, forecasters, cryptographers, radio operators, sheet metal workers, parachute riggers, link trainer instructors, bombsight maintenance specialists, aerial photograph analysts and control tower operators. They also served as mechanics, electricians, cryptologists, and photograph and map analysts among countless other duties.[1] The Allied countries utilized women in these capacities while Nazi Germany did not until too late in the war. This was one factor in the final victory for the Allies.

Over 150,000 American women such as **Dee Rouse** served in the Women's Army Corps during the war. WAC members were the first women other than nurses to serve within the ranks of the United States Army. Almost 800 Native American women served as WACs, as Women Accepted for Volunteer Emergency Service (WAVES), in the Army Nurse Corp and in the Women Marine Corps Reserve [2] More than 265,000 American women joined the Armed Forces during World War Two.[3]

In June of 1942 the Japanese seized control of the Alaskan islands Attu and Kiska. This was the only American soil that was invaded and captured during the war. American forces had to build up bases near the islands in order to attack the Japanese. This was done in the worst possible weather conditions imaginable. American air, naval, and land forces were sent to destroy the Japanese garrisons. This was accomplished on Attu by May of 1943 and Kiska was occupied in August.

America continued to build up military forces in the Aleutian Islands until the end of the war. **Don Preston** and **Louie Melendez** were part of this American force that protected the islands. American bombers used some of the Aleutian Islands as bases from which to fly missions against the Japanese home islands.

The Home Front

Chuck Williams

My cousin and good friend Elsie Bacon told me about her nephew Chuck Williams. Chuck is of Yurok ancestry and he served in the Army Air Corps as an instructor during the war. I sat down with him and his wife Pat at their house in Crescent City on October 21, 2003.

I was born in 1922 on February 18 down on the south side of the Klamath River. My father was Harry Williams and he was from the same place. He was adopted and raised by my grandparents. He wasn't Indian; he was of Greek ancestry.

How did he get adopted?

Well, my grandmother Annie lost a child during the birth and almost lost her life; they barely pulled her through. So the first opportunity they had they adopted. That's how my dad was adopted.

What tribe were your grandparents?

Yurok. They were from a village right down by the mouth of the river. There's a cemetery by it. We don't tell people exactly where because we don't want them messing around near it. Their responsibility was to perform the prayers over the spring salmon. You couldn't eat that fish until this was done.

They caught that first fish and brought it into a sweathouse. They cut it into little chunks; my mother saw this the first year she was married. As a matter of fact she said this was the last time that was ever performed.

She said the fish was still gasping when they took it to the sweathouse. They cut that fish into little chunks and put it back in this basket. After this two guys ran it back down to the mouth in the basket.

They had one of the older men from that same little village that finished this prayer and they threw it back into the river. They had young guys around to keep the seagulls away. Then the old man came back to the sweathouse. Then you could catch the spring salmon and eat them, otherwise it wasn't permitted. The first fish that was caught had this prayer performed over it.

What was your mother's name?

She was a Jones from Weitchpec. Her name was Ethel Marie Jones. My father was of Greek ancestry and raised by the Yurok. He was very fluent in the language; I used to see my mother ask him how to say something, even though she was born and raised in the language itself.

What type of work did your dad do?

He fished and he worked on the roads. He worked on houses. At first he was a ship builder in the Humboldt Harbor but he didn't like living there so he came home. I had two brothers and three sisters. We lost a sister when she was a little girl. I'm the oldest boy and had two older sisters.

I grew up on the mouth of the river. We were the last ones at that place. We had gardens and we had a dairy before a flood took the ranch. We all knew how to work hard! We hunted and fished and caught eels. I was pretty good at it but I think my dad was better!

Did you have any basket weavers in your family?

My mother and all her older sisters were. We used to go help my grandma cut the roots when she got old. We'd build a fire on the beach and she'd cook them. She'd cook them in the sand and split and scrap them.

When you were very young was the Yurok language the first language you learned?

Well, we picked it up because grandma would always talk to us. My grandpa would always scold her. He said 'They can't go to work in a bank and talk our Native language because how many customers would come in that they could speak to?'

He was big on getting an education because he didn't have any. He was wise beyond description! I wish I had listened to him more; you'd have to call me 'Mr. Williams!'

I will anyway!

Thank you!

When you were young did other Yurok people speak the language when they visited?

Oh yeah, especially gram and grandpa's friends.

When was the earliest time when you went to a Brush Dance?

Gosh, I can't remember. I went when I was a little kid. Mom and both my Grandma McCovey and Grandma Williams would be there. Us kids would go down and stay at the Gensaw house. It was really something for me.

What was it like to attend a Jump Dance?

Oh, it was strict; that and the Deerskin Dance. The Brush Dance is more of a fun Dance compared to those two.

There are a lot of rules to follow for both the men and women...

Oh yeah, and especially for the kids! You had to be brought up with that being taught to you. I danced with my grandpa. I was just a little boy. I could dance with my grandfather but I couldn't dance with my father. At that time that was a rule but I don't know if they changed it.

They always wanted my dad to sing because my grandpa knew all those songs. Dad would sing like hell out in a boat when no one was around but he wouldn't sing in the Brush Dance!

Where did you go to elementary school?

There was a little school down by the bottom past our village where my father went and we went. As a matter of fact my sister and brother were the last two students there because they closed school down. You couldn't have a school with just two or three kids there.

We really didn't know what it was like to go hungry. We were giving stuff away to people who were hungry.

This was near Requa?

Yes, straight across the river. You'd be in the water there now.

Were the school teachers Indian?

No. I went there about six-and-a-half years. I helped the teacher. She'd go out of the room and I was in charge. By Christmas time I'd have my whole year's school work done. The teacher was very nice. We had real nice teachers but I do remember one time I went to school with patches on my pants. This was common during the Depression.

So the teacher sent me home. She said I had a better pair of pants. So I went home and there was grandpa. He was strict about getting an education. He wanted to know why I wasn't in school. I told him the teacher sent me home.

So we went over to the school. He wanted to know why she sent me home. He asked if she liked her job because his son was on the school board there. She said yes, she liked the job and she liked the kids. So he told her she better have room for me there that day! She said yes and that was that!

Your father was involved on the school board?

He was the head of the school board. I guess the other people in the area wanted him to do that.

You mentioned your generation went through the Depression, did you understand about the Depression when you were young?

We really didn't know what it was like to go hungry. We were giving stuff away to people who were hungry. Sometimes my aunt and uncle would come down the river. My dad would give them potatoes and they'd give us these good tomatoes. We'd trade back and forth.

Was that a traditional thing among the Yurok?

I would say that. They didn't have mussels or clams or surf fish or seaweed. We used to call gram's sister 'Up-the-river-gram;' she owned that place where Billy Pearson's store is. This was way before that store was there. She'd bring hazelnuts or pine nuts and we'd trade.

Where would you get your acorns?

We'd go up to the hills, maybe to Gasquet or to Bald Hill up that road. We'd make a special trip to get acorns. You had to get the ones with no worm holes in them! I never cared for acorns unless I had smoked fish!

I remember when my aunt and grandma would dig a pit near these water springs up at Notchko; we had to get a certain type of gravel and we'd pack it up. My aunt would put some in the bottom and then she'd put some acorns in. The closer she came to the top then she'd put some in with no shells.

Chuck Williams ca. 1942-3
Photo courtesy of Chuck Williams.

Then she'd put a layer of that gravel and the water would seep through them. They'd leave them in there for about seven months; it would depend on how big the nuts were. They'd use acorns for soup and cook them with hot rocks. They'd take the meat and dry it then they'd grind it with rocks.

When you were young did anybody live in or use any of the old redwood plank housing?

No, the last one I knew of was that one where they had that ceremony.

Where did you go to high school?

We rode a bus from Klamath and came up here to Crescent City to high school. We studied both ways! All the people around Klamath had to come. I graduated in 1939.

Did they ever talk about the Indian history or the Indian people in the classroom?

Well, we did amongst ourselves but they didn't talk about the Indians. They'd just say 'The Indian was there and they had to put up with him.' It wasn't too popular to be an Indian in those days.

Were you treated different at the school or in the community?

I was always a novelty wherever we went and I was treated excellent.

Can you tell me that story about your first plane ride?

This guy had landed down on the river and taxied up. My uncle and everybody came over to look at the airplane; there weren't very many around in those days. He stayed with us for two days. He slept in the barn and said he appreciated us watching his airplane. This is when we lived at Notchko after we lost the ranch.

What type of plane was it?

It was an old seaplane, the type that lands in the water like a boat.

And how did your plane ride happen?

Oh, he asked if I wanted to go for a ride and I said heck yeah I'd go! I got in and we flew up around the bridge and then came back and landed. It was about two miles or so to the bridge. It was three miles by road to the old bridge and on into town.

So what was it like to be on that plane?

Oh man, I knew that's what I wanted to do when I grew up! That's what I did; I was lucky enough to qualify for it.

How old were you when you took that plane ride?

I was six or seven. I was pretty little.

You were probably one of the first, if not the first, Yurok to see the river from the air...

There weren't too many, I don't think!

After you graduated from high school where did you go?

I went down to Sherman and learned to weld. I lived down there and then I went into the Air Force. I worked in a shipyard there in Long Beach across the channel from San Pedro.

Why did you choose to go to Sherman?

I wanted to learn to be a welder. I had other relatives that went down there. They said they had a good welding school. Archie Thompson and I went there at the same time. He went in the Navy. As a matter of fact I had to pay him; I had bet him 10 bucks that I'd be in the Air Force before he'd be in the Navy! Well, they called Archie!

I went to Sherman in the fall. It was six or seven months before I took the test. I wanted to make damn sure I passed it. The bedding was clean and we had our own laundry there. We also worked in the poultry plant by there. Some of my aunts were there and some of my McCovey cousins were there.

Was that the farthest away from home you'd ever been?

At the time yes. I knew a lot of the people there. It was kind of like being at home. I had friends like Archie and Kenny Sanderson there.

Did you meet with other tribal people there?

Yeah, we'd tell them what we did and they'd tell us what they did. We'd talk about the different foods. Later when I grew up and went hunting in the mountains I realized how good we had it here.

Those guys are tough where you're from! We went hunting 10 days in a row and it never got warmer than 10 below! We had a lot of rain here but it was never that cold.

What was the process like to learn how to weld?

You just practiced until you were good enough to pass the test. Arch and I both passed and he went in the Navy and I stayed there. It was six or eight months before there was an opening in the Air Corps.

So you volunteered?

Yeah, and I went to boot camp and then I went to Missoula, Montana. I went to Montana State to get the extra math I needed to go through flight school. We went right to the university and stayed in the dorms for the Air Force guys.

There were two of us to a room. I studied aerodynamics and wing loading and all that kind of stuff. One day they called me up and said they wanted me on the parade grounds. They said they were going to pick out cadet officers.

They wanted me to go up there and shout out these orders. They had a staff major in charge. I had read the little handbook on the military. I had read that forward and backwards. They made me a flight commander; I was in charge of two dozen students. I ended up being a squadron commander.

Did they ever ask about your ethnicity and did it matter?

It didn't matter but I was asked about it. I wanted to get out and wanted to come home. Colonel Bates told me 'You realize you're one of the very few, you have too much ability to throw it all away. You realize what you'd be for your people? I'm proud of you guys, aren't you proud of who you are?'

I told him I was never ashamed that I was half-Indian. He said 'You have a responsibility to the rest of them coming up behind you. I'll give you two weeks.' I stayed there for maybe two-and-a-half months until we got through all the classes.

Those classes were pretty advanced for that time...

For that time yes. I didn't have any problems. I felt sorry for some of those guys who had a hard time. We'd tutor them down in the restroom because the lights didn't go out there until 10. They went out in the rooms at nine.

After your time there where did you go?

From there I went to Thunderbird Field by the reservoir in Phoenix. I qualified for all three (pilot, navigator, bombardier). I qualified higher in navigation than I did in piloting but I wanted to be a pilot. This is where I drove the planes.

Chuck Williams

Was it a military base?

Yeah. You never knew if you were going to be there the next day or not, it was tough! I think I was the second guy to solo. I was walking around like I was 10 feet tall! There was a trainer there who used to fly mail in Denver.

He asked where I was from. I said in northern California, almost by the Oregon border. He asked what I did. I was getting kind of angry, but I said we had a ranch. He was mean, but finally he asked if I was a rancher or a farmer.

I said I guess we were farmers. He said 'I thought you were a damn farmer, now get in that damn airplane!' So I got in that airplane and flew it around and made a landing. He made me do that again. I did it six times. He used to laugh about that.

What type of plane was that?

It was a Stearman; it was just an old two-wing biplane. We learned to fly that. It's still a good airplane.

I went from Thunderbird Field and went to basic just northwest of Bakersfield. From there I went to Williams Field in Chandler, Arizona just 20 or 30 miles from Phoenix.

Did you train on the same type of plane at all those different bases?

No, there was a BT-13 that had flaps that let you land slower and it had enclosed canopies. We flew with the instructor and then we flew by ourselves. We had wonderful weather in Arizona and in Bakersfield.

We probably stayed two months at basic training. We did four months of advanced training at Chandler Field. We got into the AT-6 there, which had quite a bit more horsepower and retractable landing gear just like the planes we were going to be in. We trained for almost four months.

They had a Chinese general there, and the pilots respected that guy more than they respected the general because he had shot down 13 Zeroes.

They split us up after we got into advanced. They had the B-25 which was a light bomber, then they had heavy bombers, and I was stuck in the training command! I signed my name on a shipping list once and almost got court-martialed for that, so I didn't do that anymore!

They wanted you to be an instructor...

Yeah, I was doomed to that...I couldn't help it. I said I didn't get in there for that. Then every day I had to come in and stand at attention for 10 days in front of the Colonel. He'd tell the secretary he didn't want to be disturbed. I finally told him to do what he was going to do to me, I wasn't a baby; I was a grown man.

He asked if I learned anything, and I said I had stepped out of line. He shook my hand and that was it. He was one of those guys who went to West Point. He was a neat man.

After your training at Chandler Field where did you go?

They sent us to instructor school at Randolph Field in Texas. I think we stayed there for a little over a month that first time. I went through there three or four times. The last time I went there a First Lieutenant from South Carolina and I did research on spins. We spun the AT-6 every way you could spin it.

We had to write this book on it. After that I taught ground school to the other pilots. I guess you could say I had it pretty good but I didn't think so. I wanted to fly those pursuit ships. That's why I got in there.

You wanted to fly the other planes...

The best they had...the P-38 and the P-47. The P-40 was the older one of all those pursuit ships. They had sent us some Chinese officers. I was one of the instructors for their first class. They had some guys that could drive!

This one guy shot down 13 Zeroes. They had a Chinese general there, and the pilots respected that guy more than they respected the general because he had shot down 13 Zeroes. He was flying in a kite compared to the Zero!

What would be a typical day at that base in Texas?

Well, we did a lot of pencil work; we'd fly a couple hours and record the reactions of the airplanes. We had to write out our day. We'd fly until noon and then write how the plane reacted under certain circumstances. Sometime we'd write into the night.

As the instructor, did you spend more time in the plane or in an actual classroom?

We spent time in the planes and in the rooms by ourselves reporting to a staff that was above us. I was a Second Lieutenant. They promised me a lot to stay in but I was ready to come home. I can't recall when I left but the war was over. I think I was in the service a little over three years. I was in 14 months as a cadet and then I was commissioned.

After your time in Texas did you rotate to different bases?

No, I taught at Williams Field; that's where I was commissioned. Then they needed some instructors down at Marana Army Air Base; that was just 36 miles north of Tuscon out in the desert. I instructed there until I got out.

Anytime you go in the plane it's dangerous, what would your flight check look for in terms of safety?

You check your stick or the wheel, and wiggle your brakes and check to make sure the lids were tight on your fuel tanks. You made sure there were no oil leaks on your hydraulic system, and you made sure that your drop would change pitch when you first start. It might need more or less air. It was an interesting life, I enjoyed it!

Did you ever instruct any black pilots or any Indian pilots?

No black pilots, but there were Indians. I never got to know any of them but they were there. They qualified as bombardiers and such.

The U.S. military segregated black soldiers so why do you think the U.S. military integrated the Indian men?

I really don't understand that because those guys were great flyers. They're getting their proper recognition now.

You were always treated with respect?

Yeah, I never did have any problems. The worst that happened to me was one day I was sitting in the officer's club reading the sports page to the paper. This colored captain asked if he could read my financial sheet. I said sure.

Whenever he would go to a table these Texans would always leave. They didn't want to be there with him. So asked him if it bothered him the way he was treated. I said I was half-Indian so I knew about persecution.

He said 'Lieutenant, my grandfather told me to treat other people how you'd like to be treated. I always remembered that. He said to always be a gentleman and this always worked for me.' He smiled and shook my hand. I thought 'What a lesson!' He and his wife came from Howard University. He was a music professor but he wasn't a pilot.

Was there a big difference in terms of the types of planes when you first went in the service and when you left?

Oh yeah, the advancements were terrific. It was like getting into a Model T and coming out in an F-150! There was that much advancement. Of course everybody had to go to school for that.

They had Chinese students that we taught at P-51 school in Colorado. We couldn't get in the airplane and here they were flying the planes! Man, I wanted to get in one of those things so bad I could taste it!

Probably because you were too valuable as an instructor...

That's the way they might have felt, but I didn't feel that way.

Did you make some good friends while you were there?

Oh yeah, there were some good guys. One time five of us flew airplanes to Santa Ana and we stayed at a really fancy place. We went to this bar and the bartender asked us what we wanted. I didn't drink so I asked for a glass of orange juice.

He brought everybody their drinks. One of the guys was my buddy who was a doctor before he became a pilot. He asked the bartender why he didn't bring my drink.

That guy said 'He knows better, he can't drink here.' Before he knew it my friend grabbed him by the neck and pulled him over the bar. At that time two bouncers came over and settled things. The manager asked what was wrong. That bartender said 'This guy grabbed me by the neck and tried to choke me.'

My friend said 'They should have left me alone and I would have choked you.' He said that! He said to the manager 'My buddy here asked for nothing but a glass of orange juice and two times this guy didn't bring it. I was going to make damn sure he brought it the third time.'

That manager turned around and told that bartender 'Your check will be ready in 10 minutes. Anybody that comes in here with a uniform on that serves our nation; don't forget they're doing that so you have a decent place to live. Now go get your check, get the hell out of here, and don't ever come back.' I said I didn't want to see that guy lose his job. The manager said he didn't deserve it.

That's a great story to share, because you sacrificed your time for your country, and a lot of Indian men from your generation did that; why do you think so many Indian people chose to go into the service?

Well, I think a lot of us felt it was our duty to be there. Really! That might sound cheap, but that isn't the case. Everybody wanted to do what they could for their country because in those days we were damn proud of our country. I'm beginning to think that sometimes it isn't that way anymore.

You mentioned that you knew some of these Indian guys who served in the First World War, did any of them talk about their time in that war?

No, they never talked about it. I can remember my dad talked to Walter McCovey by our family cemetery and Walter said he was going over there and my dad said he would pray for him. But they never talked about it. I knew several Yurok guys. Bill Horn was one. I was just a little kid.

Then they needed some instructors down at Marana Army Air Base; that was just 36 miles north of Tuscon out in the desert. I instructed there until I got out.

There is a bond that exists between people who've served, can you explain that?

Well, it's the knowledge that you both shared in the same beliefs. You were proud of your nation and you were willing to give your life for it. You can't give anything more than your life for your belief.

You've been very involved in the Yurok culture; what would you tell younger kids today?

Be proud of what they are, and who they are, and be proud of their past. Never be ashamed. We were always taught that when we were little kids.

When you see the American flag what does it represent to you?

(Chuck points to his heart). That's what I think of it...I'm a pretty proud American. If they need me I'll go right now! Everyone always laughs when I say that, but if they need me to get in one of these new fighters I would! Of course I'd have to go to school, but someone else would have to tell my wife, because I'd be gone!

Well, thank you very much for sharing with me...

Thank you for allowing me to express myself.

Have you ever been interviewed about your time in the service?

No.

Why did you choose to do that today with me?

I figured you were interested enough to want to know and I would help you any way I could. I'm proud to say I think you're doing a damn good job!

Chuck worked as a timber faller and then as a fisherman for several decades after the war. He and his wife Pat have been married for over 50 years and raised their family in Crescent City. Chuck continues to teach his Yurok language, culture and history to those who are interested.

Vernon Numan

I met with Vernon Numan at his home near Sparks, Nevada on June 6, 2003. He is of Paiute and Shoshone ancestry. Vernon was someone I remembered from the Veterans' Reunions and I was very happy to sit and listen to him share about his time in the 4th Air Force during the war.

I was born in Lovelock in 1925 but when I was a little kid we moved to Susanville. We lived there until my mother and father split up then I came to Reno. My brother stayed in Susanville and I came to Reno with my dad Bert Numan.

He was from Pyramid Lake; he was Paiute. My mother's maiden name was Lucille Wasson. She spent most of her life in Susanville; she was Paiute and Shoshone.

So you're related to Sharon Wasson?

We're first cousins. My mother and his father were sister and brother. I'm also related to Mervin Evans. I have one brother and one sister.

When you were a little guy where did you go to school?

Mostly in Reno. They had a small school on the Colony that went through four grades and then we had to the public school in town. We had to walk one mile.

We squeaked by with my dad's military pension; we got 12 dollars a month and that sure helped at that time.

That school on the Indian Colony was just for the Indian kids?

Yeah, it was mostly all Indian kids for all four grades. They were all in the same classroom!

When you were growing up here were there a lot of ranches?

Yeah, Reno and Sparks were three miles apart at that time. There was a lot of work for Indians on the ranches at that time. In fact, I used to work on a ranch in the summer. I used to watch the bombers come in on the airport there when I was working out in the fields. I never thought I'd be on one of them later on!

What type of work did your father do?

He was mostly a laborer; he worked on the railroad, and on golf courses, and on ranches. His father's name was John and his mother's name was Daisy. They used to live in Pyramid Lake and then they moved to Reno.

The Indians used to live on the hill in the back of the University before they had the Colony. Later on the government bought those 18 acres where the Reno-Sparks Indian Colony is now and the people moved there.

When you went to public school were there any other Indian kids there?

There were very few.

Were you treated any different because you were Indian?

I had a few fights at school in the class and some on the playground. I went to high school and had just started my junior year when I went in the service. While I was in the service they graduated so I never got to go to the prom or graduation. I guess that happened to a lot of guys.

Was your family affected by the Depression?

Yeah, there were no jobs. We squeaked by with my dad's military pension; we got 12 dollars a month and that sure helped at that time. The Indians got commodities from somewhere; they'd get flour and sugar and beans.

Vernon Numan ca. 1944-5
Photo courtesy of Vernon Numan.

Did you ever go to the Stewart Indian School?

I went to Stewart after I got out of the service just to go to welding and mechanic school. It was a good trade school.

Did you have anybody in the family who served in the First World War?

My dad served in France for a year. My uncle Irving was in the service but he didn't go overseas. I think he was stationed in San Francisco. There were quite a few of the fellows in the service at that time who didn't go overseas. I know three or four that stayed in the states.

Did your father ever talk about what he did over there?

He was on a gun crew; one of those big 12-inch cannons. A dozen men probably had to man that thing. He was on that crew all during the war.

Did he talk about any of the places he saw?

They were in Verdun. At the end of the war they paraded through Paris.

So he got to go through Paris...

I don't know if you've seen those films where they parade through the main streets in Paris on Armistice Day? I guess it was a big deal at that time. He got to go through Paris.

Did he ever say if he was treated any different because he was Indian?

No. I've never heard of any veterans who were treated different. About the only thing I heard was some of the Indian fellows who were stationed in some of the Southern states like Georgia or Alabama had to sit in the back of the bus with the blacks. I was never stationed down there so I don't know about it firsthand.

Do you remember where you were when Pearl Harbor was attacked?

Yeah, I was in high school. We heard it on the radio. My cousin George Kane was stationed at Hickam Field when the Japanese hit. He was in the Army before he went into the Air Force and stationed at Hickam Field.

Where is Hickam Field?

It's right there in Honolulu.

What was the impression of the students in your class when that happened?

I know they hated the Japanese for that attack. I always wondered why they (the United States government) rounded up the Japanese and put them into concentration camps when they didn't do that to the Germans and Italians.

I always wondered about that. Just like the atomic bomb they dropped on Japan; if those were white people instead of Japanese would they have dropped that bomb? I always wondered about that. They killed thousands of people with those two bombs.

How old were you when you went into the service?

I had just turned 18. I didn't volunteer; I waited until they called me in 1943. I went to basic training at Buckley Field in Denver, Colorado. We had poison gas training, target shooting and marching. From there they sent me to Kansas State to study aviation. I got to fly a little 90-horsepower plane.

I'd never been in the air before! That first time the instructor took me up to about 10,000 feet in that little and put it in a stall with the nose straight down. He said to count the turns. All I could see was the earth spinning, I couldn't count anything! That was my first plane ride! I guess they do that to see how you take it.

I was there in Denver almost a year. We mostly studied aeronautics and map reading for navigation. I took a lot of tests to be a pilot, bombardier or navigator. I did that for almost a year-and-a-half. Then the war started winding down and I wound up as a crewman on one of the bombers. As the war was winding down I went into radio school.

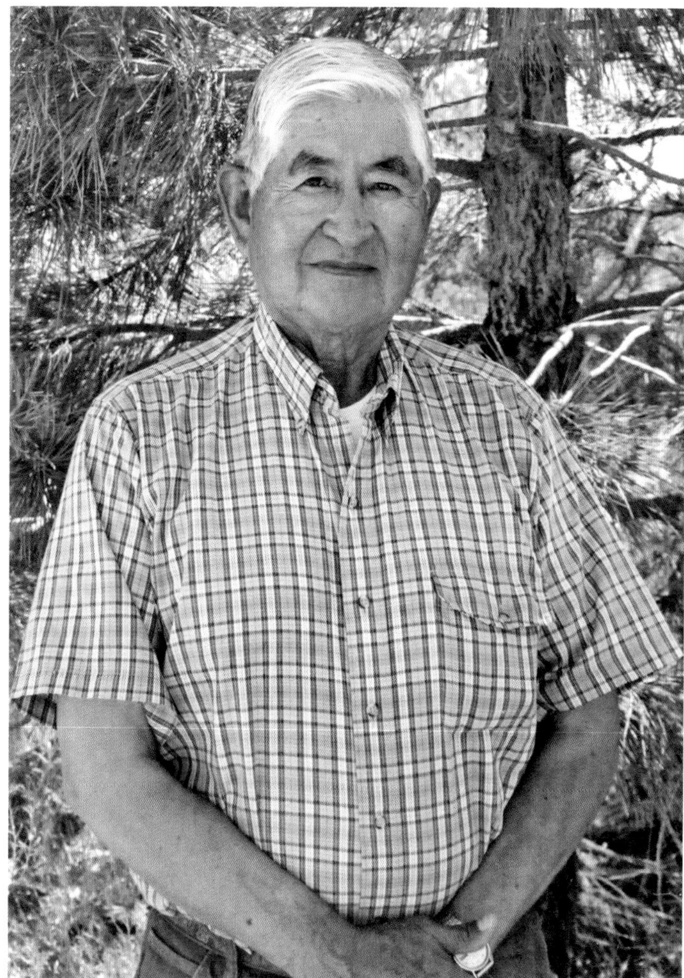

Vernon Numan

I was a radio man on a B-24. That's a four-engine bomber. We were based in Tonopah, Nevada. We went on two or three dozen training flights.

Can you describe where you were in the plane?

I was right in the middle. There was a little room where all the radio equipment was. We had one of those lamps where you could send Morse code to another plane. The only thing they didn't have on that plane was a toilet!

Every new air base I went to I always looked for another Indian fellow. I'd usually find one or two. There's just something about finding another Indian.

How long were you based in Tonopah?

Until sometime in 1945. Most of our training was almost done, but the war ended before we finished our training.

Do you know if they were training you for the European

or the Pacific Front?

Probably the Pacific because the B-24 had a little longer range than the B-17s. I don't know for sure but that's my feeling. They gave us a lot of training into those little rubber rafts. Every crew member had to learn how to swim.

What was it like for you to be away from home?

That's when you find out there's no place like home! A lot of those guys in Iraq are finding out there's no place like home. I was discharged in 1946.

Did you have any other relatives who served in the war?

In World War One those fellows weren't even U.S. citizens when they were in the service.

Uncle Mervin was in the Navy and my brother was in the Navy. My cousins from Pyramid Lake went into the Marines.

What were their names?

My cousin Stanley Winnemucca was killed at Tarawa. The first island they hit was Guadalcanal and the second one was Tarawa.

There were quite a few Indian people from this area that served, why do you think that was so?

I don't know. I remember when I was still in high school the entire Stewart football team joined. I remember the whole team signed up for different branches of the service.

After your time in the service what type of work did you do?

I worked in the Forest Service for 30 years. We worked from Hallelujah Junction all the way to Bridgeport. It was mostly in the field. I used to find grinding stones and arrowheads out in the field.

Did anyone in your family make baskets?

My mother made this baby basket over there. My mother spoke both Shoshone and Paiute and my dad spoke Paiute. They spoke quite a bit when we were young and that's how I learned it. But I never learned Shoshone because I wasn't around my mother that much. My grandparents both spoke Paiute.

Are there still people that know that language?

Not too many.

There are a lot of Paiute bands from a wide-ranging area…

We're from Pyramid Lake and by Walker River and over in Bishop. Carson City had mostly Washoe but there were some Paiute there. They go all the way into Oregon and there are some in Idaho. There are Southern Paiute in Las Vegas.

Where are the Shoshone people from?

From Fallon and farther east.

Knowing the history of what happened to our Native people, why do you think so many Native people have served in the military over the years?

In World War One those fellows weren't even U.S. citizens when they were in the service. Indian servicemen have been in the wars in the entire U.S. history. What really bothered me was how they treated the Navajo Code Talkers. They finally gave them medals but 90 percent of them were gone.

Have you ever seen any book or project about the Indian veterans from this area?

No. The Reno Colony has a list of all the tribal veterans at their office.

When did you start attending the Veteran Reunions in Susanville?

About six years ago. Brady Johnson and Gary McCloud from the Colony would go with me.

Is there anything about your time in the service you'd like to share?

Well, whenever they do the history of war veterans it seems like it's always the white people they have big write-ups in the papers, and you hardly ever hear about Indian veterans.

So it would be a good thing for other people to hear the stories?

They don't hear enough. I'd like the see the Indian Veteran's Organization get a little bigger and better.

What would you encourage young Native people today to do?

The first thing they need to do is learn to speak and understand the language of their tribe. That's the biggest downfall I've seen. There aren't too many fluent speakers. I've been to a lot of meetings held by the National Congress of American Indians and not too many people can speak their own language.

It's important for their culture and their history. They need to know who they are and where they came from. The people here used to have hand game tournaments. My grandfather was one of the last medicine men here and he used to have his own sweathouse. I used to go in there with him.

Vernon Numan has four sons, one daughter, several grandchildren and one-great grandchild. He resides near Sparks, Nevada and enjoys attending Indian gatherings.

Dee Rouse

1914-2005

Dee Rouse was of Yurok ancestry. Her older brother Barry Phillips and her uncle Henry Jackson served in World War One in France. Dee and three of her brothers served in World War Two. My friend Gloria Shuster put me in touch with Dee, who is her stepmother. We met on June 6, 2002 at her home in Eureka, Ca.

When I walked in her door Dee teased me, 'I hope

you weren't expecting to see a young lady from the war.' I laughed and teased back saying yes, I was. After we talked about my family she showed me some pictures and we began our interview. She was a Private First Class in the Women's Army Corp.

I was born July 1, 1914 in Arcata. My parents were Maggie and John Phillips. I was raised in the Arcata Bottoms. My father did repair work on ranches. I had a total of 13 brothers and sisters. There were seven of us kids in the family.

My real father John died when I was very young. When my mother married Henry Griffin there were seven more kids in the family. I was the last of the Phillips children. My father was full-blood Yurok. My mother was half Yurok. My father came from Trinidad and my mother came from Blue Creek.

I lived in Arcata until I went to high school. Then I had to leave, that was when they took us out of school. A couple of government people came to our house. The man's name was Marztoff. I remember that name even though it's been so many years, because we were so frightened of him.

He told my mother that she had too many children and she might get on welfare, so he was going to take two of her daughters away from her and have them work for the rich people in San Francisco. So that's where we wound up; my sister Gertrude was in Oakland and I was in San Francisco. We hardly ever got to see each other.

Being misplaced so fast, it was mind-boggling for me. My sister was the same way. We didn't get to see each other very much. They just loved to separate families, you know. That was one of the things they did.

That man told my mother that she was not to teach us our own language, because if she did, they would take all of the kids away. So she would never allow us to learn anything of our own culture. So when we lived in Arcata we didn't know half the things that the people back on the reservation knew. My mother was frightened! They scared her! So we didn't learn our own language.

You mentioned that some Yurok women would visit you when you were younger...

Yes, the older people came from Blue Creek. It was Sealy Griffin, and Nellie. There was another lady named Fanny. Every once in a while they would sit with my mother and speak the language and make baskets.

They made beautiful baskets. That's how they visited. But we weren't allowed to visit, because they were speaking the language.

How old were you when you had to move away?

I was in my first year of high school; I was probably 16 years old because I went to school late. I stayed with one family for about a year. They lived in Alameda. Then I stayed with another family in San Francisco. Those people in Alameda lost most of their money in the Depression. Could you turn the recorder off?

Sure. (After a short pause). How long did you stay in San Francisco?

When I came back to San Francisco I stayed with a Jewish family. I don't know how long I stayed there. They moved away, so I stayed with a military family. This man was a priest. There were two kids and me, the preacher and his wife. Then they wanted to move to Los Angeles. They wanted me to go with them, and who was I to say no? So I went with them.

Dee Rouse ca. 1943-4
Photo courtesy of Dee Rouse.

What was it like living in San Francisco?

It was scary! I had never been on a streetcar in my life! You had to go everyplace on a streetcar. You had to change cars, and you had to do it by yourself, and you better know where you're going.

That was frightening to me at first, but after a little while you could get used to it. It took quite a bit of time to do all that and also take care of all these people while knowing that they didn't like you. That was the worst part. They didn't really care for us as Indians.

What was it like to live in Los Angeles?

It was twice as hard, because it was twice as big as San Francisco! I didn't stay there very long.

When did you come back up to Arcata?

During the Depression, in the early '30s. They said I had to go to work, but I was used to that. There was a sewing class, and we had to make clothing for people coming in from Oklahoma. That's when I met Gloria's father.

His wife had passed away. That's when I married him. Then I went to work for the Chicago Bridge and Iron and worked on the dry docks for the Navy in Eureka. My marriage didn't last very long, about six years.

In '41 when the war started my brothers were all volunteers. They all wanted to go. So I said I would go too. So I did. I stayed in for two years. First I was at Camp Kohler. Then I went to Camp Beale.

Did you volunteer here in Eureka?

Yes, they said they'd take me. But they said I needed a birth certificate, but when would I get a birth certificate? We were all born at home. So I had to wait a week to get that, and have somebody to sign that so I could get in the service, and who could be more American than me?

Before you went into the service, what was the atmosphere like, were people afraid, did they talk about Japan or Germany?

Yes, they were scared to death because of the Japanese people. It was such a sneak attack, so everybody was scared.

Everybody was just running and screaming and hollering, 'The war is over, the war is over!' Everybody was pretty happy.

Where did you go after you volunteered?

We were recruited to Des Moines, Iowa. That's where we did our basic training. When I first went into the service, I told myself, 'If anybody calls me a damn Indian I'm going to punch them right in the nose!' But they didn't do that, they were all good to me. They were nice to me.

I remember when we came to the place to go into the gas chamber. I said, 'I have my whole race on my shoulders, I've got to do this, I have got to do this.' It was the real stuff, you go into this building and by the count of 10 you walk through and unfasten your mask and put it on before you go out.

So I did and I thought if I failed I would just die. So I was in there and oops, I got a smell! Boy, four, five, six, seven sure went by fast! I almost fell; it felt like somebody put a knife up your nose! Anyway, I came out. Boy was I ever happy! I knew I had my whole race on my shoulders.

Because they were all watching you...

That's right. I passed.

After basic, did you come back to California?

Yes, we were all on a train and I went to open the window and I said, 'Hey ladies, wake up! We're in California!' They said I was crazy, so I told them to ask the porter. They did and he said we had just entered California!

I just about cried, because I could feel the difference from opening the window! It was so desolate in Des Moines. I don't know how anybody can live away from the ocean. I think that's something very important.

What did you do while you were at Camp Kohler?

I transported medical supplies. That was where our soldiers were separating (into divisions). We had prisoners of war there, too. Some of them, they were just kids. They were just kids. I used to drive the prisoners to their jobs.

Then I would go back and do whatever Medical wanted me to do. I would go here and there. I had a staff car and this Colonel from Hawaii was there. He said he sure liked my driving. He said every time he would come from a building the car would be surrounded (by soldiers).

He said he would call me 'Flypaper.' He went back to Hawaii. He said when his son would get done with the service he would send him to Camp Beale to say hello and he did!

Wow, do you remember the man's name?

His name was Albert. I got to learn to drive with him in the car! That was at Kohler just outside Sacramento.

Did you stay in the women's barracks?

The first time I was at Kohler they didn't have barracks for women. So they said, 'What are we going to do with her?' So they put me in the guesthouse. There was a little building there and they cleaned it all up and said this would be for the WACs who would come in. Of course they did eventually get a lot more; we had a lot of WACs there.

But for a time you were the only one?

Yes, I was the first one. It was a Signal Corps, and they said they wanted to put me in a magazine, because I was the first WAC. They didn't even have a place to put me. So what did they do? They put me up on a telephone pole and took my picture!

It said, 'First WAC from Signal Corps.' I never got that picture, but they probably have it someplace. (The article and picture appeared in the Western Signal Corps Message).

Where was Camp Beale, and what were your duties there?

It's outside of Marysville, near Yuba City. It was very large because it was a place where people came to be separated. I transported medical supplies and I also went through Sacramento when they sent convoys in.

When you transported the prisoners at Camp Kohler, were they Italian or German?

They were German.

Can you describe them?

Well, they were all shot up. Some of them were crippled. They all wanted to talk to me. Their English was pretty bad. There was one man, his name was Alfred. He used to cook for the medical personnel. He used to give me little treats all the time.

He was a lonely man, and hurt pretty bad. You have compassion for everybody who is hurt, not just the people you know. It just comes to you. One time I went with someone on a picnic instead of to the mess hall.

It was lunchtime, so I went to see Alfred and he fixed a nice little package for our picnic. He got caught, and they took him out of there. I wondered who would tell that he did that? But there were some ladies who weren't very nice at the barracks. So somebody told on him. They took him and he stayed in the middle of the compound.

One day I drove over there to see him, and they had shaved his hair off. He had the most beautiful blond curly hair, and they shaved it completely off. I felt sorry about that, but you know, that's the way they (the Germans) did things, too. Some things we did were pretty bad, also.

You were probably the first Indian person those Germans had ever seen, they were probably pretty curious to see you...

That's right. They all treated me really good. One guy, his name was August; his legs were all shot up, he could barely walk. One day when I came to pick him up, he came out and he handed me a little plastic box that he had put my name on. He decorated it all up, he could do beautiful work. That was so nice; he wanted to give me a present.

You were probably the first Indian person that a lot of the American men had ever seen at Kohler and Beale as well...

That's right.

I can't even hardly imagine that, you were like a pioneer...

A renegade, they call it! I was afraid nobody would talk to me, or call me names. I had a lot of friends, lots of friends. Then there were some persnickety people.

There's always those types...

That's right.

What was the mood like here when Japan surrendered?

Everybody was just running and screaming and hollering, 'The war is over, the war is over!' Everybody was pretty happy.

Were you happy to be done with your time in the service?

No, I really wasn't. I enjoyed every moment. I was glad that I volunteered to go because I liked the regulation. I liked all that stuff. I don't know if I would have stayed in afterwards because they let you if you wanted, but I had to come home. It was a good time. We also had fun when we went on convoys.

I'm glad you had fun too, because it seems like that was a hard time, to live during the war...

Yes, it was really a hard time. But when you're together with all the people you knew it was really fun.

Did people treat you any different because you were in uniform?

Not really, because at that time most of the people were in uniform. They all looked at me at first because there weren't very many WACs at first, but they all treated me good.

You're talking about the soldiers at the camps?

Yes, everybody came out to look at me at first! I felt so awful! They all came and said, 'We'll take you to this mess hall;' they all wanted to take me to their particular mess hall! It was fun for a while. I always got along well with everyone.

Were there ever any other Indian WACs?

No, but there were blacks, and mostly white people as WACs. There was this one Jewish WAC, I don't remember her name. She knew how to play the piano. She had come into the barrack and said she wanted to embrace me when the war was over.

Dee Rouse

So I said, 'Well, give me a hug!' Before she left she came in one day and brought me a gift. It was a 45-record with her piano music on it. There were some other nice ladies there too.

After your time at Camp Beale where did you go?

I had separated from the service after that. I was in the service from 1942 to 1945. My sisters kept calling me and said our mother wasn't well. She wanted me to come home. I had planned on going to school, but my sisters were all married and had children, and I didn't, so I came home.

I'm glad I did because I was always the one my mother could depend on. I was married then, and my mother came to live with us. My husband Don said she was a grand lady so we took care of her.

Do you think it's good for other people to read about and learn what our Indian people did in the service during the war?

Yes, of course I think so. Think of those Code Talkers, they all came home and never said anything, because an Indian wasn't supposed to be glorified.

Let's talk about your brothers and where they were in the war...

My brother James Griffin was in the Navy in the Pacific. Then my brother Harry Griffin was in the Army in Germany. He also went through France. My brother Wallace is still living, he was also in the Navy as an engineer. Harry probably went through some of the concentration camps, but he wouldn't ever tell us anything, and he wound up killing himself.

Think of those Code Talkers, they all came home and never said anything, because an Indian wasn't supposed to be glorified.

I remember Gloria told me that your mother kept four stars in her window during the war to signify the four of you in the service...Why do you think so many Indian people volunteered to go in the service?

Well, with the living conditions they were in, maybe they thought our conditions would have been worse if we had been conquered. I don't know if I could have lived if we were conquered.

Dee's family and friends are very proud of her service to her country and to her people as a member of the Women's Army Corps. For her service to her country, Dee earned the American Campaign Medal, the Good Conduct Medal and the World War Two Victory Medal.

Jimmy James

Jimmy James spoke with me at his home in Hoopa on March 13, 2003. He is of Yurok and Hupa ancestry and is a fluent speaker and teacher of the Yurok language, as well as a longtime traditional singer and dancer for ceremonies held in his homeland. Jimmy was a member of the Army Air Corps and was stationed in the American Southwest during the war.

I was born in 1914 at Blue Creek; there was no hospital and no doctor. My mother was Nora Billy and after she got married her name was Nora Billy James. She was half Hupa and half Yurok. Her father 'Hoopa' Billy was from here.

She was from the lower end of Cappel (A Yurok village). My father's name was Jimmy James. His father had an Indian name which means 'Good singer from Wautek.' I don't remember his mother's name, we just called her grandma! I had two brothers, Andrew and Jasper.

Where were you raised when you were little?

I was left in the government school right here in Hoopa. My mother died in the hospital here. There was a doctor there and he wanted to adopt me. He went to my mother and asked if he could have me. He said he would give me any education I wanted; to be a doctor, or lawyer, he would put me through.

My mom told him to wait and come back in three days. The doctor came back three days later. My mom said, 'He's an Indian, let him stay in Indian territory. They'll never really like him in the white man's territory.' That's how come I stayed Indian. When I went in the service they tried to change it to white, but no, I'm Indian!

How old were you when you first went to the school here?

I wasn't very old; my brother was still in the war somewhere. When I got out I didn't realize my mother was dead. They were burying her and I didn't know what was happening until they put her in the hole. Then I knew what happened. I must have been pretty young.

You had a brother who was in World War One?

Yes, Andrew James.

Did he come back from the war?

Yeah, he did, and so did his cousins Lawrence Mattz and Tommy Riley and Sherman Steve. They all came back.

What village were they from?

The same place; Wautek.

Did they ever tell you any stories about what they did?

I can't remember. Lawrence was a fighter, and they put him in the ring over there in France. He said he was nip and tuck with that guy, and if he had training he could have kept up with him. Come to find out that guy was the French champ! Lawrence went to the top with the gloves.

You mentioned that one of them got gassed in the war?

Yes, that was Sherman Steve. He didn't live long after he came back. Tommy was all right and Lawrence was good. Andrew was good. Just Sherman...Those guys were over there fighting for a while.

Did you ever see them in their uniforms or anything like that?

Yeah, they came home and I had a lot of pictures of them. But our house burned down, and the last pictures went in the drink during the flood.

Who taught you the Yurok language?

That was the only language I knew when I went to school. They knocked me around quite a bit. I took some rough blows for speaking my Indian language. I remember I got hit and slapped and knocked over to the wall because I was speaking my language. They were trying to break us from it.

Can you describe what the school looked like here in Hoopa?

The first time when I went in they had the boy's building down on the lower side. That's way down there by that baseball ground. That's where we lived. The girls were way up on this side. They had a big laundry in there, and a lot of wood piled up.

The girls had their buildings there, but they burnt that building down so they moved the girls into the buildings that we were staying in. They built new buildings and gee, they were cold! The cracks in the walls were wide. They finally got it in good shape and that's where we stayed.

Did you have to wear a uniform?

In school? Yeah! We'd march and drill with wooden guns and salute the flag every morning. But we couldn't speak our Indian language. And I'm the one who took an awful beating because I couldn't speak any other language. I finally learned to speak English, but it was broken. I would know the Indian word that would make the sentence right and I'd really get popped for that. They were rough.

You stayed in a separate building with the boys; do you remember any of the names of the boys?

There were boys from Smith River and from way up the river; the Wilders and the Godfreys. Down in Riverside I ran into a lot of them.

What would a typical day be like for you in the school?

This one here was all academic, but when we got to Riverside it was half-a-day education and half-a-day vocational. Somehow the kids all worked real hard at it. I had to because my English was all broken up.

Now they're teaching the Indian language and it doesn't sound like the language to me. The only guys I can talk good with are Harold Blake and Earl Griffith. The other old people are gone. The people who teach it now don't sound like the Yurok language.

Do you think that's because they learned English first?

That's what happened. I went to school by Johnson's too. The people went according to Indian law and they abided by it. They helped one another and really loved one another. I saw them kill a deer down on the river bar and I sat and watched from up on the hill.

They cut it all up and divided it. They would give it to their neighbors and everybody got a piece. Nobody went without. The law was not let anyone go hungry, not let anyone be cold. Feed everybody and keep them warm. It was all based on love for our people.

What year was it when you went down to Sherman?

I went down in the '30s; I had a bad eye. They said if I wanted to save my eye I had to quit school. So they took me out of school in the middle of the year. There was no use staying down there, all I did was eat and sleep!

So they sent me home. I had an Indian doctor here work on me. My eye was all right and I went back to school for another year to get my diploma. I've used that diploma thousands of times through my life.

How did you get down to Sherman?

I went down by bus. We stopped in San Francisco and they put us on a ferry to go across the bay. There were a number of us, some were from Hoopa and some were Yurok. I wasn't afraid; the people were kind in those days.

When you were at Sherman where did you stay?

In the boy's building. That was really good because some of us had rooms. The better boys, the officers, had their own rooms.

We're all human and we're all created by the same Creator. Why should I lower myself just because my skin is brown?

What vocation did you learn?

I took the barber course. I had to go to San Francisco for the examination. It was a funny thing; I told the other boys they would ask us questions and they said 'Aw Jimmy, they won't do that!' But they did. There were 16 of us who went and eight of us passed. There were two Indian boys. They gave us our license.

What was it like for you to be in the city of San Francisco, since you came from a small village?

It didn't seem to bother me. I lived the way I had been living. When I would get around white kids I would be backward; I'd have an inferiority complex. It took me a long time but I got over that. We're all human and we're all created by the same Creator. Why should I lower myself just because my skin is brown? That's how I got out of it.

When you were younger and growing up, did your family get to visit you when you were at the Hoopa school, or down at Sherman?

No, I didn't even know them. I was kind of left alone. In the mess hall (at the Hoopa boarding school) they used to take the food away from the little boys. I would look for chickens to see where they were laying eggs.

I would take them down to the creek and boil them. All I took was salt. I used to take those crawfish out of the creek and eat them. I don't remember what part I ate, but I ate them! I used to go up on the hill and get some mushrooms and cook those on furnace coals. I was happy then.

Did anybody talk to you about when the first miners came into this area?

Yeah, they came into Cappel there and those Indians had never seen a white man in their lives. These white men came from Orleans; they were chasing Indians from Orleans and when they came to Bluff Creek the Indians went up the creek. Another time the soldiers came over from Klamath to Morek and they shot all those Indian people. I don't know how they did that. This didn't come from a book, it came from people who saw it and got away. (Morek is a Yurok village along the Klamath River).

My grandfather was one of them. He jumped in the river and went back to camp after they killed all those Indians. There were only five left. He went back and found five of his people. He told them to get boats and go downriver.

He didn't say what he was going to do. He killed the guards where they slept. They found out he was there and he jumped into the river again. He stopped at every village all night long, all the way down to Requa. They gave him a place to stay.

Then those Yurok came back and met with my grandfather up in the mountains above Weitchpec and they fought those white men again. That's the way they fought, they would fight whenever there were a few out. They would clean them out and run.

They (the miners) put I don't know how many big guns across the river from Weitchpec on the bank side. They had two to four volunteers for each gun. The (Yurok) head man called for volunteers to go way down past Martin's Ferry, and take enough dried salmon and deer meat and water because they would have to crawl under the brush.

Jimmy James ca. 1944
Photo courtesy of Jimmy James.

That's what they did. The Indians were really cleaning them (the miners) out. So they wanted to quit fighting and called for a treaty. In their letter it said they couldn't see who they were fighting and they wanted a treaty.

This was the result of it: the Indians came down from Weitchpec down that ridge by the bridge and came over and these guys were ready behind these big guns. These Indian guys were all volunteers doing this; they weren't forced to like the Army does now. At that time they gave us a treaty, and that's an un-ratified treaty. They're not even ashamed of that, of what they did.

Did any of the Indian people talk about the big water cannons the miners used?

They mined down to Johnson's here below where that school is. They mined all the way to that point. There are still big pipes in there.

The Yurok people are historically a loving, kind, people...

They are.

But when it comes down to it, they also know how to resist...

Yes, that's what came up right there.

Knowing everything that happened, why do you think that your brother and cousins and other Yurok men went into World War One?

We are people who live in a nation. We have our nation inside another nation. We live with our laws and abide by their laws.

Going back to your time at Sherman, would you say you enjoyed it?

Yeah, I did. I wasn't a fast runner, but I was strong. I only weighed 134 pounds. I could handle myself. One year I ran my uncle's ranch here. I got to wrestling with a steer! My uncle said to let him go; I couldn't throw him down, and I didn't let go.

It tore the membrane in my lung sac. I was just getting well down there at Riverside when I got in a fight and tore it open again! There was just no give up in me; I beat that guy up. Afterwards we became friends.

You mentioned you knew my grandfather Stan Lowry?

I just saw him around. There were so many there; they would talk with us. The Moores were there, and Leonard Ames. They were buddies with your grandfather.

When the attack at Pearl Harbor happened do you remember that?

I was camping in the woods so I didn't hear about it the next day. I don't remember if I was signed up already, but I had a bad eye. I could see really well with my other eye. They didn't know whether they were going to take me or not. It took them a long time before they said they'd take me. It must have been '41 or '42.

Where did you go to boot camp?

I went clear to St. Petersburg, Florida! It took us a week to get there! I didn't know where they were going! They don't tell you where you're going. We got off at New Orleans for a while then we kept going. You can't keep going much further! They let us off in St. Petersburg and that's where I took my basic training.

What was that like?

I have a crazy story on that. I knew about drilling from the Indian schools. We had a good drill sergeant. He took three days off and they put a PFC in there. He was about my size. We took a 10-minute break one day. I used to have a pamphlet in my pocket; I'd pull it out and read it to get my mind on something else.

One of those boys came over and said, 'How about it Chief?' I said, 'How about what?' He said, 'Put the gloves on against this acting drill sergeant.' He had just made my buddy run around the track until he dropped over.

I was mad, and I thought if I could get one punch on him I'd be satisfied. I said sure! So they said to everyone, 'Chief here is going to put on the gloves against the drill sergeant!' That guy got in there and in a little while he had blood on his face. I didn't stop, I knocked him through the ropes and he got up and damn near ran from the room.

I jumped between the ropes and punched him again before they grabbed me! They threw us back in the ring again and I kept thinking about my buddy and kept hitting him! The boxing coach asked if I wanted to be on the boxing team. I said 'No, I'm a street fighter, not a boxer.' He said, 'I can tell that!' He said he'd keep me out of KP and out of guard duty.

Finally I got that KP. Three o'clock in the morning and you're washing those great big pots! That was a cold night! We'd have fire drills in the morning and I was always on the tail end during drills and I asked that coach if the boxing spot was still open. He said yes, and told me to go over where the boxers train and go to sleep! I ran over there and put two benches together with a pillow and went right to sleep!

So then you were on the boxing team!

I was on the boxing team! The first guy I fought just kept hitting me! I had crowd fright. Then that guy kind of hurt me and I went after me and beat him. I had about 37 fights. I knocked out 11. I had all those pictures too. We just went to different bases and boxed.

Did you stay in Florida the whole time?

No, they put us on a train and dumped us off in New Mexico way out in the desert! The wind would blow so hard and the dust was so thick you couldn't see from here to that TV (four feet away). Oh man! One time it rained there. The water just flooded the whole area. It was wonderful country.

Did you ever meet any of the Indian people from that area?

Yeah, but I had problems with the Mexicans. They didn't like me because I couldn't speak their language. They were saying that I was one of them and ashamed of the language. I didn't go around them anymore, I stayed at the base. I used to run out in the desert. I jumped over a rattlesnake once! I didn't even stop, I kept going!

I was in the Army Air Corps. I was a driver. They gave me a jeep and I patrolled the area. I had guardhouse duty. I wanted to go over with the rest of the boys but they wouldn't let me. They said my eyesight was too bad.

Did you stay at that base the rest of the war?

No, I went just north of San Bernadino. What happened was I got hurt in a plane crash way out in the desert in New Mexico. They thought I was going to die. I told them I wasn't going to die! So they sent me to a hospital by San Bernadino.

Before this happened my job was to pick up plane crashes. We picked one up in New Mexico; it was one of those water-based planes. They couldn't make it over a little hill where there was water. It caught on fire.

One of the men had tried to crawl out but he burned up. The rest of the crew burned up inside the plane. There was a lot of that that I couldn't ever get over. They finally put a bunch of the men into the infantry. I told them I wanted to go too. I almost made it. But my partners that went....they never did come back.

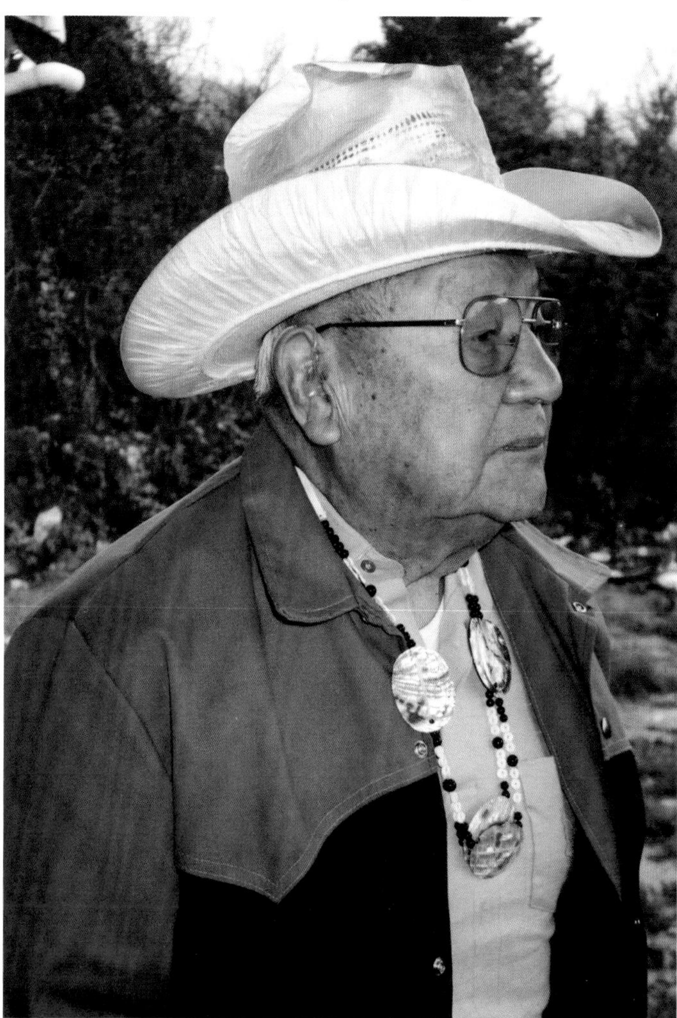

Jimmy James

After they took me out of that hospital they sent me to Santa Barbara to get well. The hardest thing was I wanted to go with those boys. I think that was the hardest thing soldiers had to live by...we knew each other and helped each other. Their money was my money and my money was their money.

So you made good friends there?

Yeah.

Did you ever meet any other Indian men in the service?

I probably did but they were in different barracks. I met a lot of Indian girls!

Did you come back to this area after the war?

Yeah, I was going to be a barber but everybody was growing long hair, nobody wanted a haircut! I had to go into the woods. I had to buy some power tools. I had a big heavy drag saw. They finally moved to lighter ones. I made pretty good money.

That was dangerous work though...

Oh yeah, I was carried out of the woods three times. One of the times was a crazy experience. I remember I was down underneath and the bar of the chainsaw got bent. I was bucking off and I got shoved down. They were carrying me out in a wire basket.

It was after the fishing season when we used to have dances there every year. I listened to what my elders said and I obeyed.

We were in a very steep area. I came to and wondered what was going on, where were they taking me? Then I passed out again. Then I heard somebody say they were taking me, they couldn't wait for an ambulance.

I came to again and heard someone talking. It was my wife. I was in a hospital bed! The doctor said I couldn't cut timber again, but I made it out there! I cut timber all along this area.

Was it mostly other Indian men that worked with you in the woods?

Yeah, I only had one white man who worked with me. I liked him, that's why I kept him on. I hired other men.

You mentioned that you worked with World War One veteran Lewis Sanderson?

Yeah, when I first worked in the woods I was a choker-setter with him. A few years later I was head rigger, and another year I was a hook-tender. Another year I was camp post. I didn't like that because you sit around too much. There were a lot of outfits running. I retired 25 years ago.

How old were you when you went to your first Brush Dance?

I was about seven or eight years old. The dance was at Requa up on the hill. It was after the fishing season when we used to have dances there every year. I listened to what my elders said and I obeyed.

I was scared of the Great Spirit if I didn't do something right. It was the same thing at the Jump Dance; you don't run around, you don't holler. You go down there to listen. When you get down the road then you can holler if you want to!

When did you first dance in the Brush Dance?

I was old; I was about 15 years old. That was at Requa. My sister Francis Roberts took me then. She married a man name Archie Roberts.

Why has it been so important for you to keep these ceremonies going?

That was the command of the Creator. It's like going to church. You'll remember what you learn every year. You listen to your elders and respect them. I used to drink a little, but no one could make me drink when I was with my elders.

How does it make you feel to see young members of your family to participate?

Some of them do, and they're doing really good. I wish all of them could. Some of them are going to the white man's church, and that's good too.

I think you do a lot of good for the Yurok people when you speak at our ceremonies, and you dance at the ceremonies...

It does make me feel good, especially when someone might come to me and say they're going to take my advice. Then the buttons on my shirt might come off, because I've swelled up! It makes me feel good. I guess I'm not too old to keep talking.

Jimmy James continues to participate at the religious ceremonies held by the Yurok people. His family is very proud of his service to his country, and they are very proud of his ability and willingness to teach the Yurok language and culture to younger generations.

Bill Evans

I spoke with Bill "Bumps" Evans on October 29, 2001 at my house in Susanville. He is Mervin Evans' nephew and fishing buddy. Bill is of Paiute and Pit River heritage and he spoke about his time in the U.S. Navy.

I was born in Litchfield right outside of Susanville in 1923. My mother's name is Hazel Sanchez and my stepfather's name was Joe Sanchez. I'm related to Mervin because his older brother was my dad. I went to school at Sherman until the eighth grade. My stepfather got sick and I came home and went to high school right here in town at Lassen.

Did you get to attend any Bear Dance ceremonies when you were young?

Oh, yes. I was pretty young when we went to them. They were near Janesville (near Susanville) and here on the Rancheria. Right where I live now they had a Bear Dance. They have them in Greenville and different places now. I remember we'd hit the bear with the wormwood or a stick for luck.

How did you get to attend Sherman?

A school bus from here in town took people from around this area and from Greenville and Alturas to go down there. It was pretty good, I liked it. They put the kids in different places.

Some were in woodwork. When you reached a higher grade that's when they let you pick where you wanted to go. I worked in the garden and did woodwork. Leonard, Stanley and Juanita were all there.

Did you play any sports when you were here at Lassen High?

I played in a lot of sports, all except tennis! I played baseball; I was the catcher. I also played basketball.

When did you join the Navy?

I joined the service in 1942 in Reno and went to Farragut, Idaho to boot camp. I went by myself. I was there in Idaho for a little over two months. I came in to San Diego on New Year's. I stayed there until about June. I learned to make torpedoes. It was just like learning mechanics, how to tear it down and build it back up again. I was a third class torpedo man.

Were there different types of torpedoes?

Oh yeah, there were aerial torpedoes, and they had submarine destroyers. I worked on aerial torpedoes that were 13 feet long. The place where we worked was just like an organized shop. They had different stands to hold different parts of the torpedoes. Usually you worked on one part for so long then you had to change and worked in another department.

I worked from 1943 until the war ended. I worked at bases at Alameda, Fort Lauderdale, and at Whidbey Island in Washington. Sometimes we'd modify a different part of the torpedo, but it more or less stayed the same. We'd check if a certain part would work right, and if it didn't, we'd have to figure out what went wrong.

About how much would an aerial torpedo weigh?

An aerial torpedo's warhead would weigh about two thousand pounds. I don't know how much the whole thing weighed. The warhead had TNT in it. There was a firing mechanism in there with a booster. There's also air in there, and when the TNT blows you have the concussion of the air just like in a hand grenade.

The Susanville Indian Warriors basketball team in the early 1950. They won so many league championships they were asked to disband. They didn't.
Athletes from upper left going to the right: Joe Evans, Gene Turner, Bob Aguilar, Francis Allen, Mervin Evans, Eugene Numan. Front row from left: Bill Foreman, Harold Dixon, Eddie Jackson, Slim Summerville, Bill Evans.
Photo courtesy of Mervin Evans.

We had the same types of torpedoes but you could set them for different depths. Certain ships will go so deep, so we figured the depth and set the torpedo. You have to work with air pressure and water pressure.

We'd go to the shop at eight in the morning. During the war the shop was open 24 hours a day. We'd work the day shift or the swing shift. I'd work the day shift.

Bill Evans

There'd be maybe 60 men on each shift. When you're working in the shop you wear the Navy blues.

Was there ever a time when you didn't have enough material to make torpedoes?

No, because anytime something on the torpedo breaks you have other parts. We always had enough parts. We had different tools for different parts of the torpedo. I never served with any other Indian men, either in boot camp or at the bases. I never felt any different than anyone else.

When you were working on the base did you have a sense of how the war was going?

Oh yes, we listened to the news. I listened to Roosevelt on the radio. I was in Seattle when the war in Germany ended. They shut the shop down when the war ended and we got a liberty.

Then they asked us if we'd like to be on shore patrol at some naval bases. I stayed down in San Francisco until the end of the war in Japan. I lived downtown, and I'd go down in the evening and go on border patrol either on foot or we'd motor around. Everybody was happy when Japan surrendered.

Do you remember the first time you and Mervin saw each other after the war ended?

Mervin was home by the time I got home. I've gone to the veteran's reunions over the years. Most of the vets are gone now, but it was always nice to see them.

Did you talk about your experiences?

Well, some of them, but most didn't talk too much about it. I worked in logging after the war. I worked in different areas in northern California for over 30 years. I've been fishing ever since!

Mervin Evans (at left) and his nephew Bill Evans proudly display the local American Legion Post Flag in Susanville, California in 2001.
The Post is named in honor of Thomas Tucker.

Bill Evans was recalled in 1952 to help re-commission a Navy destroyer in San Diego during the Korean War. He is an avid fisherman in the lakes around Susanville. He and the late Mervin Evans enjoyed attending sport events, Indian gatherings and the Bear Dance ceremonies each spring.

Don Preston

I met with Don Preston at his home on January 10, 2003. He and his wife Mary live in the small town of Alturas, which is set on traditional Pit River land. I saw Don's picture in a Susanville Indian Veterans' Reunion photograph at my great-aunt Virginia's house, and my father Ike and I made the trip to visit with Don.

I was born January 11, 1927 here in Modoc County. My father was Arthur Preston, Sr. and my mother's maiden name was Josie Townsend; her married name was Preston. My father was from here in Modoc. He and his grandmother walked from Likely near here clear up to a fort up in Oregon.

In later years when he bought an old Ford car he took that up there. My father was Pit River. My mother was from near Fort Bidwell; she was Paiute. She spoke Paiute. Her parents were from Bidwell. I had two brothers, Leonard Preston, that's him in that Navy uniform on the wall there, and Herbert Preston.

Were there a lot of Indian families that lived in this valley?

Yeah, they were mostly Pit River, and there were some Maidu near Ravendale.

Did the Pit River people have any gatherings when you were little?

Oh yeah, the older Pit River men used to get together and have meetings to talk about their lands. When I was a kid we'd have to play around outside while they were meeting. They'd send some people back to Washington to talk about things.

Do you think this country has treated Indian people fairly?

No, I don't. They still don't right to this day. I used to work with white people here on these ranches and they used to treat me good. But today some white people won't even speak to you.

When you were really little did your family ever talk about what life was like before contact with white people?

They did talk about how Captain Jack outfought the soldiers. Those soldiers took them through here. I never heard those older Indians talk about that too much, and now they're all gone.

When you were very little where were you raised?

Right here in Modoc County. We used to live on the Rancheria on the other side of town here. My dad used to have a house there. My mother died in 1939 and I went to Sherman until I went into the service.

Then I came back up here. I went to grammar school here and then went to Sherman. There were a couple of other Indian kids here.

How did you go down to Sherman?

We caught an old-style Greyhound bus and went to Reno then they transferred us to another bus. This was in 1941.

Did any other Indian kids go with you?

No, it was just me from here. We picked up some more Indian kids on the way down. I didn't have a hard time down there. Some kids down there wanted to run away but I had a good time. I liked the school.

When you got to the eighth grade they used to give us outings on the weekends. We'd work for white people and clean their yards or we'd pick oranges. We'd earn a little money then go back to school. It didn't bother me much.

What type of trade did they have you do while you were there?

Carpentry in one class and in another class we'd fix shoes. Then we went into electrician class but I didn't catch on to that! I played baseball there and we used to box in the evenings. I boxed overseas too up in Alaska. I boxed at Camp Roberts too. I boxed in the lightweight class.

Don Preston

What year was it when you joined the service?

At the end of 1943. I went into San Pedro and got inducted there then went to Camp Roberts. When we finished training they gave us a week leave. I came up here and then went to Fort Ord, California.

Everybody went their different ways. We went in a boat from Fort Ord to Fort Lewis, Washington and they trained us there as MPs (Military Police). They shipped us up to Alaska.

Where did you box in Alaska?

They had a big gym up there. This Mexican guy and I would box different guys our own age. We didn't try to get at older guys!

How old were you when you went into the service?

I was 17.

Did you volunteer?

Those guys down at Sherman said they were going in the Navy. I watched them and they never came back to school. They wrote me letters. After that I joined.

Why do you think so many Indian people volunteered to go into the service?

To do their duty for their country. That's all I did. I wanted to see some different country. I thought I was going to go to Europe but they made us stay here. Anyway, I did manage to get out of school!

Were you chosen to be in the Military Police or did you volunteer?

Cold! Cold and miserable. You had to bundle up all the time in Alaska. In camp we had those Northern Lights.

They chose our company. You had to train to shoot different kinds of weapons from pistols to carbines to machine guns. They gave us a .45 pistol. When we got to Alaska then they gave us a .38 carbine to carry around. I had four guys with me at all times. One was Mexican, one was Italian, and one guy was from Texas. We were all buddies together!

Where were you stationed in Alaska?

We were stationed in Fort Richardson by the 11th Air Force base. They'd take us out to different islands where they had air bases. We'd stay out there for three months each time then they'd bring in a different bunch and fly us to a different place.

We were all over in Alaska. We patrolled out on the beaches and patrolled the airstrips. We'd travel on a jeep. It was a rugged place. We didn't see anybody but we patrolled where they had the gun emplacements.

We mostly patrolled the airstrips and buildings. Some soldiers would want to come in and look at those P-38s and P-39s. They had B-17 bombers and C-47s there. They'd fly out and fly in. They'd show us how fast the P-38 and P-39 would go. They'd go over the base.

Did you ever see any of the Native people on those islands, and what were they like?

Oh, they were pretty good! They were Alaskan Indians. They talked with us and got along with us. They owned a store up there where we'd go.

They must have been curious about you?

Oh yeah! Especially in Fairbanks. We went there and were walking around and go into bars and these Alaskan Indians would come up and ask where I was from. I'd tell them and they'd say they were glad to have us up there.

When you were an MP were there any times when you'd have to discipline other soldiers?

Oh yeah, when we were on the base. We didn't patrol in the towns; we were out of uniform in the towns. On the base there were sometimes when guys would get loud-mouthed. We'd have to warn them and they'd be all right after that.

Did you ever see other Indian soldiers up there?

I never did see any other Indians in our Division. We were in the 761st MP battalion. We'd go to Anchorage on furlough. Or we'd go to Fairbanks. I traveled mostly on a C-47 cargo plane.

What were the winters like?

Cold! Cold and miserable. You had to bundle up all the time in Alaska. In camp we had those Northern Lights. We'd put blinds on our barracks. In the spring there were some places where the snow would melt. These little streams would have salmon in them. I never did see a polar bear!

We saw a lot of wolves and caribou and moose. It was nice in the spring. Summer wasn't that long. It seemed like winter came on quick. It would be dark for a certain time and it was windy. Sometimes we'd have to walk in snow drifts and we'd follow each other's tracks. We'd

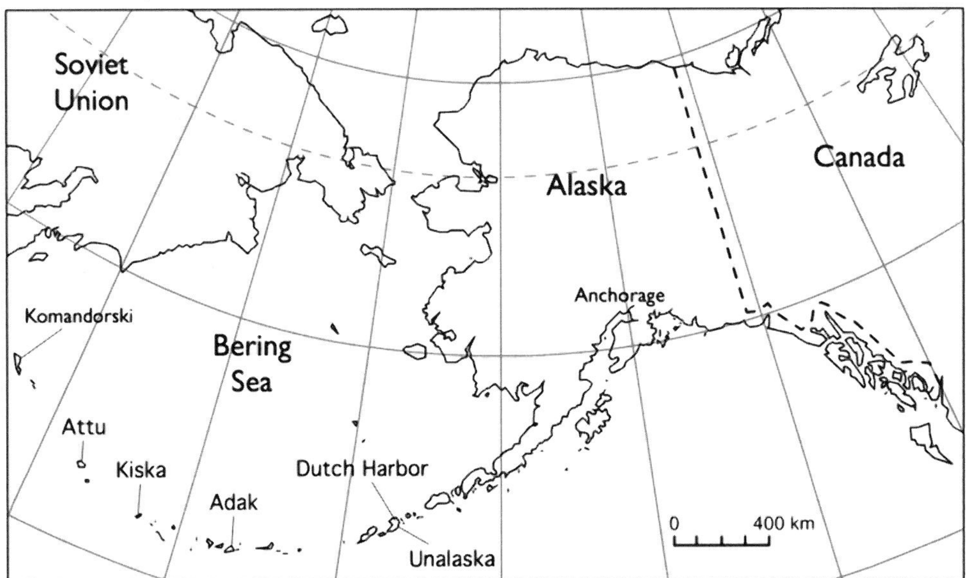

Map of Aleutian Islands.
U.S. military sources on wikepedia.com

have to walk near the shore sometimes.

The U.S. expected the Japanese to invade through the islands...

They had gotten close at one time. But those battles at Attu and Kiska happened before I got there.

How long were you stationed up in Alaska?

For around two years. I was there when the war ended. They said it was over and everybody celebrated. I got out of there on December 10, 1946. We went to Washington and got our discharge there. I went back down to Riverside. Then I came back up here. Before that I came down with rheumatoid arthritis. I had to go to the veteran's hospital in Reno for about a year.

Was your brother Leonard in the Navy during the war?

Yes, he was in a submarine. He was in Honolulu for a while there. He lived in Susanville all his life. He used to write letters to me about where he was at while I was down in Sherman in school. They transferred him to a Navy ship. He used to go on these barges that landed soldiers and Marines on islands. He would drive those for a while then he went back to his ship.

What type of work did you do after your time in the service?

I worked on all these ranches around here driving cattle. In the summer I was on a hay outfit. I baled and lifted hay. I joined the Forest Service near here because they had a program for Indians to work cutting trees and such. I drove a Forest Service engine and had a crew for a long time. After that I came here and worked at the Co-op.

What's your wife's name?

Her name is Mary; we have seven children. No great-grandchildren yet!

When did you start going to the Veteran's Reunion in Susanville?

Oh, when they first started it! Andrew Jackson got a hold of us. We'd go to see who I knew. They came from all over. They came from the coast, and from back East, and from Nevada. I missed last year's. I knew Mervin Evans and Gene Ryan. I knew Glenn Moore.

Do you think it's important for younger Indian kids to learn about their history and culture?

Oh yeah, I like to see them do that. If they don't they'll never know what the Indians did before. They have dances and are talking about getting the languages going again. I'm glad you guys came up!

Don's family is very proud of his service to his country. He and his wife Mary reside in Alturas, California.

Louie Melendez

I met with Louie and Irene Melendez at their home in Susanville June 5, 2003. Louie is of Paiute and Hispanic ancestry and served in the Army in the Aleutian Islands during the war.

I was raised in Reno, Nevada. My mother Nellie Taylor was Paiute and my father Manuel was Hispanic; that's where we get the Melendez name. He was from Mexico in the old country. His family moved into New Mexico. In those years they didn't have to have passports.

He and his brother gradually worked their way up here to Susanville and that's where he met my mother. The Joaquins are related to my grandmother Louise Harrison. She's from between here and Pyramid Lake. Years ago they used to travel back and forth. I had six brothers and five sisters. I'm the eldest!

The railroad educated me a lot, too. They sent me to engineering schools so I moved up the ladder pretty fast.

Ah, the responsible one! I'm the oldest son too!

Join the crowd!

Louie Melendez ca. 1944-5
Photo courtesy of Louie Melendez.

Where did you live in Reno?

Right there at the Colony with the other Indians. There were a lot of other Indians at that time.

Where did you go to school?

At Stewart and in Reno. I went to Stewart as a freshman. My folks sent me over there. They had a big family so that's where I ended up. I didn't stay there very long. During the summer they let you come home so I got a job on the railroad. I liked my job and I stayed there until I retired. I stayed close to a year at Stewart.

Did your father work there too?

He worked on ranches around Reno and on the railroad. He liked ranching; at that time there were a lot of ranches around in Reno but now there aren't. They were mostly farms that raised vegetables for the supermarkets.

Now there are mostly cattle ranches. A lot of the farmers sold their lands for development. We also lived way out on the Pyramid Lake Reservation. There was a railroad station by the name of Big Canyon that had men that worked on the railroad from there.

They trained us to go for days and days without water in that desert. It was hard basic training.

What was your first job working on the railroad?

Putting in ties and laying road! I liked it and stuck with it. I knew I wasn't going to do that all my life. I knew I'd work my way up the ladder in my career. The railroad educated me a lot, too.

They sent me to engineering schools so I moved up the ladder pretty fast. I belong to the Railroad Association and I was a District Manager for 300 miles of railroad when I retired.

The railroads were pretty lively back in those days. What was the cargo?

It was just about everything, but mostly timber. Everything is modern now and nothing is done by hand. It's all high-tech.

When were you born?

1923. I started working on the railroads when I was 17 or 18. I was a little kid when the Depression happened. I remember my dad working for commodities just so we could eat in those years. It was hard times. I remember I was a youngster and we'd play in the snow after the folks went to bed.

My shoes were all wet so I stuck them in the oven to dry out. My dad got up early to stoke up the stove and he wondered what was smoking in there and there were my shoes all curled up!

He didn't have any money to buy me new ones so I had to wear my damn shoes all curled up like that! I'll never forget that! I tell my wife that story and she says it's no wonder my toes are funny; it's from wearing shoes like that! But that's how hard times were during the Depression.

Did anyone on your mother's side speak their native language?

Yes, they all spoke it. Nowadays the younger people don't but they're trying to bring it back. I learned my language. I know all the words and everything that's said. It's the same with the Spanish language; I learned that while working on the railroads with Hispanic guys.

I loved to work on the railroad. If you didn't produce you were gone. My dad used to say I would never live to be an old man doing this type of work! I told him I wasn't going to work with the pick and shovel all the time, I was going to better myself.

I liked the work and the boss took an interest in me and recommended me and I worked my way up. I supported my family with that and educated my kids. They still depend on me to keep an eye out on all the railroad land here.

When the war broke out in 1941 do you remember where you were?

Irene: I don't know where you were! We didn't get married until 1942!

Louie: I was working on the railroad then. I tried to get a deferment but they wouldn't let me because they said I didn't have a responsible job at that time. A lot of the guys didn't go because they were foremen and during the war they were exempt. But I'm glad I did go in the service because I ended up with a lot of benefits I would have never had.

Louie and Irene Melendez
Photo courtesy of Ike Lowry.

Were you drafted?

Yes, I was drafted in the first part of 1943.

You mentioned you were married in 1942?

Yes, she kept insisting! I said this was a bad time for me to get married because I was going to be leaving!

So you were married and then you left for three years. Did you get to see each other at all while you were in the service?

I didn't get a furlough or anything. We didn't see each other for three years, and she was pregnant at that time.

How did the two of you meet?

Louie: You tell him!

Irene: No, you tell him!

Louie: She used to work for a ranch way out in Washoe Valley between Carson City and Reno. I met her and made all my trips in a raggedy car to court her. She said we might as well get married instead of doing that! So that's how we ended up getting married!

So how long have you been married?

A little over 60 years. They threw us a big party in Reno last year.

Irene: It was a surprise party!

That must have been fun! Where did you get married?

Louie: In Reno.

Where did you go after you were drafted in the service?

All the guys from Sparks were taken to Salt Lake City and we all took our basic training in Alabama. We had 13 weeks of basic there. From there we went to Pennsylvania. They were setting us up for that African Campaign where Rommel was.

They were killing a lot of our soldiers there. Our outfit was scheduled to go over there. They trained us to go for days and days without water in that desert. It was hard basic training. Anyway, they got us ready to ship out.

The train was there all ready. I don't know how they work these things out, but as I was getting ready to get on the troop train my name was called. I started to board the train and was halfway up the steps when they called my name again. They told me to drop out of line and I didn't go.

I didn't go with those guys and they all went over there and got killed; they wiped them all out. There was one guy with us and his name was Fredericks and he was from Schurz. He was the only survivor. So they kept me there in Pennsylvania for weeks and I felt terrible because I took all my basic with those guys.

They don't tell you where you're going to go, or why the hell they pull you out for. Out of all those guys they pulled me out. I stayed there for about a month until finally they called me. I was going to be shipped out.

They put us on a troop train going out West. I thought maybe I'd get to see home but the closest we got was Denver! We started up north and we asked the conductor where the train was going. He said to Seattle.

That's how I ended up going to the Aleutian Islands. I was lucky to go up there because maybe I wouldn't be here if I'd went with that first group I took basic with. Most of those guys were Hispanic from the L.A. area.

What was it like for you back in Alabama during basic?

We'd go to visit the town once in a while.

How were you treated by the people in that area?

That was a segregated town at that time. The black people walked in the gutter when they saw a white person coming. When they rode the bus they sat in the back. I was never told to get in the back while I was in the service. I went in the bars and places where they didn't allow blacks and I never had any trouble.

Do you think it was because you were in the service?

I don't know; I can't answer that. They treated me just like anybody else. I never had any problems like that. In the state of Washington where they had a lot of Indians they questioned me and I'd show my ID with my Hispanic last name and I could drink where they wouldn't sell to Indians. I never had that kind of trouble on account of my name. Seattle was a point of embarkation where we'd go out or come in.

Louie Melendez

You went up to the Aleutians from Seattle?

I went up on the *Sacagawea* and came back after three years on that same ship. It was loaded to capacity. I slept under the stairway way down below. When we left it was wartime and we had those little lights on the ships.

We had two destroyers on each side of us, one ahead, and a sub chaser behind us. It was some rough seas. You couldn't even stand up to eat. We had railings around the tables. I was never that seasick in my life!

I was glad to get off the ship. When you did get off

everything was wobbly for three days. That Bering Sea is one of the roughest rides in the world. Coming back was just as bad! I had a son in the Navy and he said that was the roughest ride he ever had.

I was on several of the islands. I was on Adak most of the time. I was on Amanack and briefly on Kiska. I didn't see any Eskimos! Just the grey islands. I saw the sun maybe twice in three years. There was fog and rain every day. It never stopped raining day and night. It even rained on Christmas. Right now it's probably raining there! That was a hell of a place to be.

We had 50-caliber machine guns and you'd sit there all night and all day looking at the beach. You wouldn't have a chance in the world if hundreds of them came onto the beach.

Were there barracks built when you got there?

There was no such thing as barracks! You dug your foxhole and put your tent over it.

When you went up there were the Japanese still on the islands up there?

Yeah, they were on the next island. That was Kiska and Attu at the end of the chain there.

They feared the Japanese were going to invade through that island chain…

Yeah, and they were already there. To this day they never knew how they got off that island (Kiska). When we got up there to Adak that place was like a fortress. They had 10,000 Canadians soldiers dug in there, plus all the Americans. They had the Air Force there. These big bombers were falling into the ocean because they couldn't see on account of the fog. A lot of the planes didn't come back.

You could hear them sometimes when they'd crash in the ocean. It was rough up there. When I first went up there I was with the 4th Infantry in the 7th Division. We used to have to take one or two squads at a time to watch the beaches.

That was scary. We had 50-caliber machine guns and you'd sit there all night and all day looking at the beach. You wouldn't have a chance in the world if hundreds of them came onto the beach, and they say that's the only way they would have come in.

So there was a lot of tension…

Yeah, because you knew they were out there.

How long were you in the infantry?

It wasn't too long. We'd live in tents way up on the top of this hill with the wind blowing like heck. Water would pour down. In the morning you'd wake up and your cot would be soaked in water. I had an Indian guy in my outfit from Montana who'd been in a lot of the battles. He was a veteran. He said I'd have to get used to this place!

I thought I wouldn't make it! They fed us in a canopy. You ate sea rations and powdered milk. I never saw an officer in my outfit. One time I asked this guy ahead of me who looked rugged. He had his mess gear.

I asked him 'Aren't there any officers in this outfit?' He looked at me and said 'Yeah, I'm your company com mander.' Geez, he was the captain! He said he was just one of us guys. When I went to the engineers it was entirely different. It was like moving into the Waldorf! It was so nice!

When you fill out your information about what you did in civilian life I had put down that I drove trucks in the CCC. They were short on truck drivers and I was called. They told me to pack up all my gear.

There were six of us that went. I was with the 349th Engineers. The engineers were living in Quonset huts dug under the ground. Man! I went in there and they had floors, and nice beds to sleep on with nice pillows with white sheets! I couldn't believe it! They said my bunk was in there. My stuff was all clean. We had inspections in the infantry on Fridays no matter where we were.

So I started to take apart my rifle and the guy asked what I was doing. I told him I was going to clean my gear for inspection the next day. 'Inspection, what are you talking about?' he said. 'Look at my rifle!' There were cobwebs on it!

He said 'I've never even fired one of those things!' I had to get used to their ways! We went to the mess hall and I brought my mess gear. They asked what I was doing with that. They laughed and said to throw it in the garbage.

I went in there and they had tables! And plates! And waiters! It was plush. I was there a couple days and my name was called to report to the motor pool. They assigned me to a truck and I stayed with that until the end of the war. I ended up with a good job. I was behind the wheel all the time. I took troops to their bivouacs or training. On Sundays I took them to church.

When did you work on the airfields?

That was before this. There wasn't anything out there, just the ground. We'd take these graders to the field. That airfield was for B-29s to bomb Kiska. Then I went to Fort Lewis in Washington. I went back East once. After I was done in the Aleutians I did get a furlough and I came home. Then I went back to Louisiana. I hurried to get over there on time. They dismantled everything and shipped me back to Fort Lewis, and that's where I was discharged.

Did you get to write home?

Yeah, we got to write letters.

That must have been really hard to have your new husband away for so long?

Irene: It was really hard.

Louie: They censure your letters to make sure you don't give away where you're at. When the war was over we were still under wartime orders. My outfit was traveling under wartime orders on a ship; those were a bunch of sad-sack soldiers!

They were playing that song 'Sentimental Journey.' The war was over and we were going to have to go down to the Marianas Islands. We knew if they sent us there we'd be there for years because once they send you there's no rush to bring you back!

So we were about two miles out of Hawaii and we were all out on the deck lying around. The war was over and we were a bunch of downhearted guys. The captain came over the speaker and said he had good news for us.

Our orders were changed. He gave us two choices; turn the boat around for home or go to Hawaii and spend a few days there. Everybody said to turn the boat around! I was hoping to make Hawaii because I'd never seen it!

It was in the papers that we were the only outfit they ever did that to; we had the shortest trip! When we came back they sent us to separation centers. It's harder to get out than to get in, I'll tell you that! I was there four days.

They gave you examinations. Everybody took their gear and filled the garbage can! There was a lot of new gear but no one cared! I kept my mine. They were discharging guys the whole 24 hours but there were so many. I got out at seven in the evening. It was quite an experience.

You mentioned you'd been in the Civilian Conservation Corps before the war?

Yeah, I was at the one on the Pyramid Lake Reservation, but they were all over. We went to Schurz, and to Bishop and to Lone Pine. I was at Summit Lake just out of Cedarville (near Alturas) way out in the desert. We were building fences.

Was that an all-Indian CCC camp?

They were all Indians. They were from all over; I'd say there were about 60 guys. That's how I knew a lot of those guys from Hoopa, or Warm Springs, or Schurz. I was in the CCC a couple of years.

That was a disciplined life too...

Yeah, it was. But sometimes those guys would go on some benders and fight out there in the desert! But it was mostly disciplined. I think it was a good thing because at that time jobs were scarce and it was mostly young people in these camps. It kept you out of trouble and kept you occupied.

When did you move to Susanville?

My railroad job took me to Utah for over a year. I was the foreman on this crew and whenever a job came open I'd go there. My job took me to different places. When a job opened here between Alturas and Ravendale I got it and we moved here to California. Then we went back to Utah and I was promoted.

They sent me here to Likely and then to Susanville to be a track supervisor. I was 35 years old. We've been here ever since. We had been moving all around! I worked 41 years and two months for the railroads.

Did your time in the service help you in your job and your life?

It helped in a lot of ways, especially my benefits.

Why do you think so many Native people served in the military?

I don't think they give the Native people enough credit. They ridicule Native people. I give credit to these younger people that don't put up with it. They don't have to.

You've been married over 60 years, what's the secret?

Learn how to put up with each other! Know when to keep your mouth shut!

Is there anything you'd like to share with younger Native kids?

I think they need to stay away from drugs and alcohol. Not only Native Americans have that problem. Don't even get around drugs and alcohol.

He gave us two choices; turn the boat around for home or go to Hawaii and spend a few days there.

What do you do for a hobby now?

We travel a lot. My son doesn't like it; he always calls to check where we're at!

Irene: He couldn't find us one time on our anniversary. We didn't tell him where we were going.

Louie: I told him we're over 21!

Irene: We had to go someplace on our wedding anniversary by ourselves, we didn't want anyone to know where we were!

So you ran away from them!

Louie & Irene: Yeah!

Louie and his wife Irene raised three sons. They have three grandchildren and eight great-grandchildren. They were recently honored at Lassen High School for attending every home and away football game for over 30 years.

The Arsenal for Democracy

An estimated 12,000 young Indian women left their homes to work in defense industries during World War Two. They worked as riveters, welders, mechanics, and drivers.[1] **Georgiana Trull, Edith Fogus** and **Josie Valadez** helped the war effort in this capacity. From 1940 to 1945, American workers manufactured 80,000 landing craft, 300,000 aircraft, 15 million guns, 100,000 armored vehicles and tanks, and over 40 billion rounds of ammunition.[2] Besides working in factories, many Indian women gave their time as volunteers for the American Women's Volunteer Service, Civil Defense, and the Red Cross. By 1944 Native Americans at home in America bought 50 million dollars worth of war bonds.[3]

BUY WAR BONDS

In addition to helping build the "Arsenal for Democracy" at home Native Americans also bought at least 60 million dollars worth of war bonds during World War Two.
Library of Congress, Prints and Photographs Division, (LC-USZC4-1665).

The Chicago Bridge and Iron Company came to the Humboldt Bay near Eureka, California in 1942. They were contracted by the US Navy to build a facility that could be used to create floating dry docks. After December 7, 1941, the United States Navy was in desperate need of new dry dock facilities to repair damaged ships.

The floating dry dock was designed to expose a ship's bottom for examination and repair. It could be used on islands and shortened the amount of time needed to repair the ships. Several dry docks were created and used in the Humboldt Bay. Many Native American women from local tribes worked at this dock. **Josephine Peters** was one of them. They served as welders and burners and repaired ships that carried hundreds of thousands of Marines, Army, Navy and Merchant Marine personnel during the war

Georgiana Trull

I spoke with Georgiana Trull and her husband John on January 10, 2002. She is of Yurok ancestry and her home resides next to the Klamath River on traditional Yurok territory near the villages of Sregon and Pecwan. Her husband John is a Naval veteran of World War Two.

I was born at a village on the Klamath River called Sregon in 1916. My parents were Melissa and Charlie Myers. My father was Karuk Indian and my mother was full-blooded Yurok. I went to Sherman Institute for four years.

I went down there from 1932 to 1936. We didn't have any roads here at the time, but somebody from the BIA office came and got four or five of us across the river there. We went across the river and he took us down.

My first language was the Yurok language. My grandmother stayed with us and she didn't speak English. Yurok was spoken in our home all the time. I went to most of the Brush Dances around here in Weitchpec and in Hoopa.

We'd paddle down in the boat and go to the one in Requa at the mouth of the Klamath. I danced all the time. They had the Jump Dance at Pecwan too. We also went to the Jump Dance in Hoopa. I danced here at Pecwan and also at Hoopa. It's a world renewal ceremony.

You give thanks for what the Creator has given us through the year. There were a lot of Yurok families here when I was growing up. We had quite a lot of visitors. Most of the people would come visit my grandmother or my mother, so I was around old people a lot.

I went to the Hoopa boarding school a few years and they wouldn't let us speak our language. I was there from third grade to sixth grade. We wore a uniform. It was a little dress. It had a hole for your neck and arms and the rest was just straight. We had to wear black socks and black shoes. We had to stay in the dormitory there.

What did you feel when you first arrived at Sherman?

It was a surprise to be there. I don't remember how I felt; it must have been excitement. I had a close friend who went down with me so we stayed together. Then you'd meet other people so we'd all try to stay together. My friend's name was Geraldine Van Pelt.

My brother was the first in the family to go to Sherman but he didn't stay there. The boys stayed on their side and the girls stayed on their side on the campus. We went to school for half a day then we'd go to work half a day. Some of us went to sew or do laundry or home economics.

I came home after my time at Sherman. I worked in camp as a waitress. There were big logging camps at the time so I worked as a waitress until the war started. I don't remember where I was when Pearl Harbor happened. A government worker came around and suggested we go down to Sherman to go to welding class. At first I went down to be in nursing but then I went into welding.

When this government person came through, did he ask just Indian people to go?

Yes, because he was working for the government. It was something exciting to do, and I wanted to be patriotic.

Edith Fogus (at left) and friend Georgiana Trull in welding uniforms in 1943.
Photo courtesy of Edith Fogus.

How long did it take to learn how to weld?

It took about a month. There were quite a few of us from different areas and different tribes. Then I went to San Diego. I worked at the biggest part of the Ryan Aircraft Factory. Then I worked at a place called Solar Aircraft.

There were other Indian ladies at these places. I had a friend who also came from Sherman. She worked there with me but left before the war ended. We never saw each other after that. Last year I was going to visit my grandson in Tucson, Arizona.

Glenn Moore told me that my friend lived there in Tucson. He gave me her address and phone number. So this past spring break I called her up before I went down there. After 50 years I wondered what she looked like, and she probably wondered what I looked like!

Georgiana Trull

Then we saw each other, and she lives right near where my grandson lives! Her name is Anita. We were looking at pictures of our grandsons, and my grandson knew hers from where he worked.

How long did you work at the first aircraft factory?

I worked there for a couple of years, until the war was about halfway over. Then I worked at Solar. We worked on all the different aircraft parts. We wore coveralls and boot-type shoes. I worked the swing shift while I was there.

They had three shifts when I was there. They had the day shift, the swing shift, and the night shift. We stayed in a regular apartment while we worked. San Diego was a lot of fun. We worked hard, but we had good times.

We didn't get any special time off, like Thanksgiving,

or New Year's. During the war we had to work all through that. They gave us stamps for food. We listened to President Roosevelt on the radio.

Did you ever talk with your friends about the possibility of the U.S. losing the war?

Yes, we talked about it. We dreaded the thought of Japanese rule.

What were some fun things you would do?

Oh, we'd go to the movies, or bowling, or we'd go dancing. I had roommates. One was Edith Fogus and the other was Anita. I knew Edith from Hoopa. She's younger than I am. I knew her brothers and her older sisters because I went to school with them in Hoopa.

I began working with the Yurok language a while after that. A lot of the elders didn't want to go work in the schools so they asked me to.

Where were you when the war ended?

I was still working there in San Diego. I worked as a welder for at least a year after the war ended. People were relieved when Germany surrendered. Everybody was happy.

How about when Japan surrendered?

It was the same way. The servicemen threw their hats in the air.

Did you and your friends ever wonder about what an atomic bomb was?

Yes, we wondered about it but we didn't really pay too much attention to it. We hadn't read much about it. After my time in San Diego I came home. I was living in Eureka working in the fisheries when I met my husband. We were married in 1956.

We moved up here when John got work in the woods. We were supposed to just move for the season, but here we are 50 years later! I began working with the Yurok language a while after that. A lot of the elders didn't want to go work in the schools so they asked me to. I've been working with the language for almost 30 years. It makes me feel real good when young people take an interest in the language.

Did you have any other family members who served during the war?

My uncle Donald Myers was in the Army. My nephew Dewey served in Vietnam and my son Dickie was in the service also. I'm very proud of their contributions. Even now a lot of Indians volunteer in the service.

They say this is their country too, and they are doing something for their country that they love. They feel it's their duty to protect their country.

Georgiana continues to teach the Yurok language. She has nine grandchildren and 10 great-grandchildren, and is very proud of them when they participate in their culture. She has a book titled Georgiana Trull's Yurok Language Conversation Book that was recently published and is widely used by Yurok community members.

Edith Fogus

1924- 2007

Edith Fogus met with me on Nov. 30, 2001 at her home in Hoopa, Ca. Edith is of Hupa and Redwood Creek ancestry. She has been a traditional dancer in the Brush Dance ceremony and comes from a family of traditional dancers and doctors.

I was born in 1924 and had six brothers and a sister. I graduated from eighth grade here in Hoopa. When I first started school here for the first two years it was still a boarding school and run like a military school.

We lived in a dormitory where they had all the buildings. The boys were on one side and the girls were on the other side of the campus where houses are built now. There's nothing but houses there now, but there used to be a parade ground where we used to have to march around.

We marched to the dining room and we marched back. There was a dress code. On weekends we had to dress for Sunday school; we had blue skirts, and a white blouse and a red tie. You had to have black stocking and shined shoes. We had cotton dresses during the week.

How old were you when you first started attending the Brush Dances here?

You were supposed to be a teenager to dance. They have younger kids in them now. I was a teenager when I first danced. My father's folks were ceremonial dance leaders. My father was Maynard Baldy and my mother was Nellie. She was Redwood Creek Indian and my father was Hupa.

What other ceremonies have you attended?

I go to the Deerskin Dance and the Jump Dance here in Hoopa. I leach acorns for them, and when I'm able I help them cook it. I'm kind of a consultant with Melody (her grandniece) in learning the Hupa language. She's good at it.

How did you learn the Hupa language?

We spoke it at home. We used both English and the Indian language. Redwood Creek is similar to the Hupa language. My first languages were Hupa and Redwood Creek.

Were you allowed to speak your Indian language at the boarding school?

No.

Did they ever punish kids for doing that?

Yes, you had to work for your punishment. You had to wax floors with a mop on your hands and knees until it shined. They made your work like that for punishment. My baby brother died when I was in boarding school.

Some of us at school were confined to one dormitory because we all had mumps. I didn't get to go to my baby brother's funeral. Most of the kids that lived here, their folks came after them on weekends and took them home. They had to be back in school by Monday.

After it turned into a public school they used the same buildings. Later on they tore some of them down. I left after the eighth grade and went to Riverside, California. I went to Sherman Institute. I liked it and I even stayed there one summer.

The students who stayed there worked for people around Riverside. There were a lot of ranchers growing oranges. There was nothing but orange groves around the place. The streetcar came by the school so there was transportation to downtown Riverside. I was in the band so I got to travel with the football team. We got to travel and I liked that part of it.

Edith Fogus in welding uniform in 1943.
Photo courtesy of Edith Fogus.

Can you describe what Sherman looked like?

There were different buildings for older boys and older girls. Younger boys stayed together and younger girls stayed together. Down on one end of the grounds they had all the shops where you could learn the trade.

Boys did all the cooking at the school. The girls did all the laundry. We went to school in the mornings and in the afternoon we would do laundry. There was a hospital there so some of them took nursing and some took cosmetology.

There were different workshops and I took welding. I went to welding school there. I think it was six months and you had to pass a test. I passed my test so six months after my senior year I went to San Diego to work for Solar Aircraft in an aircraft factory.

Why did you decide to do that?

Well, it was the same subject. I could have gone back and graduated but I didn't. I took a test there and they sent it to the Army and the Navy. They went over it with a fine-tooth comb to see how good you were. I rented a room on Union Street at a boarding house. Georgiana Trull did the same thing and we roomed together.

Did you know Georgiana before that?

Yeah, I knew of her and her brother Everett.

What would be a typical day for you at the factory?

I worked from four until 11 at night. I would go home or go to a movie. But the next night you better be good at your welding! You might drop asleep because everything was the same every time. You did the same thing over and over again.

You had to wear a badge to get through the gate and got Saturday and Sunday off. I did the acetylene welding. I welded together parts for airplanes. I worked on B-24s and P-38s. I worked on mostly the manifolds for them. You had to weld it just right.

It had to be strong with no pinholes otherwise they brought it back to you and you had to do it over again. There was a guy who would walk around with a cart. He would stack those parts on a table and you had to weld them together. It was kind of a monotonous job.

We had a stamp at the end of the job, it was kind of like a little chisel, and we'd put our stamp on the part so they would know whose it was. It went through the sandblaster after that and then went to where they tested it.

You had to have a really steady hand and not be nervous. You had goggles when you used the torch. We also had a hairnet. The flux that you put on before you weld the seam, every once in a while your torch would make it pop and all the sparks would fly all over you. I had holes in my uniform from that.

Were there any other Indian ladies that worked with you?

Not in my department. Long after the war they turned that aircraft factory back into a tractor factory.

Would you and Georgiana talk about your work?

We didn't talk about the work! We talked about where we'd go have dinner or something. We'd go to the zoo, something to take our mind off work. I worked there for two years, from 1943 to 1945.

You had to have stamps to get meat, butter, and all that stuff. We would go to Tijuana, Mexico if we wanted a good steak dinner, or to get nylon stockings. We went to Mexico to go shopping. On our days off we would go to the park.

You had to have stamps to get meat, butter, and all that stuff. We would go to Tijuana, Mexico if we wanted a good steak dinner, or to get nylon stockings.

What would you wear at the aircraft factory?

We had a uniform. We had a shield on our sleeve and wore a badge. You could bring your own lunch and they had snack bar where you could buy fruit if you could afford it. I don't remember how much we made, but it wasn't very much.

It was enough to pay your room and board, which was expensive. We were close enough so I could run down the hill to work. I'd go through the Italian section of town. A lot of fishermen were there, it was right close to the beach. The aircraft factory was across the highway that came into town. We'd go across the highway to work.

Was San Diego a big place back then?

Well, when the servicemen were there it was. There was a Marine Corps base not far from there. Off the coast there was an island and on one end there was a Navy base. I don't know about the Army, but Camp Pendleton wasn't far away. On the weekend the town was just full of Navy personnel and Marines.

Edith Fogus

Where were you when the war ended?

I was home here living in Eureka. My sister lived in Eureka because her husband worked on the docks. Everybody was pretty happy the war was over. The hard times were over with. You had to go without a lot of things.

Why do you think so many Indian people served in the military?

I don't know, it seemed to me like they didn't have to. A lot of them volunteered. Some were drafted, but two of my brothers volunteered; they were in the Navy. I grew up with five brothers and one sister so I was kind of a tomboy!

Edith Fogus lived in Hoopa and attended the White Deerskin and Jump Dance ceremonies along with her family. She also worked with the Hupa language as much as possible. Her family is proud of her contributions to the Hupa culture.

Josie Valadez

I spoke with Josie and Al Valadez at their home on June 5, 2003. During my interview with Al we looked at some family albums and I noticed that Josie had spent time as a welder during the war. She agreed to talk and share about some of her experiences during World War Two.

I was born and raised here in Susanville. My mother's maiden name was Grace Joaquin and my step-dad's name was Felix Guiterrez. My mother was born and raised here too. She was mostly Paiute and part Pit River and Maidu.

They bought my uncle's cabin here on the Rancheria in the early 1930s. I had four brothers and one sister. Clyde was the oldest; I was next, then Ramona, Leo, Budge and Bob.

What did your step-father do?

He was a logger and worked in the woods. My mother stayed home and took care of kids and did housework for other families.

Were there any other Indian families nearby when you were growing up?

Yes, there were the Calvins, the Dixons and some others.

What type of food did you eat when you were growing up?

Beans and tortillas, and my mother also made fry bread and biscuits like most people. My brothers used to go and hunt jackrabbits. We had family all over the place here and in Nevada. My mother spoke Paiute when my family came over. The aunts all spoke Paiute. My mother went to Stewart because her mother and father died.

Did she ever talk about what it was like?

No, not too much. She never talked about it. She spoke Paiute until the day she died. People still speak the language. I understood some of it but I never could speak it.

What year were you born?

Al: Ha! That's the question you should never ask!

I tried to sneak it in there!

Josie: 1924. I guess it's nothing to be ashamed of!

No, not at all. The reason I ask is I was wondering what life was like for your family during the Depression in the 1930s...

We never had much anyway. As long as we had food

on the table we were all satisfied. We were all born here in Susanville. We went to Washington Elementary School. There were two stone buildings where Credence is now. I went there until I went to eighth grade over by where the swimming pool is. Then I went to Sherman.

Were there any other Indian kids at the school here in Susanville?

The only one I remember was my cousin but she's passed away.

How did you go to Sherman?

I had relatives that were going there and they said it was nice. So I told my mother I wanted to go too. She found out how to get me over there. They had a bus driver here and he used to take a lot of kids from this area to Riverside. The government paid him.

Did you go by yourself?

No, there were other kids.

So it wasn't that scary?

No, they had a fixed lunch for us on the bus. We were just like any bunch of kids all talking and laughing. There were a lot of older kids there. It was exciting to see another part of the country. I was in my early teens.

I went to Sherman for about five years. We'd come home every summer. I stayed in the girls' dorm. They had the younger ones in one building and juniors and seniors in another building. They had it divided into units with six or seven beds to a unit. Then they had a small room where our counselor stayed.

You could work in the kitchen, and they had sewing, or you could work in the hospital or day care center. My favorite was the kitchen! We learned more in cooking class. It all depended on if you liked it.

You probably made some good friends while you were there?

Oh yeah, I had two good buddies and we went from seventh grade through the 12th grade. One was a mission gal, here name was Alma Coda; she was from the lower part of California. The other one was Edith Preston from Alturas.

What grade were you in when the war started?

I was a senior. We heard it on the radio. They started different programs like welding because we were at war. They set that up for anybody that wanted to volunteer. It was voluntary.

Why did you choose to volunteer for something like that?

It was something I'd never done before and it seemed interesting. All of my friends and my cousin went for it. You signed up and they took you in. You had to take a test after being there for so long.

After you pass the test they find a job for you. A lot of us ended up in San Diego. They made arrangements whenever somebody passed the test to do the welding. They'd find a place for us to stay.

What were some of the tools you'd use?

It was mostly welding-type tools, like an acetylene torch with different heads. We mostly worked with light metal because we worked with on parts for airplanes. That was all light welding, it wasn't heavy welding.

Al: You guys didn't get to weld tanks did you?

Josie: No, it was all light welding.

Did you wear the protective gear?

We had goggles and our hair was tied up. We couldn't have anything hanging down. We wore nets and bandanas.

Did you get to stay with other Indian women while you were there?

Yeah. We stayed in private homes. This elderly woman and her husband had a two story home. We ate out a lot because all she did was rent out bedrooms. That's where most of us stayed.

Did your two friends also work in welding?

We all did.

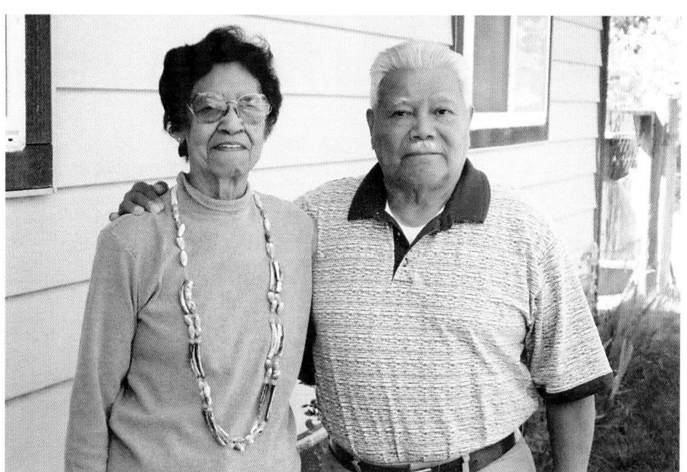

Al and Josie Valadez

Did you work in a hangar, or a warehouse?

No, we worked in a factory. It was a big building where they made parts for planes. We worked for Solar Aircraft. They had benches where they'd place you. They had parts delivered to your one desk.

Did you work on one specific part or on many different parts?

There were a lot of different shapes; it was a variety. I remember being on the swing shift and I remember being on the graveyard shift. They changed every once in a while. I was on all three shifts. We worked on all the small parts, but I don't remember which type of planes.

There were thousands of our men that flew in planes that you helped build. When you think of that what do you feel?

Well, at least I did something! I couldn't hold a gun

but we helped in some way.

Did you follow the war or talk about it with your friends?

No, we were mostly working. We came home before the war ended. Alma and I worked out at Herlong dipping boxes in oil and they used this to pack bombs.

So you were still working for the war effort, but just out at the military base in Herlong?

Yes, I don't remember, but we did that for about two years. We were there when the war ended. Maude Peconam and Alma and I worked there.

You had one brother, Clyde Northrup, who was in the service during the war...

Yeah, Leo and Budge went in afterwards. Clyde wasn't much of a writer. He was a tank operator in the Third Army.

Josie Valadez (second from right) and fellow welding students at the Sherman Indian Boarding School. ca. 1942-43
Photo courtesy of Al and Josie Valdez.

When the war ended, did you stop work out at Herlong?

After a while I quit and Alma went back home. I ended up working in a box factory until we moved to Gallup (New Mexico), and I didn't work after that, I raised the kids.

Well, that's work in itself! How did you know Al?

We knew their family for a long time. My mother knew their family for years. I went to school with his sister at Sherman. We have three children, five grandchildren, and four great-grandchilren.

So you have a big family! When did you move to this house?

Well, we've stayed near here with my mother off and on. We moved into this house in 1965. There were already homes up here. When I was younger I lived here before this was a Rancheria. This was the second round of houses that we moved into. They had a first round of smaller houses built and ours was in the second.

So you and your family have sure seen a lot of change in this area...

Oh yeah, we saw it when it was nothing but rocks and sage brush!

Al: Rocks and sage brush!

Both of your families have been here before Susanville was even a town...

Josie: Yes, back when they were kicking us around and treating us like dogs.

Al: They never thought Indians were Americans even though they came over and kicked us around. It makes me a little angry; it doesn't make me a little angry, it makes me madder than hell.

It's hard, and you both have seen your share...

Josie: We've seen our share of change!

Looking back, you both helped to defend American society...

Josie: We did our share, anyways, regardless. I think a lot of Indians did that regardless of how they were being treated. They went in and did their share.

Why do you think so many Native people have served in the U.S. military?

Al: They're doing their duty as the first Americans. It's our country.

The United States government has treated Native people so bad and for so long, what do you think could be done?

Al: Treat them better, not as someone of a different color or background...They still do it to this day. Some may think it isn't like this. That color barrier is still there. We're the first Americans. I would like to be treated as a citizen like anyone else.

Josie: Give us the right to be proud of our blood, as Indians. We were here when they came over. They should look at us in the eye. Indians have to fight for whatever they get. We are fighting for our rights.

Al Valadez, Sr. worked for over 20 years as an engineer in the Four Corners Area after his time in the war. He and his wife Josie reside in Susanville and they enjoy taking care of their grandchildren. Their family is very proud of their service to their country.

Josephine Peters

Josephine Peters is of Karuk and Shasta ancestry. She worked at the Chicago Bridge and Iron Works dry dock facility in Eureka, California during the war. I met with her at her house on May 21, 2001.

My maiden name was Josephine Grant; now it's Peters. I was born on March 8, 1923 in Somes Bar on the Salmon River in Siskiyou County. It's about three miles up the Salmon from where it empties into the Klamath River. We had 20 acres there.

The place was called the *Three Dollar Bar.* I was born at home there. I went to grammar school at Junction School. We had to walk about three miles down and back a trail. I went from first to eighth grade there.

I had five brothers and four sisters. We had to do a lot of hard work. We raised all our vegetables. We had fruit trees and canned. We had pigs, chicken, cattle, an old mule, a horse and a donkey! My mother's name was Maggie Bennett-Grant and my dad was Frank Alexander Grant.

He was born up around the Salmon. My grandfather had bought a ranch called Butler Ranch between the Forks of Salmon and Somes Bar. They had a big two-story house with a big corral and fields. The pack train would stop there for the night. My grandmother would cook for them and the next morning they'd go up the Forks.

My mother was from the Forks of Salmon. She was part of the Bennett family. Her mother was Louise Nelson and her father was John Bennett. My dad's mother's was Ellen Bruzel. She married Hugh Grant, who came from Nova Scotia to mine.

So you're Karuk from both sides of the family?

Yes, and part Shasta. My great-grandmother Jenny Red Cap was part Shasta.

Where did your grandfather Hugh Grant used to mine?

He used to mine all around the homestead at Butler's. He mined around the rivers. My dad used to mine too. He also built homes and fireplaces for people. Then he worked for the bureau of public roads.

He built framework piers for the bridges all up and down the Klamath. He also worked in Lassen County in the park area where he built monuments and gateways. He used to tell us, '100 years from now you'll go by and say Pop built this bridge!'

So what was life like during the Depression?

It didn't hit us very hard. The only thing we had to buy was flour and sugar. Everything else we canned and raised on the farm.

Did you have any basket weavers in your family?

My great-grandma Red Cap, but she died when I was only four. I used to watch her. Then I had two great-aunts, Aunt Mary from Butler and Aunt Minnie Ruben from Sandy Bar. Both of them used to make baskets when I was young.

I used to go pick sticks for them. They always made me a basket in return. Mary moved to Somes Bar across from the store. I'd get out of school early and go sit and watch her. She showed me how to make *lap-sa* plates, and how to make handle baskets. I never went into basketry much until I moved to Hoopa here. Lucy Smith lived by me and she and I used to work together making baskets.

When your great-grandma Red Cap made baskets what language did they speak?

It was mixed because some of them were Karuk and some were Shasta. My mother spoke both really well. She only spoke it when her mother or her two brothers were around. I used to sit and listen; I knew what they were talking about!

Did you learn any of it?

Some of it. Mostly the bad words, so when I went to school the teacher couldn't understand it!

The only thing I didn't like was when they put me down into a little tiny space in the floor to weld! I was kind of small and I could fit in those places.

Where did you go to school after that?

I went to Red Bluff for a year then I came back to Etna. After a year I moved to Eureka and took care of a baby for a family.

When did you first hear about World War Two?

I was back in Somes Bar when it came over the radio that war had broken out. So I immediately went back to Eureka to see what could be done and where I should go and what I should do.

How did you become involved at the shipyard?

I went there to weld. I welded on those dry-docks. They were big metal things. The only thing I didn't like was when they put me down into a little tiny space in the floor to weld! I was kind of small and could fit in those places. I kind of panicked sometimes; it would get so hot in there!

So you volunteered to work at the shipyard?

Yes.

Why did you do that?

Just to help out. There were several of us from this area (Hoopa). That's when I met the Risling family at the shipyards. Then in 1942 I married one of the boys I had met in Etna. His name was Gercia Thomas.

When war broke out they picked up all their equipment and took them to different islands where they made bases and landing fields. After he left I went back to Eureka to work in the shipyard. My husband didn't make it back. He was killed in the Battle of the Coral Sea.

Can you describe what you felt when they announced the war?

I don't know, it didn't seem to hit me at first. My dad was really upset because he was in World War One. He gave us all kinds of warnings. He was a carpenter so when he was in France had made caskets. He knew what happened all around him over there. But three of my brothers joined the Navy.

Josephine Peters with ceremonial dress.

Josephine Peters in 1942-3.
Photo courtesy of Josephine Peters.

How did it make you feel to have your brothers in the service?

Well, I had them (in the service), and I had three uncles who were all in the service. I'm very proud of them, very proud.

Josephine Peters is a prolific basket weaver and has given lectures on her knowledge of medicinal plants and herbs to universities and museums throughout the West. She enjoys attending basket weaving conferences and workshops throughout California. Her family is very proud of her contributions to her culture and her people.

The Pacific Theater

In December of 1941 the Allies had only 350,000 ground troops, less than 100 warships and around 1,000 aircraft in the Pacific. The Japanese military had 2,400,000 men, another 3,000,000 in reserve, 200 warships and over 7,000 aircraft.[1] From December 7, 1941 to the final surrender of Japan on August 15, 1945, over 268,000,000 tons of cargo left United States ports.

Imports during the war ran to 200,000,000 tons of

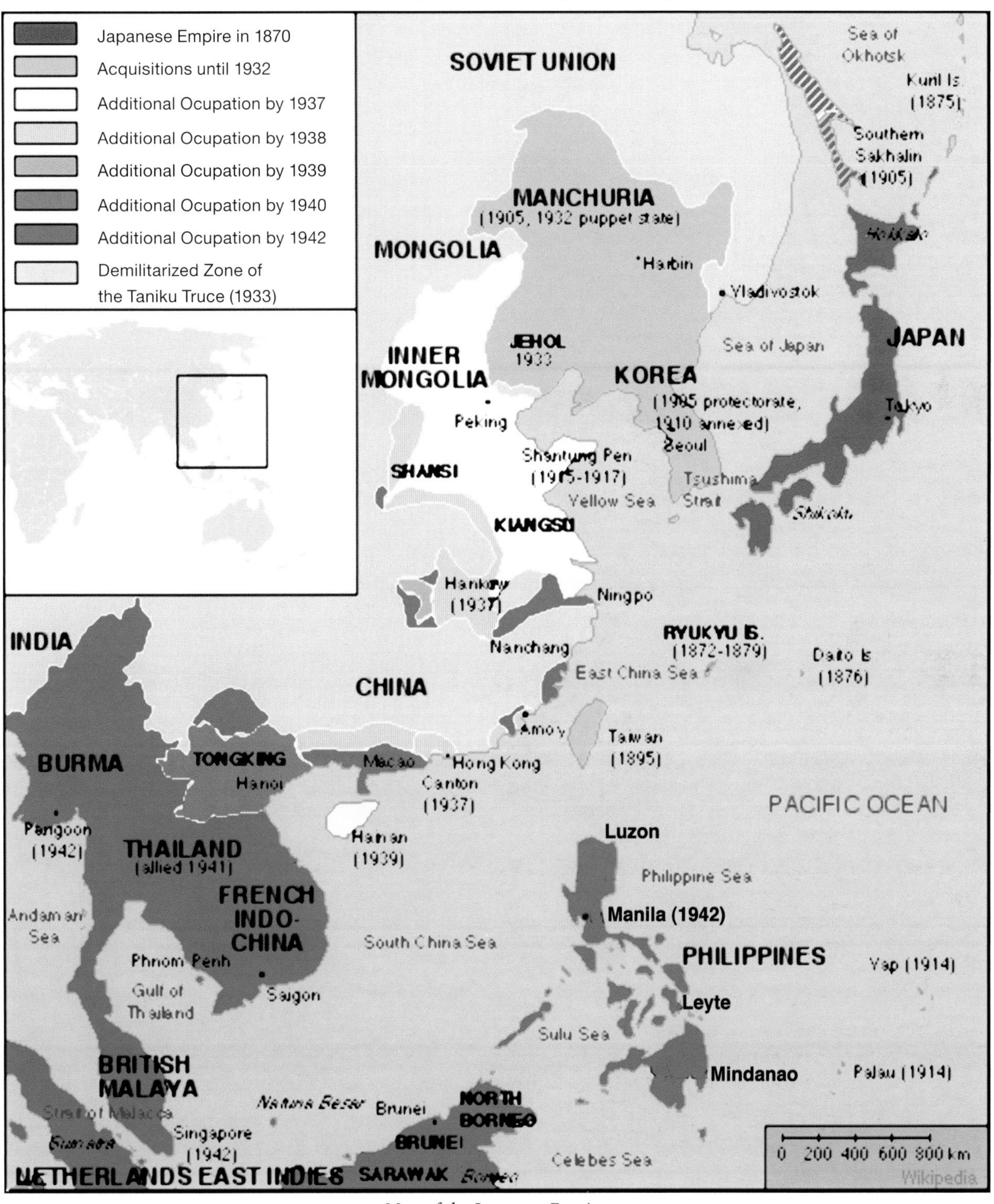

Map of the Japanese Empire.
From U.S. militery sources through wikipedia.com

dry cargo and over 64,000,000 tons of liquid cargo such as oil and lubricants.[2] Most of this cargo was brought in on ships defended by Armed Guards such as **Mervin Evans** and **Francis Allen.** From the outbreak of war to November 30, 1945 over 7,000,000 Army personnel and more than 140,000 civilians were transported overseas. Many were carried in Army and Navy transports and many were carried in Merchant Marine ships. The Armed Guard defended the Merchant Marine ships and the Army and Navy transports. During this same period over 4,000,000 military personnel were returned to the United States.[3]

Navajo Code Talkers were first used at Guadalcanal. They did not just speak in their language; they developed a dictionary and code words at Camp Pendleton, California in May of 1942.

Guadalcanal is one of the Solomon Islands, located 1,200 miles from Australia. It is about 90 miles long and 25 miles wide. Japanese forces were constructing an airfield to use in attacks on Australia. On August 7, 1942, 19,000 men of the First Marine Division, supported by Navy warships and Coast Guard personnel, invaded the island as part of Operation Watchtower. This was the first fully offensive ground attack by the United States in the Pacific. Diseases such as malaria took a tremendous toll on American service members on the island.[4]

Eventual victory at Guadalcanal was a tremendous morale boost for the U.S. and the Allies and a harbinger of doom for the Japanese. Both sides saw the battle as crucial to future success in the Pacific conflict. The First Marine Division had staged an emphatic stand and won hard-fought battles in the island jungle against Japanese reinforcements. The Second Marine Division reinforced the island in the later part of 1942 through early 1943. **Ned Crutcher** was part of this force. The Second Marine Division was formally activated in February of 1941. Elements of the Second Marine Division saw action all across the Pacific. They fought at Tarawa, Saipan, Tinian and Okinawa. Elements of the division eventually landed on Japan itself at the end of the war for occupation duty.

Navajo Code Talkers were first used at Guadalcanal. They did not just speak in their language; they developed a dictionary and code words at Camp Pendleton, California in May of 1942. The Code Talker's primary job was to transmit information on tactics and troop movements, orders and other vital battlefield communications over phone lines and radios. They also performed other Marine duties. Over 400 Navajo Code Talkers had served by the end of the war.[5]

The Japanese never broke the Navajo code, which remained classified until 1968. This was the only code never broken during the war. Code Talkers took part in almost every assault the U.S. Marines conducted in the Pacific from 1942 to 1945. This code and the successful relays by Navajo Code Talkers were a crucial element in the success of the American war effort in the Pacific. Before World War Two broke out Germany had sent teams of anthropologists to America in an attempt to study and translate American Indian languages. Fortunately, the Japanese did not attempt this, and the Germans were not successful in their efforts to translate indigenous languages in America at that time.[6]

After the attack at Pearl Harbor the United States Navy began to build up and repair its fleet; aircraft carriers, destroyers, cruisers, battleships, submarines, Liberty ships, minelayers, landing craft, patrol torpedo boats and other vessels were the main weapons used by the Navy on a front that stretched over thousands of miles of ocean. Naval air power was also a decisive tool in the eventual American victory in the Pacific. Fighter planes, scout bombers, observation scouts, patrol bombers, seaplanes, transport and utility planes were all used during the fighting.

Les Ammon served on the destroyer USS *Porterfield,* **Grant Hillman** served aboard the cruiser USS *Mobile,* **Wally Griffin** served aboard the aircraft carrier USS *Antietam,* **Darrell McCovey** served aboard an aircraft carrier, **Harold Blake** served on a battleship and an auxiliary ship and **Gene Ryan** served aboard several different ships during the war.

Confrontations such as the Battle of the Coral Sea in May of 1942 and Midway in June of 1942 checked the Japanese advance at sea. The Coral Sea is located south of the Solomon Islands. A joint force of American and Australian ships fought the Japanese Navy to a standstill. Both sides took losses, but it was the first time Japan was forced to abandon an attack. **James Campbell, Sr.** was part of the American force at the Battle of the Coral Sea.

The Battle of Midway saw the Japanese Navy lose four carriers, almost 300 planes and 3,500 men to American forces. The Americans lost 150 aircraft, a destroyer, and over 300 men. The carrier *Yorktown* was badly damaged in the fight and was sunk by an enemy submarine two days later. The Japanese loss of their aircraft carriers removed their most potent weapon in the Pacific theater. The Americans were able to learn Japanese intentions at Midway through intercepts of radio messages [7]

The Aleutian Islands campaign was originally designed by the Japanese High Command to be a diversionary feint prior to the attack at Midway. It was hoped that the Americans would send the bulk of their fleet north to counter this threat. When that didn't happen the Japanese overwhelmed the small American force at Dutch Harbor on the island of Unalaska and then occupied the islands of Attu and Kiska. This occurred on June 3-7 in 1942.

There was some fear in America that the Japanese might try to invade through these islands, and there was strong sentiment to re-capture the territory. American forces built bases on the island chain while battling sub-freezing temperatures, thick fog, gale-force winds and icy ocean waters. Many American crew members lost their lives while flying bombing missions in terrible weather in this campaign.

In May of 1943 elements of the Seventh Infantry Division invaded Attu and fought in bitter cold against 3,000 well-entrenched Japanese soldiers. Only 28 Japanese surrendered and the Americans suffered more than 500 killed and over 1,100 wounded before Attu was taken back. In August of 1943 the island of Kiska was bombarded by Navy ships and then invaded by American forces, but the entire Japanese garrison of over 5,000 men had already been secretly evacuated.[9]

Lee Hover served aboard the USS *Dewey* during both the Midway and the Aleutian campaigns, among others. The USS *Dewey* (DD349) was built at Bath Iron Works and commissioned on October 4, 1934. She weighed 1,375 tons and carried a crew of 251. The USS *Dewey* was a Farragut-class Destroyer.

Sailors such as **Archie Thompson** and **Wilbur Smith** played a crucial role in the fast repair of Navy ships at dry docks and island bases throughout the Pacific. This kept an ever-growing number of Navy ships in combat-readiness. After the Marines and the Army took over an island combat engineers such as **Rueben Green** were put to work building vital airstrips, bunkers, headquarters buildings, watchtowers, fuel lines, barracks, and other structures. Combat engineers often worked during battles as well. Men such as **Bill Rossig** and **Kenny Childs** were part of American garrisons on these islands who stayed vigil and protected the bases against potential Japanese threats.

The United States Merchant Marine was the link between the production army at home and the fighting forces around the world in the war. The prewar total of 55,000 experienced mariners was increased to over 215,000 through U.S. Maritime Service training programs. Merchant ships faced danger from submarines, mines, armed raiders and destroyers, aircraft, kamikaze attacks and the weather. Over 8,000 Mariners were killed at sea and 12,000 were wounded.[9] **Frank Grant** served in the Merchant Marines.

The battle for the Tarawa atoll began on November 20, 1943. Betio is the name of the main island in the Tarawa atoll located in the Gilbert Island archipelago. Betio was subjected to an intense air bombardment before the invasion, and it was thought the Japanese defenders were all but wiped out. The operation, codenamed Galvanic, saw 18,000 men of the Second Marine Division take part in an amphibious landing.

The first waves of Marines, among them **Jack Madero,** had to wade through a half-mile of waist-deep water in the only accessible lagoon under withering Japanese fire. There were 5,000 Japanese soldiers deeply entrenched on the island. In 76 hellish hours the Marines lost over 1,000 killed and over 2,000 wounded. The entire Japanese garrison was wiped out. Betio is three miles long and a half-mile wide.[10]

The Third Marine Division was activated in September 1942 at Camp Elliot, California. They were deployed from January through February of 1943 to Auckland, New Zealand. They participated in the following World War II campaigns: Bougainville; the Northern Solomons; Guam; and Iwo Jima. **Kenny Sanderson** was a member of the Third Marine Division.

Operation Forager was the code name given to the U.S. Navy's invasion of Saipan, Tinian, and Guam in June of 1944. Capture of the islands would provide the Pacific Fleet with bases from which they could strike other Japanese-held islands. The Army Air Corps also needed new bases from which its new long-range bomber, the B-29, could make non-stop strikes on the Japanese home islands.

Up until that time, the U.S. sent more Marines to Iwo Jima than to any other battle; 110,000 Marines in 880 ships. In 36 days of fighting there were 25,851 U.S. Marine and Navy casualties.

The American forces landed on Saipan in June of 1944 and immediately came under heavy fire. There were 29,000 Japanese defenders on Saipan and few survived the battle, which officially ended in early July of 1944. U.S. casualties numbered more than 16,500, including over 3,400 killed in action.[11] Among the Japanese casualties was Vice Admiral Chuichi Nagumo, who led the attack at Pearl Harbor. He and his staff committed ritual suicide before the end of the battle. **Willard Carlson** saw action on Saipan and was later wounded at the battle for Tinian.

The Seabees were created in 1942. They were part of the Navy Civil Engineers Corps and were given military and construction training and followed Marine units into combat. They were not an offensive group but could be counted on to fight if the need arose. They built airfields, roads, fuel lines, barracks, and everything else needed in the war. **Jack Risling** was a Navy Seabee who served during the Battle at Iwo Jima.

Iwo Jima is an island of about 8 square miles. Mount Suribachi is the highest point on the island and is an extinct volcano. The United States needed to have land airfields as close as possible to Japan for B-29 bomber missions, so on February 19, 1945 30,000 Marines landed on Iwo Jima. The island was honeycombed with Japanese pillboxes, underground bunkers, and 16 miles of tunnels.

The Japanese commander of Iwo Jima was General Tadamichi Kuribayashi. He was educated in Canada and had toured the U.S. He based his strategy on the hope that America would not stand for heavy casualties in battle. Each Japanese soldier was to kill 10 Americans before being killed. Of the 22,000 Japanese defenders at Iwo Jima only a few survived.

Up until that time, the U.S. sent more Marines to Iwo Jima than to any other battle; 110,000 Marines in 880 ships. In 36 days of fighting there were 25,851 U.S. Marine and Navy casualties. Of these, 6,825 Americans were killed. Iwo Jima was Japanese home soil, only 650 miles from Tokyo. No foreign army in Japan's 5000-year history had stepped foot on Japanese soil. **Dave Risling's** PT boat was at Iwo Jima. By the end of the war 2,400 B-29 bombers carrying 27,000 crew members had made emergency landings on Iwo Jima.[12]

The Japanese invaded New Guinea in 1942, triggering one of the hardest-fought series of battles in World War Two. New Guinea is the world's second-largest island and contains towering mountains and hot, humid jungle. Australian and American forces fought against fanatical Japanese soldiers with few supplies and support.

In August of 1945 United States President Harry Truman ordered the only two atomic bombs to be flown from the U.S. to the B-29 air base on Saipan to use against Japan.

Exhausted soldiers fought each other at places such as Buna, Gona, and the Kokoda Trail. They also had to fight against myriad diseases as well. **Ed Mitchell** saw action as part of the 33rd Infantry Division here, **Elmer Rossig** received a Purple Heart for wounds in action as part of the 32nd Infantry Division, and my great-uncle Leonard Lowry commanded men in combat as part of the 32nd Infantry Division on New Guinea and elsewhere. The fighting did not stop in New Guinea until the end of the war.

The 11th Airborne Division was activated at Camp Mackall, North Carolina on February, 1943. Members from the Division fought in several battles in the Philippines from 1944 to 1945 and liberated several internment camps. The division moved to Okinawa to escort General MacArthur into Japan in August of 1945. They remained on occupation duty until 1949. **Charlie Bowen** was a member of this honor guard in Tokyo.

In August of 1945 United States President Harry Truman ordered the only two atomic bombs to be flown from the U.S. to the B-29 air base on Saipan to use against Japan. On August 6, 1945, the B-29 *Enola Gay* set out from the island of Tinian with the atomic bomb called "Little Boy." At 8:15 am it was released over the city of Hiroshima. The city was utterly destroyed; at least 140,000 people died from the blast and radiation sickness. After Japan refused to surrender President Truman ordered a second bomb called "Fat Man" to be used. On August 9, at 11:01 am the B-29 *Bock's Car* released the bomb over the city of Nagasaki. Almost half the city was destroyed and at least 75,000 people died from the blast and radiation sickness.[13]

On September 2, 1945 at 9 am the Japanese signed the documents of surrender on the deck of the battleship *USS Missouri*. V-J (Victory in Japan) Day is celebrated on August 15th, the day Japan announced its surrender. American troops had already landed in Japan and were taking control before the surrender ceremony. General Douglas MacArthur was appointed Supreme Commander, Allied Powers and was the new military governor of Japan.

Over 15 million Allied soldiers lost their lives in World War Two. Over 50 million civilians from Allied countries died. From the Axis countries almost seven million soldiers died and almost four million civilians perished during the war. These are estimated numbers; no one can ever know for certain exactly how many people died in World War Two.

Mervin Evans

1921- 2004

Mervin Evans is my relative on my father's side. He and my grandfather Stan are cousins. Mervin served in the U.S. Navy during the war. Mervin and his late wife Ida babysat me when I was a young boy. I always looked up to him as a very special person. He is the first person I asked to do an interview. Had he said no, I probably wouldn't have continued with this book. As it was, he said yes, and during his first interview he went into his bedroom and returned with a photograph of himself with several buddies on leave in Egypt during the war. They were in front of a pyramid and the Great Sphinx. This photograph absolutely stunned me.

Mervin Evans ca. 1942-3
Photo courtesy of Mervin Evans.

I had only known Mervin through interacting with him in the small town of Susanville. I had no knowledge of him being part of this epic in history known as World

War Two. Where else had he gone? And what did my other family members do during the war? I sat down with him on a cold winter day in January 28 and again on April 15 of 2000. I am honored to say that my first name is Mervin; I was named after this man.

On my dad's side I'm Pit River; my mother's Shoshone. Their names are George and Maggie Evans. The Pit River people came from near Alturas to down by Eagle Lake and that's as far as they came.

John was the only full brother I had. Then there was Willis, Oliver, Tom and Les, Lucy, Mabel, Harriet and Ora. I graduated from Sherman Indian School in 1941. I was in Sherman there on December 7 when the Japanese bombed Pearl Harbor. And old Billy Beck and I went to San Bernardino.

We were going to sign up for the Navy. My dad wouldn't OK for me to sign up. He wanted me to come home first. So Beck went in and I didn't. I was lucky because my dad died that summer. Then I went one year at junior college here in Susanville.

How come your dad didn't want you to sign up?

The only thing I can figure is he knew he wasn't going to live much longer. My mother died the year before in 1940. He was just grieving so bad; I guess he knew he didn't have much longer. He said 'I want you to come home first before you go into the Navy.' So I came home after I graduated then he died that summer.

Before the war happened, growing up here in Susanville, were there any times you were treated different because you were Indian?

Mervin's brother Johnny Evans in early 1945. Photo courtesy of Virginia Aguilar.

Well, not here in Susanville, everybody knew me, and knew all the Indian boys here. If you ever left town then you could see the difference. Like if you ever went to Reno or San Francisco or something like that.

Then they were prejudiced people, you know. I know when we were growing up my brother and I went to San Francisco for about three months to go to school and all we did over there was fight because they'd call us names and everything like that. But here in Susanville, everybody respected us here. But when you left town that was different.

I would go to the beach and watch the ships come in and out all the time. So I decided that's what I'm going to do if I ever go in the service; join the Navy.

None of that happened during the war?

No, not in the service.

Why did you want to be part of the Navy?

I didn't like the thought of sleeping in those foxholes and eating that hardtack. I always did like water. Every time we went to San Francisco with my mother and dad I would go to the beach and watch the ships come in and out all the time.

I'd just stand there and watch them come in and out. So I decided that's what I'm going to do if I ever go in the service; join the Navy. It was either that or go in the Army.

When I was going to junior college here in Susanville they were drafting boys right and left out of school. We had a football team and had to cancel our games because most of the boys were in the service. We didn't have enough to field a team. And as soon as school let out the Army was right there waiting for me. So right after I graduated junior college here that summer in June I went right straight to Reno, Nevada and signed up. Within two weeks I was in San Diego in boot camp.

Then they put us aboard ship. I was a gunner aboard these merchant ships. They call it the Armed Guard. I think there were 28 of us gunners on board each ship. That was our job, to man all the guns on them.

In the Navy we had a clean sack to get into, you know, you had your three meals a day; you didn't have to eat out of cans and stuff. That's one reason I liked the Navy, you had a place to sleep; a good clean bed. The only thing was if your ship sunk, well, you better be a good swimmer. You had a long way to swim!

And I got torpedoed off our first ship, off of Australia. We got torpedoed out there; lay adrift for three days. Our ship didn't sink. They hit what they call the number five hole, the cargo space.

It blew from the keel to the main deck. Just blew that whole compartment out. But we had wool in the bottom hole, that's what saved the ship from busting out and sinking. We lay adrift there for three days until they found us and towed us into Sydney, Australia.

Did you spend any time in Australia, on any of the islands there?

Well, just in Sydney. We stayed there in Sydney after we got towed back. I was there a little over a month. Then they shipped us back. After we got a ship, a troop ship took us; Navy, Marines and Army soldiers. Guys that had enough time overseas, they took them home.

Were you as an American welcome in Australia?

Oh yeah! The only bad time was these three great big transports; the *Queen Mary,* the *Aquitania* and one other big troop ship came in. They brought these Australians back from somewhere. Those guys had dropped these leaflets saying the Americans were going with your women while you guys are all over here fighting.

So we had a big, I didn't get into it, I had duty that day, but there were a lot of men fighting at the park. They just met right there. They threatened the Americans to leave or that's it.

Mervin Evans (far right on donkey) and ship mates touring the Sphinx and the Great Pyramids in Egypt in 1943.
Photo courtesy of Mervin Evans.

So they had a big free-for-all out there! Then after that things got pretty hot there. You had to walk around in groups, otherwise they would jump you. But otherwise it was good. They were good people. You can't blame them. When those guys dropped those leaflets and said what the Americans were doing over there that kind of riled them up.

How many years did you serve in the war?

I think it was a little over three-and-a-half years.

Were there any other countries that you visited?

Oh yeah, the second ship I caught and went back to Australia. Then I went around the world; I went to the Indian Ocean, the Red Sea and the Mediterranean. Then I went to New York, then to Boston, from there to Greenland and cut across over to Europe. We had airplane parts and tank parts to take over there.

So your ship supplied both fronts, the Pacific and in Europe?

Yeah, the Pacific and the Atlantic. Then the last ship I caught was a Victory ship. We had a suicide dive on that one off of Okinawa. That was in early '45, when we had that suicide dive on it. We didn't sink; he hit the after mast. We lost three; two sailors and one merchant marine got killed on that one.

Did you ever feel afraid at any time in the service?

Afraid? No, that never entered my mind at any time. I don't think a guy thinks about that. Maybe some do, but I just never thought that way. I figured I was going to come home and that would be it, you know. I never figured I'd get killed.

I had some narrow escapes, but I never figured that something like that would happen. We had one kid aboard ship; he said he could see he was going to get killed. And sure as heck, when we got that suicide dive, he was one of them.

Right up there (Mervin points to a shelf in his house) is a piece of a bomb. I took a hacksaw; it's got Japanese writing on it. I cut that off. My buddy took another piece. It was a tail section of a 500-pound bomb.

They had three 500-pound bombs drop aboard that Betty, they called them. So he took a hacksaw and cut it off, right on there it was stamped 'Made in the USA.' Before the war we shipped all our metal over there and they were making bombs out of all of it.

I cut that piece there. A man told me that it's supposed to mean 'Death to the Americans.' I had to hide that because you couldn't bring anything back. I brought it home.

Did you bring anything else?

All these little pieces from Cairo, Egypt. (Mervin is pointing to small white replicas of pyramids and a sphinx.) That little sphinx is from over there in Cairo, over by the pyramids. I brought those back; those are the only things I brought back from overseas.

So you got to see the pyramids?

Yeah, we rode camels over there! Oh, that was something to see. Then we'd go down in those tombs where they buried people. It's nice and cold down in there.

Yeah, we went all along, all through the pyramids and a couple of tombs that were open, and walk down in them. It's where the Pharaohs were. That was the last part of '43.

Did you ever get a sense of how the overall war was going, or were you just concerned with your job?

No, we were too busy with what we had to do. We didn't know anything about what was going on. All we did was come back to the States and load up with tanks and airplane parts and stuff; then we'd take them overseas, drop them off, turn around, come back and get another load and head back overseas again.

Then I was on a tanker. We carried heavy crude oil for this battle wagon. And this tanker was 500 feet long. We'd go through the Panama Canal into the Atlantic. There's a little island there. We'd fuel up, go back through the lots and go over to the Marshall Islands. We'd fuel up two Navy tankers, then the battle wagon, then heavy cruisers. I spent almost a year on that tanker.

Was there ever any talk about America losing the war?

No, we never heard anything about losing it. Everybody listened to old Tokyo Rose; we listened to her on the radio. Boy, she'd say the Americans are getting slaughtered here and there, you know.

And we just laughed at her, you know. But every day she'd come on. We were overseas there. And you could turn on the radio and here she'd come on. I can't remember what time it was in the afternoon.

And she would play some all-American music, you know. And then she'd tell us that we lost this ship, that ship, this ship. 'Our Navy is sinking all your ships. All your soldiers are getting killed.' It was really just the opposite.

So it seems like there was a lot of propaganda.

Oh yeah, a lot of propaganda. You could hear all kinds of different things.

Can you name any other Indian people that you knew that served during the war?

Leonard Lowry, Stan, Jack Madero...that's from Susanville here. Bill Evans, Ed Jackson, all the Indian boys here my age went into the service. Most of them were in the Army, some went in the Marines, some in the Navy. Like Bill Evans, he was in the Navy. He made torpedoes, he worked on torpedoes.

I was wondering, when you were in the service, was there any boxing?

I did box on that first ship I was on. It was a troop ship. We carried 1,500 troops; soldiers and Marines. That's the one I lost, that I got torpedoed on. We used to have a smoker every night on that number five hole back there.

We'd box back there. I'll tell you a good one; this Marine, I guess he was a tough guy, meaner than heck. We had a Mexican kid who did a little fighting himself. He got up there to fight and this Marine tore him all up.

I had the watch from four to eight in the afternoon. Well this friend of mine said, 'I got a friend that will fight him.' He called me, 'Hey Chief, come on down and box this guy.'

I loved to box, I said OK. I took my headphones off and gave them to another guy to stand watch for me. So I went down to box this Marine. We had a chaplain who was the referee.

'Just an exhibition,' he said, 'Just go out and take it easy on each other.' I said OK. But I watched that Marine; he had no mercy on whoever he fought.

So when we started; boy, the first thing he did, he threw a right hand, and I went under. I ducked it. I thought, 'Uh oh, we're going to go at it now.'

We were on that big Liberty; there were these groundswells, and the ship would roll, back and forth. Well, as soon as the ship would come up like this, I'd turn him, and I'd get on the high side; I'd come down and just pound the hell out of him. When the ship rolled back this way I'd turn him and get him below me. And I just pounded the heck out of him for three rounds.

And what made me feel so good, after the chaplain raised my hand, you know, as the winner, all those Marines ran over there and picked me up and put me on their shoulders, and carried me back to the mess hall! I never expected that!

We had a suicide dive on that one off of Okinawa. That was in early '45, when we had that suicide dive on it. We didn't sink; he hit the after mast.

I thought they'd be madder than heck at me for beating their Marine! They said, 'Oh we're glad you beat him up so bad!' He did that to them, he used to beat them up. But that surprised me; a bunch of Marines just picked me up and carried me on their shoulders.

That made me feel good, you know! After that, I went back on watch the next day, and they were boxing, but that Marine never did go back in there to box. Then, in New Zealand, we were in a bar having a few beers.

Here comes about four or five New Zealanders walking in there. We were sitting at a table, our bunch. This guy got up and said, 'I'm the middleweight champion of New Zealand, anybody want to box me?'

Sure enough, my old buddy says, 'Yeah, I got a guy here that will fight you.' He got me in more darn trouble! So I took off my little white hat, set it on the table. We just got up, sparring around. Boy, he threw a right hand and he meant to knock me cold.

I just blocked it like that, then I came down, I knocked him colder than hell. My buddy Joe, the one who always got me in these skirmishes, said 'There's a new middleweight champ of New Zealand!' Those guys packed up their stuff and left.

I was discharged in 1945 at that little island over there in between Oakland and San Francisco. They had a Navy station right there. That's where they dropped me off. Then from there I went to Livermore. That's where I got my discharge. Then I came home.

How did you come home, did you drive?

No, I hitchhiked. In those days, a serviceman, they'd pick you up just then. You didn't have to stand out there for hours and hours. A car would come by and they'd see you and just pick you right up. So that's the way most of the boys would do it.

What was the reaction of the people when you got home, were they glad and happy?

Oh yeah, everybody was happy. Yeah, we pulled in

and Leonard Lowry was here; and Stan, and Jack Madero. We all went out and had a great time, all of us.

Did you have any other relatives that served in World War Two?

Oh yeah, my brother John, just a year-and-a-half older than me. He went in the Army. And Les Evans; he went in but they let him out after he was too old. He was in the Air Force for a while on a ground crew.

But then they sent him home because he was up in his forties. John was in the Army. He was playing softball or baseball in England. He got hit in the shin and got a bone bruise; then TB set in on the bone.

Mervin Evans

They didn't know what the hell was wrong with him. They operated on him. Then they finally realized he had TB on the bone. By that time it was all through him. He passed away here. They shipped him to the States down there at Livermore. He passed away at a sanitarium there. That was early '45.

Did you get to see him before he passed on?

Yes, I got home. I was on Treasure Island getting ready to ship out and my sister called and said he was real bad. I got a 10-day emergency leave then I hitch-hiked from Long Beach to Livermore. I stayed with him for those 10 days.

I went back to Treasure Island then I got word that he passed away. I told my commanding officer my brother just died and I need another leave. He said we can't give you anymore. I told him 'If I don't get it I'll just go over the hill. The first Liberty boat I see I'll get on.'

So I told the chaplain. I said the first Liberty I get, I'm gone. They can come get me in Susanville; I'll be there with my brother. So the chaplain talked to the officer; he got me an extra 10 days. I got to come home and bury him. Then I went back.

What year did your brother go in the service?

1941 I think. They drafted him. He was 25 when he passed away.

Did you ever go through any kind of an emotional letdown? During the war, you have this intense level of emotions...

No, that was one good thing. I never had to worry about that. I had some narrow escapes, like I said, I was torpedoed off Australia and had a suicide dive off Okinawa.

I was just missed by two torpedoes going back on the second ship. They just missed us. I was on watch. I watched those two torpedoes go across the bow. But as far as getting a letdown emotionally, it didn't bother me that way. I just figured I had a job to do.

Was there any difference here in Susanville after the war?

I didn't see any difference other than the town grew a lot faster after. People started moving out of the cities and coming here. I was born and raised here.

You've stayed active in veteran's affairs and gatherings, when did those start happening? Did you meet every year?

When I joined the VFW (Veterans of Foreign Wars), they met every month. I got out in '45 then we made an all-Indian reunion. We sent out letters all over. All the Indians that were in the service would come here every year. We've been doing that every year.

When they first started, how did they start, was it you and Grandpa Stan and some other people get together, and start it?

Yeah, we just started talking and decided we'll have an all-Indian veterans reunion. Any Indian that was in the service; men or women. If they came over we had a big dinner and had Indian dancing; Indian drums, singing.

Then we'd have a big meeting. You'd talk about which service you were in, how long you were in, stuff like that. Then we'd have a nice big dinner. Then the next Sunday morning we'd have a big breakfast. Then everybody would head home.

Can you tell me the names of some of the people who helped organize that?

Well, there was Leonard, Stan, and two of the boys from Reno; Ned Crutcher from Herlong. Andy Jackson was the one that was more or less in charge of sending flyers out to all the Indian boys. He travels all over, Andy does.

He goes to all the veterans, and service groups, their funerals. He more or less knew all the different Indians from the country. We had quite a little organization here that would meet, get it all set up, and send out the flyer. Andy would set a date then all the boys and their wives would come to it, you know.

When you got together with other Indian veterans, you talked about what, your experiences?

Yeah, we talked about the experiences we had, the places we've been.

That was probably a very good way to deal with the emotions and history...

Yeah, best to let it out instead of holding it in. That's the worst thing you can do, is hold things inside of you. You can talk it out and it helps.

Mervin Evans worked in the logging industry as a timber faller for over 30 years in the forests near Susanville. He retired in 1988. He enjoyed fishing in the lakes near Susanville and watching basketball games. He participated in veteran's parades and all-Indian gatherings. He liked to attend the Mountain Maidu religious ceremony called the Bear Dance. Mervin once dressed to represent the bear in ceremony when he was young.

Ned Crutcher

1919-2006

I spoke with Ned and his wife Wilma at their home in Herlong, Ca. It was a cold wintry day on November 30, 2000 and we talked about Ned's involvement in the Pacific during the war. Ned is of Shoshone and Paiute ancestry.

I was born in Paradise Valley north of Winnemucca but I've always been registered as being born on the McDermott Indian Reservation; that's where I belong. My mother's name was Lizzie Crutcher. I went to Stewart Indian School. I stayed there until I graduated from high school. I did miss a year of school. I went to McDermott and caught typhoid fever. They put me in a sanitarium there at the school for a year. I lost all my hair.

Was English your first language?

I know how to speak Paiute; that was my first language. I speak Shoshone, American Samoan and a little Italian.

Who taught you the Paiute language?

My grandmother. I lived with my grandmother and grandfather because my mother died when I was little and my father didn't claim us. There were three of us, me, my brother Ben and sister Birdie.

My grandmother was Jenny and my grandfather was Jack Crutcher. They raised me, then I went to Stewart and Stewart raised me! I don't regret anything about Stewart because if it hadn't been for Stewart I probably wouldn't even know English. It gave me a start, it gave me a boost.

Were there any other students at Stewart who knew the Paiute language?

Oh yes, a lot of them did. To begin with we weren't allowed to speak our own language. If you got caught speaking your own language they'd punish you.

How would they punish you?

Oh, there were a lot of methods. A new person came there from South Dakota and the severity of corporal punishment wasn't there anymore.

Did you ever see any of your fellow students be punished because of their language?

I was told that some girls were punished.

How many years did you go to Stewart?

I was there from 1932 to 1940.

When you first went there, what would your day be like?

First thing in the morning you learn to clean, make your bed. Then you go to breakfast. When you're very young you go to school all day. Later, from eighth grade on, you do your school training in the morning and then you take vocational in the afternoon.

My vocation in the beginning was house painting. At that time they used to use turpentine to thin the paint and wash the brushes. I couldn't take that because of the fumes. Maybe it was my asthma. Then I went to plumbing shop. I worked in plumbing. I alternated between plumbing shop and the dairy; that way I could drink all the milk I wanted. I was a milk freak!

A new person came there from South Dakota and the severity of corporal punishment wasn't there anymore.

I was assigned to carpentry shop one time and I didn't like it because the man there was pretty grumpy. He was an Indian fellow. I should have stayed; all of the fellows he turned out had gone to the outside to compete in the outside world.

Did they make you wear a uniform at Sherman?

They discontinued that while I was in the sanitarium. That was in 1932. I remember how it ended. People used to visit me at the hospital. They would give me clothes and stuff, and talk through the window there.

Anyway, they had a fellow there. He was a Sioux Indian. He said 'We don't need this BS.' From then on it changed, but the discipline was still the same. I was appreciative about the school, even though people say they did this to you and that; if it wasn't for Stewart I'd probably be dead a long time ago and wouldn't have had even a high school education. I appreciated it very much. It was my home.

Did you make a lot of friends?

Oh yes, you always have fellows that you buddy around with; friends for life. I boxed there from the first part of '35. The first time I boxed it was for the Golden Gloves in Reno. There was a university student there named Ray Smith from the family that owned the Harrold's Club (in Reno).

Ned Crutcher ca. 1943-4.
Photo courtesy of Ned Crutcher.

I was sort of afraid of him; he was a little bit bigger than I was. Anyway, I went out there and the first three punches I knocked him down. He never did get up! But from then on he and I were friends.

We were friends for years until he passed away. We used to go to San Francisco for Pacific Coast Tournaments. I went to the finals one time there. I boxed there for about five years in a row. I got a belt buckle for that. When I was in Stewart I gave it to a girl. That was the last time I saw that belt buckle!

What year did you graduate from Stewart?

1940. After that I was desperate for a job. I went to Salt Lake City with another Indian fellow. I hitchhiked over there. While we were there he was purchasing some clothes. As we were walking out, there was a recruiting station there.

It said to come on in. We went in there and talked to them and they signed us up. There were three of us; one white guy and us two. So they sent us to Sacramento then to San Francisco. They housed us there in order to get 14 people together to send to the recruit depot down at San Diego. So we stayed there about a week and we were sworn in as Marines. Some of the guys were cocky, a Marine there said, 'Wait until you get through boot camp, then you'll be a Marine.'

When we got there I remember this Sergeant, and pardon my language, but he said, 'Your asses belonged to your mother before, now it belongs to me for the next 14 weeks. And get your goddamn asses onto that bus. I've got you now.'

Why did you choose to be in the Marines?

I saw the uniform. I liked the uniform. The fellow at Salt Lake City was an older Marine. He had a nice story about if you enlist now you'd go to the Fourth Marine Division in China. Oh boy, that sounded good, so we signed up and were going to go to China after boot camp.

So where did you go to boot camp?

San Diego. We lived in a parade ground in two-man tents. I was with a fellow from South Dakota named Bobby. He told me, 'I don't like Indians.' So I told him, 'What the hell makes you think I like you?'

We became friends. It took 14 weeks to get through boot camp. That was rough. The discipline I learned in boarding school… I knew how to get along with people. Some of the youngsters at boot camp had never been away from momma and daddy and they had a hell of a time. They couldn't stand anyone yelling at them.

Discipline was really it at the time. If you were used to discipline like I was at Stewart it wasn't hard at all. I remember the second week I was there I dropped my rifle. A Corporal came over to me and said, 'You goddamn Indian, if you can't handle that rifle I'll get you a bow and arrow.'

What kind of weapons were you trained to use in boot camp?

They were called a Springfield 30-ought-six bolt action. I think you could put five shells in the clip. A lot of discipline was really the thing. Most of us survived, anyway. I went to Camp Elliott outside of San Diego.

They were picking fellows to go to China and Iceland. A lot of the fellows I knew went to Iceland. A friend and I were picked to go to scout sniper school. That was the end of China! That was a learning experience too.

It was a lot of work. To begin with, you learned to shoot a moving target with a scope. You either learn or you flunk. I was used to shooting guns from when I was a youngster. We were there for a month.

The funny part of that was there were pomegranate trees nearby and we'd go raid them at night. This Japanese farmer had a great big tomato patch there. This place was located where the Jack Murphy football stadium is. Anyway, we used to go out there at night. We would eventually end up having tomato fights. You had to get up in the morning and scrub all the tomatoes off!

One night the warrant officer there came out to check on us. I imagine the farmer had complained to him. He was coming along there with a flashlight. Somebody let him have it right in the mug with a ripe tomato. Boy, we scattered!

We were a bunch of kids. I think the oldest man there was 19 or 20. They made us stop going there after that. We used to take salt and eat tomatoes until you got sick. Anyway, that's part of the experience.

That's a great story. Where did you go after that?

They shipped us to the Philippines to begin with. After that they sent us back to Pearl Harbor. From Pearl Harbor we were shipped back to San Diego on the aircraft carrier the *Saratoga*. We hit in San Diego and went back to Camp Elliott.

Less than a week later the Japanese bombed Pearl Harbor. I remember a friend of mine said, 'The Japanese just bombed Pearl Harbor really bad.' I didn't believe it. So we went into the guard shack and listened to the radio and they were still bombing it.

How did you feel hearing that on the radio?

I think a lot of the fellows said 'It's here, it's happened.' So you hate the Japanese because of that. I hated the people for doing it because they killed a whole bunch of fellows that I knew on the battleship *Nevada*; the *Tennessee* was also hit. Real close friends, like brothers, like family. So that made me hate the Japanese for doing it.

One night they came in and said, 'The Japanese are going to invade the Pacific Coast.' I don't believe you'll read this in history books but they set us up down along the coast between the Mexican border and San Diego.

We spent about a week there. After that they shipped us to American Samoa. That was right after Pearl Harbor. It was January when we got there. The Samoa Island is 14 miles long and about eight miles wide at the widest. Two days before we got there the Japanese had shelled the place.

We were always on alert. We were there quite a while. I got to know the island pretty good. I learned to speak the language. It was like my Indian language. You had to work with the people, you know.

A lot of them didn't speak English, especially the older people. So you learned to talk the language in order to survive there. We were then shipped to New Caledonia and practiced landing there. The First Division had landed on Guadalcanal already. We practiced at New Caledonia and went on to Guadalcanal.

He told me, 'I don't like Indians.' So I told him, 'What the hell makes you think I like you?' We became friends.

When you were shipped over to Guadalcanal what was your rank?

I was a sergeant. I was a sergeant at Camp Elliott.

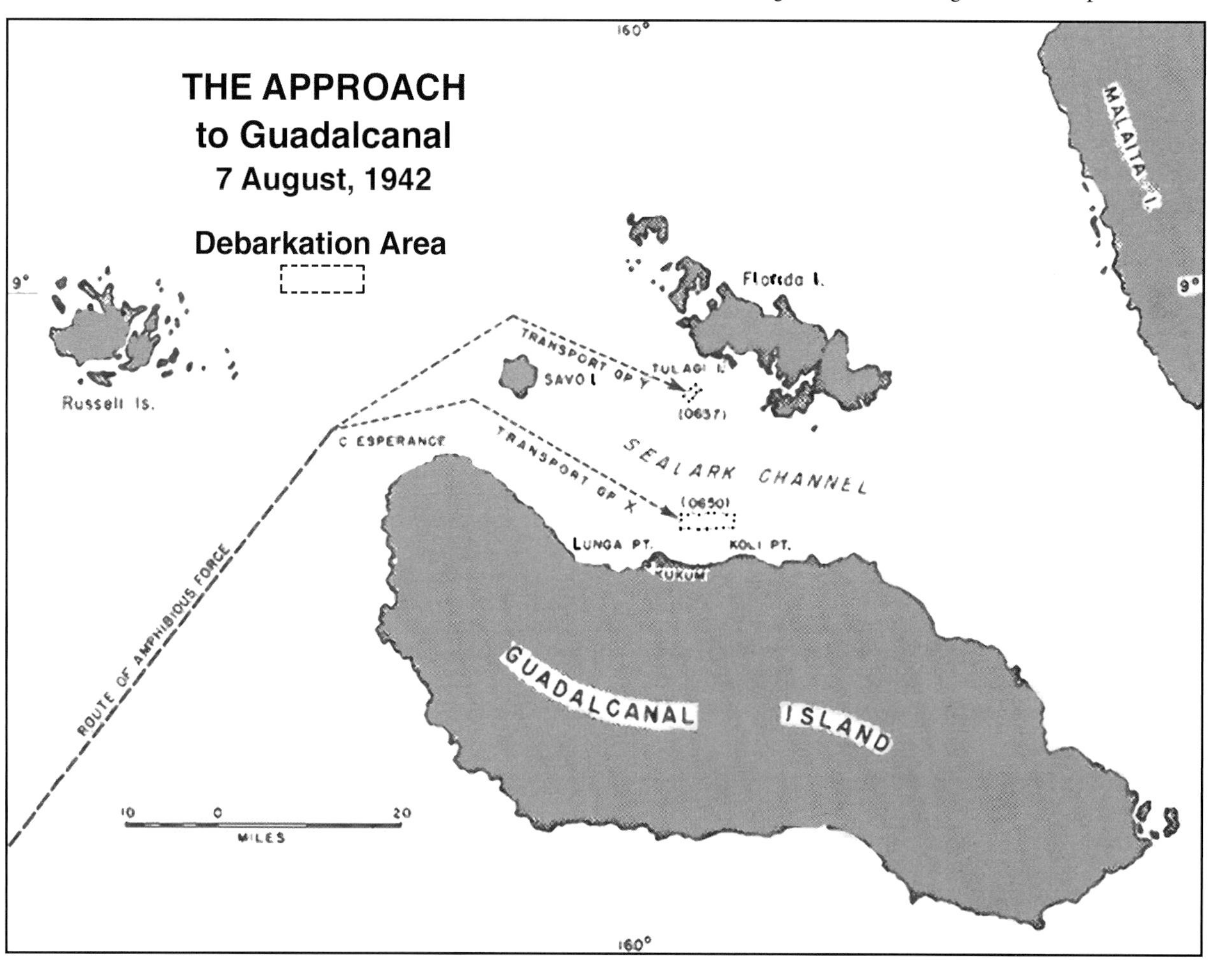

Map of Approach at Guadalcanal.
From U.S. military sources through wikipedia.com

How did they train you for hand-to-hand combat?

It was explained to you day after day. Eventually you practiced against an expert. They trained you in jujitsu at first. Then judo came in. You learned how to parry, how to knock someone down with your rifle.

We trained with a scabbard on the bayonet. That's how you learn. I remember running into a Jap by a bridge while on patrol. He was a real small person. Good thing I had training. The Japanese had a hook down below where the bayonet handle is on the rifle and they'd hook your rifle or bayonet, then they'd flip you.

I was in the Second Division, in the Third Battalion, Eighth Marines, I Company when I went to Guadalcanal... On patrol, I got bayoneted, it happened so fast.

I ran into this character in Guadalcanal. He jumped out at me; he was going to kill me. He stopped and hooked the bayonet; I had years of training and he was real light; instead of him flipping me I flipped him as he held onto his rifle.

I had to, it was no play like in a football game where you tackle a guy then let him up. You let him up he'll kill you. So you shoot him and that's it. It made me feel bad because at that time he reminded me of an Indian. Black hair and the complexion almost the same. It bothered me the first time it happened like that. Then eventually you think, well, that guy was trained to kill you. Survival of the fittest, I guess.

Ned Crutcher (at left) recruits Native men for the Marine Corps at the Stewart Indian Boarding School ca. 1943-4. The men's names (from left) are Edmond Dick, unknown, unknown, and Les Miller.
Photo courtesy of Ned Crutcher.

Was that the first time that happened?

Yes, it happened after that, but not that close. It was always at a distance. They shoot at you and miss if you see them; they were very adept at concealment but you shot back. I don't know what their instructions were; maybe to kill one or two guys before getting killed, because the majority of the time that's what happened.

They would shoot a guy or shoot at a guy and then their concealment is gone and they would get killed. That was a rough deal. You think about it later on; you think that's the most useless thing.

Ned and Wilma Crutcher

What division were you in?

I was in the Second Division, in the Third Battalion, Eighth Marines, I Company when I went to Guadalcanal. The Japanese had moved back into the hills, although they'd sneak down to where we were sometimes. On patrol, I got bayoneted, it happened so fast.

It felt like somebody hit me in the face with a rifle butt. But he hit me with a bayonet right through the face here. I remember feeling the hob-kneel shoe on my face. The Jap was trying to pull the bayonet out of me. A fellow that was with me shot him from behind before he did any more damage to me. So I have a scar from it.

While I was there at Guadalcanal a funny thing happened to me. They had a small compound for Japanese prisoners. Our Captain said to me, 'You will accompany this pharmacist to the Jap compound. He's going to treat some of the Japanese and you'll guard him.'

He went in and I stayed outside the compound. There was a big fence made out of Japanese material. When I was standing there this Japanese prisoner walked up to me and said 'You're a dumb son-of-a-bitch.'

I was thinking what I should have done. He hadn't done anything to me or touched me, what should I do, you know? He said, 'What the hell are they going to give you this time? Maybe they'll give you a new reservation! Maybe they'll give you the orange groves from southern California!'

He said this in plain English! I guess he was from up around Oregon or Washington to begin with. Later the physician said the guy had gone over to Japan to visit his great-grandparents before the war and he was conscripted into the Army.

Anyway, that was crazy. I never did see that guy again. He knew all about the reservations. There was an intelligence officer that went down to interview him. He wasn't for the Japanese; he wanted to go home I guess.

We were in Guadalcanal for 84 days. We were sent on patrols. I never had any delight in killing another person. You do it because he's there to kill you, you know. He isn't there to play.

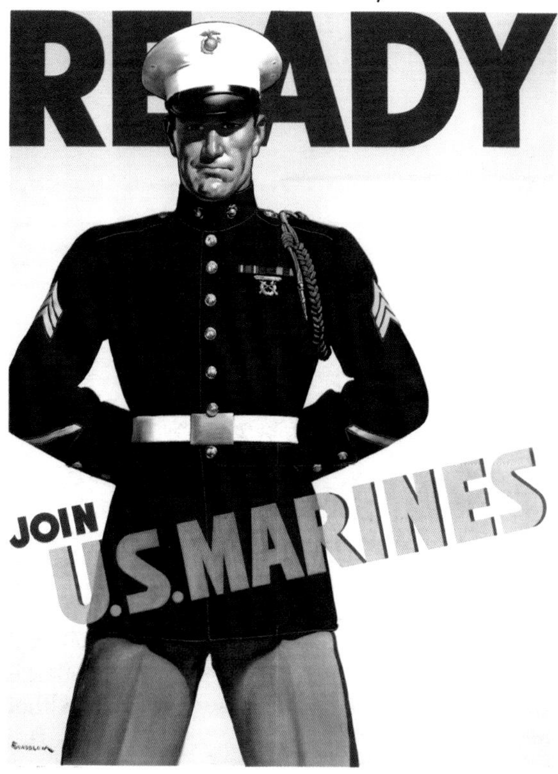

READY
JOIN
U.S. MARINES
APPLY, OR WRITE, TO NEAREST RECRUITING STATION

Recruiting poster.
Library of Congress, Prints and Photographs Division, (LC-USZC4-2092).

Every now and then you have the fear before your turn comes up to go on patrol. Someone would say, 'Well, so-and-so got bumped off today.' Or they would bring his body in, or a couple of bodies in. That was disheartening in a way and you have that natural human fear that maybe it was your turn this time.

People that say they weren't scared in combat like that are damn liars, because if you're human, you're afraid and you're scared. You don't want to die anymore than anyone else.

Were there other Indian Marines where you served?

There were a lot of part-Indian boys. But not many that showed it, you know. The only Indian fellow I knew was a guy named Grant McCloud from Yerington. He's gone now. He was in a different company.

He found out I was nearby and he'd sneak over to visit me. You relieved the tension by being kids. There's tension not amongst the Marines, it's that tension that's out there. People were afraid but there was never any tension against other Marines.

Ned Crutcher

After that I went to New Zealand. I got on a regiment that needed boxers. This fellow named Shephard was a professional boxer; he contacted the company I was in. A fellow named Leo and I were picked to give tryouts. Leo was part Indian from Biloxi, Mississippi.

We made it. There were a lot of people in both weight classes. We survived, both of us, and went on the regimental boxing team. We went to all the major cities, it was fun. I won a Silver Cup while boxing there. It's at the Stewart museum.

I fought other Marines and a lot of the New Zealand Armed Forces had teams, and also some civilians. We just traveled from city to city and town to town. It was easy duty, you know. I was scheduled to go to Tarawa but didn't go; my whole outfit got hit really bad.

I wasn't happy, but I had malaria and really bad asthma so I was going home to the States when that took place. We were probably 100 miles away from Tarawa. I was glad to come home although I lost a lot of buddies. You know, you get to serve with people for three or four years you become like family. If one guy has money everybody has money. It was great to be taught that way.

One guy told me, 'I'm Indian and I don't stand a chance.' I told him, 'If you get a diploma nobody can take it away from you. You're just as good as anybody...

There was never any dissension. I was the only Indian in the outfit; the only one that claimed it, anyway. I never felt discrimination, not once. You just become one of the guys. What was nice about it was you all dress alike. At Camp Elliott, guys would say, 'Crutcher, you have an extra pair of pants?'

Sometimes we'd switch pants, things like that. Camaraderie was the theme; it was taught to you in boot camp. And you stay that way when you get out. To this day I have a friend that I made in the service who was from Illinois. We were friends for 56 years. He died last year. I first met him in when I went in the Marine Corps. I still call his wife Mary. His name was Frank Andrews; he was part Indian.

When you were sent home did you stay in America for the rest of the war?

Yes, first I went to the Naval Hospital in San Diego. I had a sister who lived nearby. She originally worked for Sherman Indian School. She was working for the Air Force at the time I came in. Then I was in a Naval Hospital in the south side of Riverside for a long time. I was discharged from the hospital in July of 1944.

When did you first hear about the atomic bomb that dropped on Japan?

I was at Stewart when that happened. I heard it on a car radio and couldn't believe it. I heard they had tested an atomic bomb in New Mexico and that was a terrible thing, they said. I never dreamed of a time when they would drop it on people like that.

After all, they were people. In the long run though, it saved a lot of lives. It killed a lot of people unnecessarily, like children, women and old people when it was dropped. It had to be done some way. I don't know how long we would have had to fight those people before it ended. It's a terrible thing anyway. You shudder to think about it; those people, they're human beings.

How did you feel when the war ended?

Great. It was so great. You feel like a load off your back. I'd been there and thought that's great. We don't have to kill each other anymore.

Wilma: We were in Stewart and had gone to Reno that night. They announced it and Virginia Street just got all clogged with people.

Ned: Everybody was out in the street having a good time!

Wilma: We had been married in March of '45 and the war ended in August of '45.

How did you meet each other?

Wilma: My dad was the boxing coach at Stewart and my mother worked there too. We lived there. Dad would have the team over to eat after the boxing match, he'd bring them over to our apartment and I would be helping to serve the sandwiches and whatever.

That's when I first knew Ned. We didn't see each other until he came back and was on disability leave from the Marine Corps. We got married in Carson City. We stayed there for three years. He moved here to Herlong in '48.

Ned: I had worked at Stewart as a boys' advisor, boxing coach and football coach.

When you moved to Herlong what did you do?

I worked in the ammunition surveillance division. I retired in 1974.

Have you gone to any Stewart reunions?

I went to one. I had to work and I didn't take the time for it. I had a chance to go but I didn't. I went to one and I got to see a lot of the guys. When I was the boys' advisor I pushed a lot of them real hard to make it.

One guy told me, 'I'm Indian and I don't stand a chance.' I told him, 'If you get a diploma nobody can take it away from you. You're just as good as anybody, if you know what you're doing and put your nose to the grindstone you can do it.'

When did you first meet my grandfather Stan and great-uncle Leonard?

I met Stan at Stewart. He went to Stewart before he went to Riverside. That's where I knew him, Leonard too. Later on Leonard boxed. He was straightforward and a nice person. Those guys always treated me like I'm one of them; that's what I liked about them.

If you could talk to all Indian kids here in America, what would you encourage them to do?

I think it depends on where they are. At Stewart you would encourage them; 'Don't hang your head when you're walking. You're as good as anybody if you train and get a diploma nobody can take it away from you.'

You can do anything, you can be anybody, do anything you want to do. Some places it's hard on Indian children. Today, what do you suppose the dropout rate is for Indian students? It's way up. My thing is, you can train yourself and you can do anything you want.

Ned once drank with Ira Hayes at a Marine Corps base and they talked about the hardships of war. Ned Crutcher's family is very proud of his service to his country and to his people.

Lee McCardie

Lee McCardie was very excited to talk to me about his time in the U.S. Navy during the war. I met him on March 21, 2002 at his home in Hoopa. After our interview he invited me to lunch at the Senior Center in town. Lee is now the oldest living Hupa veteran.

I was born on November 15, 1913.

You were born on November 15? That's my birthday! I was born in 1974.

Really? I was born at home. My father was Oscar McCardie and my mother's name was Lena McCardie. I was raised here in Hoopa; the only time I left was to go to school and the service. I had five brothers and one sister.

My great-grandmother on my mother's side was a doctor. My father was Yurok from Cappell. My mother was from Trinidad. A lot of the Trinidad people came to Hoopa. My grandmother had a laundry here when the soldiers were here.

Did they ever talk about when Fort Gaston existed here in Hoopa, and the soldiers were here?

Well, when the soldiers first came in here there were a lot of Indians killed.

Did you have any family that attended the Hoopa Valley Boarding School?

I did from 1924 to '25. We stayed at the school and they never let us speak our language. If they caught us speaking we were penalized. We had to go down to the marching place and march for an hour. I remember working on the milk crew.

We'd get up at four in the morning to milk the cows. That was the big chore. My mother knew the Yurok language. The Yurok people would come up here a lot and trade back and forth. They brought us seafood and we'd give them what we had.

When you were very young did your family attend the Brush Dances?

Oh yes, my dad made his own songs. At that time, if you wanted to use someone's song you had to ask them to use it. They don't do that anymore, they just use it. The person who made the song isn't here anymore.

Where did you go to high school?

I went to high school in Corning in the late '20s. I went to Sherman Institute for more schooling. I graduated from there in 1934. I had two brothers, Hilton and Harvey McCardie, who went with me. I studied building construction. There were a lot of people at the school; Navajo and Hopi, and from all over the United States.

I stayed at Sherman two years. Contractors used to come up from Los Angeles to pick who they wanted for construction. Ben House and I were picked and we went to work in Los Angeles. We worked in Beverly Hills. We worked on Ginger Rogers' house. I didn't really like what I was doing. In late '34 I came back to Hoopa and went to work for the BIA (Bureau of Indian Affairs) police.

I stayed there until '39 and then went in the Navy. I took an examination, and I was put in the Air Force. It was a funny thing, if you asked to be in a particular area, they wouldn't let you. I took that examination and they sent me to Alameda Air Force station. I trained young pilots how to land at night.

We landed at night. I think the Seabees went in there first and fixed things up. We went in there and built bomb shelters under heavy fire.

Flying at night and trying to land on water is most difficult. You have to have exceptional vision; we had these SOCs, we didn't have much. An SOC (Scout-Observation Plane) is a one-prop plane that's double winged. It has water landing gear and is used for patrol.

What was it like to fly?

Well, this big plane had wings that were flopping and that was kind of scary! It was a water-landing plane. You put these rubber boots on the wheels and take it out on the water. I did a lot of observation; four of us were in the plane. We did a lot of patrol work up and down the coast.

I didn't stay there very long. In '41 we were mustering and got the news in the morning that Pearl Harbor was bombed. My squadron took quite a bit of training after that. We went through the Marine training; that's a tough course. In the middle of '42 they shipped us out to Guadalcanal right after the Coral Sea battle. That's where the five Sullivan brothers were killed.

What was your experience like at Guadalcanal?

We landed at night. We had to make our own foxholes with this small shovel. That was right on the beach there. The Japanese had planes firing on us. They had an airfield there, I think the Seabees went in there first and fixed things up. We went in there and built bomb shelters under heavy fire.

Guadalcanal was a big island. When we first got there, there were dead Japs all along the beach. We had to wait to get some bulldozers in there. I don't know how long that took. They dug a trench and just bulldozed the Japs into there.

There were quite a lot of Japs still alive on the island too. They had planes that would come down and shoot at us, and bomb. You don't pay much attention to it until it's over. You're doing what you're doing, you don't pay much attention. I had some close buddies there too.

What type of weapon did you carry?

I carried a .45 carbine. We did a lot of shooting, mostly at night. You couldn't see very well, but they were there. In the daytime the Japs hid out pretty well. They had flame-throwers for the caves.

Were you part of a particular division?

Squadron two was our call sign. I got hurt in the last part of '43. There was a big hospital there and it was full. I had malaria really bad. Malaria was the big killer; I heard it was seven to one. The Japs killed one, malaria killed seven.

Lee McCardie

What was it like to have malaria?

You get heated up, you get high fever, and then you freeze. You get cold, and need covers. There was no cure. Quinine was what they used, but they ran out of that. They gave us something that made you yellow.

I was shipped back to a hospital in Oakland and I was there for two years. I had it bad. I was pretty sick. I don't know why I lived but I did. I made it.

Did you have any family members in the service?

Oh yes, I had two brothers that were in. My brother Harvey was in the Army with Patton's tanks. My brother Hilton was in shipping.

What did you do after your time in the hospital?

I came back here in '46. I stayed in San Francisco for a while. I worked in construction for a short time. I got 45 cents an hour.

Were you ever married?

I was married three times. I have six children. I have a lot of grandchildren and great-grandchildren too!

Do you think it's important for young people to know that Indians served in the war?

I think so. They felt it was their duty. They had to have good hearts about it. You have to forgive; you can't have a grudge. You can't live with hate. Hate is a cancer.

Lee McCardie is a life member of the Veterans of Foreign Wars. He spends his time at home and enjoys visits from his family and friends. His family is very proud of his service to his people and his country.

Lee Hover

Lee Hover and his wife Helen met with me on April 22, 2001. Lee is of Karuk ancestry. He and I spoke on the phone for six months prior to this interview about traditional carving techniques used by the Yurok and Karuk people. We then discovered that we lived one mile apart from each other.

I was born on April 13, 1924 in Eureka. My mother Elsie Hover was a teacher. She was formerly a Starritt from Orleans and descended from Emma Perch. In 1932 she taught at Denny (in northern California) until 1938. The school was small and she taught all eight grades.

We had a good school time. My father was Paul Hover and he was an excellent carpenter. In 1938 we came to Arcata and went to school there. That's where I met my wife, I threw rocks at her! I got her attention and we've been together ever since!

When did you graduate from high school?

I didn't graduate. When 1941 came up December the seventh happened and I went down and volunteered for the Navy. I missed graduation by that much. My dad and I got up early that morning on December seventh and went to Elk River to a friend's place. We went there to fish.

That evening, I don't remember how late it was, but we came back into town and the first thing we saw was the Standard paper with a big red headline. I couldn't believe it. I rushed right down to the Navy recruiting station!

There were three of us that went down and I was the only one that passed. I left by train and went to San Francisco and was sworn in there. I went to San Diego and was there for four-and-a-half days. I was there long enough to get my uniform and learn to stand in line. They sent me to San Francisco and then shipped me to Pearl Harbor.

At Pearl Harbor I was taken to this field. They lined 5,000 of us sailors up and on the other side they had all our gear with our names. I don't know how they got it there, but they told everyone to find their gear. With 5,000 guys we had quite a time.

Finally we got a call to get in crews. They stopped at the letter G. The rest of us stayed on the island. I was sent to West Loch, which was a Marine encampment. I served there as a train guard. They had some trains that ran out through the cane fields. They gave us a rifle and orders. How they knew I could handle a rifle, I don't know, because I never had any training but I had learned here at home.

So they gave me orders and they said if you see movement, shoot it, because I was sitting on an ammunition train. You shoot first and ask questions afterward. The train always left in the evening. I did that for three or four nights. Two things about that; they had a man on each car on top, and the man in front of me saw something move and he started shooting.

That livened everything up because he was in the middle of a Marine encampment! You never saw such a sight, but the whole island went to general quarters because we were still expecting the Japanese to invade. That black cat caused a lot of uproar!

The other incident was that morning they had sent me to a little encampment where submariners came in for R-and-R. They put me on a truck, gave me my rifle, and told me I was to escort these Japanese prisoners back to West Loch! Here I am, 17 years old and looking at a bunch of Japs and wondering what I could do about it. That woke me up to the fact that we were really into something.

They transferred me from West Loch to a submarine base on an island. My duty at that time was they took me up this mountain to a cave that was full of ammunition for the ships. They had it all set to be blown up. There were several of us there.

What we were to do in case of invasion, even without orders, was to run up the mountain and blow it up. I asked this fellow where were we supposed to go after that and he said not to worry about it!

That's what I did there. I went back to West Loch and waited for my ship to come in. One evening I was out having dinner on liberty. I came back and everyone was gone but the sergeant. I asked him what happened. He said the ship came and they were going to send a boat back for me.

That's how I came aboard the *Dewey.* It had been out to sea for quite a while and the guys were kind of raunchy. I saw three fights between the quarterdeck and the galley as I stepped on the ship. It scared me half to death; they were rough people!

They assigned me to a bunk that was in the forward end of the galley. They had a dishwasher there that overflowed. I had the lower deck with just room enough for my shoes to float underneath as the water swished back and forth. I lasted there for a week then I moved up on deck and didn't tell anybody. In those days the bunks were stacked five or seven high. There was just room enough to crawl in on your stomach or you back.

I struck for gunner's mate and I made gunner's mate apprentice. The first battle I was in was Midway. I had never heard a big gun go off. When it went off I about jumped out of my shoes! I got a pretty good initiation there. We came back and went down to Guadalcanal for the invasion.

We were the first ship down the slot; we led the fleet in. As we were just approaching Guadalcanal a small Japanese tanker came from Tulagi right across our bow. We thought for sure they had radioed something about our fleet coming in, so the skipper said to sink it. So we sunk it, right out in front of Tulagi and Guadalcanal.

The Japanese fleet was coming down as we moved out. We could see them but they couldn't see us. It was hard… to leave our men.

It wasn't seen, thank heavens. By the way, I've read afterward on several occasions that tanker was sunk by dive-bombers. I never saw a dive-bomber; I don't know how that story got started. We sunk it with our forward guns.

We moved onto the beach and commenced firing for the occupation. The troopships came in behind us. There were two or three cruisers; I don't think there were any battlewagons, and five destroyers. At that time we didn't have a big fleet, we had a handful of ships. Our target was the barracks and the headquarters on the airfield.

A report came back to us after it was over that we had accomplished our mission. We had destroyed the barracks and headquarters and killed over 1,000 Japanese and opened that part for invasion. The troopships moved in on the beach and sent the troops in. They had a rough go of it. We stayed there and gave them fire support for three days.

During those three days, we suffered high-altitude bomber attacks, dive-bomber attacks, and torpedo attacks. We fought in the first battle of Iron Bottom Bay over by Tulagi where we sunk the five ships in that night battle.

When we came back to protect the other ships we didn't have anything, so we parked the destroyer right in front of the troopship. They finally decided we should get out of there. As we did we came under a dive-bomber attack and we disappeared around the point of the island from the rest of the fleet, so they reported us sunk.

Actually, we weren't sunk we were just around the corner hiding! That evening we started out. The Japanese fleet was coming down as we moved out. We could see them but they couldn't see us. It was hard… to leave our men.

From there we went to an island. We were supposed to receive mail, food and ammunition, but we didn't. The report had come in that we were sunk so we didn't have anything. During this time we had no food.

I never ate so much hardtack in my life. The hardtack

was so bad you'd crack it open to let the weevils get out before you ate it. So we bummed from other ships and got enough to finally get back to Pearl Harbor and then to San Francisco. We had a seven-day leave and went back to sea again. That was Guadalcanal for me.

Where were you positioned on the Dewey?

Their dive-bombers were really experienced warriors. They would come out of the sky and they wouldn't stop.

During the fighting in Guadalcanal, I was on the 20-millimeter amidships. That was my battle station. At that time I was a gunner's mate striker. Well, I lost that when I got back to San Francisco because I was a bad boy, so when we went back out to sea I heard they were short of sonar men. I struck for that and got it.

I became a sonar man. My duties ranged from underwater sonar to surface radar to aircraft radar. I worked off the bridge all the time. But my battle station was always on the gun. I was gun captain on the twin-40s, mid-ship on the port side, up until Iwo Jima. At Iwo Jima they traded me off of that to the combat information center where you did the plotting for the boys on the beach. We'll get into that later.

Was there any other time when you didn't have enough food?

There was one other time where they'd missed giving us our supplies. We had pulled up next to this battleship to get rations. They sent us ice cream! Of all the damn things, you're starving to death and then have to eat ice cream!

What was the experience like when you were being attacked by dive- bombers?

Well, I'll tell you, I was 17. All of my buddies were all young people. We were fighting against experienced warriors that had been fighting China and at different places for 10 years or more. Their pilots were superb.

When they would come in on a torpedo mission, they came three at a time in a triangle pattern. You could shoot any one of those three out and the others would not vary their position. They came at you regardless, and when they went out they strafed the back of you as they went.

Their dive-bombers were really experienced warriors. They would come out of the sky and they wouldn't stop. The high-altitude bombers were so high up you could hardly see them. They were not accurate at all.

Anywhere within five miles was pretty good for them. But the dive-bombers and torpedo planes were something else. Toward the end of the war, they'd used up all their experienced pilots; they had novices, even people who hadn't flown a plan, flying their planes. They'd get scared and disappear.

Could you describe what their planes looked like?

To me, they were just a dark color. But they had that sun on them. There was one we had shot down at Guadalcanal. It landed in the water. There were five men in the plane. This was when I was on the 20-millimeter on the starboard side. After the battle, the skipper said to go pick the men up. They were floating arm-in-arm in a circle.

The skipper leaned over the bridge and made a motion for them to surrender and we would pick them up. One of them, who was the pilot, pulled a pistol out of the water and took a shot at him. That ended the five of them right there, they were shot with 60 rounds of 20-millimeter.

There was no giving up; they weren't that type of people. They would fight to the last drop. Later on toward the end of the war we picked up another pilot. He turned out to be 16 years old and scared to death.

There was a big difference in those first pilots in the initial group of battles, like at Coral Sea and Midway and Guadalcanal. The Marines had a terrible time on the ground. The Japanese just wouldn't quit, they'd be beaten and they wouldn't quit. We had to learn to compensate for that.

How would you compensate for that?

Just by getting meaner and meaner.

Lee Hover ca. 1942-3
Photo courtesy of Lee and Helen Hover.

Where are the other places you went?

After Guadalcanal we came into Mare Island for repairs. We were going to go to the South Pacific. We got just outside San Francisco and they changed our orders to go to Alaska. Here we were with summer gear going north! They did issue us with cold weather gear. We were up there nine months.

Our mission was to start at Dutch Harbor and go island to island until we took the last one, which was Attu. It was a rough winter, it was cold and windy. The boys on the beaches had a hard time. We lost our sister ship the *Worden* on one of the invasions of Amchitka. The tides up there are very high and low.

We went in and she led the troopship in. They were going to land this troopship in and use it as headquarters for the Army. So she led the way in and when she came back out a wave dropped out from under her and she landed atop a big rock and broke in half. We had a rescue mission to do there, and we accomplished that.

Some of the boys were real heroes. There was one man in charge of a smaller boat who saw some of the men on the other side of the *Worden* on the island side. He waited until the bow of the *Worden* lifted up and he went underneath. He picked those people up and came back the same way before it came down. That man was an Indian from the Dakotas. We rescued quite a few people, but we lost several that night. The next day we had a sea burial.

We went to Attu after that. There was real heavy fog and the Navy had no charts of the bottom, so we had to operate the underwater sound gear. We took the landing craft off the *Dewey* and put them in the water and they followed us like little ducks.

We went to the beach like that. We had one battleship with us. When we got in close to the beach she opened fire. The concussion from those big guns cleared an area in the bright sunlight about two miles around. So there we sat right on the beach in the full sunlight! That scared us, boy! We got out of there in good shape.

They sent us around to Massacre Bay to do some bombarding. We were by ourselves. On the way we had three dive-bombers come from someplace. They each dropped two torpedoes. All the torpedoes broke when they hit the water. The bombers were too high. If they'd come down lower that would have been the end of us.

From there we came back to Kiska. That was a heavily fortified island. We'd bypassed it at first. It had an airstrip and a harbor and it had to be taken care of. So we went there and we put up a patrol. We flew airplanes over the island so we knew where to go. There were gun emplacements and supposedly thousands of troops there.

So we stayed out quite a ways and did some bombarding and didn't get any return fire. We moved in about half a mile and bombarded some more and still didn't get any return fire. So they said to go right up to the beach. I knew that was the end of it!

We bombarded some more and nothing happened. They called for a few of the landing craft to go in. They went in and found the barracks. There were all kinds of signs of occupation but no people. We called that, not our gold star, not our silver star, but our cellophane star, because there was no fighting!

There were no people to fight, they'd disappeared almost overnight. There was a lot of speculation about where they went. But that was the end of the Aleutian campaign for us. That took nine months. We came back in April and went down south to San Diego. We connected with the troop ships for the landing at the Gilbert Islands.

Our objective at first was Little Makin. They were going take on all three islands (Tarawa, Makin, Little Makin). At Little Makin they ran into opposition from a sunken ship that the Japs had made into a fort out in the harbor.

They sent us around to Massacre Bay to do some bombarding. We were by ourselves. On the way we had three dive-bombers come from someplace. They each dropped two torpedoes.

It had a steep roof and a little hole in the front with a gun sticking out. The dive-bombers couldn't do anything with it; no one could, but they were holding up the whole war with those three or four little guns in there.

So they called the *Dewey* to come in front of it and try to neutralize it. I was on the starboard side guns and we came in with the portside to them, so I didn't get to do any shooting in that one. They finally got some shells into that slot and opened up so they could do the landing.

They were having a lot of trouble at Tarawa so they sent us there to help. We got over there and did a lot of bombarding to try and help the boys out on the island. After that we went out to sea. We went south to a place called Humboldt Bay on New Guinea. We did some bombarding and landing of troops there.

From there we went to the Marshall Islands. Our particular mission on that one was we landed troops on Enewetak and moved immediately to Kwajalein and landed troops on that island. This took several days because things don't go real smooth. So we had those islands under our belt. From there we went to the Philippines on Luzon. My uncle Paul Starritt was with the Army Engineers on the island. I don't know how I found out, but I asked my skipper if I could find him and he said go ahead.

So I went to this little town and went out in the boondocks. I was going along on this long, quiet stretch among the sugar cane and here these two great big Filipino guys stepped out in front of me and scared me to death! They were guerillas, and they were big, mean, tough-looking boys. Anyway, they went with me to where Paul's camp had been. They had moved away that morning! So I missed them.

After we left Luzon we went through a typhoon. We went right into it and lost two sister ships in that typhoon. We lost over 700 men from the fleet and lost three or four ships from damage. We are the only ship in naval history to roll in excess of 80 degrees and come back. I spent most of my time during the typhoon on the bridge.

I was up there on watch when it became so bad you couldn't leave to go back to your bunk. I spent around 36 hours on the bridge. The storm started three days before we entered the typhoon. Once we got into the typhoon that lasted less than 24 hours. Then we had three more days to get out of the storm.

We had waves in excess of 100 feet. The tops of those waves were sheared off by winds in excess of 120 miles an hour. Visibility was cut to 100 yards. When we got through I felt like I was sandblasted by all the mist. I had taken off my undershirt in the middle of the typhoon and wrapped it around my head to filter the water out. This fine mist just made mincemeat out of you.

But the skipper had done his homework when he found out we were going through a typhoon area. He studied three different books that told what to do and so forth. He actually saved our ship. Two of our sister ships identical to us went down. He had us cut away ammunition boxes, torpedo tubes and the spotlight. It took away all the excess weight from the topside. We also transferred the fuel from one side to the other to keep it from flipping over.

The USS Dewey.
Photo courtesy of Lee and Helen Hover.

We had some pretty heroic men on board. They were engineers and firemen and they really saved the ship. At the start of the typhoon we made a roll of probably 70 degrees and it dipped water into our stack. The people down there in the fire room stuck with it and got the burners all turned off before the water hit them. If the water hit them the ship blows up.

Those boys were real survivors. The skipper did a great job of staying on the bridge and giving orders. We lost our forward stack. A high wind came along and the stack went over and wrapped itself around the ship like a big piece of paper.

I was standing right there when it happened. Then a whistle went off. It sounded like the world was coming to an end. Then we rolled way over. I was strapped to something on the starboard side just after the con room. I was standing right beside the radar and sonar room. When we'd roll over I would be submerged in the ocean. It was a funny feeling because I didn't go in feet first or head first, I went in lying down.

It would go down and down and down and you'd just about be ready to cut your belt loose to go up top, when you feel the whole ship shake. Then it would start back up. It did that several times. After Captain Calhoun retired he wrote a book about the typhoon. It describes everything. When we got through the typhoon our ship was like a stripped hull. There was no gun, no torpedoes, it was just a hull.

I did not know it at the time, but we passed through the eye of the storm two times. We didn't lose anybody overboard, but we had some bruised up people. In the eye, the sea wasn't flat, but there was no wind. It's quiet. It's quite a feeling, but you're standing there thinking you have to go out the other side!

We had men on board that should have received the highest award. Those engineers and firemen did a tremendous job. We had an officer down below that was in charge of the engine room that did an outstanding job of keeping the morale up. When the ship was rolling people were getting hurt. They'd freeze up, so he would wade through the water and talk to them. He did this several times. The pressure inside that ship was terrific.

We had one man who lost his senses. He never did come back. The first time I saw him after the storm he was walking on the deck to the chow hall. He was carrying the blue jacket manual on a belt over his shoulder like he was going to school.

This went on until we got to port and they sent him back to San Diego. I don't know if he ever made it back or not. We had a lot of people who were hurt. I was lucky, I was strapped in. A couple times I was about out of air.

We started looking for survivors because we heard other ships calling for help. Finally they called us off because we were so damaged they thought we'd sink. We went to the island of Ulithi. We were happy because we thought we were going home.

There in the harbor was a destroyer dry dock made in Eureka, California! They put us in that thing, closed the door, raised us out of the water, and we repaired our own ship. That took some time. I didn't get to come home that time!

Something I want to mention, my wife asked me if I ever dream about what happened. I don't. I dreamt about it before it happened. I dreamt of it when I was in high school. I dreamt of it when I was in grade school. I dreamt of being smothered in water. After the typhoon, I never had that dream again.

The next step was Guam and Saipan. Those were some pretty rough assignments. We were assigned to the island of Guam to do the pre-bombardment and land the troops. Then we moved to Saipan. They were having a lot of trouble there. There was more resistance there so we did a lot more bombarding. Then we moved to Rota to neutralize the airfield.

We heard there was a carrier fleet coming in to land planes on Rota to neutralize our forces, so we went down and did away with that airfield. Then we moved out to sea toward the Philippines.

Then we got the call to muster up with the largest fleet I've ever seen. We ran into over a thousand warships; destroyers by the squadron, cruisers, battleships, aircraft carriers, the whole bit. Everybody was segregated, and getting into place where they were supposed to be. I just can't describe it to you, but to see a thousand warships, in one huddle, it made me feel good!

We sailed by the Japanese fleet that day and there wasn't a shot fired. The next day was the day of the great turkey shoot. We didn't do anything; we just sailed along and had a peaceful, sunny day. But our air pilots had a hell of a battle. Our pilots shot down over 200 planes that day, I think. We broke their back because that took away their carrier protection.

Where did you go after that battle?

From there the Dewey went to Iwo Jima. We escorted the troopships and made the landing. In that battle I was assigned to the combat information center.

I was in contact with a Marine division on the island. This Marine would call for fire here, or fire there, and I'd plot it. His name was Charlie-Two-Four-One. We talked for a while, and I think it was the third day, but he said there was a counter-attack coming. We started firing. He said to come lower, he kept saying come lower.

He said, 'They're 15 yards out, drop five!'

Then he said, 'Drop five!' That brought it down to 10 yards from him. Then he said, 'Drop five!' Then he said, 'Drop five!'...That was the last I heard from him.

Did you see anything on the island?

I did see our flag go up! Our ship was right underneath and I saw it. We were right up against the high mountain (Suribachi). We were sitting on the ship right underneath when the flag went up. We didn't know at that time that there were thousands of Jap troops in caves. There was still some terrible fighting that went on.

But it was a good feeling to see the flag. And this here is the flag that we flew (on the ship) in that battle. (Lee unfolds an American flag.) I got that from the quartermaster. We had six men wounded by shells exploding on the deck. There were so many ships around that island shooting at airplanes; what comes up must come down. So we had some casualties by our own firepower.

Lee Hover

What does the American flag mean to you?

I fought for it. I respect it. I respect the thoughts behind the flag. I may not respect some of the things we do in the name of the flag, but I respect our flag, to the utmost.

Where did you go after this?

From there we went on to Okinawa. We landed there and on the twenty-first day we were assigned picket duty toward Japan. We were to warn the fleet if anyone was coming. We had lost a lot of destroyers in 21 days on picket duty.

We were all pretty tense. But we didn't get any suicide attacks on us. The one that we did pick up was 16 years old and scared to death. He was all dressed in black with a black sash.

Did you ever watch a suicide attack come at you?

There's nothing you can do about it. You just watch it and do your best to bring them down. I forget which battle it was, but there was a dive-bomber coming around behind us. It was a difficult situation because there were some of our ships on the other side. If you open up with your guns you might hit your own ships.

We were to be in the third wave, and they expected the first seven waves to be annihilated.

If you don't open fire he's going to go back up. So you promptly pull the trigger and hope you don't hit anybody but him. He was coming at us from the stern and strafed us. He put bullets through the stacks. All of a sudden he turned to the side and just went in the water.

We were on picket duty between Iwo Jima and Japan when the atomic bomb dropped. When our planes flew off of Guam to bomb Japan they flew over Iwo Jima, which was an emergency landing area.

If anything happened to them in between we were there to pick them up. That's where we were when we heard about the bomb dropping. We also had orders at the time to prepare for the invasion of Japan.

We were to be in the third wave, and they expected the first seven waves to be annihilated. That was going to be rough. But by that time I learned they always told you the worst, so I took everything with a grain of salt. There was a lot of hollering and whooping going on when we heard the war was over!

Did you ever hear Tokyo Rose on the radio?

Oh yes. Tokyo Rose would say she knew where we were. Then they'd play some songs from the United States.

How did you and your crewmates respond to her?

Oh, we enjoyed it. That was just a lot of fun. That was about the only thing we did hear. Another thing about being our at sea is you lose all contact with music. Coming back to the States and going into a bar you'd hear new music that didn't sound good, it didn't sound right at all.

The *Dewey* was coming to San Diego after the war and my skipper said it didn't make sense to ride clear to Boston to decommission the ship then come cross-country to get home. He said to take a 30-day leave.

So I did and came home for 30 days. Then I went to Treasure Island to get my discharge and guess what? They had lost my service records and I couldn't get discharged. Let's say you needed 10 points to get discharged. I had around 40. I couldn't get out. I went from office to office to office for a month.

One night someone shook me by the shoulders and said I was going to Japan for occupation duty. I said they weren't sending me anyplace because they didn't have my sea bag, my records or anything.

A couple days later I was wandering around screaming at people. I happened to go into Rear Admiral Black's office. I was giving his yeoman hell and pretty soon a voice came from the back room, 'Who in the hell is out there! The yeoman told him and he said to come back there.

I went in and met Admiral Black. He talked to me and asked me where I'd been and who was my Captain. We talked for about an hour. Finally, he pushed a button and the yeoman came in. He said, 'You find this man's sea bag and his records and I want him out that gate by 4:30 today.'

And guess what? I was out that gate by 4:30! It's all in who you know! I came by bus to get home. My wife was staying with a friend. I went down there and there she was. You can't believe that you're home. The hard part is figuring out that you're staying.

How long were you in the service?

I was in for three years and 10 months. It was all overseas duty. I had real good friends in the service. I also had enemies in the service. You can't serve for that long on a ship without getting into altercations. So you get into little groups of your friends.

Were you aware of how many Indian people were in the service from your area?

We sent our share of boys from this area. Most of them saw action. I know a lot of people from Eureka and Arcata who never went any further than San Diego. But most Indian boys saw action. The Indian boys did their part.

Lee is retired and lives with his wife Helen near Arcata, California. His family is very proud of his service to his country. He enjoys attending Karuk ceremonies and other Native gatherings.

Gene Ryan

Gene Ryan is of Maidu, Washoe and Pit River ancestry. Gene served in the U.S. Navy during the war. He and my grandfather Stan are first cousins. We had our interview on November 19, 2001.

I was born March 2, 1926 in San Francisco. My uncle Joe Lowry brought me to Susanville after six months. That was my mother's brother. He brought me to my grandmother and my grandmother raised me. She came from a big family and she was the oldest.

It was a hard life; they were very poor. We had a

tough time. My grandmother's name was Lena Peconam. She was married to Billy Lowry. He was pretty wild! She was Maidu and Washoe. Her husband was Maidu and Pit River. I have lots of relations, lots of family. Indians are very close to their family.

Did you have any brothers or sisters?

I had one half-brother and one half-sister. I was raised on a little farm off Shasta Street in Susanville, but during the Depression we lost that. Then we moved right off the Indian reservation into a little house. That was right down from your grandfather's place.

You mentioned the Depression, were you old enough to know what that was?

Well, we heard about it on the radio. We were so poor that we put cardboard in our shoes to make them last longer. We'd go in the five-and-dime store and get rubber soles and glue them on. I remember that.

When you were little did you play with my Grandpa Stan and Uncle Leonard?

Yeah, but they were a little older than me. Mervin Evans and I went to Indian school together. I was a little younger than Mervin. He and I had rubber-gun wars! We had a lot of fun. There were hard times but we had fun too.

I knew Mervin's dad and his mother well. We used to go up to their house. The land that the cemetery in Susanville is on was donated by Mervin's dad. There were a few Pit River graves already in there. The Maidu have 15 or 16 burial grounds in Susanville that nobody knows about. We had big families back in those days.

Gene Ryan in 1943-4.
Photo courtesy of Gene Ryan.

We always went to the Bear Dances; they had them all over. We used to go to them at Lake Almanor and in Susanville, and there were a couple on the reservation there. Most of them were held east of Susanville around Bass Hill and by the Janesville grade.

The Dance is supposed to give everybody a good heart and good feeling. From what I remember, it kind of got out of hand from people drinking, but now they're going back to the old way, which is good for all Indians. You try to get this spiritual ceremony going again.

It was sad because no matter what Indian school I went to they didn't want your tribal identity, you had to learn the 'Christian way.' So when I grew up I didn't think that was right. I think the Indian way is better.

What were your impressions of the Bear Dance when you were young?

Oh, I thought it was great. It was only once a year and people got together with lots of good food. When you're done dancing you had this wormwood, and after you chase the bear around, you go down to the creek and wash yourself for good health and wisdom among the people. You have to have a lot of good thoughts. That's what I remember.

What was it like to see the Bear?

Well, in those days it looked real, the way those guys covered themselves up. The way I understood it, the ceremony was for your health and a new year. This is what I remember; other people might remember it different. The Bear Dance was for the different bands of the tribes from all over. I still see Pit River people come down for it today.

Where did you go to elementary school?

I went to Susanville for a while then I went to Stewart, Nevada. My brother Joey Hill and I went together. He was my half-brother. He died very young at 49 years old. We went to the Stewart Indian boarding school but they messed up our paperwork and sent us back. After I got a little older I went to Sherman. I had some family at Sherman so they sent me there.

I was seven or eight years old when I went to Stewart. I remember they put you on a bus and took you by bus. It was the same way for Sherman. They sent a bus and took all the Indian kids in a bus.

When you were growing up, did your grandmother speak her Indian language?

Oh yes. She spoke the Maidu language. I learned a few words, especially the cuss words! I didn't really want to go to Stewart but there was no money. Now that I'm grown up I realize it was hard times then.

It was sad because no matter what Indian school I went to they didn't want your tribal identity, you had to learn the 'Christian way.' So when I grew up I didn't think that was right. I think the Indian way is better. If Indians can, they should go back to the old ways and try to pick up what they lost.

When you were at Stewart did you have to wear a uniform or certain style of clothing?

Yes, I wore blue jeans and a blue denim shirt. We also had Sunday clothes. I had a pretty hard time at Stewart because I'm pretty fair-skinned. I had a lot of fights. I was real little there. There were some Indians from Susanville that knew me.

Our ship got hit in the Marshalls and we were sent to Pearl Harbor to work on it, but Pearl Harbor couldn't handle it so we were sent to the States.

The Calvins were there and they guided me around because I was so small. That's about all I remember there. We did have good food there. I was only there a short time.

How old were you when you attended the Sherman boarding school?

I was in junior high; that would have been around 1939. I didn't finish school. I had one more year to go but I went into the service. I knew Charlie Bowen at Sherman, and I knew Mervin, Jack Madero and Leland Washoe came there later on.

I also went to school with the Moores from around Weitchpec on the coast. I knew Glenn and Don Moore. There were some other Maidu from Redding that came. I started out in the little boys' dormitory but ended in the older boy's dorm. I also knew Darrell McCovey and Billy Pratt. I ended up in the Navy with them but I went on a different ship.

What was your trade when you were at Sherman?

First I took up the dairy, which wasn't very much. Then I got into painting so I was a painter. A lot of Indians got into that to paint houses. I did that on the outside for a while. I also took up cooking for a while.

When you were at Sherman did they have you march, or do drills?

Not in my time, not when I was there. They had that in earlier times. They were just changing that when I was down there. Then in 1941, it was after we ate on a Sunday when they said the war broke out. I remember when the war broke out. I was just a kid. I was 15 when the war came. I went in the service and I was almost 17. My mother helped me out.

Did you see my Grandpa Stan and Leonard at Sherman?

No, they were already in the service by then. When I got there they were just leaving. When your grandfather and Leonard came back, usually Leonard came back and visited the school before the war really got going.

He was dressed in his uniform and it impressed a lot of us. I thought that was pretty nice. I decided to go in the Navy to be different. I went to San Francisco to sign up with Perry Allen from Alturas.

I went to boot camp in Farragut, Idaho. Training was six weeks then I went to Tacoma, Washington. I caught a ship and went to Canada, then came back and got on a small carrier. We went to the Hawaiian Islands, then during the war we were in the Gilbert Islands and the Marshall Islands.

Our ship got hit in the Marshalls and we were sent to Pearl Harbor to work on it, but Pearl Harbor couldn't handle it so we were sent to the States. I think the ship was called the *Manila Bay.* They sent other ships to help us because we were crippled.

Then I was transferred to another ship called the *White Plains* and went back overseas again and I ended up in the Philippines in a gulf battle. Then we went up north to Luzon. Then I was transferred to another ship, an LST, which is a landing craft.

They haul trucks and tanks to islands then turn around and leave. After the war ended I really got transferred around because they would fill in on other ships. I ended by serving on the *Topeka,* and then they transferred me to the *Chicago.* That was the new *Chicago* because the old *Chicago* was sunk.

What were some of your duties on these ships?

Well, I started out as a seaman. I ended up a second class petty officer, gunner's mate. I started out as a cook but got transferred. I started out on the 20-millimeter gun and went up to the 40-millimeter.

I ended up on the five-inch 38-dual purpose twins. That was a little bigger gun. I gave orders to the crew on that. You had this little lookout on top of the gun house and tell the crew when to shoot at planes and things like that.

Can you describe that gulf battle?

During that battle in the gulf the Japanese were gone. We had ships out looking for them and a few ships were left behind. We didn't know it but the Japanese came in behind us and crippled us up pretty bad and we lost a lot of ships. But then they got caught in the north. It's been a long time since I've talked about that.

Were there times when your ship was dive-bombed?

Oh yeah, that was scary. When I was on the LST a plane sent two torpedoes at us but they didn't hit us, they went underneath. During that battle I was in I was on the 40-millimeter. I was the pointer; I did the firing.

We had the pointer and the trainer and the loader in the crew. There was so much firing going on, this plane that tried to hit us was coming real low and we hit it, then it twisted into the water. I don't know if we hit it but it was pretty close to us when it went into the water.

Where did you sleep on the ships?

I slept on the middle bunk so I could jump out quick. There were about four battles I was in; I don't know what could be considered a major battle. But we had to face submarines and air attack.

They had kamikaze planes too. We were hit on one side on the USS *White Plains*. We weren't hit badly, but it damaged us. We couldn't balance the ship out.

Did you ever hear Tokyo Rose on the radio?

Yeah, I remember that. She'd tell us all kinds of stuff. She probably drove a lot of guys crazy. She was telling us to give up, or go home, or our wife was with somebody else. That's a trick of the war, you know. Some people didn't realize that.

What year did you go in the service?

I went in 1942 and came out in 1947. One time when I was on leave I came in to the States. We were in San Diego around Christmas time but they called us back in! That was some bad luck. They did give us a turkey dinner.

The food was good in the Navy. At first everything was powdered. Eventually it got better. I imagine the Army and Marines had it pretty bad too, they didn't get as good of food as we did. About two weeks after the war ended we went to Japan.

We were in that big bay where the Americans sunk all those ships. I got to see Osaka after all that bombing and I was in Yokohama. It was heavily bombed, it was horrible. They just leveled it. There's stuff that was unbelievable. They use a lot of motorcycles over there, and they were just melted. The buildings were knocked down.

Do you remember where you were when you heard the atomic bomb was used and the war was over?

I was back in the Philippines and everybody celebrated. We used sick bay alcohol for drinks! That stuff was 160-proof. Talk about getting sick!

It was a relief the war was over. They messed up and had me as missing in action because I came home a year-and-a-half later. It was good to come home. That's when your grandfather Stanley and I ran around for a while.

He mentioned about that time when the two of you went to a bar in Susanville...

Ha, ha! We were in this Italian bar there and just sitting there. These other guys were fighting at the other end. Stanley said he would go buy them a drink and tell them to quit fighting.

One of those guys was the biggest I've ever seen. I don't know what happened, the next thing I knew they were fighting, so then I had to jump in! We tore up that whole bar.

He also mentioned about that time when you went to a bar and saw that sign that said 'No Indians or dogs allowed.'

Oh yeah, that was discrimination there. The only thing I remember is they had that sign that said you couldn't go in there if you were Indian. I remember another time when I was in a bar and they told me to get out because they knew I was Indian.

Did you ever face any type of discrimination in the service?

No, not really. I faced it more when we played basketball. I was in a tournament and they wouldn't let us eat in a restaurant there. This was before the war. There was discrimination against Indians in the military, but the Navy was different.

There were a lot of Indian sailors. I was kind of a loner. I went to town by myself. I didn't drink too much then. But I did after the service. I think there was a period where we all started drinking hard, and you either pulled out of it or you didn't. I drank until I was 65. I quit in 1995. But many Indians drank and it ruined our culture.

Gene Ryan

This is a hard question to ask, but why do you think men of your generation drank so much, was it because of the war?

No, people drank before the war. Everyone was poor, and most of us had it pretty rough, with the Indian schools and everything else. It was a way out. What really hurts to this day, everybody could come to this country and have their own religion, but the American Indian was told he couldn't have his religion.

I think that's sad. That's real discrimination, as far as I'm concerned. There's a lot of hurt there. We couldn't speak our language. Everybody else could come here and speak their own language.

At that time they said American Indians couldn't have their own language. And your religion was no good, and I think the Indian religions are the best in the world if you just analyze it and use common sense. I'm glad some tribes kept their religions.

California Indians had it pretty rough because of gold. It was the end of the West, you know. Everybody got it better than the Indians. I know Mexicans have Indian blood in them, but they were considered better than Indians.

It's hard when you're the lowest on the totem pole. There's a lot of hurt. My mother went through that time; she went to Sherman and to Chemawa, Oregon. There's a lot of hurt.

Knowing all of that, why do you think so many Indian people volunteered to go in the service for this country?

That's what kept my grandmother going, she walked everywhere. She didn't ride in a car until she was over 100 years old.

I think that they never had opportunities. Indians were never hired and there was discrimination. They were the last to get hired and the first to get fired. It was that way in the service after the war. They found what they could to kick Indians out of the military, but they used them in the war because they were good fighters.

I think it's because they already went through hard times. Most of the Indians could get through boot camp, but a lot of other people couldn't. They couldn't take it. In my point of view, Indian people had it pretty tough.

Those Indian schools did help them because they did grow up with marching and wearing a uniform. They had to learn to make their bed. You had to learn to make your bed right at the Indian school or when the guy came by he'd tear it all up, just like in the military. I think it helped the Indians that way, for going in the military, because they already knew how to do that.

I think that's why some Indians really got ahead in the service. Some became officers and went up through the ranks. It's hard for any person to go up in rank and become an officer, so any enlisted man that became an officer was really something. Indians never got any recognition either. I don't know why that is, but on any TV show you never see an American Indian fighting in the service. It's always somebody else.

What did you do after the war?

I worked near Susanville in lumber. I stayed in those camps out there. Then I went to work for the Navy. I was what you'd call a weekend warrior. I worked for the government for about 38 years. I lived around the Bay Area.

When I retired I lived up in the mountains near Antelope Lake. That was pretty nice but I moved because people were breaking into my house. I had to park my car at the bottom of a hill and ski to the house in the winter.

I liked to cross-country ski but I'm getting older now. I still golf. I can't see, but I can still play it! I play in those big Indian tournaments. I just went to a big tournament in Shasta. They have Indian tournaments all over the country.

When I was younger I played baseball and basketball. I remember in Susanville they had two Indian basketball teams, the Braves and the Ramblers. The Ramblers died out but the Braves kept going and won a couple championships. We had a lot of fun. At that time they had quite a few Indian basketball teams. It's the same way today; they have teams in Covello and on the coast.

Do you feel it would be important for our media to recognize the contributions of our Indian veterans, not just from World War Two but from all conflicts?

I think so. I think they should be put on television like anyone else. They always leave the Indians out. It did ruin one guy. That Indian guy who helped raise the flag at Iwo Jima. Here was a guy (Ira Hayes) who didn't drink when he was on the reservation.

But something happened and he started drinking, and ended up dying in a gutter. That's sad. I think before Leonard passed away he told people not to drink like he did. He had sugar diabetes and tried to get away with it. Indians get sugar diabetes easy. Years ago Indians hunted and walked everywhere.

They used to walk and travel and eat wild game. As time went on in these reservations they had to eat macaroni and other foods, and they'd sit around. They don't get enough exercise. That's what kept my grandmother going, she walked everywhere. She didn't ride in a car until she was over 100 years old.

How do you feel about Indian education?

Well, when I was growing up my grandmother couldn't read, so I didn't do much homework. I just took it home then took it back to school. I try to advise my sons and daughter that education means a lot. One of my sons passed away last year. Another thing, I always told my kids when you're among different tribes you treat them the same. You never know who you're related to!

Gene Ryan enjoys attending the Bear Dance and Lowry family reunions in Greenville. His family is very proud of his service to his people and to his country.

Frank Grant

I was able to meet Frank Grant on July 11, 2002. He is of Karuk ancestry and was a member of the Merchant Marines during the war. His granddaughter Marlette put me in touch with him for this interview.

I was born on July 1, 1921 between Somes Bar and the Forks of Salmon. There was a doctor that used to ride on a horse in that area. My mother was Maggie Bennett and my dad was Frank Grant, Sr. They were both born in that area too.

My dad's side is the Karuk and my grandmother on my dad's side was from Cecilville. I think that group was pretty wiped out when the white men first came in. She spoke a different language than my mother did but they could understand each other.

My mother could understand Karuk, but I never heard her speak it. I was raised in that area through grammar school. I can remember when I was a little fellow there were no automobile roads like we have today. There were just the old 49 trails, and I can remember the pack train.

They used to have a pack train that would go up over

Frank Grant in 1945.
Photo courtesy of Frank Grant.

the hill and you could hear the bell coming down the trail. These two men would have a mail sack and come by our property, we had 20 acres then, and they'd put the mail in this sack that we hung from a Madrone tree. Sometimes I'd run up there and they'd hand it to me and I'd bring it back.

My dad had met my mother when they started building a road between Somes and the Forks of Salmon right after World War One. My dad contracted to build a section of that road. That was somewhere in the 1920s. When I started grammar school they had completed the road all the way through. It was still pretty rough.

So before the road came through everyone was on horseback?

That's right, we had a horse and I had a donkey. We used to have a little saddle and I rode the donkey. Then when we went to school I rode on the back of my dad's horse.

Did you have any brothers or sisters?

I'm the oldest, and there were five girls and six boys.

Did your family ever have any stories about when the first miners came through the area?

My mother used to talk about when the Chinese came in. They discovered gold in there and they moved the water in the river this way, and worked the bottom, then they moved it back and forth and worked the bottom all the way up. I never heard of them killing or shooting anybody.

They used to have a pack train that would go up over the hill and you could hear the bell coming down the trail.

What type of food did your family have while growing up?

Well, like I say, we had 20 acres so we had a big garden. My dad had a horse to plow the field and plant potatoes. My job was to put the seed in as he opened the ground. Then my mother canned all kinds of vegetables.

We dried and canned peaches, apples and plums. We also had a cow for milk and made our own butter. My mother and dad would go back in the Marble Mountains on hunting trips and they'd come back with a buck or something.

It sounds like you ate well, where did you go to elementary school?

Junction School at Somes Bar. The old school isn't there anymore. When I first started there was on teacher and a one-room school. There was a stove for heat and all eight grades were there. There were just enough kids to keep the school going.

But during the Depression a lot of city people moved in to mine along the rivers to make a living. Then there were a lot of children and they hired two teachers and built a two-room school. That's what they had there when I left in 1935.

What was Somes Bar like then?

It was just a store that had general groceries. You

could get certain drugs on the shelf and flour; just staples. There was also a post office. My aunt and uncle owned the store. Their names were Karl and Melissa Langford. That was my dad's sister. I believe there's still a descendant running that store now.

Across the river from us was the Tripp family. Some of those boys would travel across the river down to the school and we'd meet there. I remember some older women coming by and stay overnight and then they'd go on. We'd have cousins come visit. We were isolated so we had to make our own toys to play with.

What was the winter like?

Oh, it was cold. I can remember we had 30 inches of snow one year. There were a lot of bears out there too. They'd come in and eat the apples off the apple tree. We also had lots of raccoons; I used to shoot some, skin and dry them, and send it off to St. Louis. You'd get maybe a dollar for them, and I don't know what they'd do with the hide.

We sailed out under the Golden Gate Bridge. They always sail out at night. It was dusk. You could look out there and the Golden Gate is getting further and further away.

What was it like to be around the Salmon River?

It was clear water. We'd go swimming in it. In the summer you could drive over certain areas but in the winter it was much higher. I can remember down at Ishi Pishi Falls on the Klamath they used to dip nets for fish. My dad would get some fish and we'd salt it and can it.

Where did you go after elementary school?

I had an aunt who lived in Yreka. This was in '35 or '36; I went out there my freshman year. I went one year there. Then they moved to Red Bluff. I went to high school in Red Bluff. Boy that was hot there!

The summer after I went to high school I worked in a store, then I went to Humboldt. I paid seven dollars a month for a room near the school. Tuition was something like seven dollars, not like it is nowadays!

All they had was Founder's Hall and there were 400 or so kids going to school there. Some of the buildings they have now are named after some of the professors from when I was going. I had an uncle who worked for the Forest Service so I was taking forestry courses.

They only gave two years of courses then you had to transfer to the University of California or Corvallis, Oregon. I didn't have the money to do that so I took some other subjects. I think I took every lower-division class they had at Humboldt!

I got married right after World War Two was declared. I had to work and try to go to school. I have three children from that marriage; there's Frank the third, Zane and Laura Lee. I worked with the generator at the barrel factory in Arcata. I got one deferment and then they told me I had to go in. My boss said I should go in the Merchant Marine. In the middle of my junior year is when I went in the service. You always see the advertisement with the guy carrying his duffel bag on his shoulder.

At the beginning of the war submarines were sinking all the merchant ships. There weren't enough ships and men. They built all these Liberty ships and the Navy at that time took it over. You went in under the Navy M-1 program, which was Naval reserve on merchant ships. So I got in there.

After that they sent me to Catalina to train for 13 weeks. At Catalina you could go into the engine room on deck, the steward's department or the radio operations. After three weeks you had to decide where you were going to go. I went in the engine room since I had worked around generators and power.

During those 13 weeks they train you on a tugboat. They feed you a nice big steak and you get down around that oil and steam, and you lost all that steak! But you know I never got seasick after that! That helped, I guess. They also trained you in case of fire. They put oil on top of the water and lit the fire. You get up about 30 feet and bail off into that fire. You learned how to swim out of that.

Then they assigned you to a ship back in San Francisco. They put me on as a wiper. There are two wipers on a ship and a fireman, plus three oilers. It depended on your grade if you were to be picked as a wiper.

This friend of mine and I went on a ship together. It was called the *Richard Marsh Hoe*. These always named these Liberty ships after someone. So we took this ship across the Bay and the Navy took it over. I spent eight weeks on that ship. I got on a ship called the SS *Lyman Beecher*. We loaded up and they put planes on the deck and these amphibious-type ducks that could go in water and on land.

We sailed out under the Golden Gate Bridge. They always sail out at night. It was dusk. You could look out there and the Golden Gate is getting further and further away. You get up in the morning and you're out in the water.

That's a funny feeling the first time. You get out about two or three days and the seagulls were following. After that they went back to land. These old Liberty ships were triple expansion engines with two boilers and one engine. They topped at about eight knots per hour, and that was slow. They don't tell you where you're going either. I think we were 45 days at sea. We went down to Auckland, New Zealand.

We unloaded and they sent us down to Chile. We loaded nitrates there. They made explosives out of nitrates. When we were loading there was no smoking on deck because that stuff will burn better than gasoline. From there we brought in back to Long Beach and loaded it. That was about four months and I thought that was pretty good.

I wanted to see how the wife and my boy were doing. They gave me three days off then I met them in San

Francisco to get on that same ship. We were gone 14 months! We went to the South Pacific.

We went down to the southern tip of New Guinea. Going in there were a lot of reefs. They had it all marked but we got stuck for three days. They brought two tugs and pulled, and finally a wind came up and we kind of bounced off.

We didn't know if we had a hole in the bottom so they sent us to Newcastle in Australia to check the bottom. It was all right so they sent us to New Guinea. Then we moved troops. We'd take a whole battalion at a time. We kept moving up to all these different bays. We did that for 14 months. Then they sent us back to Chile and loaded up with nitrates. I think we took that to New Orleans.

I had enough time to apply for officer's candidate school so I applied and was accepted. That was in Alameda. I went to school there for four months. I got my third engineer's license. On the West Coast we had sailor unions but in the East Coast they had SMU, that's what they called it.

It was mixed crews. You could have different people. On the West Coast crews everybody spoke the same language. I was assigned to this ship and the fireman was from Columbia and he spoke Spanish. Then I had an oiler who was from San Lucia who spoke French. But you could talk to them and they'd understand. But if we got in trouble and started talking we didn't know anything! That was quite a trip. We went to the Pacific and loaded mostly food.

Then we came back and got another load of nitrates in Chile and took that to Brest, France and unloaded it. When we came back I signed off of that ship. They dropped me off in New York and from there I went to Chicago then to San Francisco on trains. Then I came home a little while.

My wife and I went to San Francisco and thought we'd have a week or so. I went to the Marine Engineers Association and they said they needed an engineer right then. It was a first engineer job with an increase in pay so I told my wife I had a chance to make more money so she went home.

That ship was warmed up ready to go when I got on! I went down to the engine room, put on my clothes and we took off. We went up to Vancouver and loaded wheat. When you load wheat they put boards in between the wheat otherwise it could shift and turn the ship over.

The ship worked good going up. Then with the load on, boy, it had been in dry dock and they didn't pack the high-pressure cylinder very good. That steamer was trying to get out there and they didn't stop, we had to keep going. That engine room was hot!

When we came into Panama City we dropped anchor. The third engineer and I had to work on that cylinder. We repacked it and it worked all right. Then we went through the Panama Canal. I've been through the Canal three times going either east to west or west to east.

Can you describe the process going through the Canal?

I think there're three locks on the Pacific level. They run you into this lock that's big; I don't know if two ships can fit in or not, but then they'll close the gate behind you. Then they'll open the gate in front of you and the water floods in and raises you.

They had donkeys, iron mules they called them, that would catch onto the ship and pull it into the next lock. Then you close the gate and open the next lock. The water rises up and then you go on through. In the middle there's a big lake that's fed by a river. That's where they get the water.

Frank Grant

After you get through the locks you're on your own until you get to that lake. Then you lay in there until you get clearance to go on through the other side. After you get to the other side they run you in, close the gate in front of you and let the water out until you get to sea level.

How long does that whole process take?

All day. Maybe they can put you through faster but there's always ships coming this way and you have to wait your turn.

After you went through where did you go?

For this trip we had wheat. We took that over to Antwerp, Belgium. We had gone up through the North Atlantic. It was cold and I could see the waves come clear over the ship. It was rough that time so we had to stand throttle watch.

We went through the English Channel and then up a river through Belgium to get to Antwerp. You could see the stacks where they had sunk all the ships, so you had to weave your way through there.

Now a throttle watch is when the bow of the ship comes up and you open up the steam and it gives it a push. Then when the bow goes down the stern comes up and the propeller comes out of the water and it speeds up. So you have to slow it down.

So you stay on the throttle watch and go back and forth like that. They say if it speeds up too fast it could break that propeller and you'd be stuck out there. I've stood throttle watch for a week at a time going across there.

We went through the English Channel and then up a river through Belgium to get to Antwerp. You could see the stacks where they had sunk all the ships, so you had to weave your way through there. On that trip to Brest, France we went to England.

We stayed in London. Wherever we went I always paid a guide to show me through. We went out to a castle and I went to Buckingham; I watched the changing of the guard. From London we went over to Wales. I didn't visit through Brest; the town was all shattered, it looked like somebody took a hammer and beat it all down.

That was a 14-month trip we took. We dropped anchor in what they call Humboldt Bay. We were 45 days on anchor there, just drifting around. More ships kept coming in. Finally one day we took off to the Philippines to Leyte Gulf.

While we were there unloading there was a big tanker across the bay. Next to that tanker was a little Navy personnel ship, the kind where they carried small groups of troops. A Zero came right over the top of our ship; he was after that tanker but he hit into that Navy ship and there were a bunch killed there. When he hit there was a big ball of fire.

Was there ever a time when you were threatened by a sub?

No, we never saw a sub. They might have been out there. Most of that sub stuff was on the Atlantic side.

Do you remember where you were when Germany surrendered?

Out in the Pacific! I think we were coming back to the States. I don't know where I was when Japan surrendered. The last ship I was on was the *SS James Kimball.* That's the one we went to Antwerp in.

We came back to New Orleans. The war was over with and there were all these extra ships. They just kind of tied them together. I stayed there three weeks waiting for somebody to relieve me but nobody did. Finally I just left ship! Then I came home.

What was the atmosphere like when the war was over?

I don't know. We didn't get back until way later. It took a little while for those old ships to make any headway! But looking back, I've seen tapes on TV where they had a big party, but it must have been all over with when I got back.

Will you tell me how you heard about Pearl Harbor being attacked when you were at school?

They called an assembly after they heard Pearl Harbor was hit. We listened to Roosevelt's speech. It was quiet; I started thinking I would have to go. Right at the beginning they put a watch up there in Founder's Hall. There's a tower up there with a room; they converted that room into a watch. You could watch for planes. I stood some watches up there.

You mentioned your brother was in the war?

Yes, my brother Reginald was in the Navy during the war. He lives in Hoopa. All my brothers were in the service except the youngest that was killed in a car accident. My dad was in World War One in the Army. He went over to France.

He landed in Brest, France, so when I came over and told him I was there he remembered all that. He always told us not to go in the Army. He said you'd sleep in the mud, so all my brothers were in the Navy or the Naval Reserve.

Frank Grant and his wife Eleanor reside in Eureka, CA. Frank was the president of the American Merchant Marines Veterans Association in Eureka during 2002. He is a retired process control supervisor and belongs to the local Masonic lodge.

James Campbell, Sr.

1921- 2003

I met with James Campbell, Sr. at his home on Dec. 20, 2002. His daughter Gina arranged for our interview. It was a cold, wet, rainy day during our interview. Mr. Campbell was patiently waiting for me and we sat down and he spoke about his time in the U.S. Navy.

I was born in Santa Ana, California on March 30, 1921. My mother was Clara Hostler from here in Hoopa; she passed away in 1945 when I was in the Philippines. She was from this place right here. Her allotment was right next door.

She inherited this land here. My dad's mother was a full-blooded Hupa Indian. She was a Quimby, I believe. His father came here from Kentucky somewhere in the mid-1800's. My dad James Monroe Campbell was born in Salyer in 1875 and he passed away in 1952.

They used to own Campbell Field and Campbell Creek on the Campbell ranch but they sold it. During the Depression he had a job with his relatives; they had a concrete business. He would have summers off then we'd come to Hoopa to stay. In '37 we came here and stayed and never went back.

My mother told me part of the valley was settled by the Campbells before it became a reservation. There was another group of people who worked for the Campbells on that ranch and they gave them their last name, so they're known as Campbells too. My dad had five sisters so I had quite a few cousins. I'm the only Campbell from my dad's side. I have a sister Gearldine in Blue Lake who isn't doing well. I had one brother and four sisters. They're all gone.

So your family moved to Hoopa in 1937; how old were you then?

I was 16; I finished high school here. I got out in the spring of '40 and went down south to work. I came back here a couple months before the war started. I think I came back here in October of '41. Then the war came along and right after Pearl Harbor my cousin wanted me to join the Navy with him.

The USS Atlanta.
Photo courtesy of James Campbell.

We were going to get drafted. So I went down with him to San Francisco and they had so many people they sent us home. Then they called us a few days later and we went back on Friday the 13th in February, I believe. There were three Friday the 13ths that year. After we were sworn in they sent us home again, then they called us in two weeks and we went to San Diego. I was there for three weeks. Then they sent a bunch of us to San Francisco on a train.

We stayed there on a big ocean liner. We left there on my birthday, March the 30th in '42 and went to Peal Harbor. I was assigned to an ammunition depot for a few days, and then I got on a ship. It was the *USS Atlanta* (CL-51). It was a light cruiser.

That's a picture of it there (on his wall). Then that's where the fun began, I guess! It was a new ship; it was still under shake down. After a few days of going out and learning to fire the guns and everything we went down to New Caledonia and over to the Coral Sea.

We met the fleet coming out of there after the first Coral Sea battle. There were a couple of carriers there; I think it was the *Saratoga* and the *Enterprise.* They lost the *Lexington.* They came out and we went back to Pearl Harbor for one day. They had loaded some of the ships again.

> *They were just pushing planes over the side to get them out of the way on the Enterprise to let other planes land.*

Some of the ships were still lying there sunk. By the time we got there it was maybe four months after the attack at Pearl Harbor. We got there in early April. They had a lot of it cleaned up and the aircraft were flying out of Ford Island.

We went in and fueled up and re-stored then we went north up to Midway. By then it was the first of June. Then the Midway battle happened on the fourth of June. We lost the *Yorktown* there. We were still with the Enterprise.

We had lots of planes trying to make it to where the *Enterprise* was. They were out of gas. If they couldn't make it on the first pass they'd ditch them in the ocean. They were just pushing planes over the side to get them out of the way on the *Enterprise* to let other planes land. The pilot was more valuable than the plane, you know. We turned the searchlights on toward nighttime to guide the planes where we were. It was a mess.

What were your ship's duties?

It was an anti-aircraft cruiser. It was 538 feet long and had 16 five-inch 38 guns on it. I don't know if you're familiar with the Navy guns. It was a short barrel fast-shooting gun that could fire lots of shells from a turret. We also had eight 20-millimeter guns and three sets of tom-tom guns. It also had eight torpedo tubes. It was fast, almost as fast as a destroyer.

What were your duties on the ship?

I was on a turret for a while. When you first go on they put you everywhere to try to find a place for you. I ended up in the number five turret. I was there up until the battle we got sunk in. One day we were practicing on a dummy-loading machine.

They had a dummy shell or powder can made out of maple wood. It had an iron ring on the back of it and it was heavy. They pointed that dummy down, and I had on leather asbestos gloves. They were big, thick, heavy gloves.

The old battleships from Pearl Harbor dug in the beach right below us!

I tried to catch that powder can and it just hit my hand and the blood came right out of that glove. The gun captain knew what happened and he stopped them. It smashed all my fingers here on my hand. See it? It's all flat. It smashed the meat out and broke it.

So I couldn't be in the turret anymore so they put me in the upper handling room. About 10 days later that ship got sunk and that turret got hit. There were 13 guys in there and everybody was killed but one person. I have a citation here someplace that says our ship was hit by 49 shells and a torpedo.

So your ship was sunk in battle?

Well, they blew it up. We had to leave; it was dead in the water. The *Portland* was damaged too. There was a big fleet of Japanese ships coming so we had to blow it up. This was in Guadalcanal.

After the Midway battle we'd gone back to Pearl Harbor then we went up to the Aleutians for a while but couldn't see anything there. It was foggy. So we went back to Pearl Harbor for a couple weeks. Then we went down to New Caledonia. We picked up six transports loaded with Marines. We had four destroyers with us.

We cruised around out there for a while before we went into Guadalcanal on August 8th of '42. One morning we were supposed to go in and bombard some gun emplacements the Japanese had up in the hills. We were supposed to go in there for an hour or so but we stayed in there and fired around 5,000 rounds of those 5-inch 39 projectiles. We were there until daylight ended.

The Marines really thought a lot of us when we went ashore. They told us we saved them. We were about 25 miles from the beachhead when they had what they call the Battle of Savo. We were hit once.

Some of the guys jumped in the water because the boat was burning. I stayed and went topside. I got the fire extinguisher and grabbed the ladder; I squirted that stuff on the guy that was in the turret gun and then they put salt water on it. We secured everything and did what we were supposed to do in our area, but everybody else ran!

We finally got the fire out about daylight. This all started about midnight on November the 12th. In the morning it was Friday the 13th! We all pitched in; there were the wounded to take care of. But some of those guys were really worthless. The guys from the East Coast were the worst. The ones from New York were real smart-alecks.

When you went in at Guadalcanal did you go on the island itself?

Yeah, I went in. I was down on the beach with a gun. That was after we got sunk. The first night Japanese battleships came in and they were shelling the airstrip. We were in a tent lying there. We were so tired; we never had anything to eat for 44 hours. I had one orange.

That last week before we got sunk we had been up in general quarters. They brought us sandwiches and coffee. Then that last day they let half of us go to take a shower, get clean clothes and go to the mess hall to eat. Then they let the other half go. They must have known something was coming because then we went to general quarters and stayed there. That was the last meal we had.

How long were you on Guadalcanal, and what did the beach look like?

It was a plantation. All the trees were planted in straight lines. Everywhere you looked the trees were in straight lines. That surprised me, you know. After our ship was sunk and we left the ship it was dark when we got to the beach.

We found a tent and bedded up around the tent. We were all worn out. Then those ships came in and started shelling. The tent I was in was near some slit trenches the Marines had dug. They were just big enough to lie in. But everyone just said, 'If they're going to kill us, they'll kill us wherever we go.' There wasn't anyplace to go.

They shelled a long time. There was an airplane flying around sending flares. They shelled the airstrip. It had ramps that had holes in them. They were trying to tear that up. They had a big fleet coming in to take the place back.

The Japanese finally left. The next day somebody took us to the airport and we got a 37-millimeter anti-aircraft gun. We got these canister shells, like shotgun shells, that had these balls in them. We had 10 clips for it.

There were six of us. They put us down on the beach at the mouth of the river. The Marines had pulled back on one side of the river to shorten the beachhead. Around dark this Marine captain came down. We had rifles and helmets. He came around and said they didn't have any bayonets for us. He said there were 400 soldiers in a trench behind us back about 50 or 60 yards. He told us this is where the Japanese were going to hit if they came through.

Anyhow, everybody went to bed. I was sitting by that gun and the Marine was sitting in the other seat. We were sitting there just talking. And then, it must have been midnight; there was a big flash out on the horizon.

We thought, 'Oh, here it comes. They're coming now.' We didn't have anything out there to stop them. We waited for shells to come in and hit the beach. Pretty soon there was firing both ways on the horizon. It turned out, I think it was the *Washington* and the *South Dakota* had come in from someplace.

They were battleships, and they intercepted that fleet out there and tore it up. I don't know what happened. The next morning at daylight we saw there was one of the old battleships from Pearl Harbor dug in the beach right below us!

It opened up and fired big shots down the beach about a mile. There was a Japanese transport. They'd run it right up on the beach. A little farther up there was another one. There were three of them; they'd run them right up on the beach.

Our airplanes went after them. They got some dive-bombers on them. Then some planes came in from about 400 miles away. They blew those ships up, but I guess a lot of guys got out.

When you were on shore at Guadalcanal did you ever have to fight against the Japanese, or did you ever see any of that?

No, I never did where we were. They pulled us back across the river so if there was any attack they'd have to cross the river. They had cut some protective lines where they could machine gun this way and have a cross fire. I was within a few hundred yards where they were though. We were right there until about the end of November. I'm just guessing. They took us down to New Caledonia again.

We got some new clothes, and then they reassigned a bunch of us back up to Tulagi at Guadalcanal. Then I got on with a torpedo boat. We went ashore on an island, I can't think of the name, and visited a Native village. They said to post sentries.

The chief radioman was in charge and he put a black guy as sentry to mess with him. In those days all the black guys did was serve officers. So he put him on as guard. About midnight there was a shot. Everybody got up and ran over there.

That black guy said there was somebody in where the men were sleeping. Nobody was missing. Pretty soon they found that radioman shot right through his Adam's apple. He might have sat up in his bed. That guy was from Georgia. He used to tell me he was from Georgia and he didn't like black people at all. That first night there, that guy shot him.

I didn't think of it at the time, but they might have had words and that guy shot him. That was at this island by Tulagi. I told that black guy to give me his rifle. He did, and there was another shell in there ready to fire. I unloaded it and gave it back to him. Maybe they had words, nobody ever knew. They fined him and transferred him.

What did you do after you were on that island?

I was assigned to torpedo boat squadron two and three, which were remnants. Kennedy was there; I don't know what squadron he was in. They had about 80 boats at Tulagi. There was a full squadron and some remnants.

Some of those guys were from the Philippines. They took the officers and left the enlisted people when they brought McArthur out. They've written books and made movies about some of the people I met there!

There was a guy, the chief torpedo man, who had been left in the Philippines. He and some other guys fixed up an old broke-down plane and flew it to Australia. They made it out. I went back to the Philippines with him in Squadron 39.

James Campbell, Sr.

So this was when you were on Tulagi?

Yeah, and the funny thing too, before I was on that ship I was left at the liberty dock one evening. We had to be back onboard before sundown to get back to Tulagi. I was talking to a torpedo man from the torpedo squadron in Peal Harbor.

I asked him how they got those torpedoes off those boats after what happened at Pearl. He said they fired them off. They had a powder charge on the torpedoes. They would hit it with a mallet and it made a big flash that lit up the sky.

I told him I thought they had clamps! After I got with the torpedo boats in Tulagi they had torpedo clamps; we'd build them right there. I always knew that was my idea. They said somebody in the Pacific came up with this idea. They sent some people to Maryland to develop them. I know that was my idea because I spoke with that man with the torpedo boats at Pearl.

Your entire time at Tulagi was spent working on PT boats?

One of the first boats I worked on was Kennedy's boat. They brought it to the docks someplace to replace something. It was a mahogany shell about an inch thick. I talked to Kennedy.

Yeah, that's what I did. I was a carpenter before I went in. On the way to Tulagi I met this guy from Happy Camp and they had us run the laundry on the ship. There were six or eight ladies from an island.

They did all the work washing and we bagged and wrapped the clothes for the guys. We got extra pay for that. Then on the island we got into the carpenter's shop. We were both seamen but they needed carpenters. They had quite a few boats that needed a lot of work. They'd hit reefs or something.

They brought us some guys from the Seabees because we still needed more carpenters. They worked for me and my friend, and we were seamen first. Those guys had a second class rating or better. When they saw that they didn't like it. They hollered and so they had to give us a rate. They still out-rated us but it was better.

One of the first boats I worked on was Kennedy's boat. They brought it to the docks someplace to replace something. It was a mahogany shell about an inch thick. I talked to Kennedy. He was a good guy, I thought. He was the skipper, the captain. There were other boats, and they had one of the original 77-foot boats. They came out with an 80-footer with a little more horsepower.

When Kennedy became President did you think back to that time when you met him?

Oh yeah, he was a good person. Everybody in the torpedo boats and all the officers were just common people. I worked side by side with guys who had two-and-a-half stripes. We had to get 150 gallons of gas every morning before breakfast.

There would be two officers there. One was a full lieutenant. They'd roll those drums just like we would. Every morning we did that. I was there on Tulagi for nearly two years. I must have got away from there around December of '43.

I was back in San Francisco for a few weeks. They let us go for 48 hours on liberty in San Francisco. Then I got delayed orders to the East Coast. I came back here to Hoopa for a week or so then I went to Los Angeles to see my sister. I took a train to the East Coast. I was assigned from Tulagi to the East Coast to a training center.

I misread my orders and thought I needed to be there by noon. I left Los Angeles, went to Chicago and stayed overnight, then got on a train to New York, then to Providence about 10 at night. That base was about 15 miles away.

I had to take a bus to get there. I thought my orders were for the next day. I stayed the night and had something to eat. I got to the base the next day about noon. The duty officer told me I was over leave. They put me in a squadron. I got 20 percent more pay. It was a good place to be. We had a squadron of about eight boats that new people were learning to run and dock. They'd go out and fire torpedoes.

I was there for about a year. I put in for a new squadron in early '45. I got assigned to Squadron 38 or 39. I went down to New York and went back to the Philippines. We had four boat divisions there. It was good duty and we ate good!

Did you ever have a moment during the war when you thought you might be killed?

I don't know, I never did think they were going to kill me. After the battle on our ship we looked at it. It had shell holes and even had machine gun bullet holes in it. They were that close to us. The citation we received said 49 shells hit the ship.

Our own ships hit us too. It was the *San Francisco.* I picked up a spent eight-inch projectile. It had American writing on it! I showed it to other seamen and we took it to the gunnery officer. He looked at it and said it was from the *San Francisco.*

They might have done some damage to our ship. I've read accounts of that battle that said there were three of our destroyers ahead of us and one behind us. The three ahead of us all went down. There was a guy in Willow Creek who I met that was a survivor of that. He said he was 16 years old when he enlisted.

How old were you when you went into the service?

The day we left San Francisco for Pearl Harbor it was my birthday. I was 21 years old on March the 30th. My cousin that went in with me was Oswald Bussel. He died years ago. He also went in the Navy.

Why did you guys choose to go in the Navy?

Ha! I always thought it would be better than flogging around in the mud someplace. But going back to thinking about being in danger; I never did think I was going to get killed. The first thing I did after I got out of that battle station, we were burning, and I saw other ships blowing up and exploding; I went up to the boat deck and I took my shirt off.

I took that grease we used to put on the screws of bolts on motor launches, I took that grease and put it all over my belt on my shoulders then I put my shirt back on. I got some line, about 25 feet or so, and I put it around my waist. I had to go in the water and there were no lifejackets and no life rafts.

They had whaleboats hanging there on the ship, and they had a couple small 40-foot boats, but these were all gone because they had blown up. They had medical supplies on them with water and crackers and things for you in case the ship sinks. It was supposed to be there.

There was nothing to get away in, everything got blown away. I thought that grease would protect me from getting cold in the water. I was going to tie myself to something. That's what I was thinking. Before that I never worried about anything. I always thought I'd make it.

Did you ever see other Indian men?

Not from around the coast here. I saw a doctor on a cruiser who was from Eureka, and Vernon Clarke was on there. He was from that Carson family, but he was killed in that battle. I don't remember the doctor's name.

I went to him after the war. I did meet a white guy on Tulagi whose mother was a teacher from here. He was an officer. I was walking along and he was walking with some other officers. I said hello to him and we talked a little bit.

How'd you guys get your news about how the war was going?

Every day on that cruiser they'd post it. They had a printed account of what was going on. They also had posted our position, where the nearest land was. That was in case we needed to swim I guess!

Did you ever write home or did anyone in your family write to you?

Oh yeah, my mother wrote to me all the time. My dad wrote to me too. But I've seen some of the stuff I wrote, and the censors had cut it all to pieces.

Do you remember where you were when the atomic bomb was used to end the war?

I was in Samar in the south Philippines. That was right across from Leyte. I read a book on the way to Samar. It took us 34 days to get there unescorted. I found this book on atomic power.

It said they could make bombs using atomic energy, but they hadn't done it yet. So when they dropped the bomb I was the only one who knew anything about atomic energy because I read that book! It was interesting.

How did you finally come home?

I came back on a Navy transport. That was the only time I had to stand up to eat, because they were holding so many people!

Did you come back here to Hoopa after your discharge?

Yeah. I'd gotten married. We had six children altogether, but lost a few over the years. I have around 10 grandchildren. I got into electrical maintenance. I worked for the mills, then a few years on my own.

You mentioned that you were active with the veterans here in Willow Creek?

Yeah, we started a post. The Indians couldn't buy a bottle of beer. We couldn't even buy a can of beer in a grocery store. We used to go to Willow Creek and I could buy for myself because I was a little bit lighter than the other guys were. We had a three-day meeting in Eureka. I was the quartermaster-adjutant of the post.

The commander was from Montana. He really looked Indian. They took everybody down to the restaurant Lazio's downtown to have a crab feed. We all went down there and filled the place up. The waitress came around and we ordered.

They asked what we wanted to drink. The foreman was from San Francisco. He and his wife were from San Francisco and they ordered a beer. The commander had been an alcoholic and didn't drink anymore, so he ordered coffee.

My wife ordered coffee and I ordered a Budweiser. That waitress went around the table and asked again what I wanted. I said a Budweiser. She asked me again what I wanted to drink. That guy from San Francisco told her, "What's the matter with you, woman, can't you hear, he wants a Budweiser!"

She turned and stomped away and I looked over. She was talking to someone. Then I knew what was wrong; she had recognized me as Indian and wasn't going to serve me. She brought the beer and I might have drunk two bottles. We were sitting there talking and that guy from San Francisco asked what that was all about. We couldn't buy a bottle of beer, even in a grocery store.

That guy said, 'You've been fighting in a war for four years, and you can't even buy a bottle of beer?' So we got a resolution against this and sent it down to Long Beach. I took that resolution and they passed it at our meeting. It wasn't long after when Congress repealed that law against selling liquor to Indians. It used to make me so mad. I wasn't into drinking; I always knew when to quit. I never missed a day's work from drinking.

When our ship was hit, and fire came down on us, those guys ran. They actually ran. I was the only one that stayed.

Did you ever have any other instances where you weren't treated right because you were Indian?

No.

Why do you think so many Hupa men served in the war?

Well, a lot were drafted. We lost several that were killed in the war in Europe. There might have been one who was killed at Pearl Harbor. There were many who left before I did. Several were killed outright. I had a good friend who served in a tank, but he died a few years ago.

Do you think it would be a good thing for other people to learn about what our Indian men did in the war?

Yes, there was an Indian guy I knew who went to Vietnam. They had him as a point man all the time. He would have to lead the other guys into hot spots all the time. He thought it was some kind of discrimination.

I always thought to myself about that time when our ship was hit. The commander always said not to leave. When our ship was hit, and fire came down on us, those guys ran. They actually ran. I was the only one that stayed.

James "Skee" Campbell, Sr. is proudly remembered by his family for his service to his people and to his country. He was preceded in death by his wife Ida Jean Johnson Campbell.

Archie Thompson

I was able to meet with Yurok elder Archie Thompson at his home in Crescent City on January 16, 2002. Archie is a veteran of the U.S. Navy and a keeper of the Yurok language.

I was born at Wautek in a smokehouse. I wasn't born in a hospital; I was born in a smokehouse! That's where they smoke a lot of fish. My mother's name was Delia Thompson. She was from the village of Wautek too. I had several half-brothers and half-sisters. I have one brother and one sister who are still alive.

I went to the government school in Hoopa when I was little. I was there in kindergarten. I stayed there for three years and then went to live with my grandmother on the Klamath River. My grandmother raised me; she was my mother and my father.

What was her name?

Rosie Jack Happell. We still hold that land down there. It was supposed to be 25 acres down there, but it's been whittled down to about 17 now. The county has their surveyors, and we have to go by their lines.

It's good to learn your own language! You should never lose it. It's something handed down by your forefathers.

Jimmy Jack was my uncle and he went with the surveyors. One corner stake was way up the hill, but now they have it down in the middle of the road. They did pay my grandmother for the right of way to put that bridge they have.

I remember when I was little they didn't have a bridge, they had a ferry there. I also remember when I was little I would stay near Requa and in Trinidad. I remember they used to bring big whales up on the dock, like they do with big logs. They would saw them up and sell the blubber. Boy that stunk!

What was it like when you were at the boarding school in Hoopa?

I was really young. They didn't put me in the boys building the first few weeks. I had to stay with the girls, in the girls' building! I don't remember that, but that's what they said. They give you government-issue clothes, because I don't remember having any clothes but what they gave me.

It got real cold up there. It gets cold in Hoopa. Later, I remember going to live with my grandmother and going to school in Klamath. There was an old school house there. We had to walk two miles to get to school. There were two or three of us kids and we would play on the way there and back, and we'd get back home around dark.

We had a barn, a pig pen and a place where we'd separate the milk and cream. There was an outhouse, a smokehouse and a garage. There was a church there. We also had three or four buildings that we rented out to people. The 1955 flood washed it all away. In my spare time I used to go up all the creeks and catch salmon. We'd smoke them.

Where did you learn the Yurok language?

My grandmother spoke it. She couldn't speak English. She just spoke in Yurok. I had learned it really well, but when I went to the school in Hoopa they wouldn't let you speak it. I lost it all. They made you speak English.

Archie Thompson ca. 1942.
Photo courtesy of Archie Thompson.

When I came back my grandmother would try to speak English but she would say words wrong. I can understand when someone speaks Yurok. I know what they're talking about; when Jimmy James or whomever prays in Yurok I know exactly what they're talking about.

I'm a language teacher now. I go there just to verify what people say. These younger people didn't grow up with these things. They say there are only 65 Yurok people over 80 years old. They're dying off. I see these little Mexican kids, just little guys, talking away in their language! I'd like to see the Yurok kids do that. The language is something private. White people don't know what you're saying!

In the war they had Indians talking, and the Japanese couldn't understand it! It's good to learn your own language! You should never lose it. It's something handed down by your forefathers.

They've been on this land for a long time; they know exactly what's happening. They know when the salmon go up the river; and the sturgeon and the eels. They know all these things. There's a certain time for everything.

I used to catch eels in the mouth of the river with a hook. There was an old man down there who was my grandfather, but I didn't know it. I was about nine or 10. We walked down the beach on the sand. There was an eel coming down and we both saw it, I got to it just before he did! I'll never forget that. I didn't know he was my grandfather at the time.

Where did you go to high school?

I went to Del Norte High School from 1935 to 1939. I was an outstanding athlete, and I was the only Yurok that had my name up on the coach's cup at Del Norte High. I played baseball, and track, football, and basketball.

I graduated in '39 then I went to Sherman Indian School. I was down in Klamath and a couple guys took me down there. They took a busload of us down there. I spent my time in the shop at Sherman. I learned how to weld and how to work metals. I made things and did repair work.

I stayed in the dormitory. I was the only one of my family down there. There were a lot of orange trees down there. We'd take some oranges; they were good. Every so often they would check to see if we kids had stolen some oranges, I guess the farmers would complain.

This one guy named Curly was the boss of our unit, and we opened his locker and stuffed all these oranges in it, so when they were checking lockers they found his full of oranges! And he was supposed to be our boss! They didn't do anything to him but that was funny.

That's a good story. Did you play any sports there?

I played football with Mervin Evans at Sherman. Frank Ames and Leonard Ames were also down there. The shop where I worked had a big table. You'd learn to flat-weld and so forth. I passed all three of my tests down there.

Then I joined the Navy. I signed up in Los Angeles. That's a big place! They shipped me to San Diego. I was a welder and went to shipyard school for two or three months there. Then I was shipped to Treasure Island to another shipyard school. They made me a second class petty officer and I was an instructor there. A lot of the guys didn't know what they were doing so I taught them.

When you were teaching a welding class how many students did you have?

I had maybe 15 or 20 or so. They were from all over the States. They were mostly white people, but we did have a couple Indians from Oklahoma. Their name was Thompson, too! What made it interesting there; we were done with classes and they called out people's names. They would say this person, this person and this person is going to New York, or this person and this person is going to someplace else.

We didn't know where we were going. We were all excited. You'd get packed up and the bus would take you. They finally called my name with three others. We got packed up and went to Mare Island, about 30 miles away!

Archie Thompson

We stayed four months or so. We didn't have to do anything. We would have roll call in the morning and go to town. Our only job was moving these sugar sacks around. We made money doing that.

Then we were shipped to New Caledonia. We didn't have any news about what was going on. When we crossed the equator they initiated us by getting us all wet. When we got to New Caledonia we worked at a dry dock. The dry dock would lift the boats out of the water and we would repair them. We overhauled different parts of the ship. Every ship you go on there's something to do.

What would a ship with torpedo damage look like?

Most of the time either the front or rear end was where you have to put all-new metal on there. Most of the time we dealt with a lot of crops in the ship. A ship would get into shallow water and hit corral and that corral would eat the crop right up.

Sometimes there would be something leaking. We would also steam clean all the barnacles off the ship and paint parts of the ship. There would be two shifts. There were people who worked on the dry dock and the people who did the repairs on the ships. We had a machine shop crew and a carpentry crew.

What was your responsibility?

'You guys are foreigners to me.' I told them, 'I'm a true American, you guys are just foreigners.' They backed up; they didn't know what to do. I was just telling them the truth, you know!

I had to make things of iron or repair leaks. One time a guy brought in his gas tanks. That was a bad job. If you seal up a gas tank it could blow up. So when this guy brought these in you'd think, 'Oh man.'

I stayed there about a year. I'd go on liberty each week. That's a French colony, so there was nothing but French people there. From there I moved up to Ulithi. After that I went to Guam. On the way to Guam we went through a typhoon.

This was close to the end of the war. But Ulithi, man, there was nowhere to go. We'd just go on the beach. There were ships all over the place. Battleships, carriers, destroyers, liberty ships, every ship you can imagine. That place was chock full of ships.

It was like a big town, but it was all ships. You'd take your little boat to each ship for something. Sometimes we'd get beer and the guys would get plastered, and start jumping off a ship. We'd go and pick them up.

At Guam I was in charge of the shop. We got our own bedroom and dresser. Usually we'd stay four deep in cots in a room. We got served our own meals by a colored man. I stayed there about two months.

The war was over and I had enough points to go home. I got on a Liberty ship and there were six guys in cots on top of each other! It was packed. I don't know how I slept. When I was discharged I was a metal-smith first class.

It must have been a good feeling to know the war was over...

Oh yeah, it was a relief. I was in Ulithi when the war was over. They were going to make the final push to go into Japan when they dropped the bomb and Japan surrendered.

I bet there was a lot of celebrating when they heard that...

Oh yeah. Everybody was throwing their hat in the air and breaking out the beer. That was a big celebration. I know people were dancing in the streets here and we didn't know that, but we had a pretty good time too.

When you were in the Navy, was there ever a time when you were treated any different because you were Indian?

No. I was the only Indian onboard on my ship. There were black people, Mexican people, people from the South, some Jews. Nobody would say anything to me. I used to box all the time. When we were aboard ship me and another guy went to this place on New Caledonia where they boxed on the base.

I boxed and whipped this guy, and my friend got a draw. They gave us five cases of beer for fighting that night. I think I made two or three hundred dollars that night. Those Army guys wanted to buy my beer right there so I sold it to them.

So it's fair to say that people were treated pretty well?

It seems to me they were. We were all there for one cause, to fight the Japanese. The only thing that happened to me; I was going to San Francisco this one time. I was on a bus and there were a couple of guys on it that were going to attack me. They thought I was Japanese. They were going to try to lay me low.

I told them, 'I'm Indian, I'm not Japanese. I was here before you guys were. You guys are foreigners to me.' I told them, 'I'm a true American, you guys are just foreigners.' They backed up; they didn't know what to do. I was just telling them the truth, you know!

What did you do after the service?

I came to Klamath and got a job in the mill. I was helping the blacksmith out. Pretty soon the head welder quit and I got his job. My brother Willard came home early from the war, he was a Marine.

He was younger than I was; he was 17 when he joined the Marines. He came along and we started drinking for a while. I never went back to that job, but I should have. That's something I regretted.

Were you ever married?

Yes, my wife's name was Elda. I met her at Somes Bar (near Orleans). I have eight children, 25 grandchildren and 20 great-grandchildren. I have a tribe of my own!

Archie Thompson continues to work to teach and preserve the Yurok language. His family is very proud of his service to his country and to his Yurok people.

Jack Madero

1921-2004

Jack Madero was of Paiute and Mountain Maidu ancestry. He was born in 1921 to Willis Joaquin and Edith Peconam. I was able to meet Jack through his daughter Carol, who is married to my father. Jack's clearest memories at that time were of the Sherman Indian boarding school and his time as a member of the Second Marine Division during the war.

Jack was just six years old when taken to Sherman; he was not allowed to visit home for six years. Apparently the teachers forgot he was there, or perhaps they didn't care if he visited his family. Jack thoroughly enjoyed viewing the pictures of the other veterans whom I had interviewed, and agreed to talk a little about his time at Sherman and as a Marine.

I was born here in Susanville. I knew Billy Bumps and Mervin. I was about six years old when I went to Sherman. My mother was having a hard time. She worked for some people by the name of Roseberry. I stayed in the *Hiawatha* building for little boys (at Sherman). We were all bed-wetters!

We were mostly all young kids. I think they fixed us up with uniforms. I remember them buttoning up the collars. It was like the military then. We had some good men there.

Did you have to do some marching?

Yes, we had to march every time we got ready to go eat. They made sure we got in step. We had to march in good cadence. Sherman back then was more like a military school. I stayed at Sherman about ten or 12 years. Oh, there's the picture of Charlie Bowen, he went to school with me (at Sherman). There's Ed Jackson, too, he was a Marine.

What type of trade did you learn at Sherman?

I learned auto mechanics. I liked it; there were a couple of older guys and our instructor that schooled us quite a bit. I liked it. I liked it when Sherman would loan us out to different employers. We made some good money.

When did you start boxing at Sherman?

I worked out almost every day. I started because so many of those Indian guys were working out. I used to put on an exhibition. I remember Glenn and Don Moore, they were fighters.

You used to box with my Grandpa Stan?

Oh, Stan was a great boxer. He used to kick Leonard's butt! Leonard didn't like it! Stan was a pretty tough man. He and I went to Oregon to work. Times were tough then. We got a good job there.

We worked with the CCC boys. That was before the war. I remember at Sherman there was a guy employed there named Beamus Pierce. He was the head of all the agricultural stuff. He went to school with Jim Thorpe, the great one.

That was a government school too. They played football together. There was a lot of jealousy over Jim Thorpe. He could do anything. He was over there visiting this King who admired him. Jim Thorpe could play any sport better than anybody. I often think of Carlisle, they must have had some terrific athletes.

I had to wade through the water. There were also times I had to go right down under the mud because the Japanese would have shot us if they'd seen us. There were some harrowing times with the Japanese.

When did you go into the Marines?

I volunteered for the Marines when I was pretty young.

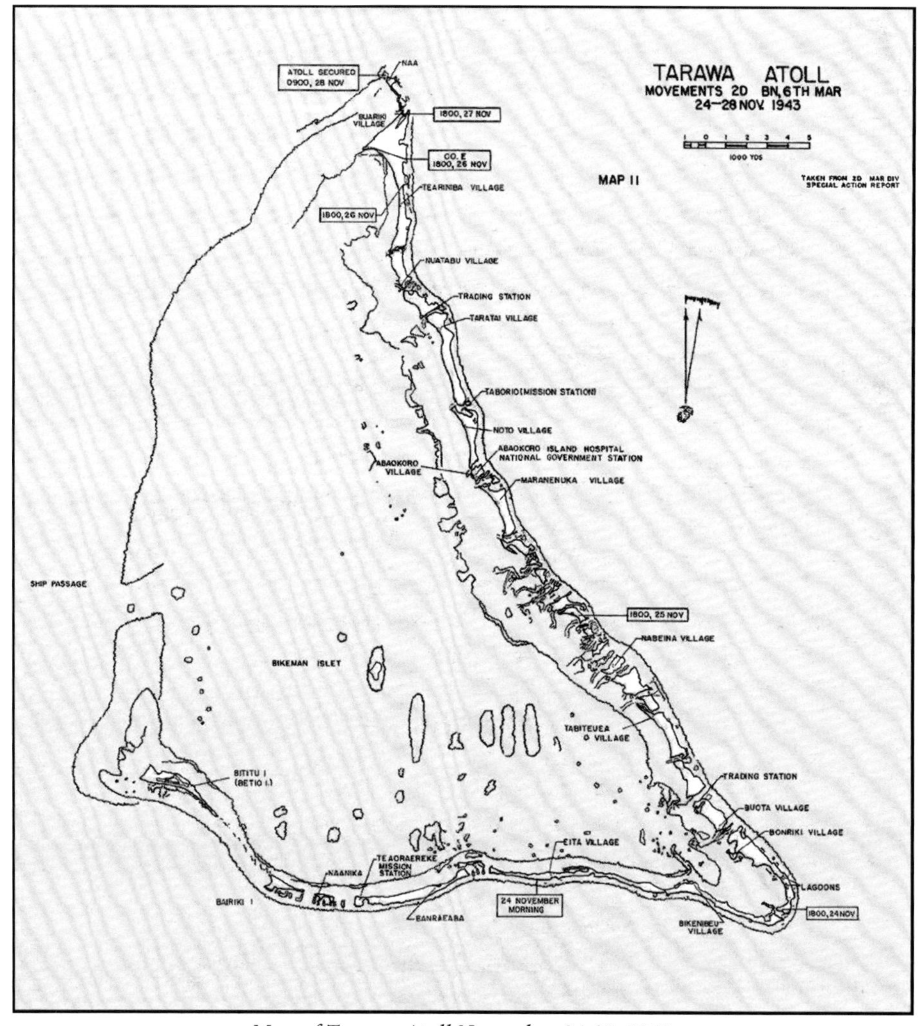

Map of Tarawa Atoll November 24-28, 1943.
From U.S. Marine Corps historical web site.

They took me in. I joined the Marines after things started happening. I joined the Second Marine Division. I wanted to be a Marine. Everybody was getting ready to fight.

Where are some of the places you went during the war?

The big one was Tarawa. That was the main one. It was pretty rough, there was quite a bit of killing going on. We were against the Japanese. I had an M1 rifle. I remember the Indian guys I was with.

Jack Madero

I had to wade through the water. There were also times I had to go right down under the mud because the Japanese would have shot us if they'd seen us. There were some harrowing times with the Japanese. They were mean. I was lucky I made it out.

I remember when Mervin ran into me in New Zealand. His brother Johnny went overseas (in the Army) and contracted some kind of disease. He looked like a movie star. He was a damn good basketball and football player.

Why do you think so many Indian people were in the service?

I don't know; it seemed the thing to be! These pictures are sure terrific.

Jack Madero's family is very proud of his service to his country.

Jack Risling

1915-2004

I met with Jack and his wife Joy at their house in Eureka, California to talk about some of their experiences during the war. We spoke on May 31, and again in June of 2001. Jack is of Karuk, Hupa, and Yurok ancestry.

I was born in the Yurok village of Morek, down the river from Martin's Ferry in 1915. That's where I grew up. I went to the little school there until about 1925 then we moved to Hoopa. My mother was Yurok; my father was Karuk and adopted into the Hupa tribe through marriage. I'm enrolled in the Hupa tribe. My parents were David Risling, Sr. and Geneva Risling.

How old were you when you went to the Hoopa Boarding School?

Well, it was around 1926. We all went. Some of us got to go home then the new kids came in. Dave came in and Les started at school there. They all went to school there.

What would be a typical day for you?

Well, they had a routine. You get up in the morning and go have breakfast. We'd go to school about half a day. In the afternoon we worked around and had different jobs. I was 10 or 11 years old; I did a lot of furnace work. They had to build fires in each one of the bigger schoolhouses or dormitories. It was our job to keep the heat up.

We had to watch the water, if it got too hot it would blow the furnace up. But that half a day we worked. I remember they had Model-T Fords that belonged to the government. We worked on cars.

Every two months they'd change the routine. I remember a guy would cut meat and I would take a cart down to the mess hall where they cooked. They took the cart and gave me half a loaf of bread covered in syrup. I would take the cart back and all the little kids used to come around for a treat!

How long did you go to the school?

Until they changed it over to the regular high school that's still going now. The old school is torn down. The new school is closer to the highway. I don't know if the old dormitory is still there. The place was an Army camp at first. They had soldiers from Fort Gaston there. After they moved out they made a school out of it.

They had a drilling place out there. There were two of them, one for the boys and one for the girls. We had to march there for a while. On Friday the girls would drill and the boys would drill just like we were in the Army.

When you were at the school did you have to wear a uniform?

It would be like in the Army or Navy; during the daytime we wore overalls and we had a uniform for church or for graduation. Everybody had to go to school, what could you do? They had to send us.

I realize today that a lot of kids didn't like that school. It's true, we had to march and all that, but what else could they have done? There were a lot of things that we didn't like but you have to do them.

Do you think this experience helped you when you went in the Navy?

Well, yes, it did. I knew how to line up and I knew when to right face, left face. They did different drills in the Navy.

What was life like during the Depression?

It so happened that during the Depression they were building the highway through Hoopa. We were pretty busy then. We had a little sawmill and furnished lumber for all the culverts and all the bridges, even the big bridge. So we were pretty busy during the Depression. The highway stabilized the economy there, so we were lucky.

When did you first hear about things that were happening in Germany and Japan?

We never paid much attention to it until they bombed Pearl Harbor. I was going down to San Francisco for a job when I heard. The news was all over. They were building an Army base there so we knew what was going on.

I went in the service in 1942. I was drafted, but I joined the Navy before they drafted me so I could choose where I wanted to go. I was exempt a couple of times because I was working for the defense building powder magazines.

When I went to join the Navy the people at the base said to come back over to the base for the duration of the war. I went there and started talking to the recruiter. He said he could do better than that, so I got a rating right off the bat because I was working as a foreman at the Naval base. So I joined the Navy and went to Rhode Island for boot camp.

One thing was kind of interesting. When they drafted us, we were all 'white' on the paper. We were Indian again after the war. After the war I found out we weren't supposed to even carry weapons! But we were Indian again after we got out.

I didn't think they should take things away from us. Indian guys who drank liquor, I didn't drink, but they said these guys couldn't do that anymore. There were things like that that I didn't think was right.

When did your brothers join up?

Dave was in college at Columbia University in New York. He became an officer in the Navy. Then Baron joined the Air Corps and got to be a pilot. He died during the war in Texas; he crashed while testing a new plane.

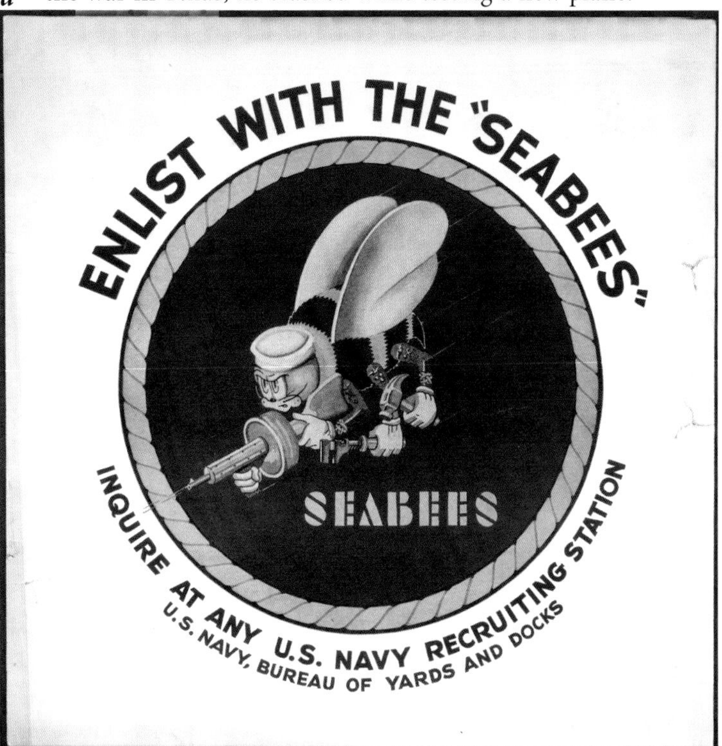

Navy recruiting poster.
Library of Congress, Prints and Photographs Division, (LC-USZC4-9618).

Then Les, who was the youngest, they sent him off to join the Army.

First he was drafted but they sent him home to grow some more whiskers! After a couple years he went in the Army. I went to Rhode Island, that's where the Seabees were. The Seabees are the same as the Army Engineers. They did a lot of building, such as road building.

After Rhode Island, the whole battalion went by train at night. We went right next to a ship and loaded up. We went to Bermuda. German submarines were pretty hot there at the time. They had civilians building barracks there.

They shipped them out and then they split the battalion. Half stayed at Bermuda and half went on. The ones that went on went to Normandy. I was lucky, they left me at Bermuda. We built airports and runways and barracks. We stayed there for a year. Then they sent us back to Rhode Island.

They gave us a two-week leave. I came home by plane. It took 27 hours! I got hung up in a couple places, in Chicago, and then New Mexico, then L.A., then finally made it San Francisco. I went back by train. I ran across Dave in New York. He was in the Navy then. We got to see New York.

We'd get together on the weekend. That was the first

time we ran across each other. We saw the Empire State Building and Madison Square Garden and quite a few other places. We had a good time. I remember the first time I went there, I got on a subway and we kept going. I didn't know where we were going, so it came to the end and went back again. At the depot I got off. I found a USO and they took me in for the night. I saw Dave the next day.

The bullets started coming in on the shore and one guy grabbed my leg and I went down. If he hadn't done that I would have probably got it!

Before we left Rhode Island the company wanted a band. I was asked if I could play in the band. So in the meantime I played in the band! I played the saxophone. I was given more liberties.

You can't argue with that!

No you can't! Our battalion stayed there a couple months. Then we came to California. We stayed there a couple of months. I was a member of the 31st Construction Battalion. From there, they took to the island of Hawaii. We stayed there for two or three months.

We were attached to the 5th Marine Division in Hawaii. We trained with them. We were all together. You practiced shooting and different maneuvers. They took us down and put us on some ships to practice invading an island. We were on Maui. We know now that it's kind of shaped like Iwo Jima.

Jack Risling ca. 1943-4.
Photo courtesy of Jack and Joy Risling.

While we were there here came Dave! He and I wrote letters all the time. Dave was an officer and had a ship. His ship came over to Hawaii from near Pearl Harbor. This warrant officer gave us this Jeep filled with gas and we got to visit.

In December we got to have Christmas dinner. In the middle of the next afternoon, it came over the loudspeakers that we were shipping out, full pack and everything, by 0600. We didn't know what was going on because they didn't tell you anything. So we got ready.

They always tell you to take all the candy you can get because you don't know where you're going. So I was so loaded with candy I could hardly get up. We went down to Hilo in trucks. We had to do some loading. They gave me half a dozen men and we had to load equipment on little platforms. We were also loading trucks and tanks. After we had all that in we had to make sure everything was lined up right so when the door opened the trucks would be able to come out.

After that I got the job that every day I would go in and check if anything was getting loose they'd give me a crew and we'd tighten everything up. We left Hilo then

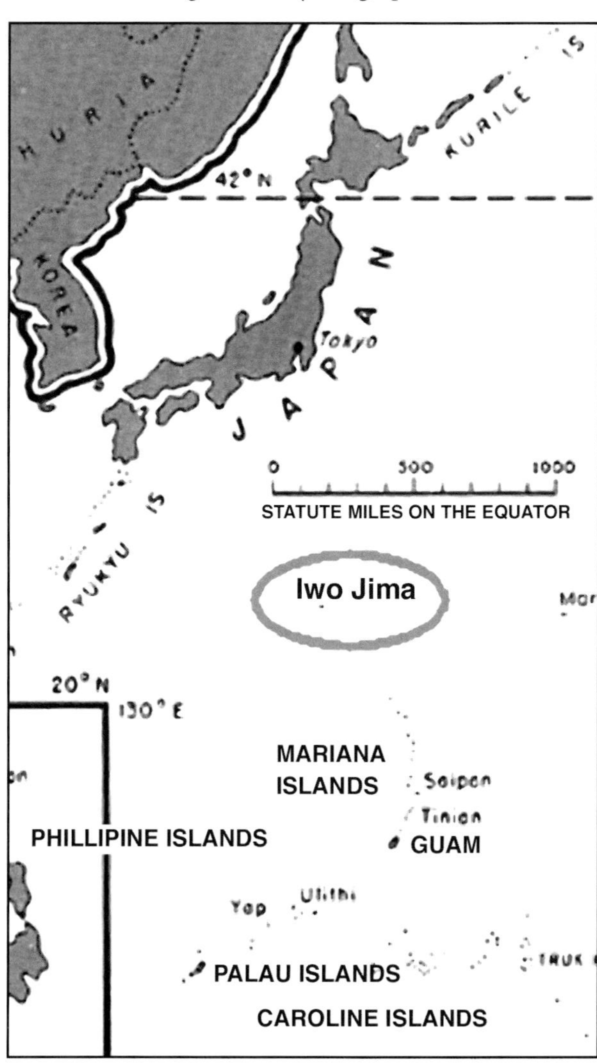

Map of location of Iwo Jima south of Japan.
From a U.S. Army historical publication on wikipedia.com

we went to Pearl Harbor. We were making a convoy I guess. This was all between Christmas and February 19 when we invaded Iwo Jima. I did look for Dave but they said his ship had already left. On some afternoons we'd catch a bus and go around Pearl Harbor and Waikiki. We'd play baseball. I don't remember how we started out of there but we got ready to go again.

They assigned me to the ship's crew after we left Pearl Harbor. Since I was a carpenter we repaired landing barges which were on the sides of the ship. We went to Saipan and picked up a bunch of Marines. We were a pretty big convoy then. It was getting pretty close to February the 19th. We always figured we were on a one-way trip!

All at once, after supper, my name came up on the loudspeaker. I went to see what they wanted. They said, 'Are you ready? I said, 'Ready for what?'

They said I was assigned to a hold there and I had a crew. I knew then what I needed. I had to be ready the next morning by four o'clock. We were to get up at three that morning, have breakfast, which was steak and eggs, and be down in the hold.

They gave me a list of what to take. The Marines would go through and I'd give them their rations. There were 3,000 Marines on that ship and they all knew my name. Then I was to take my crew and go ashore. So we gave them out their rations and whatever was on the list.

But no landing craft ever came back. The whole shore was blocked. They couldn't get the landing barges in there. It was two or three days before I could go ashore. We had a front seat; all the battle was going on.

There were planes coming down. There was a kamikaze, it hit a destroyer. It was just about the time they got to Mount Suribachi was when I went ashore. When I got there I didn't know what was going on. The bullets started coming in on the shore and one guy grabbed my leg and I went down.

If he hadn't done that I would have probably got it! While I was there I saw Dave's ship floating out there, so we were together again in a way! The rest of the company was there. You couldn't get up very far or you'd get shot.

What were you thinking at that time?

I was just with the company. I dug a foxhole. The company commander came down and shook my hand. He took me in his jeep. The big guns would be going bang, bang, bang, and about shake you out of the jeep. There were a lot of dead people laying everywhere; ours and theirs. There were a lot of dead Japanese. I don't know how long we stayed in those foxholes, but we did move to the other side.

People hadn't shaved. No one took a bath, there was hardly any water. We stayed on guard in the foxholes. I remember the first night, if the Japs came in we'd have

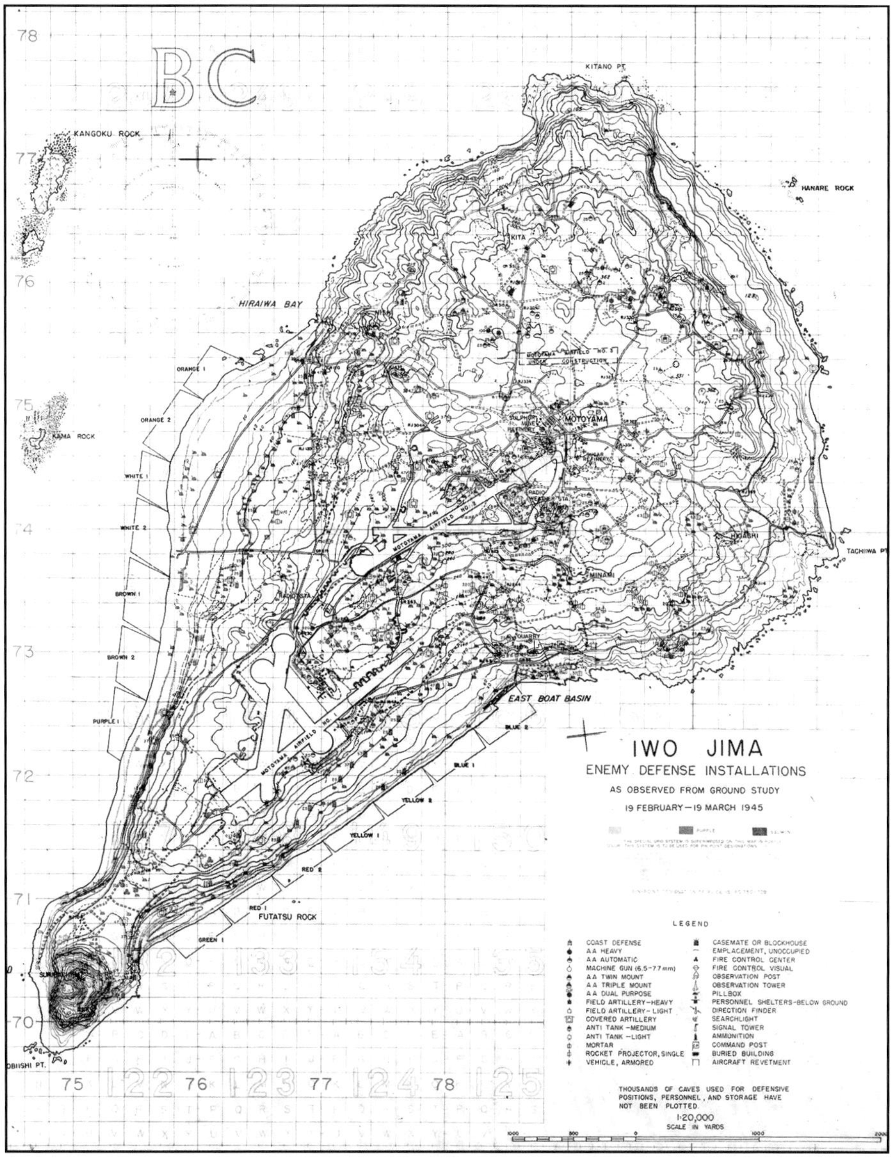

Map of Iwo Jima.
From U.S. Navy hisorical web site: www.history.navy.mil.

to fight. We could see these bullets coming in and we all jumped down into a hole there. I jumped right into a rotting Japanese corpse. Boy, I stank. I had to wear those clothes the rest of the day.

Another time, we were next to an ammunition dump that was hit. It blew up and boy, we didn't know if the Japs were coming or what. This was in the daytime. We were working at this one place and the Japanese would swim out to this big rock and shoot at where we were.

Dave (at left) and Jack Risling together on Iwo Jima in 1945. Photo courtesy of Jack and Joy Risling.

I went up and got some telephone lines and some stuff to barricade from them. You fired your rifle at anything that moves. Some guys were scared and would shoot anything and the Japs could see where they were shooting from.

I know this is a hard question to answer, but what were you thinking when you saw the people that had died lying there?

Well, we knew there were a lot of casualties. They were just there; Marines and we (the Seabees) had some too. There's been some talk since about how the Japanese would do things to our dead, cut them up or something. But we did the same thing.

The next night I saw some people had pieces of Japanese on string. It was done on both sides. We used to have these little sacks, gunpowder sacks, they call them. But some people had these little sacks full of teeth from the Japanese. Toward the end of the battle you could see the moldy bodies of dead Japanese. It's bad but you try not to notice it. You were taught to be a different guy, you were just around it and that was it.

How long were you at Iwo Jima?

February 19, that was the invasion. Then we were getting ready for the invasion of Japan. That's when they dropped the atomic bomb. In between that time, B-29s would leave Guam and bomb Japan. Planes that were shot up, with maybe two motors going, would stop and land on Iwo Jima.

It seemed like there were a bunch of planes coming in on one side and a bunch leaving the other side. It was a busy place. I was there at Iwo Jima until I came home in September of 1945. The whole island was flattened out with bulldozers. Except for the lower end which was full of caves.

Joy Risling: Can I ask a question? After the battle, was there a grave detail?

Jack: Yes, I was part of it.

Joy: Did the other services participate?

Jack: I don't know, but they brought them back. I originally saw where they had to dig big trenches and they had instruments and they put all the bodies in blankets and buried them with markers. Afterwards, they dug them up and sent them home. The Army did that.

Joy: Did they fly the injured out right away?

Jack: Yeah, they flew the injured out to Guam.

Joy: I never ask him about Iwo.

What did they do with the Japanese dead?

They buried them, but I don't know how they marked them. We used to go through the caves and see the moldy bodies.

In the meantime, Dave had come over with the enlisted men and stayed on the island. I'd go out on the ship and stay with him too.

What did that mean to you, to be able to stay with your brother?

It meant quite a bit. Dave was a captain and his ship was nearby ours at Iwo Jima. At first with all the shooting and such we couldn't visit, but after it was kind of secured we would visit with each other on weekends. He would always come visit me and have meals, I didn't have to go to the officer's quarters.

We used to argue ever since we were kids, and we were arguing once on the ship and it was getting late at night. Somebody hollered from the next bunk, 'Pull your rank on that guy!' Dave said, 'I can't, he's my older brother!'"

That was kind of funny! We used to go through the caves together. The caves were probably six feet high. There was a lot of stuff on the floors and there were a lot of swords. A lot of people sent swords and flags home, but I didn't.

It was kind of cruel, but you get to hate them. You see the Japanese and you hate him. He's going to shoot you or you'll shoot him, so you hate him. So when they went through some guys would cut through the uniforms and take the flag. When I came home I brought some Japanese grenades.

Where were you when you heard about the atomic bomb being dropped?

I was at Iwo Jima. We heard about it but it didn't mean anything until they surrendered. But when Germany surrendered, we were at Iwo Jima and everybody celebrated and shot out over the sea and everything. But there were ships out there, our own! The next morning the main guy wanted to get all the names of the ones that shot. So they came to me and asked.

I said I didn't know. So they had some gunsmiths and they were going to check the guns to see who was shooting. I had shot too! So they took down all the names of people who had shot. So we were all there when the guy came around, but he said lose it, so we lost the list!

Jack and Joy Risling

We were just happy and were celebrating.

How about when Japan surrendered?

Nobody shot! They were going to freeze us there, but we had so many points we had to go home.

Joy: So they'd gone past their tour of duty.

You must have been really happy when the war was over...

Yeah, we were already getting ready to make the invasion of Japan. Everything was being checked over, but then we didn't have to. We were ready to go home. One thing about this experience is kind of funny. I never used to lace my shoes.

One night we were sitting there. All of a sudden these bullets came in. The tracers would come in this way then they'd go that way. Then we could hear those darn planes come in. Japanese planes were coming right towards us.

There was a Japanese hole right below us. We didn't know if they were still in there or not. The planes were getting closer and closer. Anyway, we ran down to the

Jack Risling

hole there, and I didn't even have my shoes! My shoes came off. I didn't have a gun or anything! But they shot those planes down.

Joy: And he laces his shoes to this day! He ties them!

Jack: That was funny!

That's a good story. Did any of the Japanese surrender?

Yeah, because they had these wire fences. We were mixed up with the 5th Marine Division. We had the job of getting ammunition up. When we had to get the darn airfield up again we were pretty busy. But I remember seeing the POWs.

Joy: The Seabees were older men. When the Army

came in they were young so the Seabees were like older brothers.

Jack: They did have young guys in the Seabees too. But we were a little older. They always say that the Marines were tough, and they were, but they were scared too. You could see them shaking.

What was your rank when you got out of the service?

The radio was on, the news was that the 5th Marine Division had landed on Iwo and the casualties were running heavy, and they were shipping the wounded to Hawaii. Then I knew where he was.

I was a carpenter's mate first class when I got out. The Army was there toward the end and a troopship came through. People that had so many points could go home.

I had more than enough points. We came right to San Francisco. There was an island out there and we circled it. So I threw all my stuff overboard. We came in the next day. That same night I was on my way home. I had sent Joy a card to meet me at the station, but there was no one there.

Joy: He sent a telegram!

Jack: I beat the telegram!

Joy: I got the telegram afterwards. And he threw everything overboard. He came home to rationing, and he threw away Levis, and work clothes....

You were just happy to be home!

Jack: I was just happy to be home! But things keep coming up after that battle. In the foxholes, there were crabs that used to come in. You would hear them digging all the time and you didn't know if someone was trying to dig in or what.

We would fill up mats and put sand over it and put them there. Sometimes when you were looking at night you'd light a match and see where you are. Japs would come through the lines every now and then.

That was the hardest part, not knowing where you were. But we lived in those holes. We would have a guard and they would let us go in the ocean and wash off! We only had a couple canteens of water to cook with or drink. You think about that.

Do you recall when President Roosevelt died in office?

We were still at Iwo Jima when I heard. We didn't get too much news over there.

Joy: We listened to the fireside chats here at home. Everybody listened to the radio; it was all we had at that time.

What did you do after the war?

I was a carpenter before I went in. I built three little dams near Alturas while working for the government. I also helped the Rancheria at Rohnerverville and out at Quartz Valley with their water systems. Then I joined the union.

I came back to Eureka and worked. This was all before the war. After the war I went to work in this area. I was a foreman with a contractor until 1968. Then I worked at Humboldt State over there. I was the foreman when we built the library and part of Founder's Hall. I built Morris Graves' house. I retired in 1976. We did quite a bit of traveling all over the United States.

When did you get married?

January of 1941 in Carson City. Joy went to school in Hoopa.

What was it like for you to have Jack go off to the service?

Joy: Well, he had different ways of letting me know where he was. Some of the letters he wrote would be blacked out. Wherever he was, he would send home a souvenir and it would have a name on it and I would know where he was.

But I particularly remember Iwo because we had a son; he was six months old. The radio was on, the news was that the 5th Marine Division had landed on Iwo and the casualties were running heavy, and they were shipping the wounded to Hawaii. Then I knew where he was. But no word came from him.

But he had a good friend named Gene; right in the midst of the battle Gene was shipped back to the States from Iwo to go to school. It wasn't very many days after that I got a phone call. It was Gene, he told me that Jack's all right, and that he would send me a letter from Jack.

I did get a letter, Gene had worn it out in his shoe. I still have that letter. But when I heard that news about Iwo, I had this baby in my arms. I can almost feel the baby in my arms now, because I knew where he was but I didn't know if he was all right.

You were both strong in your own way.

Joy: You just had to be because there wasn't anything you could do about it.

Jack: That's how the whole thing was anyhow, you just had to adapt to it.

Joy: Well, you can't collapse, because that just doesn't help. You just have to tough it through. Everyone else was going through the same thing.

How did you get to know Lee Hover?

Jack: He was a carpenter too. We worked together quite a few times.

When did you first know that he was at Iwo Jima too?

I didn't. There was an article that came out in a magazine about Iwo Jima and I was interviewed. I believe that Lee saw that.

Joy: Nobody ever talks about it. It's only in the last couple years that they're talking. So Lee saw that article and he said he was there too! And they worked together all these years.

What would you tell our Indian youth today?

I see that they are advancing through school more now. Just keep advancing. And keep up their culture, so it doesn't get lost.

Jack Risling's family is very proud of his service to his country as a Seabee in World War Two.

Harold Blake

1913-2003

Harold Blake is of Yurok heritage. He was in the U.S. Navy and the Merchant Marines during the war. I was able to meet him at his home in Hoopa on August 1, 2002.

I was born on January 6, 1913 in Klamath at the Blake property. We had 100 acres where I was raised. I went to school there until eighth grade. I had to paddle back and forth the river to get to school.

A lot of times I couldn't get across if it was stormy weather or I was sick. That's the rough part I had. I wanted to go but couldn't sometimes. I was the only child.

What were your parent's names?

My mother was May Blake and she wasn't married to my father, who was Otto Hodge. My mother was Yurok; she was born and raised in Terwer, which is three miles upriver from Klamath. They had a Yurok village there. My father was also Yurok from Requa, which is at the mouth of the river.

I was raised on a dairy ranch and we had milk and butter and there was a creamery there where we sold it and they shipped it all out. That's the experience I had with the food we could get. I fished a little and the rest of the family fished, but we were mostly on the ranch. We cured and smoked the fish for ourselves. We had a big family; there were eight in the family.

Tell me about the school...

I remember they put pressure on us not to speak our language. They didn't want us to talk, but we continued every chance we could get. That's all I spoke at home. It didn't make any difference; I continued every chance I could get.

My grandmother didn't speak English and she's the one that kept talking to us in the Indian language. Some of her relatives were from Orleans and they spoke (the Karuk language). I learned a little of that but not too much. We just spoke the Yurok language.

How would they punish you for speaking your language?

Well, they would make us do extra chores, or something to make us stop talking. I don't know if they thought we were going to pull something on them or what. That's the only thing I can think of.

Looking back, how does that make you feel?

Well, it was work that you didn't have to do. It was punishment for speaking your language.

When did you go to the Sherman boarding school?

I went one year at Sherman then I left. I wanted to go to Haskell but for some reason I couldn't get in. I didn't care too much for Sherman on account I was pretty young. I remember one guy, he worked me over once for no reason at all.

When I went there I knocked on a door. This guy opened the door and busted me right in the face. I couldn't fight because I had never learned. That's what started me learning how to fight. Before I could get that guy someone killed him. But I continued boxing. When I was about 16 I left.

I lied about my age and joined the Navy. I was kicked out for being over leave and shortly after I was kicked out the war started. So I volunteered again and went in with a group of 15,000. There were three passenger liners with 5,000 men on each. I think there were seven escorts; they were destroyers and one heavy cruiser. We went over and delivered those guys.

> *We were in the Marshall Islands and the Marianas... I didn't have that fear; I knew I was going to make it or I wouldn't.*

I stayed in the Navy for two-and-a-half years. We traveled a lot. I was on a battleship first. Then I was transferred to a freighter. We picked up survivors and delivered supplies whenever they hit an island. We would come and go all the time.

We'd get in there and deliver things and get out. We took a lot of chances but that's war. We were in the Marshall Islands and the Marianas. I ended as a third engineer; I stuck in the engineering department because it was something I liked. I didn't have that fear; I knew I was going to make it or I wouldn't.

Was your ship ever attacked?

Yeah, I remember our ship was attacked and they knocked out the front end. They shot holes in it. I remember on that I volunteered to take ammunition to the guns.

What was the food like?

It seemed like we had plenty of what we needed. I don't remember us being short of anything. We'd be coming and going all the time.

Did you ever listen to Tokyo Rose?

I never paid attention to her. It didn't mean anything to me because we were fighting them anyway. We were after (the Japanese), they were just the enemy.

Did you stay in the Pacific the whole time?

We were transferred and shipped back to fight the Germans. We spent eight-and-a-half months in the Mediterranean. Wherever they needed help they'd send us. That was where the military needed reinforcements. That was when I was on that battleship. I don't remember the name of it. I did a lot of boxing on that ship.

Can you describe how you boxed?

Well, there were two different divisions. I was on the

below deck because that's where I worked. The seamen were up on top so we'd box each other. Then we'd box on other ships when we went to different ports.

I didn't look for it but whenever they wanted it I was ready. I was always in shape and ready to fight. I never cared to be a bully though. We used to go to a foreign territory in the Pacific and we'd do a lot of boxing there, but I can't think of the name of it. I boxed against the Marines.

Harold Blake

What did you do after the war?

I had two boys, George and Butch, during the war. After the war I wanted to continue sailing, but it was too hard for my wife to be alone. I came home to help and we had seven children. My wife's name was Ellen Nixon.

She went to Sherman; that's where I first met her. I used to drop in there at different times during the war when I was on leave. After the war I worked in the woods as a logger. I did the falling and fell redwood. It was hard work but I didn't mind it. You get used to it.

Were there other Indian men who worked with you in the woods?

Yes, usually most of our tribe was doing that. I wanted to keep sailing, but I didn't go back because I didn't want to leave my wife and children. I stayed home and worked and continued raising my family.

Are you proud of your time in the service?

Yes. Everything I did I volunteered for.

Did you have friends when you on the ships?

Yes, I had friends; I was boxing with them all the time. I always liked sports. We used to play the stick games when I was young. That's what we did, those tribal games. I used to go all the way back to the Forks of Salmon to play the stick games.

What position did you play in the stick games?

Well, I didn't have the speed of some but I had the strength to hold someone. You have three men playing; I was the anchor. I'd pick the fastest man the other team had and that's who I would hold. I had a lot of wind and used to do my part easy.

Would they have the games after they had a Brush Dance?

Yes, in the morning. That's when they would see what team is the best of the tribe. It went right on up the river like that.

When you were younger you were in the Brush Dances?

Yes, I was a background singer. I couldn't say that I could sing a song but a lot of guys could. There are certain guys who can sing and you'd help them along and build them up. Mostly it was getting together; that was the main thing.

I also liked running. One man I always wanted to meet was Jim Thorpe. I met him. I found out that my uncle Bill Hodge was with him on a ship during the wartime. He knew and fought with Jim against the enemy.

Jim Thorpe came to Eureka when I ran. He was there. This was before the war. I ran from Eureka to Arcata; I think it was 12 miles. I won that race when he was there. But he wasn't there when I raced from the Klamath Glen to Crescent City, which is 26 miles. I won that too.

It would always end up that only two or three guys would finish. Everybody else would drop out! Then the guy didn't pay me what he was supposed to, but it didn't make any difference to me. I just wanted to prove I could do it.

Did the people in Eureka or at Klamath line up to watch you?

Oh yeah, it was quite a crowd.

Did they cheer for you when you won?

Yeah.

That must have been a good feeling.

Oh yeah, you just prove what you can do. That's the feeling, and boxing was the same way.

Harold Blake's large family is very proud of his service to his country and to his people. His son George 'Pordie' Blake served in the Vietnam War.

Les Ammon

I was fortunate to meet Les Ammon at his house on January 14, 2002. He is of Hupa ancestry. Les and his twin brother Wes both served in the U.S. Navy during the war. During my time researching this book I had many people express the hope that I would talk with Les.

I was born in February of 1926 in Washington. My parents were Chan and Ruth Ammon. They were both born here in the Willow Creek area. I had six brothers. I went to elementary school in Salyer. I went to high school for three years here at Hoopa then I went in the service.

Afterwards I graduated in Eureka by taking a test. I was 17 when I went in the service.

I'm Hupa but we weren't put on the roll because my grandparents didn't have an allotment number. We went to court in San Francisco in the '80s. There were others like this too. They didn't put us on the Hupa roll; they put us on the Yurok roll.

Do you remember where you were when the bombing at Pearl Harbor happened?

Yes, I was at South Fork. That's where I lived. I heard it on the radio. It was a couple years later when I enlisted. I enlisted in June 1943. There's a picture of boot camp on the wall with me and my twin brother in Farragut, Idaho. That's my brother Wes. He was five minutes older than I was. All my other brothers were younger. There was Jube; he was in the Navy after the war. Then Junie was in the Navy during Korea. Toby was in the Air Force at the same time. The next brother Phillip was drafted and went to Europe during the Cold War. And the youngest was John, he is a teacher.

Did you and your brother enlist at the same time?

Yeah, we enlisted in Eureka. We went to San Francisco and then to Idaho. They were just building the camp there. We went in June so the weather was fine. I knew people who enlisted in the wintertime, and we didn't want any of that. There was eight weeks of basic training. After that I was assigned to a ship, the *Porterfield.* We went back to San Francisco then down to Long Beach and caught the ship there. It was a new destroyer. I have a picture of it over there. I went aboard it on Halloween of 1943.

Where did your brother go?

He went to San Diego. In the Pacific he was on the USS *Sargent Bay,* a small aircraft carrier.

What were your duties on the Porterfield?

I worked with motorboats and stationary machines. Later I ended up in the fire room. I did everything down there. You started off on the burners and keep the steam adjusted. You had to keep water in this tube for so long, that's what caused the super-heated steam. We had four boilers in each space and two engine rooms. There were probably nine or 10 men to each shift. You'd be on a four-hour shift and then off eight and on another four. In wartime it was usually four hours on and four off. You didn't get much sleep.

Les Ammon

Where did your ship first travel?

We broke it in at Long Beach, and in January of '44 we went over to the Marshall Island engagements. We were part of a convoy. We would steam around bigger convoys and look for submarines. We supported the landings at Kwajalein and some other places.

Did your ship ever come under attack?

Oh yeah. It wasn't very damn good, I'll tell you. At the end of the war near Okinawa there were all the suicide attacks. There were lots of tense moments. It was mostly suicide planes that came against us. We listened to Tokyo Rose. She was pretty close on her stuff; they knew where we were going. I made some close friends during that time. There are reunions. I've been to every reunion except I don't think I'll go this year. My health might not let me make it. The reunions started in 1977. The first one was in San Diego.

Les Ammon (at left) and twin brother Wes ca. 1942.
Photo courtesy of Dena Magdaleno

Why would you make the trip to attend the reunions?

Just to see all my old buddies. My best friend only made one reunion. One of my shipmates has a brother who lives up in Salyer there.

Can you tell me about the times when you were between assignments?

Sometimes we'd go back to Pearl Harbor and get repairs and stock up on stores. The food wasn't bad, considering. It would get pretty skimpy the longer we'd stay out. We were near New Guinea and then Peleliu, and our ship was also nearer to Japan when Iwo Jima took place.

Where was your ship located when the war ended?

We were up in Washington at a dry dock. We'd been back in the States for 10 days. A plane had lit up in our wake and it knocked our starboard system out of balance. Just before we came back went to Ulithi for a month, but it didn't work so we came back.

Did your ship ever perform rescue operations?

Yes, we picked up a lot of pilots. There were rescues all over. I was always down below, though. If you got to the pilots you were lucky. A lot of times there would be nothing left.

What did you do after your time in the service?

A little bit of everything. I worked on the power line they put in here and I worked in logging. I finally retired as an equipment operator.

Are you proud of the way you, your brother, and your other family members served in the military?

Oh yeah, they served when they were needed. My brother was in the South Pacific and he made it home, although he passed away four years ago. It was special to have a twin brother, and we got to spend all of boot camp together.

Why do you think so many Indian people chose to serve during the war?

Well, it still shows up that way in all these conflicts. Indian people have done their share. I don't know why. They couldn't vote and weren't citizens until 1924. My dad served in World War One, and I had several uncles that served. I had one great-uncle that died in France. They buried him there then they sent him over here to be buried. His headstone says, 'Full-blooded Indian killed in France.' His name was Harry Saxey.

The USS Porterfield.
Photo courtesy of Les Ammon.

Les Ammon spends much of his time at his home near Hoopa. He is much admired in the Hoopa community for his service to this country.

Elmer Rossig

Elmer Rossig met with me on December 5, 2002 at the Table Bluff Reservation-Wiyot Tribe's library in Loleta, California. Elmer is of Wiyot ancestry and he served in the Army in the Pacific during the war.

I was born in 1919 on February 17 right down on the mud flats in Bucksport. My father was Arthur Rossig and my mother's maiden name was Jessie Logan. My mother and father were Wiyot. I was conceived, born and raised in Bucksport! You can write that down!

I was born in a little house on the hill. I had one brother, William, a half-brother, and two half-sisters. I went to school here in Eureka until the eighth grade and then my mother moved to McKinleyville.

What was life like for your family during the Depression?

Good! I didn't know any other life. I stayed with my father at that time in Bucksport right by the railroad tracks. I remember he'd send me up a couple times to get a loaf of bread and beans, but that was it.

You didn't know any different. My father was a jack-of-all-trades for a while, then he went to work as a clean up man at this shop and then he retired after that. My mother stayed at home. In the spring we weeded in Loleta and picked spuds. We picked up a deer here and there.

Where we used to live there's nothing but commercial things now. Our nearest neighbor was 100 yard away on the sand dunes. It was all just field and brush. When we were young we'd go to the mud flats and get a crab here and there. Those damn crabs would grab you by the toes!

Did your mother ever talk about what life was like for the Wiyot?

No, no. That was a closed thing for some reason. I don't know why. The only thing I know is my grandmother Winnie owned some property down in Ferndale. She had the deed. Those white people took her and sent her to Hoopa. I don't know how long she stayed there. That was my father's mother.

Do you think maybe one of the reasons why they didn't speak of it was because of what happened on Indian Island?

It's possible...My grandmother might have been in Ferndale at that time. That's wasn't the thing to talk about in those days. In fact, I had to read about it in a book so I would know what happened.

Where did you go to high school?

We were staying in McKinleyville and I rode the bus to Arcata High. I went to school with Axel Lindgren and Chuck Lindgren. I graduated in 1937! I can remember things way back then! I went looking for a job and came back and stayed with my father down in Bucksport. I couldn't find one so I went to the CCC camp. Do you know what that is?

The Civilian Conservation Corps.

There you go! I went there one year; I stayed down in Willits and then halfway between Willits and Fort Bragg. Believe it or not I was the cook there for two weeks. We had salmon from a crick down there where I got a couple one day. I must have volunteered for that!

Then we went to Laytonville to fight fires. I stayed in the CCC camp for one year. We stayed in barracks just south of Willits. That one halfway between Willits and Fort Bragg only had two or three cabins because there were only 10 or 12 guys there. We cut brush and cut trees. That's where I first learned to cut timber.

You didn't know where to run, you might run right under where the fire would drop! It was a red blaze going through the trees. We fought fires and made roads.

Then we went and fought fires, and if you think fighting fires isn't scary you're full of it! You'd go out in the evening and the wind would come up and that fire would come through the redwoods...You didn't know where to run, you might run right under where the fire would drop! It was a red blaze going through the trees. We fought fires and made roads.

Then I came back and stayed with my dad. The first couple times I had to go across to Samoa and they put an office in Eureka. I went every morning for about three months for a job. Then one day I thought I would go to the library. I came back and dad asked where I was. I told him I was at the library, and he said there was a guy there that had a job for me!

I did get the job. I worked on the railroad in the woods. I straightened railroad ties, pulled ties out and put new ones in. I put gravel underneath it and all that. I did that for about six months. The railroads carried logs.

I ran into some fellows that came over from the old countries. These rails would have 30 or 40 people on them. Once a rail fell and cut this guy's fingers off. The boss was Portuguese and he said to go to the hospital. But that guy wouldn't go; he thought he was going to get fired.

That must have been pretty tough work...

I was young and full of it. I graduated to peeling bark off redwood trees. If you think that's not work you're full of it! A partner and I decided to do this to make more money. They gave you a long bar. We'd start at the butt of the tree and go up.

Then my partner slipped and just missed me! That was the last time we started from the butt up! You're supposed to start from the top and go down! It's a wonder we didn't kill ourselves, it was terrible. I was only there about three months before I graduated to falling timber with a drag saw.

That saw has a V-shape with a motor on it. You can see one at the museum. Those things only weighed about

200 pounds without the saw blade! The saw blade could go from four feet to 16 feet. You had to change the blade for different lengths. I worked in the redwoods until I retired. I'm one of those guys that the environmentalists growl at when they ask what I did for a living!

Were you working in the woods when you enlisted?

No, I was on the railroad at that time.

Elmer Rossig

You enlisted on December 9 in 1941…

I went down to Santa Rosa and from there I went to Fort Ord. The war broke out when I was just in. When the war started they asked us who wanted to join the regular Army so I joined. I wanted to get paid first! All the people in the regular Army got paid first. I don't remember how much we got.

For some reason I thought the war wouldn't last through my enlistment. I don't know why I thought that! I went to Camp Roberts after that. It was hot, dry and dusty. From there we went on a ship across the ocean. We were supposed to go to Hawaii but at that time there were still Jap subs around so we missed it.

We ended up going to Adelaide at the southern part of Australia. It's way down there on the bottom. The ship didn't bother me. I didn't get sick for some reason. Adelaide was wonderful! We didn't do much but dig holes and march around. We had Quonset huts. They looked like a big metal pipe cut in half.

What were the Australians like?

Very good! I have no reason not to like those people. I thought they were excellent. I didn't drink or smoke at that time. That's what got people into trouble, was the boozing. If you have somebody come in there half-drunk you're going to kick them out!

Then we went over to Brisbane; it was just another Army camp to me. I was in the 32nd Division at that time. Then we went to Sydney and from there we went to New Guinea. We just got on the boat and didn't think about it.

What type of weapons did you train with?

A shovel! No, they had the old Springfield rifle from World War One. Then they gave us new weapons. At some point I became a marksman; there was nothing to it. So they gave me the marksmanship gizmo to put on your dress uniform.

Elmer Rossig ca. 1943.
Photo courtesy of Elmer Rossig.

What was the climate like on New Guinea?

Hot! You're in the tropics down there. There were lots of Native people. They outnumbered the whites five or six to one. We were supposed to go to Buna; Moresby and Buna are on different coasts. The Japanese were supposedly near Moresby and we were supposed to chase them back to Buna.

Your notes say that you walked over 30 days...

Yes, we'd gone back and forth across the country. We were the select few! When we came near Buna we could hear them shooting. Nothing happened the first day. The second day was where I got my first wound.

The Japanese had those little mortars; I heard they'd put it on their knee and let it go. It would go about 100 yards and spread shrapnel around. It got me on the arms. I don't know how it missed my body.

Did you have a corpsman help you?

Hell no! I just had a couple buddies tell me I was hit and to go sit under a tree. It must have been the wrong tree because I got shot right there in the leg.

Did you know someone was shooting at you?

I still don't know how he hit me; I was sitting on the ground. He must have been up in the tree. He got me! Then they sent me back maybe 200 yards back and shoved me into an airplane and evacuated me out.

When you were hit did your buddies try and help?

One guy came and tried to stop the stop the flow of blood. He couldn't stop it and by that time they were shooting near there and he had to go. I don't know how I made it to the airplane; they must have carried me.

How old were you at that time?

22 or 23. I stayed in Townsend until I got well. Then I went back to good old Sydney. Then I worked on motors for torpedo boats. They were wood. I was pretty good at working with wood.

I did that for months until I hurt my back for some reason. I picked up a piece of plywood and that was it. Then I was sent back to the States. I got volunteered again! We were in a hospital training unit in San Francisco. You don't see that boat outfit on my discharge papers and I always wondered why that was so.

And you were discharged at Camp Beale...

It was in September or October of '45. Everybody said hoorah, especially the girls! That's where I saw my first mini-skirt!

Did you come back here after the war?

I had to stay in San Francisco for about a year and then my back healed. My dad said 'Glad to see you son.' That was it! Indian's aren't much for showing emotions!

I think you show your emotions pretty well! After you came back did you work in the woods?

Yeah. I worked in the woods until I retired. I was there for a long while. I worked from Crescent City to Garberville and the farthest east I got was Burney.

Have you ever been married?

Ever? I've been married so long it's pitiful! I've been married twice. I have one son and one granddaughter, and one great-grand child. My wife's name is Mearl.

You've been in this area for a long time...

All except for the war.

What are your thoughts on the Wiyot people trying to get Indian Island returned to them?

If they can get it so much the better! It makes me feel good because I don't know too much about the history of our people. I used to know a little of our language. My grandmother used to speak it. The only word I remember is the cuss word!

I just had a couple buddies tell me I was hit and to go sit under a tree. It must have been the wrong tree because I got shot right there in the leg.

Did you ever see any Indian guys in the service?

I never saw one that I would recognize as Indian.

Is there anything else about your time in the service I didn't ask you about?

No, those things are hidden!

Elmer Rossig was awarded a Purple Heart for wounds received in combat on New Guinea on December 5, 1942. This interview was the first time he ever shared some of his experiences about the war to someone other than family.

Ed Mitchell

I met with Ed Mitchell at his home in Hoopa on February 11, 2003. Ed is of Yurok ancestry and he served in the Army during the war.

I was born on May 27, 1922 down at Martin's Ferry by the Klamath River. My father was Ed Mitchell; I'm Junior. My mother's maiden name was Teresa Billy. She was from Weitchpec.

My father was from Martin's Ferry. They were both Yurok. She went to live with him on the mountain where he was from. We had property up there and lived there up until 1944. They made improvements and everything.

Then the government told my mom that she was trespassing and didn't belong there. I was away in the service at that time, so we lost it. I often think about it; we had acres and acres fenced in and we raised cattle and hogs. That's where I was living when I was drafted into the Army.

Where did you go to elementary school?

At Martin's Ferry; there was a little school there. The building is still there. My brothers are gone, but I have one half-brother and one older sister who are still living. We lived about two miles from the school.

We had to walk up and down the mountain. The average attendance was around 15 or 20 pupils. We were all in the same class; one teacher would teach first through eighth grade.

When you were in that school did they ever talk about the Indian people, or the Indian history of the area?

No, they didn't, and that's a big factor in my life that's

been a big hurt to me. I had an aunt who was very dominant in the family, and she didn't want any of us to learn or participate in any of our culture, and not to speak our language or anything.

She said we were going into a different way of life and it wasn't good for us to retain any of that. At first I didn't think anything about it, but after I got older…it's a big void to me. I know I would have felt much stronger and felt much better about myself had I known what I should have known.

Were there other members of your family that lived nearby?

There were some on my father's side that lived there, and some still live there.

How many years did you go to that school?

I went until the eighth grade.

What type of work did your father do?

Outside of farming he worked in the woods falling timber. My mom stayed at home. Back in those days we raised everything to eat. It's not like now. Now they get welfare, but back in those days you didn't have anything like that coming in. We raised cattle, pigs, chicken; we ate everything we raised.

You had to do things a certain way. You'd have to come to attention and salute and all that but I didn't have any problem with it.

In the summer time we had big gardens and we canned carrots and tomatoes. We stored potatoes in the barn. We had potatoes all year round and we used to thrash beans. We raised everything or we wouldn't eat. We mostly hunted deer.

So your family had food during the Depression…

Oh yeah, the Depression didn't make any difference to us. Stock people would come and buy the cattle. My aunt had an automobile and we'd go up and down the river to sell meat.

Did anybody in your family make baskets?

Yeah, my mom made different kinds. We used to go to certain places to pick hazel sticks. We'd take a day or two just to pick sticks and then peel them.

Another type we used to pick was willow. She used to like hazel because they were more flexible. The hazel should be burnt. When they burned it all these new shoots would come up.

Was the timber industry pretty big back then?

My dad went down to the coast and fell redwood. There was no logging when I was a youngster. A couple years after the war started they came in and started logging Port Orford cedar. They were using this cedar to make battery casings or something like that for airplanes. That's what they logged.

Did any of the families use the old-style redwood canoes to get around?

They used those to set nets and so forth. We did a lot of fishing with nets back in those days. I've done it in recent years but not lately.

What did you do after the eighth grade?

I started to come here to Hoopa. I had a long way to go off that mountain. It was two miles down the mountain then I'd catch a car ride. At night it was the same. It was very tiring and I had chores to do in the evening.

I could read so I gave up school. My sister went down to Riverside to Sherman. I wanted to go but I was kind of the head of the ranch. I had to get the cattle in and feed the hogs. I didn't have much liberty.

Did you parents ever tell you about when the gold miners came through?

I felt like asking for information about that but I didn't because I was afraid of what I might hear. They didn't tell me either. Maybe they didn't want me to know.

Did you hear what was going on in Japan or in Europe in the 1930s and early 1940s?

They had some news about the war, but all we had was a battery radio. We didn't have electricity where we lived. We had a telephone. Back in those days the Forest Service put a phone in people's home in order to combat forest fires.

It was one of those old phones you'd crank. It had batteries in it and our number was one short and four long! Now I have a phone that tells who's phoning, where they're phoning from and what their number is!

So you were drafted…

I was drafted. I probably would have enlisted. I didn't want to leave my mom because I knew how she'd feel about losing me. I was drafted in 1942 and they shipped me down to Camp Roberts for basic training and from there they shipped me to New Guinea.

When you went down to Camp Roberts what was that like?

We stayed in a barrack and ate in the mess hall. We'd get up early in the morning and do our thing.

Did you come across any other Indian men?

I don't remember having done so. I may have seen some but I didn't approach them and they didn't approach me.

What type of rifle did you train with?

We trained with two different types. One was an old bolt-action that they used in World War One. The other was newer and was a semi-automatic. They were heavy. We trained with mortars and machine guns and submachine guns.

What was the discipline like?

You had to do things a certain way. You'd have to come to attention and salute and all that but I didn't have any problem with it.

Were you treated any different because you were Indian?

No, I don't think so.

After basic at Camp Roberts where did you go?

We went to New Guinea. We were on a troop transport. I didn't mind it but I saw many guys were seasick.

Do you and the guys do anything fun to pass the time?

We'd play cards but that was it.

Did they have boxing matches or anything like that?

Not on the ship but on New Guinea they did, and they did back at Camp Roberts. I used to box before I went into the Army. They used to having boxing and I was on the middleweight team.

After you came to New Guinea what did you do?

We were placed in a replacement camp. I was there for a short time and then I was assigned to the 33rd Infantry Division. That's where I stayed until we landed in Japan. We used to go out in the jungle.

They were probably going to train you to invade Japan...

That's what we thought until they dropped the bomb. I was also on the front for quite a while on Luzon in the Philippines. I was hit four times there.

So you went from New Guinea to Luzon in the Philippines?

First they sent us to a little island by the name of Morotai. We'd go out into the jungle and run into Japanese and fight a little bit. We weren't there too long then we went on to Luzon.

When you were on Morotai and went into the jungle would you go out in a company?

We'd go out in squads. There were maybe 10 or 15 people in a squad, I guess. I had a machine gun. It was fairly reliable but it would jam once in a while. You'd have to knock the shell out.

It must have been pretty intense when you were in the jungle in the Philippines...

Oh yeah, it was. You never knew, those Japanese were pretty good at camouflage. I was raised on the mountains here. We might be holding a particular hill and a lot of times the guys would ask me to look at something to see if I would recognize something. Take a leaf on the hillside; when the wind is blowing they should all go one way. But when you see one or two flop back the other way and you can see the bottom side of them then you know something did that.

That's what I used to recognize. As soon as I saw that I knew something went through there or someone was behind it. I could see pretty well at night. I'd be sleeping in my foxhole and they'd wake me up to look at this or that. Lucky they did because a couple times there would be a Jap trying to creep up on us and drop a grenade!

Were your friends with people in your unit?

I was, but as far as having a buddy I never really felt that. I had a buddy here but he passed away. We'd go hunting.

Can you describe Luzon more?

Well, they'd been fighting there for a while before we got there. I don't know what outfit we relieved but we went to push into this little summer resort near Baggio. That's where we were going when I got hit.

We weren't in the jungle. We were up on a hill and we were holding it. We had foxholes all the way around and every now and then we'd receive machine gun fire and mortar fire. I don't think it was artillery I think it was mortar fire. I was hit by this mortar fire three times in my leg and once in my shoulder.

Now I can't raise my arm that well. I was conscious most of the time. The medics put me on a stretcher and took me out of there. They evacuated me back to Leyte to the hospital for quite a while.

It was like going down over some rapids. It's a big thrill to go over those rapids; you're taking a big chance. That's the way it is in combat.

I didn't want the war to end, can you believe that? You get the war into you. It works into your being. I remember the first Jap fall while I was shooting at him. I remember wondering what that soldier's mother would think; what would go through her mind? She's going to wonder how he died. I think that's what my mom would have done with me. That stuff gets to working on you and it turns you into an animal. It really does, it turns you into an animal.

I didn't want the war to end even though I might eventually be killed. It was like going down over some rapids. It's a big thrill to go over those rapids; you're taking a big chance. That's the way it is in combat. I used to volunteer to scout. The Japanese would drill holes into hills that would come out the other side.

I used to go in there, and it's dark. That's crazy! I captured two soldiers like that once. I had this flashlight and heard something and they were standing there. If they didn't have their hands up where I could see them I'd have blasted them. We came out the other side and I took them back to camp with me. I got a letter from the commanding officer for having done that.

Do you remember what they were dressed like?

They were just dressed like a regular Japanese soldier. You'd see them lying around here and there. They were young. I got in trouble in the hospital there in Leyte. I used to smoke at the time and my cigarettes were disappearing.

One night I caught this Philippine ward boy going through my stuff and I hit him in the head. They were going to give me a court-martial so I asked my doctor to ship me back to my unit. That's what he did. It wasn't too long after that when they dropped the bomb.

We were the first troops into the southern part of Honshu where they dropped that bomb. They didn't warn us about the dangers of exposing ourselves to where that bomb had landed. Three other guys and I went in there and everything was devastated and flattened out. We were looking around and went back to our camp.

My teeth got loose; I could move them around. All my teeth were loose, I guess from radiation. I thought they were going to fall out but they didn't. They solidified after two or three days.

Ed Mitchell

When you went into Japan which city did you enter?

It was Hiroshima. We saw devastation, a whole lot of devastation. We went through one city that wasn't bombed. They said it was an old city. But when we came to this place where they dropped the bomb...it was terrible. I can imagine all the women and children who perished there.

The guy up in the plane doesn't realize what he's doing. It really affected me. I got to thinking about that. It's different when you're out there fighting with soldiers. You think about killing them. But I love little kids.

Dropping that bomb snuffed them out and took their life away. They never got to live. That's what's happening now in Iraq. What did they do? They're going to condemn a bunch of women and kids for something that guy (Saddam Hussein) might do. I think it's for the oil. If you get that oil you can tell other countries what to do. But innocent people are going to suffer for that, and I just can't see it.

Did you only spend one day going through Hiroshima?

Yes, I remember going through there and thinking of how devastating it was to so many people that I didn't care to go back. We stayed in Japan for some time.

Did you get to see the Japanese civilians, and what was their attitude toward you and the other American soldiers?

Well, the ones that I knew were very friendly. They were much more friendly than I would have been had I been in their place. When we first went in there I felt like someone was going to whack me on the head at any time.

After a while you forget all about that. One thing you didn't see for a number of days were the women. They were hiding out, I guess. The children were reluctant to get close to you but after a while they were like any other kids.

When did you leave Japan?

In the latter part of '45. I wasn't over there a long time. Some people were over there for a long time. I came home on a troop ship. We were pretty joyous; everybody was happy about coming home.

We came into San Francisco. I came to Eureka on a Greyhound bus. My mom was still alive, and she was very happy to see me. She was expecting me because I told her I was coming.

Did it take time for you to adjust to being out of the war?

Oh yes. In fact, it still bothers me. It's hard for me. I guess for some people it didn't bother them. I'd get to drinking and that thing would rise up in me...

There were a lot of Indian vets from your generation, how do you feel about that?

Well, I feel it was necessary. Maybe we weren't as well appreciated as some of the other people, but this is still our home, and you have to do something to defend it.

Do you think it's important that younger Indian kids know what your generation did during the war?

I think it will stimulate a certain degree of pride in themselves and in their people, and they need that.

What type of work did you do after the war?

I worked in the woods as a rigging man and I logged timber. Then I went to work in construction. I gave up logging because it bothered me. From our ranch where I lived we used to take a day and a half to travel to the headwaters above Blue Creek. We'd stay out there for a week fishing and having fun.

One time I was out there falling timber. This was after the war. I admired that country so much when I was a kid. I had just cut this big fir tree and I stepped on the stump to look around. My son was my falling partner. It hit me like a bolt of lightning.

Here I was out there causing this devastation to the country I admired. I told my son I was quitting. I came back and the next day I went to Eureka and went to work with the union building and fixing roads. I cut trees after that, but for roads, and that didn't bother me.

How do you feel when you see young Indian kids take an interest in their culture today?

I admire them. I think it's wonderful. I think they should be encouraged to do that, and try to abide by the teachings they receive from their culture. It can only be good for them. That's what I think.

Have you ever been interviewed about your time in the service?

No.

Is there any particular reason why you chose to share with me today?

My daughter told me you were coming, and you've shown me all these nice pictures, and told me you were going to write a book. I think that would be a great thing for the Indian people; not just here, but all over. They should be exposed to something like this and it may give them a sense of belonging, which can only be good. That's what I think!

Ed Mitchell and his wife had six children and have lots of grandchildren and great-grandchildren. Ed enjoys watching all the different sports events in Hoopa in his spare time.

Kenny Childs

I met with Kenny Childs at his home in the small town of Orick, California on October 22, 2003. Kenny was a member of the Army Air Corps during the war.

I was born on July 16 in 1927 in Arcata down at the mouth of the Mad River in a barn! My mother and father used to weed, that was the only job available back then, so that's where I was born.

My father's name was William, but everybody called him Sandy. He was Yurok from around the Klamath River. My mother Dorothy was white and she was from around here. I was mostly raised around Trinidad and Blue Lake. From Blue Lake I went into the service.

My father drowned when I was five years old and my mother never remarried. She had four of us kids. We had a place that my father built on the Rancheria in Trinidad. We could never have a vehicle because the welfare people would never let her have anything. If she bought it they took it. She was never allowed to have anything.

You were raised during the Depression...

My father used to fish in the Klamath River. A boat tipped over and my father jumped in to help but drowned. We did have a garden with carrots and tomatoes and bean and peas. We had plenty to eat but we didn't have meat too often.

We grew up under welfare and they came along and gave us two pairs of pants. You had to keep those clean or wear rags! I think my mother did a good job, she held the four of us together! Nobody was taken away. She used to make sure that we saw one movie. We'd hitchhike to Arcata once a month or so.

Do you know what village your father was from?

Metta. My auntie Bell Paige and all of them came from there.

Where did you go to school as a young boy?

I started out in Trinidad. We walked from the Rancheria to Trinidad. My grandmother came from that village on the beach in Trinidad. It was us and a lot of the Lindgren kids that went to the school there. They were in the service too.

Kenny Childs

Did the teachers treat you all right?

Yeah, I think so. My aunt said when she went to school they treated them terrible. They wouldn't let them speak their own language. I never had much trouble in Trinidad but after I went to Blue Lake...the kids would segregate themselves. The teachers wouldn't do it but the kids would. The white kids would be here and the Indian kids would be there.

I was darker-complexioned and my brother was light-complexioned. I went to school there until the seventh grade then I went to Sherman for a year. I went down by bus. There was a guy going around talking to Indian people and he knew my mother had four kids. She talked to my brother and I and we were glad to go to the school.

On the way to Hawaii we hit a typhoon. They made everybody go down below. You could hear the water hitting. That was scarier than anything I did!

Then my brother and someone else were caught drinking and they sent them home but I stayed the rest of the year. After school or on weekends we could make extra money picking oranges or walnuts to go to the movies. I liked it but I didn't really want to go back. I missed home!

It was good down there because you could learn things. At first I stayed in the kitchen and then I worked with the cattle. I could go out there and whistle and those cows would come! I learned to box at Sherman but didn't box until I went in the service.

There were Yurok and Hupa there. After I left more Indians from other places came in. I came home and went to Arcata High School. I only went through the second year. It wasn't very big then, not like it is now! I liked all my teachers.

How old were you when you went into the service?

I was 18. I quit high school and started working in Eureka. I knew some of the guys who worked in the Merchant Marines and I thought I'd go do that. I didn't weigh enough but I went three times. The guy was going to see that I got in but I got drafted.

I went to Camp Beale and then I went to Camp McQuaide. That was a school by San Francisco. After that they shipped me to Baltimore for training. We stopped in Utah on the way back and they needed Air Force people. My buddy talked me into doing that. We didn't go to school for flying; we were clerks. I only went on a plane five or six times the whole time I was overseas.

How did you get to Luzon?

On the way to Hawaii we hit a typhoon. They made everybody go down below. Those bunks are inches apart; you couldn't get thrown down if you wanted to! You could hear the water hitting. That was scarier than anything I did!

As long as I was on the deck I figured I could swim, but down there it was scary. Then we went to the Philippines. We checked all these caves in the jungle and we were on guard duty. That was on Luzon. When we first got there we had to stay in two-man tents. One time we could hear these guys on guard hollering and pretty soon they started shooting. Then everything stopped. Everyone was looking outside.

We waited until the next morning and looked and there were a bunch of dead caribou! Sometimes the Japs would come in and take clothes. They didn't bother us. We had to guard the Japs who surrendered. They would catch these Japanese who walked right to our chow line. After my time there I went to Tinian and then came home to be discharged.

Did you ever run across any other Indian guys in the service?

Oh yeah, I knew Jack Basset. He was a good friend of mine who was Choctaw Indian. I knew some others and some Japanese-Hawaiian boys. There were a lot of Indian boys there.

Why do you think they were there?

They didn't have any choice, they were drafted. But now if they're in they're there because they want to be.

Your brother Bill was in the service, what did he do?

He was in the 82nd Airborne in Germany.

And you were a logger when you came back from the service?

Yeah, I was in Eureka until I got married to Pearl 53 years ago. I was a choker-setter. The hook tender would tell the head choker-setter what he needed to do. Then you'd take however many chokers you needed and tie them to the back of a CAT.

Sometimes the boss would let you ride the CAT into the woods and sometimes they wouldn't. You'd have to use eight or 10 chokers depending on the size of the log. You take three or four logs at a time in. While that CAT is gone with that set of logs you set chokers so when he comes back you can hook him up with those chokers.

I was always on the high lead. They would tie the line and you'd only have one choker on the line. They'd drag it out to you in the woods. They'd whistle for what you needed. There'd be a whistle for slack, or a certain number of whistles for tight lines, or six whistles in case somebody got hurt.

Where there a lot of Indian people who worked in the woods with you?

Yeah. I met some of the guys I knew from Sherman. It seemed like many of the Indian boys worked out in the woods. They liked to be out in the woods.

How many years did you work in the woods?

Probably 40 years. When I got out of the service all these big outfits had jobs in the woods. I mostly logged fir and some redwood.

Since you've been retired you've been active with the Yurok Tribe, why is that?

It's just something I like to do. I'd like to learn more about it. See, when I was growing up I wasn't around the elders because my mother was white. She was with my grandma and my aunt but not around on the river.

At that time the Indians didn't care for the whites

too much. My grandma liked my mom though. There were kids in Blue Lake who didn't like Indian kids. I just never let it bother me.

If you could speak to young Indian kids today what would you tell them to do?

Always pay attention to their elders. They won't learn anything by themselves. Whenever I go to any meeting that's what these elders say. It doesn't make any difference if they're Indian or white; listen to the elders because they've been there!

Kenny and his wife Pearl raised a family and are great-grandparents. They reside in Orick and he continues to stay involved with local veteran gatherings and the Yurok Tribe's Culture Committee.

David Risling, Jr.

1921-2005

I met with Dave and Barbara Risling at their home on October 26, 2002. Dave was in the U.S. Navy as a commissioned officer during the war. He is Jack Risling's younger brother. They had two other brothers, Baron and Leslie, who also served in World War Two.

I was born in 1921 at the same place as my brother on the Klamath River. It was below Weitchpec and Martin's Ferry; it was the village of Morek. Our father David's dad was German and his mother Maggie Charley was Karuk.

Maggie and my dad moved to Hoopa with a Hupa man and he became a member of the Hupa Tribe. That's how come we're members of the Hupa Tribe. My mother Geneva was English and Scottish and Yurok on her mother's side. The Karuk side of the family was from Sahwuram which is up by Orleans. There were eight of us kids in the family. Anthony was the oldest, then Vivian, Jack, Roselyn, Viola, myself, Baron and Leslie.

Did your mother speak her Indian language?

Yes. When I was little that's all the older people spoke. Us kids knew it when they talked to us. I was four or five when we moved to Hoopa. When I went to boarding school no one was supposed to speak their language.

I was there in 1926. When we moved to Hoopa we moved in a little house at the end of the valley. In the meantime my dad was putting together a little sawmill up near Hostler Creek.

What did the school look like?

They had the boys at one end of the school and the girls at the other end. The first thing they did was give you the same clothes. We had certain clothes for school and for play and for church. I always wondered what they did with the clothes we wore when we came in!

There was a heavyset woman who was pretty good; she'd spank us every once in a while. She was Russian. I didn't get in trouble very often. Once in a while but not too often! I thought she was pretty good; it wasn't like a lot of the schools where they'd beat you up and whip you.

Our batch of kids got along pretty good. We'd get to play in the brush and that's when the kids would talk the language. There were Karuk and Hupa and Yurok and there were some from Ukiah. There were some from Round Valley. They had to stay all summer long but we got to go home.

About how many kids would be in a classroom?

About 20 on average. Some might have had 15 or a dozen. When we were in class we had to learn English and math. They'd tell stories for history, and we had drawing. We had to learn how to be quiet.

Did you ever have any Indian teachers there?

No. I never did have an Indian teacher.

Never?

Never!

Was the school split into half a day of school and half a day of vocational?

Not for the little ones. It was about the fifth or sixth grade before we started the work.

Did any of your brothers or sisters go to the school with you?

Viola was a year-and-a-half older than me and she did. But we couldn't talk to the girls. We were on our side and weren't supposed to go to their side. Jack and Anthony were ahead of me.

The big problem was the kids weren't told to go to college. We were lucky to graduate. But my dad said we had a right to learn otherwise we'd get kicked around.

At that time my dad had his kids come home. Jack would have to go home. In the wintertime he'd have to paddle across the river. One time the river was going so fast he went down over the riffles! He had to walk about two miles to get to school.

I remember when Anthony and Vivian graduated from the eighth grade. I was little at that time. We stayed in a dormitory. The girls had a basement for the showers and storage. It was two stories for both.

When I was there they had an eating place and they had cooks. I didn't think the food was bad. We had mush. But first we had to march. In the fourth grade we had to march and drill. We'd have to change clothes to march.

Then after that we changed into school clothes. When we were eating we had two older kids on each end. We'd stand and say prayers, then sit down. They'd ring a bell and you could eat and talk.

A lot of the people came from homes where we ate acorns and salmon and those kinds of things and then we had to learn to eat different stuff. The big problem was the kids weren't told to go to college. We were lucky to graduate. But my dad said we had a right to learn otherwise we'd get kicked around.

When you had to drill and march who would be in charge, was it one of the men there?

At the start, but after a while they had some kids from the seventh or eighth grade who would help. We marched just like soldiers. As a matter of fact, when I was in midshipman's school they had us guys march. That was one thing I learned!

Were you allowed to speak your language in the class at all?

Back around 1931 my dad was fighting the government and the BIA. My dad was pretty smart and he knew these lawyers who would come from Washington.

Oh no, if you spoke your language and they knew about it you got a licking. You had to speak just English. We had already learned English so it wasn't a major problem, but for some of them it was really rough. I remember some little kids who came there; they'd cry.

One time Jack got to go home and I guess I started crying! I hadn't been home for a while. I was homesick and it just came out of me. A number of kids were put in there from broken homes. Most of the kids came from Klamath or the Trinity River.

Did you ever witness any of the kids get punished for speaking?

No, by the time we got there we knew better. It was really bad before my time. That school's gone now. My dad went there and they kicked him out because he was speaking Hupa at that time. So he was always in trouble. At that time they were always in trouble for that. I was in the next generation.

Did your dad attend the Chemawa boarding school?

Yeah, because they kicked him out of school. He wouldn't agree with the teachers. Back then he was one that spoke the language and did the singing in the ceremonies. My dad was little but he was a fighter! He'd carry rocks and hit somebody! He wouldn't mind the teachers. They finally sent him to Chemawa to the school there.

Did he stay at Chemawa for long?

He ran away five different times and broke out of five different jails! The sixth time he didn't break out of jail, he went north for about 10 years. This was when he was a kid; I don't know how old he was. He only made it to the third grade but he worked in a blacksmith shop.

He had one friend at Chemawa; you have his picture there. Lewis Sanderson and he would run away together. That last time Sanderson didn't want to go north. When my dad came back he knew five different Indian languages. He already knew Yurok, Karuk, and Hupa when he left and he learned two more up there.

How old was he when he came back down from up North?

I don't know but he had worked his way up as a welder. He learned to break horses and went to the reservations and worked and learned their languages. He kept moving around because he didn't want to get caught.

Were they looking for him?

I don't think so but there were some notices out. He finally went up to Canada and worked on the railroads. He learned a lot about machinery and that's how come he started that sawmill. As a little guy I used to work there and my job was to oil the engines. Vivian and Rose and my dad would cut the trees down and Anthony and Jack would saw the logs.

All we ever did was work. That's how come I do what I do today; as long as you're not asleep you do something. When the war came along that was it for the sawmill. It was old anyway. So they moved down and rebuilt another one. They had some support from some companies and it was more modern. This was after the war.

Did you have any family in World War One, or did they know anyone who served in that war?

My dad was telling me that Lewis Sanderson told him they were in trenches 100 yard away from the Germans. He came out OK. My mother's uncle Sherman Young was

Dave Risling in 1943.
Photo courtesy of Dave and Barbara Risling.

there and he fought in the trenches. He used to tell us about the airplane fights. He said at least they had something to watch besides killing each other!

How many years did you go to the boarding school?

Until it ended. Back around 1931 my dad was fighting the government and the BIA. My dad was pretty smart and he knew these lawyers who would come from Washington. I remember he used to take me around when I was little.

I didn't know what he was doing, but later on in life I figured it was no wonder I did these things; here was my dad who didn't finish third grade and he'd meet with these lawyers and congressmen, and that's when local people took over the boarding school.

In the meantime we were going to a little tiny school with two rooms in it. It was across the street from the hospital. That's where we went to school and there were 20 or 30 kids. They were from this group who were going to be on a school board that would take over this school. These people were the ones who fought against the school.

So this was when they started the transition at Hoopa from a boarding school to a regular school?

Yes. The regular school building was two stories. When they took over I was in the fourth grade. In the fifth grade I was in that little school across from the hospital. In the sixth grade I was back in the regular school.

I graduated in the eighth grade from there. It was also a high school and I graduated from there in 1939. I started playing sports when high school started.

When the high school started we played a lot of baseball. We used to run races amongst ourselves. I was slow but Anthony was the one who ran fast. We also boxed. I played everything and when I boxed I won a lot.

Tell me that story about the first time you Indian guys from the Hoopa High School played football...

That first time we played was against Ferndale. The only person we had who knew about football was Herbie O'Neill because he'd played it down at Sherman. Our principal was our coach.

We didn't know much about the game. We had won the game and we didn't even know we won! That O'Neill told us to push these two guys apart so he could block a kick. So we did, and he blocked the kick and fell on the ball and got a touchdown but we didn't know it!

The coach told us we won but we didn't believe it! We won our first game and that was the only one we won all season! The next year was 1938. We were learning and got a coach in there and he was really good. We did pretty well.

We didn't have a basketball court or anything there at the school but we had a tennis court. It rained every day. We did a lot of passing and didn't have many good shooters. We'd pass the ball this way and that way. We did have one guy who was a good shooter. He made 20 points one game. We didn't win many games; I think we beat Weaverville and South Fork.

So that's the origin of basketball in Hoopa...

That's the origin! It was a lot of fun. They had boxing tournaments and we won three championships there. Anthony used to box up in Seattle and he was rated tenth in the country in these magazines. So when he came back down he taught us how to box.

I used to fight anybody! I fought heavyweights or anyone. Every guy I fought in my weight I won by TKO. We fought in Eureka and we fought against the CCC camp guys. This one guy at the CCC I boxed was really mad because I won the decision against him. Later on I found out he was a professional!

In the meantime we were going to a little tiny school with two rooms in it. It was across the street from the hospital. That's where we went to school and there were 20 or 30 kids.

This was during high school?

Yes. After that I boxed down at San Francisco State. The only time I was beat was when I fought this guy who used to be a heavyweight. I'd beat him before and all these Indian guys were yelling for me so I thought I'd try to knock him out! I thought I'd get him in the solar plexus. I never got there! This guy knocked me flat. But I won all my other fights.

Dave and Jack's brother Baron Risling perished during the war while test-piloting a fighter plane in Texas.
Photo courtesy of Dave and Barbara Risling.

Did you ever play in the stick games?

Yeah. Anthony and I and some guys from Hoopa would practice behind our house. There was a sandbar there. When I was in high school I'd play with the bigger guys. I was a slow runner but I could wrestle. I played on the end. The biggest game I played was on the Fourth of July. Oscar Taylor was there from downriver and he was the best. No one wanted to play against him.

They signed me up against his team. That was like

playing the champion of the world! Who do you think lost the game? I hung with him for a while but once he'd get away and started running I couldn't catch him.

About 30 years later Oscar Taylor was here in Sacramento putting on a demonstration Brush Dance and he pointed to me and said 'That's the guy I learned something from. He gave me the best stick game.' He was making me feel good! He was a nice guy and became my close friend.

When did you first meet Barbara?

I met her when I went to a summer dance up above Willow Creek in the Salyer area. I liked to dance and somebody told me this girl was going to go to Hoopa. I don't know if we talked but that was the first time I saw her.

She went to Hoopa and I got to know her at school. One time we were going to ride this bus to Humboldt State and she wrote me a note wanting to ride with me but I was with the guys and didn't respond. On the way back this other girl sat with me and Barbara teases me about that!

Dave Risling's Ship PC 1139.
Photo courtesy of Dave and Barbara Risling.

After you graduated from Hoopa High School where did you go?

Humboldt State offered me a scholarship but I went down to Cal Poly San Louis Obispo. I had gone down earlier to Cal Poly with some kids representing Humboldt in the Future Farmers. When I was down there these guys signed me up to fight this college guy who was the best boxer down there!

I boxed and got a decision on him, but he hit me hard that first round. I later found out that guy had a brother who fought for the world championship twice! That guy I fought went on to box in the service. So when I was down there at Cal Poly they took us around and showed us the different things they were doing.

I had a few pigs I had raised and I sold them to go to school. They were top-rated pigs and I think I got maybe $60 for them. That was all the money I had so I bought some clothes at a second-hand store with it. I caught a ride down to Cal Poly and worked down there while I went to school. I remember the first two days were hot and I worked with the animals.

So I took a test and then was paid 20 cents an hour! I went to Cal Poly for a year and that second year at Christmas I came home. I got hurt while working; I hurt my back. I went back down to Cal Poly but they said I had to go to the hospital to get a cast. Jack was down there and he was living 10 miles west of the college there.

He brought me back up to Hoopa. They took me to the hospital at Christmas time and I didn't get out until June! Barbara had graduated that summer so I got out in time to see that. I came back to Cal Poly after that. I didn't finish at Cal Poly until after the war. The war started and four of us went to San Francisco and one signed up for the Air Force and three of us signed up for the Navy.

Where were you when you heard about Pearl Harbor?

We heard on the radio about Pearl Harbor. That's when we learned about it. We knew sooner or later we'd be going off to the war. That's when I decided I'd sign up to be in the Navy. They let us finish out the last part of our semester. I only needed three or four courses after that and I would have been done.

Where did you go after that?

I went to UCLA. They gave us the physicals and we went through the boot camp. Down there we wore the sailor's outfits. They told us what to study. We took astronomy, navigation and advanced mathematics. We had some history and mechanics. We were there for about four months. From there we went back to North Fork, Virginia.

After about two weeks we went up to New York on an old train. It took us two days to get there because everything was fouled up because of the war. We stayed there four months. We studied one hour on and one hour off. Then you'd have to study in your room. There'd be a guy who would walk through to check you all the time. But we had a good time together, too.

We'd look at some of the famous buildings in New York and see a show or something. That's when Frank Sinatra and these famous people had shows. We stayed in New York at Columbia University for four months. I came back to California for 10 days and we got married in Hoopa on April 28, 1944.

I had to go back to the Great Lakes to learn gunnery on ships. Barbara didn't go with me because she was getting everything put away from the wedding. I stayed there about six weeks and from there I went down to Miami. Barbara came there after a couple months. That was for potential captains of ships.

They gave you these tests for leadership. We would go out on ships and we took classes in navigation and electrical stuff. You had to know about the engine room and the gunnery and the navigation. You worked your way up to be a captain and that's what this was for. We had a lot of classes. It was easy for me except for that Morse code! I was more interested in Barbara at that time!

Barbara: It was all my fault!

Dave: After that we came back to San Francisco and they gave us orders but didn't tell you where you're going. We were going to Hawaii on a small aircraft carrier.

And were your brothers Baron and Leslie in the service by that time?

I think Baron was and Leslie might have come in a little later.

And your sisters were all working on the dock at Humboldt...

Yeah, they moved to Eureka. All three of them were there. They welded and made floating dry docks. They were towed out to where we were.

And your brother Anthony was too old to be in the service?

No, but they only allowed four from a family to be in the service; you remember those five Sullivan brothers that died? Anthony worked down in the Bay Area on things that had to do with the war.

Dave and Jack's brother Leslie Risling served in the Army and saw combat in the Battle of the Bulge.
Photo courtesy of Mary Risling.

How did your parents feel about having their whole family work on behalf of the war effort?

I don't think there was a problem. Everybody had to do it at that time. You're at war. It wasn't the United States taking away something. The Japanese wanted to take us over and they wanted to take the white people over.

Do you think that's why it was OK for Indian people to go in the service?

Well, it was more than just OK. You had to go anyway so you might as well sign in to have a choice. If you don't and get drafted they put you where they want.

One of the things we learned in midshipman's school was to learn how to find your own way to places.

Do you think the Indian men might have been proud to be in the service?

I don't know. Some were drafted. I joined so I could do something I would like to do. I didn't want to be in the trenches like my uncle and like my dad's friend I told you about. Leslie got in and was trained with tanks and heavy stuff.

While you were in school and training to be an officer did you ever come across any other Indian men?

Not that I can remember. There could have been some other people from other tribes that were light-complexioned.

Barbara: At that period people didn't mention if they were Indian. There was a lot of hate.

When did you become a captain?

I think it was around the time at Iwo Jima. We got on this plane at a certain time and we were to go to PC-1139. I had no idea where this was. The plane went to Guadalcanal but we stopped at Tarawa first. That was where my buddy Ozzie Bussel was. One of the things we learned in midshipman's school was to learn how to find your own way to places.

The battle was over at Tarawa and I found my friend Ozzie there! From there I flew down to Guadalcanal. They put me aboard a ship and took us to a campground. It rained a lot down there. There were a bunch of tents there and they cooked this spam. That spam was the same all the time! I checked for that PC ship but couldn't find it. Everybody told me that was a good excuse to go to New Zealand or Australia.

My job was to find this ship. I was to replace someone who had been in the war so I said no, and continued looking for the ship. Everything was secret because if the enemy found out...I asked if these guys ever saw the PC ship and they said it was in Kwajalein. I didn't know where that was but they said it was there. The ship was there but it was being repaired. I flew to the Marshall Islands and sure enough, it was there.

How many men were in the crew?

About 80 or 90. They'd been around to all these different islands.

And that's when you became the captain?

No, not there. You had to work yourself up. I was in charge of the eating place for the officers and the sonar men. We'd figure out if the sound hit a whale or a submarine. I had to do these things until another guy was transferred. I worked with the gunnery and then as the navigator and finally as the second to the captain. At Iwo Jima I was the captain. That was when Jack was there at Iwo Jima too.

We did pick up flyers. We had submarines and destroyers who did this too. These were planes that couldn't land because they were so shot up.

So you were the captain while the ship was at Iwo Jima; what were your ship's duties?

We had to worry about the Japanese submarines. We'd escort our ships out to sea and then they were on their own. We did a lot of that. We did pick up flyers. We had submarines and destroyers who did this too. These were planes that couldn't land because they were so shot up.

Do you remember a particular time when you picked up a pilot?

Oh yeah, this one guy had come back from Japan and couldn't steer well because their gear was shot up. They had to fly around to get everyone out with parachutes. Our boat was there and the plane was getting lower and lower and finally this last guy jumped out. Our guys went swimming out to save him. This guy had run that plane...it was just amazing. He had gone to school in Santa Barbara.

He was probably pretty happy to see you...

Oh, he was just about dead when they pulled him out of the water. But that was what we did. When the war ended the Marines brought all these guns from the Japanese and we would pull out and dump all these guns in the ocean. After we got through there my job was to bring the boat through the other islands. I remember one time they had the USO singers and dancers and that was fun! This was on a little island.

We played softball against each other. The Japanese were still there. The war was over but a lot of them didn't know it. But these two gave up and they brought them in to this sergeant. This Marine sergeant turned around and just shot them. We were in shock because these were human beings. That sergeant said 'We don't save these guys because they could have killed all of us.' There were things like that that went on.

When you went onto Iwo Jima how long did you stay?

There were still a few Japanese left when I went ashore to visit with Jack. They had these tunnels all through there. Some of the guys took me through there to show me. There were some dead people still in there. There were some Marines that would take their teeth out.

I didn't want to see any more of that so I left. Those pictures you have was when the war was still on. They had tents there on the island and I'd eat there. Some of the guys would get excited because I was an officer and I ate with them. I don't know if I should tell you that, they might put me in jail!

Jack had mentioned that he was able to visit you out on your ship...

He was able to visit but not all that often. Jack was still on Iwo Jima after the war was over. He used to take me all over. He built the first memorial on top of Mount Suribachi. That was the first monument.

There was an officer in charge of it but Jack was the one who with his crew did the work. That officer was from Harvard or Yale or something and he'd tell them what to do but he didn't know how to do it! Anyway, I went up there to see it. It was made out of wood and it had writing on it. Later on a hurricane or something blew that monument away so they built a new one.

I know this is tough or maybe even morbid to ask this but I'd like you to describe more about going through the tunnels on Iwo Jima...

Well, you had to put your head down at the opening. You could travel through and come out at another place. They had their guns to shoot at ships and they had cement there. I didn't go into too many because there were bodies in them. A Marine took me through there. The war had ended and some of the guys off my ship brought me that rifle Jack's holding (in his picture). They brought me lots of stuff.

Did you get to observe the entire battle at Iwo Jima from your ship?

We weren't there all the time. Sometimes we'd bring ships in and go out.

How did you maintain discipline on your ship?

That was no problem at all. In the Navy they have to do exactly what you tell them to do. Some people were rougher but I was easygoing. I always gave credit to people for what they did. When we went to Hawaii you're only supposed to give one-third of the crew some time off but I would give two-thirds of them the day off.

They would rest and I always gave them as much of whatever as I could. After the war was over some of them got to go to Japan. These planes were flying by at Iwo Jima. I'd take some of the guys and let them get on those planes to visit Japan. I got along with all of them.

What were the armaments on your ship?

We had these bombs that we'd shoot to get submarines. We'd shoot them out and if they hit a sub they'd explode. With depth charges we'd drop them and if they hit something they'd explode. They had destroyers and we'd call them because they had more gear. We didn't have to do that too often because the Japanese were almost done.

Did your ship ever get strafed or hit by a bomb?

We got hit by one U.S. bomb because they thought we were something else.

How did you hear that the war ended?

I think we heard it on the radio. Everyone was excited.

Did you or anyone on your crew have any idea of what an atomic bomb was?

I think we think it was something big because they said they dropped a bomb.

Barbara: You were pretty much in the dark about a lot that went on?

Dave: Pretty much.

Did you write letters to each other?

Barbara: Oh yeah, all the time. I wrote to him almost every night.

How about from your family, did you ever hear from Leslie?

Yeah, he wrote once from Europe. He was in the Battle of the Bulge and all that. Baron was killed during the war. I got a letter he had written the day before. He was having a problem while diving. His plane would go from here to there but they blacked out nine times out of 10.

He had written me that day before and said he only had one more time to go before he'd have some time off. He would black out and almost never pulled out of the dive. That next day he blacked out and didn't make it. It was close to the end of the war. I had a call on my ship and it was kind of odd because nobody wanted to tell me what happened. I don't know if I was the commanding officer or the second in command.

They all got together to tell me. It was pretty bad. To me Baron was the smartest one in the family. Everything was so easy for him even when he was a kid. He was real smart, smarter than I am. He was working down in welding during the war and then he went to flight school at the University of Alabama. He was number one there.

Barbara: He was in officer training school and had a 4.0 in school.

Dave: Baron was much smarter than I was. People might think I could do this or that but Baron could do twice as much as I could do.

It was rare for you to be able to visit with your brother Jack during the war, what did that mean to you?

He was the only one I got to visit with. Jack was back in Connecticut when I was in New York and we'd write and visit two or three times. It was nice to see him! We were back in Hawaii practicing the landing and he was with the 5th Marines. We got to visit there too. We knew these boats were practicing landing and Jack was there. I don't know how I found him!

Where was the final place that you docked your ship?

At first we went to Hawaii. Then from Pearl Harbor we went to the United States. We kept having lots of problems so we came in a day late to Astoria, Oregon. We came through the Columbia River and then came in to the dry docks in Portland.

Barbara, can you tell me when you went on the ship?

Barbara: That was after they went from Astoria to the dry docks. One day he decided to take me aboard and show me around. I got to eat down with the enlisted men and Dave did too. He decided I could stay over because there was no one else in the cabin with him. When I was driven back that morning all these sailors whistled and hooted at me! I was only 21 at the time.

Dave Risling

How did it feel for you to have your new husband go off to war?

Barbara: Well, nobody likes that kind of thing. I had to keep myself busy. I went back to art school for a while and I had a job coloring photographs in Oakland. I did that until I knew he was coming back from the war. I took a train up north to meet him.

Tell me about that time when you saw him on leave from New York...

Barbara: He had taken the train from L.A. up to San Francisco and he took a bus to Chico and then up north to visit family before he had to leave again. So he stopped and visited with me. I was living with a woman who had two kids and her husband was a doctor. I was living with her and helping her with her kids while I went to school.

So we had a few hours before he had to go. I thought about him and thought gee, I really should marry this guy! We knew each other for a long time and our families knew each other.

I sent him a telegram and I made sure it was only 10 words. It cost a certain amount if you sent 10 words and with any more you had to pay more. So I wrote 'If I say yes can we be married this week?' He hadn't asked me!

Dave: I had these other two girls I was going to visit so I had to say sorry I couldn't because my orders were changed!

That's a good story! How many years did you serve in the Navy?

Dave: From 1941 to 1946.

You mentioned when you started working with different congressmen that a lot of them were veterans as well...

We live in two worlds. If you are an Indian you better learn about who your ancestors were. They lived here for thousands of years.

Yeah, most of them were. One of my successes was that I befriended people in education. In education it's not who's the smartest, it's who controls the money and who can send the bills. For Indians, Republicans are against you immediately.

I would start with someone I knew and we'd talk about the war and our kids. Then they'd say to call if I ever needed them. It was the same with people here in the state. Most were service people.

I'm curious about why you spent so many years of your life working on behalf of Native American law and education?

I was an Indian, and because I saw what my dad was able to do with that boarding school in Hoopa. He was without an education but he was a smart guy and knew how to meet people. All my life we always worked. Even as little kids we worked, worked, worked. Everybody had a job to do.

Why have you been involved with the religious ceremonies?

Before I went to college my dad brought me into the woodshed. It was a Sunday morning. My dad had a stick in his hand. The woodshed was empty because it was summertime. He drew a circle and put dots in it.

He asked me what that was. I said it was a circle with some dots. He said there was a lot I needed to do in life. He said I was going to college and asked what I planned on taking. I hadn't thought about it and I said maybe I would take law. He drew a flag next to the circle.

He said, 'The dot in the circle are the Indians and the big circle represents the white people. To do anything you have to fight 100-to-one. We have to outsmart these guys. They don't know anything about Indians.'

'You have to outsmart these guys. Do you think you can get very far on a wagon wheel with just one spoke?' That's when he explained this was a wagon wheel. He said, 'You have to have all the spokes to travel. The problem with Indians is they might only have one spoke.'

He pointed to one of the spokes and said 'That's who you are; it's your Indian-ness. That's why they have these ceremonies. The most important thing is your spirituality.' He went on and pointed out all these things, education, politics, to have a whole wheel.

'When you have the whole wheel together, then you can win.' He said 'When you go off to college if you forget who you are don't bother coming home.' I wanted to come home! I didn't really understand it until I was older.

And you've been coming home ever since. Tell me about how you feel to see your kids or grandkids participate in the ceremonies.

They all did it in their later years. I feel great because Barbara and I never pushed them to do this or that. I learned from my mom and dad.

If you had the opportunity to speak to every Indian kid in America what would you tell them?

The first thing I would tell them is who we are, and how we existed as Indian people before Europeans came, and how we are going to live in society today. We live in two worlds. If you are an Indian you better learn about who your ancestors were. They lived here for thousands of years.

David Risling's family is very proud of his service to his country and his service on behalf of Native Americans in education.

Kenny Sanderson

Kenny Sanderson and I met because Willard Carlson mentioned his name to me. Kenny is of Yurok ancestry and he was in the Marine Corps during the war. We met at his home on August 16, 2002. Kenny had written out a prepared statement that he read for the interview. I then asked him some questions.

"'I'm from the Klamath area and lived here almost all my life except for the years I attended an Indian boarding school in Riverside called the Sherman Institute. I was active in sports such as boxing, wrestling, and football. In 1940 I wrestled for the Olympic tryouts at the Oakland YMCA gym.

Then on December 12, 1941 I went to join the Marine Corps. I didn't have my folks' consent to join. I was too young. What I did was I wrote my own letter saying it was OK for me to join. Then I was in the Marine Corps.

I learned a lot. I did three years and four months overseas. I enjoyed my years of adventure. I saw action at Guam and at Midway, and I was at Pearl Harbor just after the Japanese struck. There were 4,500 of us Marines and I don't think any were over 25 years old. We were going on and we didn't know where. Wherever they sent us was where we had to go!

After I got out of the Marine Corps I became a professional boxer. I boxed around here, in Eureka, San

Francisco, Portland and Crescent City. I fought in the main event every time. When I was in the Marine Corps I fought over in Honolulu. I fought all over the island. I was what you would call an entertainer.

There were 10 or 12 of us. They'd put us aboard a plane and flew us from island to island. We boxed and entertained the troops. In 1945 I was down in Guam; I was with the 3rd Marine Division. Then came the rotation system. They came to me and said, 'Corporal Sanderson, you're going home. You have enough points so you're one of the first eligible boys to leave from here.'

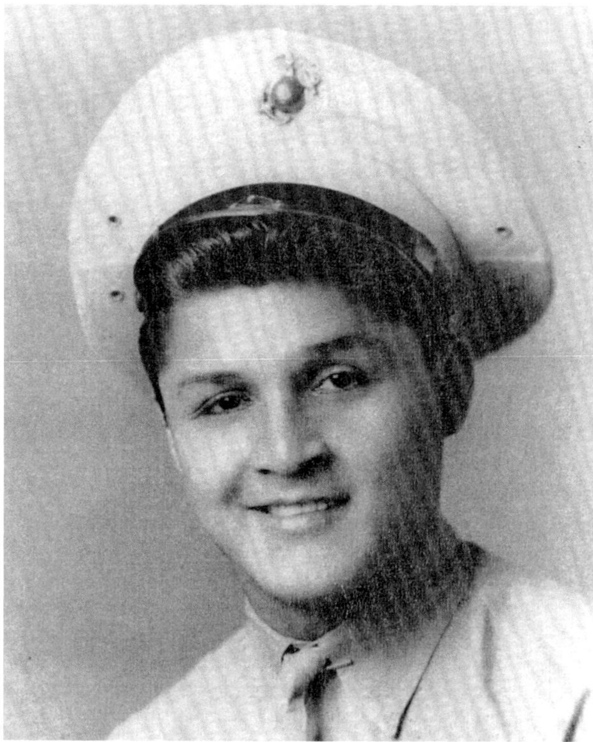

Kenny Sanderson ca. 1943-4.
Photo courtesy of Kenny Sanderson.

So I boarded a ship. It wasn't clean. It was oily, and dirty, but the chow was good! Then I got down here to San Diego. When we were overseas I was around colonels and other big officers. We didn't have to salute; we talked to them just like I'm talking to you.

But when we got back to the States one of these shavetails that was in for maybe 30 days said, 'Hey Marine you know who I am, I'm a lieutenant, you salute me.' I said, 'Sir, we were overseas and we had colonels, lieutenants, and officers and we were all together.' He didn't say anything, then he said to salute him anyway, so I said I would, sir. So then I got out.

I came back to Klamath. My dad Lewis Sanderson was a logger. He was working for the Simpson timber company in 1945 and '46. When I joined the Marine Corps I did not tell my mother or my father. I just wrote a letter and gave it to the superintendent at Sherman. It said it was all right for me to join the service and two weeks later I was in! In other words I volunteered."

And how old were you?

I turned 17 about 16 days before I went in.

What was your mother's name?

Lydia Pilgrim-Sanderson. She came from Terep. We had a place up there too. We used to go to school there and Mr. Blake used to be the bus driver. He had an old Ford bus. In the wintertime he'd come up the river in high water in a gas boat. He'd take us down to Blake's landing; we'd board the bus, go to school at Requa then at three we'd come back.

The Japanese were still on Guam. We had to fight them. I was a machine-gunner.

We didn't think anything of it. He was a great pilot. He knew where the channels were and stuff like that. After that I went down to Sherman. I went down to Sherman for ninth and tenth grade. I was just in eleventh grade when I decided I'd join the Marine Corps. I enjoyed my time there.

I saw guys that faltered along the way but they pushed them on and on. There were these big 200-pound guys, when they went in to get their tetanus shot they'd pass out! They'd go right down and hit the floor!

Where did you go to boot camp?

I went to boot camp in San Diego, California. Then I went to Pearl Harbor. At the time I came into Pearl we had to zigzag through the ships. There was still smoke and steam coming out of them. I would say the sailors aboard the ships, the ones that were still alive entombed; I would say they're the heroes of 1941.

I would say they were the heroes, not us guys who came later. They didn't know what was coming. I understand that in Hawaii some people thought the Japanese were coming, but the big shots didn't believe them. They thought they were on maneuvers. Then we heard that Pearl was hit.

I was a machine-gunner at Pearl after it was attacked. I was at a place they called Ford Island; it's an island that had steel nets to keep submarines out. But when the Japs attacked Pearl Harbor they had flown right over this place and dropped their torpedoes from the air. That's how they attacked us at Pearl.

After your time at Pearl where did you go?

I went to Guam and then I hit Midway. I was attached to the Third Marine Division. The Japanese were still on Guam. We had to fight them. I was a machine-gunner. I was guarding the north end of the island and I saw a Japanese come along about a thousand feet in front of me. I just let him come along, and come along, until he was about 300 feet away from me. Then I just opened up with my machine gun and it seemed like I cut him right in half. I didn't go over and look, but that was that.

How long were you at Guam?

I was at Guam for about three months. We were getting ready to hit the island of Japan. But we heard early in the morning we got the word the war was over. They dropped the A-bomb on Japan.

And the other island you were on was Midway?

Yes, I came on that island in a C-54. That's a transport. We were about 10 miles from the island and it looked like a little speck in the water. I wondered how the heck could we land on that? But then we got closer and landed. Our 5th Marine defense was out there. We were there for a while, then I was shipped to Honolulu, and from there I was shipped to San Diego, then from there I came home.

Kenny Sanderson

What was it like to be a Marine?

Well, to be part of the Marine Corps…when I was down at Sherman I used to box a lot, and I was kind of a smarty guy. But when I went in the Marine Corps they teach you discipline and how to respect your elders. They would say, 'As long as you're in the Marine Corps I'm your mother and your dad, and what I say goes, you do it.' That's what they told me, just like that. I did what they told me and got along pretty well.

Did you like the uniform?

The uniform was perfect! I loved it. I had khakis. When I came back overseas I bought some blues. I hitch-hiked home from San Francisco up to Klamath. At that time in '45, they said, 'Look at that Marine standing there!' I had no trouble getting a ride.

Did you ever serve with other Indian men?

Yes, there were two or three of us from Sherman Institute all in the same platoon. One was from Arkansas, another was from Ukiah. Paul Jackson was his name. When we came back from the war we were at Camp Elliott. They were trying out a bomb, and there were lots of Marines there. They gave us dark glasses and told us not to look at the explosion.

When were you discharged?

Well, I had come home to Klamath to visit. I got back to base two days late, so they got me for that. They put me in solitary confinement for two weeks. Then a 4th Marine Division officer came along. I'd never seen this officer before in my life. He bailed me out. 'PFC Kenny Sanderson,' he said, 'I'm bailing you out and you're on your own now.' I got out with an honorable discharge and everything was fine.

How long were you at Sherman?

I went down there in '37. I was there three years. I knew Frank and Leonard Ames, and Glenn Moore, and a whole bunch of the guys. I also knew some of the women from Hoopa, and Morek, and other places. Glenn and I wrestled along with Frank and Leonard and Delbert Sharp.

What was your trade at Sherman?

I took up cooking, baking, engineering, shoe-shop, farming and dairy. At that time Sherman was the best boarding school I could go to. Everybody got along and everybody tried to help each other out. We all got along fine.

How did you know my grandpa Stan Lowry?

He was in the same dormitory with me. I boxed with him. You know Clyde Johnny? I boxed with him and Darrell McCovey and a bunch of other guys.

What weight class were you in boxing?

Lightweight; 135 to 138 pounds. My strategy when I boxed; I was short and the other guy was tall. In order to get to my opponent I had to do a lot of infighting. I'd bob and weave and get in close.

Who did you box against when you were in the Marines?

We fought Army, we fought Navy and we fought civilians from Honolulu. I fought in the Honolulu Bowl. It seated 2,400 people at that time.

That's a pretty big crowd…

It's a big crowd. When you're fighting it seemed like you would go deaf. I couldn't hear anybody hollering or anything. I just boxed and boxed. The longest matches I had were eight rounds. I met George Avers and Joe Louis and I met a guy from San Francisco who was a champ but I forgot his name.

Were there any other Indian guys that boxed?

Oh, there were some, but they weren't California Indians. They were from other states. There were four or five other Indian guys besides me.

What tribe are you?

I'm Yurok, but my dad Lewis is part Karuk. There's a bunch of Sandersons up in Orleans. My mother Lydia was from Terep here on the Klamath. Henry Pilgrim was her father. I was born in November of 1924.

So you're related to Aileen Pilgrim Figueroa?

Yes, she's my aunt.

Growing up, did you speak the Yurok language?

Yes, we all did. That was my first language. We'd stay with our grandma and she'd teach us. It's hard to speak because it's been so long now. I did a lot of hunting around Terep and Red Mountain. I killed my first bear up there. I call my dog out here, his name is Bear!

What does the American flag mean to you?

The American flag shows who were the first people here. In the flag it's red. That's us red men, we were here first. Then the white for the white men. The blue is for everybody else.

Did you ever talk about your experiences in the service with anyone else?

I never have. It's in me but I don't talk about it.

Did you have any relatives that served in the war?

I had one, Floyd Pilgrim, killed in Normandy. He was an uncle.

Is there anything else you'd like to share?

I can say this about the Marine Corps, they taught you discipline. When they say 'Jump' you jump. I appreciate it; they made a man out of me. I was only 17, but they made a man out of me. That's what the young kids need today; they need to be taught discipline. They need to be taught to respect their elders. I would say the whole world needs more discipline to get along with each other.

Why do you think so many Indian people were in the service?

Well, we weren't recognized as people in 1917 when my father went in the service. They were citizens after that. We made a name for ourselves but you don't hear about it. It seemed like they didn't want to let other people know that Indian people were in the Marine Corps or anything like that. They just didn't give them the recognition.

You mentioned your father was in the service in World War One...

He went over to France. One time he said there was snow in France, and one of the guys chopped a Germans' leg off and they started a fire with it. I don't know if he was kidding or not. He didn't talk about anything else.

What did you do after your time in the service?

For a time I didn't know what to do with myself here. Finally I got a job with the Simpson timber company. I started working in the woods when I was 12 years old. I retired about four years ago.

What have you done with your spare time?

In my spare time, believe it or not, I'm a songwriter. I have songs by Keith Bradford from Nashville, he plays them.

Thank you very much...

I appreciate talking to you. God bless everybody; all the Indians that I know up and down the river.

I can say this about the Marine Corps, they taught you discipline. When they say 'Jump' you jump. I appreciate it; they made a man out of me.

Kenny Sanderson was the 2002 grand marshal for the Salmon Festival Parade held by the Yurok Tribe. His country song Wreck of the Old '97 can be found on the Whiskey River: Keepin' It Country album and his song Linebackers and Quarterbacks can be found on the New Sounds in the Country Volume 5 album.

Bill Rossig

Bill Rossig is of Wiyot ancestry and is a member of the Table Bluff Reservation-Wiyot Tribe's tribal council. I sat down with Bill at his home on January 17, 2003 to talk about his time in the Coast Guard Artillery during the war.

What year were you born?

1916.

What was Bucksport like when you were little?

It was a town, it wasn't part of Eureka. We lived down there by Standard Oil. My brother Elmer and I used to go fishing in the Humboldt Bay a lot of times. One time my brother fell in from the redwood planks. He fell in and I just barely got to him.

We did a lot of fishing. We got a lot of sea trout and perch. The environment's changed. Nowadays the kids get in trouble. What can they do? They have to get permits to fish. We used to fish all the time. We got all the crab we wanted. We used to use mud worms to fish.

Did your family ever talk about what happened to the Wiyot people at Indian Island?

No. I don't remember hearing my mother say anything. Irene, who is my aunt, stayed with the grandmother. She could hear them talking in the Indian language. I never did hang onto it. They're trying to learn it now at Table Bluff, and I'm on the language committee. I do it because they need someone there.

Does that make you feel good to see they're trying to get the language back?

Oh yeah, but it's hard. U.S. citizens are supposed to speak English. You never know what the government is going to say though. Now the best thing that's happened to Indians are these casinos but now the government wants to take a bite out of that. A lot of people think we get a lot of money from the government, but we don't. The agreement a long time ago was they were to take care of Indians.

I lived with my dad all during my school years here in Eureka and I stayed with my mom during other times. I went to the high school in Eureka when it was two stories high, but it was torn down. I graduated from there in '36.

They put me in the Coast Guard Artillery. Hardly anybody knew they had such a thing.

I was part of the wonder team, I don't know if you ever heard of it, but we were never scored upon in football! I was right half. My brother Elmer played for Arcata at the left end, and my mother always swore I was trying to hurt him! The Eureka guys would brag about beating these smaller schools but I didn't.

I stayed with my mother until I was 38 years old. Her name was Jessie Lamberson. She was born at Mad River. I lived with her for 38 years until I got married and I can't remember having an argument.

My step-dad Fred Lamberson was a good worker. He was a Yurok; his dad owned a place up in Orleans. We worked around in the fields in the Arcata Bottoms for farmers. We got 10 cents a row and you couldn't see the other end! That's what we used to say.

I helped the farmers pick potatoes and hay. That's how we got through the Depression. During the Depression we delivered fish to people all the way up to Orleans. I remember we used to have to back up hills because that's when the gas tanks sat in front. You had to back up to force the gas in the engine!

Every weekend we'd end up on the river camping out someplace. I applied for one job in all my life. When I got out of high school there was a kid whose dad worked at the Hammond Lumber Company. He said to sign up. That was it. I worked hard all my life and every job came to me. I guess I was a good worker.

During the war I got a job with my step-dad at Pacific Lumber. I thought for sure I was going into the infantry. But when I graduated, my brother had this friend with a motorcycle, and he wanted me to help him work on it.

This was at our house in McKinleyville. I asked my mother if there was any gas in the motorcycle tank and she said no, it had been parked there for some time. I shook the tank and heard some gas in it. So I poured it out into a coffee can and then poured it onto the ground. I lit a match on it and poof! It burned the gas.

There was an inch-and-a-half of gas left in the can. I went to pour it onto the ground and I got burned. My clothes caught fire. My brother caught up with me and put the fire out. In those days, the first thing they did was put butter on the burns.

So they put butter on my burns and I felt good. But my mom wanted me to go to the hospital so I said OK. The hospital was about five miles away. When I got there I could feel it. They put me on a gurney but I fell off it because I was moving around so much. Oh man! The next morning I had blisters on my legs like balloons. Don't mess around with fire!

I wanted to go to college; I was going to play sports because that's what got me through high school. I was going to go to HSU but that fire ended that. Anyway, I was at PL when the war broke out. I got in my car and went to San Diego. I thought I was going into the infantry because I had three years of infantry experience already.

Bill Rossig as a member of the California National Guard in 1934.
Photo courtesy of Bill Rossig.

Were you drafted or did you volunteer?

Well, I volunteered after they drafted me! They put me in the Coast Guard Artillery. Hardly anybody knew they had such a thing. We trained on old French guns from France! They sent me to Fort Warden, Washington. That's by Seattle.

I stayed up there for a year. I went up the rank from PFC to corporal, then to sergeant in charge of the guns. We had stationary guns and the ones next to us had guns that would shoot then go down. Anyway, I was sergeant for two weeks then I had a disagreement with the lieutenant, so I got broke down to corporal!

After a while I got tired of the weather there so I asked for a transfer, and they sent me to a boot camp nearby. It was where all the bad boys were sent. I got along good with the commanding officer there, and was put in charge of these guys.

I'd take these guys to a store about two miles away. They'd ask if they could buy beer but I told them I didn't want to see it if they did. We'd always salute if anyone came by, and there were no complaints. During parades we were always complimented about how we addressed ourselves.

What race or nationality were those guys?

Those guys were mostly all white. I don't remember any Indians up there. That was mostly in '42. But I wanted to get transferred again. I went to San Francisco and then to Honolulu. We were on the east side of Honolulu.

All we did was play ball. That's when I met Pee Wee Reese and some other guys. Pee Wee Reese told me I should come out and try out with them after the war was out but I never did. I wasn't interested in playing baseball. At that time there weren't any colored people playing. I always remember these colored guys who played with us; they were good players.

After Honolulu I went to another island there. I almost died there. The people there have cockfights and the loser gets eaten! They invited me to have some chicken. I got really sick and passed out. Two days later I woke up in the hospital. I don't remember if I went back to the same outfit or not, but we went to a couple of islands in the south. I don't remember their names.

Bill Rossig in 1942. Note the World War I helmet and uniform.
Photo courtesy of Bill Rossig.

When we reached one we could see these big mines floating next to our ship. We could see our planes bombarding the hills. That was as close as I got...when we landed on one island I saw one Jap. I was down at the beach one day on the rocks.

We must have gone to about five islands or something like that. We always had two guns. I was on one of those islands when the war ended.

I saw something move up by a cave. We knew there were Japs around in the caves but they wouldn't bother us. They would steal something to eat at night but they wouldn't bother us. I told the sergeant about it and he got me and four others to go over there to those caves. Sure enough, that guy was lying there.

The sergeant said something to him and he turned over. The sergeant had a Tommy gun and I think he emptied the whole clip into him. He said he thought he had a gun. He got some citation for that. I thought that was a joke. But that was the only thing I ever saw. We'd go to these islands and put up our guns and that was it. There was nothing exciting for me except for other people training and I played baseball! I mostly played second base and a little at third.

That must have been traumatic to see that guy get shot like that...

Oh yeah, I'll never forget it. And he didn't have a gun. He had a few supplies and a blanket. I imagine that happened a lot.

Were you attached to a particular division at this time?

Well, the islands were already taken. We would go in after and set up our guns that had a range of 22 miles for defense. We were told that if we needed to, we could turn around and support the infantry, but we never did.

What type of guns did you take care of?

They were portable. They were called Long-Toms. Ever since I went in I was the gun pointer. You sat along side the gun and they had instruments for range. Another guy sat at the instruments for horizontals. I was on the range to move the gun up and down. We never fired very many shells, and nothing against an enemy ship.

We must have gone to about five islands or something like that. We always had two guns. I was on one of those islands when the war ended. It took us a year to get home. The ship we were on broke down and the captain kept us on it! We waited for months to get home. I didn't get home until late '46.

Going back to before the war, you were active in the National Guard. What year did you start that?

I'm not sure, 1936 or '37.

How did you decide to join the Guard here in Eureka?

I'm not sure. My friend and his brother also joined at the same time. We'd go down to San Luis Obispo every summer to train. That was infantry training. You'd crawl around and shoot with a rifle. I'll always remember the heat down there; it was terrible in the desert. We were in tents.

Bill Rossig

In those days it was all foot soldiers, all infantry. I was an expert with the rifle. It was from World War One! That's what we trained with. Then in World War Two they had newer rifles. The old gun you loaded by hand. The newer gun had a clip. I was in the Guard for three years. I was stationed here in Eureka. My first train rides were when I'd go down all the way down by San Diego for the National Guard.

When did you first get involved at the Table Bluff Reservation?

At first I was on the housing committee back when it was the old reservation. That new site they have is sure nice; it's a beautiful piece of land. They elected me to be on the council so asked my wife Sylvia and she said it was up to me. I've been on the council around four years now.

I don't know if they'll elect me again because I'll be 90 when that term is up! We have a really smart council. For a long time I was the only man on the council. I also belong to five other clubs. I have a life membership in the VFW. I've worked with Little League baseball for over 40 years.

What would it mean for you if the Wiyot people were to get all of Indian Island back?

Oh, that would really be something. We bought a section of it. I've never been on it myself.

You've been pretty active during your life, what's given you this energy?

I don't smoke and I don't drink. I like slow-pitch softball. Another sport I liked was soccer. I bowl and played lots of baseball. I remember about four years ago I was still playing ball at 82 years old. One game I stole second, third and home! Anytime they said go I would. I didn't know I could run that fast! One time I did get called out and my son was the umpire! I know I was safe!

Bill Rossig's family is very proud of his service to his country and to his Wiyot people. He continues to volunteer his time for community organizations.

Willard Carlson

Willard Carlson is Archie Thompson's brother. He is of Yurok ancestry and agreed to meet with me on August 13, 2002. Willard was in the U.S. Marine Corps during the war. We sat on his front porch and talked while several of his grandchildren played in the front yard.

I was born in 1926 in Eureka, California. I went to school in Eureka. My father's name was Milton Carlton and my mother's was Delia Thompson. There were two other Indian kids in my class. I went to school there about six years then I went to Stewart, Nevada for a couple years.

I came back home and Delmar, he's another Marine, but he's dead now; he wanted to go join the Marines. I was only 16 and he was 17, so he was old enough. So I went with him to San Francisco on the first of February in 1943. So one guy signed him up and then they signed me up. They told us to come back in a couple weeks and we'd go in the Marines.

Two weeks later we came back and we got sworn in on February 18, 1943 in San Francisco. We took the train on down to San Diego; it was hot in that train so we rolled down all the windows. We went through this tunnel and all that soot came in the train! We got all dirty!

Anyhow, we finally got to Los Angeles and boarded another train, the *Santa Fe Chief*, and took that to San

Diego. There was a bus waiting there to take us to the recruit depot. We got there and we had this long hair.

All these Marines came by and took their hats off, they had shaved heads, they said, 'You'll be sorry, you'll be sorry you even got to this place!' Anyway, we were at the boot camp there, and there was a rifle range there.

I got sick at that rifle range; I had the flu, so they let me get in with a New York outfit. The first outfit I was in was mostly California, Washington and Oregon guys. They were an all 17-year-old unit, everybody was 17; I was 16. Everybody was about the same age.

So I remember going overseas and all the soldiers were grown men. They said, 'These Marines are nothing but boys, look at them.' We were all small, and didn't have to shave. So they put us in Pearl Harbor for a while. Then they sent us to a place almost by the Equator. Then they shipped us back to the Hawaiian Islands to guard some ammunition places.

Then in '44 they sent us down with the 2nd Marine Division. We went out to sea and didn't know where we were going. They were sending us to a place called Saipan. So we came to Saipan; we didn't go in the first wave, but eventually we went in.

We were the Second Marine Division. We went in there and saw combat. I don't remember how many days we fought there. I saw thousands and thousands of dead Japanese bodies. We shot I don't know how many. I shot one guy about 18 feet away. I had a BAR and blew him full of holes.

I felt bad about that, you know. I don't know how many, but I shot a lot more. If anyone ever asked, I'd say 'I do not know, I do not know.' But I shot a lot of people. And we took Saipan. Then we went to Tinian, which was close by. It was another Japanese island.

That's where they built the B-29 base that bombed Japan. We fought there about eight or nine days and I finally got shot. I got shot in the leg. Tinian had big flat sugarcane fields; that's where they built the base. So I went back to Saipan.

They eventually flew me to the Hawaiian Islands. I stayed there a while and took a ship to San Francisco. We got there and they had three bands playing, an Army band, a Navy band and a Marine band. Then they had these big ambulances and took us to a hospital. Then I went to the Santa Cruz Naval convalescent hospital. I stayed there until the end of the war. July 24, 1945 is when they discharged me. I came home and worked in the woods. I logged all my life.

Did you ever serve with any other Indian men in the service?

Yes, Delmer was in the service. I saw a whole platoon of Navajo Indians come in. They were all so poor they had bib overalls on with a blue shirt. They had these shoes that you could buy for 50 cents apiece.

Other than that, my friend Delmer and I went in together. He was a Wiyot; he's dead now, I think he died in '92. I used to write him letters all the time. I wrote him a letter and three months later I wondered if he was alive or dead. Then his letter came in at the end of the war; he was wounded in the battle at Okinawa in the last battle of the Pacific. He made it home too.

I had other Stewart classmates like Floyd Osborne; he was killed in the battle at Pelileu, and Art Case, another buddy where we went to school together; he was killed at Saipan. I didn't know he was in my outfit, but he got killed there.

My friend Wilfred Albers was shot up in the Philippines someplace. He'd gone now, too. I think all those guys were in the same class. We all got Purple Hearts, and three of us came back and two didn't come back. That's casualties of war.

Willard Carlson

When you were at Stewart did you do any boxing?

No, I was pretty young there. I left when I was about 13 years old. I came home and got a job. When I was 15 I had a job in construction and bought a car better than my dad's. I went over to Stewart to get Delmer and he said I was rich or something! Johnny Erickson was another veteran who went to Stewart. He's dead now. He was wounded in the Philippines. He was in the Army.

It sounds like you made some close friends at Stewart...

Yeah, and they got killed. Another friend of mine who was wounded was Herbert Orcutt. Quite a few of us guys got wounded.

Do you remember where you were when Pearl Harbor happened?

Stewart, Nevada. All the older boys started leaving the next day to join the service. So I left to come home and got a job in '42. I bought my car and got my friend Delmar. Then in '43 we joined the Marines.

Sometimes the artillery would be shooting at us and ours would be shooting over at them and you're just lying in the ground. That's your protection. If you stand up you get killed

You mentioned at Saipan you carried a BAR, what type of weapon is that?

That's a Browning Automatic Rifle; it has 20 rounds in the magazine. I packed 270 rounds in an ammunition belt around me, plus other stuff like hand grenades and knives. It was so heavy the ammunition belt had little straps and they cut into me.

I only weighed 135 pounds. I went to this Mexican guy named Francisco De La Cruz, he was a mortar man. They had big, wide, heavy straps to pack their heavy mortars, so I got some mortar straps from him. Then I was comfortable with the BAR. Those thin straps would cut me so I got some mortar straps from my friend.

When you were in combat in Saipan, were you in a jungle?

No, it wasn't like that. There were sugarcane fields. They had a sugar mill there. The island is about 15 miles long and maybe five or six miles wide. There were 30,000 Japanese there and I think we fought 30 days. I think we killed 30,000 in 30 days. We lost 4,000 of ours killed and 12,000 wounded. We had 16,000 casualties there.

Where would you sleep at night?

In a hole in the ground; you had a foxhole. You had to sleep in the ground. If you don't you get killed; there were mortars going every night. They shelled and everything. You dug a hole and you stayed there. Then we had a 50-percent watch; one guy would stay awake an hour and the other guy sleeps.

You do that all night long. You expect an attack 100 percent! You stay awake all night long! That's life for you. You don't go to sleep in that foxhole. Your buddy guards you or you guard him. Those mortars came day and night. Especially at nighttime; boom, they'd hit around you.

We'd shoot back at them. Sometimes the artillery would be shooting at us and ours would be shooting over at them and you're just lying in the ground. That's your protection. If you stand up you get killed. Nobody stands up at night in the Marine Corps. If anyone stands up you kill them, even if it's your brother. That's the Marine Corps for you.

You had to be pretty tough to be in the Marines...

I don't know if it's you're tough or what! You can live through it. It wasn't if you were tough. You're lucky to be here today.

Willard Carlson ca. 1943-4.
Photo courtesy of Willard Carlson.

Why do you think so many Indian people joined the service?

I really don't know. They wanted to go to war I guess. Everybody volunteered, you know. Everybody was patriotic in those days, to get in the service.

Your brother Archie was in the Navy...

Yeah, he was down at Ulithi repairing ships. He wrote a letter to me that said he was repairing ships that were all shot full of holes. Those guys welded four hours on, four hours off. We said he wished he was in the Marines. I thought, not where I'm at. They had the life; they slept in nice beds and everything. The Marines, we sleep in the dirt on the ground.

When you were at Saipan what type of food did you eat?

We just ate rations. They told us not to eat their food because the people over there used human manure. They said not to touch it. We just ate K-rations.

Was there ever a time you lacked water?

Oh no. We had jeep cans full of water. We brought our own water from Hawaii. They would bring it up to the front lines for our canteens.

You mentioned after your time in Saipan you went to Tinian and were wounded, could you describe that?

We were pinned down and this guy on the hill was shooting at me. I didn't even see him, and bang! I told my partner I was hit. He went after a corpsman. This Mexican guy was the corpsman. The first thing he did was cut my sleeve and gave me morphine. Then he looked where I was shot at, patched me up, put me on his back and ran about 100 yards and flipped me into a ditch.

I don't know if he was killed or not. The Japs were shooting cannons down there trying to hit our half-tracks. The shells were landing all around. Finally a jeep came and picked up the wounded guys. We were happy to get out. The troops on the front line didn't have a smile on their face in combat like in the movies. You're grim.

How many days were you fighting at Tinian before you got wounded?

About nine days.

That must have been pretty traumatic to be in that type of combat?

Well, yes it is. I saw a lot of dead people, lots of dead bodies.

Was there ever a time you thought you might die?

Nope. But all those guys were so young. See, the average age of a Marine in the Second World War was about 20 years old. All those young guys would say, 'God, wouldn't it be happy if we could live to be 21 years old? We've seen everything and done everything! You didn't worry about getting killed. You worried about cracking up.

Have you ever talked about your time in the service for any interviews, other than just around your family?

No, not really, and not even hardly to my family. Usually veterans don't talk too much about what they've seen…

Because you lived through and saw some pretty terrible things…

Yeah, when I hit the island of Tinian we were on this half-track going down this road…there was a dead guy's legs lying there, just his pants and his legs. We went down about two or three hundred feet further and there were his shoulders and head lying there.

We looked at him; a direct hit from our Navy ship must have just… boom. The Japanese guy didn't even know what hit him. It cut right through him. We saw guy's brains blown out and all kinds of horrible stuff… dead people.

So you were right up close to the Japanese soldiers…

Oh yes.

Did you see what type of uniform they had on?

Kind of a brownish uniform. At Tinian there was a lot of mortar fire, and I looked over and I saw one Marine sitting there pulling flesh off his face. He took this flesh and threw it off. I went by him and went to the front lines by myself.

I saw all these guys, about 50, come down to this place down this hill. It was getting dark and I couldn't distinguish them. So this lieutenant came up and said, 'Kill all the sons of bitches.'

He and I cut loose on those Japs; I don't know how many I got, I never went down and looked. Oh, yeah, I've been close to them and I even saw one Japanese guy's teeth, because I shot his knees out with my BAR.

We were pinned down and this guy on the hill was shooting at me. I didn't even see him, and bang! I told my partner I was hit.

Did you ever see any Japanese with their swords?

Yeah, but I never got one. One guy had one of those Japanese sabers. It was an old one, all nicked up. The only thing I ever got off a Japanese was a pistol. I went in there and this guy had it around his neck. I saw these two, they were sitting up, they were dead and I was getting ready to blast them with my BAR.

I went over there, I guess a shell must have hit close by, the concussion might have killed them. I didn't see any visual wounds or anything. Maybe they killed themselves, I don't know. So I took the cord off and took the pistol off one's neck.

I came out of there like a kid with a toy. Everybody said, 'You're lucky, you're lucky.' I said, 'Look what I've got.' I eventually traded it. An Army guy came down and gave us a bottle of rum, so I gave him the pistol.

Were you on a troopship when you moved island to island?

Oh yes, I've been in troopships. It was just cramped up. I've been on LSTs too. I've been on a lot of ships.

Did you have other family members in the service?

Just my brother, and I had cousins in the Navy, but they didn't see combat.

Where were you discharged?

At a place called Mare Island. I hitchhiked home. I sent my sea bags up by express and thumbed home to my sister's place in Eureka. They were happy to see me. Then I went to work with my brother-in-law in the woods.

What do you think about the American flag when you see it?

Well, we grew up saluting it. They teach you that when you're in grade school with the Pledge of Allegiance.

When you were in boarding school at Sherman did you have to wear a uniform?

No, just regular clothes.

Did you have a trade there?

I worked on the dairy, and I worked in the paint

shop learning how to mix paints. They didn't have much. It was cold in the wintertime. I don't know how it was in the summer because we came home. If you could go home in the summer you could, but some kids stayed there from the first grade to when they graduated.

How do you feel about your time in the service?

I'm kind of glad I was in the service. I'm glad I did a little time there. I saw a lot of ocean and met a lot of people. A lot of them are probably dead now.

You were just a young, young boy...

I know. I was 16 when I went in 1943. I was 18 when I came out.

You earned a Purple Heart; did they give it to you at a particular time?

Yes, when I was at the hospital they had the service. Everybody stood at attention and the officers awarded me the Purple Heart.

How did you feel to get a Purple Heart?

Well, a Purple Heart's a Purple Heart. People ask if I'm proud of it and I'll say I guess so. But I lost it a long time ago.

Is there anything else about your time in the service you'd like to share that I haven't asked about?

No, not that I can think of.

Well, thank you very much for talking with me.

Sure, I like that recorder you've got there.

Willard Carlson worked as a logger for several decades in Humboldt County. He lives in Blue Lake, California with his family. He is well-known and respected among the Native community for his service in the Marine Corps.

Darrell McCovey

After my talk with Alfred McCovey I set out to find his brother Darrell up in the very small town of Orleans. Orleans is set on traditional Karuk territory. It was a hot day as I made the journey inland. Just outside of Orleans is a bridge that spans the Klamath River. I crossed over this bridge three times while searching for Darrell's house.

When I found his house there was a note attached to the door that read, 'To talk with Darrell come down below the bridge on this side of the river.' I was enjoying this adventure of finding my relative, and I made my way down under the bridge.

There was Darrell and his family. The grandkids were playing in the river and Darrell was sitting on the sand. I introduced myself to nine relatives I had never met on that day. Darrell was in the U.S. Navy during the war.

I was born in 1921 right across the river from Requa. I had five brothers and six sisters. I was the sixth one born. I'm the oldest McCovey male living right now. I went to school at Pecwan. It was a one-room school with one teacher. When I was in the fourth grade they built two new schoolhouses. I went there until eighth grade then I went to Sherman.

What was it like living on the river when you were very young?

It was rough but we made it all right. My dad worked during the summer months. He was hurt working in the woods and he was crippled up his last few years. They used to have commercial fishing for Indians at the mouth of the river and I was born in the fish camp. My grandmother Elsie McCovey was my doctor.

When you were young did you attend the Brush Dances?

They wouldn't have the really young kids stay up all night, so in the early morning is when I went. I really liked them. I didn't dance, but I liked to watch them. I watched the Deerskin Dance in Hoopa; they didn't have that dance in Pecwan.

They had the Jump Dance at Pecwan, and I saw one Brush Dance at Johnson's, which is about a mile below Pecwan. The Jump Dance was slow, with one singer. The Brush Dance is livelier, with more singers.

Can you tell me about the McCovey family history?

It's a big family. My dad was Charles Jr. His dad was Charles Alfred McCovey. That's Big Boy's name too. What I heard about Charles Alfred is that he joined the Merchant Marine when he was 14 or so from back East. His stepfather didn't treat him well, so he made his way here somehow. He married a full-blooded Yurok lady, but I didn't know her.

What about your uncles?

There was Uncle Ike, and Uncle Bill and Uncle Walt. There were four boys. Their sisters all died off. Uncle Ike lived down at Notchko. That's where old man McCovey settled, that's where all his family was raised.

Uncle Bill used to be a deputy sheriff in Klamath for years. Uncle Walt was my favorite. He had kids my age. He lived above the river about five miles. I used to stay with him in the summer months. He was in the service during World War One.

He used to play stick games...

Yeah, they say he was one of the best stick players. I played sticks too. That's all we did. There were big sandbars and we used to go there and play. That was our favorite game.

What position did you play?

Well, the fastest guy stayed on the end where they could run straight through. I guess I was the fastest, I was on the end. I would play with my brothers and everybody. I used to play with older kids. We played against Hoopa too. There was a Jump Dance and after that we played sticks and beat them.

How did you get to Sherman?

Well, most kids went to Sherman. My two sisters went down there. I liked it down there. I didn't play any sports, I was pretty little. I think I was 14 when I went down there. I was supposed to graduate in '42 so it was around 1938 when I went down there. I worked in the mill and cabinet shop. They had all these machines there and you had to be pretty careful.

You mentioned you knew Mervin Evans, and you recognized my grandfather Stan?

Yeah, I knew Mervin pretty well. Stan was postgraduate and I was just a scrawny freshman, so I don't know if he noticed me. There were a lot of Indians from all over. Most of the students of the same tribe stuck together.

When you were in school did you hear anything about the war in Europe?

Yeah, but I didn't pay too much attention to it. Hoopa had a boxing tournament and they were going to bring in soldiers to box. My uncle came down to Sherman and picked a couple of us up to box in Hoopa.

We had to hitchhike back to school! People in Hoopa were pretty mad about that, that we had to hitchhike in winter. The servicemen couldn't make it because the war broke out.

What year did you go in the service?

I went in June of '43. I stayed there for three years. I was drafted and went to boot camp in Farragut, Idaho. That's a little east of Spokane. There was a busload of us from Humboldt County that were drafted and went to get our physicals in San Francisco. Most of those guys were sent to Idaho too so I was with people from Humboldt.

Were any of those guys Indian?

No, there were just two Indians. Billy Pratt and I were the only two. Boot camp was eight weeks then I went to Washington for four months. I was assigned to a small aircraft carrier.

They built them in Washington and they put them in commission in Oregon. I was in Oregon for two months, then they put the ship into commission and we went down to San Francisco for fuel and ammunition. Then we went overseas. We went to Hawaii and then went down to the south Pacific.

When you went to Hawaii did you dock at Pearl Harbor?

Yes, they hadn't raised some of the ships yet. They were lying on their sides. It was pretty sad to see.

That must have been really hard to see. Did you visit any part of the island?

Yeah, we visited! There were no Japs there. We got four beers apiece when we went. God, there were some big poker games! These guys would be big winners; they'd win a thousand dollars!

Where did you go after Hawaii?

The first island I went to in the Gilberts was called Tarawa. That was a real knockout for the Marines. I went to all those islands. I remember one time I was on gun watch and I was just ending; I was going to pick up my breakfast and the general quarters bell started clanging.

I left my food and went to my gun station. I looked out on the horizon. You could see for miles. I saw all these ships out there, and I thought they were ours. They passed the word over the PA system that all the planes on those ships were attacking, and that's when all hell broke loose. God, they just knocked the hell out of us.

Darrell McCovey

There was a cloud hanging by us, and pretty soon seven Japanese planes came out of it and began shooting at us, but they missed us. Then these other suicide planes came in. They didn't hit us, but they came so close it rocked everything and bent the screws on the ship. We couldn't go very fast after that. They sank five of our ships in two-and-a-half-hours, but we were lucky and didn't get hit.

After one of the suicide planes missed our ship and blew up, some of our guys went and pulled out some of the remains. They found fingers and pieces of the scalp.

It had black hair on it. They asked me if I wanted a souvenir, if I wanted a piece of that Jap, but I said no. What would I do with that? It was scattered all over the place.

It was scary to see the suicide planes. Two of them dove on a ship right next to us and they hit where the elevator was where they keep all the ammunition, and that ship blew up and sunk. We watched the guys abandon ship way out there, and I don't know if they made it or not. This all happened in the Philippines.

What type of gun did you use?

We had a 40-millimeter cannon. We had one 5-inch gun on the tail and the rest were 20-millimeters. I don't know if I ever hit any planes, but I shot a lot of ammunition! Oh, boy, they were loud. After that one time I joked they might as well finish with an air raid siren. I also served as a deck aid. That's what they called them. We tied up the ship and that was our duty.

I don't know if I ever hit any planes, but I shot a lot of ammunition!

Going back to your time at Tarawa, can you describe that?

Oh yeah, we went in after the battle. I don't know how the Japs survived, everything was bombed out. The trees were just stubs. It was just a small island, too.

After your time in the Philippines where did you go?

I transferred to another ship called a destroyer escort. It was a small ship. We went back out to the South Pacific but didn't see anything. We were kind of patrolling out there. We also gave cover for troops going in on certain islands.

At Saipan we got fired on from the shore. I forget which island I was at when the war ended. It was sure good news though. I was on the ship when they announced over the loudspeaker the war was over. Everyone was hollering.

Did you ever listen to Tokyo Rose?

Yeah, I listened to her, God she was funny! She'd talk about how your girlfriend is with these 4-Fs and all that. I used to like to listen to her, that was funny, but jeez, some of those guys, it went to their heads. They would cuss around. I guess they took her prisoner after the war. She went to school someplace down in southern California and spoke real good English.

When they announced the war was over, did they mention that an atomic bomb was used?

Yeah, I didn't even know they were going to do that. Nobody knew what it was, they just said they used a big bomb. We didn't even know what kind of bomb it was, to tell you the truth.

Are you glad you were in the Navy?

Yes, but sometimes I wished I went in the Army. You know my brother Big Boy was in the Army and he saw all those foreign countries, and all I saw was water! Water and some islands!

Other than Big Boy, what other family members of yours were in the service?

My brother Allen was in the Army but he didn't go overseas. My brother Card was in the Navy too. Stanley was his name but we called him Card. When I was just in the service and we were pulling into Pearl Harbor I was reading my letter from my mom.

I used to read mom's letter first out of all of them. She wrote to me which ship he was on. I was sitting on the back part of the ship. The battleship *Maryland* came steaming by. That was Stanley's ship! They tied up down a ways. I asked permission to leave ship and go down there. I ran all the way down there and saluted and asked permission to come aboard.

I said I had a brother on the ship. They asked what his name was and I said, 'Seaman McCovey.' I didn't call him Card right then! So they passed the word and called the quarterdeck. He was on a work detail, but here he came! So we had dinner and everything before I had to go back. A couple months later he came over to see me on my ship. I got to see him twice at Pearl Harbor.

Darrell McCovey ca. 1942-3.
Photo courtesy of Dee Reed.

That must have been a happy time, to see your brother...

Oh, yeah. We didn't have too much to catch up on

though. He was only 16. He gave our grandmother's name down as his mother when he joined up. That put his age up a couple years. When I was on leave I came all the way back to Notchko. Our family was pretty happy.

When you were in the service, were you treated any different because you were Indian?

Boy, they respected me! I was kind of a tough guy. They were kind of scared of me. The crew treated me real good. I was discharged in 1946 in Norman, Oklahoma. After the war ended this buddy of mine from Oklahoma told me to write my mom that was going with him to Oklahoma. We bought a little car first. I was back there almost four months.

I damn near stayed there, geez there were a lot of pretty girls! I damn near stayed there! I left out of Oklahoma City. I started to hitchhike. The first ride I got was to Amarillo, Texas. I thought I had it made. I hired a cab to take me west. We started out and the cabby asked me where I was going. I told him and he turned around and took me back to the town! So I caught a slow train to Oakland. I caught a bus in San Francisco.

What did you do after your time in the service?

I went to work in the woods. I worked on the rigging. I worked here in the woods and rafted logs out of Pecwan for eight or nine years. That was the best job I ever had. I worked on the water. Then the logging petered out there. I got married to my wife Mavis and moved here to Orleans. There was a Christian guy in town here.

I went to church one night and asked him for a job. He said if he needed me he'd come get me, and the next day he came for me! I worked for him for eight years. I've lived here in Orleans since '65. They had that big flood that washed everything out in Pecwan so we moved up here. There was no work anyway and Orleans was kind of a boomtown then.

Why do you think so many Indian people served in the war?

I think a lot of them were drafted just like me. My brother is about the only one I can think of that volunteered.

I really appreciate talking to you…

Sure, I was glad to.

It's really great to meet another relative!

Oh yeah, that's right!

Darrell McCovey resides in Orleans, Ca. He enjoys spending his time with his family and visiting friends, and he continues to attend the Brush Dance ceremonies. His family is very proud of his service to his country.

Wilbur Smith

Wilbur Smith is of Maidu, Pit River and Paiute ancestry. He lives near Pyramid Lake in western Nevada about two hours from Susanville. He was a very young member of the U. S. Navy during the war. He is also one of the first Indian entrepreneurs of his generation and he owns the Pyramid Lake Store. Wilbur was very kind and met with me on January 9, 2003 at his home.

I was born January 8, 1926, my birthday is tomorrow! I'll be 77.

Happy early birthday! Where were you born?

I was born along the Sacramento River. I can't tell you the exact town, but my birth certificate says Butte County. My father's name was Harry Smith. He was Northern Paiute from the Pyramid Lake Reservation. His father's name was Johnny Smith and he lived in Pyramid.

My mother's name was Lorena Wiltse. She was Maidu and Pit River and she was born in Milford. There was a little area there where some of the Natives lived and that's where she was born. Her father was Jack Wiltse and her mother's name was Susie Washoe before she became a Wiltse.

Susie was from the Greenville area. Jack was Washoe, and he was born in the area known as Red Rock off of Highway 295. I have three sisters. One is deceased and two are living. My youngest sister lives in Monterey; she's a retired school teacher. My full sister is retired in Salt Lake City.

My grandmother was a healer. I was exposed to the native plants and herbs. That was pretty interesting, to go out at certain times of the seasons and pick certain things.

Where were you raised?

We were kind of a migrant type of people. What I understand is that my father followed the hay route. They would work from ranch to ranch during hay season. They'd go up into Oregon and back around to the area around here. I was more or less raised by a single parent.

We had a ranch around the Doyle area, but when I grew to school age my grandmother Susie and my step-grandfather Albert Mitchell lived in the community of Loyalton. He was a Wintun from down by Colusa, and he worked for the Western Pacific Railroad there. So they sent me to live there and go to school in Loyalton.

What was it like living with them?

It was great living in town! There were very few Indian people there but we got along fine with the general public. We lived right in the community in town. In those days we ate basic foods; potatoes, rice, beans and more game than today. As I got older I got to hunt.

My grandmother was a healer. I was exposed to the native plants and herbs. That was pretty interesting, to go out at certain times of the seasons and pick certain things. She was a healer, but I was a little too young to understand.

Did your grandmother speak her native language?

She spoke in several Native languages. She was a traveler and we went a lot of different places and she seemed to fit in with whichever tribe we were around. The tribes in the Loyalton area were mainly Washoe, but of course there were Paiute and Maidu and Pit River there, but the main ones were Washoe and Paiute.

Did your grandmother make baskets?

She made some little baskets, but mainly she made harvest-type baskets. We'd go out and harvest plants. The baskets were cone shaped and she would line them for different kinds of seeds. She made one basket with a handle to knock seeds into the baskets.

I know we went to Susanville for a gathering there. We went to Lake Almanor where they had the Bear Dance in the spring.

Were you raised in baby baskets?

The basket I was raised in was a Wintun basket. I have a picture of myself in it somewhere. It wasn't made like the type around here. It was made of something more solid, but it did have the hood on it. It looked like it had abalone shells on the side of it. My sisters were raised in the traditional Paiute and Washoe baskets.

Did your family ever go to traditional ceremonies or gatherings when you were little?

We went to several different places. I know we went to Susanville for a gathering there. We went to Lake Almanor where they had the Bear Dance in the spring. We came to Pyramid for some holiday. They had bucking horses and a lot of hand games and card games. The other ceremony I remember was out in Sierra Valley. At a certain time of the year the Washoe would have a rabbit drive.

The people gathered out there in a camping area and they'd go out and hunt jackrabbits. They'd clean them and they'd have a certain way they'd cut the hide of the jackrabbits. Then they'd put it on a type of spinner and it would make a type of string.

Then they'd put that on a frame and make a blanket out of it. They'd put patchwork coverings over it and it would be like a comforter. I can remember we went out several evenings to watch that. Then they would have some of their round dances and card games. They don't have that anymore that I know of.

What were the hand games like?

Oh, they were pretty competitive. They'd play all night! Whoever had the bones were the singers. They'd sing to confuse the other side. Once you guessed the bones, or the sticks, then the singing would go on the other side.

So you'd have to guess how many bones the other person had?

Two people would have two bones, one clear bone and one striped bone. If you guessed that one person had the bones and then guessed who else had the bones it would switch sides.

How long did you live with your grandmother and Albert?

I lived with them four years. My mother came to town and I went to live with her and my sister. I went to Loyalton until the sixth grade. Then in seventh grade I went to Sherman.

How did you get to Sherman that first time?

I got free transportation to Reno. They put me on another bus to Los Angeles. Then they put me on another bus to Riverside. That's how I migrated. The first time I went I met some kids that were coming from the east part of Nevada. So we all helped each other out to get to school.

So you were by yourself at first. Were you afraid?

I was more excited than afraid. In fact, I was the one that wanted to go rather than being sent. The reason I wanted to go was we went to Reno one time. A friend's niece had just graduated from Sherman and she had her school book. We were looking at that and I liked what I saw. I told my mother I wouldn't mind going there.

When we got back to Loyalton and the grammar school principal was a friend of my mother's. She called the Sacramento office and arranged for me to get to Sherman. The following year when I came back I told my sister and my cousin Lester Wilson about it. He had stayed with my mother and sister when I was gone. I told them how I liked Sherman and so the next year the three of us went down there.

Where did you stay that first year at Sherman?

They had two dormitories for the boys and two for the girls. They had the small boy's building and the large boy's building. The small boy's building was the *Wigwam*. Being a small boy, that's where I stayed. I think the school population was around 500 boys and girls from different tribes. It was nice; there were tribes from all over the country. There wasn't a dominant tribe so that made it a lot easier than say at Stewart, where there were a lot of Washoe and Paiute, and you had to kind of stay with your tribe.

You also went to high school at Sherman?

Yes, I eventually did. I did come home most summers. We didn't have time off for holidays like Christmas and Thanksgiving. So we put in a full semester and got out of school a little earlier. Back then in junior high school you had to go into a different trade every nine weeks so you had the full spectrum of the trades.

I think it was when you were a junior or a senior you could declare what you wanted to study as a trade. At that time I liked baking and printing. I eventually did become a printer. Everybody liked the cooking. You could get a little extra to eat! But you had to try all of them to get an idea of what you liked.

And how about the girls?

They had their own dormitory. The main school

building was set between the girls' and the boys' dormitories. The school was built Spanish-style and it had archways where our driveways were. It was quite unique. It's not like that today. I first went down there in the fall of 1939.

At that time we didn't have the uniform code that they did have prior to that. I don't know when they changed the dress code. We were issued some clothes there, and every year we'd get one or two pairs of shoes.

Did you ever get to visit the outlying area?

Yes, the older you got the more lenient they were about letting you off the campus. You had certain time limits to be back which was good. That way they could keep track of the kids.

Did they have any Indian teachers while you were there?

Oh yeah, they had some Indian teachers when I was there. In fact, my printing instructor was a Cherokee from North Carolina. The assistant instructor was also Indian. We did have Indians there in the different trades, it wasn't all Anglos.

What type of sports did you play while you were there?

When you go to a smaller school like that you have an opportunity to play more than one sport. It isn't like today where you kind of have to specialize to be an athlete. You got to try just about anything. Some you made, some you didn't. It was great.

We had quite a few sports for such a small school. In the spring we had track, cross-country and baseball. In the fall we had football and one of the top wrestling teams in southern California. I ended up playing basketball, baseball and football. Football was my main sport.

What position did you play?

I played linebacker, but I was more of a right guard. Back then we could play both ways if you had the ability. We played a pretty good schedule for a small school. The year I became a junior I was captain of the football team and we won the league that year. We played some of the bigger schools like Poly Tech High, Hemet and others.

We usually played each team twice. When I played we still had leather helmets. They just started coming out with plastic helmets. In those days you didn't have a nose guard either! We had a letterman's club to qualify for and that initiation was something!

So it sounds like you had a good time at Sherman...

Personally, I think I did. Now somebody else might not have the same feelings I have. It seemed while going through life I started pretty early doing what I wanted to do. I think I made mostly the right choices.

When you were at school there you got to know a lot of people. Did you get to know my grandpa Stan?

No, but he and Leonard came to the school one time and I found out who they were. They were master sergeants. Leonard went to officer's training school and Stan had a battlefield commission.

Do you remember where you were when Pearl Harbor was attacked?

I remember exactly where I was at. There were three or four of us on a Sunday. We were in one of the older boys' rooms. We were listening to the radio; we used to listen to a music program out of Los Angeles a lot. That was the big band era back then. Then they mentioned Pearl Harbor. We all quieted down and listened to it. That was it; I'll never forget the day we listened to the radio. I was 14.

Wilbur Smith

How old were you when you joined the Navy?

I was still 16, just turning 17. I went in December of '43. I had to get my mother's permission to go. She gave me that permission.

Did you talk about it with anybody before you decided to join?

Not really, but I could see we had a lot of older people going to school that were leaving all the time. I looked around and all my friends were disappearing! One day I was running a little late to school and I thought I would go down to see the Navy. It just popped into my head! So

I turned around and took my books back to my room and went to a streetcar.

At that time Magnolia Avenue ran in front of the school to the town of Riverside. So I got in the streetcar and went to the recruitment office for the Navy. He told me what I had to do. I said all right and went to see my mother and she said OK, so I took that back to him and joined up.

Was there any particular reason why you wanted to join the Navy out of all the branches of service?

Not really. Well, I thought as long as I was afloat I'd have a clean bed and something good to eat! They picked me up from Riverside and went to Los Angeles for my physical, and from there to San Diego to a Naval training base. At that time they were pushing us through pretty fast so I went through boot camp in 28 days.

I had an eight-hour leave and then I was sent to a destroyer base in San Diego. From there they shipped me up to Treasure Island. I spent three days there then they put me on a sea-going tug in the Bay. I spent about a week or so there then they shipped us out. It was pretty choppy!

I've never seen so many ships. There were ships as far as you could see. There were battlewagons and carriers with destroyer escorts.

I'll never forget that first meal; it was baked pork chops and sauerkraut. It was all pretty greasy! The way our tug was listing you had to stand up to eat. So we went out of the Bay and got out in the ocean and traveled up the coast to Washington. I lucked out, I never did get seasick.

Once we got up there we picked up these dry-dock sections. There were three sections to a floating dry dock. So there were three tugs and we each latched onto a section and went to the South Pacific. We went 51 days without seeing land. We went past Guadalcanal and just above New Guinea to a little group of islands called Los Negres Islands.

That's where we stopped, and it's also where Task Force 58 was forming for the second battle for the Philippines. I've never seen so many ships. There were ships as far as you could see. There were battlewagons and carriers with destroyer escorts. It was something to see. We didn't make that battle because the auxiliary went out in our motor so we had to stay for repairs.

The dry-dock sections we brought in were put together and they could put a destroyer in them and raise them out of the water to repair them. It was kind of interesting to be in that part of the world. We could see some of the Natives from the islands. Some of them would come out in canoes and try to trade with us. The main thing they wanted were mattress covers. It was pretty neat down there.

After that we went to Kwajalein and Eniwetok and I finally came home for a seven day furlough. They shipped me to Oxnard to go back overseas. While we were there I got word that James Washoe was up in Santa Barbara in a hospital. He had broken his leg on a jump; he was a paratrooper. So I hitchhiked up there to visit him.

When it was time to leave we loaded up on an attack-transport to head for Okinawa. We hadn't taken Okinawa yet. We ended up in Pearl Harbor on Easter Sunday. The officers got to go to church on the beach and the enlisted men stayed on the ship. We stayed there for a couple of days and then ended up in Saipan. We stayed there and didn't make it to Okinawa. I put 13 months on Saipan.

That's a long time on one island!

Well, when you're young...there were just parts of buildings and rubble. There was some different equipment in the water and tanks that didn't make it to shore. It was just an island with nothing much on it except for the airstrip we built for bombers. It was mainly an Army base until we took over then it was a Navy base. Our strip there was more like a regular air terminal. The planes that came through there were mostly transport planes carrying people or cargo.

I was in charge of a crew of 12 or 13 men to maintain the area there. I was a boatman's mate, which would be a third-class petty officer. So I had a crew to take care of. We had some Red Cross workers there. We still had some Japanese in the jungle up there. We'd be watching a movie on the beach or something and we'd see these big lights come on near the dumps or something and then rat-tat-tat-tat!

Those machine guns would go off. We were in tent city when we first got there and they eventually built Quonset huts. In the morning we'd wake up and look in the sand and see where the Japanese had wandered through at night. After we left there I had enough points to be discharged.

They put us on an LST and shipped us to Guam. We made it and got off the ship. They had a converted liner there called the USS *Hermitage.* We boarded that. There were three USO shows and there were doctors and nurses. When we were north of Hawaii we ran into a tidal wave. Everybody was ready and you could feel that ship raising and raising, then finally going down. We finally made it into San Francisco. That shoreline looked pretty good that evening!

Did you ever talk with other crewmates about how the war was going?

We knew we were winning. We were getting news all the time. We could see these B-17s take off. It was kind of neat watching them. There was a flat top on the hill before you went over the ocean. The planes would take off with their bombs on the strip and hit the end of the runway. We'd see them drop down before they started to rise up.

We always thought one would hit the water because some got down pretty close to the water. They had rescue ships out there. There was another island called Tinian which was bigger than Saipan. That's the way they would go. What always fascinated me was when these planes would come back. It always seemed like the inside motor that wasn't running when they came back! I flew from Saipan to Guam and back but never went on a mission.

Was there ever a time when you came across other Indian men in the service?

Yeah, when I was on Saipan there was one fellow named Calvin Sisk. He went to Sherman and he was already on the island when I got there. So I got to meet him there. He was from around the Redding area but I've heard he passed away. One day I was driving a truck hauling tents that were being replaced with Quonset huts.

I kept passing this one truck. I thought I knew that guy! So I waited for him at this one spot. He came passing by and stopped. He was one of the classmates I went to school with! He was in the Marines. When I was coming home he was going to China. I met with some Indians from other places too.

Wilbur Smith ca. 1942-3.
Photo courtesy of Wilbur Smith.

You were very young to be in the service. Were you ever treated any different because you were so young?

I just fit right in! One thing was I couldn't go into bars or stuff like that. But I had some fun times! One place I remember was in Pasadena. There was one guy who I went to boot camp with from Kansas City. I'll never forget him; his name was Toby. He said he owned a cleaning establishment at that time in Kansas City.

Well, after we got out of boot camp he had his girlfriend bring his car to this destroyer base. It was a convertible and she was staying at a pretty fancy hotel in San Diego. We had another friend, a big tall white guy from Arkansas. He was a semi-pro baseball and basketball player. A few days later I shipped out and they stayed there. After I came back from the islands I ran into them and they were both still there! They never left! That was a kick.

I was too young to know anything. I was never homesick. It was like when I went to boot camp, having gone to Sherman I learned how to wash your clothes, make your bed and sweep the floor. So when I went to boot camp it was like Sherman but with different people. You'd hear some of those boys crying at night. A lot of that at Sherman prepared you for a military life and made it easier on you.

What year was it when you came back home?

We got into San Francisco and then to Treasure Island. We drew some pay and got a liberty. We went to San Francisco and the first thing I had was steak with sliced tomatoes and onions! Then we went out and partied that night! I still wasn't 21! The next morning we went to a health club for a steam bath and massage.

We came back to Treasure Island and they took us to Oakland by bus. Then we headed to Los Angeles and then to San Pedro. I asked to be discharged down there. This was in April of 46'. They discharged me and I went to Riverside and told them I was coming back. I went home for summer and came back to school in fall.

Your mother must have been pretty happy!

Oh, you know how mothers are! She always let me do what I wanted. I never got in trouble. I was never a drinker.

So you went back to Sherman. How much more time did you have?

I went for one year and finished my senior year. Then I went to work in Los Angeles as a printer for four years.

When you were at Sherman there were other guys who were also veterans. It must have been a completely different experience?

Yes, a lot of us were still kids at heart. We ended up having a basketball and football team made up of veterans. We were too old to play varsity so we played against junior colleges and we even played against the prison at Chino one year. We were invited to play football against them.

They were super-nice and we had dinner with them! The school charged us for room and board and it came out to about half the money we'd get each month. I had a friend who had a car and that gave us more mobility.

Do you remember the names of any of those veterans who came back to Sherman with you?

There was Lester Wilson, who was my cousin. The names come and go with me know. I'm a life member of the VFW and I'm a past commander of my post. My post doesn't exist anymore because the membership dropped so low and they moved it.

How long have you lived in this area?

Going on 20 years. We built the store here the year before I moved over here. I lived in Loyalton and would come over here on weekends. I would tie up flies at night after work and bring them over to the store. I would stay here Friday night; I slept on the floor for a year in the store in my sleeping bag.

I would go home Sunday night. Then I decided I might as well retire. I had worked in demolition on the demolition grounds out at Herlong. I was one of the only Indian guys there. I commuted from Loyalton.

Were you ever married?

I was married one time. I have four children, three girls and a boy. I have four grandchildren.

In our Indian community we know who our veterans are, but why do you think Indian veterans from this area haven't publicly shared about their experiences?

Well, things like this don't really come up unless you have a crisis. Indian people don't wave their flag. We don't go out and say this and that. We're a laid-back kind of people. Our veterans volunteered. We're not one to really wave the flag. We don't look for a handout.

We're a laid-back kind of people. Our veterans volunteered. We're not one to really wave the flag. We don't look for a handout.

I think I'm a simple person. I don't need a lot of money, I don't need fancy clothes, or rings or diamonds. I think a lot of our people are like that. The only thing we like is to see another member of our race no matter what tribe or where you're from. I like to learn more about their culture.

Through your time here at the store you've probably met lots of different people?

Yeah, and sometimes Indian people have had conferences near here so I get to talk to them. I used to be kind of a shy person, but I like to talk one-on-one. I had a good life in the service. I've been a lucky person. I think I've made fairly good choices. At my age, every day is a holiday!

Well, thank you very much for sharing with me.

That's all right. You're one of the few I'll do this with.

Wilbur Smith still helps run his store in Pyramid Lake. He enjoys hearing about other Native tribes and cultures and visiting with customers. His family is very proud of his service to the country.

Reuben Green

I met with Reuben and Bea Green on February 16, 2001 at his step-daughter's home in Crescent City. Reuben is an enrolled member with the Elk Valley Rancheria and is of Tolowa ancestry.

I was born in 1921 in Crescent City. My parents were Edward Green, Sr. and Josephine Green. I had several brothers and sisters but they're all gone. I was raised around this area. My dad worked at a ranch called the Miller Ranch. Then in the 1930s we moved away from here. I went to school at Pine Grove and then went to Crescent Elk. My father worked in the woods and on a dairy ranch.

Did you ever help your dad with his work?

I started out milking cows then I went to work in the woods. I did a little bit of everything. Life was good. It was hard times, but everyone was having them.

When you were growing up did anyone in your family speak an Indian language?

My mother could speak three or four different languages. She could hear another language two or three times then she could speak it. My grandfather used to run a pack train at a place called Big Flat. A panther had jumped onto one of his packhorses and his horse reared up and something went through his stomach and killed him. My parents never referred to it, that they were Indian. My dad never did. His background was something I didn't know about. He was adopted by a family that used to own half of Del Norte County!

My parents divorced in 1927 and I stayed with my mother and one of my brothers. When I went to work in the woods we had to stay in logging camps. It was good. It was the only life I knew. You get up and go to work. You eat good. That was in 1936.

Did you ever hear or read anything about what was going on in Europe or Asia?

Not too much. We'd work in the woods every day and never pay any attention. The only thing we heard about was Pearl Harbor.

Do you remember where you were when Pearl Harbor happened?

Oh yes, I was falling timber by the Van Duzen River. I don't remember if the word was by radio, or the paper, or an individual, but we were all talking about it. It was the talk of the country, you know.

What did you feel when you heard about it?

Oh, it made me wonder. The draft was going on. My two brothers got drafted. I thought to myself, 'They can't get ahead of me,' so I went to Crescent City and told them I wanted to join. I would have been drafted anyway. My brothers went in two weeks ahead of me.

What were their names?

Kenneth and Billy. Kenneth was in the Army infantry and my brother Bill was in the quartermaster's.

What branch did you join?

The Combat Engineers in the Army. I went to boot camp in Hawaii. I got 37 months in the service and had 37 months overseas.

What was it like to travel to Hawaii?

It was strange. You wonder what the next day's going to bring you.

Were there any other Indian people in boot camp with you?

Yes, there were some, but you don't go around asking people their nationalities. But one man from here who stayed three or four tents down from me was Brady McVeigh.

What was boot camp like for you?

We stayed in a place called Tent City. They just gave us basic training. The weather was nice sometimes, but it would rain. The mud would get on your clothes and you couldn't get it off. We trained with an M-1 rifle.

When did you get to go into the combat engineers?

I don't know who does it, but they call your name after boot camp and tell you which area to go to. That's how I went to the 34th Combat Engineers. As far as I know, we were under the 27th Division, but I might be off there. We went a mile from where we took our basic training and that's where they had their barracks.

For a while we worked on ammunition dumps. Then one day I got on KP! This is kind of comical. In those days, I had to keep going. Most of the other guys my age would come back and lay on their bunk. I'd go up to the kitchen and take some food. Finally the mess sergeant came to me and asked if I wanted to cook.

He said, 'We need a cook, you get one day on and two days off.'

I said sure and they sent me to baking school. I came back and got the head-baking job. I had two helpers; they knew more about baking than I ever did or ever will! They knew how to bake! They were foreigners and couldn't get our mathematics down, so I helped them. I did that for a while.

They moved our outfit down off Waikiki. One day they took three of us and detached us to the 807th Aviation Engineers. They put us on a plane and flew us to Baker Island. We stayed there for six months.

What did you do on Baker Island?

Not very much of anything! There had a landing base. They used Baker as a refueling station.

What type of planes would land there?

B-24s. We kept the landing strip in shape. If a plane came in all shot up we would clear it out so other planes could come in. We kept things operating. The planes were going to the Marshall Islands to bomb. This was about 1943.

After your six months at Baker where did you go?

They sent us back to our regular outfit. I had worked on a cat on Baker and when I came back they put me on a cat at Saipan until the war ended.

What was it like on Saipan for you?

Well, when we got there we were unloading, and about half our company had unloaded. I was just about ready to unload when they said to seal up. They stopped unloading and sealed the ship. We stayed out there for seven or eight days. That was the time when the Japanese Navy was going to come in and raise hell with us. I don't know if we were a decoy or what. Then we went back in. Our crew that had unloaded looked pretty beat-up.

Reuben Green

The island was tropical. I never saw too much jungle because I wasn't a foot soldier. I was on equipment all the time. If jungle was in the way I'd bull-doze it out of the way. I was also on graders and helped grade roads. Then I got on a ditch-digger and started building big ditches.

I also ran a big crane and helped unload ships that came in.

So you were on Saipan after it was taken over by the U.S.?

No, we got there on D-day. We left seven days and came back in. The Marines were there.

So there were still Japanese on the island?

Oh yes, they were all around. One time we had to dig our foxholes to fall asleep and a guard shot one about 10 feet from me where I was sleeping. They were all over.

That must have been very traumatic.

Yes, but you don't think of it that way. You're there with your buddies. See, everyone was your buddy. It was a different atmosphere. We stayed there roughly seven or eight months. After that we loaded our boat up and headed for Okinawa. It was near dark when we went in there.

We could see the red tracers coming in from every direction, and planes overhead. I saw one plane look like it was going to try and hit our ship. It was one of those suicide planes.

We could see the red tracers coming in from every direction, and planes overhead. I saw one plane look like it was going to try and hit our ship. It was one of those suicide planes. On Okinawa I ran a bulldozer. One time I was grading near the mess hall. A buddy of mine taught me how. Like I said, I always had to keep going. I worked all day. That night the master sergeant told me to get a guard and go grade. So I grabbed a buddy and asked if he'd be my guard. He said yeah, and we went out.

So you had to have a guard when you went out to work?

You always had to have a guard.

Did any Japanese ever fire on you when you were working in the machines?

Not that I know of. One time I was grading on the side of a mountain. A mortar came over us; then another one went over and crashed into the jungle. We jumped into a foxhole. We took off out of there. We would get strafed damn near every night in our area. One of our guys was standing near a tent in the doorway and he got killed right there.

I couldn't figure it out though, we'd get strafed two or three times and hardly anybody would get killed. It scared you! You'd get out and dig your foxhole a little deeper. I was on Okinawa for eight or nine months. I worked on quite a few airstrips. We built roads on the front lines. We worked wherever they needed us.

Did you ever get treated any different because you were Indian?

No, but I was in charge of the heavy equipment toward the end of my time in the service. There were a bunch of us in the tent and someone said something about an Indian one time. About three guys jumped out of their bunk and said, 'What'd you say?' That guy said, 'I take it back.' They said, 'You better.'

That was the only time anything was said about that. I was going through tank school when the war ended. Our captain said I would be in charge of the motor pool because there was a master sergeant that never showed up. I had a good time there. I just had the guys tell me where they went. They always did right to the 'T.' I was a technician sergeant.

When you were on the islands was there concern about diseases?

There was quite a bit of malaria. They made you put your nets down and the guard would come and make sure they were down. I was on Okinawa and there was an outdoor movie showing. We were on a ridge just heading down there when we heard someone shouting the war was over.

About that time it looked like the war started, everyone started shooting! We were up there on that ridge and there were ricochets all around us. I dove under a vehicle. I told my guys, 'If the war is done I'm not going to get killed now.' We heard some guys got killed by wild ricochets.

Where did you come to port after the war?

Los Angeles. We anchored there for seven days. Guys would talk to me and say they lived on the hills that we could see from the ship. That hurt them worse than anything because they could see it! I came up by train to camp by Riverside. They gave us a coming home dinner. We were served by Italian prisoners. Boy, you should have heard some of our guys yelling at them. 'So this is the way you fight the war!'

I got my discharge at a camp by Marysville. My two brothers made it back. Bill went to Alaska and Kenneth was in the Philippines somewhere. I had other relatives in the war too. There was John Green, Rufus Green, Earl Green and Harry Green. My oldest brother Eddie went to the recruiter and said he wanted to go. They said there were enough of the Green family in the service and sent him home.

How long did you work in the woods after the war?

Well, I started in 1936 and retired in 1993. I did odd jobs at the end. Out of all that time I only took a month off, other than my time in the service.

What does the American flag represent to you as a veteran?

Respect it.

Are you proud of the way you served your country?

Yes, I am. When I went in the war, the owner of the small logging outfit I worked in said he could have got me a deferment. I told him I didn't want one. My brothers were in and no one was going to call me a slacker or anything! It's important that younger people know what we were doing.

Reuben and his wife Bea currently live in Crescent City. Reuben enjoys working outdoors. He and Bea also enjoy working around their house. His family and his community are very proud of his service to his country.

Grant Hillman

I met with Grant Hillman at his home in Orleans on March 21, 2003. Grant served in the U.S. Navy during the war. He is of Karuk ancestry, and his home is situated on traditional Karuk territory near the Salmon River.

I was born in 1927 right down here by the river in Orleans! There was no doctor but there was a mid-wife; her name was Vivian Wilder, she was Ben Wilder's wife. He was a lieutenant in the First World War. I think she delivered a lot of kids here on the river back then. Nobody went to hospitals in those days.

My mother's name was Maddy Tenet. She was from Somes Bar across from Ishi Pishi. That's where she was raised. She went to the Carlisle Indian School in Pennsylvania. She was at the school the same time that Jim Thorpe was there.

She went back there to school for four years and stayed there. In my time they had Indian schools out here. They had Chemawa in Oregon; I had one sister go there, they had Stewart in Nevada and they had Sherman Institute. I had brothers and sisters go down there. If you wanted to continue your education you went.

Otherwise when you finished the eighth grade you were done with school if you were needed at home. At Sherman you came home every year in between. A bus would pick you up and take you back. But you couldn't go on to higher education.

This was how the government kept their foot on you. When you have people with a higher education it's pretty hard to hold them down. The government's way of controlling people was through education. When you went to school at Sherman in Riverside you went to school half a day and worked half a day. Indians weren't allowed to go to a public school and a lot of people don't realize this.

My father's name is the same as mine; Grant. He was from Nebraska. He came to this area in 1916. He was on a crew that built the first bridge here in Orleans. He met my mother and stayed here. They bought a ranch. This house is on the upper end of the ranch. In our family there were four boys and four girls. Most went to Sherman and one went to Chemawa.

What did your mother share about her time at Carlisle?

It was the same as going to Sherman. You couldn't go on to college. When she came back here she worked as a matron at the school in Hoopa. It's not like this anymore. The first time I went to public school was at the high school in Eureka. There were about 15 Indian kids there at that time. After we were there about a month it came over the PA system that all the Indian kids were to report to the study hall at one o'clock.

So we did, and this guy who came around to take kids to the Indian school was there, and he told us kids, 'You know you don't belong here. This is a public school and Indian kids don't belong in public schools. You come up here and sign these papers and the bus here will ship you out.'

Nobody signed. That was the beginning of the ending of the suppression here in this county. I think that was about the time the Second World War started because I was in high school when the war started.

Do you remember the names of any of those kids that were there?

Yes, there was Axel Erickson, and Nadine Starritt and my sister Vivian was there, and those are the ones from Orleans that I recall. I look back on this and think that most people don't realize how the Indians were suppressed. If you tell them something like that they can't visualize it. They think everything's been a certain way.

What was life like for you when you were a really young boy in Orleans?

Well, you really enjoyed it. You were born and raised on the river so this is all you knew. I think the younger generation of Indians has the belief that our culture was lost 100 years ago. This is not so. We probably lost most of our culture during the 1930s. When I was a kid we still did the same things. You could see the old Indian women going out with their big burden baskets to gather their mushrooms and acorns in the fall. We did a lot of burning; around every three years.

When fire suppression started this is when our culture changed completely. This is when the brush began to grow. So this did away with our hunting places and our acorn and mushroom gathering places.

The reason our culture changed was when Roosevelt was elected President. We were in a deep Depression. He started the CCCs, the Civilian Conservation Corps. These guys wore Army uniforms, had reveille and had caps. They didn't have weapons. There weren't any Indians in the CCC camp here. They had one over in Gasquet and they had them all over.

They had the Indian CCC camp down in Willits. All the Indians from here were sent to Willits. I had two brothers go there. We weren't integrated. Integration came later. Once they had the CCC camp here they built a lot of roads. This is when fire suppression started.

When fire suppression started this is when our culture changed completely. This is when the brush began to grow. There were no natural fires because they put them out. So this did away with our hunting places and our acorn and mushroom gathering places. This changed the Indian culture.

It was a slow process of change all through the '30s.

Before that everything was pretty much the same. The Forest Service had no more than a half a dozen people here at the time and they were local. They really didn't have control until the fire suppression started and then the Forest Service became stronger and stronger. They were the main cause of us losing our culture.

So how have you felt during the last few years when we'd have these huge forest fires because of decades of fire suppression?

They're short-sighted. They can say what they want about cooperating with the Indians, but the only time they cooperate is when they've been forced to. For example, when they had the Dillon Fire going toward Elk Valley; they wanted to put a fire camp in Elk Valley.

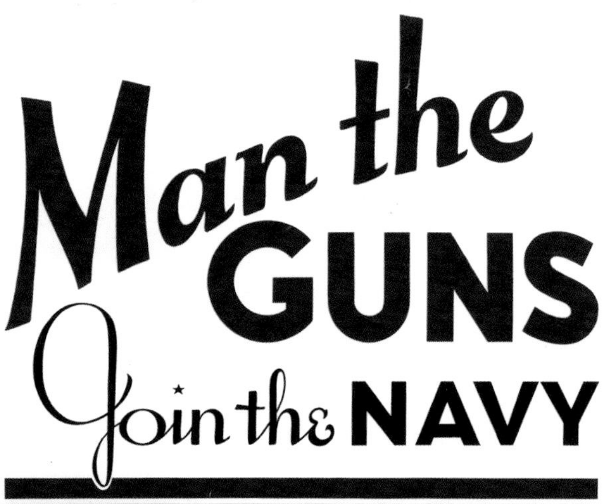

Recruiting poster.
Library of Congress, Prints and Photographs Division, (LC-USZC4-2009).

My boy was against that. That place is culturally significant to many Indian groups including the Karuk. He said to let the fire go through there. A camp of three or four hundred guys in Elk Valley would cause more damage with their trucks and machines than any natural fire would. The local Indians had to barricade the road to keep them from going into Elk Valley.

When I was a young fellow I knew people like Herb Orcutt and Paul and Calvin Starritt; they did a lot of burning in the fall. The Forest Service would lock these people up during the fire season. This is the Forest Service! Then they had these lookouts, and they figured they would hire these people for the lookouts instead of lock them up.

Any change in Forest Service policy had to be forced, and it's still the same way. If Indian people want anything done they have to be unified against the Forest Service in order to make change. The Forest Service's long range plans are for five years.

Five years is like the blink of an eye in our cultural ways. Our cultural ways go back thousands of years. A five year plan is nothing. You can't accomplish anything in five years. It's like what the country is facing now. They think they can solve the fire hazards in the short term.

You can't; it's something that goes on and on. The programs here have no connection to Indian culture. The game and fish are our culture. The long range plan for the Forest Service should be to put the country back the way it was. If you look at all of our regalia it has to do with the elk. Before our time there were a lot of elk here. They had to be re-introduced because of Forest Service policies.

When you were a young boy did anyone in your family gather basket material or create baskets?

Yes, my mother spoke Indian and all the old Indians would come visit and they'd speak in Karuk. That big basket there was made by Nettie Ruben who was a relation of mine. That basket is well over 100 years old. She was probably one of the best basket weavers on the river. You go to any museum and you'll see a picture of her. I think we have a really good basket program here in Orleans right now. The young girls are doing some really fine work and it's being run by LaVerne Glaze.

Why is it important that this tradition continue?

I think any of our culture should be saved. The Forest Service will allow them to burn small spots here and there, but we have to go through them to do it. This is not right. Your willows and hazel sticks are the same way. If they're burned they grow long and fast that first year. But they have to be kept cut and burned. Then you don't have the bugs in them. If you don't cut and burn you don't have hazel sticks, and it's the same with the bear grass.

As long as we have young people learning to gather roots, and bear grass and hazel sticks to make these things there will be a certain amount of burning going on. It should be controlled by our culture, not by what the Forest Service thinks. As long as we have young people learning this it puts the pressure on them to widen this. This is my way of thinking!

Nettie Ruben used to live close to here and I was

close to her. She would tell me whenever I wanted to go hunting in the fall to tell her and she would make medicine for me. She'd tell me when to go, and right where to go, and I'd get a deer. When I was in the Navy I used to think about this. I'd be lying in my sack.

There had to be some way...how could they have that kind of power? It finally came to me. I'd see those ladies go to gather their acorns. They'd burn every three years. There was a spring down below where they'd leech them. There were lots of reasons to burn, there were no bugs and it gave them room to move around to get mushrooms.

Those deer don't like buggy acorns either. So they would come in near those women who gathered every day. So they knew when the deer would come to feed. They knew all about them. I figured that out lying in a sack aboard ship! I was really a believer in our Indian ways. That's the way it was.

Do you think that whole process you just described, that connection to the land and that connection to the animals, that this is medicine?

That is medicine. There's nothing superstitious about it. It wasn't power, it was their knowledge of the land.

Do you have any knowledge of when the miners came through?

Our country seems to run on money. They concentrate on money. In the mining days gold was what was important so they used hydraulics to push land into the river to get at the gold underneath. This wasn't good for our fish. I can remember as a kid this river used to run red from all the silt build up.

I witnessed hydraulic mining when they washed a ranch near here into the river. It takes a long time for it to flow out. They washed out a lot of village sites. They finally saw that the mining was doing a lot of harm so they stopped. Then they started logging for money. Then there was nothing but logging trucks going through. Then they decided that was hurting the country and they stopped. It was either full bore or nothing, there was no in-between.

You were talking about the Karuk people who served in World War One, can you tell me anything else about them?

Well, there was Ike Ferris and Orvel Allen and Ben Wilder. He was a lieutenant. There was Chris Larson from across the river. There were a lot of Karuk who served in that war.

You were a young man and you knew these vets, did they make any kind of impression on you, or did they talk about it much?

They didn't talk about it too much. Ben Wilder used to live right by here. He was a good mechanic. He told me one time that the government gave him a raise on his World War One pension; the way he saw it the government wanted the vets to use that extra money to drink themselves to death, then they'd actually save money, but he was going to fool them and he quit drinking! He was probably right, there were some that did drink themselves to death with that extra money. He was a funny guy and well-educated. He lived until he was 90.

Do you remember where you were when Peal Harbor happened?

I was in junior high school in Eureka. The principal announced that everybody was to go to the auditorium and listen to the President. This was a couple days later when they declared war on the Japanese. In the late '30s we used to have these big iron scrap drives. All this scrap was gathered for the Japanese because they were buying it.

I remember these old-timers say 'Well, these Japanese are going to be shooting this scrap back at us.' They were right! But they thought we'd wipe them out in a couple of weeks. That was a long couple of weeks! I'll never forget that! Funny how things like that stay with you.

What year was it when you went into the service?

I went in in 1943. I wasn't quite 17 yet, but you could get in if you knew somebody like a preacher who could write how old you were. They'd take his word for it. That's how a lot of young guys 16 years old did it.

So that's how you got in?

Yeah.

And you volunteered?

Yeah. I volunteered in Eureka then we went to San Diego for boot camp. When you're young like that you want to see excitement or you're missing out on something! You had friends that you went to school with that were already in there, so you wanted to be in there too.

On about the third day was when they sent these kamikazes, the suicide planes. Then it was really serious. You either get them or they get you.

Junior Orcutt and John Erickson and a lot of young fellows from here were in the service. I had one brother, Orel, who was in the Army. He went in the year before I did. I think he was in the Pacific. That's where I was too.

When you went to boot camp was that the farthest away from home you'd ever been?

At that time it was. It was like the end of the world! That was a big adventure! I'd never been to a big city before. At that time I had good hearing. You went through different tests. If you had good hearing they wanted to put you into communications, but I wanted sea duty. I wanted adventure!

So I went aboard the USS *Mobile;* that's a light cruiser. On my 17th birthday I was at Leyte in the Phillipines. From there we went to Okinawa. That was on April Fools' Day in 1945. That was like a turkey shoot for about three days.

I'll always remember that it was really nice weather. We just bombarded the beach before a landing. On about the third day was when they sent these kamikazes, the suicide planes. Then it was really serious. You either get them or they get you.

I think our ship had 13 planes to its credit. I was on the twin 40-millimeter. The twin-40 could put out 250 rounds in a minute. There were quad-40s but I was on a twin. There were two twins on the tail and I think there were two sets of quads on the starboard and port on the main deck. There were two twins up high on the super structure and that's where I was at.

You could rest about four hours and then you were on for four hours unless planes were coming in then you were on all the time. So they tried to wear you down to where you can't think too well. This happens through fatigue. They'd come within 20 miles and we'd pick them up on the radar, then they'd turn back. By that time you're wide awake. You never knew when they'd come within range.

This was the way they psychologically worked on your mind. You don't get any sleep. You'd go back, lay down, and by the time you were almost asleep you'd have to go again. This was continual with no rest. When they did come in there were 40-millimeters on a lot of ships out there along with the five-inch guns. These were the most effective anti-aircraft guns. The 20-millimeter didn't explode and make a curtain out there, it just had regular bullets.

You'd see where they were going with tracers. Right before they came into range we'd just blacken the horizon with flack. If they thought they could get through they'd try to come through. If they could come through under the radar close to the water then they could get right in on you. When you were shooting at them and just lining them up a five-inch would fire, and if it was a little off to the left or the right it would explode and blow the plane sideways.

Then you're off again! I think we could have done better if it wasn't for the five-inch doing that, because it made the plane look like it was dodging. We were hit once on the number two turret. They took us down to the Philippines and put new barrels on.

You were hit by a plane or by a bomb?

By a plane. There were lots of close misses when they'd come right over the bow and crash.

What were your emotions during those times, what were you feeling?

Either you get them or they get you. You have no place to run. You're ship's pretty narrow! You're not going to jump over the side! You've got to stay! That's the only bad thing about the Navy; you've got no place to go! A fire was always the spookiest thing. You really have to get it put out or you've lost your home and you're in the drink.

A lot of the time our sea engagements were at night. I don't know why. I don't think the Japanese radar was as good as ours, so they might have depended on the night. We'd have our destroyers out in front, then the cruisers then the battleships. It depends on the range of the guns as to where your battleships were positioned. They could fire 20 miles so they're way back there.

This is how you come into range. Your position is different. We'd steam out and we'd know something was up. The captain would come and he'd tell you how many ships they had and what kind, and how many ships we had and what kind, and the time we were supposed to meet. We were supposed to meet about midnight. This was just before dusk.

Their planes would come in to try to soften us up and our planes would do the same to them before we made contact. So everybody was on standby. Sure enough here they come. You'd see your planes go over to them. There'd be about three hours before we made contact. Probably half your crew is writing letters; why, I don't know! If you get sunk your letters aren't going anyplace!

But half your crew is sitting and nobody is talking. It's real quiet then. Everybody carries a knife so the other half of the crew is sharpening their knives. You're thinking if you get in a sea engagement and you get sunk, the chances are they're going to get sunk too, and we'll all be in the water. This is the only weapon you have, so half your crew is sharpening your knife and half is writing letters home. I was always sharpening my knife! That's a real tense time.

How long was the Mobile near Okinawa?

Probably two months. We'd come in and bombard during the day and go out to sea at night. The Japanese had what were called Q-boats. These were suicide boats. If you stayed in close they'd come out with dynamite aboard and try to get you.

The suicide planes were the worst. I think on Okinawa the Navy probably suffered more casualties because of this. You have to protect the carriers in your group at all cost. They're sitting in the middle and they're surrounded by the cruisers and the battleships in a radar picket. They're the ones who take a beating. They'd try to take out those pickets who were on patrol.

It's just like when guys would go out on patrol on foot. These pickets are the same thing; they're out on patrol to let you know what's coming. So the Japanese would try to knock them off. They're the ones who took the biggest hits. A lot of times ships would put out smoke screens and you'd stay in the smoke.

They'd be looking down and all they'd see was smoke. Our radar wasn't really perfected. Ours was jerky, but even under this smoke we'd follow the planes. The waiting was always the worst to me. It was hurry up and wait. This waiting gets to you really bad! There were too many things going on in your head.

The concept of a suicide plane was a new weapon; did your crew ever talk about this after seeing them?

You kind of had to make up your own mind about it.

You know the Mitsubishi car? You carry so much hate... Mitsubishi was the name of the Japanese plane. We'd study their silhouettes on screens...this was a Zero, this was a Mitsubishi...so you could pick them out. Yet right to this day they sell Mitsubishis here!

Whenever I see that name it kind of pisses me off. It takes a long time to get that hate out of you when you've seen your friends get killed. You can't fight unless you have this hate in you. The more hate the more you can fight. I think this is what happened in Vietnam. The people here didn't have the hate.

What brought the hate on in World War Two was when the Japanese bombed Pearl Harbor and killed a couple thousand guys. The hate was instant. You've got to go on this hate and it becomes stronger and stronger. Until you can create this hate you can't fight.

I drive a Nissan car and pickup, and I would say for about 40 years after I got out of the service it made me kind of mad and I wouldn't buy anything that said 'Japan' on it. Now I drive two of them. So this hate eventually gets out of you. When I see this Mitsubishi car I still think of the war. How can they put out a car with that name? I know I wouldn't buy a Mitsubishi car!

The USS Mobile.
Photo courtesy of Grant Hillman.

After Okinawa where did your ship go?

After Okinawa we went back to the Philippines for R-and-R to wait for the invasion of Japan itself. They were really softening up Japan at that time. We were getting ready; we knew it was coming. During the day they took us to the beach like we were little kids. There was a river and a fence where you couldn't get out of this compound. They had basketball courts there for the thousands of guys.

You'd stand in line and get two cans of beer then you'd go down to the beach and drink this beer and relax. When you're young two beers just doesn't do it! At five in the evening they'd have loudspeakers tell you to go by these palm trees to line up and go back to your ship at night.

They had officers across this river; they got to watch movies, and I imagine they got to eat a little better than the enlisted men, too. There was always a little friction; you didn't see them sitting on the beach with two cans of beer! I had a friend who was a real gambler; there were three of us who ran around all the time. We would always talk us into pooling our beer and he would go to a poker game. He'd lose day after day! I think he only won one time!

We were still there when they dropped the atomic bomb on Hiroshima. We didn't know what an atomic bomb was. But before that, when we were back on Okinawa ,Roosevelt had died. I could remember Roosevelt being the President since I was a kid, and I suppose three-quarters of the crew were my age and didn't know anything but Roosevelt, too.

We was like a god to us, and he dies. Boy, what a blow...what were we going to do? They said Truman would be President. Who in the hell was Truman, we never heard of the guy! It was like your life depended on Roosevelt, he was the one and only leader.

When Truman ordered the atomic bomb to be dropped where were you?

We were still at this recreation area, and after the second one the Japanese quit. You can't believe it. What were we going to do? What's going to happen now? It's kind of funny when you look back on it. You knew it was good the war was over.

There was so much hate built up that you can hardly believe this was happening. We were supposed to go on fighting. Before they disarmed it was really spooky. There were a couple carriers, some destroyers and our cruiser and we were escorting a hospital ship to Nagasaki, where the second bomb was dropped to get some prisoners of war out of there.

This was before the surrender was signed and they had quit; to go in we had to pass two Japanese destroyers on the way out. We'd go to a general alarm and to our battle stations when they were within range. There was no trust. The war was over but they hadn't disarmed yet. What were they going to do?

Their way of surrendering was to pull their man-of-war flag down and fly the merchant flag. They had two flags; the rising sun and the merchant flag, the white one with the red dot. They had to fly the merchant flag and kept their barrels elevated to about a 25-degree angle and pointed straight ahead. They had a big white cross painted on their stacks.

When they would pass us all of our guns were trained on them. This was how they surrendered, but you're still right on them! You can't believe it! We got to this harbor with a narrow entrance and hills on both sides. Each gun position was given a map. We were going into the harbor with the hospital ship; the aircraft carrier stayed outside with the destroyers.

These Japanese soldiers weren't under occupation yet; everybody was still armed. It was really spooky. We were given this map to this entrance of the harbor where their gun emplacements were. You had certain territory to focus on as you went in that harbor. You stayed focused on that gun.

We knew once we went in that harbor if they fired on us we were dead; there wasn't any getting out. So we went in there. Most of the prisoners of war were Burmese. There were a few Australians and Americans. The white soldiers were like skin over bones. A lot of them couldn't even walk. The ones who couldn't walk went aboard the hospital ship at the dock.

Grant Hillman with Brush Dance regalia.

The ones who could walk they brought out to us. We moved up on the deck and slept on the deck. They got the beds. They were all full of dysentery and they could barely walk. The Burmese were in a lot better shape than the white soldiers. They were starving to death, like skeletons. They gave them new uniforms and they were like sacks on them. We'd help them down below; they crapped all over. They couldn't even get to the edge. It was a mess all over.

Every once in while, every three or four minutes, there would be a P-51 come through the harbor. VROOM! You could look down from where my gun turret was; you could see the pilot. Boy that made you feel good! That's what it was, a show. It would come back through, VROOM! You could see the Japanese soldiers on the dock packing their rifles up.

We took those prisoners of war to Okinawa and dropped them off and went to Sabo for more prisoners of war. The Japanese were still walking around; I don't think they disarmed them for seven or 10 days. The first time we got to go on a beach we'd go 50 in a group.

At Nagasaki on the waterfront those big iron beams were just melted. I don't how big the city was, and I don't know how many people died there, about 70,000 or something, but the streets were there. You'd go down the streets and you could tell where the factories were because there'd be long rows of leis lying there. The people wouldn't look at you. They'd look away as we went by. We were armed.

When we went into Sasebo you could go into the stores and take what you wanted. They would jabber something and you'd give them a hard look. There was some looting until they brought in the occupation troops. There was that hate.

Those occupation troops were young guys. I was probably 18-and-a-half, maybe 19, but these guys looked like they were right out of school. The Japanese are very polite people. You can't put soldiers in there who've been fighting them for years; there's too much hate. So they had to rush in all these troops from the States.

Those Japanese would bow to them and these young guys ate that up and they thought there was nothing wrong with these people. You have so much hate in you that you begin to hate your own people. They believed in how polite the Japanese were.

So after two or three weeks you didn't like those guys who didn't have that hate, so they had to get you out of there as soon as they could. So far in Iraq we've only had 13 or 14 guys killed over there. The more they kill the more hate these guys will have. You can't fight war without hate, and the more killing that goes on the more that hate is created.

Do you think that's why some veterans drank when they came back to the States?

I think so. I also think that maybe we don't hate the white people, but we don't trust them either. There's a lot of old (Indian) people that hand this down. They weren't even citizens; they were a number, a roll number. Why did the government give us roll numbers? We didn't have names, we had roll numbers.

A lot of white people don't even know this. We couldn't

go to public schools…I can remember on Second Street in Eureka there would be a bar with a sign that said 'No dogs or Indians allowed.'

You don't forget this, so you tell your kids. They believe you. They might not believe you if they haven't seen it, but if you don't tell them this history might be lost. I came home on leave one time and went out with my brother. He was lighter complexioned. At that time in Eureka if you were dark complexioned you didn't go in a bar. It was against the law for Indians to drink or be served.

During the Second World War when you went out you went out in full uniform or you were a deserter. So I was in uniform and my brother and I went to have a drink. We went into a bar where they didn't serve Indians, even during the war. My brother ordered a drink and so did I, and they served him but not me. You never forget stuff like this. I'll probably remember it until I die.

So many Native people, and probably every Karuk family, had someone who served, and you came back to a country that still didn't fully respect you. What are your thoughts on that?

They're not good thoughts. But those thoughts changed over time. At that time I was kind of bitter. You don't forget bitterness, it's just like hate.

Knowing all of this, and knowing that during World War One Indian soldiers weren't even citizens, why do you think so many Native people chose to fight for the U.S.?

This was still our country. We're fighting for right here, and I don't think we'll ever stop fighting for right here! Through education and unity we can move ahead. I think that we want something better for our kids.

This is ingrained in Indian people just like everyone else. I'm a firm believer that this has to come through education. I'm a strong believer in our education too, our way of life. We can't lose it. They tried to squeeze it out of us over the years. I see it's coming back. It makes a person feel good.

Grant and his late wife Lorraine were married for over 40 years and had four children, numerous grandchildren and one great-grandchild. Grant worked as a construction foreman and superintendent, working on roads just like this father before him. His family is very proud of his service to his country and his Karuk people.

Francis Allen, Jr.

Francis Allen, Jr. is another Indian veteran whom I heard about while growing up. I was able to contact him through his daughter Christine Law. Francis is a veteran of the U.S. Navy in World War Two and was perhaps the only California Indian Naval deep sea diver in the 1950s and 1960s. He is of Pomo ancestry. We sat in the basement of the Susanville Veteran's building on the morning of October 12, 2002, which was the day of that year's Indian Veteran's Reunion.

I was born August 12, 1926, in Santa Rosa, California. My father was Francis Allen, Sr., and my mother was Lena Cordova. My father and mother were both Pomo. My mother was born in Cloverdale and my dad was born in Ukiah, in California. I had three sisters and later my mother remarried and had more children. I was raised in Santa Rosa, Hopland, Cloverdale…my parents were migrant workers.

We all had to wear coveralls and black lace shoes. We were furnished clothing and stayed in dormitories.

They'd work with fruit and hops wherever they could find work. It was the Depression and it was really hard on them. My sister Ramona and I goofed around as children. We played by the riverbanks or in the hop fields. We ate the grapes or prunes that they were picking. I knew my grandmother on my father's side. Her name was Daisy Meyers, and my mother's mother's name was Lucy. Her mother was Trudy Arnold. They're both buried in an Indian burial ground in Cloverdale.

Did anyone in your family speak their Native language?

Oh yeah, my mother spoke fluently. My great-grandmother spoke too. But they didn't want to teach us because we were learning the white man's ways. At that time there was such discrimination against Indians. It was horrendous.

So it was almost a way of protecting you, not learning the language?

Yes, then the culture was gone. But let me say this, my aunt Elsie Allen has some basket work in the Smithsonian.

When did you attend the Stewart Indian School?

It's kind of hazy, but it was around the second grade. I remember before going to Stewart that I was playing around in some grass with my cousin, and I stepped on an old corn beef can and it almost severed my big toe. When I went to Stewart it was all festered, and almost turned to gangrene. They took care of it over there. I was about seven or eight.

Did you have to wear any type of uniform?

We all had to wear coveralls and black lace shoes. We were furnished clothing and stayed in dormitories. I don't remember how many children there were, but it was kindergarten through sixth grade. Then you were sent to the big boy's side. They lived in cottages four to a room. I ended up over there.

What was the schedule like at that first dormitory when you were little?

You know what, I don't remember. We'd get up

around seven o'clock then we'd go wash up, get dressed, brush our teeth then line up in formation to march to the dining room hall. Different meals were the same way. It was run on a military-style schedule.

Everything was by height. We lined up by height. We had to learn to make our own bunks, even the little guys. The big guys wouldn't help them. The hygiene was really good there. We had glasses if you needed them. When I was smaller we had some heroes. I can't think of their names now, but there was a guy called Norris who was a pole-vaulter. They guys would box or play football or basketball. We'd watch and want to be like them and finally it happened!

So it was good to have older Indian kids to look up to?

Oh yeah, and we didn't know it at that time but we were different people, different tribes. It wasn't that important, it was just boys together. I made some good friends there growing up throughout the years. I had a cousin there, Louie Arnold. He came later.

I started out a lightweight, at 135. When I went in the service I boxed at 147 then ended up a middleweight.

My other cousin Marie Arnold was there and my sister Ramona was there. She's two years younger than I am. The girls had the same deal that we did, except in another dormitory. They were treated in the same military fashion. They had their own uniforms they dressed in too.

When you were older and moved to the other dormitory what was a typical day like for you?

Well, when we were on the little boy's side we'd all have chores. We'd have laundry for the whole dorm and have to fold it and put it in cubicles. Each person had a number for their clothes. When we got on the other side we had other chores.

Of course we had to clean our rooms, but being from the little boy's section we knew all this. We went to different shops. They had every kind of vocational trade. There was a big farm that had a big dairy, and chickens, pigs and cattle. Some guys worked there because they wanted to be farmers. There was plumbing, auto mechanics, bakery, electricians, cooks...anything.

Did you like the regimented style of life?

After you got used to it, it really didn't matter. I remember we had a lot of freedom. We'd run around in the sagebrush or go to a river. We'd go to Carson City to the movies. As long as we were there for checkups or meals. I think now that the training I had then really did me good when I went in the service. Every Friday night we'd watch a movie at Stewart, unless you were punished.

What was the punishment system like?

Just keeping away from the extras. They'd make you scrub the bathroom with a brush. That kind of thing.

Did you play any sports?

I played football and I boxed. This was before I joined the service. This was in the spring of 1943. I boxed the Golden Gloves in Reno, Nevada. I was the runner-up. I played football and was a two-year letterman. We played against Reno, Sparks, Fallon, Gardnerville and Susanville.

Those were all-white teams?

Yeah, but around Fallon and Sparks they had Indian boys on their teams too.

When you boxed, what weight class were you in?

I started out a lightweight, at 135. When I went in the service I boxed at 147 then ended up a middleweight.

Francis Allen's boxing pose ca. 1941-2.
Photo courtesy of Virginia Aguilar.

They must have had some good boxing teams there...

At Stewart, oh yes. I forgot how many years running they took the team trophy.

Were there any Indian teachers at Stewart when you were there?

Yes, the auto mechanic instructor was, and the superintendent was an Indian from Oklahoma. There was a fourth grade teacher who was Indian, and I think the guy who ran the plumbing shop was probably Washoe Indian.

Do you remember where you were when the war broke out?

When I heard about it I was in Jack's Valley working on one of those vocational deals. They came in and told us about the war and had a radio. At that age I didn't really comprehend what going to war meant. That was in '41, so I was about 15. Two years later I went in.

I was watching the movie *North Atlantic* with Humphrey Bogard about the Armed Guard. That's what I wanted to be, on a ship. Sure enough, that's where I ended up! Another guy did that too; Mervin Evans. His ship was torpedoed. My ship was on the West Coast.

When the war broke out, did the older boys at Stewart immediately join the service?

A lot of them did.

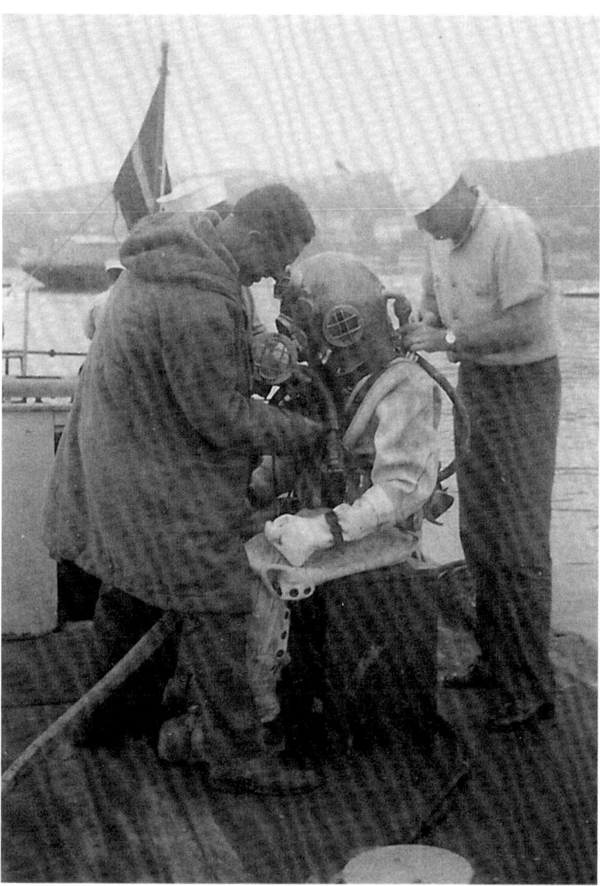

Francis Allen preparing for a deep-sea dive ca. 1953-4.
Photo courtesy of Francis Allen.

Why do you think they did that?

Probably personal reasons...patriotism. At that time, I don't really know why I went in! Probably to be an Armed Guard on a ship, and patriotism, too.

What recruiting station did you go to?

Reno, and all I had on was a white t-shirt, a letterman sweater, levis, and argyle socks and loafers. I remember that! Two other guys went with me; I talked them into coming. There were George Nixon and Milton Lotchis. We went together. We went to Salt Lake on a train, then to Farragut, Idaho for boot camp.

What tribe were those other two?

One was Hupa and the other was Klamath. We were all together. They were my friends. They were boxers too. When we went up to boot camp there were three Indians and the rest of the guys were white. So we were looked at with a little discrimination until one guy came around asking for boxers.

We all went in and won camp boxing championships! So they looked at us differently then! They were afraid we might kick the shit out of them! We all went separate ways after camp.

Where did you go?

They sent me to San Diego to gunnery school. I think that was six weeks. Then I finally ended up on a Liberty ship in San Francisco. That thing was huge to me. There were 26 of us. We had different rates. We took cargo to New Guinea. We stayed anchored at some islands in the Marshalls for 90 days.

Francis Allen ca. 1953-4.
Photo courtesy of Francis Allen.

From there we went to Leyte in the Philippines. That's where we saw a Japanese bomber come right over us. There were a lot of ships in the harbor and they were all shooting at it. They didn't even think of the fallout, they were just shooting in the air. It went unscathed. It flew right on through and bombed an ammunition depot on the shore, then took off. It waved its wings before it took off.

After that we went to Newcastle, Australia. Then we went to New Caledonia, then back to the States. That all took about 13 months. I ended up at the naval air station at Alameda. I was one of the seamen that mopped the decks at the barracks. That was my duty until I was discharged. After that I went back to Stewart and asked them if I could finish my education. They said all right but put me in with the seniors. There were quite a few veterans who came back from the Army, Navy and Marines.

You probably had some stories to tell!

Yeah! Then we'd BS the young people! We were veterans of foreign wars! They looked up to us.

I must have been really different for you to go back to Stewart after the war?

Yeah, it was. We grew up. I also think we missed out a lot. Other people grew up dancing and listening to the jukebox but we missed out on that. When we came back it was good. When football came that was great. We'd take girlfriends to the movies and things like that. Me and my sister always talk about Stewart.

The scariest time I had was one time on a mission I was down about 180 feet and my air ran out. There was no air.

When you were serving on that Liberty ship what were you transferring?

It was a lot of cargo. There was a lot of service supplies; candy, cigarettes, beer and a lot of fuel.

After you were discharged what did you do?

I was discharged in May of '46. After Stewart I met Lorraine, who was from Susanville. After graduation I came up here to visit her and we got married and I stayed. I worked for the Paul Bunyon lumber company. In 1950 I went back during the Korean conflict. They put me in a cargo-handling battalion for months.

That was for loading and off-loading ships. After you were trained you were sent to Kwajalein. It was just an airstrip with a couple of barracks. I wanted to get off that island! All you did was sit there and drink beer and wish you were back home. A circular came out calling for divers for the Navy.

I think I wanted to get off that island so bad that's why I volunteered to go into the diving corps! I became a deep-sea diver for the United States Navy and I did that for 16 years. I went to New Jersey to learn at salvage diving school. At first it was scary. You cannot get claustrophobic! A couple of the guys, after they got dressed and put the helmet on them, they went berserk. After a couple of months of training they put me on a ship. It was the USS *Dixie AD14*.

What was the training like for deep-sea diving?

Well, there was a lot of classroom work. After a while we had sea training.

Can you describe the first time you went underwater in your suit?

Yeah! In New Jersey you had about 20 feet of silt in the river bottom there. It was all black. All you had was a lifeline. After you get orientated it was all right. But it was always scary to go down. At that time the limit for salvage was around 50 feet. The limit for deep sea diving was 300 feet. The Navy today is very different.

I went to underwater swimming school in Key West, Florida after that. I was six weeks of running up and down sandy beaches with bottles on your back. It was hot, humid weather. But I came out with the certificate so that was that!

Francis Allen ca. 1953-4.
Photo courtesy of Francis Allen.

The scariest time I had was one time on a mission I was down about 180 feet and my air ran out. There was no air. When I shot to the surface I bypassed the decompression stop. So they grabbed me and threw me into the decompression chamber and I stayed there 72 hours. When that big door slams shut all you hear is the hiss of the air coming in.

They take you down to the pressure you were and bring you up gradually so you won't get the bends. Then they watch you for any pains. I would describe it like arthritic pains. I've been decompressed three times. They used to call us bubbleheads because they said some of the nitrogen bubbles were still there and we weren't right, but that was just joking!

Was there a time limit on your dives?

It would depend on the depth. The longer you stay down the longer you took to decompress. I remember one time I was down looking for an anchor; the current was running against me. We could speak over transmitters to the top. I saw the anchor and was dragging a line to it. They called and said it was time to come up.

I said I was almost there. I finally got there and put the line over it in a half-hitch. Then I went up. I think I went over my limit by about three minutes. So I had to stay a little longer to decompress. One time on the *Dixie* we were going to Taiwan. I was in my bunk early in the morning. I heard this high-pitched scream.

A fishing boat had tried to come across our bow. They believed it was good luck to cross in front of a ship. Only they capsized. I was the only one at that time that had underwater experience with scuba gear. They called me to the bridge and asked me to check the ship, so I did. The chief in charge, instead of putting lifts under and raising it up, decided to turn the ship over and raise it like that. I had to pull out nine bodies. They were covered in oil and so slippery it was hard to hold them. That wasn't very good.

Over the years we went on different ships. We worked on submarines changing screws and doing some cutting and welding. We also worked on destroyers. The *Dixie* was a destroyer tender so we'd take care of destroyers when they came into port. I was also on the USS *Sperry AS12,* which was a submarine tender.

A lot of times we'd check everything under the bottom. There might be a big dent and we'd have to change the screws underwater instead of taking it to a dry dock. We got hazard duty pay. It was fun, especially in San Diego. I remember one time we were wearing facemasks with a line. I went underwater and came up under the bow.

This guy was on the side on a scaffold painting the ship. He was maybe six or eight inches off the water. I reached up and grabbed his foot, then swam back under. That evening I was on liberty at this bar and he came walking in. 'You SOB, I thought a monster got me!' he said. He never went on the side again!

He never expected that. One time at lunch this guy was fishing on our diving boat. We had sardines and crackers. So I took a sardine can and went underwater and tied it to his line and gave it a pull. Then I swam back up and those guys were telling him to play the fish good. That can was moving everywhere. Then bam, he pulled up the can! He looked at me and said, 'You SOB!'

You were in the Navy until when?

Clear up until Vietnam. We stayed in four teams. During Vietnam we'd go over there for a quarter then another team would go over. They sank a Liberty ship and we stayed nine months to get it out. That was a bad one. The current runs so strong near Vietnam. They had put explosives on a boat and ran it into the side of this ship right near the engine room.

I think there were eight people that were wiped out. We had to go down in all this oil and everything. Those guys had been in there for I don't know how long. Oh man, the smell of death…that's something bad. We had to put them in body bags.

Francis Allen

Why did you choose to stay in the service so long?

I really don't know. I had a wife and four children. They'd move to wherever I was at.

It seemed to me that the men of your generation who were in the service had a special bond. Does it seem that way to you?

Yes we do. When I come up here I know the guys, Mervin, Ned Crutcher and the Jackson brothers.

How many years have you been attending these reunions?

I've been to every one except the first one. I enjoy seeing other vets, but it's sad because it's dwindling. Those World War One and most World War Two veterans are gone. We have a few Gulf War veterans. I do like to see my family when I'm here.

When you were young did you ever think you'd be working in the water so much?

I never did. I liked to swim for entertainment. I didn't think about diving. The training was immense. I think it was in 1939 when they started with the diving. They had a copper hood that would fall off. Then they created the suit.

Now they have guys go down 1,000 feet. I retired from the service in January of 1972. I went to school on the GI Bill, and bought a home on the GI Bill. I've been retired ever since. One thing about retirement, you don't have to worry about vacations!

Francis Allen earned many commendations for his time in the Navy, among them are: The Good Conduct Medal, American Campaign Medal, Asiatic Pacific Campaign Victory Medal, Philippine Liberation Medal, World War Two Victory Medal, Korean Service Medal, National Defense Medal with Bronze Star, Naval Unit Commendation Medal, Vietnam Service Medal, and the Republic of Vietnam Campaign Medal. His family is very proud of his service to his country.

Charlie Bowen

1921-2001

Charlie Bowen was of Pit River, Mountain Maidu and Welsh ancestry. Charlie and his late wife Audree made their home near Crescent City which is set on the traditional land of the Tolowa people. Charlie and my grandfather Stan are cousins. Charlie sat down with me in May of 2000 to talk about his time as a paratrooper in the war.

I went to basic training down at Camp Roberts, California. I was talking to a couple of guys down there who were going to volunteer to join the paratroopers when they got out of basic training. I don't know how come, but that's when I first decided to become a paratrooper. After basic training they never even gave us a furlough, they just sent us to Fort Benning, Georgia.

We trained up there, and man, they trained us and trained us and trained us. We were in good shape and well trained.

That's when my second daughter Junie was born. I got to see her one time before I left. She was just a baby. Audree came down to San Francisco, I got a chance to see Junie on a three day weekend pass. I never saw her after that until she was two or three years old.

What division were you in?

Well, that came after I shipped overseas. We weren't attached until we shipped over. When I got out of jump school they gave us a furlough. That was the first furlough I had since I got in. They started shipping everybody to England for the invasion of Normandy. Me and my buddy, two of us out of this whole darn group got sent up to North Carolina to Camp McCall. That's where I first lucked out in the service. I never got sent to England.

Those paratroopers in the first invasion, they went through all kinds of things. They were only training a regiment of us at Camp McCall. They trained us up there for five months, I guess. It seemed like a long time. We trained up there, and man, they trained us and trained us and trained us. We were in good shape and well trained.

Every Monday morning they would jump us out someplace. We'd stay out in the field all week, training about different tactics. Then come Friday we'd head back to camp. Monday morning they'd jump us out someplace else. I don't know; they were training us for some special duty.

That's the only thing anyone could figure out. They had different branches of the service, but all paratroopers. I don't really know what they were training us for, but for some special duty. But that's where I first lucked out otherwise I probably wouldn't have made it in Europe.

Were there any other Indians that you trained with, or at the camp?

Jump school is where I first met John. He's the only guy I knew, Johnny Smith. He was a paratrooper too. We were going home one night, catching a bus there in Columbus, Georgia going back to camp; he's the only one I ever met.

He was a paratrooper. He was the only one. But there were quite a few Indians there, but none from the West that I met. Most of the Indians that I did meet were from back East. There were quite a few paratroopers that were Indians.

Can you remember the first time you ever jumped out of a plane?

Oh yeah, I'll never forget that. They trained us for four weeks, I think. The first week is just getting into shape, teaching you how to jump off different places, how to fall and all that kind of stuff, physical training mostly for the first week. Then they started with the rest, especially jumping off different heights so you learn how to fall.

And we jumped off towers with harnesses on, on a cable. You jumped out a door and everything else like an airplane. You'd go down, and that would catch you, the cable. They taught you how to do that part of it, and how to land, and of course physical training all the time.

Then the last week of training they taught you how to fold 'chutes. When you got ready to jump you had to fold your own 'chute when you were going to jump. The last jump was a night jump. You had to fold your own 'chute if you jumped that night. Then after that night jump the next day you headed to camp. Up at Camp McCall we jumped every Monday morning.

What were you thinking when you're coming down on a parachute?

You had to check your equipment if you had something to get loose from quickly. There were a lot of things like that you had to know. You had whatever you needed. Different sections of the Army would have different weapons. You never packed anything really big. It would have to be strapped to you somewhere. Or those short carbines, they folded up short.

You couldn't jump with a lot of stuff. They experimented with different ways, too, with extra weight on a rope. You had a long rope, when you jumped out and were coming down you had to let it down. You could pack extra weight that way, ammunition or whatever.

Of course you'd be coming down faster with that extra weight on that long rope. It would hang way down there. As soon as it hit the ground you'd cut it loose. Then you'd ease up, you wouldn't hit as hard as if you had that on you. They had a lot of different ways like that.

I still would like to know what we were training for there; some special service. But it never got to that point in the war. They got a pretty good hold by the time they would have needed us. See, we were still training when they landed in Europe for the Normandy Invasion. So they pretty well had things in hand so they evidently didn't need us. Of course they were still fighting the Japanese so that's where they sent us instead of sending us to Europe.

Charlie Bowen in 1945 in Japan.
Photo courtesy of Charlene Storr.

What countries did you go to?

The Philippines and Japan. I was in the 11th Airborne Division. We joined them over there. That was in the Philippines. We were there I don't know how long when we heard the war ended. I can't remember how long it was.

Were you drafted?

Yeah. I was working at the Mare Navy Yard in Vallejo. I graduated in '41. I put in my application for work. When they came around to it I got different papers back and I got one from Mare Island Navy Yard. I decided to take that one because it was the better job.

The Philippines and Japan. I was in the 11th Airborne Division. We joined them over there.

The work that I learned down there at school was welding; I was a welder. So that's where I went to work. Then the war started in December right after we graduated. I'd already graduated but I went back to finish my training as a welder and wait for a job.

Charlene was born in '42; after I went to work at Mare Island that's when Audree and I decided to get married. She was working, when she left school she did the same as me, we both went back to further our training. She did secretarial and bookkeeping.

She got a job with the government service in Sales, Arizona. She went out to a reservation in Sales and worked there. She was working there while I was working at Mare Island. Of course the war came along then too. Anyway, we decided to get married and that's when we got married.

How many years did you go to Sherman Indian School?

Four years. I went there as a freshman then I graduated.

How did you decide to go to Sherman?

Well, just like all the rest of them there in Susanville, we all went to Fort Bidwell. All of us, the whole kaboodle. We went as first-graders. Mervin, me, there must have been others. I was born in Susanville.

What part of Susanville were you born?

That house is still there where I was born. You know where the old Lowry place is. My dad had that house built. I was born there. I don't know how long we lived there. It had a front porch and it's still that way, still the same thing. Every time we go by there we show the kids or whoever's with us. I had one brother and five sisters. I'm the youngest one.

Why do you still participate in the Bear Dance? What

does it mean to you?

I'm Indian enough to know what I want, what I need, and what I'm here for. I'm still Indian enough with my own thoughts as far as I'm concerned. I need the Bear Dance because I believe it.

What were your parent's names?

Charlie and Ida Bowen.

Were they born in Susanville?

No. My dad, the story is,it isn't written down, this is what he told us; in Pittville (near Susanville) there was a big village. This is way back during the Modoc War. The soldiers were killing all the Indians near Alturas; they tried to get rid of all the Indians.

Well, that's what they did to this village near Pittville. The story is that when the soldiers came and started slaughtering the people, some got away and somebody grabbed my dad. He was just a baby. They got away and headed toward Susanville, I guess, because that's where he ended up.

A lot of the people in that country were Pit River and they did the same thing, they escaped south. Probably your great-grandpa too, him and my dad are first cousins. That's how come I'm related to Leonard and Stan, we're second cousins.

How long did you live in Milford? You must have been pretty young.

Oh yeah, but I can remember. I was born in Susanville. We did live there at that time. It must have been a few years after that when we moved to Milford. The Lowry place is right there. I can remember I must have been four or five years old.

I remember Stanley shot himself through the fingers. He was down by the apple trees there. I can remember that like it happened five minutes ago. I don't remember how old I was when we all headed for Fort Bidwell. That was in '28. My brother didn't go. Leonard and Stanley were there.

How long did you stay at Bidwell?

One year.

Did you have to wear a uniform?

Yeah, I think so. Seem to me like we did. I think so.

Do you remember how many other kids were there? Were the boys separated from the girls?

Yeah, there were quite a few and they were separated just like at Sherman. I think one reason I went there was that all of us ran around together, played together. Mervin and I were in the same grade. Anyway, that was in '28. When we left up there in '28 my sister Esther went up there too. She never went to the boarding school. She went to school in town. She stayed with my sister. But Esther went to school downtown.

What did they have you learn when you were at the school?

Just like any other boarding school. You had to learn how to take care of your stuff. That was the first grade. Then we went back to Susanville. Shortly after that we moved to Portola. I stayed in Portola until I was a senior, that's when I went to Sherman.

How did you meet your wife Audree?

We were in the same grade.

Where was your mother from?

Genesee. (Genesee Valley is located next to Greenville). My mother's father was a Welshman, he came from Wales. My dad went to the Indian mission school in Greenville. There used to be a school there. So he was pretty much raised there.

We used to go to town once in a while, then we'd leave Milford, then when you get to those little hills where the dump is, when he went up the hill on this side, he'd always point back up to that little valley there. He said that's where he was raised, on a ranch up there. Evidently some white rancher took him.

That's evidently where the name Bowen came in. Of course no one knows for sure. But that's where he said he was raised as a baby. Then when he grew up they sent him to that school. I don't know how he got there. I remember looking at a museum in Taylorsville there and seeing his picture.

What year did you go in the service?

It had to have been '43, I think. They kind of suspected the war in '41. Then bang, everything was go. They had to build ships and repair ships not just at Mare Island, but Hunter's Point, Bethlehem Steel and all of them in the Bay Area there.

When the war started I thought I would be in the Navy, I was working for the Navy, might as well go in the Navy. They wouldn't let me go. I could have quit and walked off, but they wouldn't even let me go. Later, when things slacked off, that's when I was drafted.

What regiment were you in?

I was in the 187th Regiment of the 11th Airborne Division. When the war ended, it ended so darn fast. They had to have had this all planned. We were in kind of a permanent camp in the Philippines, in the jungle. There wasn't much action. Things were pretty much under control. Well, they had a screen up, and we were sitting there watching a picture show. It was sitting up on a little deck.

We were sitting on the ground watching that darn show. Pretty soon here came a guy just hollering, he jumped on that deck, he was going wild! Man! That really scared the life out of us! We just knew the Japanese were coming. Everybody jumped up, finally he calmed down and hollered 'The war is over, the war is over!'

They had heard that they had dropped that second bomb. It happened that morning; then later they got word from Japan that they surrendered. We were probably the first ones to hear the war was over. After that all happened, we went on back and went to sleep, if you could sleep! Not many people slept you know, the war was over!

The next morning this guy came around with a list of names on a piece of paper. He came over to me and said take your bag and report over to that tent over there. So I grabbed all my worldly belongings and went over there. A couple of other guys came over too. We were wondering what they wanted us for now that the war was over.

We sat on the ground and waited. Pretty soon two officers came over. They said get your bags, we have trucks over here, go load up, we're going to Japan. Just like that. The war just ended 10 minutes ago! We're going to Japan? We can't be going to Japan! We just got done shooting at them!

I just could not believe it. I don't know if half the Japanese soldiers knew the war was over and here we were going to Japan. What happened, that's why I say this must have been all planned beforehand by the big guys, we headed south to Manila. We went to an airstrip there and we loaded up and took off.

You know we just could not figure out what in the world was going on, because they never told us anything. Anyway, we flew in to the largest island of Japan. Here came other airplanes just like us; all of us paratroopers. They gathered us up and fed us. That night it started to rain, one of those terrible typhoon-type storms they have there.

It grounded us there for maybe three days. We did find out that what happened was the 11th Airborne had a pretty good reputation. The Japanese were afraid of paratroopers; they didn't want anything to do with paratroopers.

We were going straight to the Okinawa airstrip. That didn't sound very good because the war was barely over! They also told us we were designated as honor guards for General MacArthur. We were there to make sure, I don't know how we were to make sure, it was just a regiment of paratroopers in the middle of Japan, to stay there and make sure that the Japanese had surrendered. The officers said we were going to go to Yokohama. There was a big American hotel right there on the Tokyo Bay.

To become a paratrooper they had limits. You couldn't be over six foot, I'm six foot; you couldn't weigh over a 180 pounds, I weighed 180 pounds. That's the way it was with all of us, we were all the same size and we had the same baggy pants and the boots.

The 11th had quite a name over there; they were scared of paratroopers. Anway, that's how the paratroopers got that honor, or whatever you want to call it, but we were sent there as guards for MacArthur and that's what we did. When we got there, they put us on trucks and we headed down the road clear into Yokohama.

All along this road they had Japanese soldiers. They had rifles, I don't know if they had shells in the rifles, but they were standing with their backs to the road while we went by. I don't know if they were guarding to make sure we didn't get hurt or what, but we just knew somebody somewhere was going to get a last shot! That's what you think, you know.

That never happened?

Nothing happened like that, that I ever heard of. We went on in to Yokohama. We went in to that hotel, it was nice, but Yokohama and Tokyo were just practically leveled, burned out. Tokyo itself, the only place that really wasn't burnt out and leveled was a couple dozen streets, the main street and the big area where the Emperor's Palace was. But everything else was just burnt out. Yokohama was the same way.

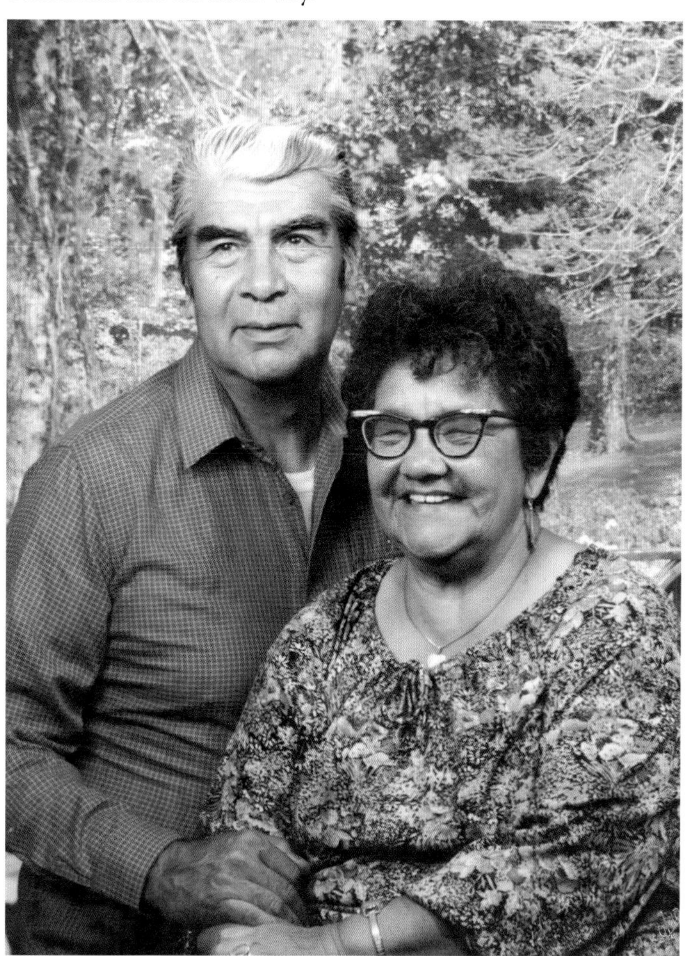

Charlie and Audree Bowen in 1983.
Photo courtesy of Charlene Storr.

Did you see people there?

Oh, a lot of people all over the place. But that sure was a scary situation, because we just knew there was someone mad enough to...you know there's millions of people there, you can't possibly watch everyone. You just knew that somewhere somebody is going to get a last shot at you. But I never heard of anything happening like that.

When you were in Japan how did the civilians act?

They just looked at you is all, just curiosity. The kids

would run around and look at you like that. Just curious. The Japanese had nothing, you know the general population, they had nothing. Just rags on. They had nothing. I don't know how they survived as well as they did. I don't even know what they ate.

So it was really an honor for you to be part of that guard?

I would think so, just for the division. They were scared of the paratroopers. That's why they wanted us all to be the same size, a really sharp looking outfit; which we were, actually. We stayed in that hotel, man, I can't remember.

You don't know what a feeling it is to be in something like that, it was really something. Just that part was unbelievable, as I think back about it.

We were there more than a week before anybody showed up. Finally, some ships came in because some personnel showed up. We stayed until MacArthur showed up about the second or third week we were there.

Then we stayed there for maybe four weeks in that hotel. Then we moved up on a hill, to what they called the American sector of Yokohama. It was where the Americans used to live, it had a fancy racetrack. All we had were rations to eat.

Did you ever see General MacArthur?

Oh yeah.

What was he like?

He was a real soldier, a real soldier, just what you would expect from a person like that. One night I happened to pull duty at the front door and he came by. He said hello while I saluted. All told, I think we were there in Yokohama for maybe a couple months then we were relieved.

Our outfit was clear up on the north end of Honshu Island, which is the main island of Japan. Sendai was the name of the town up there. That's where the 11th Airborne was situated. We stayed there a few months. Even up there where we were that town was leveled.

They really bombed Japan even before we went in. Then we moved from there to Hokkaido, the next island above the main island. They ferried us there. We were there a day, came back to Tokyo and then came home.

Did you come in to San Francisco?

No, when we left Tokyo we traveled the northern route right to Seattle. About halfway there we hit the most terrible storm ever. Man that was a storm! I knew we weren't going to make it! And that was a big boat. Up on the top deck you could look way down there at the dock. But that darn storm, the waves were breaking clear over the top of the ship. That boat just creaked and groaned, I just knew, the war's over and I'm going home and I'm never going to make it!

That was scary! Of course, I wasn't a sailor so there might have been worse storms than that, but man I would never like to have been in one. We finally made it back to Seattle. Coming in there on that boat, boy it felt good. I was overseas over a year. A little boat met us quite a ways out of Seattle.

There were dancing girls and music on there, man, our boat about tipped over; everybody rushed over to one side to look! We finally docked up in Seattle. Talk about a good feeling! You never know what it's like unless you go through something like that; the feelings you get, the situations you are in and out of. Oh man, it took a long time to get off that boat and step on the ground. Then down on the dock they had these push carts with cartons of milk.

Oh man, I bet I drank two gallons of milk. First glass of milk I had since we left the United States. Talk about a good feeling, people were dancing and singing and music was going. You don't know what a feeling it is to be in something like that, it was really something. Just that part was unbelievable, as I think back about it.

We stayed overnight there then we took a train to a camp near Marysville. Then I went over to San Francisco and had to wait all night to catch a bus back to Crescent City. I got to ride that bus right up to the house. I would have had to walk the five miles from Crescent to the house, but the driver dropped me off right where my road is. I had my pack and was walking to the house; nobody knew I was coming home.

Audree didn't know, she knew I was coming but had no idea when. So I walked to the house that's there now. I walked up there, the door was open, it was summertime. I just about got to the door and somebody looked out and saw me, and hollered.....boy, what a feeling. Going through life, you have so many different feelings, different things that happen to you, some good and some bad. But to get a good feeling like that…it's just, you know, it's just unbelievable. You never forget something like that. That was quite an experience of life.

If you could tell young kids today what it meant to you to go through that, what would you say?

Things today, everything changes. Something like that I don't think could ever happen again at a caliber of which it did. That was two world wars at one time, in Europe and the Pacific. Things are different, they're not going to send a bunch of guys over there and have them killed, there's a guy over here that will push a button and kill them. We're in a different world.

Even in my lifetime, I've lived probably three different lives, it's changed that drastically….life used to be fairly simple, but not anymore. You've still got to protect your family and your country, there's always somebody trying to take it. Younger generations actually… they'll never realize what they missed. Life used to be simple with no problems. The only problems were the ones you made.

You must be very proud of how you served your country.

Oh yeah, when somebody hits you, you've got to hit back, to protect yourself. You just had to protect yourself. This is kind of a good little story I'll tell you about. It was in Manila. I'm not positive but I think it was Clarke field there in Manila. When the Japanese took over that was where they put their prisoners. They had a prison camp there in Clarke field. Mostly civilians but there might have been some soldiers.

There was a civilian; he worked at a naval yard southwest of Manila. This man was taken prisoner when the Japanese first started taking over the islands there. He was a prisoner for years at Clarke Field. When the 11th Airborne went through there, they liberated that prison camp.

They jumped some 11th Airborne there and they liberated that place. In 1947 I went down to San Francisco. I thought I would get reinstated in the civil service. I wanted a job at Hunter's Point across from Candlestick. So I went into this office to apply for a job. When I went into the main office to apply for the job the boss was in there. He recognized me from Mare Island.

He said he recognized me; I didn't have to take the test for a job. He handled the paperwork and sent me down the hall to the local foreman. I walked in that office. There was a guy sitting at the desk there. I handed him my papers and he started looking at them. While he was looking at them he asked me if I was ever in the service, I said yes. He asked me what outfit I was with.

I was just standing there in front of his desk. I said I was in the 11th Airborne. The words '11th Airborne' barely came out of my mouth when that guy ran around the end of his table, ran up to me and just grabbed me. I was standing there; I didn't know what to do! It was like he just went wild. He just hugged me like that, and he hung on, he wouldn't let me go, he just hung on me!

I didn't know what to do, I didn't want to hit him; he wasn't hurting me, you know. The man was just hugging me, for quite a while there, until finally he came to. He said, 'I'm sorry, I just couldn't control myself.' He said, 'You're the first 11th Airborne man I've seen since Clarke Field.' He was a prisoner. It wasn't my company that liberated that camp, but I was the first one he'd seen since then. He was just so darn happy that he finally got to meet someone from the 11th Airborne!

Prior to their passing, Charlie and Audree Bowen raised nine children together. Charlie worked in the logging industry in northwestern California and southern Oregon the majority of his life. His family is very proud of his service to his country.

Wallace Griffin

1922-2004

Wally Griffin was of Yurok ancestry. He and Dee Rouse are siblings and she arranged for the two of us to meet at her house on June 18, 2002. Wally was a veteran of the U.S. Navy. He brought several pictures of his brothers in World War Two and a certificate recognizing his contribution during Operation Ivy, the super secret American mission to create and test the world's first hydrogen bomb.

I was born in 1922 in Arcata. I knew Charles Lindgren and I went to school with his brother Axel. I knew Wally Scott too; he and I played football together. I also ran track. My position in football was the running guard. I liked that position because you got to be in every play!

The war started after I got out of high school. After I graduated from high school I decided to join the Navy in 1941. I went to boot camp in San Diego and once I got out of boot camp I was coming home on leave and that's when the Japanese attacked Pearl Harbor. So I got home and turned around and came back to base.

Once I was there they sent us up to San Francisco and from there we took a ship to Honolulu. I was stationed there for quite a long time. From there I was sent back to the states and I went back to Philadelphia for new construction. That's when I got assigned to the aircraft carrier USS *Antietam.*

After we went on a shakedown tour, that's what they do with a ship, they go on a cruise to make sure everything's running all right, we went down through the Panama Canal and went to the south Pacific. When you're going through the Canal those carriers are built so they just barely fit through the locks.

When you're going through the locks you only had about this much room on both sides.

That's why the gunboats on the sides of carriers built on the East Coast couldn't be put on until they got to the West Coast, otherwise the ships would get hit coming through. When you're going through the locks you only had about this much room on both sides (he motions with his hands) and they used what they called donkeys on each side to help tow the ship into the lock.

Then they fill up the lock with water and let water out on the other side. One interesting thing about the Panama Canal is they don't have a pump anywhere in that place. It's gravity that makes the water flow from that lake that's part of the Canal. All those locks are filled with gravity-feed. There's no pumps anywhere.

Anyway, after we got our gunboats on we went out to the Pacific, but we got there too late for any action. Before the war was over they had the *Antietam* and another aircraft carrier sailing up and down the Pacific really fast so that the Japs would see us here one day and the next day we'd be 500 miles away.

That way the Japanese thought we had more carriers than we actually had! But then after the war was over we went to Japan and anchored in Tokyo Bay. They had subways over in Tokyo and they were still running all right. We used to get on a subway and the train would go way out somewhere.

Every time we would get out at a stop, the Japanese would see us and they would all step back and run. They were afraid of us. This ship went to China and we were in northern China for a long time. We were anchored there for quite a long time.

We did get a chance to go to Shanghai on leave, but the ship I was on was too large to get into port, so we would go on a destroyer. We would spend maybe 10 days and then come back. After that we went to Saipan, Formosa and Guam.

What were your duties on the carrier?

I was an engineer. I worked in the engine room. I was the chief machinist mate. I worked in the forward engine room. On the aircraft carrier you have four engines; two engines forward and two engines aft. Then you have four motors for each engine.

I think they said each engine had 75,000 horsepower. When we were out in the Pacific and we had planes taking off there had to be a certain amount of wind coming across the deck. On the *Antietam* we would get up to high speeds and we had a rooster tail flying really high on the back end! Boy, it would fly up, I used to go in the back and watch the water fly up way in the air! After we finally got back to the States is when I got my discharge. I got discharged in San Francisco.

Wally Griffin aboard the USS Saratoga *near Saipan in 1946.*
Photo courtesy of Wally Griffin.

When you took the test to become a chief what did you have to do?

They gave you all kinds of questions about the engine room. That's where you'd mostly be. They were also in the fire room. When I first made chief they transferred me out of the 'M' division. 'M' division took care of the engine. The 'A' division took care of other machinery, like the hydraulic pumps and the elevators. They transferred me to the 'A' division where I didn't know anything. You better believe I learned fast!

What type of planes did they have on the carrier?

They were all fighters. One time we had these fighter planes, I forget what they called them, but they didn't need much room to take off, they'd take off right from the deck. We had Corsairs and I don't remember the other ones.

When your carrier was at sea did you have escorts?

We had escorts all the time. We had destroyers and also cruisers. Those destroyers can't carry a lot of fuel. They'd have to come alongside the carrier to refuel all the time. On the carrier I was on we could fuel four destroyers at the same time if we had to.

One reason the destroyers liked to come and refuel was down in the galley they would make a lot of ice cream. When the ship was refueling they'd haul things back and forth; they hauled that ice cream over, so they always liked to get that ice cream for dessert!

What was the food like on the carrier?

The food was all right. When I made chief, the chiefs ate just like the officers did. In fact, on the ship I was on the chiefs ate even better than the officers. Every month every chief put in a dollar and part of it went to our main cook and the main baker.

So we always got the best pick of the food and the best cuts of the meat! You know, when we were out at sea for a long time the flour on board would get bugs in them, like weevils.

When everybody would eat bread they'd pick out all the dark spots because that was a weevil. One time in the chief quarters, there was a chief who was always crazy, we were having soup, and he picked out all the bugs and he had a big pile. Then he put them in his soup and ate the soup! He was always pulling something like that.

How many years were you in the service?

I was in for six years. We stayed on the West Coast;

we never did go back to the East Coast. We weren't in any battles because the major part of the war was over by the time we got out there.

Did you have some friends in the Navy?

Yes, in fact when I became a chief I came home on leave once and I brought a chief who was a buddy of mine. Once you became chief the guys were together all the time so you get to be buddy-buddy.

I remember one guy named Harvey from Texas, another one named Sydney from Florida and another friend who became chief the same time I did from Boston. He talked just like a Bostonian too! It didn't matter where the hell from the United States you came from, if you get to be friends, you get to be friends.

I bet they all wondered where Arcata was...

Oh yeah, some of these guys were from the South, and they don't have many trees in the South. I once told these guys, 'Where I live they have trees so big you can drive a car through them.' They said I was full of it!

So I wrote home to my mother and asked her to send some pictures. There was a place where they did have a tree where you could drive right through it and she bought a picture of it from the gift shop and sent it to me. I showed it to them and they couldn't believe it!

Did you ever listen to Tokyo Rose on the radio?

Oh yeah. She played music most of the time. Some of those guys that were married would listen to her say their wives were cheating on them, and she would pick on them. But mostly she'd play good American music.

Where were you when the war ended?

We were in the Pacific. When the war ended in Europe I was back in Philadelphia then. My brother Jimmy, he was on the East Coast all the time and his ship was in Boston. Anyway, I was in Philadelphia and I don't know what gave me the idea I was going to Boston to see Jimmy, but I made it to New York. That's when V-E Day happened, and I never did get out of New York!

The last thing I knew, these women were pulling me back off the train before it went to Boston! You never had to buy a drink. Even in Philadelphia while the war was still going on that was really a good liberty town.

When we hit Philly there were four guys in the group I was in. We didn't have much money but we went there anyway and had a hell of a time; people were buying us drinks and wanted to take you home for dinner! That was sure a good liberty town.

So you had two other brothers in the service?

Yes, Jimmy was my older brother and then Harry was my younger brother. He was in the Army. And my sister Dee was in too.

What was that like, having two brothers and a sister in the service?

Well, I felt pretty good about it. I used to think, they can't say the Griffin family wasn't patriotic! I remember when I came home on leave Dee was stationed at Camp Kohler. I took our sister and we decided we were going to visit Dee. I felt so funny; there wasn't another sailor within miles there!

Where did your brother James serve?

He was on a destroyer on the East Coast. He was a sonar man. Harry was in Europe the whole time. He never did talk too much about it; he had it pretty rough over there. He never said a damn word about it and he was in a lot of battles. James never talked about it either. James didn't come back over here after the war. He got married and stayed in Boston. He eventually opened up a TV repair shop.

Wally Griffin

Can you tell me what this certificate is about?

Oh, this is about Operation Ivy. The Navy had a civilian navy that I joined. It used to be part of the Army and they called it the Army Transport Service. They used it to transport soldiers all over. Some were troopships and others were passenger ships. I was on a combined passenger and troopship. They used our ship to haul the scientists to where they were going to have the hydrogen bomb explosion.

We were out there over four months before we came back. The scientists used our ship as a hotel. They'd go ashore and work then they'd come back at night, have dinner and sleep onboard. Before they exploded that bomb they gave us these real dark glasses to wear.

But since this was the first H-bomb they didn't know how bright the flash was going to be. They had us turn around when the bomb went off even though we had the glasses on. After the bomb exploded they told us we could take the glasses off and look.

Jesus, you should have seen that…way off on the horizon…and we were 32 miles away. There was a huge column of dust and I don't know what else just boiling straight up in the air. I don't know how wide that column was because we were so far away, but I noticed while looking up there was an Army bomber flying over. They were taking pictures. They warned us about the flash, but I guess they never thought about the noise and the shock wave that would come along after the explosion.

This will tell you how they improved the strength of the bomb, the first test we were 32 miles away, the next hydrogen bomb they exploded the ship had to be 200 miles away.

When that noise and that shock wave hit the ship it was just like being in an earthquake. That noise was so damn loud I think that caused me to lose part of my hearing. Before we were selected to go on the ship on this operation they had the FBI check out everyone. After we got down there, and after the bomb exploded, they didn't censor the mail that people were sending home!

So this one sailor on one of the ships sent a letter to a newspaper in San Jose and they had a picture of that bomb exploding. He drew a picture of the bomb exploding on the letter and boy there was a hell of a stink about that! All that security and they didn't check the mail!

When they exploded the bomb, was it already on the island, or did they drop it from a plane?

The bomb was on a tall scaffold. That's where it exploded. It wasn't on the ground; it was way up on the scaffold.

Did you ever see the bomb?

No. I imagine that bomb was taken over by a Navy ship. I never saw the bomb but those scientists had loose lips. They liked to talk about their work and they weren't supposed to. But they liked to sit around and talk and the officers ate in the same dining room where the civilians ate.

We'd sit and talk. That's when I found out it took an atomic bomb to explode a hydrogen bomb. You need something to cause that reaction. It takes explosives to explode an atomic bomb, and for a hydrogen bomb you have to have a lot of explosive power, so it took an atomic bomb to explode a hydrogen bomb. I found that out from the scientists.

What were your feelings like watching this bomb go off?

Well, I just couldn't believe it. You know, I found out later when they had built that scaffolding on that small island. That island wasn't really large. After they exploded that bomb that island wasn't there anymore. The whole island disintegrated.

You know what they found out later, all the birds in the area that were white survived, but all the dark color birds died. The heat or something killed them. That happened miles and miles away from the explosion.

That was the very first test of a hydrogen bomb. This will tell you how they improved the strength of the bomb, the first test we were 32 miles away, the next hydrogen bomb they exploded the ship had to be 200 miles away.

Before they exploded that second hydrogen bomb, and during the first one too, a lot of Japanese fishing ships were warned about it. But some were still out there. After the test they went back to shore and had to get rid of their ships because they were contaminated in the explosion.

That huge column was really something to see. Another thing, when that column was going up, what looked like steam started spreading out from horizon to horizon, then all of a sudden it was gone like that! But that noise was what really got me, and it just shook like an earthquake.

You're one of the very few people in this world that has actually witnessed the explosion of a hydrogen weapon, what do you feel about this type of weapon?

I remember thinking to myself, 'I hope they never have to use this bomb.' And the bomb I witnessed blowing up was small compared to the next one. Look how much damage they did with the atomic bombs in Japan, they wiped out almost whole cities. Luckily they never had to use the H-bomb. I'm glad they never had to use it. I don't even know why they developed it, to tell you the truth.

You mentioned the FBI did a background check, how did they talk to you?

They didn't talk to me, the reason I found out they had the FBI check me out was when I came home on leave after the test I saw this guy I went to school with. He asked me when I got out of jail. I asked him 'What?' He said the FBI was there checking me out. They went to the high school and talked with people who knew me. That's how I knew they checked me out.

Going back to during the war; did your ship ever dock on any of the islands in the Pacific, or did you dock at Hawaii?

We docked in Pearl Harbor. I've been there hundreds of times when I was in the Navy and later when I was in the merchant navy. I stayed there almost a year when we first went during the war. Every two weeks we'd go to Honolulu and back.

Did they have the memorial built yet?

No, it wasn't until after the war. After the war I saw it, they put the memorial right on top of the *Arizona*. The *Arizona* is still there, you know.

What were your feelings like when you first saw Pearl Harbor?

Well, when I first got there it was only about eight days after the Japs had attacked it. I couldn't believe all those ships lying on the bottom. They had an air base called Ford Island and then around it they had what was called Battleship Row. That's where they had all the battleships tied up. The *Arizona* was sunk, and all these other ships were sunk too...Jesus.

While I was stationed there I was assigned to a work party. They had raised the *California* and they had us working on that ship. They were going to fix it. There was mud everywhere and I thought they were never going to get it fixed, but by God they did. But one thing that made me sick, and this is the worst part, they were still taking the sailors out of the ships that were sunk and they put them in these big bags.

I happened to be on that damn work detail that day and they hauled the bodies in those bags behind the boat. They took them ashore to examine and try to find out who they were. They didn't have their dog tags. They took down the tattoos and everything to see if they could to find out who they were. And all those ships in the water were a sad sight to see.

Did it make you mad, did it make your crew mad to see that?

Well, yeah, it did. It was painful to see. You can't believe all those people that died in the attack, and so many were still in the ships, you know.

How old were you right then?

I was only 18 when I first saw those ships sitting on the bottom. I had just graduated from high school.

Has anybody ever asked you about what you did and what you saw during the war?

No, this is the first time. I've never had anybody approach me like this.

Wally Griffin worked in sawmills and the logging industry after the war for several decades. His family is very proud of his service to his country.

Leonard Lowry

1920-1999

My great-uncle Leonard Lowry is the most decorated Native American soldier in United States history. He is also one of the most decorated American soldiers in the country's history. He joined the service as a Private First Class and retired after almost 27 years in 1967 as a Lieutenant Colonel in the United States Army.

He served in World War Two in the Army's 32nd Infantry Division and saw combat as an officer in New

Leonard Lowry in 1946.
Photo courtesy of Virginia Aguilar.

Guinea and on the islands of Leyte and Luzon in the Philippines. He also saw combat during the Korean War as an officer in the Army's 2nd Infantry Division. Leonard was wounded a total of 22 times in combat.

Most of these wounds were inflicted in the throes of hand-to-hand combat. He spent time as a leadership instructor at Fort Benning, Georgia after the Korean War. Leonard also served at the Pentagon during part of the Vietnam War. He served in Australia, Japan, New Caldonia, South, Korea, Hawaii and Germany during the course of his service in the U.S. Army.

His list of honors is overwhelming. They include the Distinguished Service Cross for extraordinary heroism in action, two Silver Stars for gallantry in action, two Bronze Stars for heroic achievement in action, five Purple Hearts for wounds incurred in action, the Legion of Merit, the Army Commendation Medal, the Infantry Combat Badge with star, the U.S. Presidential Unit Citation with Oak Leaf Cluster, the Republic of The Philippines Unit Citation, the World War Two Victory Medal, the American Campaign Medal, the Good Conduct Medal, the American Defense Service Medal, the Asiatic-Pacific Campaign Medal with three stars, the Japan Occupation Medal, the Philippine Liberation Medal with two stars, the Philippine Independence Medal, the Armed Forces Reserve Medal, the National Defense Service Medal with star, the United Nations Service Medal, the Republic of Korea Unit Citation and the Korean Campaign Medal with five stars.

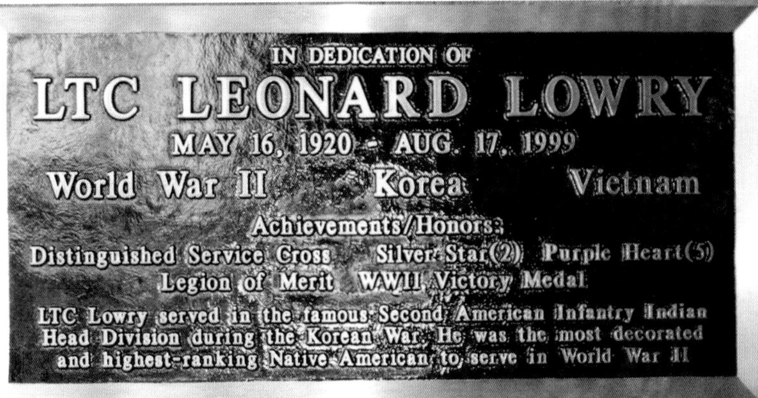

The name plate to the headquarters building at the Sierra Army Depot in Herlong, California. The building was named after Leonard in a special Army ceremony held at the base on April 4, 2004. Leonard was the most decorated and highest-ranking Native American from the state of California to serve during World War Two. Photo by Lynn Goddard, Official Photographer for the Sierra Army Depot.
Used with permission.

Leonard was nominated for the nation's highest decoration, the Medal of Honor, but did not receive it. He always told the family that those men who nominated him ended up either killed in action or missing in action, therefore the award could not be given. He was wounded by enemy rifle or machine-gun fire in New Guinea, in Leyte and once at Luzon. He was also wounded by 14 grenade fragments in a fight in Luzon. The fragments shattered his wrist and landed up and down his back, arms and legs. They also knocked out his front teeth.

In July of 1944 near Afua, New Guinea First Lieutenant Lowry was awarded his first Silver Star for gallantry in action. His force of 500 men had been halted and pinned down by heavy machine gun fire. He personally led a small party and assaulted the machine gun position, allowing the rest of the column to continue its advance. They then rejoined the main body and he led it to the successful completion of its mission.

This was the official statement given by the Army for this medal. It doesn't capture the emotions, the anger and the fear, that Leonard must have felt while leading men into harm's way. It doesn't capture the horrors of men killing other men with bullets and bayonets and knives. It doesn't capture the pain he must have felt to know that men under his command died during this offensive. It does recognize that First Lieutenant Lowry would be an exemplary combat officer and soldier.

Leonard was a front-line officer who led by example. I have several letters written by men under his command that describe him as the bravest soldier they'd ever encountered. He was calm under fire and decisive in giving direction. He obviously had that panache and élan that soldiers yearn for in their officers.

On November 30 of 1944 Leonard's Company I along with other companies of the Third Battalion was ordered to attack Hill 400 near Limon, Leyte in the Philippine Islands. The hill was the key defensive position of the Japanese First Imperial Division. Located in the upper Ormoc Valley, Hill 400 was part of the enemy's supposedly impregnable Yamashita Line; the fall of this position would contribute to the final collapse of Japanese resistance on Leyte.

There was dense undergrowth and irregular slopes that hindered the attack. A final barren stretch of 200 yards lay between the Americans and the crest of the hill. This stretch of ground offered no concealment for the troops. They faced artillery, machine guns, mortars and small arms over eight grueling days of fighting. Leonard and his men faced numerous banzai charges that at times knocked them back. But they continued to struggle and eventually overtook the crest in vicious hand-to-hand fighting. The battle was officially over, appropriately enough, on December 7, 1944.

The Third Battalion, 127th Infantry Regiment was cited for outstanding performance of duty in action against the enemy in honor of this battle. This is what the official record states. On the bottom of his copy of this record, my great-uncle Leonard wrote 'Toughest battle I was ever in.'

These are a few of the many recorded and unrecorded battles Leonard took part in. Leonard killed many men up close and personal. He kept the sabers of some Japanese officers he bested in combat during World War Two. In the early 1960s he gave them back to the officer's families in a ceremony at the Presidio in San Francisco where he served as a plans and operations officer.

Leonard was part of the Army's Second Infantry Division in 1949 and was immediately deployed to Korea in 1950 when hostilities broke out. The 'Indian Head'

Division saw vicious hand-to-hand fighting against North Korean forces in the fall of 1950. When the Chinese entered the war the division's forces took to the offensive in the battles of Chipyong-ni and Wonju. It was during this time that Leonard was awarded with the United States military's second-highest award for extraordinary heroism. The citation reads:

'The Distinguished Service Cross is presented to Leonard Lowry, Major (Infantry), U.S. Army, for extraordinary heroism in connection with military operations against an armed enemy of the United Nations while serving as Commanding Officer of Company C, 1st Battalion, 38th Infantry Regiment, 2nd Infantry Division. Major Lowry distinguished himself by extraordinary heroism in action against enemy aggressor forces in the vicinity of Hoengsong, Korea, on 12 February 1951.

On that date, Company C had the mission of covering the withdrawal of a road-bound artillery battalion along a road paralleled by enemy- infested hills and ridges. After ten consecutive hours of heavy fighting, during which Major Lowry heroically led his men in knocking out several enemy roadblocks designed to trap the battalion, the column reached the regimental assembly area and joined the 3d Battalion.

As the two battalions began assembling and reorganizing, a strong enemy force occupying positions on a ridge adjacent to the assembly area placed a heavy barrage of mortar and automatic-weapons fire on the friendly troops, inflicting numerous casualties. Quickly organizing a group of men from his company, Major Lowry personally led them in an assault on the nearest enemy held hill and succeeded in killing the enemy occupying it. Although seriously wounded during this engagement, he continued to lead his men in assaults on the others hills in the area until the entire ridge had been cleared of hostile forces.'

Headquarters, Eighth U.S. Army, Korea: General Orders No. 419 (June 10, 1951)

The severe wound Leonard incurred was a shot through the abdomen. He was shipped to a hospital in Japan and spent months recovering. He was then assigned to various posts in America and Germany through the end of the Korean War.

I remember my great-uncle as a tall man with a baritone voice. He certainly had a walk that defined him as a soldier. Before the war Leonard won the Pacific Northwest Golden Gloves Championship in Seattle. He was the only Native boxer on the team that traveled to the fight.

Leonard won boxing matches throughout California and in Nevada in the 1930s and won a 10-state tournament in his weight division in Reno, Nevada. When Leonard and my grandfather Stanley were in the Army's Seventh Infantry Division Leonard won the Seventh Infantry Heavyweight Boxing Championship in early 1941. His plans to become a professional boxer were halted due to the war.

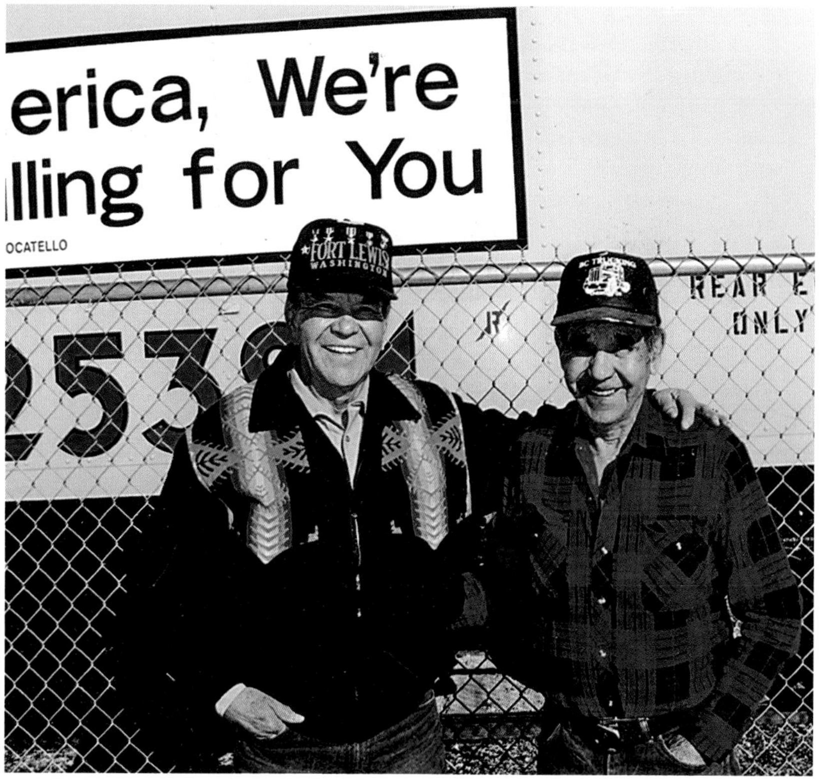

Brothers and buddies. Leonard and Stanley Lowry in 1998.
Photo courtesy of Ike Lowry.

Leonard spoke three Indian languages and taught Native American history at Lassen Community College and Feather River Community College in northern California after he retired from the service. He was very involved in Native American health and education programs for many years. When he spoke people usually listened with respect.

Leonard also suffered greatly from what he saw and did in combat in World War Two and Korea. Post-traumatic stress disorder as a medical diagnosis did not exist for his generation of combat soldiers. Like many men who lived through combat, Leonard drank alcohol to mask the pain and blur the memories.

I remember some of the times when my great-uncle Leonard drank. He became a different person, an angry and mean person who would sometime say terrible things to friends and family. The episodes would pass, but each time would hurt his body more. They also took a toll on our family as a whole. This type of hurt is part of the continual sacrifice for this country that not only soldiers, Marines, airmen and sailors give, but their families also give.

Leonard passed away in 1999. His passing helped spur me to start this book. Many of the men I interviewed shared their admiration for his accomplishments in the military. They believe, and I do as well, that Leonard deserves to be accorded with the Medal of Honor for his actions in combat as a member of the United States military. No California Native American has ever received the Medal of Honor.

Chag Lowry

Leonard (at left) and Stanley Lowry visited their younger sister Virginia at the Sherman Indian Boarding School while on leave in 1943.
Photo courtesy of Virginia Aguilar.

In Memoriam

Leroy Doolittle ca. 1942-3
Photo courtesy of Marjorie Colegrove.

Leroy Doolittle

There were seven of us in the family. Leroy was the oldest, Reatus was in the middle and Robert was the youngest. We were raised right here in Hoopa. Our father's name was Reatus and he was Indian from the Covello area and our mother was Sophie Campbell Doolittle, and she was full-blooded Hupa Indian.

We lost our mother when I was 10. She had worked in the bakery at the Hoopa boarding school. My dad worked on the telephone system here in Hoopa when we were young. We all went to the boarding school in Hoopa until the eighth grade.

Our uncle Henry Campbell served in the Navy in World War One. When he came back he talked to his nephews and all of us. Leroy and Reatus were drafted by the Army when World War Two broke out. Robert volunteered.

Leroy had told me, 'The reason I'm going is I want to keep the war from coming over here onto our reservation.' Leroy served in Italy. He stayed with an Italian family when he was on furlough. Leroy drove a tank and was hit in action.

When his tank was hit it caught on fire. He told me, 'There were three or four of us in there. Two of us went out. When I went in to get my partner I got burned. I got burned when I went back in to save him but I couldn't leave him in there.'

He got a Purple Heart for that. He was scarred for life from those burns. He looked terrible when he came back. We went to Eureka to meet him. When I saw him I didn't let the tears come although they were there. He was such a good sport about it. He didn't sit around and cry about it. He came back natural, just joking and everything. He went through several operations because of those burns.

Robert had served in the Navy. He had been adopted by May Jackson when he was little and had taken the Jackson last name. I think he served in the Pacific but was discharged because of a heart condition.

I don't remember where Reatus served but he lost an arm in the service; I know more about Leroy because we were really close buddies. They weren't guys to brag. They wanted to forget it because war wasn't good. I'm proud of my brothers.

Ruby Jarnaghan

Jack Mattz ca. 1942-3.
Photo courtesy of Lavina Bowers.

Jack Mattz

My brother Jack Edwin Mattz was born in 1921 to the late Emery and Geneva Mattz. He was of Yurok, Karuk and Tolowa ancestry. He graduated from Del Norte High School where he was a great athlete. Jack was the oldest of 10 children and was always a loving and wonderful son and brother.

The last time the family saw him he was home on leave during the war. Our family and friends came to visit; there was a lot of food and fun. The folks were very proud of Jack. Jack was a paratrooper of the 101st Airborne Division and was killed in action during Operation Market-Garden in Holland.

He posthumously received the Bronze Star and a Purple Heart for his bravery and courage on the day he died. Several years after his death one of the men in his company came to the house and told my parents what had happened the day he died.

Jack had gone before the other troops toward an enemy dugout and killed several enemy soldiers with his machine gun. When his ammunition ran out he then used hand grenades to destroy the dugout. Jack's fellow soldier told mom and dad that he saw Jack killed not two hours later.

My parents were very thankful to hear about their oldest son; it made them happy to hear about Jack but they also grew very sad at the same time. Jack was a paratrooper like many of the Indian boys that went to war; they made extra money for this dangerous duty. Jack often sent money home for the family while he was away. Jack did not marry. He always remained in the family's heart as their "hero." He was a handsome man and very caring to his family. He will always be remembered and missed.

Lavina Bowers

Harvey McCardie ca. 1942-3.
Photo courtesy of Ruth McCardie.

Harvey McCardie

I was born in Germany in Darmstadt, which is between Frankfurt and Heidelberg, in 1928. My father's name was Friedrich Boensel and my mother's name was Johanne. My father was a Social Democrat. I went to elementary school in the village of Arheilgen. We were aware that there was a new government even as little kids because we saw the storm troopers marching. In 1938 I had to join the Hitler Youth. You automatically belonged to the Hitler Youth at age 10. Your family wouldn't have dared not to have you join.

When you joined the Hitler Youth we had to say an oath. The oath was 'We pledge allegiance to our *Fuehrer* and to the Third Reich. I promise at all times to do my duty to my *Fuehrer* Adolf Hitler, my country and my flag.' We sang a song after we did the pledge that went like this- 'Our flag marches on before us. Our flag is the new order. Our flag takes us into eternity. Our flag means more to us than death.' In other words, we were taught to die as 10 year olds for Adolf Hitler. I went to high school until I was 16 and then started my training to be a preschool teacher. We had a class in racial science. That was a class where we learned that different races have different shaped heads and that we were the best there was.

There was no talk about Jews in class, the only thing I remember as a little girl was there were Jewish children in class. Then all of a sudden they were gone. I asked my teacher where my friend Sara was, and she said they went away to live by themselves. We never saw them again, of course.

I met my first husband Elden Justus after the war; he was from America, and we were married and had two children, my son Jack and daughter Rose. We came to the U.S. in 1950. He was assigned to Korea and was killed in action in December of 1950.

I met Harvey McCardie in 1952. I met him in my own apartment because he came with another girl! I liked that he had been in the invasion of Europe. He knew my country because he was stationed there for a while. We had a connection. He left the Army in November of '45. He had served with the Third Army. He crossed the Rhine River by Worms not far from my home! He was a gunner in a Sherman tank. He told me that in Metz he had stepped out of the tank and was shot in the leg and hand. He spent three months in the hospital and came back in time to cross the Rhine. Harvey knew that the war was something that had to be done. He did what he had to do. We went to Germany in 1988 and we followed the route he had come through. It is now called "The Romantic Route." Harvey said it didn't look very romantic when he first went through it!

Harvey was with a company that went through the Dachau concentration camp. He said it was very, very sad and that the people put their arms around the soldiers and cried. They were finally free. The rest of my country was also saved by the Allies.

We moved to Hoopa when we were married so I've been here 51 years. I became the Hoopa High School librarian in 1970. We were married 42 years when Harvey passed away. He was an outstanding step-father. He raised my daughter and son like they were his own and he loved his granddaughters. He was an outstanding man.

Ruth McCardie

Edwin Dixon Smith, Sr. ca. 1951-4.

Edwin Dixon Smith, Sr.

Our father's name is Edwin Dixon Smith, Sr. He was born in Round Valley in Covelo in 1931. His mother passed away when he was nine months old. His father's name was Burnam Smith. They were of Pomo, Wailaki, Yuki, Koncow Maidu and Nomalaki ancestry. He had eight brothers and one sister.

Our dad was the baby of the family. He went to the Stewart Indian Boarding School near Carson City, Nevada when he was a young boy, and then went to the Santa Rosa Junior High and High Schools until age 17. He quit school to join the Marine Corps. He served during the Korean War. His brother Richard was in the Marine Corps during World War Two. Richard served at Guadalcanal. Richard came down with yellow fever during his time in the service.

Our father served with the "Black Sheep Squadron," which was a Marine Corps fighter squadron that was commissioned during World War Two. He went through basic training down in San Diego. He was an aircraft mechanic and worked on F-4 Corsairs during his time in the Marine Corps. He served on an aircraft carrier during the Korean War. This is often called the 'Forgotten War.' He served four years. He told the family he went in as a boy and came out as a man. It's possible he joined the Marines because his brother Richard had been in World War Two.

Our first cousin Marianne Smith was in the Marine Corps during the early 1980s and our first cousin Lionel Carroll, Jr. was in the Marine Corps during the late 1970s. Edwin served in the Marine Corps for four years, from 1983 to 1987. He joined the Marine Corps because our dad did. We're very proud of our father's service in the Marine Corps. We're also very proud of our uncle's service in the Marines during World War Two.

Edwin Smith and Jo Smith

Stanley Wilder, Sr. ca. 1942-3.
Photo courtesy of George Wilder.

Stanley Wilder, Sr.

My father Stanley Martin Wilder, Sr. was born to Lillian Ferris-Wilder and Albert Wilder, Sr. in Orleans, Ca in November of 1921. His father Albert was Karuk and his mother Lillian was Yurok. He attended elementary school in Orleans and graduated from the Chemawa Indian Boarding School in Oregon.

He volunteered for the service in 1942 and was sent to Fort Ord and Camp Roberts in California, then on to Camp Hood in Texas. My father's unit was Recon Company, Second Platoon, 603rd Tank Destroyer Battalion, Sixth Armored Division, which was part of the Third Army commanded by General George S. Patton, Sr.

The 603rd Tank Destroyer Battalion left New York aboard the *Queen Mary* and arrived in Glasgow, Scotland, then on to Sherborne, England via train. The 603rd then left for Utah Beach and moved through France, Belgium and Luxembourg before crossing the Rhine River in Germany. Their motto was "Seek, Strike, Destroy."

Sergeant Stanley Wilder earned this nation's third-highest award for gallantry in action at the end of the Battle of the Bulge. His citation reads:

'By direction of the President of the United States, the Silver Star has been awarded to Sergeant Stanley M. Wilder of the U.S. Army for gallantry in action in Belgium on February 6, 1945.

Sgt. Wilder was on a mission to locate a suitable crossing of a river; Sgt. Wilder's patrol came into cross-fire from the enemy. He stood his ground and returned fire, knocking out one machine-gun nest and enabled his patrol to take cover, and then he silenced the second machine-gun nest. Sgt. Wilder's gallant action prevented serious casualties to his patrol and enabled him to successfully complete his assigned mission.'

My father joined the Army because he was patriotic and because so many of his family had served or were serving their county in the military. His uncles George Ferris and Benjamin Wilder were both veterans of World War One. His brother Leroy Wilder was a radio operator and waist-gunner on a B-17 and was killed in action over Italy in 1943. Another brother, Harry Wilder, served with the Marines in the Pacific against the Japanese. His first cousin Wilfred Ferris, Sr. was an Army Ranger who assaulted the cliffs on Omaha Beach on D-Day.

My father was married to Anne Clarke of Frazer, Montana. They had four children: Dewayne, Lillian, George and Stanley Jr. My father passed away in December of 1968. My father and the rest of my family's proud and patriotic military service had a huge impact on my life, and influenced me to volunteer for service in the U.S. Army during the Vietnam War.

George Wilder

Lawrence Reed
Photo courtesy of Sandra Lowry.

Lawrence Reed

My husband Lawrence Reed was a wonderful husband and father that loved his family very much. He worked hard all his life to support us.

Lawrence was born at Pecwan in 1925 to Sophie Reed and lived on Pecwan Hill with his grandmother Nellie along with his brother Joseph and sister Nellie. He attended the Sherman Institute for a while then he enlisted in the service with the Army at a young age in 1943. He served in the Philippines as a member of the 149th Infantry Regiment. He fought at Luzon and served as a scout for his company.

He earned a Bronze Star and the Combat Infantryman Badge during his time in the Pacific. Like many of his men he came down with malaria and it stayed with him even after he returned home. He came home in 1946.

He worked as a logger for many years and also worked in construction. He helped build Martin's Ferry Bridge. He also worked in Hoopa and in Burney Falls. Lawrence was also a beautiful mechanic, and everybody came to him to work on their cars. His brother Joseph also served in the Army during the war.

He was my friend and husband, and I sure miss him. We were married for over 50 years. We had seven children and now have 106 grandchildren, great-grandchildren and great-great grandchildren. The family is all over the country.

Dee Reed

Gus Riecke, Jr. ca. 1942-3
Photo courtesy of Jeanne Riecke.

Gus Riecke

Our uncle Gus Riecke was the son of August and Fanny Gaston Riecke of Trinidad, California. He was born in Blue Lake, California on November 26, 1917. His father was a carpenter who worked on local bridge projects, and his mother came from the Yurok village of Cautep along the Klamath River.

He had two older brothers, Fred and Leslie, and an older sister named Gertie. He attended the Indian School on the Hoopa Reservation and also attended the Chemawa Indian School in Oregon along with his brother Leslie. Gus was inducted into the Army Air Corps on March 11, 1942 at the Presidio in Monterey during World War Two.

Gus began training at Blythe, California and ended his third phase in Peyote, Texas. He was a member of Crew 30. On May 10th of 1943 he was assigned to a B-17F known as the "Jackie Ellen" of the Eighth Air Force, 367th Heavy Bombardment Squadron, 306th Bomber Group. Also known as the "Clay Pigeons" his squadron was based in Thurleigh, England.

At about 1400 hours on October 14, 1943, while on the way to bomb ball-bearing factories in Schweinfurt, Germany on Mission 115, his formation was hit by dozens of enemy fighters and received heavy damage to the plane's horizontal fuselage. The plane went down and only one member of the crew survived; Technical Sergeant Joseph Bocelli, who was the radio operator.

Now known in World War Two history as "Black Thursday", over 70 B-17 bombers were shot down or severely damaged and over 600 crew members died or were captured as prisoners on this mission. Gus' dog tags and remains were found in a Belgian village cemetery in 1950. He was re-interred in Arcata's Greenwood cemetery near other Yurok veterans of World War Two.

Jeanne Riecke and Paul Joseph Riecke

In Remembrance

The following is a partial list of Northern California Indian veterans of World War Two who have passed away since the end of the war. If you are a family member of a California Native American veteran of World War Two and would like to include their photo, name and tribal affiliation to this list for a future book printing please email at ova@humboldt1.com or write to Post Office Box 185, Eureka, California 95501.

Robert 'Bob' Aguilar
(Paiute)
United States Navy

Ernie M. Alton, Jr.
(Tolowa)
United States Navy
Killed in action aboard the USS *Arizona* on December 7, 1941.

J. Benjamin Bristol
(Hupa)
United States Army
Killed in action in Italy.

George Dowd
(Yurok)
United States Army

Johnny Evans (Pit River/Shoshone)
United States Army

Wilfred Ferris
(Yurok)
United States Army

James Griffin
(Yurok)
United States Navy

Harry Griffin
(Yurok)
United States Army

Archie Hess
(Pit River)
United States Navy

Orrell Hillman
(Karuk)
United States Army

Henry Hodge
(Yurok)
Unites States Navy

James Hodge
(Yurok)
United States Army

Otto Hodge
(Yurok)
Killed in action in Italy.

Edna Pearch Ichelson
(Karuk)
United States Navy
Women Accepted for Volunteer Emergency Service (WAVES)

Ed Jackson
(Maidu/Pit River)
United States Marine Corps

Peter Jackson
(Hupa)
United States Army Air Corps

Marie Jake
(Yurok)
United States Army Women's Army Corps

Eugene Lewis
(Yurok)
United States Marine Corps
Killed in action on Iwo Jima.

Fred Maddux
(Karuk)
United States Army

Allen McCovey
(Yurok)
United States Army

Howard McCovey
(Yurok)
United States Army

Stanley McCovey
(Yurok)
United States Navy

Bennett Moore
(Yurok)
United States Army
Killed in action on New Guinea.

Edward Moore
(Yurok)
United States Navy

Grover Moore
(Yurok)
United States Army

Romaldo Natt
(Yurok)
United States Army
Killed in action in Germany.

Clyde Northrup
(Paiute/Maidu)
United States Army

Herbert O'Neill
(Yurok)
United States Army

Floyd Pilgrim
(Yurok)
United States Army
Killed in action in France.

Leonard Preston
(Pit River/Paiute)
United States Navy

William Quimby, Jr.
(Hupa)
United States Navy

Grover Reed
(Yurok)
United States Army

Joseph Reed
(Yurok)
United States Army

Baron Risling
(Yurok/Karuk/Hupa)
Killed in action in Texas.

Leslie Risling
(Yurok/Karuk/Hupa)
United States Army

Paul Stone
(Paiute)
United States Army
Killed in action on Okinawa.

Julius Tripp
(Karuk)
United States Navy

Glen Wasson
(Paiute/Shoshone)
United States Marine Corps

Leroy Wilder
(Karuk)
United States Army Air Corps
Killed in action over Western Europe.

Donald Wilson
(Hupa)
United States Army
Killed in action in Italy.

If you are a family member of a veteran you can submit Standard Form 180 and write to the National Personnel Records Service in St. Louis to request a copy of their personnel or medical records. To access the Standard Form 180 go to this link on the Internet: www.archives.gov.

National Personnel Records Center
Military Personnel Records
9700 Page Avenue
St. Louis, MO 63132-5100
Contact Information
Telephone: 314-801-0800
E-mail: MPR.center@nara.gov *
Status Check: mprstatus@nara.gov *
Fax: 314 801-9195

This information was retrieved from www.archives.gov/st-louis/military-personnel/index.html on 11-19-06.

"No Answer"

At the Indian Veterans' Reunions the names of all present veterans are put into this soldier's helmet. When a person's name is called they say "Present," and people will smile and greet them. When the name of a recently deceased veteran is called, there is a moment of silence, then a veteran replies, in grave dignity, "No answer." The photo in the background is of Thomas Tucker.

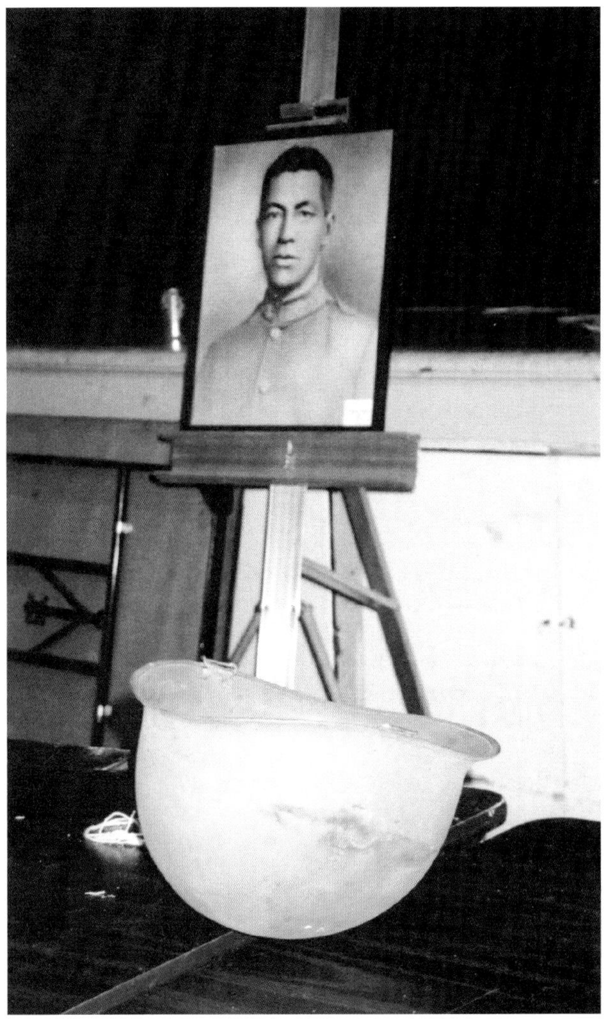

Epilogue

I always had a fascination with World War Two. I began reading books about it in the third grade. Perhaps this was a subconscious reaction to my own families' involvement in the war, I don't know. I do remember that my grandfather Stan Lowry gave me a book when I was in the seventh grade. It was the only book he ever gave me and it was titled *Inside the Third Reich* by Albert Speer. He said I could learn some history from it. So I took it home and started reading.

Speer was Hitler's favorite architect and he was the Reich's Minister of Armaments in the later part of the war. After the war he was sentenced to prison for several decades and it was there he reflected on the crimes of Hitler's regime and wrote his book. I continued to read more about the war as I grew older.

Andrew Jackson (Mountain Maidu/Pit River) during a Memorial Day service in 2001 at the Susanville Pioneer Cemetery in Susanville, California. Mr. Jackson is a decorated combat veteran of the Korean War. He helped found the Susanville Indian Veterans' Reunions and has been in charge of organizing them for many years.
Mr. Jackson worked for the Forest Service for several decades after the Korean War. He has attended countless services for World War Two, Korean and Vietnam-era Marines, soldiers, sailors and airmen. Andrew Jackson encouraged me to write this book. I thank him for always being there for our Native American service men and women.

The only histories I found about Native Americans in the war were of the Navajo Code Talkers and the story about Ira Hayes. I still don't believe the Code Talkers have received their full due. The code they designed while serving in the Marine Corps helped win the Pacific War for the United States and the Allies.

On Iwo Jima alone Code Talkers successfully relayed over 800 messages. The Navajo Code Talker's successful use of their code to transmit vital intelligence and instructions during combat literally saved the lives of tens of thousands, perhaps hundreds of thousands, of American men in the Pacific. Imagine how many more American Marines, soldiers and sailors would have died during those island battles without this code. Allied forces were able to break both Japanese and German codes throughout the war and this was a crucial part of their success.

The Navajo Code was the only unbreakable code used in the war. But the Code Talkers were not the only Native people who served in the conflict. There were Native people from dozens of Tribes across the country. There were also Native people from Tribes in Canada that fought in the Canadian forces for the Allies. Indigenous people from around the world fought and died for the Allied cause.

The only story I ever read about a Native American in World War One or in World War Two was of Ira Hayes. He was a Pima Indian from Arizona who helped raise the United States flag along with other Marines during the battle at Iwo Jima. Their efforts were captured on camera and the image is the most famous of the war. He was hailed as a hero. He and others flag raisers were sent on a bond tour and treated as celebrities. Ira suffered a lot during and after the war and became an alcoholic. He ended up dying after a night of heavy drinking in the 1950s.

Our people had to endure a lot, and many veterans drank because of what they saw or because of what they had to do. But Ira Hayes does not represent every Native American soldier. He was just one person thrust into an extraordinary role. My people struggled and survived as best they could in an often racist society.

Yes, many Native veterans drank when they came home, and this in turn affected their relationships with their wives, their children, and their grandchildren. Add the stress of returning from combat to the stress of being Native in a racist society and it's easy to see why this happened. This is part of the sacrifice our Native people gave to this country. But many veterans from all backgrounds drank after the war. There was no such thing as post-traumatic stress disorder for these veterans. There were no counseling programs. They were simply expected to rejoin society and cope.

Exactly what type of life did returning Native veterans face when they came home to America? That's a question that definitely deserves more scholarship. Here in northern California a booming timber industry meant that many found employment in the woods. This dangerous work was socially acceptable for Native men.

The Reservation and Rancheria systems where many of these men lived soon came under attack. The United States carried out one of its most destructive policies regarding Native rights eight years after World War Two ended. It was a policy called termination and it lasted from 1953 to 1962. Termination meant that Tribes across the country lost their federal trust status. Tribes now had to try to fight in court to protect their water, mineral, health, education, and housing rights.

In 1958 in California 48 different Rancherias were terminated. This included several in northern California. It took several decades of hard political fighting by Native people before some Rancherias and Tribes were reinstated with federal trust status. During that time timber and mineral companies stripped a lot of natural resources out of northern California indigenous lands. It's safe to say this betrayal of trust led to bitterness among Native people from northern California.

Writing about Native history and culture is difficult because events are always interlocked. Part of my awe regarding these veterans comes from the fact that during the California Gold Rush so many indigenous people were murdered. They didn't die of disease and they weren't moved to another state, they were killed. The California State government and the United States federal government paid bounty hunters and militia members to murder Native people throughout California. This is fact. This genocide occurred among the grandparents and parents of these World War Two veterans. For them to then go out and risk their lives, and many gave their lives, for this country is astonishing to me. I still can't believe they did this, but perhaps that is due to my upbringing.

I was born in 1974 and raised right after the Vietnam War ended. I believe many in my generation were taught to question the government and the military. It was different in 1941. America had helped win World War One only 27 years prior. Often I would be looking through photographs with a veteran and they would show me a picture of a family member who served in the First World War. I'm sure those family veterans made a big impression on young Native people who then served in World War Two. So I tried my best not to interject my own bias into this book. I tried to stay objective and I did learn that it was a different time and a different value system during World War Two for many Native people. They were, and are, patriots and I respect that.

Most of these veterans attended boarding schools when they were young. There isn't much written information available about California's Indian boarding schools or their drastic effects on our indigenous cultures. These boarding schools changed everything from our language to our diets. These places represented an evil that most people can't understand. The idea that you can force little kids to assimilate into another culture is sickening. These were small, defenseless children.

To take away a person's childhood and their education must be two of the worst sins imaginable, and that is exactly what these places attempted to do. In many cases they succeeded, but there were those who resisted by running away or secretly remembering their native language and customs.

You'll notice that some of these men and women shared good and bad memories of their times at these places. They attended at a time of extreme change within the boarding schools in the 1930s when attempts were made to clean up the system. The military-style regimen at these schools in the late 1930s even helped many men when they attended boot camp.

They were used to being away from home and listening to people who yelled at them. I have to smile at that because these stories show how our people are strong and adaptable. Native Americans have a very different view of the U.S. public education system due to this history of boarding schools. Again, these places were ruled by terror and fear, and cultural knowledge was lost through the generations that attended.

There has been a tremendous amount of positive social change that's occurred here in northern California since the time of the boarding schools and termination. Many of these veterans and former riveters have helped revitalize our Native languages and our religious ceremonies. They've served on tribal councils, health boards and education committees. They have become a generation of elders and historians that our communities rely on for guidance.

Why did I include my questions within the interviews? In every book I've ever read regarding Native American history and culture I've never come across an author who has included the questions they might have asked to gain information about a tribe. This omission is quite dangerous, in my opinion. It allows authors and scholars to present their interpretations of history and their interpretations of culture. Notice I stated they've never included the questions they might have asked. How do we know if they asked questions at all?

If you can't view the questions or read about the methods that a person uses to glean information regarding an indigenous culture, how can you be sure they are presenting the truth, and not just their own perspective? This has been the case for too long within the field of Native American Studies. Go back and read any books you might have about Native people. Who is telling the story? Is it the people themselves, or is it the non-Native author? Even a Native author must include their methods of gathering information somewhere in their publications. Our people should demand this and students of Native American history should demand this.

Our Native elders and veterans are the experts in their own culture and history. Their words must be respected and viewed as the primary source of information about their cultures. This is why I chose to present the interviews verbatim.

I and others did edit for grammar in each interview, and I did frame the interviews in a linear format for easier reading. For instance, most interviews begin with the veteran stating when they were born, where they went to school, and so on. But sometimes those questions weren't asked in that order.

I could not force a veteran to conform to a linear line of questioning. That would be disrespectful, and it would not be a comfortable process. Sometimes we took breaks and I did interview several veterans twice because they wanted to speak to me again. I then merged those interviews together. I also gave a transcription of the interview to each veteran before I printed this book and gave them the opportunity to edit anything they saw fit. Including the veterans in the editing process was the respectful thing to do. In almost all cases the only edits were of a grammatical nature.

You can easily critique my questions and you are reading first-hand accounts of Native history and World War Two history. I'm not suggesting these interviews give the entire history of either genre, but you can take comfort in knowing that these are the real accounts of real people and I did my utmost to corroborate their experiences with literature reviews and Internet research. As I stated in the prologue, any mistakes in this book belong to me alone.

These northern California indigenous cultures are all based on oral histories. In order for our history to continue elders must verbally share information. They are conforming to their cultural mores by doing this. But they are only sharing it; they are not giving it away.

So the theft of our histories in the name of academics must stop. The way to do this is to compel scholars to include their methods of how they treated Native people while conducting research. They must disclose why they want to conduct research, how they will conduct research, where they will conduct research, how long they want to conduct research, and when they will conduct research. Most importantly, they must disclose who owns their research when it's completed. Do the Native people own it, or does some non-Native institution?

The ability to present history represents a power structure, and the power structure in America regarding Native American history continues to favor non-Native universities, museums and institutions. I'm not trying to invalidate all non-Native people who want to help present Native history. I'm just writing this to attempt to find ways to bridge a gap between cultures.

You'll notice I relied on several publications about Native American history written by non-Native people. But the time has come for Native American Tribes and institutions to start encouraging, training and hiring their own young people to work with their own elders to present their own histories. I am very proud of the fact that several Tribes supported this book.

This book is Native written, edited and produced. I presented my material to the tribal councils of each Tribe listed as a sponsor. They sponsored my book idea with the hope that young people regardless of ethnicity will learn from these veterans and elders. Many of these council members were raised by veterans, and many are veterans.

I relied on family members and community members from each culture to help guide me to the people whom I spoke with. I often asked a son or daughter if their father or mother would share with me. I also made poster boards of previous interviews and showed them to each veteran. They would see a familiar face and it made them feel more at ease. The important thing to note is these veterans were ready on some level to share. They didn't do it because I told them to; they did it because they were ready and because they saw that I am Native just like them. I believe they trusted me on a cultural and an academic level.

I never started an interview by asking directly about the war. I always started with easier questions, such as when and where the person was born. The war questions weren't asked until later in the interview, although some of the men wanted to talk about that first. I allowed each person to dictate the pace, the length and the type of questions for each interview.

I learned very quickly how important that would be. One man was speaking about his time at a battle, and he had never shared about it. I could sense a change come over him and his eyes became kind of glossed over. He was reliving the experience, not just telling about it. He became very emotional and I quickly asked a totally different question to bring him out of it. It was a scary learning experience for me. I had to judge when a person was going into that state, and learn how to prevent that from happening.

I also had to learn not to keep all these war stories bottled up inside me. I shared with my family and friends. Sometimes I would have to stay in bed all day after an intense interview. I would also have to take time off from writing because of what I had learned. It wasn't always an easy or an exciting experience.

I originally thought I would interview three or four family members and be done. I just wanted to help Native veterans tell their stories and share their histories. They have more than earned this right. It is important to remember that veterans must be ready to share what they've gone through. No one has the right to expect them to relive such stressful, often painful memories for any reason. It took many members of this World War Two generation over 50 years to come to terms with their wartime experiences.

So what was that connection between the men I had observed at those reunions as a little boy? I found it was a silent measure of respect amongst each other for living through a momentous period in history. They never bragged about it.

I wanted to touch on the subject of Native Americans who serve today in the United States military. I know many Native families have strong military histories. My own family is one of them. I had a total of 14 family members who served in World War Two. My cousin Warren Gorbet served in the Marine Corps in the late 1950s.

My late uncle Mike served two tours in the Army in Vietnam. My cousins Dugan Aguilar and Richard Aguilar served in Vietnam in the Marine Corps and the Army. My father-in-law Len Haff served in the Marine Corps. So I respect those Native people who have served, and I respect those Native people who continue to serve.

I've also observed what policies the United States government continues to practice regarding Native sovereignty and culture. It isn't a good record. There's still too much deception. Our political, religious, land and water rights are under continuous assault by either state or federal policies. Our ceremonial sites are in constant danger of being developed by mineral, timber or tourism companies. We are the only ethnic group in America that is continually asked or told to dig up our ancestor's remains so that developers can put up another building, house or shopping mall, or for academics to study us like objects.

I have this to say to any young Native person who might think of joining the military: If you choose to enlist, strive to be the best that you can. Be aware that your indigenous people are counting on your safe return to your homeland. You can apply the skills you learn in the service among your own communities. Above all else, be aware that Native people walked before you in that uniform. Your actions will be remembered in all ways.

Native people do have an array of dignified, respectable positions available to us in today's society. It doesn't have to be in the military. You can be a good parent, a good husband, a good wife, a teacher, a traditional singer, a basket weaver, a construction worker, an educator, a traditional dancer, a firefighter, a tribal employee, a tribal council member, a ceremonial regalia maker, an academic, a lawyer, a health care worker, a doctor, or any one of a hundred other professions.

It took me six years to complete this journey. I crisscrossed northern California more times than I can count in search of my Native veterans, eventually driving over 40,000 miles. I can remember as a young boy we'd have family gatherings with my grandfather Stan from the 99th Army Division, my great-uncle Leonard from the 32nd Army Division, my great-uncle Bob Aguilar from the Navy Seabees, my cousin Mervin Evans from the Naval Armed Guard, and my cousin John Peconam from the Army Military Police all together at once.

These memories always inspired me to do more research and to speak with more veterans. I felt like I was honoring these family members by writing this book. I didn't realize how many veterans and Indian families knew my grandfather and his brother until I started this project. Having the same last name as them really helped!

I learned a lot about my own family through this book, and that was an unexpected bonus I'll always cherish. Those bonds between boarding school mates, veterans and Indian men are all combined in this generation. These guys are close. I have always yearned be a part of that bond, and every time I sat with those men I felt it.

Two other events in my life helped convince me I should write this book. The first occurred when I was 14 years old and we attended one of the Veteran's Reunions in Susanville. I was alone in the men's bathroom washing my hands when an old Indian man came up beside me. He was in his 80s or even his 90s. He washed his hands in the sink next to mine. He spoke to me. 'We sure cleared out those German fighters from the sky,' he said.

His face was weathered and old, but his dark brown eyes had a sparkle in them. I didn't know who he was or why he said that, so I just looked at him and nodded. He smiled and I walked out very curious. I decided to sit just outside the door and see who this man was with. I waited for about 10 minutes and he didn't come out. I finally got up and went back into the bathroom. No one was there. The man had vanished.

The second event occurred the first time I went to vote. It was in 1993 and I was 18 years old. I went to vote at the Calvary Baptist Church, which is located right behind the Susanville Indian Rancheria. Across from the church lies an Indian cemetery. This cemetery is located on ancient Maidu land, and Native people from several tribes rest in peace there today.

As I walked into the church I was excited about my opportunity to vote. Entering the church I noticed that the volunteers were all old veterans. These men wore their Veterans of Foreign Wars caps and were very nice to me.

As I wrote my name in the record book to vote I noticed that several of my family members had already voted. There was my grandfather Stan among them.

I thought it special that I could add my name among theirs in this book. I finished signing and started with my ballot toward the voting area. My grandfather Stan emerged from a booth.

He saw me and said, 'Hi Chagamem,' which is my full name. He continued walking by me toward the door to leave.

I said, 'Hello Grandpa,' as we passed.

Just before I opened the voting booth to go in, I looked back at my grandfather. He was just walking past the veterans who were manning this voting station.They all stood up as he walked by, raised their arms and saluted. My grandfather's back stiffened, and he saluted back in mid-stride.

Had I not looked back I would have missed this entirely. There was no one else there to witness this silent communication of respect. I went in to vote.

As I walked back out the door of that church I looked around in the bright sunshine, but Grandpa Stan wasn't there anymore. I continued walking out into the world he had protected.

Stan Lowry at a Bear Dance in 1998.
Photo courtesy of Ike Lowry.

Notes

California Gold Rush

1. Clifford E. Trafzer and Joel R. Hyer, *Exterminate Them! Written Accounts of the Murder, Rape, and Enslavement of Native Americans during the California Gold Rush* (Michigan: Michigan State University Press, 1999), 7.
2. Pratap Chatterjee, *Gold, Greed and Genocide* (Berkeley, CA: Project Underground, 1998), 19.
3. Kimberly Johnston-Dodds, *Early California Laws and Policies Related to California Indians,* special report prepared at the request of Senator John L. Burton, President pro Tempore, (California Research Bureau, 2002), 1.
4. H.W. Brands, *The Age of Gold* (New York: Doubleday, 2002), 277.
5. Dodds, "Early California Laws," 5.
6. Ibid.
7. Robert F. Heizer, *They Were Only Diggers; A Collection of Articles from California Newspapers, 1851-1866, on Indian and White Relations,* (Ramona, CA: Ballena Press, 1974), 87-88.
8. Jack Norton, *Genocide in Northwestern California,* 2nd ed. (San Francisco: The Indian Historian Press, Inc., 1997), 45-46.
9. Robert F. Heizer, *The Destruction of California Indians,* (Lincoln, NE: University of Nebraska Press, 1993), 219.
10. Dodds, "Early California Laws," 5.
11. Norton, "Genocide in Northwestern," 140-141.
12. Dodds, "Early California Laws," 18.
13. Chag Lowry. "The Price of Gold," (Original Voices, 1999), http://www.originalvoices.org/PriceOfGoldEight.html.
14. Dolan H. Eargle, Jr., *Native California Guide: Weaving the Past & Present* (San Francisco: Trees Company Press, 2002), 33.
15. James J. Rawls, *Indians of California: The Changing Image* (Norman, OK: University of Oklahoma Press, 1984), 141-147.

Indian Boarding Schools

1. Margaret L. Archuleta, Brenda J. Child, and K. Tsianina Lomawaima, *Away from Home: American Indian Boarding School Experiences* (Phoenix, AZ: Heard Museum, 2000), 16.
2. Ibid., 38-39.
3. Byron Nelson, Jr., *Our Home Forever: The Hupa Indians of Northern California* (Hoopa, CA: The Hupa Tribe, 1994), 134.
4. Sherman Indian High School, "Sherman History," http://www.sihs.net/history.html (accessed June 1, 2006).
5. The California State Military Museum, "Historic California Posts: Fort Bidwell," http://www.militarymuseum.org/FtBidwell.html (accessed May 1, 2006).
6. The Chemawa Indian School, "Chemawa History," http://www.chemawa.bia.edu/history.html (accessed June 5, 2006).
7. The Nevada State Museum, "Division of Museums and History: Stewart Indian School," http://dmla.clan.lib.nv.us/docs/museums/cc/Exhibits/stewart/index.html (accessed May 10, 2006).

Reservations and Political Definitions

1. Stephen L. Pevar, *The Rights of Indians and Tribes,* 2nd ed. (Carbondale IL: Southern University Press, 1992), 19.
2. Rawls, "Indians of California," 211.
3. Pevar, "The Rights of Indians," 37.

World War One

1. Hew Strachan, *The Oxford Illustrated History of the First World War,* (Oxford: Oxford University Press, 1998), 9.
2. H.P. Willmott, *World War I,* (New York: DK Publishing Inc, 2003), 26.
3. Ibid., 196.
4. Ibid., 200
5. Ibid., 198.
6. Thomas A. Britten, *American Indians in World War I: At War and At Home,* (Albuquerque, NM: University of New Mexico Press, 1997), 51.
7. Ibid., 58.
8. Ibid., 99-101.
9. Ibid., 75-81.
10. Ibid., 106-107.
11. Ibid., 82.
12. David Hurst Thomas, *Skull Wars,* (New York, NY: Basic Books, 2000), 67.
13. Clifford E. Trafzer, *As Long as the Grass Shall Grow and Rivers Flow: A History of Native Americans,* (Belmont, CA: Wadsworth Group/Thomson Learning, 2000), 529.
14. Thomas, "Skull Wars," 67.
15. Ibid., 67-8.

The Origin of World War Two

1. Laurence Rees, *The Nazis,* (New York, NY: The New Press, 1997), 17.
2. H.P. Willmott, Robin Cross, and Charles Messenger, *World War II,* (New York, NY: DK Publishing, Inc, 2004), 10.
3. Joachim C. Fest, *Hitler,* (New York, NY: Random House, 1975), 200-216.
4. Chris Bishop, SS: *Hell on the Western Front,* (St. Paul, MN: MBI Publishing Company, 2003), 7-12.
5. Rees "The Nazis," 73.
6. Ibid., 75-8.
7. Willmott, Cross, and Messenger, "World War II," 42.
8. Iris Chang, *The Rape of Nanking,* (New York, NY: Penguin Books, 1997), 3-7.
9. Willmott, Cross, and Messenger, "World War II," 106-114.
10. Ibid., 114.

The European Theater

1. Samuel W. Mitcham, Jr. and Gene Mueller, *Hitler's Commanders,* (New York, NY: Cooper Square Press, 2000), 178.
2. Stephen E. Ambrose, *The Good Fight,* (New York, NY: Athenum Books for Young Readers, 2001), 44.
3. Chris Chant, *Aircraft of World War II,* (New York, NY: Barnes & Noble, Inc., 1999), 89.
4. Richard Collier, *The War in the Desert,* (Alexandria, VA: Time-Life Books, 1977), 154.
5. Ambrose, "The Good Fight," 32.
6. Robert Wallace, *The Italian Campaign,* (Alexandria, VA: Time-Life Books, 1981), 179-82.
7. U.S. Department of Defense, *World War II Informational Fact Sheets,* (Washington, DC: USA 50th Anniversary Commemoration Committee, 1995), 76-7.
8. Ibid.
9. Ibid., 24.
10. Willmott, Cross, and Messenger, "World War II," 232.
11. TIME, *V-E Day: America's Greatest Generation and Their WWII Triumph,* (New York, NY: TIME Books, 2005), 45-53.
12. Willmott, Cross, and Messenger, "World War II," 270.
13. Don & Petie Kladstrup, Wine & War, (New York, NY: Broadway Books, 2002), 198-203.
14. Ambrose, "The Good Fight," 68.

The Home Front

1. U.S. Department of Defense, "World War II Informational Fact Sheets," 23-24.
2. Ibid., 16.
3. Ibid., 23.

The Arsenal for Democracy

1. Jere' Bishop Franco, *Crossing the Pond: The Native American Effort in World War II,* (Denton, TX: University of North Texas Press, 1999), 82.
2. Willmott, Cross, and Messenger, "World War II," 125.
3. Franco, "Crossing the Pond," 101.

The Pacific Theater

1. Mitchell G. Bard, *The Complete Idiot's Guide to World War Two,* (Indianapolis, IN: Alpha Books, 1999), 133.
2. United State Merchant Marine, "American Merchant Marine at War," (US Maritime Service Veterans, 2006), htpp://www.usmm.org (accessed June 13, 2006).
3. Naval Historical Center, "Naval Armed Guard Service in World War Two," (Department of the Navy, 2006), http://www.http://www.history.navy.mil/faqs/faq104-1.html.
4. U.S. Department of Defense, "World War II Informational Fact Sheets," 65-66.
5. Alison R. Bernstein, *American Indians and World War II,* (Norman, OK: University of Oklahoma Press, 1991), 49.
6. U.S. Department of Defense, "World War II Informational Fact Sheets," 16.
7. Martin Marix Evans, *Battles of World War II,* (Shrewsbury, England: Airlife Publishing Ltd., 2002), 90-91.
8. U.S. Department of Defense, "World War II Informational Fact Sheets," 63-4.
9. United State Merchant Marine, "US Merchant Marine in World War II," (US Maritime Service Veterans, 2006), htpp://www. http://www.usmm.org/ww2.html (accessed June 13, 2006).
10. U.S. Department of Defense, "World War II Informational Fact Sheets," 75.
11. Willmott, Cross, and Messenger, "World War II," 211-213.
12. TIME, *V-J Day: America's World War II Triumph in the Pacific,* (New York, NY: TIME Books, 2005), 78-85.
13. Willmott, Cross, and Messenger, "World War II," 292.

Bibliography

Ailsby, Christopher. *SS: Hell on the Eastern Front.* Osceola, WI: MBI Publishing Company, 1998.

Alford, Kenneth D. *Great Treasure Stories of World War II.* Mason City, IA: Savas Publishing Company, 2000.

Ambrose, Stephen E. *The Good Fight: How World War II Was Won.* New York, NY: Athenum Books for Young Readers, 2001.

Archuleta, Margaret L., Brenda J. Child, and K. Tsianina Lomawaima. *Away From Home: American Indian Boarding School Experiences.* Santa Fe, NM: Heard Museum, 2000.

Bard, Mitchell G. *The Complete Idiot's Guide to World War II.* Indianapolis, IN: AlphaBooks, 1999.

Bernstein, Alison R. *American Indians and World War II: Toward a New Era in Indian Affairs.* Norman, OK: University of Oklahoma Press, 1991.

Bishop, Chris. *SS: Hell on the Western Front.* St. Paul, MN: MBI Publishing Company, 2003.

Blakeley, W. H. *The 32nd Infantry Division in World War II.* Reprint, Nashville, TN: The Battery Press, 2000.

Bradley, James, and Ron Powers. *Flags of Our Fathers.* New York, NY: Bantam Books, 2000.

Brands, W. H. *The Age of Gold.* New York, NY: Doubleday, 2002.

Britten, Thomas A. *American Indians in World War I.* Albuquerque, NM: University of New Mexico Press, 1997.

Brown, John S. *Draftee Division: The 88th Infantry Division in World War II.* Reprint, Novato, CA: Presidio Press, 1998.

Botting, Douglas. *The D-Day Invasion: World War II.* Alexandria, VA: Time-Life Books, 1978.

Chang, Iris. *The Rape of Nanking.* Reprint, New York, NY: Penguin Books, 1998.

Chant, Chris. *Aircraft of World War II.* New York, NY: Barnes & Noble, Inc., 1999.

Cohen, Stan. *The Tree Army: A Pictorial History of the Civilian Conservation Corps, 1933-1942.* Reprint, Missoula MT: Pictorial Histories Publishing Company, Inc., 2003.

Collier, Richard. *The War in the Desert: World War II.* Alexandria, VA: Time-Life Books, 1977.

Costo, Rupert, and Jeannette Henry Costo. *The Missions of California: A Legacy of Genocide.* San Francisco, CA: Indian Historian Press, 1987.

Department of Defense. *World War II Informational Fact Sheets.* Washington, DC: USA 50th Anniversary Commemoration Committee, Department of Defense, 1995.

Dodds-Johnston, Kimberly. *Early California Laws and Policies Related to California Indians.* Sacramento, CA: California Research Bureau, 2002.

Dunnigan, James F., and Albert A. Nofi. *Dirty Little Secrets of World War II.* New York, NY: Quill, 1994.

Eargle, Dolan H. *Native California Guide: Weaving the Past & Present.* San Francisco, CA: Trees Company Press, 2000.

Evans, Martin M. *Battles of World War II.* Shrewsbury, England: Airlife Publishing Ltd., 2002.

Essame, H. *Patton.* Reprint, Conshohocken, PA: Combined Publishing, 1998.

Fest, Joachim C. *Hitler.* Reprint, New York, NY: Vintage Books, 1975.

Franco, Jere' Bishop. *Crossing the Pond: The Native American Effort in World War II.* Denton, TX: University of North Texas Press, 1999.

Frank, Richard B. *Downfall: The End of the Imperial Japanese Empire.* New York, NY: Penguin Books, 1999.

Garfield, Brian. *The Thousand-Mile War: World War II in Alaska and the Aleutians.* Reprint, Garden City, NY: Nelson Doubleday, Inc., 1983.

Goolrick, William K. and Ogden Tanner. *The Battle of the Bulge: World War II.* Alexandria, VA: Time-Life Books, 1979.

Heizer, Robert F. *The Destruction of California Indians.* Reprint, Nelson, NE: University of Nebraska Press, 1993.

Heizer, Robert F. *They Were Only Diggers: A Collection of Articles from California Newspapers, 1851-1866, on Indian and White Relations.* Ramona, CA: Ballena Press, 1974.

Herzstein, Robert Edwin. *The Nazis: World War II.* Alexandria, VA: Time-Life Books, 1980

Horner, David. *The Second World War: The Pacific.* Osceola, WI: Osprey Publishing Limited, 2002.

Hoyt, Edwin P. *The Kamikazes.* Short Hills, NJ: Burford Books, 1983.

Kladstrup, Don and Petie Kladstrup. *Wine & War.* New York, NY: Broadway Books, 2001.

Laur, Walter E. *Battle Babies: The Story of the 99th Infantry Division in World War II.* Reprint, Nashville, TN: The Battery Press, 1985.

Levy, Alan. Nazi Hunter: *The Wiesenthal File.* New York, NY: Carrol & Graf Publishers, 2002.

Los Alamos Historical Society. *Los Alamos.* Reprint, Los Alamos, NM: Los Alamos Historical Society, 2002.

Manchester, William. *Goodbye, Darkness: A Memoir of the Pacific War.* Boston, MA: Little, Brown and Company, 1980.

McClain, Sally. *Navajo Weapon: The Navajo Code Talkers.* Tucson, AZ: Rio Nuevo Publishers, 2001.

Mitcham, Jr., Samuel W. and Gene Mueller. *Hitler's Commanders.* New York, NY: Cooper Square Press, 2000.

Nelson, Byron. *Our Home Forever: The Hupa Indians of Northern California.* Hoopa, CA: Hupa Tribe, 1994.

Nies, Judith. *Native American History.* New York, NY: Ballantine Books, 1996.

Norton, Jack. *Genocide in Northwestern California.* San Francisco, CA: The Indian Historian Press, 1997.

Parker, Danny S. *Battle of the Bulge: Hitler's Ardennes Offensive, 1944-1945.* Philadelphia, PA: Combined Books, 1991.

Paul, Doris A. *The Navajo Code Talkers.* Pittsburgh, PA: Dorrance Publishing Company Inc., 1973.

Pevar, Stephen L. *The Rights of Indians and Tribes.* Second Edition, Carbondale and Edwardsville, ILL: University of Illinois Press, 1992.

Prior, Robin and Trevor Wilson. *The First World War.* London, England: Cassell & Company, 2001.

Rawls, James J. *Indians of California: The Changing Image.* Norman, OK: University of Oklahoma Press, 1984.

Rees, Laurence. *The Nazis: A Warning from History.* New York, NY: The New Press, 1997.

Rhodes, Richard. *Masters of Death: The SS-Einsatzgruppen and the Invention of the Holocaust.* New York, NY: Alfred A. Knopf, 2002.

Sebag-Montefiore, Hugh. *Enigma: The Battle for the Code.* New York, NY: John Wiley & Sons, Inc., 2000.

Smith, Jim and Malcolm McConnell. *The Last Mission: The Secret History of World War II's Final Battle.* New York, NY: Broadway Books, 2002.

Speer, Albert. *Inside the Third Reich.* Toronto, Canada: The Macmillan Company, 1970.

Stannard, David E. *American Holocaust.* New York, NY: Oxford University Press, 1992.

Steinberg, Rafael. *Island Fighting: World War II.* Alexandria, VA: Time-Life Books, 1978.

Strachan, Hew. *The Oxford Illustrated History of the First World War.* New York, NY: Oxford University Press, 1998.

Thomas, David Hurst. *Skull Wars: Kennewick Man, Archaeology, and The Battle for Native American Identity.* New York, NY: Basic Books, 2000.

TIME Books. *V-E Day: America's Greatest Generation and Their WWII Triumph.* New York, NY: TIME Books, 2005.

TIME Books. *V-J Day: America's World War II Triumph in the Pacific.* New York, NY: TIME Books, 2005.

Tobin, James. *Ernie Pyle's War.* Lawrence, KS: University of Kansas Press, 1997.

Toland, John. *The Last 100 Days.* New York, NY: The Modern Library, 2003.

Trafzer, Clifford E. *As Long as the Grass Shall Grow and Rivers Flow.* Belmont, CA: Wadsworth Group/Thompson Learning, 2000.

Trafzer, Clifford E. and Joel R. Hyers. *Exterminate Them! Written Accounts of the Murder, Rape, and Enslavement of Native Americans during the California Gold Rush.* East Lansing, MI: Michigan State University Press, 1999.

Townsend, Kenneth William. *World War II and the American Indian.* Albuquerque, NM: University of New Mexico Press, 2000.

Wallace, Robert. *The Italian Campaign: World War II:* Alexandria, VA: Time-Life Books, 1981.

Whitlock, Flint. *The Fighting First: The Untold Story of the Big Red One on D-Day.* Boulder, CO: Westview Press, 2004.

Willmott, H.P. *World War I.* New York, NY: Dorling Kindersley Publishing Inc., 2003.

Willmott, H.P., Robin Cross and Charles Messenger. *World War II.* New York, NY: Dorling Kindersley Publishing Inc., 2004.

Unpublished Works

U.S. Department of the Interior. *Indians at Work.* Chicago, ILL: U.S. Department of the Interior, 1945.

Related Web Sites

The California State Military Museum
www.militarymuseum.org

National Archives and Records Administration
www.nara.gov

Navy Historical Center
www.history.navy.mil/

National Museum of the Marine Corps
www.usmcmuseum.org/

United States Holocaust Memorial Museum
www.ushmm.org

U.S. Maritime Service
www.usmm.org

About the Author

Chag Lowry is of Yurok, Mountain Maidu and Pit River ancestry. He was born and raised among his father's people in Susanville, California. He has an MA in Education and a BA in Journalism from Humboldt State University. He lives with his wife Rebecca and their son Trey in northern California.

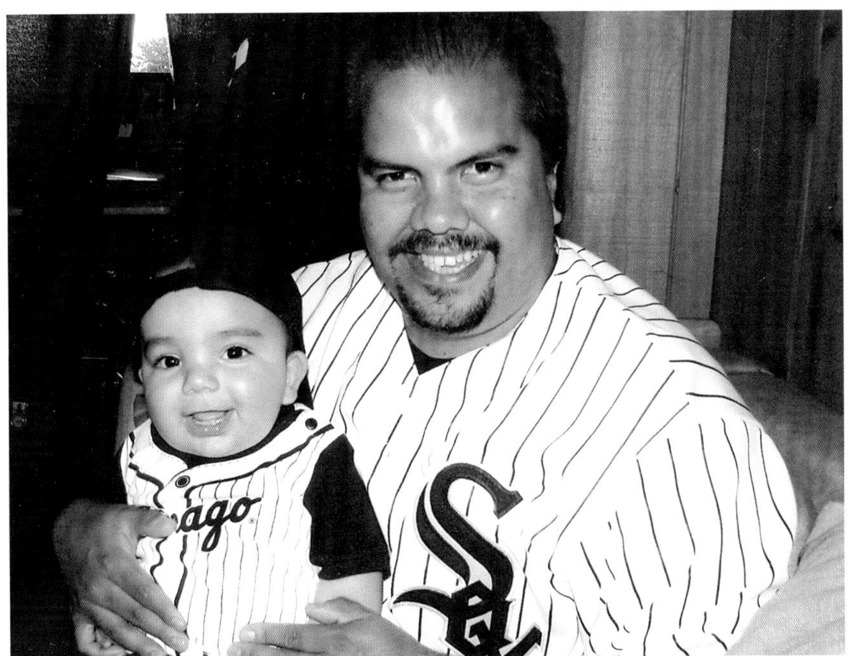

Photo by Rebecca Lowry.